BONHOEFFER AND KING

Their Life and Theology Documented
in Christian News 1963-2011

A Fifty Year Battle vs. Intellectual Laziness

Herman Otten, Editor

BONHOEFFER AND KING
Their Life and Theology Documented in Christian News 1963-2011
A Fifty Year Battle vs. Intellectual Laziness

Copyright 2011 © Lutheran News, Inc. All Rights Reserved.
No Portion of this book may be reproduced in any form, except for quotations in reviews, articles, and speeches, without permission from the publisher.

Library of Congress Card
Lutheran News, Inc.
684 Luther Lane
New Haven, MO 63068
Published 2011
Printed in the United States of America,
Lightning Source Inc., La Vergne, TN
ISBN 978-0-9832409-0-7

Quotes about
BONHOEFFER AND KING

"*Dietrich Bonhoeffer and Martin Luther King, Jr., must be numbered among the most prominent and influential Christians of the Twentieth Century.*"
—**Stephen R. Hayes in "King and Bonhoeffer as Protestant Giants," Fortress Press**

"*So persuasive is his (Bonhoeffer's) influence that Lutheran Church Historian Martin Marty once suggested dividing the theological world into two groups: those who admit their debt to Bonhoeffer and those who borrow his ideas without acknowledgement.*"
—*Time*

"*Although he claimed to be a Lutheran and is so-called in the literature of our day, Bonhoeffer was not Lutheran, for he rejected and abandoned the theology and teaching of the Book of Concord.*"
—**Raymond Surburg, Concordia Seminary, Ft. Wayne**

"*The most influential theologian of the Twentieth Century.*"
—**Matthew Becker, *Concordia Journal,* Concordia Seminary, St. Louis**

"*He was a confessional Lutheran.*"
—**Uwe Simeon Netto, *Lutheran Witness* (LCMS) and *Issues, Etc.***

"*May well be perhaps the most important Lutheran theologian since Martin Luther.*"
—**Concordia Seminary, St. Louis**

"*Dietrich Bonhoeffer rejected the deity of Christ.*"
—**Cardinal Carberry, *St. Louis Roman Catholic Review***

"*Though most evangelicals probably do not know it, most Bonhoeffer scholars dismissively reject the idea that Bonhoeffer's theology is compatible with American evangelical theology.*"
—**Richard Weikart, California State University, Stanislaus.**

Martin Luther King "*is first of all a committed Christian.*"
—***The Lutheran Witness*, LCMS.**

"To him (King) the traditional issues of theology – sin and salvation, the divinity of Christ, His virgin birth, His bodily resurrection are peripheral. Love is central."
—The National Observer in **"The Theology of Martin Luther King."**

"His affairs had been an open secret for years, but two weeks after his birthday, King confessed to one of them to his wife Coretta."
—Time

"He doubted the truth of the literal resurrection of Jesus."
—Rufas Burrow, Jr., Westminster John Knox Press

"How else could we speak of the young earth except in the language of fairy tales?"
—Dietrich Bonhoeffer

"But, we ask, if the words of Genesis 1-3 are the language of myth and fairy tales, [as Bonhoeffer says] what conceivable warrant is there for saying that they also have a capacity as the Word of God? Do the Grecian myths have a capacity as the Word of God?"
—Edward J. Young, Professor of Old Testament, Westminster Theological Seminary.

"There's going to be a drama this year. And the hero is not Martin Luther, but 20th Century Dietrich Bonhoeffer."
—Detroit Free Press, 1965.

"Bonhoeffer left no school of disciples, but he has nonetheless become the most frequently quoted theologian of his generation. For better or worse, his idea of a 'religionless Christianity' has been taken up by today's Death-of-God thinkers."
—Time, 1966.

"Dietrich Bonhoeffer has been called the most distinguished Christian martyr of the twentieth century."
—LCA Sunday Church School Series BONHOEFFER

"Bonhoeffer notes that man has, step by step, conquered his environment, until there is allegedly no room for God, as historically understood, in the framing or articulation of the culture modern man has created."
—Harold P. Kuhn, "Still Adolescent?" in *Christianity Today*, May 17, 1967

". . . the Christ of Bonhoeffer is not the Christ of the Scriptures, is not the Christ of the Reformers. . ."
—Dr. Cornelius Van Til, *Westminster Theological Journal*, May, 1972.

"Before God he states that the New Testament never identified Jesus as God (p. 50); he fails to affirm the bodily resurrection of Christ (p. 108) he equates the Holy Spirit with the Risen Christ (p. 109); and he declares that 'the miracles were often not so much stories of what Jesus once did, but symbols of what he still can do' (p. 450)."
—Blue-Print, March 29, 1977

"The quotation from Bonhoeffer sounded good. Certainly a good sounding quotation by a man widely recognized as evil would not be used in a Christian publication. Yet here is displayed favorably a quote by a theologian who viciously attacks the Bible and the Christian faith."
—**Bolton Davidheiser**

"Paul W. Powell, a Southern Baptist leader in Texas, claims that 'Dietrich Bonhoeffer was a great Christian if there ever was one.'"
—*Southern Baptist Leader*

"For him teaching was living the message of Christ. His students learned by watching Christ grow in themselves and in their teacher."
—*Lutheran Forum*

"The post-humously published Letters and Papers from Prison has become a 20th-century classic of Christian ethics."
—*The Lutheran*

"He had no faith in the physical resurrection of Christ. Bonhoeffer believed the 'historicity' of the Resurrection was in 'the realm of ambiguity,' and that it was one of the 'mythological' elements of Christianity that 'must be interpreted in such a way as not to make religion a pre-condition of faith.' He also believed that 'the Resurrection is not the solution of the problem of death,' and that such things as miracles and the ascension of Christ were 'mythological conceptions' as well."
—*Biblical Discernment Ministries*

"Most of Bonhoeffer's writings, which run to 16 volumes, are still in print in more that a dozen languages. His 'Letters and Papers from Prison' and 'Ethics' are stables in courses in mainline Protestant and Catholic seminaries today."
—*St. Louis Post Dispatch*

"Bonhoeffer never sets forth the true doctrine of justification by faith and its implications for the Christian life."
—**Raymond Surburg**

"Bonhoeffer's Christology is not what the New Testament sets forth, but was the product of his philosophical thinking."
—**Raymond Surburg**

"The liberal, Modernist Protestant power elite in Germany have made Bonhoeffer into a type of church father. Not only have streets and schools been named to honor Bonhoeffer, but even Lutheran churches bear his name."
—**LaMarr Blecker**

"In his book The Cost of Discipleship, *Bonhoeffer paints a vivid picture of how to be true to the Christian faith under a hostile regime."*
—**Charles Colson**

"In his writings, though, he plainly rejected such doctrines as the virgin birth, physical resurrection, and substitutionary atonement of Jesus Christ. According to Bonhoeffer, it is a 'cardinal error' to regard Christianity as a religion of salvation."
—**David Cloud**

"And because he lived where and when he did--in the bowels of a gangster state-- Bonhoeffer was thwarted in his attempt to fashion a new understanding of Christian belief."
—**Rabbi A. James Rudin**

"Much more good would be accomplished for the promotion of true Christianity if the AAL would spend all the money it did financing the movie on Bonhoeffer to help produce a movie on some orthodox and anti-Communist churchmen as C.F.W. Walther, Walter A. Maier, Alfred Rehwinkel, Robert Preus, Kurt Marquart, or Raymond Surburg."
—**AAL Movie on Bonhoeffer**

"The historical Bonhoeffer was a serious and intellectual theologian. The AAL Bonhoeffer was a muddleheaded aristocrat, who seemed to be led by the nose by his brother-in-law, Hans von Dohnanyi, who was a noted German jurist and early opponent of the Third Reich."
—**LaMarr Blecker**

"So Bonhoeffer rejected classical Christology, had a low view of the Bible, denied the deity of Christ, denied the sinlessness of Christ, and doubted the physical resurrection of Christ."
—**David Becker**

"The Lutheran Church-Missouri Synod's Concordia Publishing House recently published **'Till the Night Be Past-The Life and Times of Dietrich Bonhoeffer'** *by Theodore J. Kleinhans. The 171 page book is available from Concordia Publishing House, 3558 S. Jefferson Ave., St. Louis, MO 63118-3808. 1-800-325-3040. The CPH book presents Bonhoeffer as a great Christian."*
—*Christian News*

"When Martin Buber spoke of 'Eclipse of God' in the twentieth century, he was thinking of 'the conceptual letting go of God,' of the confinement of God to man's subjectivity by modern philosophers and psychologists. With Bonhoeffer and the death-of-God 'school', theology itself began to contribute to this eclipse."
—**Franklin L. Baumer**

"With the airings on public television of the film Bonhoeffer: Agent of Grace, *and the advent of Martin Doblmeier's 2003 documentary,* Bonhoeffer, *individuals may wish to take a more in-depth look at the most influential Lutheran theologian of the twentieth century."*
—**Matthew Becker,** *Concordia Journal,* **Concordia Seminary, St. Louis**

"Dr. Uwe Simeon Netto in his CPH published book The Fabricated Luther *refers to Bonhoeffer as 'theologically an orthodox Lutheran'."*
—**Uwe Simeon Netto**

"One hundred years after Dietrich Bonhoeffer's birth, and more than six decades after his violent death, it is high time for Lutherans to reclaim their greatest martyr."
—**Uwe Simeon Netto, *Issues Etc., The Lutheran Witness***

"Yes, Dietrich Bonhoeffer was a strong sinner in this sense of the word, for he was a confessional Lutheran."
—**Uwe Simeon Netto, *Issues Etc., The Lutheran Witness***

"Does the faculty really believe that Bonhoeffer is 'perhaps the most important theologian since Martin Luther' and that 'Dietrich Bonhoeffer may well be the most widely admired and respected Christian theologian among Christian pastors and theologians in the USA?'"
—**Concordia Seminary, St. Louis**

"In the Review, *Oct. 31, 1969, Father John Zupez, S.J., stated that Cardinal Carberry was incorrect in stating in his talk to the Teachers' Institute that Dietrich Bonhoeffer rejected the divinity of Christ.*

"Quite surely Cardinal Carberry had no desire to injure the reputation of a man of undoubted sincerity and courage. He merely wanted to warn the faithful, as is his duty, of the danger of secularism, which denies the supernatural destiny of man, and of the distortion of Christianity by modern followers of Bonhoeffer into an agnostic humanism."
—**Hugh J. O'Connell, C.S.S.R**

"In his book Existentialism and Christian Belief, *author Milton D. Hunnex, reluctantly admits that Bonhoeffer was a 'secular theologian' (p. 94) who taught a 'religionless Christianity,' (p. 96) whose writings have 'become the rallying cry for a wholesome defection from the Christian faith' (p. 98)."*
—**Fundamentalist Digest**

"From what we have learned of Bonhoeffer we see that his Christ as Center is to all intents and purposes the same as the Christ-Event of the new hermeneutic, of the new quest of the theology as history. In all of these the historic Protestant hermeneutic is rejected as rational-determinist and irrational-indeterminist. In all of these the text of Scripture is interpreted in terms of hermeneutical principles based on the epistemology of Kant and his followers."
—**Cornelius Van Til**

"Dietrich Bonhoeffer was 'a man of the word of God,' says Eric A. Andrae in an article published in the January, 2008 Concordia Theological Quarterly *of Concordia Theological Seminary, Ft. Wayne, Indiana."*
—**Concordia Theological Quarterly**

"This week, CN, which applies the same standard to 'friend and foe,' in its report of Rev. Matthew Harrison's recent book 'A Little Book on Joy' notes that the book includes about 10 quotations from Dietrich Bonhoeffer leaving the impression that Bonhoeffer was some great Christian theologian."
—**Matthew Harrison**

"At the heart of Bonhoeffer's theology was the mystery of the incarnation. In a circular letter he wrote, 'No priest, no theologian stood at the cradle in Bethlehem. And yet, all Christian theology has its origin in the wonder of all wonders that God became man. Alongside the brilliance of holy night there burns the fire of the unfathomable mystery of Christian theology.'"
—**Eric Metaxas**

"Today the 2009 CPH catalog lists 10 books by Bonhoeffer and one book about him, which was published by CPH. All are now available from CPH. The CPH catalog lists no book by Maier."
—***Christian News***

"As the Holocaust religion grows, do not be surprised that the Bonhoeffer myth will continue to grow."
—***Christian News***

"This year's Advent Preaching Seminar will examine critically the Advent preaching of three German theologians/preachers: Dietrich Bonhoeffer, Helmut Thielicke and Gerhard Ebeling. Drawing on their work, suggested outlines and illustrations will be offered for a midweek Advent series as well as the Sundays of Advent."
—**Concordia Theological Seminary, Ft. Wayne**

"*Christian News* has yet to find one person who has actually read what Surburg and Van Til wrote about Bonhoeffer's theology who still maintains that Bonhoeffer was a Christian whose Christ was the Christ of the Bible and that Bonhoeffer accepted such Christian doctrines as the physical resurrection of Christ."
—***Christian News***

"Together with likenesses of Saint Elizabeth of Russia, Archbishop Oscar Romero, and others, their statues now properly grace the façade of Westminster Abbey in the heart of London. Just above the Great West Door, Bonhoeffer and King symbolically bless those going into, but also those coming out of, the historic church."
—**Timothy Jackson**

"According to Bonhoeffer, the resurrection and other events in the Bible are thus not true as empirical facts of history."
—**Richard Weikart**

"Thus Bonhoeffer saw all biblical language as problematic and in need of demythologizing. The entire Bible is myth, not just miracles."
—**Richard Weikart**

"At the present time CPH is helping to mislead the LCMS about Bonhoeffer and praising him as the greatest theologian since Martin Luther, a theologian who denied the resurrection of Christ as an event which took place in real calendar history. Praising and following Bonhoeffer will help continue the LCMS down the road to becoming one more of America's 'anything goes' denominations."
—**Herman Otten,** ***Christian News***

"Bonhoeffer is more like a theologically conservative evangelical than anything else. He was as orthodox as Saint Paul or Isaiah, from his teen years all the way to his last day on earth."
—**Eric Metaxas in Christianity Today**

"In a lecture in 1928 Bonhoeffer stated that the Bible is filled with material that is historically unreliable. Even the life of Jesus is 'overgrown with legends' and myth so that we know little about the life of Jesus."
—**Richard Weikart**

"By preachment and by action Dr. King has demonstrated that he is a committed humans rights leader but is first of all a committed Christian."
—***The Lutheran Witness***

"To him the traditional issues of theology—sin and salvation, the divinity of Christ, His virgin birth, His bodily resurrection—are peripheral. Love is central."
—***National Observer***

"...says Methodist Bishop John Wesley Lord of Washington, D.C., Dr. King is nothing less than the 'moral leader of the nation'."
—***National Observer***

"Lutheran pastors should be more interested in reading everything by Martin Luther King Jr. than by Martin Luther, a California clergyman told a convocation of American Lutheran Church pastors today in St. Paul."
—***Minneapolis Star***

"Dr. Martin Luther King has himself recorded his indebtedness to Walter Rauschenbusch (THE CHRISTIAN CENTURY, April 13, 1960, p. 440). Now who was Rauschenbusch? He was the real founder of the Social Gospel in America. His 'theology' was simply a religiously sugarcoated socialism."
—**Kurt Marquart**

"King (foremost personality in the civil-rights movement) is notorious for his association with communists, communist fronters communist organizations, and moral degenerates connected with communist causes."
—***Dan Smoot Report***

"For myself, I am perfectly willing to grant his brilliance, his basic sincerity, his charismatic effect upon sperhaps hundreds of thousands of Americans – and still regretfully conclude that primarily Martin Luther King left his country a legacy of lawlessness."
—**Lionel Lokos**

"Martin Luther King whom the Communists say heads the 'civil rights' revolution has sparked such insurrection under the guise of peace and non-violence. King is publicized on every occasion, put on television programs and on university platforms to stir hate against the respectable Negro people who are law abiding citizens, and who speak out against his kind."
—**Julia Brown, a patriotic black American**

"It is well known that Fosdick rejected such Christian doctrines as the deity of Christ, Christ's virgin birth and His physical resurrection from the dead. King did the same. Fosdick and King both rejected historic Christianity. Their god was not the God of historic Christianity."
—**Christian News**

"*The new* Lutheran Book of Worship *used by the Lutheran Church in America, the American Lutheran Church, and the Association of Evangelical Lutheran Churches has a special day set aside for King, who is featured as a great Christian saint in the LBW.*"
—**Christian News**

"In letters. . . Sullivan claimed....four other solid grounds for the probe (of King): embezzlement, employing prostitutes, alienating wives affections from their husbands and violation of the Mann Act.... King, for instance, had embezzled or misapplied substantial amounts of money contributed to the civil rights movement. King also had violated prostitution laws in numerous places."
—**Conservative Digest**

"Those of us who received the grace of working with Martin Luther King, Jr., know how profoundly his life and work were empowered by religious faith."
—**Father Richard Neuhaus**

"For that reason, Mr. King went from an 'integrationist' who tried to reform the system to a 'revolutionary, and said in private that he was a Marxist,' Mr. Cone said. 'If white people knew what King was about, they would have never named a holiday for him'."
—**Religious News Service**

"Let me be personal. I didn't look up to him. I didn't agree with him. His life was not a life I would be proud to have led. I wouldn't even expect his views on any subject to be very interesting. I did admire his courage, but I admire the courage of many people. And I think that most Americans feel the same way I do."
—**Joseph Sobran**

"Of course, only God knows those who are genuine Christians, but we know, according to the Bible, that one is not a Christian unless he believes in the substitutionary death of Christ and His bodily resurrection. King did not accept either tenet."
—**Don Boys**

"At the age of 13 I shocked my Sunday school class by denying the bodily resurrection of Jesus. From the age of thirteen on, doubts began to spring forth unrelentingly."
—**Martin Luther King**

"This book by an admirer of King shows that King did not accept historic Christianity, led an immoral lifestyle, does not deserve to have a national holiday named after him, and should be removed from the calendar of saints in The Lutheran Book of Worship."
—**Review of** *Faith Pilgrimage of Martin Luther King* **by Frederick L. Downing**

"...one of Christianity's great knights of faith."
—**Donald Capps**

"The betrayal of the black pulpit in America is King's legacy."
—**Geoffrey Thomas,** *Banner of Truth***, England**

"Three hundred educators concluding a three-day 'mini-summit' here today are pushing to have materials related to the Rev. Martin Luther King Jr. included in the curriculum of the nation's schools."
—**Washington Times.**

"...King is the greatest American of this century."
—**Sun Myung Moon**

"And, recall, there were liberals a 'plenty in Washington who snickered at the tapes when they were played behind closed doors-vile and scabrous material gathered on the orders of a liberal Attorney General and distributed by liberal President Lyndon Johnson. 'G-damn it,' David Garrow quotes L.B.J., 'if only you could hear what that hypocritical preacher does sexually.'"
—*Christian News*

"Let steps be now taken to repeal the act of Congress authorizing the Federal holiday."
—**Carl McIntire, President of the International Council of Churches**

"FBI records back up the Rev. Ralph David Abernathy's newly published claims that Dr. Martin Luther King Jr. had extramarital affairs, including liaisons the week he was slain, says a former U.S. attorney who had access to the files."
—*Huntsville Times*

"One of the hoaxes that CN *has repeatedly exposed is the hoax that prominent churchmen who live in adultery, such as Paul Tillich, Martin Luther King and Karl Barth were great **Christian** leaders. The 'new morality' defended by liberal churchmen allows for the adultery of such great church leaders as King, Tillich and Barth. God tells us that unrepentant adulterers go to hell."*
—**Editor,** *Christian News*

"What kind of message is the Lutheran Witness *and all the other denominational publications praising King sending to America's youth, particularly black youth, when they praise King and refuse to condemn his well known disgusting adulterous life style? This is the message: 'Extra-marital and premarital sex is O.K. boys and girls.'"*
—*Christian News*

"The U.S. does not need a special day for a Marxist adulterer. Let's have a Booker T. Washington Day rather than a Martin Luther King Jr. Day."
—*Christian News*

"Why is a man once reviled by the Right now celebrated by it as a hero? The answer partly lies in the fact that the mainstream Right has gradually moved to the left since King's death."
—**Marcus Epstein**

"I for one am thankful for Martin Luther King's work and I would echo and affirm these comments by Dr. Alfred Mohler."
—**Paul McCain of CPH**

"Once again CN *says: 'Down with all racism. Defend the oppressed and persecuted. Celebrate a Booker T. Washington Day and not a Martin Luther King Day.'"*
—*Christian News*

"He disclosed to her (his wife Coretta) the one mistress who meant most to him since 1963 – with intensity almost like a second family even though she lived in Los Angeles – a married alumna of Fisk, of dignified bearing like Coretta, but different."
—*Time*

"For example, he doubted the truth of the literal bodily resurrection of Jesus. He recalled growing increasingly 'skeptical of Sunday-school Christianity' and was embarrassed by the 'unbridled emotionalism' in his father's church."
—**Rufus Burrow Jr.,** *Martin Luther King Jr. For Armchair Theologians.*

Read this book to find out who is the real Dietrich Bonhoeffer and Martin Luther King

TABLE OF CONTENTS

PREFACE	1
The Theology of Dietrich Bonhoeffer	4
'New Reformer' Ousts Dr. Luther at Rally	6
Bonhoeffer's Influence	9
A Review and Analysis of the LCA Sunday Church School Series BONHOEFFER	10
Still Adolescent?	11
The Great Debate Today	13
Van Til's Analysis of Bonhoeffer's Theology	14
Dietrich Bonhoeffer and Jimmy Carter	14
Bonhoeffer and the Council on Biblical Inerrancy	15
Dietrich Bonhoeffer (1906-1945) The BDM Letter Of Biblical Discernment Ministries	21
An Evaluation of Dietrich Bonhoeffer's Life and Theology after Half of a Century	23
Wer Ist Bonhoeffer?	33
Dietrich Bonhoeffer, Fundamental Baptist News Service	36
The Man Behind the Bonhoeffer Legend	37
AAL Helps Create Film on Bonhoeffer	40
The Theology of Dietrich Bonhoeffer	41
Bonhoeffer-Agent of Grace	44
Dietrich Bonhoeffer Rejected Classical Christology	46
Oesch and Burgdorf-Not Bonhoeffer	49
LCMS's CPH Publish Book Praising Bonhoeffer as A Great Christian	50
"Draws One Closer to The One True Faith"	53
Bonhoeffer: "The Most Influential Theologian Of The Twentieth Century"	55
Sixty Years Later, Bonhoeffer a Christian Hero To Both Left and Right	57
The Lutheran Witness Did Not Publish This Letter on Bonhoeffer	62
The Most Widely Admired and Respected Theologian In America	63
Not the Christ of the Bible	68
Dietrich Bonhoeffer (Review Article by CorneliusVan Til) Westminister Theological Journal	71
Refusing to Read Evidence	86
Theological Hero #1	87

Teilhard de Chardin and Dietrich Bonhoeffer	88
Bonhoeffer: "A Man of the Word of God"	90
A Call for Evidence on Bonhoeffer	94
Bonhoeffer – Pastor-Martyr-Prophet, Spy	97
The Growing Bonhoeffer Myth	104
Claim Bonhoeffer Was An Orthodox Christian	107
Bonhoeffer and King	112
Surburg, Maier, Bonhoeffer, and the Holocaust	114
Bonhoeffer: Denied Resurrection of Christ	118
Bonhoeffer Denied the Resurrection and Deity of Jesus Christ	121
Scripture and Myth in Dietrich Bonhoeffer	128
Saffen's Bonhoeffer House	140
Bonhoeffer, Thielicke and Ebeling Repudiated Historic Christianity	142

MARTIN LUTHER KING JR.   145

There is Reason to Thank God for the Like of Martin Luther King	146
The Theology of Martin Luther King	147
Religious Socialism	150
King's Christian Ethics	153
It's Very Simple	154
The Southern Conference Educational Fund	155
Color-Communism-And Common Sense	157
Wave of Rioting Hits U.S. Cities Schiotz Urges Lutherans to Back King	158
Black and Conservative	162
King and the WCC	164
Reverend Martin Luther King	165
King and The King of Kings	166
House Divided-The Life and Legacy Of Martin Luther King	168
Ministerial Students and Their Role in Community	171
King and Fosdick	174
Saint King-Martyr of the Church	176
The Inspired Community: A Glance at Canon History	178
A Response to Black Theology	178
The FBI and Martin Luther King Jr.	180
Americans, Stop Thinking Like Communists	183
Folk Singer Seeger and Wife Win Reconciliation	186

A Marxist Is No Saint	188
Black Church Leaders Told They Fail to Teach Gospel	189
The Double Standard of the Liberals	192
The Faith Pilgrimage of Martin Luther King, Jr.	197
Bearing the Cross: Martin Luther King, Jr. and the Southern Christian Leadership Conference	204
Rescind the Martin Luther King, Jr. Federal Holiday	211
Can Unrepentant Adulterers Get to Heaven?	215
Better Late Than Never	217
King "Preaches" at Valparaiso University	222
Catholic Bishops Want Vatican to Name King a Martyr	224
Says King Was a Communist Traitor	225
Will LCMS Give $250,000 For Martin Luther King National Memorial?	226
Myths of Martin Luther King	228
An International Church	232
READ-READ-READ	233
ELCA Published Book Defending Cone's Black Theology	234
A Booker T. Washington Day Rather Than Martin Luther King Jr. Day	239
A Booker T. Washington and George Washington Carver Day	241
Response To McCain's "Happy Martin Luther King Day"	247
APPENDIX	251

Christian News Challenges the Concordia University System and All Christian Youth – Work for A 21st Century Reformation

FIGHT FOR THE FAITH

By Herman Otten, Pastor
Trinity Lutheran Church
Editor, *Christian News* and *An American Translation of the Bible*
Concordia University, Wisconsin, February 3, 2011

Preface

Dietrich Bonhoeffer and Martin Luther King Jr. may be the two most highly regarded "churchmen, martyrs and Christian saints" of modern times. A press release from the Lutheran Church-Missouri Synod's Concordia Seminary, St. Louis said that Bonhoeffer was perhaps the greatest Lutheran theologian since Martin Luther. Concordia Theological Seminary, Ft. Wayne had similar praise for Bonhoeffer. Seminaries throughout the nation are teaching America's future pastors that Bonhoeffer and King are great Christian Saints, follow their theology and example!

When this editor attended Concordia Seminary, St. Louis, during the 1950s neither liberal nor conservative professors said much about Bonhoeffer. *The Lutheran Cyclopedia* published by the LCMS's Concordia Publishing House in 1950 said nothing about Bonhoeffer. The *Index to Concordia Theological Monthly 1930-1959* has no listing for Bonhoeffer. The Bonhoeffer myth has grown with the story of the six million Jews exterminated by the Germans during World War II which neither Winston Churchill nor Dwight Eisenhower mention in their voluminous writings about World War II.

Bonhoeffer and King Their Legacies and Import for Christian Social Thought published in 2010 by the Evangelical Lutheran Church in America's Fortress Press includes portraits of King and Bonhoeffer with the title: "King and Bonhoeffer as Protestant Saints." They are referred to as among "the most prominent and influential Christian Saints of the twentieth century" (21). This book from a Lutheran publisher says that "Both Bonhoeffer and King were committed to following the way of the incarnate Jesus – and followed him to death" (204). "Both Bonhoeffer and King were murdered in April of the year when they had reached age thirty-nine, depriving us of the leadership we so badly needed for healing our shame, and for recovery from authoritarianism and domination" (pp. 204-205).

The editor of *Christian News* is basing his views of Bonhoeffer and King on their own writings and actions and on what many others have written about them. He never spoke with Bonhoeffer or King. His home church in New York City was close to Union Seminary where Bonhoeffer studied. However, Bonhoeffer never attended this church or any other confessional Lutheran Church in New York. The *National Observer* published "The Theology of Martin Luther King" in 1964. The editor wrote to King and his Southern Christian leadership conference to find out if King had been misrepresented by this newsweekly sister journal of the *Wall Street Journal* when it reported that King did not affirm such Christian doctrines as the virgin birth and resurrection of Christ. The *National Observer* told *Christian News* that neither King nor his Southern Christian Leadership Conference registered any complaint about the article.

This book includes some of the hundreds of articles which appeared in *Christian News* from 1963 to 2010 about Bonhoeffer and King. Some are from those who highly praised both Bonhoeffer and King as great Christians and others by those who contend that both Bonhoeffer and King repudiated the historic Christian faith and denied such Christian doctrines as the virgin birth, deity and resurrection of Christ. Readers can judge for themselves who is telling the truth about Bonhoeffer and King.

Through the years *Christian News* has repeatedly invited those who defend Bonhoeffer and King as great Christians to respond to articles by such Christian scholars as Raymond Surburg, Cornelius Van Til and Richard Weikart who showed that Bonhoeffer in his own writings rejected the resurrection of Jesus Christ and other doctrines. The articles on Bonhoeffer's theology in this book by Surburg, Van Til, and Weikart were never refuted by any Bonhoeffer defender. No King fan has ever shown where *Christian News* misrepresented King's theology. *CN* has repeatedly found that those who defend the theology of Bonhoeffer and King refuse to read what *CN* has reported about Bonhoeffer and King.

The editor has been accused of being a racist and anti-Semite because he has long taken sharp issue with the anti-Christian theology of Bonhoeffer and King. Ever since his youth growing up in New York City and working in Harlem, the editor has opposed racism of all kinds. Blacks in Harlem loved "Painter Herman," the editor's father.

LCMS Bureaucrats at the 2010 LCMS convention banned an overture from the editor's congregation calling for a firm Christian stand against all kinds of racism. The organized conservatives who want *CN* to cease registered no complaint. *CN* has noted that theological liberals and skeptics are the real anti-Semites because they undermine faith in the God of the Old Testament, the book of the Jews. Bonhoeffer and King were among those who insisted that both the Old and New Testament were books filled with myths, Moses did not write the Old Testament and it is not God's directly revealed and inerrant Word.

Rather than teaching their students to regard Bonhoeffer as perhaps the greatest Lutheran after Luther, a man of the Word of God and the most influential Lutheran since Martin Luther, the professors who shun *Christian News* should be urging their students to read the editor's *Baal or God* published in 1965. It cites real scholars, including Jews, who repudiated the J-E-D-P source hypothesis as fiction. *Baal or God* defended the historicity of both the Old and New Testament which Bonhoeffer and King, along with Rudolph Bultmann, rejected. The great LCMS Bonhoeffer and King praising scholars should be telling their students to read *Who Really Wrote the Bible? And Why It Should Be Taken Seriously Again* by Eyal Rav-Noy and Gil Weinreich.

Eyal Rav-Noy, a native of Israel, is director of the Jewish Learning Academy, where he specializes in textual analysis and biblical criticism. He shows that skeptics like Bonhoeffer who rejected the Mosaic authorship of the first five books of the Bible are guilty of "intellectual laziness."

How dare a mere country pastor like the editor of *Christian News* challenge the great scholars in all of the major denominations, including the Roman Catholic Church and Orthodox Church, who accept the prevailing view about Bonhoeffer and King? Jewish scholars Eyal Rav-Noy and Gil Weinreich write in *Who Really Wrote The Bible?*:

"We argue that most contemporary biblical criticism is a fraud, an exercise in futility, and a model of lemming-like conformity. On balance, the academic study of the Bible has not contributed to a better understanding of the text. Rather, the field seems to be devoted to the circular task of proving itself correct" (27).

"Despite this rather pompous dismissal of any dissent, it is the academic critics of the single authorship of the Bible who are short on objective evidence, and it is the documentary hypothesis that is unscholarly and cannot withstand logical scrutiny" (24).

This book maintains that the best evidence clearly shows that both Bonhoeffer and King repudiated the resurrection of Christ and the historic Christian faith regardless of the prevailing opinion among the great scholars. One chapter in *Who Really wrote the Bible?* is titled "Intellectual Laziness" and another "Creation, Plagues and a Talking Donkey: The Bible Critics Make Asses of Themselves." The same could be said about the great Bonhoeffer and King champions who refuse to read the kind of evidence arrayed in this book. The book exposes the intellectual laziness of the Bonhoeffer and King defenders in the Lutheran Church-Missouri Synod who refuse to read *Christian News* even though it was sent to their church. The subtitle of the book is "A Fifty Year Battle vs. Intellectual Laziness."

LCMS professors are members of LCMS congregations receiving *CN*. There is no excuse for any real scholar in the LCMS to say that he never saw any evidence that Bonhoeffer and King rejected the historic Christian faith. Articles in *CN* referring to Bonhoeffer and King cover almost 50 years. This explains frequent use of various quotations. Some of what *CN* has published about King and Bonhoeffer was repeated several times.

This book on Bonhoeffer and King not only shows that their theology is not Christian but also exposes the lack of true scholarship of professors, church bureaucrats, and others who insist that the theology of Bonhoeffer and King was Christian and that Bonhoeffer was the greatest Lutheran since Martin Luther.

The Appendix, pp. 251-296, "Christian News Challenges the Concordia University System and All Christian Youth - Work for a 21st Century Reformation - FIGHT FOR THE FAITH" was prepared for presentation at Concordia University, Wisconsin on Febrary 3, 2011. It calls for the highest standards of Christian scholarship which include examining the evidence about the theology of Dietrich Bonhoeffer and Martin Luther King. The evidence is in this book.

Fortress Press has announced it will publish *Power, Politics and the Missouri Synod-A Conflict that Changed American Christianity* by Dr. James Burkee, with a foreward by Dr. Martin Marty on February 1, two days before the editor of *Christian News* will present the essay in the Appendix. Dr. Burkee is chair of the faculty of Concordia University, Wisconsin. The Fortress book mentions accusations of racism, anti-semitism and kookishness made against the editor of *Christian News*. The Fortress book also reports that the editor of *Christian News* filed charges of false doctrine vs. Dr. Marty and includes some quotations from Marty's writings included in *Christian News*. The reader can judge for himself if the editor of *Christian News* is a racist because of what he has said about Dr. Martin Luther King, if he has misrepresented Dr. Marty, is anti-semitic and embodies kookishness. Power, Politics, and the Missouri Synod by Dr. James is available from *Christian News*. Defenders of Martin Luther King and Dietrich Bonhoeffer are invited to show where *Christian News* has misrepresented King and Bonhoeffer. *CN* will publish their response and include it in any reprinting of *Bonhoeffer and King-Their Life and Theology In Christian News 1963-2011*.

The Theology of Dietrich Bonhoeffer
(Editorial)
November 15, 1965

LUTHERAN NEWS has received a number of inquiries concerning the theology of Dietrich Bonhoeffer. Lutheran pastors and laymen in Michigan have expressed concern that, instead of the usual worship in observance of Reformation Day, Missouri Synod Lutherans in Detroit sponsored a play based on the life of Dietrich Bonhoeffer. While some Lutherans have endorsed Bonhoeffer's theology, it should be noted that THE ORDER OF SERVICE FOR REFORMATION 1965, distributed at the Detroit Reformation Festival, said: "The full theology expressed by Bonhoeffer is not necessarily endorsed by Concordia College or The Chapel Players or The Lutheran Center Association."

Although Bonhoeffer did use orthodox terminology at times, particularly in his earlier works, the views he expressed just prior to his death in 1945 are certainly not in harmony with historic Christianity. The quotations listed below are taken from Bonhoeffer's LETTERS AND PAPERS FROM PRISON, Fontana Books, S.C.M. Press, Great Britain, 1953. We suggest interested readers study this volume for themselves.

Bonhoeffer Wrote

"Kierkegaard said more than a century ago that if Luther were alive then he would have said the exact opposite of what he said in the sixteenth century. I believe he was right-CUM GRANO SALIS" (pp. 31-32).

No Religion of Salvation

"To resume our reflections on the Old Testament. Unlike the other oriental religions, the faith of the Old Testament is not a religion of salvation. Christianity, it is true, has always been regarded as a religion of salvation. But isn't this a cardinal error, which divorces Christ from the Old Testament and interprets him in the light of the myths of salvation? Of course it could be argued that under Egyptian and later, Babylonian influence, the idea of salvation became just as prominent in the Old Testament--e.g. Deutero-Isaiah. The answer is the Old Testament speaks of HISTORICAL redemption, i.e. redemption on this side of death, whereas the myths of salvation are concerned to offer men deliverance from death. Israel is redeemed out of Egypt in order to live before God on earth. The salvation myths deny history in the interests of an eternity after death. Sheol and Hades are not metaphysical theories, but images which imply that the past, while it still exists, has only a shadowy existence in the present. It is said that the distinctive feature of Christianity is its proclamation of the resurrection hope, and that this means the establishment of a genuine religion of salvation, in the sense of release from this world. The emphasis falls upon the far side of the boundary drawn by death. But this seems to me to be just the mistake and the danger. Salvation means salvation from cares and need, from fears and longing, from sin and death into a better world beyond the grave. But is this really the distinctive feature of Christianity as proclaimed in the Gospels and St. Paul? I am sure it is not. The difference between the Christian hope of resurrection and a mythological hope is that the Christian hope sends a man back to his life on earth in a wholly new way which is even more sharply defined than it is in the Old Testament.

"The Christian, unlike the devotees of the salvation myths, does not need a last refuge in the eternal from earthly tasks and difficulties" (p. 112).

Resurrection Mythology

Concerning the "mythological" elements of Christianity, Bonhoeffer wrote: "I am of the view that the full content, including mythological concepts, must be maintained. The New Testament is not a mythological gambling of the universal truth, this mythology (resurrection and so on) is the thing itself-but the concepts must be interpreted in such a way as not to make religion a pre-condition of faith (cf. circumcision in St. Paul)(p. 110).

"A bit more about 'religionlessness.' I expect you remember Bultmann's paper on the demythologizing of the New Testament? My view of it today would be not that he went too far, as most people seem to think, but that he did not go far enough. It is not only the mythological conceptions, such as miracles, the ascension and the like (which are not in principle separate from the conceptions of God, faith and so on) that are problematic, but the 'religious' conceptions themselves" (p. 94).

"The thing that keeps coming back to me is, what IS Christianity, and indeed what IS Christ, for us today? The time when men could be told everything by means of words whether theological or simply pious, is over, and so is the time of religion as such. We are proceeding towards a time of no religion at all: men as they are now simply cannot be religious any more" (p. 91).

Getting Along Without God

"God is teaching us that we must live as men who can get along very well without him. The God who is with us is the God who forsakes us (Mark 15:34)" (p. 122).

God Superfluous

"Belief in the Resurrection is not the solution of the problem of death" (p. 93).

"I should like to write a book not more than 1200 pages long, and with three chapters . . Chapter 1 to deal with: . . .

"(b) the decay of religion in a world that has come of age. 'God' as a working hypothesis, as a stop-gap for our embarrassments, now superfluous (as already intimated)."

"CHAPTER 2

"(a) 'Worldliness' and God.

"(b) What do we mean by 'God'?

"Not in the first place an abstract belief in his omnipotence, etc. That is not a genuine experience of God, but a partial extension of the world. . . Our relation to God not a religious relationship to a supreme Being, absolute in power and goodness, which is a spurious conception of transcendence, but a new life for others, through participation in the Being of God. ..

"c) This as the starting point for the reinterpretation of biblical terminology. (Creation, fall, atonement, repentance, faith, the new life, the last things.)" (pp. 163-165).

In his book CREATION AND FALL, Bonhoeffer says that the book of Genesis presents " . . . the ancient world picture in all its scientific naiveté." He says the book of Genesis contains myths.

Missouri Synod Lutherans are defending Bonhoeffer's theology because Bonhoeffer had something to say about Christian living in this world. We haven't found anything good in Bonhoeffer's works that hasn't been said by orthodox Christian theologians before him. Such theologians as Luther, Gerhard, Chemnitz, Pieper, and Walther, not only emphasized sound Christian living but also affirmed their faith in Christ's physical resurrection and the great doctrines of the Christian faith. It seems to us that a drama based on the life of a Christian theologian would be far more fitting for a Reformation Festival than a drama based on the life of a modern skeptic, who rejected many of the truths of historic Christianity.

WORD OF MAN OF GOD?

From an undated clipping received from William F. Beck shortly after the publication of Bonhoeffer's *Creation and Fall*.

Creation and Fall – A Theological Interpretation of Genesis 1-3, by Dietrich Bonhoeffer (Macmillan, 1959, 96 pp., $1.50), is reviewed by Edward J. Young, Professor of Old Testament, Westminster Theological Seminary.

One peruses this work with a feeling of sadness. The author, we understand, lost his life at the hands of Hitler's henchman, Heinrich Himmler. We have in this book lectures delivered at the University of Berlin during the winter semester 1932-33.

The author's purpose is to give a theological interpretation of the first three chapters of Genesis. This is not to say that he gives a serious exposition of the words of Genesis. Far from it. They present ". .. the ancient world picture in all its scientific naiveté" (p. 26), for they are simply a myth ". . . just as irrelevant or meaningful as any other myth" (p. 44). "How else could we speak of the young earth except in the language of fairy tales?" (p. 47).

The author does concede that the language of Genesis has a capacity as the Word of God (p. 44). But, we ask, if the words of Genesis 1-3 are the language of myth and fairy tales, what conceivable warrant is there for saying that they also have a capacity as the Word of God? Do the Grecian myths have a capacity as the Word of God? Do the fables of Aesop? *Alice in Wonderland*? It is about time for some adherent of irrationalism to explain why the "erroneous," "human" words of the Bible have anything to do with the Word of God. And we should like the answer couched in straightforward language, not in the "it is, yet it isn't" type of explanation,. . .

'New Reformer' Ousts Dr. Luther at Rally
Lutheran News, November 15, 1965
Faulstick says Michigan Lutherans should not feature a theological liberal at Reformation Festival.

Photographed from the October 30, 1965, DETROIT FREE PRESS.

You run into the name Dietrich Bonhoeffer everywhere.

And Sunday there'll be proof of his popularity at the annual Missouri-Synod Lutheran Reformation Festival at Ford Auditorium.

There's going to be a drama this year. And the hero is not Martin Luther, but 20th Century Dietrich Bonhoeffer.

Bonhoeffer, martyred by the Nazis, 20 years ago, preaches to Protestant and Catholic alike from beyond the grave. As Luther stirred up Christianity with his ideas for reform beginning with his 95 points of debate in Wittenberg, Oct. 31, 1517, so Bonhoeffer is stirring up Catholic and Protestant thought today.

The National Catholic Reporter and *Commonweal*, Catholic publications, recently featured Bonhoeffer. The Vatican council's schema, Church in the Modern World, reflects some of Bonhoeffer's concern that the church must come to grips with specific modern problems.

Bonhoeffer is claimed by "saints" and "sinners" alike. The current "death of God" theologians, who say you can't talk of a God out there any more or even use His name for it is meaningless, hail Bonhoeffer, just as much as the Sunday school teacher who expounds on his life of sacrifice and "costly" faith versus "cheap" easy faith.

Controversial Anglican Bishop John Robinson looked to Bonhoeffer for his inspiration to help change the language of the church.

Why Bonhoeffer?

Bonhoeffer is the apostle of "religionless" Christianity.

Why, then, in the "Cup of Trembling", a play by a Californian Presbyterian, in the Lutheran Reformation rally at 3 p.m. Sunday will Bonhoeffer be the hero?

Detroit Missouri Synod Lutheran pastors were asked what they thought of this replacing of the historic reformer by the modern controversial theologian.

Some of the older Lutheran clergy were less enthusiastic about the drama, but support it. "Times are changing," said one Detroit Missouri Synod pastor. Another: "I'm more concerned about the use of drama, than about Bonhoeffer," said one about Bonhoeffer: "I'm, not really up with it, but I go along with the committee."

Younger Men Speak

It was left to the younger clergy to explain the presence of Bonhoeffer in Sunday's rally.

Said Professor Robert Lehmann, of Concordia College, Ann Arbor, who's directing the drama: "Bonhoeffer has something to say about Christian living. . . One has to be able to come to grips with his conscience."

Bonhoeffer, who said the church doesn't always have to be right, but ought always be specific and outspoken on all issues, was hanged at Flossenburg, Germany, on April 9, 1945, a few days before the town was liberated.

The drama Sunday opens with a noose hanging symbolically on the Ford Auditorium stage, as the drama moves into a flashback of Bonhoeffer's life as a scholar who studied and taught on both sides of the Atlantic, but whose conscience made him return to his native but hostile Germany.

"He wants Christianity to be Christianity and evangelistic, not self contained," said Lehmann.

"He propelled the church into social areas and would do so today into the area of civil rights and other areas. Luther took the church out of the cloister and put it where it belonged, with the people. So does Bonhoeffer."

No Pleasant Seminary

Said another younger pastor, the Rev. Edward Rauff, of St. John's Lutheran Church, 4950 Oakman, "even apart from his theology, which is sometimes questioned, Bonhoeffer's life is important. He did not choose to survive in some pleasant seminary, but was willing to die for his faith. This also tends to reflect his theology – he talks about the grace of God, but it is not a cheap grace."

Said Ronald Starenko, of Faith Lutheran, Livonia: "For Bonhoeffer, God is imminent. Worship of a God out there is subject to considerable question.

"Bonhoeffer's not in conflict at all with Luther, although he didn't grapple with the same question. "Luther was not only concerned with man's relation to God by faith but as much concerned about love and relation with one's fellow man.

"For Luther, too, God is not out there, but present in every act of love."

Playing the part of Bonhoeffer, who is called Erich Friedhoffer in the play, is Concordia ministerial student David Conrad, 19, of Alliance, O.

He will step out of his role once in a while to preach at a nearby lectern in the play. So there is something for everyone--preaching, for the older generation more accustomed to it, and drama, for the younger.

Michigan Congregation Leaves LCMS
Charges That Missouri Synod Tolerates Attacks on Bible - Officials Disagree - Defend Seminary Professors
Lutheran News, November 15, 1965

Wayland, Michigan, October 31 -- Trinity Lutheran Church voted here this evening by a better than two-thirds majority to sever all ties with The Lutheran Church-Missouri Synod after it heard officials of the Synod attempt to refute their pastor's charge that The Lutheran Church-Missouri Synod tolerates false doctrine...

The congregation also invited the editor of LUTHERAN NEWS to the meeting to appear before Missouri Synod officials and to defend the position taken by the paper that The Lutheran Church-Missouri Synod tolerates professors who teach doctrines contrary to historic Christianity. The editor attended the meeting and explained that he was not present to tell the congregation how to vote but to demonstrate that the Missouri Synod does tolerate false doctrine and to answer any charges officials might have concerning LUTHERAN NEWS. Pastor Faulstick has written a number of articles for LUTHERAN NEWS. When officials were asked if they knew of any errors published in LUTHERAN NEWS, they replied that they knew of none. Most of the pastors and teachers in the Missouri Synod receive LUTHERAN NEWS. Two of these officials present said they receive LUTHERAN NEWS.

Faulstick also read "'New Reformer' Ousts Dr. Luther at Rally" from the October 30, 1965, DETROIT FREE PRESS. (Reproduced on this page, ed.) The Wayland pastor said that Lutheran congregations in the Michigan District should not feature a drama at a Reformation Festival with Dietrich Bonhoeffer as the hero. He said that Bonhoeffer was a theological liberal and that such "outspoken liberals" as Anglican Bishop John Robinson derived much of their inspiration from Bonhoeffer. THE DETROIT FREE PRESS quoted Rev. Ronald Starenko of Livonia as saying: "For Bonhoeffer, God is imminent. Worship of a god out there is subject to considerable question." Faulstick still believes there is "a God out there." Bishop John Robinson, who writes that "any notion that God really exists 'out there' must be dismissed" (HONEST TO GOD, p. 31-32), claims to have received many of his thoughts from Paul Tillich, Rudolf Bultmann, and Dietrich Bonhoeffer.

Situation Ethics
Lutheran News, May 30, 1966

SITUATION ETHICS. By Joseph Fletcher. The Westminster Press, Philadelphia, 1966. 176 pages. $1.95

Joseph Fletcher is one of the foremost spokesmen for "The New Morality." While we have frequently taken issue with Fletcher and "The New Morality," we urge readers interested in "The New Morality" to secure a copy of SITUATION ETHICS....

He asserts: "With Dietrich Bonhoeffer we say, 'Principles are only tools in God's hands, soon to be thrown away as unserviceable.'" (28). According to Fletcher, "If a lie is told unlovingly it is wrong, evil; if it is told in love it is good, right" (65). Fletcher's constant theme is: "ONLY ONE THING IS INTRINSICALLY GOOD, NAMELY, LOVE; NOTHING ELSE AT ALL" (68).

Bonhoeffer's Influence
Lutheran News, June 27, 1966

"If asked to name the most influential work of modern Christian thought, older Protestant divines might point to Karl Barth's powerful commentary on THE EPISTLE TO THE ROMANS or Paul Tillich's SYSTEMATIC THEOLOGY. Younger ministers, on the other hand, would be far more likely to cite a book that is scarcely more than an elliptical fragment of theology, since it was never intended for publication at all. It is the LETTERS AND PAPERS FROM PRISON by Dietrich Bonhoeffer, the now famed German Lutheran pastor who was arrested and later executed by the Nazis."

"Bonhoeffer left no school of disciples, but he has nonetheless become the most frequently quoted theologian of his generation. For better or worse, his idea of a 'religionless Christianity' has been taken up by today's Death-of-God thinkers. His belief that the church must exist to serve the world is axiomatic to activist ministers. So persuasive is his influence that Lutheran Church Historian Martin Marty once suggested dividing the theological world into two groups: those who admit their debt to Bonhoeffer and those who borrow his ideas without acknowledgement" (TIME, May 27, 1966, p. 58-61).

(COMMENT: Here are a few quotations from Bonhoeffer's LETTERS AND PAPERS FROM PRISON: "To resume our reflections on the Old Testament. Unlike the other oriental religions the faith of the Old Testament is not a religion of salvation. Christianity, it is true, has always been regarded as a religion of salvation?" But isn't this a cardinal error, which divorces Christ from the Old Testament and interprets him in the light of the myths of salvation?" "The Christian, unlike the devotees of the salvation myths, does not need a last refuge in the eternal from earthly tasks and difficulties" (112). Concerning the "mythological" elements of Christianity, Bonhoeffer wrote: "I am of the view that the full content, including mythological concepts, must be maintained" (110). He refers to the resurrection as "mythology." "A bit more about 'religionlessness.' I expect you remember Bultmann's paper on the demythologizing of the New Testament, my view of it today would be not that he went too far, as most people think, but that he did not go far enough. It is not only the mythological conceptions, such as miracles, the ascension and the like (which are not in principle separated from the conceptions of God, faith and so on) that are problematic, but the 'religious' conceptions themselves" (94). "We are proceeding towards a time of no religion at all: men as they are now simply cannot be religious any more" (91). "God is teaching us that we must live as men who can get along very well without him. The God who is with us is the God who forsakes us (Mark 15:34)" (122). "Belief in the Resurrection is not the solution of the problem of death" (93). "I should like to write a book more than 100 pages long, and with three chapters . . . Chapter 1 to deal with:. . .

"(b) the decay of religion in a world that has come to age. 'God' as a working hypothesis, as a stop gap for our embarrassments, now superfluous (as already intimated)" (8). Bonhoeffer repudiated the Christian faith in his later writings. He has been widely hailed by Lutheran youth leaders who have featured him in ARENA and ONE. Orthodox Christians obviously do not fit into either of Marty's "two groups" mentioned in TIME. The "God is Dead" theologians rightly acknowledge their debt to Dietrich Bonhoeffer. Ed.

A Review and Analysis of the LCA Sunday Church School Series
BONHOEFFER
Lutheran News, September 19, 1966

A. LCA Curriculum

"An example of 'seed on good soil' may be seen in Dietrich Bonhoeffer. He was a young Lutheran pastor in Germany who was hanged by the Nazis at the close of World War II. He was a brilliant Christian thinker, but he did not live long enough to develop his thought in full detail. Yet his few books and letters from prison have been like seed. They influence many persons today who seek to explain the Christian faith for our times" (THE GOSPEL STORY OF JESUS, Teacher's Guide, p. 131).

"Dietrich Bonhoeffer has been called the most distinguished Christian martyr of the twentieth century. What makes his martyrdom outstanding is not the pain he had to suffer, but the fact that he accepted martyrdom as part of his discipleship" (IBID., p. 311).

"Bonhoeffer's friend, the Bishop of Chichester, summed up his life with these words, 'He saw the truth and spoke it with complete absence of fear.'" (AS ONE WHO SERVES, p. 48).

B. Bonhoeffer's Later Position

Bonhoeffer's last writings indicate that he completely repudiated historic Christianity. The quotations listed below are taken from his LETTERS AND PAPERS FROM PRISON, Fontana Books, S.C.M. Press, Great Britain, 1953. "Unlike the other oriental religions that faith of the Old Testament is not a religion of salvation. Christianity, it is true, has always been regarded as a religion of salvation. But isn't this a cardinal error, which divorces Christ from the Old Testament and interprets him in the light of the myths of salvation. Of course it could be argued that under Egyptian and later, Babylonian influence, the idea of salvation became just as prominent in the Old Testament - e.g. Deutero-Isaiah. The answer is, the Old Testament speaks of HISTORICAL redemption, i.e. redemption on this side of death, whereas the myths of salvation are concerned to offer man deliverance from death. . .

"The Christian, unlike the devotees of the salvation myths, does not need a last refuge in the eternal from earthly tasks and difficulties" (1120.

Concerning the "mythological" elements of Christianity, Bonhoeffer wrote: "I am of the view that the full content, including mythological concepts, must be maintained. The New Testament is not a mythological garbing of the universal truth, this mythology (resurrection and so on) is the thing itself-but the concepts must be interpreted in such a way as not to make religion a precondition of faith (cf. circumcision in St. Paul)

(110).

"A bit more about 'religionlessness." I expect you remember Bultmann's paper on the demythologizing of the New Testament. My view of it today would be not that he went too far, as most people seem to think, but that he did not go far enough. It is not only the mythological conceptions, such as miracles, the ascension and the like (which are not in principle different from the conceptions of God, faith and so on) that are problematic, but the 'religions' conceptions themselves" (94).

"God is teaching us that we must live as men who can get along very well without him. The God who is with us is the God who forsakes us (Mark 15:34)" (122). "Belief in the Resurrection is not the solution of the problem of death" (93). For views similar to the "God is Dead" theologians see pages 163-5.

Bonhoeffer denied such Christian doctrines as the virgin birth and resurrection of Christ. We doubt whether this religious skeptic should be referred to as a CHRISTIAN martyr and brilliant CHRISTIAN thinker.

Still Adolescent?
By Harold P. Kuhn
Christianity Today, May 17, 1967

Much that has been said in the recent past about man's "coming of age" has been inspired by the prison statements of Dietrich Bonhoeffer, popularized by Bishop Robinson in *Honest to God*. The most frequently quoted passages from Bonhoeffer's writings are excerpts from the series of *Briefen an einen Freund* (Letters to a Friend), especially those written between June 8 and July 16, 1944.

It is not surprising that Bonhoeffer's theological statements are woolly and contradictory, since he wrote from prison, with the Gestapo waiting to close in upon him; he realistically expected at any moment to hear the knock at his cell door from the seedy characters who would bid him accompany them – to the gallows. Yet these writings need to be studied for what they are and what they say, so that their truth or non-truth is judged from their intrinsic meaning, and not by the aura of the heroic that surrounds their author.

Like a refrain comes Bonhoeffer's reiteration of the theme of the *Mündigkeit der Welt und des Menschen* (the of-age-ness of the world and of man). He sees this as the end-result of a process that had its roots in the scientific movements of the fourteenth and fifteenth centuries and has continued steadily to the point at which man no longer needs God as a constitutive factor for his thinking, whether moral, political, or scientific (see letter for July 16, 1944, in Richard Grunow, ed., *Bonhoeffer Auswahl*, p. 589).

Bonhoeffer notes that man has, step by step, conquered his environment, until there is allegedly no room for God, as historically understood, in the framing or articulation of the culture modern man has created. Bonhoeffer assures us *(ibid*., p. 577) that man has learned to manage or at least to cope with all the important factors and elements that confront him without recourse to God as a working hypothesis. Man simply must learn to get along without God.

Perhaps this will suffice for the present as a statement of Bonhoeffer's thesis, if we add that at the end of his letter of July 16, 1944, he speaks of God as powerlessly permitting himself to be crowded out of the world and onto the cross. This view has quite evident affinity with the "radical theology" of Thomas Altizer.

The theme of man's coming of age is a tempting one that derives a degree of plausibility from the immense strides science has made in conquering nature. Man stands at the threshold of the conquest of space: lunar exploration today, interplanetary travel later. The question remains, however: Does this capability imply as much as modern man thinks it does?

As one considers man's coming of age, one troublesome facet of experience presents itself. Perhaps never again does a person feel so grown-up and so capable of managing his own affairs as he felt at the onset of adolescence. This period in life, so easily forgotten by adults, has as one of its signs a false and foolish sense of autonomy and self-sufficiency. Thus, to understand the present status of the race, as it imagines itself to be "of age," he may well recall some of the traits of mind that accompany the puberty crisis....

We Can't Save Ourselves
By George C. Reese
The Lutheran, December 4, 1968

Genuine Christian living is not claimed, but shared. The church exists primarily to serve others. A martyred German pastor sparked this trend in current religious thought.

There is a reformation of the churches in our time. The new reformation is the church's reaction to the present-day world. It is a reaction in large part to the findings of modern science and the self-reliance of modern culture. The church, therefore, is trying to speak and act in ways appropriate to the present setting.

Among the earliest voices of the new reformation, none was more effective or more influential than the voice of Dietrich Bonhoeffer, a German Lutheran pastor who was executed in one of Hitler's prisons. He reinterpreted the Christian Gospel in words both sharp and clear. His theology was developed in the crucible of a dramatic personal and political experience....

The old gospel in new clothing
is not always easy to accept.
But no one can deny that we are
Seeing a reformation in our day.

SERVICE AT UNION MARKS THE LIFE OF BONHOEFFER
By Religious News Service
April 9, 1970

New York (RNS) - Union Theological Seminary faculty and students joined here in paying tribute to a former member of their community who by leaving the safety of the school went to martyrdom under Hitler.

In a service of worship, they thanked God for Dietrich Bonhoeffer, hanged by the

Nazis at Flossenburg on April 9, 1945. He was a major shaper of contemporary theology. . . .

Because of his courage, his emphasis on concerns of the world and his jovial disposition, Bonhoeffer is a favorite among seminary students today.

Dr. Mottu said Bonhoeffer is a theologian "we need today." He warned against an "infantile temptation" to identify too completely with him. "We have a lot of things to think and do" to catch up with the Lutheran professor, said Dr. Mottu.

He said that Bonhoeffer was never really understood. "He was considered a fanatic during his activity with the Confessing Church (beginning In 1935), a traitor when he was involved in the plot against Hitler, and an atheist when 'Letters and Papers from Prison' appeared."

The book mentioned contained the last part of Bonhoeffer's theological writing and in it is found the phrase "religion less Christianity" which is seen as a forerunner of modern secular themes in the church. His influence has been greatest in the U.S., England, and Eastern Europe.

THE GREAT DEBATE TODAY
Lutheran News, June 7, 1971

The Great Debate Today. By Cornelius Van Til. Nutley, New Jersey, Presbyterian and Reformed Publishing Co. 07110, 1970. 239 pages. $4.50.

Van Til, a leading Orthodox Presbyterian theologian, here shows the radical difference between the Christ of some prominent modern theologians and the Christ of Scripture. . .

Van Til is equally critical of Dietrich Bonhoeffer. He contends that the Christ of Bonhoeffer is not the Christ of Scripture and can hardly be distinguished from the Christ of Karl Barth (42-47). Van Til says: "The ecumenical significance of all this is far-reaching. Bonhoeffer was quite consistent with his own theology and with that of the post-Kantian, neo-Protestant tradition when he did his best to further the cause of modern ecumenism. Why should not Lutherans, Calvinists, and Armenians unite under the banner of the new primacy of a new Christ-projection? Surely all of us want to make the message of the saving grace of God relevant to the needs of modern man. So we must all demythologize and then re-mythologize or allegorize, not only the Genesis narrative, but the New Testament as well. After that we must give an existential interpretation of its message in terms of the ideal man, calling him Christ, and interpreting all reality in terms of him as its center.

"While neo-orthodox Protestant theology is thus developing its Kantian Christ-mythology, there is something very similar to this going on in Roman Catholic circles" (47-48). . . .

We recommend this book particularly for evangelical pastors and professors who maintain that such theologians as Barth, Bonhoeffer, Pannenberg, Cullmann, Moltmann, Kierkegaard, and Kueng at least affirm the fundamental doctrines of historic Christianity. While we do not agree with Van Til's strict Calvinism, we know of few theologians who possess a better insight into modern theology than Cornelius Van Til.

VAN TIL'S ANALYSIS OF BONHOEFFER'S THEOLOGY
One of the Best
Christian News, **September 11, 1972**

". . . the Christ of Bonhoeffer is not the Christ of the Scriptures, is not the Christ of the Reformers. . ." says Dr. Cornelius Van Til in THE WESTMINSTER THEOLOGICAL JOURNAL, May, 1972.

Van Til writes in a review article on Bonhoeffer: "The Christ of Bonhoeffer, in contrast to the Christ of Calvin, is constructed in terms of post-Kantian philosophy and theology. This is factually incontrovertible. The consequence of this fact implies a reinterpretation, and UMDEUTUNG, of every word of the vocabulary of biblical and confessional teaching. However much evangelical--and notably, Reformed--Christians may wish to incorporate Bonhoeffer in the list of their heroes of the faith, together with Calvin, Kuyper, Bavinck, Hodge, Warfield, and Vos, they have no right to do so. Bonhoeffer must be placed in the line of Kant, of Schleiermacher, of Ritschl, and of Barth. It is the theological descendants of such men as these who rightfully claim Bonhoeffer as their own.

"Modern, neo-orthodox theologians know that the two Christs, the Christ of Luther and Calvin and the Christ of Bonhoeffer stand mutually opposed to one another."

Van Til documents his article with quotations from the writings of Bonhoeffer to show that Bonhoeffer's Christ is not the Christ of the Bible. Bonhoeffer has been highly praised by such Lutheran liberals as Martin Marty and in parts of the Lutheran Church-Missouri Synod's Mission: Life curriculum. THE WESTMINSTER THEOLOGICAL JOURNAL is published by Westminster Theological Seminary, Chestnut Hill, Philadelphia, Pennsylvania 19118, $7.50 per year, $2.50 a copy. Van Til's analysis of Bonhoeffer's theology is one of the most perceptive we have seen.

DIETRICH BONHOEFFER AND JIMMY CARTER
Blu-Print, March 29, 1977

During the 1976 election campaign candidate Jimmy Carter testified that his four favorite theologians were: Reinhold Niebuhr, Karl Barth, Paul Tillich and Dietrich Bonhoeffer. Not one of these four men holds to the Christian faith which is confessed by Jimmy Carter's Southern Baptists in their famous 1925 confession of faith. In fact, all four vehemently reject the Christian Faith. A couple in New York, upon hearing of the honor Jimmy Carter placed on Bonhoeffer, decided to secure several books by this theologian in Germany. The first thing they discovered is that he didn't die for the Christian faith, but rather for participating in one of the plots to assassinate Hitler.

They found in his book "Creation and Fall" that he held that both were myths and fairy tales. In his book "No Rusty Swords" they found on page 318: "the New Testament bears witness in both doctrine and history, it is nothing in itself but bears witness of something less. . . Its words and statements are not in themselves true and eternal and holy. The whole New Testament in all its parts is meant to be expounded as witness, not as a book of wisdom, a teaching book, a book of eternal truth." On page 317, he wrote "The New Testament is not a book which contains eternal truths, doctrines, norms."

In a letter written on July 16, 1944, Bonhoeffer wrote: "There is no longer any need for God as a working hypothesis, whether in morals, politics, or science. Nor is there any need for such a God in religion or philosophy. In the name of intellectual honesty these working hypotheses should be dropped or dispensed with as far as possible. The only way is that of Matthew 18:3, i.e. through repentance, through ultimate honesty. And the only way to be honest is to recognize that we have to live in the world. And this is just what we do see—before God. So, our coming of age forces us to a true recognition of our situation vis a vis God. God is teaching us that we must learn to live as men who can get along very well without him. The God who is with us is the God who forsakes us (Mark 15:34). The God who makes us live in this world without using him as a working hypothesis is the God before whom we are ever standing." Before God he states that the New Testament never identified Jesus as God (p. 50); he fails to affirm the bodily resurrection of Christ (p. 108) he equates the Holy Spirit with the Risen Christ (p. 109); and he declares that 'the miracles were often not so much stories of what Jesus once did, but symbols of what he still can do' (p. 450)." We are amazed at the appalling ignorance of one who claims to be a N.T. scholar. For starters he might read: John 1:1; Heb. 1:8; Romans 9:5; Titus 2:13; John 20:28

Bonhoeffer And the Council on Biblical Inerrancy

13530 Fonseca Ave.
La Mirada, CA 90638
July 29, 1982
Editor, *Christian News*
Sir:

The Spring, 1982, issue of Update, a periodical of the International Council on Biblical Inerrancy reported that the San Diego Conference of the Bible was attended by more than 2500 pastors and laymen who gathered "to affirm their faith in an inerrant Bible" and we are told that "the roster of speakers and seminar leaders read like a 'Who's Who' of evangelical figures prominently identified with what has become popularly known as the 'battle' for the view that the Bible is true and authoritative on every matter about which it speaks."

Prominently displayed on the second page is a quotation from Dietrich Bonhoeffer. This is most inappropriate for a report on such a conference and in a publication of an organization with its declared objective. Making an inquiry, we are informed that to date, nearly five months after the conference, not a single person receiving the periodical, the noted speakers, the sixteen members of the Council, or the fifty persons on the Advisory Board offered an objection.

The quotation from Bonhoeffer sounded good. Certainly a good sounding quotation by a man widely recognized as evil would not be used in a Christian publication. Yet here is displayed favorably a quote by a theologian who viciously attacks the Bible and the Christian faith.

Here are some quotations which reveal the real and mature thinking of the man. They are from the 1967 edition of his *Letters and Papers From Prison*, Macmillan, edited by his friend Eberhard Bethge. He was in prison and was executed by the Nazis because he was involved in two conspiracies to assassinate Adolf Hitler.

"God is being increasingly pushed out of a world that has come of age, out of the spheres of our knowledge and life, and . . . Since Kant has been relegated to a realm beyond the world of experience. Theology has on the one hand resisted this development with apologetics, and has taken up arms — in vain — against Darwinism, etc." page 341.

"God as a working hypothesis in morals, politics, or science, has been surmounted and abolished; and the same thing has happened in philosophy and religion for the sake of the intellectual honesty, that working hypothesis should be dropped, or as far as possible eliminated," page 360.

"Man has learned to deal with himself in all questions of importance without recourse to the 'working hypothesis' called 'God.' In questions of science, art, and ethics this has become an understood thing at which one now hardly dares to tilt. But for the last hundred years or so it has also become increasingly true of religious question; it is becoming evident that everything gets along without 'God'--and, in fact, just as well as before," page 325.

"If in fact the frontiers of knowledge are being pushed further and further back (and that is bound to be the case), then God is being pushed back with them, and is therefore (constantly) in retreat" page 311.

"I expect you remember Bultmann's essay on 'demythologizing; of the New Testament? My view of it today would be, not that he went 'too far,' as most people thought but that he didn't go far enough" page 285.

"The Christian is not a homo religiosus, but simply a man, as Jesus was a man. . ." page 369.

"It's true that Christianity has always been regarded as a religion of redemption. But isn't that a cardinal error, which separates Christ from the Old Testament and interprets him on the lines of the myths about redemption?" page 336.

"Belief in the resurrection is not the 'solution' of the problem of death," page 282.

"The God of Jesus Christ has nothing to do with what God, as we imagine him, could do or aught to do," page 391.

Sincerely,
Bolton Davidheiser
La Mirada, California

A GREAT CHRISTIAN
December 24, 1984

The December *The Lutheran* of the Lutheran Church in America includes an Advent sermon by Dietrich Bonhoeffer which is reprinted from *Sojourners*.

While we can understand why so many praise Bonhoeffer as a great Christian, by this time clergymen should at least be familiar with the fact that in his last writings Bonhoeffer clearly repudiated historic Christianity. He even argued that such a skeptic as Rudolf Bultmann did not go far enough in his demythologizing. *CN* reviewed Bonhoeffer's letters from prison a good number of years ago and quoted from them at considerable length so that our readers could judge for themselves whether or not

Bonhoeffer accepted historic Christianity and the Christ of the Bible.

Paul W. Powell, a Southern Baptist leader in Texas, claims that "Dietrich Bonhoeffer was a great Christian if there ever was one." Robert Summer, editor of the *Biblical Evangelical*, says in a review of Paul Powell's *Dynamic Discipleship* (Broadman) and I Like Being a Christian in the December 7, 1984 *Biblical Evangelist*:

"Alas, our enthusiastic comments must be tempered to a lament we made in our review of his work *I Like Being a Christian* (reviewed January 6, 1984): *we do not like some of the men he praises*! In this one, not only does he praise men like E. Stanley Jones, but he says about the Neo-Orthodox Bonhoeffer: 'Dietrich Bonhoeffer was a great Christian if there ever was one.' This makes us temporarily wonder if the author knows what a Christian is! Bonhoeffer, a disciple of Karl Barth, was not a Christian at all, to say nothing of a 'great' one, join our judgment. He was one of the fathers of the 'death of God' philosophy and wrote, 'There is no longer any need for a God as a working hypothesis, whether in morals, politics, or science. Nor is there any need for such a God in religion or philosophy. In the name of intellectual honesty these working hypothesis should be dropped or dispensed with as far as possible.'

"He described the story of creation and the fall as myths and said about Rudolf Bultmann's efforts to remove myths from the Bible: 'I expect you remember Bultmann's essay on "Demythologizing" of the New Testament? My view of it today would be, not that he went "too far," as most people thought, but that he didn't go far enough."

"In fact, since Powell is concerned about souls, perhaps he is not aware that Bonhoeffer wrote: 'Individualistic concern for personal salvation has almost completely left us all . . . There are more important things than bothering about such a matter.'"

Come, O Rescuer
The Lutheran, December, 1984

German Lutheran theologian Dietrich Bonhoeffer preached this Advent sermon about a year after Adolf Hitler came to power. It still speaks powerfully to victims of oppression.

By Dietrich Bonhoeffer

You know what a mine disaster is.

The moment even the most courageous miner has dreaded his whole life long is here. It is no use running into the walls, the silence all around him remains. He knows people are crowding together on the surface; but the way out for him is blocked.

Bonhoeffer and the Confirmation Class
Lutheran Forum, Pentecost 1985

Bonhoeffer was a man constantly unsettled by the impact of Christ in his life. He had a view of religious education that far exceeded any mere classroom pedagogy. For him teaching was living the message of Christ. His students learned by watching Christ grow in themselves and in their teacher.

Liberating Faith: Bonhoeffer's Message for Today
By Geffrey B. Kelly. Augsburg, 206 pages. $10.95.
The Christian Century, April 10, 1985

Forty Years after his death, Dietrich Bonhoeffer continues to inspire people of amazingly diverse backgrounds and perspectives. In the introduction to this extraordinary contribution to the steadily growing Bonhoeffer literature, Eberhard Bethge, the man who knows Bonhoeffer best and who has done the most to make him known, writes: "We have now before us the first book by an American that combines accurate analysis with the creation of valuable guidelines for further discussion of the critical implications of Bonhoeffer's life and theology." On the strength of that word alone, anyone interested in Bonhoeffer should read Geffrey Kelly's presentation.

Bonhoeffer's Paradox and Ours
The Christian Century, April 10, 1985

Today this German Christian's struggle has become our own. It is the struggle to move through ambiguity to analysis, to go beyond paradox to perception, to answer vexing dilemmas with courageous decisions. In Bonhoeffer, we confront the high stakes of life's moral choices. As perilous as the issues of our time may seem, Bonhoeffer's legacy reminds us that we must take sides, that indifference is the worst form of immorality. Every one of us must enter the crucible of moral deliberation. To refuse is to invite the paralyzation of our consciences and the free reign of evil.

Bonhoeffer Witnesses to Third World
The Lutheran, May 15, 1985

Lutheran theologian Dietrich Bonhoeffer was killed by the Nazis 40 years ago, but he speaks to liberation theologians today. Dr. John Godsey, Wesley Theological Seminary, Washington, said that Bonhoeffer relates "to today's Third World theologians because he spoke to the condition of life which they face."
Also speaking at the convocation was Dr. James Burtness of Luther Northwestern Seminary, St. Paul, Minn. He said Bonhoeffer's ethics were Christ-centered, but added that "Bonhoeffer handles Lutheran tradition in a creative and sometimes radical way."

Bonhoeffer Biographer Will Speak Here
St. Louis Lutheran, March 15, 1992

Dietrich Bonhoeffer (1906-1945) was a leading opponent of Nazism among Lutheran theologians in Germany. He was executed just one month before the end of World War II, and much of his life story and writings might have been lost had they not been preserved by his former student and best friend, Eberhard Bethge.

Bethge and his wife Renate will be in St. Louis April 13 and 14 to make several presentations on the life and times of Bonhoeffer. Their visit to St. Louis is sponsored by The Bonhoeffer Study Group of Saint Louis, Concordia Seminary, and The Goethe Institute.

The Lutheran Bonhoeffer
The Rabbi of Berlin
By Ruth Zerner
Lutheran Forum, August, 1993

> Caged before the end,
> you are ready, for death or life.
> Hope upon your horizon,
> Maria searches for you,
> calling you to life.
> Lean, sturdy, noble and loving,
> she does not find you.
> Your letter promises:
> "Our marriage shall be
>   a yes to God's earth."

The (newest) Book
By Linda-Marie Delloff
The Lutheran, November 1993

Bonhoeffer anniversary

November marks the 50th anniversary of Dietrich Bonhoeffer's first prison letter to his friend, Eberhard Bethge. Bonhoeffer was the German Confessing Church pastor whose fight against the Nazis ended with his execution in 1945. The post-humously published *Letters and Papers from Prison* has become a 20th-century classic of Christian ethics.

The Lutheran Seminary at Philadelphia has been marking this anniversary with a fall lecture series. It also held a special hymn festival devoted to hymns that reflect Bonhoeffer's views. The centerpiece was Bonhoeffer's own hymn, *By Gracious Powers*, based on the prison letters.

But the observance did not end there. The International Bonhoeffer Society chose the seminary as the site for its Dietrich Bonhoeffer Works Translation Project. Over the next decade scholars will translate the new 16-volume German critical edition of Bonhoeffer's works into English. Augsburg Fortress, the Evangelical Lutheran Church in America publishing house, will publish the books.

Helpful reading
The Lutheran, April, 1995

Books by Bonhoeffer
Available from Augsburg Fortress:

The Cost of Discipleship, Collier Books. A searching meditation on the Sermon on the Mount and Jesus' call to discipleship.

Creation and Fall. Temptation: Two Biblical Studies, Collier Books. Examines the early chapters of Genesis.

Ethics, Collier Books. Written at the time of his political resistance.

Letters and Paper from Prison, Collier Books. Theological and personal reflections during his imprisonment.

Life Together, Harper. A warm, yet searching look at Christian fellowship.

About Bonhoeffer

Dietrich Bonhoeffer: A Life in Pictures, Translated by John Bowden, Fortress. An excellent introduction for general readers. Contains the best available photos of the man and the places of his life.

Dietrich Bonhoeffer: Man of Vision, Man of Courage, Eberhard Bethge, Harper & Row. The definitive biography.

Dietrich Bonhoeffer: Memories and Perspectives, 90-minute documentary video with study guide, Trinity Films. Includes interviews with his family and co-workers, (800) 523-0226.

Dietrich Bonhoeffer: Witness to Jesus Christ, by John deGruchy, editor, Fortress. Bonhoeffer's key ideas, written for the general reader.

The Cup of Wrath, by Mary Glazenger, F.C. Beil, A gripping account of Bonhoeffer's involvement in the resistance movement.

The Church for Others
The Lutheran, April, 1995

50 years ago the Nazis hanged a young German pastor for his resistance work. His words still call us to costly discipleship.

By Wayne Whitson Floyd Jr.

Who could have guessed that his influence toward faithful Christian discipleship would be greater 50 years later than it ever was in his own lifetime? Who could have known we would still be listening to the witness of his life and the theology which guided it?

Four themes in Bonhoeffer's writings are especially worth recalling as we commemorate the 50th anniversary of his death:. . .

Dietrich Bonhoeffer (1906-1945)
The BDM Letter, A Publication of Biblical Discernment Ministries, July/August 1995

Dietrich Bonhoeffer was a neo-orthodox German theologian, pastor, preacher, radio broadcaster, and prolific writer in the 1930s and early 1940s, during the rise, rule, and downfall of Adolf Hitler. (Active in the anti-Hitler resistance movement, Bonhoeffer was imprisoned in 1943 and was hanged by the Nazis at Flossenburg on April 9, 1945.) He was greatly fascinated with neo-orthodox thought, theology, and terminology, and was greatly influenced by the major theologian of neo-orthodoxy, Karl Barth (1886-1968).

Bonhoeffer's writings are credited with helping to father the "Death of God" theology which was popularized by the Anglican Bishop John A.T. Robinson in the 1960s decade. Bonhoeffer was in reality a practical atheist and a religious humanist who denied virtually every cardinal doctrine of the historic Christian faith (*Letters and Papers from Prison*, ed. Eberhard Bethge, New York: Macmillan Co., 1972, pp. 9-12).

Bonhoeffer readily acknowledged "the debt he owes to liberal theology." Declaring that it was impossible to know the objective truth about Christ's real nature and essence, Bonhoeffer proclaimed that God was dead. Moreover, Bonhoeffer believed that the true Christian was the confessing believer who totally immersed his life in the secular world, becoming a secular Christian. Rejecting the objective unalterable moral standards of the Bible, Bonhoeffer proclaimed a situational ethics--that right and wrong are determined solely by the "loving obligations of the moment" (*Letter and Papers from Prison*, Macmillan, pp. 9-12, 378; *Ethics*, pp. 38,186; *No Rusty Swords*, pp. 44-45).

Bonhoeffer presented his own strain of neo-orthodox existentialism. Nevertheless, many evangelicals have been taken in by his warm-hearted piety and by his high sounding devotion to Christ and call to suffer for His sake. There are those today who continue to present Dietrich Bonhoeffer as a genuine Christian hero (e.g., Don Matzat, Chuck Colson, and the editorial board of *Christianity Today*). Grand Rapids Baptist College (GARBC) scheduled a play in the fall of 1991 which extolled Bonhoeffer's memory. And Dr. John F. MacArthur, Jr., has favorably quoted from Bonhoeffer to expound on the nature of true Christian fellowship ("The Riches and Responsibilities of Fellowship," *The Master's Current*, Winter 1994, p. 2). All such accolades to Bonhoeffer are clearly unwarranted.

The following is a summary of the beliefs and influences of Dietrich Bonhoeffer:

1. He believed that "God is teaching us that we must live as men who can get along very well without Him. The God who is with us is the God who forsakes us." He also believed that the concept of God as a "supreme Being, absolute in power and goodness," was a "spurious Being, absolute in power and goodness," was a "spurious conception of transcendence" (*Letters and Papers from Prison*, S.C.M. Press edition, Great Britain: Fontana Books, 1953, pp. 122, 164).

2. He refused to discuss the origin of Christ, His relationship to the Father, His two natures, or even the relationship of the two natures. Bonhoeffer was adamant in his belief that it was impossible to know the objective truth about the real essence of Christ's being-nature (*Christ the Center*, pp. 30, 88, 100-101).

3. He questioned the Virgin Birth, and in reality denied it (*Cost of Discipleship*, p. 215).

4. He denied the deity of Christ; he advocated that "Jesus Christ Today" is not a real person and being, but a "corporate presence" (*Testimony to Freedom,* pp. 75-76; *Christ the Center*, p. 58).

5. He denied the sinlessness of Christ's human nature and further questioned the sinlessness of His earthly behavior (*Christ the Center*, pp. 108-109).

6. He believed that Christ exists in three "revelatory forms" – as Word, as sacrament, and as church. From asserting that Christ is the church, he followed that all persons in the church are identical with Christ (*Christ the Center*, p. 58; *Cost of Discipleship*, p. 217). This amounts to pantheism!

7. He believed that Christianity is not exclusive, i.e. that Christ is not the only way to God (*Testimony to Freedom*, pp. 55-56).

8. He was one of the early promoters of the modern ecumenical movement (*Testimony to Freedom*, pp. 22, 212, 568). He was also an evolutionist (*No Rusty Swords,* p. 143), and believed the book of Genesis was scientifically naïve and full of myths (*Creation and Fall*).

9. He adhered to neo-orthodox theology and terminology concerning salvation (*Testimony to Freedom*, p. 130), was a sacramentalist (*Life Together*, p. 122; *The Way to Freedom*, pp. 115, 153), believed in regenerational infant baptism (*Letters and Papers from Prison*, Macmillan, pp. 142-143) as well as adult baptismal regeneration (*The Way to Freedom*, p. 151), equated church membership with salvation (*The Way to Freedom*, p. 93), and denied a personal/individualistic salvation (*Letters and Papers from Prison*, Macmillan, p. 156).

10. He denied the verbal-plenary inspiration of Scripture, believing that the Bible was only a "witness" to the Word of God and becomes the Word of God only when it "speaks" to an individual; otherwise, it was simply the word of man/men (*Testimony to Freedom*, pp. 9, 104; *No Rusty Swords*, p. 118; *Sanctorum Communio,* p. 161). He also believed in the value of higher criticism/historical criticism, which is denial of the inerrancy and authenticity of the Bible (*Christ the Center*, pp. 73-74).

11. He had no faith in the physical resurrection of Christ. Bonhoeffer believed the "historicity" of the Resurrection was in "the realm of ambiguity," and that it was one of the "mythological" elements of Christianity that "must be interpreted in such a way as not to make religion a pre-condition of faith." He also believed that "the Resurrection is not the solution of the problem of death," and that such things as miracles and the ascension of Christ were "mythological conceptions" as well (*Christ the Center*, p. 112; *Letters and Papers from Prison,* Fontana Books, pp. 93-94, 110).

Dr. G. Archer Weniger declared, "If there is wholesome food in a garbage can, then one can find some good things in Bonhoeffer, but if it be dangerous to expect to find nourishment in a garbage can, then Bonhoeffer must be totally rejected and repudiated as blasphemy. It is worse that garbage" (*FBF Information Bulletin*, May 1977, p. 12).

[The above article was adapted in part from a paper by Don Jasmin (*Fundamentalist Digest,* P.O. Box 2322, Elkton, MD 21922-2322). See also the 9/13/93 *Christian News,* p. 21; and the Oct. Dec 1991 *Bibliotheca Sacra*, pp. 399-408.]

Who Am I?
Whoever I am, thou knowest, O God,...
The Lutheran, September, 1995

Bonhoeffer, a well-known German Lutheran pastor and theologian, was hanged in the Flossenburg concentration camp April 9, 1945 by special order of Gestapo director Heinrich Himmler.

"Who Am I?" is reprinted from Letters and Papers from Prison, *by arrangements with Scribner, a division of Simon and Schuster.*

The Courageous Message of Bonhoeffer
Christian News, September 11, 1995

"The Courageous Message of Dietrich Bonhoeffer - Victim of Nazis Taught Christ's Love Must Be Shared," a major article in the August 26 *St. Louis Post-Dispatch* says that "Robert W. Bertram will teach courses on Bonhoeffer's life and thought at Washington University and St. Louis University next week. Bertram is a Seminex professor emeritus of theology at the Lutheran School of Theology in Chicago."

"Most of Bonhoeffer's writings, which run to 16 volumes, are still in print in more that a dozen languages. His *Letters and Papers from Prison* and *Ethics* are stables in courses in mainline Protestant and Catholic seminaries today." Bonhoeffer in his final "Letters and Papers From Prison" repudiated the historic Christian faith. He rejected what the Bible and Luther teach about the deity of Christ, the resurrection of Christ, and justification by faith alone. See *The Christian News Encyclopedia* (3466, 31, 1900, 2190) for quotations from Bonhoeffer showing that he repudiated Christianity and at the end adopted a demythologizing of the Bible even more radical than Rudolph Bultmann. *CN* has noted that it is amazing that even some Lutherans who consider themselves orthodox regard Bonhoeffer as some great guru. When space permits *CN* will publish an analysis by Dr. Raymond Surburg on Bonhoeffer's theology. Hopefully, it will convince at least the confessional Lutherans, who continue to believe that Bonhoeffer was a true Lutheran, that Bonhoeffer repudiated historic Christianity.

An Evaluation of Dietrich Bonhoeffer's Life and Theology After Half of a Century
By Raymond F. Surburg
Christian News, September 18, 1995

On April 9, 1995 certain Christians observed the 50th anniversary of the execution by hanging of Dietrich Bonhoeffer, who did not even reach the 40th year of his life.[1] It is averred that he was only active as a theologian for about less than 15 years and despite this brevity he has exercised a great influence on Protestants, Roman Catholics and other religionists ever since his premature death. Webster of Toronto College claimed that Bonhoeffer remains one of the most provocative voices in contemporary Christianity despite the fragmentary and occasional character of much of his writings.[2] Martin E. Marty and Dean Peerman in their *Handbook of Christian Theologians* discussed him with such recent theologians as Anders Nygren, Gustav Aulen, C.H. Dodd, Oscar Cullmann, Reinhold Niebuhr, Karl Barth, Emil Brunner, Friedrich Gogarten, Rudolf Bultmann, Paul Tillich.[3] Franklin Sherman, Lutheran Tutor at Oxford University, wrote: "Since his death in 1945 and largely due to the impact of his posthumous published *Letters from Prison and Other Papers* and fragmentary *Ethics*, his influence has spread throughout the Christian world.[4]

How great a Lutheran theologian was Bonhoeffer? Did he have a correct understanding of Christianity and the purpose of human existence? Since on a number of occasions members of The Lutheran Church-Missouri Synod have honored Bonhoeffer and commemorated him and his theology, it might be profitable to examine his life and theology.[5]

A Survey of the Life of Bonhoeffer

Dietrich Bonhoeffer was born in Breslau on February 4, 1906, the son of a university professor and leading authority on psychiatry and neurology.[6] He could boast that in his previous lineage there were theologians, professors, a great church historian (Carl von Hase), artists and some even had aristocratic blood in their veins. Dietrich had three brothers, a twin sister, and three other sisters. Leibholz claimed that from "his father Dietrich Bonhoeffer inherited goodness, fairness, self-control, and ability; from his mother his great human understanding and sympathy, his devotion to the cause of the oppressed, his unshakeable steadfastness." In Breslau and Berlin Dietrich's parents raised their offspring "in that Christian humanitarianism and liberal tradition which was to Bonhoeffer as native as the air he breathed. It was that spirit which determined Dietrich Bonhoeffer's life from the beginning.[7]

Already at 14 he planned on becoming a theologian. He attended lectures at Tuebingen in 1923-1924 but came back to Berlin where he completed his education. Here he encountered the liberal Troeltsch and also had opportunity to study under Harnack and had opportunity to listen to Lietzmann's New Testament lectures.[8] Gradually he felt himself drawn to Karl Barth's theology. Bonhoeffer visited America, and attended Union Theological Seminary, New York, where he imbibed some of the religious and political ideas of Reinhold Niebuhr. After a year internship in a German-speaking congregation in Barcelona, he was appointed as lecturer (Privatdozent) in theology at Berlin (1930). After a year at Union Seminary in New York, he served in Berlin both as lecturer at the university and as pastor to the students of the School of Technology. The year 1933 found Bonhoeffer as pastor of two German-speaking congregations in London. While in London there began a life-long friendship with Bishop of Chichester, G.K.A. Bell. When Hitler came to power he at once opposed National Socialism and its attempt to use the Church for political purposes. In 1935 Bonhoeffer was back in Germany and joined the Confessing Church Movement, representing one third of Protestantism. With Martin Niemoeller he became a leader in the Confessing Church Movement which protested the inroads of Nazism on German Christianity.

Karl Barth was the principal author of the *Barmen Declaration*, a document to which Bonhoeffer contributed. He became director of a short-lived seminary, founded to prepare pastors for the Confessing Church. His license to teach was revoked in 1936 and Himmler closed the seminary in 1937. Bonhoeffer traveled a lot to apprise other Christians of the dangers of Nazism. He did secret work for the churches and traveled to Sweden and Switzerland and had dealings with church officials outside of Germany.

He joined the Resistance Movement and once was involved in a plot to prevail upon the British to accept a conditional German surrender, but the British demanded unconditional surrender. His brother-in-law Dohnany brought him into the anti-Nazi resistance movement and served as a double agent in the German military office. For aiding 14 Jews to escape he was imprisoned, as well as for his anti-government activities and speeches. Bonhoeffer spent a little over two years as a Nazi prisoner (1943-1945). He was confined for 18 months in the Tegel Military Prison, near Berlin. When it was discovered that he had participated in the plot which unsuccessfully attempted to kill Hitler on July 20, 1944, he was removed to the Maximum prison and executed by hanging on April 9, 1945,[12] just a few days before the liberation of the Flossenberg prison. On April 5, 1945 his sister and Dohnany were executed by the Gestapo.

Although Bonhoeffer did not reach 40 when he died, he is supposed to have exercised a great influence on his contemporaries in the 50 years since his death. His writings, both before and after his imprisonment, are alleged to have exercised a great influence on certain individuals. He has also been gratefully remembered for opposing Nazism on its Jewish extermination policy and for the fact that he aided the smuggling out of Germany of 14 Jewish people, for which he was imprisoned. Outside of Germany Bonhoeffer was hailed as a martyr.

Bonhoeffer's political and religious ideas were determined by the fact that he saw everything through the glasses of the political developments in Germany. His books also did not fail to reflect his parental training, his university experiences and the thinking of the great theologians of the day. His writings contain divergent views. In his *Sanctorum Communio*, his doctoral dissertation, he endeavored to bridge the theology of revelation as held by Barth and the philosophy of sociology,[14] a work which reflected Troeltsch, in that Bonhoeffer tried to center the church concept in its corporate life. This thesis is said to have set forth in germ form some of his future ideas appearing in his *Ethics*, *Christology* and *Letters from Prison*.

While Bonhoeffer lectured at the University of Berlin, he issued *Creation and the Fall*, a writing dealing with Genesis 1-3. In this book the German opponent of Nazism claimed that Genesis presents the "ancient world picture in all its scientific naiveté." Genesis he averred "contains myths." Bonhoeffer was an exponent of higher criticism. Bonhoeffer's Christology was different from the traditional Christology as set forth by Roman Catholicism, Lutheranism and for the most part of Calvinism. In his Christology he showed the influence of Karl Barth. His Christology is totally removed from Luther and the Lutheran Confessions. During his directorship of the seminary for the Confessing Church at Finkenwalde, he published *Life Together* and *The Cost of Discipleship*.

Bonhoeffer and the Ecumenical Movement

Leibholz claimed that Dietrich Bonhoeffer after October 1933, after six months of the Church struggle, realized that the situation in which the world and the Churches found themselves in the 1930s that nothing was to be gained any longer for the churches by citing their old Creeds as statements.[15] He believed that the ecumenical movement was the only way to unite the various churches of the body of Christ. Bonhoeffer believed that the Christian Church needed to listen to a new message of the Bible and place them in the context of the whole Church. Even before this he had become a member of the Youth Commission of the World Council of Churches and of the World Alliance for International Friendship through the Churches. He was elected (with Praeses Koch) to be a member of the Ecumenical Council for life and Work at Froena, Denmark in 1943. Bonhoeffer tried to use the ecumenical movement to oppose Hitler's Nazification of the Christian Church. Together with Niemoeller (1892-1894) he organized the First Synod of Barmen in the Buhr. *The Barmen Declaration* was directed at the "German Christians" movement, which fostered extreme nationalism and anti-Semitism, to which was also added a liberal theological stance. Represented at Barmen were both Lutherans and Reformed. Douglas claimed: "The declaration did not purport to be a comprehensive statement against common deviations; it stressed the headship and finality of Christ, and the pre-eminence of Scripture belief and practical actions for Christians. There was a pointed repudiation of the German Christians subordination of Christ's Church to the State."[17]

An Evaluation of Bonhoeffer's Theology

Although he claimed to be a Lutheran and is so-called in the literature of our day, Bonhoeffer was not a Lutheran, for he rejected and abandoned the theology and teachings of the Book of Concord. Luther was opposed to unionism, to wrong ecumenical altar and pulpit fellowship which Bonhoeffer advocated. When one reads the religious writings of Bonhoeffer one finds that there is not much they have in common with Luther's Small Catechism, "the layman's Bible." The fact that the Lutheran, Reformed and Enthusiasts have diametrical differences, did not disturb Bonhoeffer. Although he knew the concept of "purity of doctrine," which he himself used, he was totally unconcerned with it. He agreed with the "melancholy Dane of Denmark, Soren Kierkegaard, who in the early 1900s averred that if Luther had lived later, he would have completely abandoned his views." With this erroneous judgement Bonhoeffer agreed. One might retort: How does any person hundreds of years after, know what Luther would have done? They are ascribing to Luther apostasies of which they are guilty.

In *The Cost of Discipleship* Bonhoeffer constantly refers to many Bible verses, hundreds of Bible passages are employed and he seems to insist upon the importance of following Christ. A portion of this writing was an exposition of the Sermon on the Mount (Matthew 5-7). While much in it sounds orthodox and Biblical, Bonhoeffer looked at religion through his spectacles of opposing Hitlerism and the people's worship of the German Chancellor as God. The followers of Christ must take a stand at all costs against National Socialism and if necessary be willing to die in opposing it.

The Cost of Discipleship denounces the doctrine of the churches as a hindrance to attracting the unchurched to Christ.[21] He accused the Protestant Churches of offering "cheap grace." Under the cover of Luther's doctrine of justification by faith alone, he charges, believers have been relieved of the obligations of discipleship.[22] Even though he quotes from Romans, Bonhoeffer never sets forth the true doctrine of justification by faith and its implications for the Christian life. Here is Dietrich's famous statement about "cheap grace": "Cheap grace" means grace as a doctrine, a principle, a system, it means forgiveness of sins proclaimed as a general truth, the love of God taught as the Christian "conception" of God. . . The church which holds the correct doctrine of grace has, it is supposed, *ipso facto* a part in that grace. In such a Church the world finds a cheap covering for its sins; no contrition is required, still less any real desire to be delivered from sin.[23] Bonhoeffer claimed that "costly grace" accompanies a life of discipleship. Here he fails to distinguish properly between justification and sanctification! His misunderstanding of faith and works is further shown by his claim that the Church has wrongly insisted that obedience follows faith. Bonhoeffer challenged the following statement: "Only he who believes is obedient (i.e. only works done in faith are truly good)." Dietrich, by contrast, puts it this way: "Only he who is obedient believes (only a faith expressed in good works is truly faith.)[24]

Bonhoeffer's Concepts of The Church

Already in his doctoral dissertation, already alluded to, he tried to emphasize the fact of the social character of the Church. Sherman pointed out hat Bonhoeffer held 'that if man's very nature as a created being is social, "the fall" is equally communal. The doctrine of original sin implies the solidarity of the guilt of the whole human race. Hence man's redemption must be equally corporate in character; and so it is, since it consists precisely in the creation of a community of the redeemed. In Jesus Christ as "a collective person" "as deputy" or "representative for all mankind," the humanity of Adam is transformed into the humanity of Christ.[25] Through his life, death and resurrection, the communion of saints is realized. Bonhoeffer identified the Church with Christ. Thus he wrote: "the Church is the presence of God." Adapting the phrase from Hegel, Bonhoeffer claimed that the church was "Christ as existing community."[26]

Bonhoeffer's Christology

He wrote a series of lectures on Christology which were lost, but his friend Bethgen has reconstructed Bonhoeffer's views from student's notebooks and are now found in Volume 3 of his *Gesammelt Schriften*. His Christology is considerably different from that found in Luther and in the Lutheran Confessions. He divided his Christology into the following topics: The contemporary Christ, the historical Christ and the eternal Christ.[27] Instead of beginning with the eternal, followed by the historical he began his Christology with the contemporary, namely, with Christ as existing as the Church. Relative to the historical Christ he averred that Christ did not exist for himself but as a Christ "for me." "This is the deputyship that he assumed not only for me but for the whole of nature and of history," Bonhoeffer's Christology is not what the New Testament sets forth, but was the product of his philosophical thinking. For one thing, he made a strong distinction between Christ's humiliation and his incarnation. Thus the German theologian claimed "that humiliation pertains to the fallen, creation, the incarnation to primal creation. The humiliation was temporary, but the incarnation is permanent. With the return of Christ to the Father, humanity has been assumed into the eternal life of God himself."[28] The doctrine of the communication of attributes was ignored by him. Only the son now has His human nature, but The Father and Holy Spirit are spirit, and do not have a body.

In *The Cost of Discipleship* Bonhoeffer made this assertion: "As they contemplated the miracle of the Incarnation, the early Fathers passionately were wrong to say that God took human nature upon him, it was fallacious to say that God chose as perfect individual man and united himself to him. God was made man. This means that he took upon himself our entire human nature with all of its infirmity, sinfulness, and corruption, the whole of apostate humanity."[29] This contradicts who the real human Christ was. According to Bonhoeffer, redemption involves not merely the plurality of human individuals, but rather humanity in its entirety, which meant that redemption was universal in scope. Redemption was the restoration of the "form" of man as he was originally created in God's image. In Jesus Christ the Incarnate, Crucified, and Risen One, this true image has again taken form in human history. Bonhoeffer's Christological views are pure speculation and are anti-Biblical.[30]

Van Til's Critique of Bonhoeffer's Christology

Van Til in his book, *The Great Debate Today* contended that the Christ of Bonhoeffer is not the Christ of Scripture and can hardly be distinguished from the Christ of Karl Barth (pp. 42-76 of Van Til's Book). Asserted the former Westminster professor of Christian Apologetics: "The ecumenical significance of all this is far reaching. Bonhoeffer was quite consistent with his own theology and with that of post-Kantian, neo-Barthian tradition when he did his best to further the cause of modern ecumenicist. Why should not Lutherans, Calvinists and Armenians unite under a banner of new primacy of a new Christ projection? Surely all of us want to make the message of the saving grace of Christ relevant to the needs of modern man. So we must all demythologize and then remythologize or allegorize not only the Genesis narrative but the New Testament as well. After that we must give an existential interpretation of its message in terms of the ideal man calling him Christ and interpreting all reality of him as its center."[31]

Bonhoeffer and Biblical Hermeneutics

Bonhoeffer abandoned the hermeneutics of Luther, Melanchthon, Chemnitz, the authors of the Lutheran Confessions and the theologians of the era of Lutheran Orthodoxy.[32] He utilized and reinterpreted Scriptures to fit in with his false religious and philosophical views. In Genesis 1-3 he opposed the literal meaning of the opening chapters as may be seen from *Creation and Fall: A Theological Interpretation of Genesis 1-3*. Later he adopted the Bultmann view on "mythology" of the New Testament. Concerning the mythological elements of Christianity he wrote: "I am of the view that the fall content, including mythological concepts, must be maintained. The New Testament is not a mythological garbing of universal truth, this mythology (resurrection and so on) is the thing itself--but the concept must be reinterpreted in such a way as to make religion a pre-condition of faith (cf. circumcision of Paul).[33]

In Bonhoeffer's opinion Bultmann in his mythologization of the Bible did not go far enough. Thus the German asserted: "It is not only mythological conceptions such as miracles, the ascension and the like (which in principle are not in principle separate from the conception of God, faith and so on) that are problematic, but the religious conceptions themselves."[34]

His View of the Resurrection

In one of his prison letters Bonhoeffer declared: "Belief in the resurrection is not the problem of death."[35] However, Bonhoeffer ignored all those scripture verses that speak of the blessedness of a life after death, and the statement of Christ, that on the Last Day all men will rise, either to condemnation or to eternal life. (John 5:28-29) Bonhoeffer's great error was that he concentrated on this life instead on the life to come. The subject of eschatology is absent from the purview of his theology.

Old Testament Contains No Religion of Salvation

Wrote Bonhoeffer: "To resume our reflections on the Old Testament. Unlike other oriental religions that faith of the Old Testament is not a religion of salvation. Christianity, it is true, has always been regarded a religion of salvation. But isn't a cardinal error, which divorces Christ from the Old Testament? And interprets him in the light of the myths of salvation. Of course it could be argued that under Egyptian and later Babylonian influence, the idea of salvation became just as prominent in the Old Testament e.g. Deutero-Isaiah. The answer is, the Old Testament speaks of *Historical* redemption on this side of death whereas the myths of salvation are concerned to offer men deliverance from death. Israel was redeemed out of Egypt in order to live before God on earth. The salvation myths deny history in the interest of an eternity after death. Sheol and Hades are not metaphysical theories, but images which imply that the past, while it still exists has only a shadowy existence in the present. It is said that the distinctive feature of Christianity is its proclamation of the resurrection hope, and that this means of a genuine religion of salvation, in the sense of release from the world. The emphasis falls upon the far side of the boundary drawn by death. But this seems to me to be just the mistake and danger. Salvation means salvation from cares and from fears and longing, from sin and death into a better world beyond the grave. But is this the distinctive feature of Christianity as proclaimed in the Gospels and St. Paul? I am sure it is not. The difference between the Christian hope and resurrection and a mythological hope is that the Christian hope sends a man back to life on earth in a wholly new way which is even more sharply defined that it is in the Old Testament."[36]

Bonhoeffer and the Existence of God

While in prison Bonhoeffer came to the conclusion that mankind no longer needs God. What amounts to theoretical atheism was Bonhoeffer's assertion that God is teaching us that we must live as men who can get along very well without him. "The God who is with us is the God that forsakes us (Mark 15:34)."[37]

While in prison Bonhoeffer asked: What do we mean by God? His answer was: not in the first place in an abstract belief in the omnipotence, etc. That is not a genuine experience of God is not a religious relationship to a supreme Being, absolute in power and goodness, which is a spurious conception of transcendence, but a new life for others, through the participation in the Being of God. This is the starting point for the interpretation of biblical terminology (creation, fall, atonement, repentance and faith, the new life, the last things)."[38]

Bonhoeffer's Perverse Views About God's Presence in the World

Again in prison he declared: "God is being increasingly pushed out of a world that has come of age, out of the sphere of our knowledge and life, since Kant has been relegated to a realm beyond the world of experience. Theology has on the one hand resisted this development with apologetic and has taken up arms - in vain - against Darwinism."[39] Traditional Darwinism, it should be noted was atheistic and denied God's part in creation and preservation.

No Need for God, Bonhoeffer's Claim

"God as a working hypothesis in morals, politics or science, has been surmounted and abolished and the same thing happened in philosophy and religion. For the sake of intellectual honesty, that working hypothesis should be dropped, or as far as is possible eliminated."[40]

Man No Longer Needs God

"Man has learned," so the German opponent of National Socialism claimed, "to deal with himself in all questions of importance without recourse to the 'working hypothesis' called God. In questions of science, art, and ethics this has become an understood thing at which one now hardly dares to tilt. But for the last hundred years or so it has also become increasingly true of religious questions; it is becoming evident that every thing gets along without 'God' and, in past just as well as before."[41]

"If in fact the frontiers of knowledge are being pushed further and further back and that is bound to be the case, then God is pushed with them and is therefore (constantly) in retreat. The God of Jesus has nothing to do with what God, as we imagined, could do or ought to do."[42]

Mankind No Longer Needs of Religion

Bonhoeffer argued that mankind has become of age and no longer needed religion, which is only a deceptive garment of true faith. He sought to acknowledge Christ not as an object of religion, but as in truth the Lord of the world. He spoke of Christian worldliness, which he claimed was quite different from religion, which retreats from the world into inward life and speculation. The Christian is identified not by his beliefs but by his actions, by his participation in the suffering of God in the life of the world."[43]

Bonhoeffer's Plan for the Reconstruction After the War

One writer has called Bonhoeffer "a Christian humanist."[44] A humanist was a person who emphasized the importance and centrality of man and a Christian humanist, one which utilized certain Christina ideas, but was basically anthropocentric.[45] While in prison in the Tegel Military Prison he was worried as to what would happen to the culture of Western civilization, whose demise Hitler could bring about. During his imprisonment he looked forward to the reconstruction of Christian thought after his death. He suggested the need for "a religionless Christianity."[46] While the world was going to decay, he claimed that "God had come of age." God as a concept had been used by people as a stop gap for their embarrassment, and God was superfluous, in that in Europe the world had become of age. A Christian was a man who had concern for others and that the church must be for others.[47]

Bonhoeffer's Negative Influence

Bonhoeffer's final writings, especially as reflected in views found in Letters from Prison and Other Papers, exercised a tantalizing power over thinkers since his death and have given impulse to Marxist theologians sponsoring 'liberation theology', and on those who contended that "God was dead" in the world and those wishing to promote a this-worldly social gospel.[48] Both Zerner[49] and Webster[50] endeavor to save Bonhoeffer's respectability as a Christian theologian, but Bonhoeffer's statements are too clear and explicit.

Roger Shinn of Union Theological Seminary claims that the Tegel prisoner proposed views radically different from his earlier writings.[51] *The West Minister Dictionary of Church History* asserts about Bonhoeffer's *Ethics* and *Letters and Papers in Prison*: "In these he reinterprets Biblical concepts for a world that has become of age, in which neither the usual metaphysical categories are adequate. He teaches a revolutionary understanding of Christian belief in which there is no separation of the religious realm. The Christian identifies with and suffers for the world as Christ did. Bonhoeffer's worldly commitment and execution tend to illustrate and emphasize his written ideas."[52] H.D. McDonald made this judgment of Bonhoeffer's writings: "So varied and opposing are the theories deriving from his that a meaningful sketch of his ideas presents difficulty. Among his most fruitful insights were his total rejection of natural theology, and of a 'religious apriori' in man; the reality of God's absolute self-disclosure in Christ; the historical and present Christ as God revealed incognito; Christ interpreted in terms of 'the-man-for-others'; and particularly, his much discussed and misunderstood concepts of 'religionless' and 'worldly Christianity,' and 'man come of age.'"[53]

Bonhoeffer Memorials and Eulogies

When the execution of Bonhoeffer became known in Europe and in America, there were held memorial services and eulogistic pronouncements were made for a man who had died for is opposition to National Socialism and for the exercise of humanitarianism. Leibholz made this hyperbolic statement that Bonhoeffer's death could not be measured by human standards. They felt that God himself had intervened in the most terrible struggle the world had witnessed so far by sacrificing one of his most faithful and courageous sons to expiate the crimes of a diabolical regime and to revive the spirit in which the civilization of Europe had to be rebuilt."[54] Leibholz claimed that Bonhoeffer's life and death belong to the annals of Christian martyrdom, or as Niebuhr said "to the modern Acts of the Apostles."[55] On July 27, 1945 a memorial service was held at Holy Trinity in London, sponsored by the Bishop of Chichester.

Bonhoeffer Versus Jesus and Paul on Duty to Human Government

In the **Cost of Discipleship** Bonhoeffer discussed Christ's statement on Matthew 22:21[56] and Paul's instruction on Romans 13:1-8.[57] Both Jesus and St. Paul lived in the first century A.D. Roman Empire. At their time there were 60,000,000 slaves in the Roman Empire, who were treated like chattel, with no rights.[58] Neither Christ nor Paul denounced slavery and encouraged slaves to rebel. In fact, Paul made a runaway slave, Onesimus, return to his master Philemon. Crucifixion was used as a death penalty, involving Jews and Gentiles. Neither Jesus nor Paul condemned this practice. The Jews of Palestine suffered indignities at the hands of Roman procurators. Yet neither Christ nor Paul called upon the Jewish people to revolt. Emperor worship (the deification of a man) began with Augustus and later caused the death of many Christians who refused to offer up incense to Caesar as divine. One might say that there were great similarities between the first century Roman world and 20th century Germany. Claudius banished Jews from Rome in A.D. 49.

Christ told his enemies who wanted to entrap him: "Render unto Caesar the things that are Caesar's and to God the things that are God's." Writing at the time, when Christian-murdering Nero was emperor, to the Roman congregation penned the God inspired directives: "Let every person be subject to the governing authorities. For there is no authority except from God and those that exist have been instituted by God. Therefore he who resists the authorities resists what God has appointed, and those who resist will incur judgment."[59]

Bonhoeffer joined German resistance movement and traveled on its behalf. On May, 1942, Bonhoeffer met with the Bishop of Chichester at Sigunta, Sweden, and conveyed plans for overthrowing the Nazi regime, together with proposals for the subsequent establishment of peace. Anthony Eden was given these proposals and later rejected them, demeaning unconditional surrender.[60] Bonhoeffer was also involved in a lot to assassinate Hitler, which was unsuccessful. He did the opposite of what St. Paul said Christians were to do in dealing with the government. As a churchman Bonhoeffer was using the sword to save the church, concerning which Jesus had told Peter: "Put thy sword into they sheath, for all they that take the sword shall perish by the sword" (Acts 5:29). It is true that man must obey God rather than men, when the latter demands the doing that which violate God's laws. However, when he takes a stand against the government, he must take the consequences, which Niemoeller did when he protested Jewish persecution and the anti-religious views of Hitler and his minions.[61] Niemoeller together with Bonhoeffer had been one of the writers and promoters of the **Barmen Declaration**. Niemoeller was a prisoner from 1937-1945 at Sachsenhausen and then at Dachau. But after his release he became active as a church leader in German Protestantism. The difference in the end between these two religious leaders was: one engaged in hostile activity against his constituted government, the other did not.

Footnotes

1 "Turret of the Times," ***Christian News***, July 10, 1995, p. 3.

2 J.B. Webster, "Dietrich Bonhoeffer,' Sinclair B. Ferguson, David Wright, **New Dictionary of Theology** (Downers Grove, Illinois: Intervarsity Press, 1081)p. 107.

3 Franklin Sherman, "Dietrich Bonhoeffer," in Martin Marty and Dean G. Peerman (Cleveland and New York: The World Publishing Company, 1967), pp. 464-484.

4 **Ibid.**, p. 464.

5 "Defender of God is Dead Theologian to Speak at Concordia Seminary, St. Louis," *Christian News* March 20, 1992, found also in **Christian News Encyclopedia, Vol. 5**, p. 3466. At a reformation Festival in Detroit Bonhoeffer's theology was honored, CF. *Christian News Encyclopedia V*, p. 3466. Bolton Davidheiser criticized The council of Inerrancy for utilizing Bonhoeffer,cf. *Christian News Encyclopedia, III*, p. 1900.

6 Cf. G. Leibholz, "Memoirs," Introduction to Dietrich Bonhoeffer, The Cost of Discipleship (New York: Macmillian Publishers, 1963), pp. 11ff.

7 **Ibid.**, p. 11.

8 Sherman. **Op.cit.**, pp. 464-465.

9 R. Zerner, "Dietrich Bonhoeffer," Walter A. Elwell, **Evangelical Dictionary of Theology** (Grand Rapids: Baker Book House, 1988), p. 168b.

10 J.D. D. Douglas, "Barmen Declaration, in Elwell, **op.cit.**, 76b. Also Sherman. **Op. cit.**, p. 465.

11 Roger L. Shinn; "Bonhoeffer, Dietrich," **Encyclopedia Americana** (Danbury: Grollier Incorporated, 1994), p. 208.

12 Sherman, **op. cit.**, p. 466.

13 Reinhold Niebuhr, "Death of a Martyr," **Christianity and Christ**, June 2, 1945.

14 The complete title of this dissertation was: **Sanctorum Communio: eine Dogmatische Untersuchung Zur Sociologie der Kierche**, 1930.

15 Bonhoeffer, **The Cost of Discipleship**. Revised and Unabridged Edition (Macmillian Publishing House, 1963), pp. 38-339.

16 Leibholz, "Memoir," **op. cit.**, pp. 14-15.

17 Douglas, op. cit., p. 465.

18 Cf. F.E. Mayer, **The Religious Bodies in America** (St. Louis: CPH, 1956), p. 134; 212-216.

19 Bonhoeffer, "Cum grano Salis," pp. 31,32.

20 Bonhoeffer, **The Cost of Discipleship, op. cit.**, pp. 37-352. The book is characterized by the use of many Biblical passages, cf. listing of verses cited on pp. 348-352.

21 **The Cost of Discipleship, op. cit.**, pp. 38-39.

22 **Ibid.**, pp. 45-46.

23 **Ibid.**, p. 46.

24 Thus Sherman, **op. cit.**, p. 467.

25 **Ibid.**, pp. 468-469.

26 **Ibid.**, pp. 469.

27 **Ibid.**, p. 474.

28 **Ibid.**, pp. 474-475.

29 **Ibid.**, p. 475.

30 For a correct presentation of Christology, cf. John Schallerr, **Biblical Christology, cf. John Schaller, Biblical Christology. A Study in Lutheran Dogmatics** (Milwaukee: Northwestern Publishing House, 1981), 287 pp.

31 Cornelius Van Til, **The Great Debate Today** (Nutley: Presbyterian and Reformed Publishing Company, 1970), pp. 42-47.

32 Cf. Ralph Bohlmann, **The Hermeneutics of the Lutheran Confession** (St. Louis: CPH, 1983), 163 pp. Revised Edition: Raymond F. Surburg, "The Significance of Luther's Hermeneutics for the Protestant Reformation," **Concordia Theological Monthly**, 24, 243-261, April, 1953.

33 Dietrich Bonhoeffer, **Letters and Papers from Prison** (London: SCM press, Fontana Books, 1953), p. 110.

34 **Ibid.**, p. 94.

35 **Ibid.**, p. 93.

36 **Ibid.**, p. 112.

37 **Ibid.**, p. 122.

38 **Ibid.**, p. 163-165.

39 **Ibid.**, p. 341.

40 **Ibid.**, p. 360.

41 **Ibid.**, p. 325.

42 **Ibid.**, p. 311.

43 Sherman, **op.cit.**, p. 483; **Prison Letters and Other Papers**, pp. 163ff.

44 Leibholz, **op. cit.**., p. 35.
45 Jerald C. Brauer, Editor, **The Westminster Dictionary of the Bible** (Philadelphia: The Westminster Press, 1971), Cf. article on "Humanism," pp. 415-416. Shinn, "Bonhoeffer, Dietrich,": **Encyclopedia Americana, op. cit.**, p. 208.
46 Sherman, **op. cit.**, p. 483: Bonhoeffer, **Prison Letters and Other Papers**, pp. 163-165.
47 Bonhoeffer, **Prison Letters and Other Papers**, pp. 163-165.
48 Shinn, **op., cit.**, p. 208.
49 Zerner, **op., cit.**, p. 169.
50 Webster, **op. cit.**, p. 109a.
51 Westminster Dictionary of Church History, **op. cit.**, p. 124.
53 McDonald, "Bonhoeffer, Dietrich," Douglas, Editor, **The New International Dictionary of the Christian Church**, (Grand Rapids: Zondervan Publishing House, 1974), p. 142b.
54 Leibholz, "Memoir," **op. cit.**, p. 32.
55 **Ibid.**, p. 33.
56 The Cost of Discipleship, **op. cit.**, p. 296.
57 **Ibid.**, pp. 292-296.
58 Frank E. Gaebelein, **Philemon, the Gospel of Emancipation** (New York: Our Hope Publications, 1939), p. 17.
59 **Good News for a New Life** (New York: American Bible Society, 1964-65), p. 263.
60 Sherman, **op. cit.**, pp. 465-466.
61 John P. Dever, "Niemoeller, Martin," in Douglas, **The New International Dictionary of the Christian Church, op. cit.**, p. 712a.

Wer Ist Bonhoeffer?
Christian News, November 24, 1995
By Hans Jouchim Schultz
Reviewed by LaMarr Blecker

Published by the author, 1995, paperback, 64 pages. The book is written in German and can be obtained by contacting the author whose address is Hermann-Lons-Strasze 48, D-22926 Ahrensburg, Germany. The author requests an unspecified "small contribution towards printing costs." The contribution may be sent to the author or to his bank, Vereins-und Westbank in Hamburg, Konto-Nummer 38 26260; Bankleitzahl 200 300 00 (no address given for the bank).

The book offers the theological ideas and personal observations of Dietrich Bonhoeffer, which the author obtained from published sources. The author provides adequate footnotes for his quotes attributed to Bonhoeffer.

Many believe Bonhoeffer was executed by the Nazis because of his faith. In truth, however, Bonhoeffer was arrested and charged with treason due to his anti-regime activities in the German resistance. That Bonhoeffer was a martyr to the German nation can be defended in the same way we see the Revolutionary War hero, Nathan Hale, a martyr to American liberty from Great Britain. Both men were technically traitors to the established government, and both paid for their activities with their lives. By no stretch of the imagination was Dietrich Bonhoeffer a martyr to the Christian faith, since there seems some doubt, supplied by his own words, if he was a believer.

Although we have no reason to believe Herr Schultz may have misquoted Bonhoeffer's published expressions of faith (or lack of same) or in any way "doctored" references, we see his book as quite subjective. One may believe that Bonhoeffer had a complex personality, torn between traditional Lutheran belief and the Modernism which characterized much of his published commentary. For example, moments before he was hanged, an official saw Bonhoeffer on his knees in fervent prayer. Herr Schultz dismisses Bonhoeffer's last act, one of personal piety as mere pretense (p.10). Bonhoeffer mentioned to a friend shortly before his execution, that he had reverted to Luther's practice of beginning and ending each day with the sign of the cross. However, Bonhoeffer told his friend that such a practice did not necessarily signify a change in heart from his modernist views and belief (pp. 48-49). One wonders which was the **real** Dietrich Bonhoeffer, the doubting Modernist or the man facing imminent death being called to repentance by the Holy Ghost? Herr Schultz makes some interesting speculations concerning one of Bonhoeffer's personal bad habits: Smoking (p. 18). True, smoking is an addictive habit, one which der Fuehrer roundly condemned (Hitler forbade smoking in his presence.)

Perhaps, indicative of Herr Schultz's subjectivity was his sweeping assertion, that to his knowledge, no one confessing Christ was killed by the authorities of the Third Reich! (p. 47). We have never heard of Herr Schultz prior to reviewing his book. However, unless Herr Schultz had a wide network of reliable informants or had at hand reasonably complete archives of the Third Reich, such a statement seem at best meaningless or even misleading. Given the depraved indifference of the leaders of the Third Reich toward values other than their own, it seems difficult to accept that no Christian suffered death for application of Acts 5:29 (We ought to obey God rather than man) by refusing to carry out depraved orders of higher authority for conscience's sake. In another section, Herr Schultz cites a rather trivial incident to suggest the authorities of the Third Reich protected Christians against rowdies of the Brown Shirt variety. In the city of Siegen, the police forcibly ejected SA rowdies who had discharged stink bombs at a religious meeting and heckled Christian speakers (pp. 47, 48). That at least one act of rectitude by the police under the Third Reich is cited, hardly seems sufficient to suggest the Third Reich had a policy of protecting Christians against Nazis.

Herr Schultz makes some interesting commentary on the failed July 20, 1944, Putsch against Hitler. The Putsch was primarily an attempt by mostly monarchist and conservative officers of the German Army to kill Hitler and replace the Nazi regime with one to be consistent with Romans 13, and those who lost their lives in the failed coup could hardly be construed as Christian martyr. However, the superficial Crown Prince, at least on the level of civil rectitude, would seem to have been a distinct improvement over the mad, blood thirsty Hitler and his pagan, evil regime. Herr Schultz sees the Putsch in a different light. We grant Schultz's speculation, that had the Putsch been successful, Dietrich Bonhoeffer would have been included in the Crown Prince's government in some capacity or other. However, Herr Schultz views such a prospect with horror. According to Herr Schultz, Bonhoeffer's inclusion in a non-Nazi government would have been as an enemy of God and of Christians at a top position in the state (p. 25). Although Bonhoeffer's theological positions would have duly qualified him as an "enemy of God and Christians." Schultz mentions not a word about the so-called Reichsbischof Muller, a pagan whom Hitler foisted upon the Evangelisch Keriche, giving rise to the "Bekennende Kirche." At worst, Bonhoeffer's inclusion in a German government would have replaced pagans with an apostate.

Schultz, however, seems on target with his criticism of the current Bonhoeffermania. The liberal, Modernist Protestant power elite in Germany have made Bonhoeffer into a type of church father. Not only have street and schools been named to honor Bonhoeffer, but even Lutheran churches bear his name (p. 38). The Modernists in charge of the German unionist Evangelische Kirche have made Bonhoeffer, a political martyr, into a martyr of the Christian faith. But to Modernists, the line separating politics from faith no longer seems to exist. Schultz's book is useful in exposing Bonhoeffer's Modernist beliefs and is valuable in contradicting the Zeitgeist's estimation of Bonhoeffer's positive contributions to the Christian faith, as Schultz puts it "to unsophisticated Christians." One need not wade through tomes of prose, thanks to Herr Schultz, to learn of Bonhoeffer's theology. Bonhoeffer, at least the published Bonhoeffer, was definitely not a Lutheran, and there seems to be some serious doubt whether the man was a Christian. The value of the book is diminished by the unfortunate subjectivity of Schultz on both Bonhoeffer and the author's vague suggestion, that the Nazi regime was not inimical in its reaction to the Christian faith.

Bonhoeffer Taught the Cost of Discipleship
By Charles Colson
Christian Chronicles, November 7, 1996

Half a century ago a young Lutheran pastor named Dietrich Bonhoeffer was involved in a failed plot to assassinate Adolph Hitler-and was executed by the Nazis for treason.

Astonishingly, earlier this year Bonhoeffer's reputation was resurrected when he was officially exonerated by a court in Berlin.

But Bonhoeffer was more than a leader of the Resistance under the Third Reich. He was also a powerful voice for the church.

In his book *The Cost of Discipleship*, Bonhoeffer paints a vivid picture of how to be true to the Christian faith under a hostile regime. Under persecution, Bonhoeffer discovered that even though God's grace is freely given, it also extracts a high cost.

Even in prison, Bonhoeffer's life shone with divine grace. He comforted other prisoners, who looked upon him as their chaplain. He wrote many moving letters that were later co elected in a volume called *Letters and Papers from Prison* - a book I read during my own stay behind bars, finding strength and encouragement.

On the morning of April 9, 1945 - less than a month before Hitler was defeated - Bonhoeffer knelt and prayed, and then followed his captors to the gallows, where he was hung as a traitor.

Now, 51 years later, Bonhoeffer is finally receiving the official recognition to match the spiritual veneration he has inspired in so many believers.

The late British journalist Malcolm Muggeridge wrote a tribute to Bonhoeffer in his book *The Third Testament*. Muggeridge wrote: "Looking back now across the years. . . What lives on is the memory of a man who died, not on behalf of freedom or democracy or a steadily rising gross national product, nor for any of the 20th century's counterfeit hopes or desires, but on behalf of a cross on which another man died 2,000 years before.". . .

Dietrich Bonhoeffer
February 1, 1997
Fundamental Baptist News Service,
1219 N. Harns Rd., Oak Harbor, WA 98277

– Dietrich Bonhoeffer (1906-1945), a German theologian who was executed in the closing days of World War II, is praised continually by the modernistic ecumenical movement represented by the World Council of Churches and its member denominations. The man is often mentioned, in fact, in a positive manner by Evangelical scholars today. In his writings, though, he plainly rejected such doctrines as the virgin birth, physical resurrection, and substitutionary atonement of Jesus Christ. According to Bonhoeffer, it is a "cardinal error" to regard Christianity as a religion of salvation.

The following are quotations which reveal Bonhoeffer's heretical and apostate thinking. They are from the 1967 edition of his Letters and Papers from Prison, Macmillan, edited by his close friend, Eberhard Bethge. He was imprisoned and executed by the Nazis for his involvement in two conspiracies to assassinate Adolf Hitler.

"God as a working hypothesis in morals, politics, or science, has been surmounted and abolished; and the samething has happened in philosophy and religion. For the sake of the intellectual honesty, that working hypothesis should be dropped, or as far as possible eliminated" (p. 360).

"Man has learned to deal with himself in all questions of importance without recourse to the 'working hypothesis' called 'God.' In questions of science, art, and ethics this has become an understood thing at which one now hardly dares to tilt. But for the last hundred years or so it has also become increasingly true of religious questions; it is becoming evident that everything gets along with 'God' – and, in fact, just as well as before' (p. 325).

"If in fact the frontiers of knowledge are being pushed further and further back (and that is bound to be the case), then God is being pushed back with them, and is therefore (constantly) in retreat" (p. 311).

I expect you remember Bultmann's paper on the demythologizing of the New Testament. My view of it today would be not that he went too far, as most people seem to think but that he did not go far enough. IT IS NOT ONLY THE MYTHOLOGIAL CONCEPTONS, SUCH AS MIRACLES, THE ASCENSION AND THE LIKE (WHICH ARE NOT IN PRINCIPLE DIFFERENT FROM THE CONCEPTIONS OF GOD, FAITH AND SO ON) THAT ARE PROBLEMATIC, BUT THE 'RELGIOUS' CONCEPTIONS THEMSELVES" (Letters and Papers from Prison, p. 285).

"It's true that Christianity has always been regarded as a religion of redemption. But isn't that a cardinal error, which separates Christ from the Old Testament and interprets him on the lines of the myths about redemption?" (p. 336).

"Belief in the resurrection is not the 'solution' of the problem of death" (p. 282).

"The God of Jesus Christ has nothing to do with what God, as we imagine him, could do or aught to do" (p. 391).

David Cloud
dccloud@whitbey.net
http://wayoflife.org
1219 N. Harns Rd., Oak Harbor, WA 98277
(See *The Christian News Encyclopedia* for information on Bonhoeffer's theology).

The Man Behind the Bonhoeffer Legend
By A. James Rudin
c. 1997 Religion News Service

(Rabbi Rudin is the national anti-religious affairs director of the American Jewish Committee.)

Undated - The German Lutheran pastor Dietrich Bonhoeffer -- who was not yet 40 when the Nazis executed him in Berlin in April 1945-- has emerged as the dominant figure of Christian resistance to Nazism.

Indeed in some churches and seminaries today, Bonhoeffer's name is invoked as a mantra, but usually without real knowledge of the man and his tumultuous times. Before he is totally lost in the mist of legend it's important for Christians and Jews to examine Bonhoeffer's life and legacy. In the 1930s, Bonhoeffer opposed the "German Christian" movement -- known as the "Brown Church" because many of its pastors wore Storm Trooper uniforms and espoused absolute obedience to Hitler and murderous anti-Semintism. The Nazi church stressed belief in an "Aryan Jesus," and called for the elimination of all "Jewish influences" from church life.

Bonhoeffer considered the "German Christian" movement heretical because it capitulated to Nazi ideology. But he later came to believe that all forms of Christianity were inadequate in opposing Nazism, because adherence to strict orthodoxy and doctrinal purity in the face of evil left the church paralyzed. When he recognized the church was morally bankrupt in the struggle against Hitler, Bonhoeffer did what few German clergy did during those terrible years: he crossed the line from spiritual resistance within the church to overt political action against the Nazis.

It was a fateful decision for the young pastor, one that ultimately cost him his life. Bonhoeffer was arrested in 1943 by the Gestapo and imprisoned until his execution two years later, just a month before Germany surrendered to the Allies.

Bonhoeffer's final letters from prison reveal an emerging sense of "Christian realism" and an intriguing concept he labeled "religionless Christianity."

Bonhoeffer understood that God's compassion extended far beyond the narrow confines of his church. As early as 1938, he told some seminary students that "(Not only religious) but secular freedom, too, is worth dying for." Bonhoeffer did not live long enough to evolve from a theologically sturdy Lutheran into a religious universalist. But he was definitely a pilgrim on that path. And because he lived where and when he did--in the bowels of a gangster state-- Bonhoeffer was thwarted in his attempt to fashion a new understanding of Christian belief.

Bonhoeffer's Legacy: A New Generation
By John W. DeGruchy
The Christian Century, April 2, 1997

"A brief scan of the Bonhoeffer bibliographies, regularly published and updated by the International Bonhoeffer Society, indicates the extent to which Bonhoeffer's life and thought have become the subject of serious scholarship during the past three decades."

"Bonhoeffer's insistence on 'confessing Christ concretely' was important for many who struggled against apartheid."

"There can be little doubt that Bonhoeffer's legacy has had a major impact on Christianity since his martyrdom 50 years ago."

I believe that Bonhoeffer's question about Jesus Christ remains the fundamental issue for Christian theology. But how would he approach that question now? If we take his own development seriously, we can assume that he would want to be in critical continuity with Christian tradition. I doubt that he would reject the 'negative' Christology of the patristic period, or Luther's 'theology of the cross.' At the same time he would not simply repeat past theological formulas. His answer would have a contemporary freshness and relevance. He would utter the word of God 'in a new language, perhaps quite nonreligious, but liberating and redeeming -- as was Jesus' language'" (*Letters and Papers from Prison*).

"But time and again his approach to doing theology suggests the way forward. Those who explore his writings will usually find some clue which provides a way of grappling with the issues. In this sense, it is fortunate that Bonhoeffer never completed his theological work in any systematic way. It remains open-ended, thereby inviting us to participate in an ongoing task of action and reflection."

Bonhoeffer - Why isn't Bonhoeffer honored at Yad Vashem
By Stephen A. Wise
The Christian Century, February 25, 1998

"Officials at Yad Vashem in Israel say they have no evidence that Bonhoeffer 'specifically helped Jews.'". . .

"Bonhoeffer's words and actions entitle him to a place in the pantheon of the Righteous at Yad Vashem."

Bonhoeffer and the AAL
Christian News, May 15, 2000

Now it's the Aid Association for Lutherans which is promoting Dietrich Bonhoeffer with a large gift (story on page 1).

Dr. Raymond Surburg, a retired professor at Concordia Seminary, Ft. Wayne, ably shows Bonhoeffer's anti- Christian theology, pp. 8-9

CN has exposed Bonhoeffer's liberal theology ever since 1965 when Lutherans in the Detroit area featured and praised Bonhoeffer rather than Martin Luther at a Reformation rally, p.6. *CN* quoted directly from Bonhoeffer's writings to show that Bonhoeffer denied such basic doctrines of the Christian faith as the virgin birth, deity and resurrection of Christ. Some of his statements in his final writings approach atheism.

CN has asked the AAL whether any member of the AAL's Board of Directors has voiced any concern about the AAL financed movie on Bonhoeffer. The AAL includes some pastors and leaders who are supposed to be conservative. Some may defend the

AAL by arguing that the AAL leaders and the members of its Board of Directors are not particularly known to be great theologians. If Bonhoeffer is praised at Concordia Seminary, St. Louis, and many Lutheran professors and churchmen, then why should anyone object if the AAL spends a large sum of money presenting Dietrich Bonhoeffer as a great Christian, Lutheran and martyr?

Martin Luther King, Jr., and Bonhoeffer both were killed at age 39. Both denied the resurrection of Christ and historic Christianity. King openly admitted that he was a Marxist. Both King and Bonhoeffer are now hailed by religious liberals as great Christian saints and martyrs. When such non-Christian liberals as King and Bonhoeffer are held up as great heroes of the faith even at LCMS schools, is it any wonder that eventually more students will believe that it is possible to be a famous Christian without believing in the Trinity or in such doctrines as the virgin birth, deity and resurrection of Christ?

When will the AAL finance a movie on some Christian who opposed communism and religious liberalism and who defended the basic doctrines of the Christian faith, such as the Trinity, virgin birth, deity and resurrection of Jesus Christ.

Much more good would be accomplished for the promotion of true Christianity if the AAL would spend all the money it did financing the movie on Bonhoeffer to help produce a movie on some orthodox and anti-Communist churchmen as C.F.W. Walther, Walter A. Maier, Alfred Rehwinkel, Robert Preus, Kurt Marquart, or Raymond Surburg.

When *CN* published Ron Stelzer's biography on Rehwinkel, *CN* thought about producing a video on this colorful LCMS professor. *CN* could find no major donor to produce the kind of movie which the AAL is now financing on Bonhoeffer.

All members of the AAL should read Dr. Surburg's article on Bonhoeffer's theology in this issue, send it to AAL leaders and members of the AAL Board of Directors and then ask the AAL leaders if they believe Bonhoeffer was a Christian and if they approve the promotion of a movie which portrays a skeptic who ended up almost an atheist as a Christian martyr. The large sum of money the AAL has spent promoting Bonhoeffer could have been better spent helping more of the many excellent projects of AAL branches.

Lutherans Promote Liberal Who Rejected Christianity
AAL Helps Create Film on Bonhoeffer
Christian News, May 15, 2000

Dietrich Bonhoeffer's "inner struggle between his faith and his opposition to the Nazi regime is the subject of a film created by AAL and production partners in Germany and Canada that will air on PBS in June" reports the May/June **AAL Correspondent** in an article titled "BONHOEFFER -- AGENT OF GRACE."

Dennis Clauss, second vice president of Church relations, is quoted in the correspondent: "This is a great story. It's a spy story, it's a love story and, above all, it's a story about a man of faith driven to agonizing ethical decisions." Clauss says that the film is well made and that "It was produced with powerful characterizations and striking cinematic detail. Everyone involved went to great pains to ensure its historical integrity."

The Correspondent says that "Those pains already have been recognized internationally. 'Bonhoeffer' was named the Best Film of the 40th Annual Monte Carlo Television Festival held this February in Monaco. Film companies from 70 countries were represented, and American powerhouses like MGM worldwide, Columbia Tristar, Paramount Pictures and NBC Enterprises all competed." The AAL publication observes that Bonhoeffer "has been called one of the most influential theologians of the 20th century." The entire AAL article is reproduced in this issue. When liberals in the Lutheran church have promoted Bonhoeffer during the last 40 years, *CN* has often published excerpts form Bonhoeffer's last writings to show that Bonhoeffer repudiated the Christian faith, the deity and resurrection of Christ, and the actual existence of the God of the Bible. However, some Bonhoeffer defenders maintain that it is not necessary for a good Christian to accept such doctrines.

CN asked the author of the article on Bonhoeffer, who works at the AAL home office:

"Does the film present Bonhoeffer as a Christian theologian who accepted such basic Christian doctrines as the Trinity, the deity, virgin birth and resurrection of Jesus Christ? Has any member of the Board of Directors of AAL or any AAL officer expressed any concern about Bonhoeffer's theology?"

CN asked to receive a copy of a videotape of the film and discussion guide as soon as they available.

CN received this response on May 11:

Rev. Otten:

The film "Bonhoeffer: Agent of Grace" will premier nationwide on the PBS network June 14th at 9:30 a.m. EDT/8:30 p.m. CDT. After the television premier, VHS copies of the film and an accompanying discussion guide will be made available to the Lutheran community through AAL branches.

It is expected branches will be able to begin ordering these materials in early June. You may want to contact Mr. Rickie Kloppe, a leader of Branch 181 in New Haven, MO., and tell him of your interest in this film. Mr. Kloppe's phone number 573-372-3127.

No expressions of concern about the content of this film have been shared by AAL board members and executives who have viewed the film.

There are varying opinions about the Christian witness of Dr. Bonhoeffer. I encourage you to draw conclusions about the story presented in this movie after you have seen it.

Fraternally,

Dennis A. Clauss
Second Vice-President
Church Relations

Bonhoeffer has long been presented in church circles, including the LCMS, as a faithful Lutheran theologian.

"Lutherans explain Why 'New Reformer' Ousts Dr. Luther at Rally," an article in the October 30, 1965 *Detroit Free Press* by religion editor Hiley Ward reported: "You run into the name of Dietrich Bonhoeffer every where.

"And Sunday there'll be the proof of this popularity at the annual Missouri-Synod Lutheran Reformation Festival at Ford Auditorium.

"There's going to be a drama this year. And it is not Martin Luther, but 20th Century Dietrich Bonhoeffer." (Entire article reproduced in this issue of *CN*)

The November 15, 1965 **Lutheran News** noted in an editorial on "The Theology of Dietrich Bonhoeffer":

November 15, 1965
Lutheran News
The Theology of Dietrich Bonhoeffer
(Editorial)
on pages 4-6
A Hero of Liberal Churchmen

Bonhoeffer has long been the hero of liberal churchmen who saw a far greater threat in Nazism that they ever did in Communism. Few movies have been made about Christians who suffered under Communism and churchmen who took a strong stand against Communism.

The May 27, 1966 **Time** said that "So persuasive is his (Bonhoeffer's) influence that Lutheran Church Historian Martin Marty once suggested dividing the theological world into two groups: those who admit their debt to Bonhoeffer, and those who borrow his ideas without acknowledgement." Marty has written in ELCA's **Lutheran** that the actual physical body of Christ did not rise from the dead.

A May 6, 1969 Religious News Service story reported that a new Lutheran church in Hamburg, Germany was named after Dietrich Bonhoeffer. An LCMS church at the University of Chicago under the leadership of Rev. Wayne Saffen had a Bonhoeffer House. The April 10, 1970 **Christianity Today** at the 25th anniversary of the death of Bonhoeffer said that "Bonhoeffer was a biblical expository preacher from the whole of Scripture. He practices the strictest of Christian discipline in devotions and daily life." An April 9, 1970 RNS story reported form New York: "Union Theological Seminary and students joined her in paying tribute to a former member of their community who by leaving the safety of the school went to martyrdom under Hitler. In a service of worship, they thanked God for Dietrich Bonhoeffer, hanged by the Nazis at Flossenburg on April 9, 1945. He was a major shaper of contemporary theology."

"Martyrdom of 20th Century Theologian Observed," another 1970 RNS story said: "The name of Dietrich Bonhoeffer, as one writer put it, has an 'almost unchallenged prestige among younger Roman Catholics and Protestants.'

"But older churchmen are numbered among his disciples and admirers too, and those who disagree with his ideas found in his writings rarely brush him off lightly."

Bonhoeffer was great a hero among such liberal professors at Concordia Seminary, St. Louis as Robert Bertram. "The Courageous Message of Dietrich Bonhoeffer," a story in the August 26, 1995, **St. Louis Post Dispatch** said: "Robert W. Bertram will teach courses on Bonhoeffer's thought at Washington University and St. Louis University starting next week. Bertram is Seminex professor emeritus of theology at Lutheran School of Theology in Chicago." "Bonhoeffer took a lonely and dangerous stand (like Martin Luther 400 years earlier) and paid the ultimate price, Bertram said." "Bertram noted that Bonhoeffer, like a later martyr and 'hero of conscience,' Martin Luther King Jr., was a disciple of Gandhi and his credo of non-violence.

"The two churchmen, prophets, both of their time and ahead of it, both traveled to the mountain top and were cut off prematurely at age 39 as the result of violence, Bertram said."

The St. Louis paper noted that "most of Bonhoeffer's writings, which run to 16 volumes, are still in print in more than a dozen languages. His 'Letters and Papers from Prison' and 'Ethics' are staples in courses in mainline Protestant and Catholic seminaries today. And because of his poetry and writings on the theology of justice he is also studied as a literary and philosophical figure of his time, Bertram said."

ELCA's September, 1995 **The Lutheran** reprinted "Who am I?" from Bonhoeffer's **Letters and Papers from Prison**. The ELCA's December 4, 1968 **The Lutheran** praised Bonhoeffer and his theology, comparing him with Luther and maintained that "For Bonhoeffer, Christ is absolutely crucial."

"Bonhoeffer and the Confirmation Calls," an article in the Pentecost 1985 **Lutheran Forum** by monk Brother John alert commended Bonhoeffer and his theology.

"Bonhoeffer Biographer Will Speak Here," a report in the March 15, 1996 **St. Louis Lutheran** said that Bonhoeffer's biographer and "best friend" would be speaking at Concordia Seminary, St. Louis. The visit of Eberhard Bethge and his wife to St. Louis was sponsored by The Bonhoeffer Study Group of St. Louis, Concordia Seminary and the Goethe Institute. A video on the life of Bonhoeffer was also shown at Concordia Seminary. Bonhoeffer was presented to the students and faculty at the seminary as a great Christian theologian and hero. His anti-Christian theology was not exposed and repudiated. Someone like the editor of *Christian News* who has attacked Bonhoeffer's theology has been banned from speaking at the LCMS seminary. *CN* had wanted to show the students and faculty where Bethge and the video did not tell the real truth about Bonhoeffer's theology. Some Sunday School material published by major denominations has highly praised Bonhoeffer and his theology. A curriculum published by the Lutheran Church in America (now in ELCA) said:

"An example of 'seed on good soil' may be seen in Dietrich Bonhoeffer. He was a young Lutheran pastor in Germany who was hanged by the Nazis at the close of World War II. He was a brilliant Christian thinker, but he did not live long enough to develop his thought in full detail. Yet his few books and letters from prison have been like seed. They influence many persons today who seek to explain the Christian faith for our times" (THE GOSPEL STORY OF JESUS, Teacher's Guide, p. 131).

"Dietrich Bonhoeffer has been called the most distinguished Christian martyr of the 20th Century. What makes his martyrdom outstanding is not the pain he had to suffer, but the fact that the accepted martyrdom as part of his discipleship" (IBID., p. 311).

"Bonhoeffer's friend, the Bishop of Chichester, summed up his life with these words, 'He saw the truth and spoke it with complete absence of fear." (AS ONE WHO SERVES, p. 48).

Critics of Bonhoeffer

Dr. Raymond F. Surburg, a professor at Concordia Seminary, Ft. Wayne, in "An Evaluation of Dietrich Bonhoeffer's Life and Theology After Half a Century" published in the September 18, 1995 **Christian News** and reprinted in this issue shows that Bonhoeffer's Christ was not the Christ of the Bible or Martin Luther.

Some conservative Roman Catholics have expressed concerns about Bonhoeffer's theology, Cardinal Carberry of St. Louis noted that Bonhoeffer denied the deity of Christ. See "Bonhoeffer Revisited" reprinted here from the **St. Louis Review** of the Archdiocese of St. Louis.

A February 1, 1997 Fundamental Baptist News Service report on Bonhoeffer noted: "The man is often mentioned, in fact, as a positive matter by Evangelical scholars today. In his writings, though, he plainly rejected such doctrines as the virgin birth, physical resurrection, and substitutionary atonement of Jesus Christ. According to Bonhoeffer, it is a 'cardinal error' to regard Christianity as religion of salvation."

The July/August 1995 newsletter of **Biblical Discernment Ministries** said: (on page 21).

The December 7, 1984 Biblical Evangelist said: "Bonhoeffer, a disciple of Karl Barth, was not a Christian at all, to say nothing of a 'great' one, in our judgment. He was one of the fathers of the 'death of God' philosophy and wrote: "There is no longer need for a God as a working hypothesis, whether in morals, politics, or science. Nor is there any need for such a God in religion or philosophy. In the name of intellectual honesty these working hypotheses should be dropped or dispensed with as far as possible."

Dr. G. Archer Weniger wrote in the march 29, 1977 Blu Print: "During the 1976 election campaign candidate Jimmy Carter testified that his four favorite theologians were: Reinhold Niebuhr, Karl Barth, Paul Tillich and Dietrich Bonhoeffer. . . Bonhoeffer is not only a deceiver and a wolf in sheep's clothing, but he is an atheist as is Tillich, while both Niebuhr and Barth were Unitarians at their best."

Christian News has often noted that Tillich, Barth and Niebuhr rejected such Christian doctrines as the Trinity and the resurrection of Christ.

Dietrich Bonhoeffer: Memories and Perspectives
Christian News, May 15, 2000

THE LIFE STORY OF DIETRICH BONHOEFFER is one of the great epics of courage and conviction in the twentieth century. A young pastor in Germany when Hitler came to power, Bonhoeffer was among the first of his countrymen to recognize the threat posed by Nazism to the basic human values of western civilization. A leader in the Confessing Church (that group of pastors which actively opposed the nazification of the German Lutheran Church), Bonhoeffer also played an active role in the German resistance movement. He was arrested by the Gestapo in 1943, spent two years in prison and concentration camps and was hanged at the Flossenbürg camp on April 9, 1945. He was 39 years old. Since his death, his writings and life story have continued to inspire and challenge countless men and women throughout the world.

DIETRICH BONHOEFFER: MEMORIES AND PERSPECTIVES, a documentary film in three parts, explores Bonhoeffer's life and times in chronological fashion: the American experience, the early years of the Church Struggle, Bonhoeffer's peace sermon at Fanö, the underground seminary at Finkenwalde, the flight to America in 1939, his return to Germany, work in the resistance movement and, finally, prison and death. Filmed in Germany and France over the past two years, the movie features interviews with Bonhoeffer's family, friends, and co-workers, highlighting Dr. Eberhard Bethge, Bonhoeffer's closest friend and chief biographer. These candid interviews are supported by photographs from the National Archives in Washington, D.C., the YIVO Institute for Jewish Research in New York City, as well as selections from various European sources.

In Short
The Christian Century, May 24-31, 2000

Dietrich Bonhoeffer: A Biography. *By Eberhard Bethge. Edited by Victoria J. Barnett (revised and unabridged translation). Fortress, 941 pp., $39.00 paperback.*

The new English translation of Bethge's 1970 biography, skillfully rendered by Barnett, includes all corrections and revisions of earlier editions. As a result, the edifying story of a remarkable 20th-century Christian life is now available in even greater detail. At 941 pages it's not a quick read, but Bethge offers a compelling account of a complex man. While nothing replaces the power of Bonhoeffer's own writings, Berthge's work has a poignant power of its own. For Bonhoeffer students, the most significant news may be that the endnotes have been updated. The notes now refer to the English translations of the 15-volume German edition of Bonhoeffer's complete works, which are now appearing, also from Fortress.

Bonhoeffer – Agent of Grace
(A Review)
By L. Blecker
Christian News, June 19, 2000

On Wednesday evening, June 14, 2000, the AAL production of BONHOEFFER – AGENT OF GRACE was aired on the local PBS channel. Sorry to say, the AAL production seemed to be a disjointed jumble of vignettes, loosely based on historical fact. That Rev. Dr. Dietrich Bonhoeffer was a German patriot of the highest order was not clear in the AAL production. The historical Bonhoeffer was a serious and intellectual theologian. The AAL Bonhoeffer was a muddleheaded aristocrat, who seemed to be led by the nose by his brother-in-law, Hans von Dohnanyi, who was a noted German jurist and early opponent of the Third Reich. From the AAL production, one was lent the impression that Bonhoeffer was a dilettante anti-Nazi, primarily concerned with Hitler's assault on Christianity and the Jews – until he was incarcerated by the Gestapo. It is true that Bonhoeffer was a member of the "Confessing Church," which was successful in combating Hitler's so-called German Christian Church. However, the fine point was made, that Bonhoeffer opposed the state's takeover of the Church but did not oppose the state (in deference to Romans 13). Bonhoeffer knew the Nazis made no such fine distinctions, and it is doubtful whether Bonhoeffer himself did. On ethical, if not Christian grounds, Bonhoeffer was a convinced opponent of the regime. Bonhoeffer did become an Abwehr agent (military intelligence) of Admiral Canaris. The Abwehr was a hot bed of secret political resistance to the Third Reich, and Bonhoeffer knew what he was doing by accepting an appointment to the Abwehr. According to AAL, however, only after his arrest by the Gestapo, it was as though prison had a sobering and crystallizing influence on Bonhoeffer, who then began ministering to his fellow inmates as a sort of chaplain. Not much of Bonhoeffer's unorthodox Christianity was visible in the AAL production. However toward the end of the 1- 1/2 hour production, Bonhoeffer was seen preaching in a ruined church to Captain Best of the British Secret Service, Lieutenant Kokorin of the Russian army and a former Nazi whose name escapes us (Best and Kokorin were historical characters). In this scene, Bonhoeffer made reference to a "grown up world" where there would be a "Christianity without religion."

The savagery of the Nazis was played down in the AAL production in the now familiar "banality of evil" genre. The final scene of Bonhoeffer's murder at Flossenburg was pure fantasy. One got the impression that the gallows were reserved for Bonhoeffer. However on that day, April 9, 1945, not only Bonhoeffer but Admiral Canaris, General Oster, Dr. Sack (Army Judge Advocate), Captain Strunk and Captain Gehre were hanged in assembly-line fashion, one after the other. All these men were forced to strip naked as a final humiliation and marched to their deaths, after being beaten and sentenced by drum-head, illegal SS courts martial. That Bonhoeffer, Canaris and the other were involved in anti-Hitler activity, including plotting the assassination of Hitler, is historical fact to which Bonhoeffer believed the evil of killing Hitler was the lesser of the two evils-doing evil and being evil. To Bonhoeffer, any cooperation with the regime was to be evil.

There were other historical inconsistencies in the AAL production. The scene where Bonhoeffer was offered his life in return for negotiating with the Allies for SS Chief Heinrich Himmler seems pure fiction. We do not recall reading anything in historical accounts about this proposed pact with the devil's agent Himmler. However, the scene did provide a vehicle for thought. Bonhoeffer, when offered the hope of living, was able to portray illusory hope offered by a liar and fiend as the "final temptation" in declining Himmler's offer. When Hans Oster was first introduced to Bonhoeffer as General Oster, Oster wore the uniform of a field grade officer. A bit later, it seems as though AAL was able to find a general's uniform for the Oster character. As suggested in the AAL production, Hans von Dohnanyi did indeed contract a serious infection in an effort to avoid trial. However, the AAL production shows von Dohnanyi executed on a rubble heap, defiant to the end. However, in fact, von Dohnanyi, semi-comatose from his infection, was tried and executed on a stretcher, testimony to both Nazi bumbling and savagery. There are credible reports that Bonhoeffer toward the end took to making the sign of the cross in his devotions, and immediately before his murder was seen in fervent prayer, hardly the acts of a man who doubted the existence of God. Since we cannot look into the heart of man, particularly at the moment of death, Christian charity would lead one to hope that Pastor Bonhoeffer was a Christian when he mounted the gallows, a man better than his theology. Pity AAL did not choose to portray Bonhoeffer's final moments in the light of credible history.

In seeking to do too much in a 1-1/2 hour program, AAL did little justice to Bonhoeffer as an ethical man, a German patriot as well as an unorthodox theologian. At least, AAL did give the impression that Romans 13 does have limits in the life of a Christian, even an unorthodox one, as to a Christian's duty to the state. That limit is the Christian, in the end, must obey God's Law rather than that of man. Nevertheless, Bonhoeffer was not martyred because of his Christian faith. Rather, Bonhoeffer died for his ethical resistance to an evil, foul regime translated into active political resistance against it.

Dietrich Bonhoeffer Rejected Classical Christology
By David Becker
RP Digest
Christian News, June 5, 2000

I don't mean to be critical of people, but I do want to speak the truth in love, and one of my pet peeves is when I see people, especially those who consider themselves to be, and present themselves as, theologically conservative, praise Dietrich Bonhoeffer.

Bonhoeffer espoused a so-called religionless Christianity, and expressed doubt about God as a working hypothesis. He was a father of the so-called "death of God" "fad" of a few years ago.

He wrote a lot and also wrote some things that sounded orthodox but he consistently had a low view of the Bible, considering a lot of it myth.

In his book, Christ the Center (1960, Harper & Row), Bonhoeffer wrote:

"So if we speak of Jesus Christ as God, we may not speak of him as the representative of an idea of God who possesses the properties of omniscience and omnipotence (there is no such thing as this abstract divine nature!)" (p. 108).

So Bonhoeffer didn't really believe that Jesus is God.

Bonhoeffer continued, "Strictly speaking, we should really talk, not about the Incarnation, but only about the Incarnate One. An interest in the incarnation raises the question 'How?' The question 'How?' thus underlies the hypothesis of the Virgin Birth. It is both historically and dogmatically questionable. The biblical evidence for it is uncertain. If the biblical evidence gave decisive evidence for it is uncertain. If the biblical evidence gave decisive evidence for the real fact, there might be no particular significance in the dogmatic obscurity. The doctrine of the Virgin Birth is meant to express the incarnation of God and not just the fact of the Incarnate One. But does it not miss the decisive point of the incarnation by implying that Jesus has NOT become man wholly as we are? The question remains open, just as and just because it is already open in the Bible" (p. 109).

NOTE: The *Lutheran Witness* in 1957 stated, "The doctrine of the virgin birth of Christ is a fundamental article of our faith, the denial of which makes saving faith in Christ impossible…

"A true child of God finds it no harder to believe this miracle than any other. If God in the beginning instituted natural conception through the union of husband and wife, the same almighty power enables Him to use other means. 'With God nothing shall be impossible' (Luke 1:37).

"If we do not believe this, but regard Jesus as the true, natural son of Joseph and

Mary, then we are compelled by the Holy Scripture to regard Jesus as having been born in sin like all the other sons of men (John 3:6; Eph. 2:3).

"The Virgin Birth was God's way of producing a holy child, who was also the Son of God and therefore able to fulfill the Law perfectly, suffer our punishment, and thus bring about everlasting atonement and reconciliation of the world to Himself (2 Cor. 5:19). Our Savior was God and man in one Person; that fact makes our redemption certain."

Bonhoeffer didn't think that that Jesus is sinless either. "The assertion of the sinlessness of Jesus fails if it has in mind observable acts of Jesus. His deeds are done in the likeness of flesh. They are not sinless, but ambiguous. One can and should see good and bad in them" (p. 113).

Speaking of the resurrection of Jesus Christ from the dead, Bonhoeffer said, "This is and remains a last stumbling block which the person who believes in Christ must accept in one way or the other. Empty or not empty, it remains a stumbling block. We are not sure of its historicity. The Bible itself reveals the stumbling block in showing how hard it was to prove that the disciples had not perhaps stolen the body. Even here we cannot evade the real of ambiguity" (p. 117).

Edwin H. Robertson wrote an introduction to Christ the Center, called "Bonhoeffer's Christology." According to Robertson, "The question (Bonhoeffer) is answering is not, 'What do you think of Christ?,' a question he would have rejected; but, 'How has Christ been understood and what is wrong with the classical concepts of Christology?'" (p. 10).

"The Chalcedonian Definition is cold, statue cold, and requires the warm breath of life before it can be recognized as anything to do with Jesus Christ. Bonhoeffer would have us discover the ever-present Christ in our existence, in the purpose of history and in the meaning of creation" (p. 24).

So Bonhoeffer rejected classical Christology, had a low view of the Bible, denied the deity of Christ, denied the sinlessness of Christ, and doubted the physical resurrection of Christ.

So why is Bonhoeffer being vigorously promoted by ostensibly conservative theologians like ....

Well, I'm not going to name names. The record shows who they are.

Some have said that while Bonhoeffer was shaky if not totally hertical theologically, at least he opposed Adolf Hitler. Bonhoeffer did indeed say and do some good things against Hitler, but his most well-known act was involvement in a plot to assassinate Hitler. I don't think this was in accord with Christian ethics of general civil obedience. Rescuing Jews and others and lawful opposition to Hitler is one thing, but murdering one's governor is another. As one denomination's faith statement says "Civil Government. We believe that rulers should be upheld at all times except in things opposed to the will of God," Rom. 13:1-5. Admittedly Bonhoeffer and others were in a difficult situation in Nazi Germany, but Bonhoeffer went too far in advocating the murder of Hitler. So Bonhoeffer was unsound not only doctrinally, but also in practice.

If Dietrich Bonhoeffer said some good things, surely they can be found elsewhere, preferably in the Bible itself. Bonhoeffer was a way-out theological liberal. I don't think he's a churchman whose faith and life are worthy of emulation.

Solzhenitsyn Rather Than Bonhoeffer
The AAL Spent Hundreds of Thousands Promoting a Theologian Who Rejected Christianity
Christian News, August 7, 2000

"Lutherans Promote Liberal Who Rejected Christianity – AAL HELPS CREATE FILM ON BONHOEFFER," the lead story in the May 15 **Christian News** noted that the Aid Association for Lutherans spent a huge sum of money helping to produce "Bonhoeffer-Agent of Grace." The film was shown on national television. The AAL is sending a free copy of the film to every AAL branch.

Some of the speeches by Solzhenitsyn which *CN* published are in the **Christian News Encyclopedia**. Solzhenitsyn exposed that fact that in the West many of the Communist-controlled Russian churchmen are considered to be faithful.

Rather than spending thousands of dollars promoting a liberal theologian like Bonhoeffer who did not speak out against communism and who denied such doctrines as the resurrection of Christ, the AAL should have promoted someone like Solzhenitsyn, an anti-Communist Christian.

Continue In My Word
Christian News, November 20, 2000
John 8:31

(Bulletin cover shows Martin Luther King, Pope John XXIII, Mother Teresa, and Dietrich Bonhoeffer)

Cover of the bulletin published by the Evangelical Lutheran Church in America's Augsburg Fortress Press to be used on Reformation Sunday, October 29, 2000. Martin Luther King, Jr., was a modernist who rejected the historic Christian faith. He did not affirm such Christian doctrines as the virgin birth, deity and resurrection of Jesus Christ. Even his close friends have noted that King said he was a Marxist. It is well-known that he was an impenitent adulterer who had many extramarital sexual affairs. Pope John XXIII and Mother Teresa rejected the central doctrine of the Reformation, justification by faith alone in the merits of Jesus Christ. According to Mother Teresa, pious Hindus, Muslims and other non-Christians can get to heaven without saving faith in Jesus Christ. Dietrich Bonhoeffer in his last years totally repudiated the Christian faith. He denied the resurrection of Jesus Christ and said that the entire Bible had to be demythologized since, according to this "Lutheran" theologian, it contained many myths and errors.

Oesch and Burgdorf-Not Bonhoeffer
Christian News, February 24, 2003

The Lutheran Church-Missouri Synod's Concordia Publishing House has published one more biography of Dietrich Bonhoeffer, the great hero of so many churchmen. *CN* has for years shown that Bonhoeffer repudiated historic Christianity.

Theodore Kleinhans is the author of the CPH biography of Bonhoeffer.

CPH would do the cause of confessional Lutheranism far more good if it would publish a biography and some of the writings of such orthodox Lutheran theologians as Wilhelm Oesch, Paul Burgdorf, and Raymond Surburg.

When Kleinhans mentioned some criticism of Oesch (*CN*, Jan. 3, 1983), Paul Burgdorf came to Oesch's defense. Note "Regarding the Ministry of Dr. William Oesch-Clearing the Air" by Paul Burgdorf below. Oesch was born in the U.S. But spent most of his career in Germany. *The Christian News Encyclopedia* has information on Oesch. If CPH wants to publish a biography about a German theologian it should have published one on Oesch who took issue with Barth's and Bonhoeffer's anti-scriptural theology. It appears as if those at CPH responsible for determining just what should be published believe that the really famous theologians are those who are praised by the liberals. Many of Oesch's writings can easily be found in Der Lutherische Rundblich, a scholarly journal Oesch edited.

CN previously suggested that the Schwan Foundation would be doing much more good if it financed a collection of the writings of Burgdorf and Surburg, who took sharp issue with Bonhoeffer's anti-Christian theology, than some of the other books this foundation has been helping CPH publish. At the 100th anniversary of the birth of Dr. Hermann Sasse, those in the LCMS who prefer the hierarchical position of Loehe and Grabau to that of the congregationalism of Walther, made certain it was properly observed. They were able to get the Schwan Foundation to help finance a publication of some of his writings. Sasse defended the editor of *CN* and *CN* years ago published some of his writings. However, it would have been more helpful for the LCMS if the Schwan Foundaion and CPH had published a book of the writings of Oesch, Burgdorf and Surburg, who were all strongly pro-Walther. The pro-Walther position taken by Oesch and Burgdorf may be one reason that those who were able to get the Schwan Foundation to finance the writings of Sasse had little interest in even mentioning the 100th anniversary of the births of Oesch and Burgdorf.

Last week *CN* noted in "Jesus First Should Praise the Schwan Foundation" that foundations are not interested in helping any publication, like Oesch's **Crucible** or Burgdorf's **Confessional Lutheran,** which actually name the liberals and take issue with a church's bureaucracy. It's OK to finance the "positive" "mission minded" conservatives as long as they do not cry out against and name the wolves as Burgdorf and Oesch did. There is little prestige in being associated with men like Oesch and Burgdorf and plenty of prestige in supporting those who praise skeptics like Bonhoeffer and Marty.

CPH Interim President Paul McCain has not yet answered *CN*'s letter pertaining to CPH's praise of a theologian who denied the virgin birth, deity and resurrection of Christ (p. 1).

LCMS's CPH Publish Book Praising Bonhoeffer as A Great Christian
Denied Such Doctrines as The Virgin Birth and Resurrection of Christ
Christian News, February 24, 2003

The Lutheran Church-Missouri Synod's Concordia Publishing House recently published "Till the Night Be Past-The Life and Times of Dietrich Bonhoeffer" by Theodore J. Kleinhans. The 171 page book is available from Concordia Publishing House, 3558 S. Jefferson Ave., St. Louis, MO 63118-3808. 1-800-325-3040.

The CPH book presents Bonhoeffer as a great Christian. *CN* asked Rev. Paul McCain, Interim President of CPH, on Feb. 17: "Did you express any concern that Bonhoeffer was so greatly praised by CPH even though Bonhoeffer rejected the Christian faith, including such doctrines as the virgin birth, deity and the resurrection of Jesus Christ?"

The Nov. 15, 1965, *Christian News*, in an editorial on the theology of Bonhoeffer, quoted directly from Bonhoeffer's last writings statements showing that he had repudiated the Christian faith. Dr. Raymond Surburg, a professor at Concordia Seminary, F. Wayne, Indiana, writes in "An Evaluation of Dietrich Bonhoeffer's Life and Theology After Half a Century" (*Christian News*, Sept. 18, 1995): "While in prison Bonhoeffer came to the conclusion that mankind no longer needs God. What amounts to theoretical atheism was Bonhoeffer's assertion that God is teaching us that we must live as men who can get along well without him." Bonhoeffer said that his demythologizing of the Bible went beyond Rudolf Boltmann. Surburg quoted at length from Bonhoeffer's writings.

CN published a letter from a Nebraska pastor who did extensive research on the life and theology of Bonhoeffer for a graduate degree in Religious Studies. The pastor said Surburg was correct. According to him, Bonhoeffer "was a heathen and no Christian." A book published by Yale University Press in 1977 came to the same conclusion. The June 3, 2002, *CN* quoted from this book, **Modern European Thought: Continuity and Change in Ideas, 1600-1950** by Franklin L. Baumer, Pierson College, Yale University, 1977, MacMillan Publishing Co. Inc. Many Bonhoeffer defenders seem unaware of this book. The cover of the new CPH publication on Bonhoeffer says:

"From his birth into a prominent family at Breslau to his execution by the Nazis at Folssenburg, Dietrich Bonhoeffer lived an extraordinary life. As the son of a leading psychiatrist in Berlin, Dietrich embraced the riches of European intellect and culture. Yet amid his passion for learning and adventure, he recognized and heeded Christ's calling to serve the church in a tumultuous world.

"In this moving biography, Kleinhans recounts the story of Dietrich's childhood and education, his formative years as a pastor and theologian, and the difficult years prior to and during World War II. The author paints a sympathetic, yet balanced, portrait of Bonhoeffer's work and ministry. He explores important themes of family, church and faith, and public discipleship in the midst of Nazi tyranny and propaganda.

"Although not exhaustive, this easy-to-read book addresses all the significant issues and events in Bonhoeffer's dramatic story.

"See in these pages how God's sure promise and strength would sustain this remarkable servant 'till the night be past.'

"Theodore J. Kleinhans is a retired pastor and Air Force chaplain living in Appleton, Wisconsin. He served as consultant to the PBS movie, 'Bonhoeffer: Agent of Grace,' produced by Aid Association for Lutherans. He has written nine books and is a member of the Author's Guild."

Kleinhans writes: "I was involved to a small degree with shaping a film about Bonhoeffer for broadcast on public television in the summer of 2000. The film, Dietrich Bonhoeffer: Agent of Grace, showed some of the conflict in Dietrich's personality: his practical involvement with the world of politics and at the same time his eagerness not to give up the God whom he had come to understand and live with. From the reactions to the film in Germany and in America, it is evident that Bonhoeffer was a highly respected but controversial figure" (p. 12).

Karl Barth

Several time Kleinhans mention that Karl Barth, whom the CPH author evidently believes affirmed the basic doctrines of the Christian faith, had a great influence on Bonhoeffer. He writes:

"What Bonhoeffer learned at Berlin came not only from its own faculty, but from a young Swiss professor who had begun teaching at Gottingen – Karl Barth. The whole campus at Gottingen buzzed with talk about its new theological star. Barth could even excite Dietrich's cousin, Hans Christoph von Hase, who was not a theologian, but a physicist. Summarizing the role of Karl Barth as the major theological figure of the century might take as many thousands of pages as he himself used in his seemingly endless *Christian Dogmatics*. Barth flashed on the scene like a meteor, studies and taught throughout Germany, helped write the Barmen Confession that clearly condemned the anti-Christian character of the Third Reich, then returned to teach at his native Basel. The theological movement Barth started has been labeled *Neo-Orthodoxy*, and his famous students, including Bultmann, Gogarten, Tillich, and Niebuhr, were tagged Barthians. Very simply, Barth tried to sweep away the theological debris that had accumulated for decades and to turn the church back to a pristine vision of an all-knowing and all-loving God, who purely out of goodness and mercy had revealed Himself to humankind.

"In Berlin, Dietrich Bonhoeffer had little contact with Barth. He did not even read him at any length. Yet there is little doubt that the teachings of Karl Barth were finding a ready home in the budding conscience of Dietrich Bonhoeffer. In fact, one of the early papers Dietrich wrote for Seeberg came back marked with red exclamation points and had 'Nein' scribbled all over it because, in the professor's opinion, it showed too much Barthian influence" (pp. 51-52).

Kleinhans refers to Bonhoeffer as "A disciple of Karl Barth."

"Still, Dietrich was not yet 25, too young for ordination or a lectureship. The travel in Spain and Italy had more than whetted his appetite for other cultures and new insights. He was restless. A disciple of Karl Barth, though he had never met the man, he realized he would face considerable hostility in the United States. Highly trained systematic and dogmatic theologians from Europe were not all that welcome in a church atmosphere that stressed the social gospel, which insisted on action rather than thought" (p. 67).

"Scarcely had he paid his respects to the big old house on Wangenheimstrasse than Dietrich left to seek out Karl Barth at the University of Bonn. From New York, his Swiss friend Sutz had written a letter of introduction, and Dietrich was quick to follow it up. Although Bonhoeffer had earned the rank of privatdozent, or private instructor, was a licensed lecturer, and had published two books, his name was wholly unknown to Barth. Nevertheless, the 45-year old Swiss pastor, who had suddenly become the star of German theology, quickly learned to admire the 25-year-old disciple who for three weeks joined his seminar and, unlike most of his students, always could find an apt quotation from Luther or Augustine.

"To Dietrich, the pipe-smoking Barth was highly impressive. Not one bit pompous or dogmatic, Barth showed a dedication both to faith and to reason that was unmatched by any other theological professor Dietrich had encountered. Their walks, their chats, their meals together – this was the kind of warmth herr doctor professors seldom practiced, even with interesting privatdozents. Although Barth would eventually flee to his native Switzerland, Dietrich remained a lifelong admirer and correspondent" (pp. 74, 75).

Kleinhans concludes:

"For himself at least, Dietrich finally found convincing answers after a long and painful quest. Man is God's instrument on earth, made in His image, responsible, redeemed in Christ, enlightened by God's Spirit, and self-fulfilling" (p. 170).

The Christ of Dietrich Bonhoeffer and Karl Barth is not the Christ of the Bible. Karl Barth rejected the resurrection of Jesus Christ. He did not believe in the scriptural and Christian doctrine of the Holy Trinity. This editor waded through some of Barth's ponderous writings during his student days and came to the conclusion that it was waste of time to read all of Barth's works. The *Concordia Theological Monthly* of Concordia Seminary published an article by Dr. J. T. Mueller, a professor at the seminary, showing that Barth rejected historic Christianity. Anyone who wants information about Barth's theology should check *The Christian News Encyclopedia*. CPH published Olav Valen-Sentatd's **The Word Can Never Die** which ably shows that Barth rejected the doctrine of the Holy Trinity. It appears as if most Seminary professors have never read the book. Now CPH publishes a book which commends Barth and Bonhoeffer.

Rather than praising Barth, CPH should show that this "Greatest Theologian of the Twentieth Century" who had such a great influence on Bonhoeffer, repudiated historic Christianity and led an adulterous lifestyle. **The Question of Woman – The Collected Writings of Charlotte von Kireschbaum** reviewed in the Nov. 11, 1996, *Christian News* shows that Barth had as a married man a close romantic and intellectual association with von Kirschbaum, over the vigorous protest of his wife, for 35 years. Barth not only repudiated scriptural theology but also what the Bible teaches about an adulterous relationship.

"Draws One Closer to The One True Faith"
"Hanged On a Twisted Cross? -- New Film on Bonhoeffer
Christian News, June 3, 2003

Yale University Book: Bonhoeffer Rejected Christianity - Surburg: Bonhoeffer Denied Deity and Resurrection of Christ

"Hanged On A Twisted Cross," a new film about Dietrich Bonhoeffer, according to the May 20 **Human Events** "makes it clear that Bonhoeffer gave up himself for Jesus Christ." The conservative publication says in a review of the film that "like all programs on Bonhoeffer, it must be seen." Human Events says: "Listening to the entries in Bonhoeffer's diaries and books bring one closer to one true faith of the Apostles."

Many conservatives, along with theological liberals, have often praised Bonhoeffer and said he was a true Bible believing Christian. Two years ago the Aid Association for Lutherans helped produce the film, "Bonhoeffer -- Agent of Grace". It was aired on PBS. A video of the film was widely distributed by the AAL to Lutheran congregations all over the nation. During the past 40 years *CN* has published statements from Bonhoeffer's books and diaries in which he denied such doctrines as the virgin birth, deity and resurrection of Jesus Christ. *CN* quoted directly from Bonhoeffer's last writings. The September 18, 1995, **Christian News** published "An Evaluation of Dietrich Bonhoeffer's Life and Theology After Half a Century" by Raymond Surburg, Ph.D. Th.D. Surburg quoted directly from the writings of Bonhoeffer. This professor at the Lutheran Church-Missouri Synod's Concordia Seminary, Ft. Wayne and Concordia University, Seward, Nebraska, concluded: "While in prison Bonhoeffer came to the conclusion that mankind no longer needs God. What amounts to theoretical atheism was Bonhoeffer's assertion that God is teaching us that we must live as men who can get along very well without him."

Christian News sent Surburg's articles to each member of the AAL's Board of Directors, including Rev. Thomas Zehnder, a leader of Jesus First and a former district president of the LCMS, and Dr. Gary Greenfield, president of Wisconsin Lutheran College in Milwaukee. *CN* wrote to Zehnder, Greenfield and the other members of the AAL Board of Directors: "I would like to know if the members of the Board of Directors believe that Bonhoeffer accepted such doctrines as the virgin birth, deity and physical resurrection Jesus Christ. Has any member of the Board of Directors or officer of AAL expressed any concern about Bonhoeffer's theology?" *CN* did not receive a response from Zehnder, Greenfield or any other members of the AAL Board of Directors. *CN* published a letter from a Nebraska pastor who did extensive research on the life and theology of Bonhoeffer for a graduate degree in Religious Studies. The pastor said Surburg was correct. According to him, Bonhoeffer "was a heathen and no Christian."

A book published by Yale University Press in 1977 came to the same conclusion about Bonhoeffer. Here is a section from **Modern European Thought: Continuity and Change in Ideas, 1600-1950**, Franklin L. Baumer, Pierson College, Yale University, 1977, MacMillan Publishing Co., Inc:

"Dietrich Bonhoeffer's now famous theological letters, written in a Nazi prison, describe, with agonizing clarity, the salient features of Europe's religious landscape in the first half of the twentieth century: the all but total secularization of culture; the rise of new theologies to meet this situation: and the hint -- alas there was no time for anything more, since Bonhoeffer was executed when only thirty-nine years old -- of a much more radical theology to come, of a 'religion less Christianity,' as he named it. Brought up in a secular family, which ridiculed theology, and persecuted by the German state (not, however, for his religious opinions but for his role in the Resistance), Bonhoeffer was better placed than most to appreciate the lengths to which secularism had gone. In a letter of June 8, 1944, to his friend Pastor Bethge, he wrote feelingly of the world's 'great defection from God' in the twentieth century. The secular movement, which he thought began about the twentieth century, 'has in our time reached a certain completion. Man has learned to cope with all questions of importance without recourse to God as a working hypothesis. In questions concerning science, art, and even ethics, this has become an understood thing which one scarcely dares to tilt at any more.'

". . . Bonhoeffer, by the time he wrote his last letters was critical of all forms of Christian apologetics. . . Even the Confessing Church, set up to oppose the Nazified church in Germany, and of which Bonhoeffer was a leader for a time, had lapsed into a conservative restoration of historical Christian theology. Bonhoeffer's own message, though none to clear, seemed to point beyond these theologies to a new sort of radical Christianity, characterized by complete honesty, dispensing with all 'religious jargon,' including the term God itself, which had become meaningless for most people, yet keeping the suffering Christ, and thus speaking to modern man's condition. But it remains an open question as to whether Bonhoeffer's own religionless religion did not represent a bankruptcy of the whole theological understanding, at least as that was rationally understood" (pp. 439-440).

"But Bonhoeffer was groping toward a substantially new idea. This was a secularized Christianity, completely divested of metaphysics and cut to the dimensions of the world of man. 'You would be surprised and perhaps disturbed,' he wrote to his friend Bethge in the spring of 1944, 'if you knew how my ideas on theology are taking shape.' To the end, Bonhoeffer continued, in part, to talk traditional God-language, to speak of 'being in God's hands,' of the revelation of God in Christ, even of the being and transcendence of God. But there does not seem to be much doubt that he was trying to formulate some kind of new 'secular' theology that would not require such language. Bonhoeffer's argument, partly sketched at the beginning of this chapter, was as follows. Whether we like it or not, the world has become completely secularized. The time of 'religion as such,' when men could be told everything by words, theological or pious, was over. 'Men as they are now simply cannot be religious any more.' So what was man to do? Having 'come of age,' it was neither possible nor desirable, for mankind to reclaim 'the land of childhood,' as in the Middle Ages. As 'mature' men, they must acknowledge the situation. 'God,' wrote Bonhoeffer paradoxically, 'is teaching us to get along very well without him. We can live without God, the deus ex machina who has died, but not without Christ. Christ, entirely within human ken, as God was not, signified, for Bonhoeffer, simply 'concern for others,' 'freedom from self, maintained to the point of death,' or crucifixion. Bonhoeffer's preoccupation with the crucifixion is reminiscent of 'the suffering God,' so much discussed by English theologians during and after World War I. This suffering God, weak and powerless in the world, was to be the starting point for Bonhoeffer's new 'worldly' theology.

"A radical departure from other theologies, past and present, this was almost a non-theology. It reflected the invasion of theology itself by secularism, an acceptance of secular conviction, or lack of conviction, which not even Tillich, much less Barth or

Martin, would have tolerated. It reflected, too, the fading of metaphysical vision, so noticeable also in contemporary philosophy. Carried followers the solemn styled death-of-God theologians' of Europe and America, it meant the restriction of theology to empirical statements about man and his world and the loss of any sort of transcendent Being in whom man's life could be anchored. When Martin Buber spoke of 'Eclipse of God' in the twentieth century, he was thinking of 'the conceptual letting go of God,' of the confinement of God to man's subjectivity by modern philosophers and psychologists. With Bonhoeffer and the death-of-God 'school', theology itself began to contribute to this eclipse" (pp. 454-455).

After quoting from **Modern European Thought**, David Becker of Religious Political Digest concludes:

"Last year the Aid Association for Lutherans, a pan-Lutheran insurance company sponsored an acclaimed film about Bonhoeffer, who is generally held in high esteem among 'Lutherans' in spite of his being a virtual atheist in what he believed."

BONHOEFFER: "THE MOST INFLUENTIAL THEOLOGIAN OF THE TWENTIETH CENTURY"
Matthew Becker In Concordia Journal of Concordia Seminary, St. Louis
Christian News, December 6, 2004

Dietrich Bonhoeffer, who denied such basic doctrines of historic Christianity as the deity and resurrection of Jesus Christ, was the "most influential theologian of the twentieth century," says Dr. Matthew Becker in the October, 2004 Concordia Journal. Becker, who formerly taught at Concordia River Forest, Illinois, and Concordia University, Portland, Oregon, is now a professor at Valparaiso University, Valparaiso, Indiana.

The masthead of the Concordia Journal says: "Issued by the faculty of Concordia Seminary, St. Louis, the Concordia Journal is the successor of Lehre und Wehre (1855-1929) begun by C.F.W. Walther, a founder of The Lutheran Church-Missouri Synod and its first president as well as the first president of Concordia Seminary. Lehre und Wehre was absorbed by the *Concordia Theological Monthly* (1930-1972) which was published by the faculty of Concordia Seminary as the official theological periodical of the Synod."

Becker has written for the LCMS's *Lutheran Witness*. He is asked to write for the Concordia Journal even though he denies the inerrancy of the Bible, promotes women pastors, and supports evolution. He is a strong supporter of LCMS President Kieschnick. Kieschnick appointed a lawyer, who has served as an attorney for Becker when Becker threatened action vs. *CN* for exposing his theological liberalism, to the LCMS's Commission on Constitutional Matters. *Christian News* has repeatedly documented Becker's liberal theological position. Becker has words of praise for Albert Schweitzer in an article in the journal of the St. Louis seminary even though Schweitzer repudiated Christianity and was a unitarian.

The LCMS's Concordia Publishing House in 2002 published **TILL THE NIGHT BE PAST: The Life and Times of Dietrich Bonhoeffer** by Theodore J. Kleinhans.

The book fails to point out that Bonhoeffer rejected the historic Christian faith. Matthew Becker's review of the CPH book on Bonhoeffer is reproduced in this issue of *CN* from the October, 2004 *Concordia Journal*. *CN* is also including some of the many articles *CN* has published during the last 40 years showing that Bonhoeffer repudiated Christianity. None of the "great scholars" of the LCMS who praise Bonhoeffer have ever shown where *CN* has misrepresented Bonhoeffer. "An Evaluation of Dietrich Bonhoeffer's Life and Theology After a Century" by Raymond Surburg, Ph.D. Th.D. was published in the September 19, 1995 *Christian News*. *CN* suggested that the LCMS publish a collection of writings by Surburg, including his analysis of the theology of Bonhoeffer and some of his many writings which have appeared in *Christian News*. However, CPH prefers publishing a book praising Bonhoeffer as some great Lutheran. Material commending Bonhoeffer is considered by CPH to be more helpful for LCMS pastors and laymen than the writings of Raymond Surburg published in *Christian News*.

CONCORDIA JOURNAL
Volume 30, October 2004, Number 4

TILL THE NIGHT BE PAST: *The Life and Times of Dietrich Bonhoeffer*. By Theodore J. Kleinhans. St. Louis: Concordia, 2002. 171 pages. Paper. $15.99.

With the airings on public television of the film *Bonhoeffer: Agent of Grace*, and the advent of Martin Doblmeier's 2003 documentary, *Bonhoeffer*, individuals may wish to take a more in-depth look at the most influential Lutheran theologian of the twentieth century. Of course, the standard, definitive biography is still that by Bonhoeffer's closest earthly friend, Eberhard Bethge. Bethge's *Dietrich Bonhoeffer: Theologian, Christian, Man for His Times*, rev. ed. (Minneapolis: Fortress, 2000), published in 1967and first translated into English in 1970, examines both the life and the thought of Bonhoeffer to a degree yet unmatched. But weighing in at just under 1,050 pages, Bethge's account may be too much to handle for some. Thankfully, there are lighter texts that introduce readers to the main intricacies. In addition to Renate Wind's *Dietrich Bonhoeffer: A Spoke in the Wheel* (Grand Rapids: Eerdmans, 1992; 182 pages), there is now Kleinhans' account.

Like many theologies (e.g., Augustine's, Luther's, Kierkegaards's, Barth's) but unlike many others (e.g., Origen's, Aquinas', Quenstedt's), the theology of Bonhoeffer is comprehensible only in relation to the life of its originator. The faith and order and the life and the work run together and mutually affect each other so that knowledge of the life and the actions are integral to knowledge of the faith and the theology. Indeed, the coherence between Bonhoeffer's life and thought, their fundamental integrity, makes Bonhoeffer attractive to many, both inside and outside the Christian Church.

Kleinhans' twenty-six chapters take the reader through the main events of Bonhoeffer's life, though they do not provide much analysis of the thought that was shaped in relation to these events. The reader is taken from Bonhoeffer's infancy in Breslau, through his childhood in cosmopolitan Berlin and his decision to study theology (Tubingen and Berlin), to his years as pastor (Barcelona in 1928, London in 1933-1934) and as an assistant lecturer in Berlin (1929-1930, 1933), than onward to his years spent as a participant in the Ecumenical Movement, as a radical member of the Confessing Church, as director of an illegal seminary, and eventually as a collaborator in a conspiracy to assassinate Hitler. Kleinhans ends with a summary of the "trial" and execution of Bonhoeffer at the Flossenburg extermination camp.

Though Kleinhans has obviously relied significantly upon Bethge's and others' accounts (in book and documentary forms), as he himself admits, he also provides an occasional insight of his own. Particularly interesting and enjoyable are Kleinhans' descriptions of Bonhoeffer's childhood, his university days and Barcelona escapades, the Preachers' Seminary (both at Zingst and Finkenwalde), his activities as international courier for the conspiracy, his courtship and engagement to Maria von Wedemeyer, and his final days as a prisoner. Kleinhans does not provide much insight, however, into Bonhoeffer's theology. This is a book to get a sense of Bonhoeffer's external life; it is not a book that examines his ideas to any depth. The reader must look elsewhere for summaries and analyses of Bonhoeffer's *Discipleship, Ethics,* or the famous and influential letters from prision.

There are some additional weaknesses to the book. Unlike Wind's and Bethge's texts, Kleinhans' does not contain a chronological table for Bonhoeffer's life. This would have been helpful to include, especially since the reader on occasion must struggle to learn the year and season in which Bonhoeffer did something significant. Unfortunately, the book contains some rather glaring errors: Bultmann, Gogarten, Tillich, and Reinhold Niebuhr were not "famous students" of Barth (52); they were contemporaries and fellow theologians whose ideas often conflicted with Barth's (Tillich was never labeled a Barthian!). Contrary to Kleinhans' statement (170), *Discipleship* was published during Dietrich's lifetime (in 1937).

These drawbacks aside, the book provides, a brief, straightforward, and very readable account of Bonhoeffer's life and times.

Matthew Becker
Portland, OR

Sixty Years Later, Bonhoeffer a Christian Hero to Both Left and Right
Bonhoeffer Conference At Concordia Seminary, Ft. Wayne
Ed. Bonhoeffer Rejected Resurrection of Christ
By CHRIS HERLINGER c. 2005 Religion News Service
Christian News, January 23, 2006

Ed. For information on the anti-Christian theology of Dietrich Bonhoeffer see *The Christian News Encyclopedia*, pp. 3466, 1900, *Christian News*, December 6, 2004, "An Evaluation of Dietrich Bonhoeffer's Life And Theology After Half A Century" by Raymond Surburg, *Christian News*, December 6, 2004. Bonhoeffer rejected such doctrines as the Resurrection of Jesus Christ.

Concordia Theological Seminary, Ft. Wayne, Indiana is sponsoring a Dietrich Bonhoeffer conference, February 3-4, 2006 in observance of the 100th anniversary of the birth of Bonhoeffer. Will the seminarians be asked to read "An evaluation of Dietrich Bonhoeffer's Life and Theology" by Dr. Raymond Surburg, who was a professor at Concordia Seminary for many years? He shows that Bonhoeffer rejected Christianity and the Christ of the Bible.

There is a sharp difference among good conservative Lutherans about the theology of Dietrich Bonhoeffer. Rev. Paul McCain, interim president of CPH, supports CPH's presenting of Bonhoeffer as a sound Lutheran. The Board of Directors of the AAL (now Thrivent) praised Bonhoeffer and his theology. Dr. Uwe Simeon Netto in his CPH published book **The Fabricated Luther** refers to Bonhoeffer as "theologically an orthodox Lutheran." Hopefully the Ft. Wayne Dietrich Bonhoeffer conference will include an open dialogue on the theology of Bonhoeffer where both sides will be presented and students and faculty may judge for themselves. *CN* will publish a response by anyone who would like to show where Dr. Surburg's evaluation is in error.

Luther and Bonhoeffer Misunderstood
Presented at Concordia Seminary, Ft. Wayne
By: Charles E. Ford 7216 Lindell Blvd., Saint Louis MO 63130-4405
home: 314-727-5083 - office: 314-977-2434 - e-mail: fordce@slu.edu
Christian News, July 3, 2006

Martin Luther and Dietrich Bonhoeffer have many things in common. Among them is the frequency with which their writings are misunderstood. A recent illustration of Luther being misunderstood is based on the following statement from his table talk [1], which has been cited as evidence that Luther believed that Jesus and Mary Magdalene were sexually intimate. (This is discussed by Mollie Ziegler. [2])

A Year With Dietrich Bonhoeffer
BOOK REVIEW: Theologian's Ideas, Not Heroics, Noted
By ROBERT FINN c. 2006 Religion News Service

"A Year With Dietrich Bonhoeffer" edited by Carla Barnhill (HarperSanFrancisco, 401 pages, $19.95)

(UNDATED) Dietrich Bonhoeffer was one of the authentic heroes of World War II. A German Protestant theologian who spoke out fearlessly against Hitler and participated in an assassination plot against him, Bonhoeffer was hanged on Hitler's orders three weeks before the Nazi dictator committed suicide on the eve of Germany's surrender in April 1945.

Bonhoeffer's fame today rests perhaps more on his political courage than on his theological views. In "A Year With Dietrich Bonhoeffer," one of a series drawing on the writings of significant thinkers, editor Carla Barnhill arranges spiritual exhortations from Bonhoeffer's work into a kind of Christian religious almanac, offering one item for each day of the year.

The dark and tragic political events in which Bonhoeffer was involved are kept largely offstage, alluded to only when useful for making some spiritual point. Under appropriate dates, the reader finds laconic footnotes marking the author's arrest and imprisonment and other pertinent events, but further commentary is mainly left to the liberal evangelical clergyman Jim Wallis, who contributes an insightful introduction.

All sorts of topics are considered in this bite-size format: the nature of sin and evil, love, peace, forgiveness, Christian community, authority, judgment and prayer. The tone is elevated and didactic, often highly abstract and somewhat ecumenical in tone. Non-Protestants can find much to savor, though non-Christians surely will feel that Bonhoeffer's Christian religious references and focus on Scriptural matters largely exclude them.

Taken one daily page at a time, the book doubtless will have more impact than when read straight through over a week or so. It offers a kind of secular breviary for the religiously inclined lay Christian.

Some of Bonhoeffer's bedrock personal religious convictions recur like themes in a musical work -- the need for Christians to live their faith actively in the world by tackling its toughest problems, for example. He is contemptuous of those who merely talk a good game.

Perhaps Bonhoeffer's most famous religious coinage, the term "cheap grace," is the theme for several dates. It means simply praying and going through the Christian motions; "no contrition is required, still less any real desire to be delivered from sin."

Bonhoeffer showed his contempt for "cheap grace" in the most extreme way when he passed up a post abroad to return to Hitler's Germany, well aware that he probably was signing his own death warrant. He plunged into work with the underground anti-Nazi "Confessing Church" and joined in a failed plot to kill Hitler -- surely an extreme act for a man otherwise committed to Christian nonviolence. But then, he once had written, "It is an evil time when the world lets injustice happen silently," so he knew what he had to do. A lesser man might have dodged the issue to save his skin.

The 100th anniversary of Dietrich Bonhoeffer's birth passed in February largely unnoticed. He was hanged in the Flossenburg prison camp just a couple months after his 39th birthday. (Robert Finn wrote this article for The Plain Dealer of Cleveland.)

Welcome Back, Dietrich Bonhoeffer
By Uwe Simeon-Netto
Issues, Etc.
Lutheran Witness, February, 2006

Monday, Jan. 30, the Issues etc. program of station KFUO in St. Louis will continue its series of interviews on lay vocation. This series deals with God's many callings to service in the temporal realm. With the forthcoming 100th anniversary of Dietrich Bonhoeffer's birth in mind, I shall again take up last Monday's discussion about this martyr's place in what Lutherans call the "left-hand kingdom." My following article on this subject was written for the February 2006 issue of the "*Lutheran Witness*" magazine.

One hundred years after Dietrich Bonhoeffer's birth, and more than six decades after his violent death, it is high time for Lutherans to reclaim their greatest martyr. We have allowed him to be hijacked by far too many weird theologies. Because of his jailhouse musings about "religionless Christianity" he has been portrayed as the apostle of Christian atheism, as the father of the "God is dead" movement of the 1960s. "Seldom has an author, living or dead, been so misrepresented by his commentators and translators," wrote Paul Lehmann, by no means a confessional Lutheran but one of America's most prominent liberal theologians.

Never mind that Bonhoeffer interpreted "religion" – as opposed to faith -- as a form of self-actualization and self-justification; never mind that "whatever he meant by 're-ligionless Christianity,' he certainly did not think it eclipsed the need for prayer, worship and sacrament," wrote Stephen R. Haynes in his recent book "The Bonhoeffer Phenomenon."

Left-wingers such as Father Daniel Berrigan (of questionable Vietnam-era fame) and Beatriz Melano, a Latin American sage, altered Bonhoeffer into a progenitor of liberation theology. Meanwhile Georg Huntemann, a conservative German evangelical, stripped him of his Lutheran credentials by claiming that he was actually a Calvinist of sorts. Huntemann, himself of Reformed persuasion, used his volume, The Other Bonhoeffer, to rail relentlessly against the Lutheran Two Kingdoms Doctrine, which he thoroughly distorted, clearly not realizing that Bonhoeffer's very life and death bore the markings of this doctrine as none other.

One must be grateful to Gustavo Gutierrez that at least he, the actual founder of liberation theology, did not give Bonhoeffer his imprimatur as a radical. To Gutierrez, Bonhoeffer was, though courageous, a bourgeois.

And that was true. Like most of the men and women who suffered and died resisting Hitler, Bonhoeffer hailed from the Germany's upper classes, whose very ethos the murderous Nazi thugs violated. Bonhoeffer was born Feb, 4, 1906, in Breslau, then the capital of German Silesia, now part of Poland, as the son of a celebrated psychiatrist and a noblewoman.

At that time, Europe was in peace; it was still the cultured continent that had no idea its refinement would soon be shattered by the slaughter of millions in the fratricidal first World War and then by World War II, the handiwork of Adolf Hitler. According to his biographer and friend Eberhard Bethge, Bonhoeffer considered Hitler a tool of the Antichrist, the Beowulf as Martin Luther called the Antichrist.

According to Luther, when the Beowulf enters a village, the peasants have the obligation to slay him; should they fail to do so, they will incur guilt. This was the way Bonhoeffer felt about Hitler. Before his death in 2000, Bethge told me that when his friend became involved in the plot to kill the tyrant he said, "Of course, Christ's words that those who draw the sword will die by the sword also apply to us (co-conspirators). But right now reason dictates that we must do this, and then of course we must still turn to God for forgiveness in Christ."

Then Bonhoeffer added, "Now for the first time I have understood what Luther meant when he wrote (to Philipp Melanchthon in 1521), 'Sin boldly but even more boldly believe and rejoice in Christ.'"

Yes, Dietrich Bonhoeffer was a strong sinner in this sense of the word, for he was a confessional Lutheran. He who at age 21 had earned his Ph.D. in theology, did not act in his capacity as a citizen of the spiritual right-hand kingdom – Christ's realm – when he conspired to kill Hitler. He did so in his role as resident of the secular left-hand kingdom – the realm of reason where God reigns in a hidden way. In that kingdom Bonhoeffer was not a pastor but an unpaid agent of the Abwehr, Germany's military intelligence service, which actively opposed the Nazis.

Indeed, so adamantly did he insist on making this distinction that he even insisted on having his name removed from congregational prayer lists for pastors suffering persecution for proclaiming the Gospel. As his friend Wolf-Dieter Zimmermann reported, Bonhoeffer did not want these clergymen placed in even greater danger by being thus associated with him and his conspiratorial activities.

Dietrich Bonhoeffer later coined the phrase that "suffering with God in a godless world" was the Christian's proper response to "God's show of solidarity with suffering humanity." He was prepared to suffer in the extreme as part of his citizenship in the left-hand kingdom, which is still under sin.

He could have avoided this fate. He was in New York in June 1939, trying to avoid conscription into the German military. A stellar career as a professor at Union Theological Seminary awaited him. But a daily Scripture lesson changed his mind: "Do your best to come to me before the winter." (2 Timothy 4:21). So he decided to return to Germany just before the outbreak of World War II to share his fellow-countrymen's fate. "I have made a mistake in coming to America," he wrote to U.S. theologian Reinhold Niebuhr. "I must live through this difficult period of our national history with the Christian people of Germany. Christians in Germany have the terrible alternative of either willing the defeat of their nation in order that Christian civilization may survive, or willing the victory of their nation and thereby destroying our civilization. I know which of these alternatives I must choose; but I cannot make that choice in security."

According to St. Louis mathematician Charles Ford, a leading American Bonhoeffer scholar, "Bonhoeffer returned from America because he did not want to miss his encounter with Christ, who was waiting to form in his life."

Bonhoeffer knew the cross was waiting for him, and he accepted it in true discipleship of Christ, here, in the secular realm. He was hanged April 9, 1945 in Flossenbuerg concentration camp, only days before it was liberated by American forces. He died nobly, or so the camp's physician reported later:

"I saw pastor Bonhoeffer, before taking off his prison garb, kneeling on the floor, praying fervently to his God. I was most deeply moved by the way this lovable man prayed, so devout and so certain that God heard his prayer. At the place of execution he again said a short prayer, and then climbed the steps to the gallows brave and composed."

This sounds like an almost blissful ending. It seems, though, that the doctor made up this tale in order to avoid punishment later in a war crimes trial. B. Jorgen L.F. Mogensen, a Danish diplomat imprisoned in Flossenbuerg, denied the existence of a scaffold or gallows in that camp. Mogensen is certain that Bonhoeffer died the same ghastly death his two Abwehr superiors, Adm. Wilhelm Canaris and Maj. Gen. Hans Oster, suffered. They were slowly strangled to death by a rope dangling from an iron hook that had been sunk into a wall. When they lost consciousness they were revived so that the procedure could be repeated over and over again. The man who revived them was evidently none other than the camp doctor who later made up the story about Bonhoeffer's elegant end, Mogensen insisted.

Bonhoeffer's bitter end was in a sense his personal exclamation mark behind his own, Lutheran theology of the cross. So it is time for his radical, atheist, postmodern and other weird admirers step back and hand him over to us. Welcome back, Dietrich Bonhoeffer, you are home now – finally, 100 years after your birth and nearly 61 after your death!

The Lutheran Witness Did Not Publish This Letter on Bonhoeffer
Christian News, July 3, 2006

February 20, 2006
The *Lutheran Witness*
1333 S. Kirkwood Rd.
St. Louis, MO 36122-7295

Letter to the Editor:

Some years ago the *Lutheran Witness* said Martin Luther King was a "committed Christian" and the *Lutheran Witness* Reporter hailed Albert Schweitzer as a great Christian saint. Neither affirmed such Christian doctrines as the virgin birth and resurrection of Jesus Christ.

Now the February, 2006 *Lutheran Witness* says Dietrich Bonhoeffer was a "confessional Lutheran." Bonhoeffer also did not affirm the virgin birth and resurrection of Christ.

Does the *Lutheran Witness* believe a person can be a "committed Christian" or a "confessional Lutheran" if he does not affirm the virgin birth and resurrection of Christ?

For more than 40 years *Christian News* has documented Bonhoeffer's anti-Scriptural and anti-Christian theology from his own writings. Although Bonhoeffer did at times use orthodox terminology, particularly in his earlier works, the views he expressed just prior to his death in 1945, are certainly not in harmony with historic Christianity. Interested readers should study Bonhoeffer's Letters and Papers from Prison, Fontana Books, S. C. M. Press, Great Britain, 1953. Space does not permit me to quote Bonhoeffer at great length as *Christian News* did already in the November 15, 1965 *Lutheran News* (now *Christian News*).

Bonhoeffer, whom the *Lutheran Witness* now says is a "confessional Lutheran" wrote: "Kierkegaard said more than a century ago that if Luther were alive then he would have said the exact opposite of what he said in the sixteenth century. I believe he was right - Cum Grano Salis." (pp. 31-32). Soren Kierkegaard rejected the historic Christian faith. Concerning the "mythological" elements of Christianity, Bonhoeffer wrote: "I am of the view that the full content, including mythological garbling of the universal truth, this mythology (resurrection and so on) is the thing itself - but the concepts must be interpreted is such a way as not to make religion a pre-condition of faith (cf. circumcision in St. Paul)" (p. 110).

Bonhoeffer wrote that Rudolf Bultmann did not go far enough in his demythologizing of the New Testament. "It is not only the mythological conceptions, such as miracles, the ascension and the like (which are in principle separate from the conceptions of God, faith and so on) that are problematic, but the 'religious' conceptions themselves" (p, 94). "God is teaching us that we must live as men and who can get along very well without him. The God who is with us is the God who forsakes us (Mark 15:34)" (p. 122). "Belief in the resurrection is not the solution of the problem of death" (p. 93).

Christian News published Dr. Raymond Surburg's long articles documenting the anti-Christian theology of Dietrich Bonhoeffer. Franklin L. Baumer in his Modern

European Thought: Continuity and Change in Ideas, 1600-1950. (Dierson College, Yale University, 1977, MacMillan Publishing Company) came to about the same conclusion about Bonhoeffer as Surburg.

Christian News sent Surburg's article documenting Bonhoeffer's theology with lengthy quotes from Bonhoeffer's writings to leading Lutheran defenders of Bonhoeffer. *CN* invited them to show where Surburg misrepresented Bonhoeffer. Not one of the many Bonhoeffer defenders responded. (*Christian News*, January 23, 2006).

The *Lutheran Witness* should not mislead its readers by praising the theology of such opponents of the Christ of the Bible as Martin Luther King, Albert Schweitzer, and Dietrich Bonhoeffer, regardless of how noble they were in the struggle against racism, Nazism, and poverty.

Sincerely,
Herman Otten, editor
Christian News
New Haven, Missouri

cc. Dr. Uwe-Siemon Netto Enclosed: January 23, 2006 *Christian News*, "An Evaluation of Dietrich Bonhoeffer's Life and Theology After Half a Century" by Raymond Surburg, pp. 18-20. Yale University Book: Bonhoeffer Rejected Christianity, pp. 20-21. "Dietrich Bonhoeffer Rejected Historic Christianity - Defender of God is Dead Theologian to Speak at Concordia Seminary, St. Louis." *Christian News*, March 30, 1992. "Cornelius Van Til Critiqued C. S. Lewis - Dietrich Bonhoeffer", *Christian News*, October 23, 2000.

THE MOST WIDELY ADMIRED AND RESPECTED THEOLOGIAN IN AMERICA
Concordia Seminary, St. Louis "The Most Important Lutheran Theologian Since Martin Luther"
Dietrich Bonhoeffer
Christian News, July 3, 2006

"Bonhoeffer Conference," a report on page one of the June 5, 2006 *Christian News* begins: "A Conference sponsored jointly by the Dietrich Bonhoeffer Centennial Committee of America and Concordia Seminary.

"July 19-21, 2006 Dietrich Bonhoeffer may well be the most widely admired and respected Christian theologian among Christian pastors and theologians in the USA. The scope of his appeal is exceptionally broad, spanning across virtually all Christian denominations and across perspectives ranging from the traditional to the liberal. His centennial offers a unique opportunity for activities that highlight the many remarkable aspects of his theology and life. This conference features nationally and internationally recognized experts on Bonhoeffer. These include Lutherans and members of other Christian church bodies. There will be emphasis on confessional Lutheran aspects of Bonhoeffer's thought and at the same time presentations from other Christian perspectives. It is a unique opportunity for Lutherans to highlight perhaps the most important Lutheran theologian since Martin Luther and to converse about the contributions Bonhoeffer can make to the life of the 21st Century church."

CN is not familiar with all of the many speakers who are being brought in from various sections of the U.S. and some other nations. As far as *CN* knows, no scholar or theologian who maintains that Bonhoeffer in his last years repudiated Christianity, has been invited to speak. It will be a costly conference. The news release in the June 5 *CN* lists the speakers and mentions: "Funding by Cranach Institute; Lutheran Charities Foundation Chair of Pastoral Ministry and Life Sciences; Lutheran Foundation; and private contributions."

Concordia Seminary, Ft. Wayne, sponsored a Bonhoeffer conference on February 3-4, 2006. All speakers appear to have maintained that Bonhoeffer was a solid Christian and orthodox Lutheran. See the editorial note at the end of "Sixty Years Later, Bonhoeffer a Christian Hero to Both Left and Right" (p. 23). *CN* challenged the speakers to refute what Dr. Raymond Surburg, a former member of the Ft. Wayne faculty, says in "An Evaluation of Dietrich Bonhoeffer's Life and Theology After Half of a Century" on pp. 19-21. What Surburg wrote on the basis of reading Bonhoeffer's actual writings was not even mentioned at the Ft. Wayne conference on Bonhoeffer. It appears as if Surburg's scholarly article will also be ignored at the St. Louis conference on Bonhoeffer.

"Welcome Back, Dietrich" by Uwe Siemon-Netto is reprinted from the February, 2006 *Lutheran Witness* on p. 19. A letter *CN* wrote to the *Lutheran Witness* in response to this article is on p. 1. The *Lutheran Witness* for more than 45 years has had a policy of not publishing anything from that "uncertified" pastor in New Haven, Missouri. The only time *Christian News* or the editor's congregation has been mentioned in the LCMS's official publications is when the LCMS's Council of Administrators warned members of the LCMS not to read *CN*, when the entire LCMS's Council of Presidents unanimously adopted a resolution condemning *Christian News* and each time the editor's congregation was suspended and expelled from the LCMS and then each time the LCMS's Board of Appeals ruled against the suspensions and expulsions.

The *Lutheran Witness* even refused to mention *CN*'s publication of *An American Translation of the Bible* and the publication of the first English translation of C.F.W. Walther's *Pastoral Theology*.

"'Hanged On A Twisted Cross' New Film on Bonhoeffer 'Draws One Closer to The One True Faith'" on pp. 21-22 notes that a book published by Yale University Press shows that Bonhoeffer in his final years rejected Christianity. "Luther and Bonhoeffer Misunderstood" on p. 23 by Dr. Charles Ford defends Bonhoeffer's theology.

Invite Both Sides

In the interest of hearing both sides, Concordia Seminary, St. Louis could have invited the editor of Friday Church News Notes who said in the June 5, 2006 *CN* in "Bonhoeffer Worshiped a False Christ - EVANGELICALS WHO PROMOTE UNBELEIVERS": "By denying the virgin birth, miracles, resurrection, and ascension, Bonhoeffer worshiped a false gospel. By denying the infallible inspiration of Holy Scripture, Bonhoeffer destroyed the very foundation of our faith. He was, in fact, an unbeliever. And this unbelief perverted everything he did and wrote."

"Cornelius Van Til Critiqued C.S. Lewis Dietrich Bonhoeffer" in the June 5, 2006 *CN* quoted Van Til, a well known Presbyterian theologian as writing that "For (Bonhoeffer) the Christ of historic orthodox followers of Luther and Calvin is not the living Christ... According to Bonhoeffer orthodox theology destroys the very notion of covenantal, personal relationships between God and man."

The late Cardinal Carberry of St. Louis told the Teachers' Institute in St. Louis that Bonhoeffer rejected the deity of Christ. Hugh J. O'Connell, C.SS.R in the November, 1969 *Roman Catholic St. Louis Review* (reprinted in this issue) quoted directly from Bonhoeffer's writings to show that the Roman Catholic Cardinal's evaluation of Bonhoeffer was correct.

Bonhoeffer's Theology

"Welcome Back, Dietrich" is the title of the February, 2006 *Lutheran Witness* article praising Bonhoeffer as a true confessional Lutheran. Long time readers of *Christian News* know that Bonhoeffer has been hailed by many churchmen, particularly Lutherans for decades. "Lutherans Explain Why - 'New Reformer' Ousts Dr. Luther at Rally," a story in the October 20, 1965 *Detroit Free Press*, reproduced at the time in *Christian News* said: "You run into the name of Dietrich Bonhoeffer every where. "And Sunday there'll be proof of his popularity at the annual Missouri - Synod Lutheran Reformation Festival at Ford Auditorium.

"There's going to be a drama this year. And the hero is not Martin Luther, but 20th Century Dietrich Bonhoeffer." *The Detroit Times* noted that the liberal Anglican Bishop John Robinson and the "death of God" theologians were among those looking to Bonhoeffer for inspiration and praising his theology. The Detroit paper said that "Bonhoeffer is the apostle of 'religionless' Christianity."

At the time of this Reformation rally *CN* received inquiries about the theology of Bonhoeffer. "The Theology of Dietrich Bonhoeffer," an editorial in the December 15, 1965 *Lutheran News* (*Lutheran News* became *Christian News* in 1968) quoted at some length from the writings of Bonhoeffer. *CN* recognized that: (See "Theology of Dietrich Bonhoeffer, on pages 4-6).

Anti-Semitism And the Holocaust

Bonhoeffer has long been particularly praised by Lutherans who want to let Jews and others know that they are anti-Nazi, oppose anti-Semitism, and do not deny that during World War II the Germans executed some six million Jews, most of them by gassing. Many of those who laud Bonhoeffer seldom have as much praise for any Christian martyr who opposed Communism. When *CN* visited the Holocaust memorial in Berlin and viewed the exhibits in Buchenwald showing the horrors of the Holocaust, *CN* asked some who praise Bonhoeffer and insist that the Germans exterminated six million Jews during World War II: "Where are the memorials for the many millions murdered by the Communists?" The Bonhoeffer defenders knew of no such memorials.

Bonhoeffer was executed twenty years before *CN* published its first editorial on his theology based solely on Bonhoeffer's writings. Obviously Bonhoeffer's theology has not changed since then. Hopefully Bonhoeffer repudiated his final writings and confessed faith in Jesus Christ as his Savior from sin and the Resurrected Redeemer, true God and true man. There is no record that he did this. The editor basis his views on Bonhoeffer's theology on Bonhoeffer's writings not on what others say. He never met Bonhoeffer when Bonhoeffer was in New York at Union Seminary. The editor did a little research at Union when he was a graduate student at nearby Columbia University and Columbia Teacher's College but that was years after Bonhoeffer was in New York.

Dr. Charles Ford, a speaker at the LCMS conferences praising Bonhoeffer, on p. 23 claims that the Bonhoeffer critics have misunderstood what Bonhoeffer really said.

Ford quotes what a St. Louis professor heard Dr. Hermann Sasse say about Bonhoeffer. *CN* probably has more personal letters from Sasse than any Lutheran pastor who is still living.

Both Dr. Ford and Dr. Uwe Simeon Netto have taken a sound Lutheran stand on many issues. *CN* has published some of Dr. Netto's excellent articles.

Some wanted to know if by publishing some of Dr. Netto's articles this meant that *CN* always agrees with the former UPI religion editor who is now on the staff of Concordia Seminary, St. Louis and also doing some work at Concordia, Bronxville. *CN* has a long history of publishing material from authors with whom *CN* is not always in accord. When CPH published Dr. Netto's **The Fabricated Luther - The Rise and Fall of the Shirir Myth** *CN* published a lengthy review commending the book. *CN* sold many copies. Hopefully CPH will soon publish a second edition. Yet *CN* took issue with the author when he referred to Bonhoeffer as "theologically an orthodox Lutheran." *CN*'s review is in the editor's Luther Today - What Would He do Or Say?

When Netto at the time of the death of John Paul II wrote that "He was my Pope, too," the May 2, 2005 *CN* published an editorial titled "He Was Not My Pope." Pope John Paul rejected the entire Christian doctrine of justification by faith alone, supported evolution and maintained that Muslims, Jews and other non-Christians could get to heaven without saving faith in Jesus Christ. An LCMS pastor took issue with *CN* when he published a column by Dr. Netto in which he allowed for millions of years rather than affirming a six 24 hour creation and a young earth. *CN* has always defended the young earth position and a 6-24 hour day creation. *CN* disagreed with Dr. Netto when he wrote in the March 2002 Forum Letter that Father Richard John Neuhaus and Dr. Jaroslav Pelikan "did not desert Luther" even though they left the Lutheran Church. Father Neuhaus joined the Roman Catholic Church and Dr. Pelikan the Orthodox Church. Both of these churches reject the central Christian doctrine of justification by faith alone. The June 19, 2006 *CN* reprinted "'More Going Home to Rome:' Neuhaus and Pelikan Did Desert Luther" from the March 11, 2003 *CN*. Both Pelikan and Neuhaus deserted Luther many years before they left the Lutheran Church-Missouri Synod. *CN* documented at great length their liberal theology more than 40 years ago. Both denied the inerrancy of the Bible, supported evolution, and rejected the central scriptural doctrine of justification by faith in the merits of Jesus Christ alone.

The faculty of Concordia Seminary, St. Louis, should make it clear that it does not agree with the press release from the seminary promoting the July 19-21 Bonhoeffer conference at the seminary. Does the faculty really believe that Bonhoeffer is "perhaps the most important theologian since Martin Luther" and that "Dietrich Bonhoeffer may well be the most widely admired and respected Christian theologian among Christian pastors and theologians in the USA?"

If this is true, what does it say about the theology of most U.S. pastors? What about Chemnitz, Gerhardt, Krauth, Walther, Pieper, etc? Aren't they more important than Bonhoeffer who denied the basic doctrine of the Christian faith?

Bonhoeffer Revisited
St. Louis Review (Roman Catholic), November 1969
Christian News, July 3, 2006

Editor:

In the *Review*, Oct. 31, 1969, Father John Zupez, S.J., stated that Cardinal Carberry was incorrect in stating in his talk to the Teachers' Institute that Dietrich Bonhoeffer rejected the divinity of Christ.

In his early life, Bonhoeffer was indeed an orthodox Protestant theologian. However, after long months in a Nazi prison he began to develop his doctrine of "religionless Christianity." His ideas are expressed in his *Letters and Papers from Prison*.

He states clearly that means for him a "non-religious interpretation of Biblical terminology" (217).

He attempts to work out a "worldly" interpretation in which the secular takes the place of the sacred. He says: "There is no longer any need for God as a working hypothesis whether in morals, politics or science" (218).

He makes it clear that he wants to get rid of "the religious premise, and of creeds and dogmas." "Our relation to God (is) not a religious relationship to a Supreme Being, absolute in power and goodness, which is a spurious conception participation in the Being of God" (238).

Of Christ he says: "In what way are we in a religionless and secular sense Christians. . . not conceiving of ourselves religiously as specially favored, but as wholly belonging to the world? Then Christ is no longer an object of religion, but something quite different, indeed and in truth the Lord of the world. Yet what does that signify? What is the place of worship and prayer in an entire absence or religion?" (164).

These ideas are not taken out of context. They are repeated over and over in his Letters. Such statements have made him the high priest of "religionless Christianity" and of the "Death of God" theologians.

Quite surely Cardinal Carberry had no desire to injure the reputation of a man of undoubted sincerity and courage. He merely wanted to warn the faithful, as is his duty, of the danger of secularism, which denies the supernatural destiny of man, and of the distortion of Christianity by modern followers of Bonhoeffer into an agnostic humanism.

Hugh J. O'Connell, C.S.S.R
Liguori, MO

Not The Christ Of The Bible
"Great Confessional Lutheran Scholars"
Refuse to Study Evidence Bonhoeffer's Christ
Christian News, October 16, 2006

"Confessional" Lutherans now are among those who seem to be falling all over themselves praising the theology of Dietrich Bonhoeffer. One book after another is being published commending Bonhoeffer's theology. *CN* has shown for more than 40 years that Bonhoeffer's Christ is not the Christ of the Bible. When Detroit area Lutherans decades ago had more praise for Bonhoeffer than Luther at a Reformation Rally, *CN* documented Bonhoeffer's anti- Christian theology directly from Bonhoeffer's last writings.

This year at the 100th anniversary of Bonhoeffer's birth Concordia Seminary, Ft. Wayne and Concordia Seminary, St.Louis had conferences where Bonhoeffer was held up to students and others attending the gathering as a great confessional Lutheran. A news release from Concordia Seminary, St. Louis said that Bonhoeffer is "the most important Lutheran theologian since Martin Luther" and that he is the most widely admired and respected theologian in America. (*CN*, July 3, 2006, p.1)

Christian News maintains that a theologian who denied such doctrines as the resurrection of Jesus Christ should not be considered "the most important Lutheran theologian since Martin Luther." The October 2, 2006 *Christian News* referred to C.F.W. Walther, the first president of the Lutheran Church-Missouri Synod, as "the American Luther" and Dr. Kurt Marquart, who died last month as "The International Luther." *CN* said that Concordia Seminary should have awarded Marquart a D.D. degree. *CN* claims that the writings of Walther and Marquart have been far more helpful for Christendom than any Bonhoeffer wrote.

The February, 2006 *Lutheran Witness* published an article by Dr. Uwe Simeon Netto which said that Bonhoeffer was a "confessional Lutheran." The *Lutheran Witness* refused to publish a letter from the editor of *Christian News* showing that Bonhoeffer rejected such doctrines as the resurrection of Christ. Only one side was allowed to be heard. *CN*'s letter was published in the July 3, 2006 *CN* together with the *Lutheran Witness* article which insists that Bonhoeffer was a confessional Lutheran. *CN* also published a review of a CPH book praising Bonhoeffer. The review was by Dr.Matthew Becker, a member of Jesus First who promotes evolution and women pastors.

The review appeared in the Concordia Journal of Concordia Seminary, St. Louis. The Concordia Journal would not publish an article by a Lutheran theologian who mentions that Bonhoeffer's Christ is not the Christ of the Bible but it did publish a review by a Jesus First liberal. *CN* challenged both seminaries to publish or at least respond to "An Evaluation of Dietrich Bonhoeffer's Life and Theology After Half a Century" by Dr. Raymond Surburg, who had long been a professor at Concordia Seminary, Ft. Wayne. Surburg, on the basis of Bonhoeffer's own writings, showed that Bonhoeffer's Christ was not the Christ of the Bible. Those who praised Bonhoeffer at both seminaries ignored Surburg's thoroughly documented article. It was again reprinted in the July 3, 2006 *CN*. This same issue of *CN* quoted from a book published by Yale University which showed that Bonhoeffer rejected the Christ of the Bible. When the AAL financed a movie praising Bonhoeffer and his theology, *CN* sent Surburg's article to each member of the AAL Board of Directors, including Dr. Tom Zehnder, a member of Jesus First. *CN* invited each member of the AAL Board of Directors to show where Surburg was in error and where he misquoted Bonhoeffer or quoted him out of context. Not one member of the AAL responded.

"The Most Widely Admired and Respected Theologian In America" in the July 3, 2006 *CN* noted: "Bonhoeffer has long been particularly praised by Lutherans who want to let Jews and others know that they are anti- Nazi, oppose anti- semitism, and do not deny that during World War II the Germans executed some six million Jews, most of them by gassing. Many of those who praise Bonhoeffer seldom have as much praise for any Christian martyr who opposed Communism. When *CN* visited the Holocaust memorial in Berlin and viewed the exhibits in Buchenwald showing the horrors of the Holocaust, *CN* asked some who praised Bonhoeffer and insist that the Germans exterminated six million Jews during World War II: 'Where are the memorials for the many millions murdered by the Communists?' The Bonhoeffer defenders knew of no such memorials."

CN has often insisted on the importance of studying documentation and the actual evidence. *CN* has frequently photographed as evidence articles of liberals. What a tragedy that even so many who claim to be confessional Lutherans refuse to study the evidence. They simply follow the crowd and promote what is politically correct. The "great confessional Lutheran scholars" refuse to read any evidence published in *CN* showing that Bonhoeffer's Christ is not the Christ of the Bible. The following item appeared in the September 11, 1972 *Christian News*.

"...the Christ of Bonhoeffer is not the Christ of the Scriptures, is not the Christ of the Reformers..." says Dr. Cornelius Van Til in The Westminster Theological Journal, May, 1972.

Van Til writes in a review article on Bonhoeffer: "The Christ of Bonhoeffer, in contrast to the Christ of Calvin, is constructed in terms of post- Kantian philosophy and theology. This is factually incontrovertible. The consequence of this fact implies a reinterpretation, and UMDEUTUNG, of every word of the vocabulary of biblical and confessional teaching. However much evangelical- and notably, Reformed-Christians may wish to incorporate Bonhoeffer in the list of their heroes of the faith, together with Calvin, Kuyper, Bavinck, Hodge, Warfield, and Vos, they have no right to do so. Bonhoeffer must be placed in the line of Kant, of Schleiermacher, of Ritschl, and of Barth. It is the theological descendants of such men as these who rightfully claim Bonhoeffer as their own.

"Modern, neo-orthodox theologians know that the two Christs, the Christ of Luther and Calvin and the Christ of Bonhoeffer stand mutually opposed to one another."

Van Til documents his article with quotations from the writings of Bonhoeffer to show that Bonhoeffer's Christ is not the Christ of the Bible. Bonhoeffer has been highly praised by such Lutheran liberals as Martin Marty and in parts of the Lutheran Church- Missouri Synod's Mission Life curriculum. **THE WESTMINSTER THEOLOGICAL JOURNAL** is published by Westminster Theological Seminary, Chestnut Hill, Philadelphia, Pennsylvania 19118, $7.50 per year, $2.50 a copy. Van Tils' analysis of Bonhoeffer's theology is one of the most perceptive we have seen.

* * *

The current price of The Semi-annual Westminster Theological Journal is $35.00 for institutions and $20.00 for individuals, $15.00 for students, $10.00 for a copy of the current year.

* * *

The August 7, 2006 *Christian News* published several articles showing that the Christ of Karl Barth is not the Christ of the Bible. One of the articles was "Christianity and Crisis Theology" by Cornelius Van Til. It appeared in the August, 1948 *Concordia Theological Monthly* of Concordia Seminary, St. Louis.

Bonhoeffer also greatly admired Soren Kierkegaard. The Easter **Logia** of the Luther Academy praised Kierkegaard and urged Confessional Lutherans "to follow Kierkegaard for a distinctly Lutheran and scholarly view of teaching and scholarship." *Christian News*, April 25, 2006 published what Logia said about Kierkegaard and then showed that Kierkegaard's Christ was not the Christ of the Bible. J. T. Mueller wrote in the December, 1945 of Concordia Seminary that "Kierkegaard's Christ was of his own making."

Van Til's article in the May 1972 Westminster Theological Journal showing that Bonhoeffer's Christ is not the Christ of the Bible appears below. Lutherans praising Bonhoeffer as a great Confessional Lutheran never mention what Surburg or Van Til wrote about Bonhoeffer after carefully studying Bonhoeffer's writings.

DIETRICH BONHOEFFER
A Review Article *
CORNELIUS VAN TIL
Westminster Theological Journal, May 1972
Christian News, October 16, 2006

In this book Eberhard Bethge presents us with an exhaustive and definitive story of the life and labors of Dietrich Bonhoeffer. Every page of it makes fascinating reading.

If you are primarily interested in Bonhoeffer's struggle against Adolf Hitler, you can find a "blow-by-blow" report of what happened. If you are primarily interested in Bonhoeffer's brave leadership in the Confessing Church, you will be impressed, even amazed, at the insight, the zeal, and the perseverance of the man. I could not help comparing him to Dr. Gresham Machen and his struggle in the Presbyterian Church in the United States of America. However, my primary interest is in Bonhoeffer's theological views.

There has been a good deal of debate about the question of whether Bonhoeffer's theology is orthodox or non-orthodox. Let us see what we may garner on this question from Bethge's book and then supplement this with material from Bonhoeffer's own works.

Bethge traces the development of Bonhoeffer's theology from its inception to its consummation. We shall follow his story in broad outline.

"Bonhoeffer was registered," Bethge says, "at Berlin University from June 1924 to July 1927."[1] Friedrich Schleiermacher had been the "founder" of this institution. "Adolf von Harnack's authority ... was no longer in dispute" at Berlin.[2] Harnack lived next door to the Bonhoeffers. Bonhoeffer attended the "special seminar" Harnack held in his house on "the origins and early history of the Church."[3] This took place in 1929 and after.

At about this time Bonhoeffer was already interested in Søren Kierkegaard. At this time, too, Karl Holl, the famous Luther interpreter, "made a lasting impact on him."[4] But "Bonhoeffer's favorite subject in Berlin was systematic theology, which was taught by Reinhold Seeberg...."[5] "Seeberg transmitted to him Ritschl's aversion to metaphysics."[6] Seeberg also taught him "to take the social category seriously."[7] "The key to his theology of the following five years, the concept of 'Christ existing as community', was forged here too."[8]

But from the time that he began to sit at Seeberg's feet "he had already begun to be fascinated by Barth...."[9] This explains the fact that he thought of nineteenth-century theology as an "obscuration of the Reformation."[10] Bonhoeffer admired the greatness of such men as Schleiermacher, but "the only personalities to whom he granted real authority over him were Karl Barth and Dr. Bell. . . ."[11] The latter was a British friend.

DIALECTICAL THEOLOGY

"The discovery of Barth took place ... between the summer of 1924 and that of 1925."[12] He soon "made himself a propagandist" for what his mother called "the Barth book," namely, *The Word of God and Theology*, published in 1924.[13] About this time Bonhoeffer also became acquainted with some notes of certain of Barth's lectures given during 1924-1925. It "was from these that Bonhoeffer obtained a first insight into the structure that was to be erected on the foundations of Barth's *Epistle to the Romans*."[14]

As a brilliant student of systematic theology, Bonhoeffer followed with intense interest the "bitter controversy that was the subject of universal comment, namely that between Barth and Harnack in the *Christliche Welt* of 1923; in which neither yielded an inch to the other and each proclaimed a black future for theology if the other were left in command of the field."[15]

There was, in the last analysis, no doubt as to where Bonhoeffer's sympathies lay. "With his discovery of dialectical theology, Bonhoeffer acquired a more positive direction that took the place of his previous rather restless roving. He now took a real joy in his work; it was like a liberation."[16]

Of special interest to Bonhoeffer was the fact that the new theology "removed him from the field of speculation" since it "came into being with the peculiar task of preaching -the earthly, concrete task of proving the worth of the Word of God in human terms."[17]

COMMUNIO SANCTORUM

Bonhoeffer's doctoral dissertation dealt with the subject *Communion of the Saints* (*Communio Sanctorum*). "Bonhoeffer's aim ... was no less than that of reuniting his divergent intellectual heritages, bringing sociology and the critical tradition into harmony with the theology of revelation, i.e. reconciling Troeltsch and Barth."[18]

"There was a personal impulse behind Bonhoeffer's aim of establishing the Word of God in a sociological community. In the living Church, salvation acquired its *pro me* in an *extra me* without either disappearing in favour of the other."[19]

From the time of his student days, Bonhoeffer made himself conversant with modern philosophy as well as with modern theology. He found the "tools for this ecclesiology" (that expressed in his *Communion of the Saints*) in the I-Thou personalism prevalent in those days.[20]

ACT AND BEING

"Bonhoeffer's second book *Act and Being* was written in the summer and winter of 1929."[21] In this book he seeks to build on and go beyond the Barthians. We shall presently meet this notion of going "beyond Barth" again. The direction in which Bonhoeffer wants to go beyond Barth is already set forth definitely in *Act and Being*. He wanted to persuade Barth "of his own belief in the *finitum capax infiniti* that in spite of everything God was accessible."[22] As Bethge quotes Bonhoeffer's *Act and Being*:

> In revelation it is a question less of God's freedom on the far side from us, i.e. his eternal isolation and aseity, than of his forthproceeding, his given Word, his bond in which he has bound himself, of his freedom as it is most strongly attested in his having freely bound himself to historical man, having placed himself at man's disposal. God is not free *of* man but *for* man. Christ is the Word of his freedom. God is *there*, which is to say: not in eternal non-objectivity but (looking ahead for the moment) "haveable," graspable in his Word within the Church. Here a substantial comes to supplant the formal understanding of God's freedom.[23]

Bonhoeffer fears that there is a little of "the old extreme Calvinism" left in Barth, keeping him from teaching the genuine identity of God with man in history. Barth has, thinks Bonhoeffer, identified the false idea of God's transcendence found in "the old extreme Calvinism" with that which springs from the use of "the methods of Kantian transcendentalism."[24] "To state the position in greatly over-simplified terms, while the early Barth, desiring to proclaim God's majesty, begins by removing him to a great distance, Bonhoeffer, inspired by the same desire to proclaim his majesty, begins by bringing him into close proximity."[25]

We see then that in *Act and Being* Bonhoeffer builds upon the main theme of *Sanctorum Communio*, i.e., "that the Church is the basic givenness of theology."[26] That is to say the church conceived of as "Christ existing as community" is the starting point of all proper theology. When the church is thus conceived, Bonhoeffer argues, it is in harmony with a properly personalistically and ethically conceived philosophy. "It is the reality of the Church, again conceived of as 'Christ existing as community', that makes fruitful the tension between the respective legitimate interests; of the existentialist theology of Act on the one hand, as developed theocentrically in Barth anthropocentrically in Bultmann, and on the other of the Neo-orthodox theology of Being of the 'pure doctrine'. Thus both requirements, that of contingency and of continuity of revelation, are preserved."[27]

Bethge points out in this connection that by thus using his notion of "Christ existing as community" as doing justice to both the "contingency and continuity of revelation" Bonhoeffer is already laying the foundation for the idea of "non-religious interpretation" of Christianity found in his "letters from prison fifteen years later." At every stage of his thinking it was his view of Christ that was central.

CREATION AND FALL

In his book *Creation and Fall*, based on lectures given in 1932, Bonhoeffer offered what he called a "theological interpretation" of Genesis 1-3.[28] This Bethge also calls an "eschatological interpretation."[29] This "theological or eschatological interpretation" of origins is what it is because it seeks to satisfy the idea of the correlativity of the contingency and continuity of revelation in Christ existing as community. Bethge does not deal with this book very fully. However, a brief look into it will convince the reader of the truth of what Bethge asserts about it.

To understand what is meant by "in the beginning," Bonhoeffer argues, we must presuppose the notion of pure contingency, i.e., of the ultimacy of time. Ultimate reality is purely contingent. The "freedom" of God and the free relationship between, them presuppose pure contingency as enveloping both of them. It is only in terms of pure contingency that personality, divine as well as human, can escape being reduced to the dimension of causality. We know, i.e., conceptually understand, nothing about creation "in the beginning" except in terms of revelation, and this revelation is that of Christ existing as community. And the idea of Christ existing as community involves, as it is involved in, the idea of pure contingency. "We know that we must not cease to ask about the beginning though we know that we can never ask about it. Why not? Because we can conceive of the beginning only as something temporal, therefore precisely as that which has no beginning."[30]

Says Bonhoeffer, "There can therefore be nothing more disturbing or agitating a man than to hear someone speak of the beginning as though it were not the totally ineffable, unutterably dark beyond our blind existence."[31] "No one can speak of the beginning but the one who was in the beginning," that is, God in Christ.[32]

The idea of a beginning is therefore "not a temporal distinction." If it were it would not be unique and free.[33] Accordingly, "between Creator and creature there is simply nothing: the void. For freedom happens in and through the void - Creation comes out of this void."³⁴

It is by means of this idea of pure contingency that Bonhoeffer seeks to escape speculation. With Kant, Bonhoeffer holds that man's intellectual statements are, in the nature of the case, restricted to the realm of phenomena. With Barth, Bonhoeffer holds that God is the God of pure negation. Only in terms of pure negation of all intellectual statement is there pure freedom.

But this is only one side of the story. For we must also say that only in terms of pure affirmation is there pure negation. It is man's pure freedom and with it God's pure freedom that constitute unity in the phenomenal world. Intellectual statement about God made by man in terms of himself and in terms of the cosmos reduces God to the dimension of man and the world. We cannot say that there must be a God who has a purpose for the world on the basis of the fact that we have seen purpose operating in the world. The teleological argument for the existence of God is as surely invalid as are the cosmological and the ontological.

But now if we do what is logically impossible, i.e., start from above, then everything changes. Follow Kant's principle of the primacy of the practical reason, and you find that all things in the phenomena are what they are as manifesting the purpose of God. Barth applied Kant's principle of the primacy of the practical reason and, by means of it, found that God is *wholly* revealed in the world even as he is *wholly* hidden in it. The idea of God as wholly revealed in the world is correlative to the idea of God as wholly hidden in the world. That is to say, the two are dialectically related to one another.

It is this dialectical character of revelation that sets off Barth's theology at every point from the historic Christian faith. And it is this same dialectical principle on which Bonhoeffer also builds his theology.

The idea of pure contingency stands for the idea of the wholly hidden character of revelation. If you reason according to this principle, you will, if you are consistent, deny the possibility of any direct revelation in history, either in Christ or in Scripture. If there were such a direct revelation, addressing man, whether by promise or by threat, man would not be free, and without freedom how can man be responsible?

Applied to the narrative of Genesis 1-3, this means that it cannot be historical, i.e., temporal. If we think of it as temporal we do so because we have already thought of a God who first existed and then created.³⁵ To "think" of creation properly is to think of it as unthinkable, i.e., as contingent. When we do this then we first think of God as free (contingent) and of man as free (contingent).

But then we cannot thus think of both God and man as free (contingent) unless we think of contingency as dialectically related to pure, formal unity. A pure formal oneness of all reality, including God and man, must be presupposed as correlatively related to pure contingency including God and man. This oneness must be *formal*, because if it had any content both God and man would cease to be free. As formal, the unity stands for the wholly manifested or revealed character of the freedom both of God and of man.

It is this purely formal unity as correlative to purely formal contingency that excludes the orthodox Protestant view of the self-existent God who has a plan for man and his world.

It is this dialectical or activist approach that Bonhoeffer used in order to harmonize the theology of Barth with the transcendental principles of post-Kantian personalistic philosophy. His book *Act and Being* illustrates this fact throughout.

It is this dialectical or activist approach that controls his theological or eschatological exegesis of Genesis. The idea of the resurrection of Christ is interpreted as being the formal principle of unity thought of as correlative to the idea of creation as the principle of pure contingency. "But the God of the creation and of the real beginning is, at the same time, the God of the resurrection. From the beginning the world is placed in the sign of the resurrection of Christ from the dead. Indeed it is because we know of the resurrection that we know of God's creation in the beginning, of God's creation out of nothing. The dead Jesus Christ of Good Friday - and the resurrected Kupios (Lord) of Easter Sunday; that is creation out of nothing, creation from the beginning."[36]

CHRIST THE CENTER

In 1933 Bonhoeffer gave a series of lectures on Christology. Bethge has given us the substance of these lectures. Surely Edwin H. Robertson is right when he says that "Christology is the key to Bonhoeffer's thought."[37]

In his Christology Bonhoeffer takes his starting point from that of Barth. Even so he wants again to go beyond Barth. Keeping this in mind we understand something of what Bonhoeffer means when he says:

> Jesus is the Christ present as the Crucified and Risen One. That is the first statement of Christology. "Present" is to be understood in a temporal and spatial sense, *hic et nunc*. So it is part of the definition of the person. Both come together in the concept of the church. Christ is present in the church as a person. That is the second christological definition. Only because Christ is present can we inquire of him. This presence is the presupposition for the development of the christological question.... The understanding of his presence opens the way for the understanding of the person.[38]

Like Barth, Bonhoeffer is here, as throughout his discussion of Christ, doing two things. Negatively he is getting rid of all forms of traditional Christology because, as he says, it operated with the ideas of a "God in himself" and a "man in himself." On the orthodox view "God in timeless eternity is not God."[39] Jesus limited by time is not Jesus. "The proclaimed Christ is the real Christ."[40]

Getting rid of the traditional ideas of a God *in himself* and a man *in himself* has special application with respect to the Chalcedon Creed. Here again Bonhoeffer does essentially the same thing that Barth does. Barth says that if the purpose of the Chalcedon Creed is to be realized, we must *actualize* the incarnation. The traditional view distinguished sharply between the divine and the human natures of Christ. This was stultifying in the extreme. It precluded the possibility of ever properly identifying the Jesus of history with the Christ of faith.

It was impossible on the traditional basis to assign to Christ his proper place as truly God and truly man. Bonhoeffer, as well as Barth, rejects the traditional view of the incarnation. For both men this traditional view presupposes an abstract, already existent, divine nature and an abstract, already existent, human nature bound together by conceptual manipulation.[41]

Bonhoeffer rejects the traditional view of the Chalcedon Creed in terms of what he speaks of as the "critical significance of the Chalcedonian definition."[42] We must first do away with "any thought of the Godhead and manhood as something demonstrable." Then we must do away with the "natures in isolation no longer form a startingpoint." Then we realize that "the startingpoint is the fact that the man Jesus *is* the Christ, *is* God. This *is* cannot be deduced. It is the presupposition of all thought, and cannot be constructed afterwards. After Chalcedon, the question can no longer be "How can the natures be thought of as different and the person as one?" but strictly, "Who is this man of whom it is testified that he is God?"[43]

Having rejected the traditional view of the person of Christ, Bonhoeffer also rejects the traditional view of the work of Christ. In this respect too Bonhoeffer's view is basically similar to that of Barth. Barth says that "Jesus Christ is the atonement."[44] Jesus Christ is sovereign and universal grace.

Bonhoeffer expresses the same idea of sovereign, universal grace again and again. We note only one instance. Bonhoeffer says: "When the unity of act and being in Christ is understood in this way" (i.e., in terms of the *pro me* structure of reality), "the question of his person, i.e. the question 'Who?' can be rightly put. He is the one who has bound himself to me in free existence. And he is the one who has freely preserved his contingency in his 'being-there for you'. He does not have the power of this being *pro me*, he *is* this power."[45]

Moreover, what is true for *me* is true for humanity as a whole:

> Jesus Christ is for his brethren by standing in their place. Christ stands for his new humanity before God. But if that is the case, he is the new humanity. He stands vicariously where mankind should stand, by virtue of his *pro me* structure. He is the community. Not only does he act for it, he is it, by going to the cross, bearing sin, and dying. So mankind is crucified, dies, and is judged in him.
>
> Because he acts as the new humanity, it is in him and he is in it. Because the new humanity is in him, God is gracious towards it in him.
>
> This one, whole, person, the God-man Jesus Christ, is present in the church in his *pro me* structure as Word, as sacrament and as community.
>
> To begin Christology with this statement of one who is present, has the advantage that Jesus is understood from the start as the Risen One who has ascended to heaven.[46]

We saw earlier that in *Act and Being* Bonhoeffer was seeking to support his dialectical theology with a post-Kantian personalist philosophy. We saw also that Bonhoeffer was attempting, from the start, to use this combination of personalist philosophy and dialectical theology in order to go beyond Barth.

It is fairly obvious that as early as 1933 Bonhoeffer had the vision of humanity as a whole, as well as of the church, as participant in the being and act of Christ. The Barth of *Romans* stressed a purely nominalist idea of the freedom of God. In his *Church Dogmatics* Barth continued the motif of the pure contingency of God. It was God's nature to turn wholly into the opposite of himself and to be wholly hidden in the world. But in the *Church Dogmatics* Barth saw with increasing clarity that he could not maintain his motif of pure contingency except as correlative to pure, formal universality. Accordingly, in the later volumes of this work he spoke of all men as having from all eternity been in Christ and of God as therefore wholly revealed in the world.

Bonhoeffer was ahead of Barth on this point in that he saw from the outset that purely sovereign, i.e., contingent, grace was, in the nature of the case, also universal grace.

Bonhoeffer does not think of himself as having "ever changed very much."[47] The idea of Christ as "the man for others" is clearly already implied in his notion of Christ as set forth in his 1933 lectures.

THE COST OF DISCIPLESHIP

The Cost of Discipleship "appeared in time for Advent 1937."[48] Bonhoeffer was at this time still searching "for the concrete social nature of the Body of Christ," i.e., the church. The church is "the Real Body of Christ all earth."[49] So we must deal with those who are disciples of Christ. Discipleship is "participation in Christ's suffering for others, as communion with the Crucified."[50] By "interpreting belief in Christ as discipleship, he [Bonhoeffer] succeeds in putting new life into the sawdust puppet of Christology."[51]

Bonhoeffer himself begins his book by a discussion of *costly grace*. Traditional orthodoxy operated with "cheap grace." "Cheap grace means grace as a doctrine, a principle, a system. It means forgiveness of sins as a general truth, the love of God taught as the Christian 'conception' of God."[52] On the other hand, "Costly grace is the gospel which must be *sought* again and again, the gift which must be *asked* for, the door at which man must knock."[53] Costly grace is the "Incarnation of God."[54] Cheap grace closes "the way to Christ" while costly grace opens it. Orthodoxy has a conceptually constructed and therefore an abstract Christology and cheap grace.

Such an "abstract Christology" renders "discipleship superfluous" and is "essentially inimical to the whole conception of following Christ."[55] "Christianity without the living Christ is inevitably Christianity without discipleship, and Christianity without discipleship is Christianity without Christ."[56]

Now to become disciples we must "obey a concrete demand." Without this preliminary step of obedience, our faith will only be pious humbug, and lead us to the grace that is not costly. Everything depends on the first step." This first step "is a step within everybody's capacity, for it lies within the limits of human freedom."[57] At the same time it is "through the call of Jesus [that] men become individuals." "It is no choice of their own that makes them individuals by calling them." For the Christian "the only God-given realities are those he receives from Christ."[59]

Bonhoeffer agrees with Søren Kierkegaard in thinking of Jesus Christ as the one in whom individuality, i.e., pure contingency, and universality, pure rationality, are united. With Barth he agrees that Christ is the one true man and that all other men are men by virtue of participation in Christ. It is as such that costly grace *is* the incarnate One.

Disciples of Christ do what they do because they are what they are as participant in Christ. "They are called blessed because of their visible participation in his cross."[60] The unconditional love of God to all men expresses itself in and through the disciples of Jesus.

It is obvious from what has been said that in *The Cost of Discipleship* Bonhoeffer was working out the principles of his Christology. These principles required him to reject the orthodox view of Christ as being intellectualistic and deterministic. Over against this orthodox determinism he set his principle of pure contingency. Bonhoeffer's Christology and with it his view of discipleship presuppose what Richard Kroner calls the ethical dualism of Kant. For Bonhoeffer as well as for Kant the world of space and time is the world that answers to the conceptualizing activity of man in the manner that Parmenides insisted that it must do if it was to be known at all. Then, in complete opposition to this realm of space and time, this world of phenomena, is the realm of human and divine freedom. Of this realm *nothing* can be said conceptually. In later language these two realms are set over against one another as the realm of *Historie* and the realm of *Geschichte*.

But setting the two realms over against each other is accomplished in the interest of their ultimate unification. This unification cannot be attained by means of logical subsumption. It must be done by moral postulation *instead* of by conceptualization. For this reason Kant *postulated* the primacy of the idea of teleology over that of mechanism. The ethical dualism is made subservient to an ethical monism.

Neo-orthodox theologians use this Kantian notion of the primacy of the practical over the theoretical reason in the construction of their Christ. They make the biblical terminology of man's creation, fall, and redemption subservient to the idea that man is inherently good and that the evil that is in him is unconditionally "forgiven him." Barth's notion of sovereign (free) universal grace expresses this post-Kantian view of man. Man is man as a sinner whose sins are freely forgiven in advance, i.e., in Christ.

Bonhoeffer's Christology is as true to the principles of a personalistic, Kantian philosophy as is that of Barth. The *Costly Grace* of Bonhoeffer is therefore in reality cheap grace. The "sinner" is not subject to the wrath of God. Christ did not suffer under the wrath of God as the substitute for his people.

ETHICS

In 1939 or 1940 Bonhoeffer began his work on *Ethics*. He felt as though "ethics was his life's task."[61] Says Bethge: "For a long time the Church had claimed Bonhoeffer's attention, and the world, with its insistence upon creation and history, had with good reason remained unheeded, but now it received new attention as the sphere of the *regnum Christi*."[62]

"Exclusiveness of Christ's lordship -that is the message of *The Cost of Discipleship*; the wide range of his lordship - that is the new emphasis of Ethics."[63] Bonhoeffer works out the significance of the incarnation for the whole world.

We turn to the *Ethics* briefly to see what this means. Like Barth, Bonhoeffer wants ethics to start from God as speaking to man in Christ. Love is the central subject of ethics, but "no one knows what love is except in the self-revelation of God. Love, then, is the revelation of God."[64] But this means that "all our ideas and principles relating to love are concentrated in the strictest possible manner upon the name of Jesus Christ." And this "must always be understood in the full concrete historical significance of the historical reality of a living man."[65] This man is, of course, Jesus Christ.

"Love, therefore, is the name for what God does to man in overcoming the disunion in which man lives. This deed of God is Jesus Christ, in reconciliation."[66]

"Whoever sees Jesus Christ does indeed see God and the world in one. He can henceforth no longer see God without the world or the world without God."[67] The figure of the Reconciler, of the God-man, Jesus Christ, comes between God and the world and fills the center of history."[68]

At this advanced stage of Bonhoeffer's thinking, the work of Christ in the church is for him a steppingstone toward the work of Christ for the world as a whole. "The longing of the Incarnate to take form in all men is as yet still unsatisfied. He bore the form only in a small band. These are His Church."[69]

We must therefore enlarge our vision and "speak about the way in which this form takes form amongst us ...."[70] We start again from "Jesus Christ the crucified" and see that "this means that God pronounces its final condemnation on the fallen creation."[71]

Having looked anew at Christ, I turn to myself. I now realize that "the aim of all ethical reflection is ... that I myself shall be good through my action."[72]

As a member of the church I realize that its mandate is concerned "with the eternal salvation of the whole world."[73]

The final upshot of the *Ethics* is therefore "helping people 'to share in life', it is the Christlife in the midst of the human."[74] "Bonhoeffer has now reached the position," says Bethge, "where the letters from prison come in with their surprisingly simple formulations. What begins like *The Cost of Discipleship* ends with the formulation of 'worldliness'."[75] Says Bonhoeffer: "The cross of atonement is the setting free for life before God in the midst of the godless world; it is the setting free for life in genuine worldliness."[76]

* * *

We return now to the question with which we began. Are the theology and philosophy of Dietrich Bonhoeffer orthodox or neoorthodox? There are those who affirm the former. Thus, for instance, Lester de Koster, the editor of *The Banner*, an "official organ of the Christian Reformed Church," says that there "are striking parallels between the thought of Calvin and of Bonhoeffer."[77]

Both men have, says DeKoster "an uncommon sensitivity to the significance of the visible church."

Again, "Both Calvin and Bonhoeffer experienced the Church as gathering about the Word preached.. . .."

Still further "both men wrestled with the awful ambiguities of life...."

Once more, "Both men knew what it means to 'live before the face of God' in a world which behaves 'as if God does not exist'."

All this DeKoster affirms in a review of Bethge's book. Summing up the matter, he says: "Like Calvin before him, Bonhoeffer had little time for speculation and still less appreciation for it. Above all, Bonhoeffer has shown the twentieth century...that Christ enlists in this century profound theologians in active engagement, even unto death."[78]

The following remarks must be made of this evaluation of Bonhoeffer's thinking.

In the first place, there is not the least justification for it in Bethge's book. According to Bethge, Bonhoeffer was a great admirer of Barth. But Barth had one weakness, namely, that he retained something of "the old extreme Calvinism." It was because of the leftover of this "extreme Calvinism" that Barth stressed too greatly the transcendence of God above the world at the expense of his immanence in the world. Clearing out the "old extreme Calvinism" of Barth's theology, Bonhoeffer would show forth the majesty of God by stressing his proximity.

What shall we say about these "parallels" between Calvin and Bonhoeffer? We must say that at most they are formal. So far as content is concerned, the theological positions of Bonhoeffer and Calvin are diametrically opposed to one another. We have given enough evidence in this article to substantiate this claim. Every informed Christian must choose between the two. For the orthodox Christian it should not be difficult to see the necessity for doing this.

How can it be necessary, however, to choose against a man who centered all his thinking around Christ and who gave his life out of love for Christ? Did Bonhoeffer not, like Calvin, think and live *coram deo*? Was not his motto like that of Abraham Kuyper, *pro Rege*, for the king? Did he not, again with Kuyper, seek to interpret every domain of life, even the realm of the natural or secular, in terms of Christ?

Our answer to all such questions must, of necessity, be that the Christ of Bonhoeffer is not the Christ of the Scriptures, is not the Christ of the Reformers, and, in particular, is not the Christ of Calvin. Simple honesty compels us to say this. The Christ of Bonhoeffer, in contrast to the Christ of Calvin, is constructed in terms of post-Kantian philosophy and theology. This is factually incontrovertible. The consequence of this fact implies a re-interpretation an *Umdeutung*, of every word of the vocabulary of biblical and confessional teaching. However much evangelical - and notably, Reformed - Christians may wish to incorporate Bonhoeffer in the list of their heroes of the faith, together with Calvin, Kuyper, Bavinck, Hodge, Warfield, and Vos, they have no right to do so. Bonhoeffer must be placed in the line of Kant, of Schleiermacher, of Ritschl, and of Barth. It is the theological descendants of such men as these who rightfully claim Bonhoeffer as their own.

Modern, neo-orthodox theologians know that the two Christs, the Christ of Luther and Calvin and the Christ of Bonhoeffer stand mutually opposed to one another. Moreover, such followers of Calvin as have just been mentioned claim the whole wide world, the world of science and philosophy as well as the world of theology, for their Christ. Similarly, such followers of Kant as have just been mentioned also claim the whole wide world, the world of science, the world of philosophy, as well as the world of theology, for their Christ.

Finally, both the present-day followers of Calvin, and the present-day followers of Kant know that the struggle between the two Christs is a struggle to the death. It is the battle of Armageddon that is now being waged between them, and every man is involved in it.

Why is it that many of the followers of the Christ of Scripture, the Reformers, and particularly of Calvin, do not see this alternative? It is, in large measure at least, due to the fact that they are told about such supposed parallels as Mr. DeKoster has spoken of in his review.

Well, there are parallels between the north and the south Vietnamese soldiers too. Both are Vietnamese. Both wear uniforms. Both shoot with guns, etc. Yet both are out to destroy each other. Their aims are exclusive of one another. It is a battle to the death between them.

Is the comparison far-fetched? Is it unfair to Bonhoeffer? No, Bonhoeffer would have it that way. For him the Christ of historic orthodox followers of Luther and Calvin is not the living Christ. No man can be a disciple of the living Christ so long as he finds the relationship between himself and the Christ directly in the space-time world. So long as he does this the "believer" is no longer a believer but a man in himself and his God is no longer his God, but a God in himself. According to Bonhoeffer, orthodox theology destroys the very notion of covenantal, personal relationship between God man.

On the orthodox view in general and on the historic Reformed view in particular, Christ spoke and claimed that he had spoken directly to his covenant people as the great Prophet, the great High Priest, and the great King. The Pharisees rejected him, saying that he blasphemed when he made himself out to be the Son of God. They had virtually accepted the Greek form-matter scheme, and in terms of it denied even the possibility of a direct confrontation of man with God. In terms of the Greek form-matter scheme there could be no creation-fall-redemption sequence in history as expressing the work of the Father, the Son, and the Holy Spirit.

Now the freedom-nature scheme of Kant and his followers is the direct historical descendant of the form-matter scheme of the Greeks. In both schemes apostate man assumes his ultimacy or autonomy. In both schemes man takes the place of God. In both schemes man, instead of God, is the final point of reference in all predications.

With its nature-grace scheme, Roman Catholic philosophy and theology seeks to combine the Greek and the Christian points of view. The *analogia entis* idea of much of Romanist thinking is based on the idea of human freedom in terms of pure equivocism correlative to pure univocism.

Karl Barth rejects this *analogia entis* idea in favor of the *analogia fidei* idea. Yet the latter is basically similar to the former. Barth's scheme expresses the I-thou/I-it dimensionalism of post-Kantian philosophy.

Barth is certain that his *analogie fidei* scheme enables him to start and end his thinking about all things in terms of the primacy of the Christ-Event. Barth's Christ-Event requires him, as noted, to actualize the incarnation. God is pure contingency. He is free to turn wholly into the opposite of himself and then take mankind up into participation with his own aseity. Barth therefore also actualizes the doctrine of election; Christ is the electing God and, at the same time, the elected man. Election does not pertain to individual men. There is no elect Jacob and there is no reprobate Esau. All men have a lower, an Esau, aspect, and all men have a higher, a Jacob, aspect, in them. There are not two classes of men, those who are and those who are not set free from condemnation because of Jesus' death and resurrection. There was no transition from wrath to grace that took place in the past, near Jerusalem, through Christ. To understand what took place then and there we must distinguish between *Historie* and *Geschichte*. The realm of *Historie*, the I-it dimension, the field of impersonal science, is not and cannot be the place where a person-to-person meeting of man with Christ took place. It is only the orthodox, the "friends of the speaking serpent," the *beati possidentes* who reduce the person-to-person involvement of man with Christ to a mechanica., conceptual, doctrinal, impersonal entity.

As a consequence of its failure to interpret all things in the light of the Christ-Event, orthodoxy misconstrues the nature of grace altogether. Grace is inherently sovereign grace, i.e., purely contingent grace. Grace is the free gift of the free God to the free, i.e., contingent, man. Involved in and correlative to this purely contingent relationship between the purely contingent God and the purely contingent man is the idea of all-inclusive universality. And the Christ-Event is the intersection in point of pure contingency and pure continuity. All men are what they are because they are fellow men with the one true man, Jesus. Thus grace is inherently universal as well as sovereign grace.

Now Bonhoeffer's Christ existing as community differs only in detail from this Christ-Event of Barth.

A word must be said in conclusion to make this point clear. For this purpose we look at the argument of *Act and Being* once more.

In part one of this book Bonhoeffer reviews the main philosophical attempts to answer the question of knowledge and of being. In doing so he does not question the legitimacy of philosophy's starting with man as autonomous. He assumes that the starting point and the procedure of modern philosophy are what, naturally, they would have to be. There is no such thing as apostate thought in the sense described above. A theological and eschatological interpretation of the Genesis account based on the idea of Christ as community precludes any such interpretation of the creation and fall of man. Man manifests his fallenness, his being in *Adam* as over against his being in *Christ*, by his conceptualizing, impersonal interpretation of his relation to Christ. It is he who thinks of the Christ-Event doctrinally, the way the Chalcedon theologians did and the way orthodox theologians do—it is he who is fallen *in Adam*. Of course, even he is, though he "knows" it not, *in Christ*. The "knowledge" that to be a man at all one must be *in Christ* is given by *revelation*. This knowledge inheres in all mankind.

So far Bonhoeffer's argument runs along the line of that of Barth. Bonhoeffer is in perfect agreement with Barth in saying that *nothing* can be known of God. Faith stands for Bonhoeffer, as well as for Barth, in absolute contrast to knowledge.

But then, like the men who engage in the new quest of the historical Jesus, and like the men of the new hermeneutic, Bonhoeffer thinks that Barth has overdone his negations. Barth has overdone the notion of *pure* contingency. To be sure Barth could not overdo his negations over against the *beati possidentes*. But Barth did, according to Bonhoeffer, overdo his negation in that he did not show how it, of necessity, required a new affirmation – not as though for Barth grace was not inherently universal as well as inherently sovereign, but he did not point to the historic Jesus as manifesting this grace in *Historie*.

In other words, Bonhoeffer thinks he carries out the implication of modern critical philosophy more consistently than Barth did. If Kant first set the realm of personal freedom in absolute antithesis to the realm of impersonal science, he later postulated a universal saving influence in the latter realm because of the operating presence of human freedom in it. Even Kant made room for a certain type of Christ in terms of such a philosophy. Bonhoeffer's thinking is more theological than that of Kant, but not significantly different.

Bonhoeffer offers "the Church as a unity of act and being."[79] The church is where alone *Dasein*, i.e., man in his world, is understood.[80] But "Christ is the corporate person of the Christian communion." "Christ is in the communion as the communion is in Christ."[81] "The communion is a corporate person whose name is also Christ."[82] In the communion "Christ reveals himself as. . . the new humanity itself."[83]

Now, since this is the case, "God's freedom has bound itself" to men. Precisely in this binding God's freedom comes to expression.

As a consequence of this free binding of himself to man, the communion "has at its disposal the Word of forgiveness; in the communion may not only be said, existentially, 'I have been forgiven', but also—by the Christian Church as such, in preaching and sacrament—'thou are forgiven'; furthermore, every member of the Church may and should 'become a Christ' to every other in so proclaiming the gospel."[84]

It is thus that Bonhoeffer creates a new class of *beati possidentes*. This class includes all men. All men have the Word of forgiveness at their *disposal*. But not for a second does this imply a return to the position of the orthodox *beati possidentes*. To be sure that no one understands him to advocate a return to orthodoxy, he adds, "The being of revelation does not lie in a unique occurrence in the past in an entity which in principle is at my disposal and has no direct connection with my old or my new existence...."[85] Bonhoeffer wants no return to an objectifiable ego and with it to an entitative view of revelation. What he is after with his idea of revelation as a "possession," is to make certain that the idea of contingency will bear positive fruit. This requires that one think of pure contingency as from the outset; exhaustively correlative to pure universality. Barth had failed at this point. Bonhoeffer wants a new *positivity* with respect to Christ and a new *availability* of him for mankind.

With its almost exclusive stress on the pure contingency, the otherness, of revelation, Barth's theology might lose itself in individualism.[86] As such it would not be available for mankind. Again, with its stress on the otherness of revelation, Barth's position lifts faith out of contact with man. Barth says that "man's knowing is not knowing."[87] "It is a fateful error on Barth's part to replace the Lord and creator with the concept of the subject."[88] One result of this is "that God is virtually defined as the subject of my new existence, of my theological thinking, instead of as Lord and Creator of both."[89]

This is serious criticism. Even more serious is what he adds, as follows: "But the ultimate reason for the inadequacy of Barth's explanation lies in the fact that it fails to understand God as a person."[90]

We escape these weaknesses in Barth, Bonhoeffer contends, "by thinking of the Christ-person in the community of persons called the Church."[91] Only if Christ is for us the corporate personality inclusive of all other personalities do we have direct recourse to him. "The world of entity is transcended by this personal being, which also bestows on it its character: it 'is for' man in Adam his own subjected, 'interpreted' world with the curse of death; It is for man in Christ the world delivered from the I yet newly subjected to it by God in the expectation of the new creation (Rom. 8, 19ff.); finally, it is absolutely for God, its eternal master. "[92]

Herewith, thinks Bonhoeffer, we have escaped the danger of thinking of faith as a "reflected form of faith-wishfulness. That is the danger of Barth." Barth "undermines his position by introducing reflexion into the act of faith, with the effect of casting doubt on faith itself, therefore indirectly on Christ."[93] Having taken Christ as the community as our starting point we have attained to the certainty of faith. We have, all of us have, humanity has, arrived at home. We have maintained our freedom and our unity individually and as a race.

It ought to be apparent now that the parallels between Calvin and Bonhoeffer are purely formal. Both want to begin with revelation. But what Calvin thinks of as revelation is pure speculation for Bonhoeffer. On Bonhoeffer's view, Calvin's position reduces revelation and man's response to revelation to an entitative, impersonal thing. There could on such a basis be no real revelation and no real faith. On the other hand, what Bonhoeffer thinks of as revelation and faith as response to revelation is from Calvin's standpoint pure speculation. For all its reference to revelation and to faith, Bonhoeffer's theology, like that of neo-orthodoxy and like that of the "consciousness theology" against which it militates, is still a projection theology. Bonhoeffer's starting point is basically the same as that of Kant. Bonhoeffer, like Kant, limits science and makes room for faith, i.e., for faith in a wholly indeterminate relation between a wholly unknown God and a wholly unknown man. The self-attesting, Christ of Scripture is pressed into this modern Kantian framework of philosophical speculation.

Bonhoeffer, like Calvin, attributes great importance to the church. Yes, indeed, but for Bonhoeffer the church is the "new humanity" centered in the "Man for others." The members of Bonhoeffer's church are not those who have been saved from the wrath to come because they are washed in the blood of the lamb. They are members of the "body of Christ" whether they know it or not because they participate in Christ as the new humanity.

In a pictorial album on Bonhoeffer, W. A. Visser 't Hooft speaks with great enthusiasm of Bonhoeffer's theology[94] and its significance for the ecumenical movement. This is natural. The Christ of Bonhoeffer, Christ as man for others, may well be taken as the motto for the ecumenical movement.

Westminster Theological Seminary, Philadelphia

*Review of Eberhard Bethge: *Dietrich Bonhoeffer. Man of Vision, Man of Courage.* New York and Evanston: Harper and Row, 1970. xxiv, 867. $17.95.

1 Eberhard Bethge, op. cit., p. 44.
2 Ibid., p. 45.
3 Ibid.
4 Ibid., p. 46.
5 Ibid., p. 47.
6 Ibid., p. 48.
7 Ibid.
8 Ibid.
9 Ibid.
10 Ibid., p. 49.
11 Ibid.
12 Ibid., p. 50.
13 Ibid., pp. 50-51.
14 Ibid., p. 51.
15 Ibid.
16 Ibid., p. 52.
17 Ibid.
18 Ibid., p. 59.
19 Ibid.
20 Ibid.
21 Ibid., p. 96.
22 Ibid., p. 97.
23 Ibid., p. 98.
24 Ibid.
25 Ibid.
26 Ibid.
27 Ibid.
28 Ibid., p. 162.
29 Ibid., p. 163.
30 Dietrich Bonhoeffer, *Creation and Fall: A Theological Interpretation of Genesis 1-3* (London: SCM Press, 1959), p. 13.
31 Ibid., p. 15.
32 Ibid.
33 Ibid., p. 17.
34 Ibid., p. 18.
35 Ibid., p. 16.
36 Ibid., p. 19.
37 Dietrich Bonhoeffer, *Christ the Center* (Introduced by Edwin H. Robertson and translated by John Bowden; New York: Harper and Row, 1966), p. 12.
38 Ibid., p. 43.
39 Ibid., p. 46.
40 Ibid.
41 Ibid., p. 101.
42 Ibid.
43 Ibid., p. 102.
44 Karl Barth, *Die Kirchliche Dogmatik* (Zurich: Evangelischer Verlag. 1953), IV:1, 35.
45 Bonhoeffer, *Christ the Center*, p. 48.
46 Ibid., pp. 48f.
47 Bethge, *op. cit.*, p. 153.
48 Ibid., p. 370.
49 Ibid., p. 372.
50 Ibid., p. 374.
51 Ibid., p. 378.

52 Dietrich Bonhoeffer, *The Cost of Discipleship* (New York: Macmillan, rev. ed., 1959), p. 45.
53 Ibid., p. 47.
54 Ibid., p. 48.
55 Ibid., p. 63.
56 Ibid., p. 64.
57 Ibid., p. 70.
58 Ibid., p. 105.
59 Ibid., p. 109.
60 Ibid., p. 161.
61 Bethge, *op. cit.*, p. 621.
62 *Ibid.*
63 *Ibid.*, p. 622.
64 Dietrich Bonhoeffer, *Ethics* (ed. Eberhard Bethge; New York: Macmillan, 1964), p. 50.
65 Ibid., p. 51.
66 Ibid., p. 52.
67 Ibid., p. 70.
68 Ibid.
69 Ibid., p. 83.
70 Ibid., p. 88.
71 Ibid., p. 131.
72 Ibid., p. 188.
73 Ibid., p. 211.
74 Bethge, *op. cit.*, p. 624.
75 Ibid., p. 625.
76 Ibid.
77 Lester De Koster, review of Eberhard Bethge, *Dietrich Bonhoeffer: Man of Vision, Man of Courage in The Banner*, January 15, 1971, p. 24.
78 Ibid.
79 Dietrich Bonhoeffer, *Act and Being* (Translated by Bernard Noble and introduced by Ernst Wolf; New York: Harper, 1956), p. 117.
80 Ibid., p. 118.
81 Ibid., p. 120.
82 Ibid.
83 Ibid., p. 121.
84 Ibid., p. 122.
85 Ibid., p. 123.
86 Ibid., p. 122.
87 Ibid., p. 135.
88 Ibid., p. 136.
89 Ibid.
90 Ibid., p. 137.
91 Ibid., p. 137.
92 Ibid., pp. 174f.
93 Ibid., p. 176.
94 James Martin Bailey and Douglas Gilbert, *The Steps of Bonhoeffer: A Pictorial Album* (Philadelphia: Pilgrim Press, 1969), foreword.

Refusing To Read Evidence
Intellectual Snobs
Christian News, October 16, 2006

Dr. Kurt Marquart's opposition to human regulations, making man-made by-laws and church bureaucrats is not some notion he developed in later years. When this editor was his roommate at Concordia Seminary, St. Louis, Marquart placed a plaque on the wall in our room which had a statement from Thomas Jefferson championing liberty, free speech, and opposing tyranny. Marquart did not agree with Jefferson's theology but he had the same love for liberty such American Founding Fathers as Jefferson had. Marquart said at the 2003 Walther Conference: "Our tragedy is that this absolute priority of the divine truth has become displaced in our Synodical life. By what? By organizational, bureaucratic concerns. Our disease is, you might say, 'bureaucratitis.'" "Some Writings of Professor Kurt Marquart" on pages 14-26 of the October 2, *Christian News* summarize some of the many writings of Dr. Marquart which have appeared in *Christian News* during the last 44 years.

He wrote in 1964 in "Sanctifying An Unholy Cause" (p. 18): "It was specifically guaranteed, again and again, that the synod would not have the slightest power to compel obedience to any human regulations." Now LCMS President Kieschnick wants the LCMS to have the power to assess ("tax") congregations. Support the LCMS bureaucracy or get removed from the LCMS.

Van Til on Barth and Bonhoeffer

Already during his first year at Concordia Seminary Marquart read books which the liberal intellectuals, both professors and students, acted as if they did not exist. One of them was *The New Modernism* by Cornelius Van Til, an orthodox Presbyterian scholar. Van Til in this book showed how radically such neo-Orthodox theologians as Karl Barth and Emil Brunner had departed from historic Christianity. At the time Barth, Brunner, the Niebuhrs, Aulen and Tillich were some of the great heroes of many LCMS "scholars."

Marquart wrote in 1965 that "for intellectual snobs of course facts contained in books they dislike simply don't exist." The intellectual snobs generally refused to read such books as Van Til's *The New Modernism*.

This issue of *CN* includes an article by Cornelius Van Til on the theology of Dietrich Bonhoeffer. It was published in the May, 1972 *Westminster Theological Journal*. *CN* at the time commended the article. The entire article is on pages 10 and 11 of this issue. This year both LCMS seminaries had a seminar on Bonhoeffer where his theology was praised. The St. Louis seminary said in its publicity of the Bonhoeffer seminar that Bonhoeffer is the most important Lutheran theologian since Martin Luther and that today Bonhoeffer is the most admired and respected theologian in America. *CN* published an article by Dr. Raymond Surburg, a professor at Concordia Seminary, Ft. Wayne, on the theology of Bonhoeffer. Surburg documented his article with many quotations from Bonhoeffer. He showed that Bonhoeffer rejected the Christ of the Bible and historic Christianity. *CN* suggested that the great scholars at Concordia Seminary, Ft. Wayne and Concordia Seminary, St. Louis read Surburg on Bonhoeffer and attempt to show where Surburg is in error. *CN* has shown for more than forty years where Bonhoeffer is in error. *CN* has noted during those years that intellectual snobs act as if facts contained in *Christian News* about such theologians as Barth,

Brunner, Bonhoeffer and the liberals in the LCMS simply do not exist. *CN* is now inviting the great scholars, who maintain that Bonhoeffer was the confessional Lutheran they claim he was, to read and respond to Van Til's review article on the theology of Bonhoeffer. The *Lutheran Witness* published a feature article by Uwe Simeon Netto of Concordia Seminary, St. Louis claiming Bonhoeffer was definitely a confessional Lutheran. The LCMS's Concordia Publishing House insists Bonhoeffer was a confessional Lutheran.

Intellectual snobs most likely will continue to ignore anything *CN* publishes, including the writings of Dr. Kurt Marquart, C.F.W. Walther's *Pastoral Theology,* William Beck's *An American Translation of the Bible, The Christian News Encyclopedia,* Peter Krey's *Devotions on the Apostle's Creed, Christian News,* etc. Marquart hit the nail on the head already more that 40 years ago when he wrote that "for intellectual snobs of course facts contained in books they don't like simply do not exist."

Theological Hero #1
Dietrich Bonhoeffer
The Fundamentalist Digest,
April – May 2007
Christian News, December 10, 2007

Who were these two men? First, who was Dietrich Bonhoeffer? From a positive perspective, Bonhoeffer was a German religious patriot who opposed Hitler's Nazism and who became a spy for the underground resistance movement, leading a failed assassination attempt against Hitler. He was imprisoned and later murdered by Hitler's henchmen for his resistance efforts.

As a German theologian, however, he can be credited as the unofficial father of the "God is Dead" theology. In 1992, yours truly authored a 17 page expose treatise dealing with the former Grand Rapids Baptist College & Seminary [Now Cornerstone University and Grand Rapids Theological Seminary]. This discourse was entitled *Is Grand Rapids Baptist College and Seminary [GRBCS] a New-Evangelical Institution?*

A large part of this expose was based on the fact that in Nov. 1991 the GRBCS drama department presented a play for three days on Bonhoeffer's life. In this play, Bonhoeffer was presented not just a political martyr, but also as a hero of the faith. Pages 7-16 of that treatise deal exclusively with Bonhoeffer's denial of the historic Christian faith. In preparation for this writer's expose, he read completely through all fourteen of Bonhoeffer's published books!

Bonhoeffer's *Denials of the Faith*

Bonhoeffer was the father of the "God is Dead" theology that became so popular in the 1960's decade. He said that Christianity would become alive only when it became dead, that is, when it became totally secularized and completely identified with human culture and the world's society. In simple terms, Bonhoeffer believed that for Christianity to survive in the modern world, spiritual Christianity had to die and secular Christianity had to take its place.

Consider the following quote: "The secularity of the church follows from the incarnation of Christ. The church, like Christ, has become world…it is entirely world." "Renunciation of its claims to 'purity' lead the church back to its solidarity with the sinful world ....only this kind of church is free, the church that confesses its secularity." (Testimony to Freedom, p. 92)

Bonhoeffer did not literally accept any of the historic cardinal doctrines of the faith; he denied literal belief in every vital Christian truth. Ponder these quotes by Bonhoeffer: (a) Scripture: "The N.T. ...is nothing in itself, but bears witness of something else...its words and statements are not in themselves true and holy" [*No Rusty Sword*, p. 118]; (b) Christ: "In his flesh was the law which was contrary to God's will. He was *not* the perfect good...it was he who assumed flesh with its tendency to sin and self will." [*Christ the Center*, p. 108]; (c) Christianity: "What are we to think of other religions? ...We answer that the Christian religion as religion is not of God. It is rather another example of a human way to God, like the Buddhist and others..." [*Testimony to Freedom*, p. 55].

In his book *Existentialism and Christian Belief,* author Milton D. Hunnex, reluctantly admits that Bonhoeffer was a "secular theologian" (p. 94) who taught a "religionless Christianity;" (p. 96) whose writings have "become the rallying cry for a wholesome defection from the Christian faith" (p. 98).

Both Rejected Historic Christianity
Teilhard de Chardin and Dietrich Bonhoeffer
Christian News, December 10, 2007

The October 28, 2007 *St. Louis Post Dispatch* (below) reviewed "The Jesuit and the Skull" by Amir D. Aczel. *The Christian News Encyclopedia* includes several articles on the Jesuit Teilhard de Chardin. He rejected the deity of Jesus Christ. He was an immoral, untruthful theologian who cohabited with several women. The liberal National Council of Churches used his evolutionary statements and the non-Trinitarian Statement of Faith of the United Church of Christ as its confession when the NCC celebrated its 30th anniversary. The NCC holds the copyright to the *RSV* and the *ESV* being promoted by CPH. Years ago the LCMS's *Lutheran Witness* said that the Federal Council of Churches, predecessor of the NCC, was the "most vicious agency" in Protestantism.

The November 15, 1976 *CN* (*CNE*, 1183) noted: "Teilhard de Chardin was an evolutionist who did not believe that Christ was God or rose from the dead. Teilhard admitted: 'I am on the contrary essentially pantheist in my thinking and temperament.' Paul Hallett noted in the June 1, 1969 *National Catholic Register*: 'Teihardiasm is nothing but the pantheism of Spinoza in new a dress that is sentimentalized atheism.'"

The New Catholic Encyclopedia, which says evolution is a fact, praises Teilhard de Chardin even though a pope did warn against uncritical acceptance of his views.

Cornelius Van Til in "Pierre Teilhard de Chardin" noted that Chardin's "Christ is but a vague ideal of the would be autonomous man." (*CNE*, p. 991) (From "Creation Problems In Churches" by Herman Otten, 8th Bible-Science Convention, Concordia College, River Forest, Illinois, June 25, 1980).

"Holy Hoaxer? Teilhard and Piltdown Man," an article in *Time* (*CNE*, p. 948) noted that Father Teilhard was implicated in one of the most famous scientific hoaxes: the notorious Piltdown man was presented as one of the missing links. In 1953 he was unmasked. "The remains are nothing more than a fabrication of modern human and ape bones doctored to make them the look of antiquity." Many evolutionists had accepted the Piltdown man as absolute fact.

The April 28, 1975 *Christian News* said in a review of *The New Hermeneutics* by Cornelius Van Til:

The New Hermeneutics. By Cornelius Van Til. Nutley, New Jersey: Presbyterian and Reformed, Box 185, 1974. 230 pages. $5.95.

The author, who has an amazing grasp of modern theology, shows how far the followers of the new hermeneutic have departed from historic Christianity. He covers the views of such men as Ernst Fuchs, Gerhard Ebeling, John Dillenberger, Fritz Buri, Schubert Ogden, A.D. R. Polman, H.M. Kuitert, Jurgen Moltmann, S.U. Zuidema, and Herman Wiersing.

Cornelius Van Til quotes Dietrich Bonhoeffer as writing: "As a subject for historical investigation, Jesus Christ remains an uncertain phenomenon; his historicity can neither be affirmed or denied with absolute certainty" (90). Van Til concludes his discussion of Bonhoeffer:

"From what we have learned of Bonhoeffer we see that his Christ as Center is to all intents and purposes the same as the Christ-Event of the new hermeneutic, of the new quest of the theology as history. In all of these the historic Protestant hermeneutic is rejected as rational-determinist and irrational-indeterminist. In all of these the text of Scripture is interpreted in terms of hermeneutical principles based on the epistemology of Kant and his followers. In all of these the attempt is made to go beyond Barth and beyond Bultmann in terms of a Christ-Event, i.e., of an Act-theology in which a purely formal principle of unity is more consistently than ever before made wholly correlative to a purely formal principle of diversity" (91).

Van Til shows why there is so much similarity between modern Roman Catholic and modern Protestant thinking. (pp. 91-92).

"A word may here be added about Piere Teilhard de Chardin's Christ-Mystique.

"It might be thought that the so-called essentialist philosophy of Roman Catholicism would reject the Christ-Event of modern Protestant Act-theology. Do not the proponents of Act-theology constantly set their position over against the supposedly static categories of the Greeks? Do not Roman Catholic theologians reject the philosophy of Kant and his followers because of its subjectivism?

"All this is true but something more basic is also true. The essentialist philosophy based on Aristotle and the act-philosophy of Kant are alike based on the idea of human autonomy with its concomitant notions of abstract impersonal rationality and abstract impersonal irrationality. It is this fact that accounts for the current rapprochement of modern Roman Catholic and modern Protestant thinking.

"As an illustration of this fact we call attention briefly to the similarity between the idea of Christ as the center of Bonhoeffer and of Christ as the Omega of Pierre Teilhard de Chardin.

"Teilhard de Chardin is first a scientist, second a philosopher, and third a theologian. He offers what he thinks of as a totally integrated view of man and his world by means of the process of biological and cosmic evolution. All things are working in a process of interiorization toward their apex in Christ. Teilhard's categories are as activist as are those of any Protestant Thinker" (91,92).

Concordia Theological Quarterly, Concordia Seminary, Ft. Wayne
BONHOEFFER: "A MAN OF THE WORD OF GOD"
Christian News, June 9, 2008

Dietrich Bonhoeffer was "a man of the word of God," says Eric A. Andrae in an article published in the January, 2008 *Concordia Theological Quarterly* of Concordia Theological Seminary, Ft. Wayne, Indiana.

Christian News has shown for some 45 years that Bonhoeffer in his own writings made it clear that he rejected such Christian doctrines as the resurrection and deity of Jesus Christ. He did not believe in the Holy Trinity. *CN* published a detailed documented article by Concordia Seminary, Ft. Wayne Professor Raymond Surburg showing that Bonhoeffer in his last writings promoted theoretical atheism.

While the theological journal of the Ft. Wayne seminary published many writings by Surburg, it refused to publish Surburg's article on Bonhoeffer. Now it publishes an article which says almost the exact opposite what Surburg wrote about Bonhoeffer. What Surburg wrote is simply ignored. *CN* has often noted that intellectual snobs just ignore those who disagree with their position. *CN* repeatedly challenged Bonhoeffer defenders to respond to Surburg's "An Evaluation of Dietrich Bonhoeffer's Life and Theology After Half a Century."

No Bonhoeffer defender has ever shown where Surburg misrepresented Bonhoffer. The first two pages of the *CTQ* article praising Bonhoeffer are reproduced in this issue. The *CTQ* article says that "there is much – confessional Lutherans can affirm in Bonhoeffer's writings and actions.

"After Martin Luther, Bonhoeffer may arguably be the most recognized and quoted, as well as the most misunderstood and misapplied, Lutheran theologian today." Although Bonhoeffer did not believe the Psalms were God's Word, the *CTQ* says "Bonhoeffer's interpretation of the Psalms is pervasively Christocentric." The *CTQ* claims that "Bonhoeffer, however, insists on the doctrine of justification as the touchstone and thereby interprets these Psalms in the light of Christ's forgiveness toward all." Surburg showed that the Christ of Bonhoeffer was not the Christ of the Bible and Lutheran Confessions, true God and true man. While the liberal professors at Concordia Seminary, St. Louis who eventually formed Seminex praised such liberal and neo-orthodox theologians as Karl Barth, Emil Brunner, Gustav Aulen, Anders Nygren, and others, seldom did any of them commend demythologizers Rudolf Bultmann and Dietrich Bonhoeffer who said the Bible contained myths. They were more perceptive when it comes to Dietrich Bonhoeffer than professors in the LCMS and editors at CPH who have become Bonhoeffer fans. Publicity for Bonhoeffer has grown along with stories about the ruthless Germans exterminating in gas chambers some six million Jews.

The *CTQ* commends the work of Dr. Uwe Simeon-Netto on Bonhoeffer. Dr. Simeon-Netto insists that Bonhoeffer is a confessional Lutheran in an article published in the LCMS's official *Lutheran Witness*. The *Lutheran Witness* refused to publish any letter showing that Bonhoeffer in his own words rejected historic Christianity. While *CN* has commended much of the work of Dr. Simeon-Netto, *CN* has disagreed with his evaluation of Pope John Paul II, Richard Neuhaus, Jaroslav Pelikan and the evolutionary notion of millions of years. According to this Bonhoeffer champion, Pope

John Paul II was also his pope. Although Neuhaus joined the Roman Catholic Church and Pelikan joined the Greek Orthodox Church, Simeon-Netto claims they never left Martin Luther. Both were universalists, denied the inerrancy of the Bible, justification by faith alone, and supported evolution. Neuhaus claims no one is in hell, and that such faithful Jews as his "great teacher" Rabbi Abraham Heschel are in heaven. "Is Greek Orthodox Christian?", reviewed on page one shows how far Orthodoxy has departed from historic Christianity. When Bonhoeffer's 100th birthday was celebrated at Concordia Seminary, St. Louis, a news release from the seminary said that Bonhoeffer was the most important and influential Lutheran since Martin Luther. Some wanted to know how it was possible for a seminary, which claims to be a confessional Lutheran seminary, to allow such a statement to go unrepudiated. How is it possible for a seminary to publish a review article by Dr. Matthew Becker which praises Bonhoeffer far higher than any 20th century Lutheran theologians, including men like Francis Pieper, Walter A. Maier, William Beck, etc.? Becker rejects the inerrancy of the Bible, supports evolution and the ordination of women. The latest issue of the seminary's *Concordia Journal* published reviews by two LCMS professors who support the anti-Scriptural theology of Seminex.

Reprinted here is Chapter XII from *Walter A. Maier Still Speaks – Missouri and the World Should Listen*. It is titled "Surburg, Maier, Bonhoeffer, and the Holocaust." *CN* sent a review copy of this book to the *CTQ* and the *Concordia Journal* of Concordia Seminary, St. Louis. *CN* has not yet seen any mention of the book in these journals which have a long history of generally ignoring anything published in *Christian News*.

Walter A. Maier Still Speaks - Missouri and the World Should Listen
Chapter XII Surburg, Maier, Bonhoeffer, and the Holocaust

Dr. Raymond Surburg, a Lutheran Church-Missouri Synod Old Testament scholar, who taught at Concordia University, Seward, Nebraska, and Concordia Seminary, Ft. Wayne, repeatedly defended the position Dr. Walter Maier took on the inerrancy of the Bible, the historicity of Genesis, higher criticism, evolution, the Old Testament etc.

Some of the many articles Surburg sent *Christian News* for publication are in *The Christian News Encyclopedia*. Dr. Walter Maier Jr. regularly visited and watched over Surburg during Surburg's final years. Dr. Walter Maier III preached the sermon at Surburg's funeral.

"The CTCR vs. THE LCMS – The History of Messianic Prophecy in the Lutheran Church-Missouri Synod from 1847 Till the Issuing of the CTCR's 'Prophecy and Typology' in 1996" were the title and subtitle of an article by Dr. Raymond Surburg in the September 30, 1996 *Christian News*.

The LCMS's CTCR adopted a statement in 1996 which took issue with the position on messianic prophecy which Luther, Maier, Beck and the LCMS in former years defended. It supported the position of the Concordia Publishing House Self Study Bible (*NIV*) which says in its comments on Psalm 16:9-11: "David speaks here, as in the rest of his psalms, first of all of himself." The CTCR took issue with the Apostle Peter who said that David is here not speaking about himself but only about Jesus Christ (Acts 2:25-26). Surburg wrote:

"Walter A. Maier, Sr. and Messianic Prophecy"

"Walter A. Maier, Sr. (1893-1950) followed the views on Messianic prophecy held by Luther, Walther, Stoeckhardt, L. Fuerbringer, Laetsch and other contemporaries. In his *Notes on the Genesis Seminary Course*[38] and in his *Notes of Selected Psalms*[39] he defended rectilinear prophecy and was opposed to the substitution of typological prophecy in place of rectilinear. In opposition to many scholars of his day he accepted Psalm 8 as a rectilinear prophecy dealing with Christ and not having as its purpose the praise of the greatness of man as God's creature. He vigorously defended the Christocentricity of the Old Testament.[40] In a published Christmas sermon he claimed that there were over three hundred Messianic prophecies in the Old Testament. Maier relied upon the clear statements of the New Testament for the establishment of numerous Old Testament predictions about Christ's life and work. L. Fuerbringer and Th. Laetsch were two other contemporary exegetes who agreed with Maier about rectilinear prophecy.

CN hopes to be able to publish at least some of Surburg's writings on a wide variety of subjects. One of them is "An Evaluation of Dietrich Bonhoeffer's Life and Theology After Half of a Century." Bonhoeffer was executed at the age of 39 on April 9, 1995 for his part in a plot to execute Adolf Hitler. Surburg wrote in the September 13, 1995 *Christian News*, as many Christians were marking the 50th anniversary of Bonhoeffer's death: "While in prison Bonhoeffer came to the conclusion that mankind no longer needs God. What amounts to theoretical atheism was Bonhoeffer's assertion that God is teaching us that we must live as men who can get along very well without him." Surburg based his article upon Bonhoeffer's writings, particularly his last writings. Surburg wrote: "Although he claimed to be a Lutheran and is so called in the literature of our day, Bonhoeffer was not a Lutheran, for he rejected and abandoned the theology and teachings of the Book of Concord." "His Christology is considerably different from that found in Luther and in the Lutheran Confessions." Bonhoeffer's "Christology is not what the New Testament sets forth, but was the product of his philosophical thinking." "Van Til in his book, *The Great Debate*, contended that the Christ of Bonhoeffer is not the Christ of Scripture and can hardly be distinguished from the Christ of Karl Barth (pp. 42-76 of Van Til's book.)" "Later he (Bonhoeffer) adopted the Bultmann view on 'Mythology' of the New Testament." "In Bonhoeffer's opinion Bultmann's demythologizing of the Bible did not go far enough."

Christian News has exposed the anti-scriptural and anti-Christian nature of Bonhoeffer's theology for some 45 years. No Bonhoeffer defender has shown where *CN* or Surburg misquoted Bonhoeffer. While Concordia Publishing House no longer publishes or sells any books by or about Walter Maier it sells and even publishes books by and about Bonhoeffer. While both LCMS seminaries commemorated the 100th birthday of Bonhoeffer by inviting outside speakers to praise Bonhoeffer, neither seminary had any commemoration of the 100th birthday of Maier. The LCMS's *Portals of Prayer* has quoted Bonhoeffer as some great authority who has much wisdom to offer, but does not quote Maier in the same manner. In 2006 when both LCMS seminaries had a conference marking the 100th birthday of Bonhoeffer, *CN* suggested that the conference should have at least one speaker respond to such critics of Bonhoeffer as Raymond Surburg. What Surburg wrote and what *CN* has exposed about Bonhoeffer's anti-Christian theology was totally ignored. When the *Lutheran Witness* praised Bonhoeffer as a great Christian in an article by Uwe Simeon Netto, the *Lutheran Witness* refused to publish a letter from *Christian News* telling the truth about Bonhoeffer's theology. *CN*'s letter included quotes from Bonhoeffer's writings. One of them was: "Belief in the resurrection is not the solution of the problem of death," from Bonhoeffer's *Letters and Papers From Prison*, reviewed in the November 15, 1965 *Christian News*. (The *Lutheran Witness* article and *CN*'s letter are in the special July 3, 2006 *Christian News* issue on Bonhoeffer).

When the Aid Association for Lutherans sponsored and widely distributed to Lutheran congregations a film praising Bonhoeffer as a great Christian, *Christian News* asked the members of the AAL's Board of Directors if they believed a person who denied the deity and resurrection of Christ could be considered a Christian. No member of the AAL Board of Directors responded. Several times *CN* has noted that Franklin L. Baumer in his *Modern European Thought: Continuity and Change in Ideas, 1600-1950* (Diers College, Yale University, 1977, MacMillan publishing Company) came to about the same conclusion about Bonhoeffer that Surburg did.

As the story of the Germans exterminating 6 million Jews during World War II, most of them by gassing, grew, Lutherans particularly increased their publicity and praise for Bonhoeffer. Honoring a theologian executed by the Germans was one way to make it known that Lutherans opposed Hitler and accepted as fact the ever growing story that the Germans executed six million Jews during World War. Maier did not praise Dietrich Bonhoeffer as some great Christian martyr as he is now being praised in the LCMS. It is true that he did not mention or accept as fact the six million Holocaust figure. However, Prime Minister Winston Churchill, President Dwight Eisenhower and the Red Cross, which investigated German prison camps during World War II, also did not mention the 6 million figure. During World War II when this editor went from door to door in a predominately Jewish neighborhood in the Bronx, New York, collecting newspapers for the war effort, none of the tenants of the hundreds of apartments he visited ever mentioned anything about their relatives in Eastern Europe being exterminated in gas chambers. For information on the Holocaust and Revisionism, see *The Christian News Encyclopedia*.

Those in the LCMS, who have referred to themselves as "hypereuros" or "high church," just as the Bonhoeffer enthusiasts, have also held conferences commemorating anniversaries of their heroes. But they have never conducted any such conference to preserve the memory of Walter Maier.

Christian News has asked many: "Why?" "Why Bonhoeffer and not Maier?"

Footnotes

38W. A. Maier, *Notes on the Book of Genesis* (St. Louis Concordia Mimeograph Company, 1930)

39Exegetical *Notes on the Psalms* (St. Louis: Concordia Mimeograph Company, 1930), cf. especially his arguments for rectilinear prophecy and rejection of typological prophecy in Ps. 2, 8, 16).

40Walter A. Maier, Sr., The Radio For Christ (St. Louis, Concordia Publishing House, 1939), 50 in a sermon for Christmas on Isaiah 9:6,7.

Differences Between Neuhaus and Otten
Christian News, January 19, 2009
(Excerpts)

Neuhaus	Otten
1. Denied the inerrancy of the Bible already during his seminary days (1957-58) in discussions with Otten.	1. Affirmed the inerrancy of the Bible.
17. There is no one in hell.	17. Those who die without saving faith in Christ are lost in hell.
33. Said that such liberals as Martin Luther King and Dietrich Bonhoeffer, who denied the resurrection of Christ, should be declared saints.	33. Bonhoeffer and King did not affirm the virgin birth and resurrection of Christ and should not be declared great Christian saints.
34. Invited to speak at Concordia Seminary St. Louis and Concordia Seminary, Ft. Wayne where he was hailed as a great faithful Christian theologian.	34. Banned from speaking at both LCMS seminaries.
35. At least some LCMS "high church" "hypereuros" consider it an honor to be published by Neuhaus.	35. At least some LCMS hypereuros consider it a "kiss of death" to be published in Christian News.
36. Liberals and hypereuros consider it a mark of scholarship to quote Neuhaus and First Things.	36. Liberals and hypereuros regard it a mark of ignorance to quote from or read Christian News.
37. Support the war in Iraq.	37. Follow the advice of George Washington. Build a strong defense but do not meddle in wars all over the world.
38. Considered worthy of millions of dollars from pro-Israel groups.	38. Not considered worthy of support by any major foundation.
39. Highly praised by Paul McCain of CPH.	39. McCain says Otten is a liar.
40. Otten is an anti-semite because he maintains there is no evidence that the Germans exterminated six million Jews, 3 1/2 million in Auschwitz alone, by gassing.	40. Neuhaus is not showing true love to Jews when he tells them they get to heaven without faith in Jesus Christ.

A CALL FOR EVIDENCE ON BONHOEFFER
March 15, 2010

Last week *Christian News* in its comments on the Rev. Dr. Gerald Kieschnick's *Waking the Sleeping Giant* called for evidence that Billy Graham actually referred to the LCMS as a "sleeping giant". *CN* asked Kieschnick, Paul McCain at CPH, and the Billy Graham Evangelistic Association for the evidence. The Billy Graham Evangelistic Association told *CN* it could find no evidence that Graham ever made the statement used for the title of Kieschnick's CPH book.

This week, *CN*, which applies the same standard to "friend and foe," in its report of Rev. Matthew Harrison's recent book "*A Little Book on Joy*" notes that the book includes about 10 quotations from Dietrich Bonhoeffer leaving the impression that Bonhoeffer was some great Christian theologian. *CN* is now calling for evidence to show that what *CN* has said about Bonhoeffer for almost 50 years on the basis of Bonhoeffer's writings and what Professor Raymond Surburg said in his "An Evaluation of Dietrich Bonhoeffer's Life and Theology After Half a Century" (*CN*, March 31, 2008) is in error. Bonhoeffer has been praised as a faithful Lutheran by Concordia Publishing House. He is often favorably quoted by theologians who want to be considered in step with the times. Many Lutherans want to particularly distance themselves from those accused of being anti-Semites for claiming there is no evidence the Germans exterminated some six million Jews during WWII, most of them in gas chambers.

The AAL, now Thrivent, funded a movie featuring Bonhoeffer as a faithful Christian. The *Lutheran Witness* published an article by Uwe Simeon Netto stating that Bonhoeffer was a faithful confessional Lutheran. *Christian News* has often shown, almost from its beginning in 1962, that on the basis of Bonhoeffer's own writings, Bonhoeffer repudiated historic Christianity, including such doctrines as the physical resurrection of Christ. Several times *Christian News* has published a long fully documented article by Professor Raymond Surburg of Concordia Seminary, Ft. Wayne, showing that Bonhoeffer's Christ was not the Christ of the Bible. The last time was in the March 3, 2008 *CN*. *CN* has noted that Franklin L. Baumer in his *Modern European Thought: Continuity and Change in Ideas*, 1600-1850 (Diers College, Yale University, 1977 MacMillan Publishing Company) came to about the same conclusion Surburg did. Some of what *Christian News* has published about Bonhoeffer is in *The Christian News Encyclopedia*.

When both LCMS seminaries at the 100th anniversary of Bonhoeffer's birth held events Bonhoeffer was highly praised as a great Christian and Lutheran. *CN* challenged them to respond to what Surburg of Concordia Seminary, Ft. Wayne, had written about Bonhoeffer. Invite a speaker who defends what *CN* has been saying about Bonhoeffer for almost 50 years on the basis of Bonhoeffer's writing and not on the basis of all the myths surrounding Bonhoeffer promoted by those who refuse to examine the evidence about Bonhoeffer, the Holocaust, and other matters such as the Billy Graham quote about him saying the LCMS is a "sleeping giant". (Ed. Graham may have said this even though the statement is not recorded in the minutes of the LCMS Atlantic District convention where he is supposed to have made the statement).

What Surburg had written and what *CN* has said for decades about Bonhoeffer is ignored by the great scholars who consider it beneath them to even admit that they read *Christian News*. Kurt Marquart noted that "intellectual snobs" refuse to accept as fact what is published in some newspaper they despise. It is time for the "great scholars" to examine the evidence in every area upon which they pontificate before they pass on fiction as fact. Last week *CN* said that those who pass on the Graham quote Kieschnick used for the title of his book should study the evidence. This week *CN* in all fairness again says that those who hail Bonhoeffer as a great confessional Lutheran should study the evidence. *Christian News* plays no favorites. The standards which *CN* applies to one candidate about evidence also apply to the other even though *CN* may have been opposing the one and supporting the other for years. Reprinted here from the March 31, 2008 *Christian News* is "In the Lutheran Church Missouri Synod Today – IT'S BONHOEFFER OVER MAIER:"

New Bonhoeffer Biography by Eric Metaxas Hits The Streets To Great Reviews
Warren Smith, World Magazine, April 22, 2010

Friends:

This email is a bit out of the ordinary compared to others you receive from me, but I simply couldn't resist the opportunity to let you know that there is an important new biography of Dietrich Bonhoeffer newly released.

"Bonhoeffer: Pastor, Martyr, Prophet, Spy" is written by my friend Eric Metaxas. And even if he was not my friend I would say that this is an IMPORTANT book, with new insight into one of the most fascinating figures of the 20th century.

I strongly recommend today's review of the book from the *"Wall Street Journal."* This review is written by another friend, Joe Loconte, with whom I've had the pleasure to get to know because of our mutual associations with WORLD Magazine and The King's College. Here's a link to Joe's review:

http://online.wsj.com/article/SB10001424052702303491304575189132952513158.html

So please buy this book, read it, and spread the world. To help with that process, here are a couple of other links, first to the book's page on Amazon:

www.amazon.com/Bonhoeffer-Pastor-Martyr-Prophet-Spy/dp/1595551387/ref=sr_1_1?ie=UTF8&s=books&gid=1271976314&sr=1-1

Belief in Action
In Hitler's Germany, a Lutheran pastor chooses resistance and pays with his life.
By Joseph Loconte
Wall Street Journal, April 22, 2010

In "Bonhoeffer: Pastor, Martyr, Prophet, Spy," Eric Metaxas tells Bonhoeffer's story with passion and theological sophistication, often challenging revisionist accounts that make Bonhoeffer out to be a "humanist" or ethicist for whom religious doctrine was easily disposable. In "Bonhoeffer" we meet a complex, provocative figure: an orthodox Christian who, at a grave historical moment, rejected what he called "cheap grace" – belief without bold and sacrificial action.

"Most Important and Influential Lutheran Since Luther" says St. Louis Seminary
BONHOEFFER - PASTOR- MARTYR- PROPHET, SPY
Christian News, May 10, 2010

Bonhoeffer, Pastor, Martyr, Prophet, Spy. By Eric Metaxas. Thomas Nelson Publishers, 565 Royal Parkway, Nashville, TN 37214. 2010. 591 pages. $29.99.

Dietrich Bonhoeffer is held in higher regard at many seminaries and by numerous churchmen more than any other theologian of the 20th Century. When the 100th birthday of Bonhoeffer was celebrated at Concordia Seminary, St. Louis, a press release from the seminary said that Bonhoeffer was perhaps the most important and influential Lutheran since Martin Luther. A review article by Matthew Becker in the seminary's *Concordia Journal* praised Bonhoeffer far higher than any 20th century Lutheran theologian, including men like Francis Pieper, Walter A. Maier, William Beck, etc. The LCMS's *Lutheran Witness* said that Bonhoeffer was "a confessional Lutheran."

The foreword to this biography of Bonhoeffer is by Timothy J. Keeler, New York Times Best Selling author of *The Reason for God*. Eric Metaxas is *New York Times* Best-Selling author of *Amazing Grace*. The back cover and jacket of *Bonhoeffer, Pastor, Martyr, Prophet, Spy*, says:

Praise for Bonhoeffer

"'For anyone whose faith has been strengthened by the life and witness of Dietrich Bonhoeffer, this is the biography you have always wanted. Eric Metaxas has written a rich, detailed, and beautiful account of the great pastor and theologian who gave us The Cost of Discipleship and sacrificed his life for opposing Hitler. Metaxas' Bonhoeffer is A MONUMENTAL ACHIEVEMENT AND A DEEPLY IMPORTANT WORK.'"

–Greg Thornbury, PhD, Dean of the School of Christian Studies at Union University

"'A captivating and inspiring read from start to finish. Sets the record straight on Bonhoeffer's commitment to Scripture and his unyielding passion truth that led him to give up his life in the battle to save the Jews of Europe. Buy it. THIS BOOK COULD CHANGE YOUR LIFE.'"

–James N. Lane, Founder, New Canaan Society; Former General Partner, Goldman, Sachs & Co.

"'Dietrich Bonhoeffer's great fight is that his understanding of faith in times of conflict speaks to generation after generation. Eric Metaxas' Bonhoeffer is the biography for this generation. A MASTERPIECE THAT READS LIKE A GREAT NOVEL and weaves together on one opus an understanding of Bonhoeffer's theology, the complex and tragic history of 20th century Germany, and the human struggle of a true Christian hero. Eric Metaxas is claiming is place as the pre-eminent biographer of Christianity's most courageous figures.'"

–Martin Doblmeier, Filmmaker, *Bonhoeffer*

"'With great skill, energy, and warmth, Metaxas reminds us why the life of Dietrich Bonhoeffer stands as a rebuke both to believers and sceptics. Rarely has the story of a Christian martyr been told with such realism and depth. IT'S A GEM OF A BOOK."

–Joseph Loconte, Lecturer in Politics, The King's College, New York City; Editor of *The End of Illusions: Religious Leaders Confront Hitler's Gathering Storm*

"Praise For *Bonhoeffer - Pastor, Martyr, Prophet, Spy* -- A Righteous Gentile vs. The Third Reich" a section in the front of the book has statements from the following highly praising the book: Greg Thornbury, PhD, Dean of the School of Christian Studies at Union University; Joseph Loconte, Lecturer in Politics, The King's College, New York City and editor of *The End of Illusions: Religious Leaders Confront Hitler's Gathering Storm*; Martin Doblmeier, Filmmaker, Bonhoeffer; James N. Lane, Founder, New Canaan Society, Former General Partner, Goldman, Sachs & Co.; Caleb J.D. Maskell, Associate Director, Jonathon Edwards Center, Yale University (2004-207), Department of Religion, Princeton University; Gordon Riddle Pennington, CEO, Burning Media Group; Gerald Schroeder, PhD, Israeli Physicist and Teacher at The Aish Ha Torah college of Jewish Studies in Jerusalem, Author of *Genesis and the Big Bang* and *The Science of God*.

Eric Metaxas writes:

"Although the Bonhoeffers weren't churchgoers, all their children were confirmed" (38).

"Karl (father) Bonhoeffer was wary of anything beyond what one might observe with one's senses or deduce from those observations. Concerning both psychoanalysis and religion he might be termed an agnostic" (13).

"For Dietrich the theologian to hold a prejudice in favor of Lutheranism or Protestantism, or even Christianity, would be wrong. One must consider every possibility and avoid predisposing oneself to where it would all lead. During his lifetime, Bonhoeffer brought this critical and 'scientific' attitude to all questions of faith and theology.

"But another reason he was so open to the Catholic church now had to do with Rome itself, where the best of the classical pagan world he so loved met and coexisted harmoniously with the world of Christendom. Here in Rome it was all art of some continuum" (54).

Karl Barth

"But there was another theologian who had a greater influence on Bonhoeffer than any of these and whom he would revere and respect as much as anyone in his lifetime, who would even become a mentor and a friend. This was Karl Barth of Göttingen.

"Barth was Swiss by birth and was almost certainly the most important theologian of the century, many would say of the last five centuries" (60).

"Bonhoeffer agreed with Barth, seeing the texts as 'not just historical sources, but [as] agents of revelation,' not merely 'specimens of writing, but sacred canon.' Bonhoeffer was not against doing historical and critical work on biblical texts, indeed he had learned from Harnack how to do it and could do it brilliantly" (61).

"In the next two years Bonhoeffer visited Barth often. In September 1932, just after Barth completed the first volume of his landmark Church Dogmatics, Bonhoeffer visited him on the Bergli in Switzerland" (120).

No Significant Change

"Nearly all that Bonhoeffer would say and write later in life marked a deepening and expansion of what he had earlier said and believed, but never any kind of significant theological change. He was building on what had been established, like a scientist or mathematician" (84).

Luther and the Jews

"But when it came to the Jews, Luther's legacy is confusing, not to say deeply disturbing.

"At the very end of his life, after becoming a parody of his former cranky self, Luther said and wrote some things about the Jews that, taken on their own, make him out to be a vicious anti-Semite. The Nazis exploited these last writings to the utmost, as though they represented Luther's definitive take on the matter, which is impossible, given what he'd said earlier in life" (91, 92).

"As his health declined, everything seemed to set him off. When a congregation sang anemically, he called them 'tone-deaf sluggards' and stormed out. He attacked King Henry VIII as 'effeminate' and blasted his theological opponents as 'agents of the devil' and 'whore-mongers.' His language waxed fouler and fouler. He called the pope 'the Anti-Christ' and 'a brothel-keeper above all brothel-keepers and all lewdness, including that which is not to be named.' He blasted the Catholic church's regulation of marriage and accused the church of being 'a merchant selling vulvas, genitals, and pudenda.' Expressing his contempt for the devil, he said that he would give him 'a fart for a staff.' He viciously mocked Pope Clement III's writings: 'such a great horrid flatus did the papas arse let go here! He certainly pressed with great might to let out such a thunderous flatus--it is a wonder that it did not tear his hole and belly apart!' Luther seemed to have an absolutely torrid love affair with all things scatological. Not only were his linguistic flourishes styled along such lines, but his doctors seem to have followed suit: for one of his ailments, they persuaded him to take a draught of 'garlic and horse manure,' and he infamously received an enema--in vain--moments after he had departed this world. So it is in this larger context that one has to take his attitude toward the Jews, which, like everything else in his life, unraveled along with his health.

"The troubles started in 1528 when, after a large meal of kosher food, he suffered a shattering attack of diarrhea. He concluded that the Jews had tried to poison him. By that time he was making enemies everywhere" (92, 93).

"But the tragicomedy became purest tragedy when, three years before his death, Luther advocated actions against the Jews that included, among other things, setting fire to their synagogues and schools, destroying their houses, confiscating their prayer books, taking their money, and putting them into forced labor" (93).

Nazi Theology

"One sometimes hears that Hitler was a Christian. He was certainly not, but neither was he openly anti-Christian, as most of his top lieutenants were" (165).

"Hitler's attitude toward Christianity was that it was a great heap of mystical out-of-date nonsense" (166).

"Martin Bormann and Heinrich Himmler were the most passionately anti-Christian members of Hitler's inner circle, and they didn't believe the churches should adapt or could. They wanted the clergy crushed and the churches abolished, and they encouraged Hitler along these lines whenever possible. They hoped to accelerate the timetable for open warfare with the church, but Hitler was in no hurry. Whenever he attacked the churches, his popularity waned. Unlike his top men, Hitler had an instinctive political sense of timing, and now was not the time to take on the churches directly. Now was the time to pretend to be pro-Christian" (166, 167).

"Since Hitler had no religion other than himself, his opposition to Christianity and the church was less ideological than practical. That was not the case for many leaders of the Third Reich. Alfred Rosenberg, Martin Bormann, Heinrich Himmler, Reinhard Hedrich, and others were bitterly anti-Christian and were ideologically opposed to

Christianity, and wanted to replace it with a religion of their own devising. Under their leadership, said Shirer, 'the Nazi regime intended eventually to destroy Christianity in Germany, if it could, and substitute the old paganism of the early tribal Germanic gods and the new paganism of the Nazi extremists'" (169).

Gandhi

"In any case, he had long felt that Gandhi could provide some clues for him. Gandhi was not a Christian, but he lived in a community that endeavored to live by the teachings set forth in the Sermon on the Mount. Bonhoeffer wanted Christians to live that way. So he would travel to India to see it practiced by non-Christians. At Fanø he asked the assembled Christians: 'Must we be put to shame by the non-Christian people in the East? Shall we desert the individuals who are risking their lives for this message?' (248).

Bonhoeffer Wrote to His Grandmother

"Before I tie myself down anywhere for good, I'm thinking again of going to India. I've given a good deal of thought lately to the issues there and believe that there could be important things to be learned. In any case it sometimes seems to me that there's more Christianity in their 'heathenism' than in the whole of our Reich Church" (248).

Preaching the Word

"Bonhoeffer took preaching seriously. For him a sermon was nothing less than the very word of God, a place where God would speak to his people" (272).

Lutherans and Obedience to Government

"The willingness of Lutherans to keep the church out of the world reflected an unbiblical overemphasis on Romans 13:1-5, which they had inherited from Luther. They had never been forced to deal with the boundary of this scriptural idea of obedience to worldly authorities. The early Christians stood up against Caesar and the Romans. Surely the Nuremberg Laws would force the Confessing Church to take a stand against the Nazis" (281)

Saase and "an Atrocious Piece of False Doctrine"

"But someplace in this beautiful landscape, planted like a time bomb, was a single sentence. It would soon explode and effectively obliterate every sentence around it and cause a firestorm of controversy. Bonhoeffer did not think of it that way when he wrote it, and he had never imagined that it would become a focal point of the lecture. The controversial sentence was this: 'Whoever knowingly separates himself from the Confessing Church in Germany separates himself from salvation.' The condemnations were thundering. When the lecture was published in the June issue of Evangelische Theologie, the paper quickly sold out. Bonhoeffer's essay led Hermann Sasse, who had cowritten the Bethel Confession with him, to declare that the Confessing Church as 'distinct from the confessional movement upheld by the Lutheran churches, is a sect, the worst sect in fact ever to have set foot on the soil of German Protestantism.' Merz said that Bonhoeffer's declaration was 'the ecstatic effusion of a hitherto level headed man, contradicting everything that was essential to Luther.' General Superintendent Ernst Stoltenhoff called it 'nothing more than an atrocious piece of false doctrine,'" (286,287).

"Pro-abortion defenders of Bonhoeffer seldom mention that Bonhoeffer said it was 'murder' (472).

Nazis and Homosexuality

"It must be said that the Nazi leaders, including Hitler, had no moral difficulties with homosexuality. Many of the early figures in the Nazi movement were homosexuals, Ernst Röhm and his strutting cronies chief among them. Hitler has plausibly been connected to such activity. But in the Third Reich an accusation of homosexuality was without peer in smearing someone's reputation" (305).

Union Seminary - Riverside Church -- Fosdick

"When Bonhoeffer attended Union Seminary in New York in 1939 he heard Harry Emerson Fosdick preach at Rockefeller's Riverside Church where Harry Emerson Fosdick was the preacher. In his diary he wrote 'Quite unbearable.' He noted:

'The whole thing was a respectable, self-indulgent, self-satisfied religious celebration. This sort of idolatrous religion stirs up the flesh which is accustomed to being kept in check by the Word of God. Such sermons make for libertinism, egotism, indifference. Do people not know that one can get on as well, even better, without "religion"? . . . Perhaps the Anglo-Saxons are really more religious than we are, but they are certainly not more Christian, at least, if they still have sermons like that. I have no doubt at all that one day the storm will blow with full force on this religious handout, if God himself is still anywhere on the scene . . . The tasks for a real theologian over here are immeasurable. But only an American himself can shift all this rubbish, and up till now there do not seem to be any about'" (333).

Fosdick denied the deity of Christ and the entire historical Christian faith. One of his hymns is in the LCMS's new *Lutheran Service Book*. LCMS pastor Berthold von Schenck, who received his doctorate in Germany when Rudolf Bultmann was present says in his autobiography *Lively Stone* (available from *CN* for $12.50 plus s/h), published and praised by the American Lutheran Publicity Bureau, that Fosdick was the best preacher of his day and Lutheran Hour speakers Walter Maier and Oswald Hoffmann the worst.

The Beginning of WWII

The author presents what he calls Hitler's plan to make it appear as if his attack on Poland was done in self defense.

"The plan was for the SS, dressed in Polish uniforms, to attack a German radio station on the Polish border. To make the whole thing authentic, they would need German 'causalities.' They decided to use concentration camp inmates, whom they vilely referred to as Konserve (canned goods). These victims of Germany would be dressed as German soldiers. In the end only one man was murdered for this purpose, via lethal injection, and afterward shot several times to give the appearance that he had been killed by Polish soldiers. The deliberate murder of a human being for the purposes of deceiving the world seems a perfectly fitting inaugural act for what was to follow. This took place on schedule, August 31.

"In 'retaliation,' German troops marched into Poland at dawn on September 1. Göring's Luftwaffe rained hell from the skies, deliberately killing civilians. Civilians were murdered more carefully on the ground. It was a coldly deliberate act of terror by intentional mass murder, never before seen in modern times, and it was the Poles' first bitter taste of the Nazi ruthlessness they would come to know so well" (347, 348).

The Nazi
Worldview at Home

"Just as Hitler had been planning for years to enslave the Poles and kill the Jews, he had been planning to murder every German with a disability. Now he could do just that. As early as 1929 he had publicly proposed that 700,000 of the 'weakest' Germans be 'removed' per year" (354).

"As soon as the Polish campaign was under way, a number of adult patients deemed the least 'fit' were put on buses for these 'transfers.' The places to which these poor souls were transferred would murder them. At first the method was via injection, and later on via carbon monoxide gas. The parents or relatives of these patients had no idea of these goings-on until they received a letter in the mail, informing them of the death of their loved one, who had already been cremated. The cause of death was usually given as pneumonia or a similarly common ailment, and the ashes of their loved one's remains arrived shortly thereafter" (354, 355).

What Is The Truth

"Bonhoeffer's willingness to engage in deception stemmed not from a cavalier attitude toward the truth, but from a respect for the truth that was so deep, it forced him beyond the easy legalism of truth telling" (365).

God's Chosen Jews

"And he knew that being chosen by God, as the Jews were chosen, and as the prophets were chosen, was something unfathomable. It was the highest honor, but a terrible one, one that none would ever seek" (388).

Wannsee Conference

"The extermination of 'world Jewry' under the Orwellian aegis of the Final Solution had begun. At a conference at Wannsee early in 1942, the fate of all Jews within reach of the Third Reich had been sealed" (391, 392).

"'Religionless Christianity'"

"Many know Bonhoeffer only as the one who coined the dubious concept of religionless Christianity. And ironically many in the 'God is dead' movement have regarded him as a kind of prophet" (465).

"In a nutshell, he saw a situation so bleak, by any historical measures, that he was rethinking some basic things and wondered whether modern man had moved beyond religion. What Bonhoeffer meant by 'religion' was not true Christianity, but the ersatz and abbreviated Christianity that he spent his life working against. This 'religious' Christianity had failed Germany and the West during this great time of crisis, for one thing, and he wondered whether it wasn't finally time for the lordship of Jesus Christ to move past Sunday mornings and churches and into the whole world. But this was simply an extension of his previous theology, which was dedicatedly Bible centered and Christ centered" (467).

"This was not the thin pseudo humanism of the liberal 'God is dead' theologians who would claim Bonhoeffer's mantle as their own in the decades to come, nor was it the anti-humanism of the pious and 'religious' theologians who would abdicate Bonhofffer's theology to the liberals. It was something else entirely: it was 'God's humanism, redeemed in Jesus Christ" (468).

The Heart of Bonhoeffer's Theology

"At the heart of Bonhoeffer's theology was the mystery of the incarnation. In a circular letter he wrote, 'No priest, no theologian stood at the cradle in Bethlehem. And yet, all Christian theology has its origin in the wonder of all wonders that God became man. Alongside the brilliance of holy night there burns the fire of the unfathomable mystery of Christian theology" (472).

Buchenwald

"Buchenwald was one of the Nazi centers of death. But it was not merely a place where people died; it was a place where death was celebrated and worshiped. As much as Bodelschwingh's community at Bethel had been a living embodiment of the gospel of life, where the weak were cared for and loved, Buchenwald and its equivalents throughout the Third Reich were living embodiments of the satanic worldview of the SS, where weakness was preyed upon and crushed. Human beings were sometimes murdered for their skin, which was used to make souvenir items such as wallets and knife cases for members of the SS. The heads of some prisoners were shrunken and given as gifts. Bonhoeffer had heard of these abominable practices through Dohnanyi, but few other Germans knew of them at this time. When Emmi Bonhoeffer boldly told neighbors that in some camps the fat of human beings was used to make soap, they refused to believe her, convinced such tales were anti-German propaganda" (504).

"The name Buchenwald means 'Beech Forest.' Though it was not an extermination camp per se, 56,545 people were killed there, through forced labor, shooting, hanging, or medical experiments before the Allies liberated it in April 1945"(504). "Another method was putting the 'test persons' into tanks of icy water. At the Nuremberg trials, a Dachau prisoner who had the misfortune to serve as an 'orderly' for Rascher said that as these victims froze to death, their temperature, heartbeats, and respiration were regularly recorded. In the beginning Rascher did not permit anesthesia, but 'the test persons made such a racket that it was impossible' to continue without it" (511).

"Rascher conducted four hundred such 'freezing' experiments on three hundred persons. A third froze to death. The others were gassed or shot afterward" (513).

Gas Vans

"Rascher knew whereof he spoke. The Germans had used gas vans to kill people with mental disabilities and others in the euthanasia programs since 1940. Afterward they had used them to kill Jews. These vans were so filled with people that those inside could barely breathe to begin with. When the engine was started, the exhaust was pumped directly into the interior of the van, so that by the time the van arrived at its destination, the passengers had become corpses and were unloaded straight into the crematorium ovens" (518).

Hitler's Death Sentence

"Bonhoeffer's sentence of death was almost certainly by decree of Hitler himself, as were the death sentences of Oster and Dohnanyi" (529).

Last Minutes

"A camp doctor at Ekossenburg where Bonhoeffer was hanged gave this account of Bonhoeffer's final moments:

'I was most deeply moved by the way this lovable man prayed, so devout and so certain that God heard his prayer. At the place of execution, he again said a short prayer and then climbed the steps to the gallows, brave and composed. His death ensured after a few seconds. In the almost fifty years that I worked as a doctor, I have hardly ever seen a man die so entirely submissive to the will of God'" (532)

Concordia Seminary, St. Louis: Bonhoeffer, The Most Important and Influential Lutheran Since Luther
THE GROWING BONHOEFFER MYTH
Christian News, May 10, 2010

Above is a report on a major biography of Dietrich Bonhoeffer just published by Nelson Publishing and written by a *New York Times* Bestselling award winning author. It is being praised by scholars throughout the U.S.

Theologian Bonhoeffer was hung by the Nazis in 1945 for his part in a plot to assassinate Adolph Hitler. Yet when the Lutheran Church-Missouri Synod's Concordia Publishing House published the 1160 page *Lutheran Cyclopedia* in 1954 there is no mention of Bonhoeffer.

The "Index to *Concordia Theological Monthly* 1930-1959" compiled by Theodore F. Allwardt and published by Concordia Publishing House in 1963 appears to indicate that nothing was written about Bonhoeffer by the faculty of Concordia Seminary from 1930-1959 and that none of his writings were mentioned in the seminary's theological publication. *The Twentieth Century Encyclopedia of Religious Knowledge, An Extension of The New Schaff-Herzog Encyclopedia of Religious Knowledge* published by Baker in 1955, Lefferts A. Loetscher of Princeton Seminary, Editor in Chief, does not mention Bonhoeffer. It does have articles on such Lutherans as Francis Pieper and Walter Maier, who lived during Bonhoeffer's years. The many "uninformed" editors and contributors to these encyclopedias fail to recognize that Bonhoeffer was "the most important and influential Lutheran since Luther." The 3 volume *The Encyclopedia of The Lutheran Church,* published by Augsburg in 1965 does have items on Bonhoeffer. It mentions Bonhoeffer studied at Union Seminary in New York City in 1930-31, became a student pastor in Berlin, went to London in 1933, serving two German speaking congregations. In 1935 the German "confessing church" made him the director of its theological seminary at Finkenwalde. The new biography of Bonhoeffer quotes Herman Sasse as saying that the "Confessing Church" "is a sect, the worst sect in fact ever to set foot on the soil of German Protestantism"(286, 287). He traveled to the U.S. again in 1938 but then returned. He was arrested on April 5, 1943 for taking part in a political resistance movement. "After two years of imprisonment in the concentration camp of Flossenburg he was murdered." Nothing is said about Bonhoeffer being the greatest and most influential Lutheran since Martin Luther.

What almost all Lutheran Church-Missouri Synod theologians, both conservatives and liberals, failed to recognize about Bonhoeffer's alleged greatness has drastically changed in the LCMS. The Bonhoeffer myth has grown with the myth of the six million Jews exterminated, most of them in gas chambers during WWII. While neither Winston Churchill nor Dwight Eisenhower, who wrote volumes about World War II and the investigations of the Red Cross, said anything about the six million allegedly exterminated by the Germans, today hardly any seminary professor has ever expressed any doubt about the six million figure. There are Holocaust memorials and museums in many sections of the U.S. and elsewhere. Thousands of books have been written on the Holocaust and hundreds of movies have been made to show that the Germans did exterminate some 6 million Jews. Bonhoeffer is hailed as a leading Christian defender of the Jews.

Special celebrations were held at Concordia Seminary, St. Louis and Concordia

Seminary, Ft. Wayne commemorating Bonhoeffer's 100th birthday in 2006. Concordia Seminary, St. Louis said Bonhoeffer was the most important and influential Lutheran since Martin Luther. Were former LCMS professors, who did not recognize Bonhoeffer's greatness and being next to Luther simply uniformed, ignorant and not very well read scholars?

Dietrich Bonhoeffer earned his doctorate at the University of Berlin in 1927, Henry Koch earned his doctorate at the University of Leipzig in 1919, and Walter Maier earned his doctorate at Harvard University in 1919. Three weeks later, on "June 23, approximately 70,000 people crowded into Chicago's mammoth lake front stadium, Soldier Field, to attend the quad centennial celebration of the publication of Luther's Catechism for which Dr. Maier was the featured speaker" (Paul Maier, A Man Spoke, a World Listened, p. 93). Today in the LCMS Bonhoeffer is regarded by the "great scholars," as far more highly respected and quoted more frequently than Maier or Koch.

The *CN* editor's *Walter Maier Still Speaks, Missouri and the World Should Listen* says that at the time of Maier's death in 1950, five years after Bonhoeffer died, Maier was the best known Lutheran in the world. He had a weekly audience of 20 million, was heard on over 1,236 stations in 120 countries. The Lutheran Hour was heard in some 30 languages. Maier was referred to as "the Jeremiah of the Twentieth Century." Concordia Publishing House published some 20 books by Maier, including his best selling marriage manual, *For Better Not For Worse*.

Today the 2009 CPH catalog lists 10 books by Bonhoeffer and one book about him, which was published by CPH. All are now available from CPH. The CPH catalog lists no book by Maier. *CN*'s request to reprint an updated edition of Maier's marriage manual has been denied. CPH refused to publish *Walter Maier Still Speaks – Missouri and the World Should Listen.*

Henry Koch was a pastor of a 900 member confessional Lutheran Church in Berlin where he also was a professor. His church began four other confessional Lutheran churches. Bonhoeffer had nothing to do with these confessional Lutheran churches while he was in Berlin. Koch returned to the U.S. in 1939 when Hitler's "Brown shirts" began keeping watch over him. Koch then taught Greek and Latin at the LCMS's Concordia College, Bronxville, New York. Here the *CN* editor first met him. CPH published a book which broke the Eighth Commandment against Koch by referring to him as a vocal Nazi sympathizer. CPH refused to publish Koch's *The Christian's Travel Guide to World History – In the Footsteps of Moses, Jesus, Paul, and Luther."* It shows that CPH, which now champions Bonhoeffer, did not tell the truth about Koch.

The *CN* editor knew nothing about Bonhoeffer during Bonhoeffer's years at Union Seminary, 1931-32 and then again in 1939. The editor was born in Manhattan not far from Union Seminary and years later did some research at Union Seminary. When Bonhoeffer studied in New York he was not far from some confessional Lutheran churches, such as St. Matthew Lutheran Church, the oldest continuing Lutheran Church in the U.S. Bonhoeffer showed no more interest in these true Lutheran churches than he did in the confessional Lutheran church close to where he studied in Berlin. Theologically already then Bonhoeffer was much closer to the liberal theologians Maier, Koch, and Sasse strongly opposed. Yet the LCMS's *Lutheran Witness* and CPH insist that Bonhoeffer was a confessional Lutheran.

Today among both liberals and conservatives it is considered a mark of high scholarship and being up-to-date to quote Bonhoeffer. The March 15, 2010 *CN* noted in a report on *A Little Book On Joy* that conservative Matthew Harrison in this book scatters some 10 boxed quotations from Bonhoeffer. *CN* said: "Dietrich Bonhoeffer is favorably quoted more than any other theologian other than Martin Luther. He is on pages 33, 54, 55, 70, 87, 97, 142, 151, 169, and 176." *CN* has highly recommended many of Harrison's other writings.

As the Holocaust religion grows, do not be surprised that the Bonhoeffer myth will continue to grow.

Selections From "The Bethel Confession"
By Dietrich Bonhoeffer
Lutheran Forum – Spring 2010 -
American Lutheran Publicity Bureau

Editor's Note: *The Bethel Confession*, written in August 1933 in Bethel, Germany, by Dietrich Bonhoeffer with the assistance of Hermann Sasse and other Lutheran theologians, is an exemplary piece of confessional testimony in the face of church crisis. It was an early response to the theological and political machinations of the German Christians during the Third Reich. At the same time it has a normative clarity that makes it a invaluable teaching document even in entirely different settings. For this reason we sought permission from Fortress Press to reprint selections of it here so that contemporary Lutherans learn more about it. The complete text, more information about its history, an earlier draft, and explanatory footnotes can all be found in vol. 12 of *Dietrich Bonhoeffer Works*, Berlin 1932-1933. (The December 2010 *Forum Letter* of the American Lutheran Publicity Bureau begins with a long quote from Bonhoeffer's *The Cost of Discipleship* on cheep greed.)

I. On the Holy Scriptures

The Holy Scriptures of the Old and New Testaments are the sole source and measure of the doctrine of the church. They constitute the witness, valid in its entirety, that Jesus of Nazareth, who was crucified under Pontius Pilate, is the Christ, that is, Israel's promised Messiah, the King of the Church, the Son of the living God.

All church doctrine must be measured solely by the Holy Scriptures and be revealed as pure doctrine through it alone. The Holy Scriptures alone witness to the divine revelation. They reveal a one-time, unrepeatable, and self-contained history of salvation, beginning with the promise given to the fallen Adam and culminating in the founding of the church. The church proclaims this history as God's revelatory act, meant for us. In bearing witness to these acts of God, the Scriptures are God's word to us. The church can proclaim God's revelation only by interpreting this word, which bears witness to it.

The history to which the Scriptures bear witness is salvation history, that is, the history of salvation, which God brings to the world. It does not present the people in the Bible as holy but only shows that, despite their unworthiness, they were called into the church, for the salvation God had prepared for them. The full understanding of this history begins with the New Testament, testifying to the culmination of God's plan for salvation in the incarnation, words, deeds and miracles, death and resurrection of Jesus Christ, and in the founding of the church. The Old Testament is the word of

God, because it is the one God who calls Israel to be the church, who is rejected by Israel and who founds the church of the New Covenant.

The Holy Scriptures constitute a whole. They have their unity in Jesus Christ, the Crucified and Risen One, who speaks throughout the Scriptures. We are not the judges of God's word in the Bible; instead, the Bible is given to us so that through it we may submit to Christ's judgment. Only through the Holy Spirit do we hear the word of God from the Bible. But this Spirit itself comes to us only through the word of the Holy Scriptures in their entirety, and therefore can never, except by enthusiasm, be separated from this word.

World and *Christianity Today* Join LCMS Seminaries on Bonhoeffer and Neuhaus
CLAIM BONHOEFFER WAS AN ORTHODOX CHRISTIAN
Christian News, July 12, 2010

The July 2010 World and July 2010 *Christianity Today* in reviews of *Bonhoeffer – Pastor, Martyr, Prophet, Spy* by Eric Metaxas highly praised Dietrich Bonhoeffer and Metaxas' book. Metaxas says in an interview titled "The Authentic Bonhoeffer" in the July 2010 *Christianity Today* that "Bonhoeffer is more like a theologically conservative evangelical than anything less. He was as orthodox as Saint Paul or Isaiah, from his teen years all the way to his last day on death."

Bonhoeffer, who denied the deity and resurrection of Christ, is now championed at both Lutheran Church-Missouri Synod seminaries almost more than any other theologian.

"Insights for Advent Preaching from Bonhoeffer, Thielicke and Ebeling", a notice in the July 2010 *For the Life of the World* of Concordia Seminary, Ft. Wayne, says:

"This year's Advent Preaching Seminar will examine critically the Advent preaching of three German theologians/preachers: Dietrich Bonhoeffer, Helmut Thielicke and Gerhard Ebeling. Drawing on their work, suggested outlines and illustrations will be offered for a midweek Advent series as well as the Sundays of Advent."

Bonhoeffer – Pastor, Martyr, Prophet, Spy was reviewed in the May 10, 2010 *Christian News*. The review included many statements from the book. Metaxas praises Karl Barth, who had a great influence on Bonhoeffer. He claims that at Wannsee in January, 1942, Heydrich presented plans to exterminate all the Jews of Europe. The Bonhoeffer admirers insist that the Germans exterminated 6 million Jews during WWII. Metaxas says that Buchenwald was one of the Nazi centers of death and a place where death was celebrated and worshipped. He claims that "Human beings were at times murdered for their skin which was used to make souvenir items such as wallets and knife cases for the SS. The heads of some prisoners were shrunken and given as gifts" (504).

Christianity Today and *World* together with both LCMS seminaries have also had high praise for Father Richard John Neuhaus, a former LCMS liberal pastor who became a Roman Catholic priest. The editor told Neuhaus during their student days at Concordia Seminary that Neuhaus and his friends could very well one day join the Roman Catholic Church. Neuhaus denied the inerrancy of the Bible and the historicity of the Genesis account of creation and other parts of the Bible. He rejected justification by faith alone, and was a universalist who said no one was in hell. This issue includes a letter *CN* sent to *Christianity Today* after *Christianity Today* referred to Neuhaus as "The Radical Conservative." *CT* refused to publish the letter.

"Intellectual Snobs and Envy" mentions that Kurt Marquart wrote 45 years ago that for intellectual snobs facts in publications they despise do not exist. Although *CN* has shown for almost 50 years that Bonhoeffer and Neuhaus rejected basic Christian doctrines, the intellectual snobs reject all this evidence.

"Confessional" Lutherans now are among those who seem to be falling all over themselves praising the theology of Dietrich Bonhoeffer. One book after another is being published commending Bonhoeffer's theology.

The Lutheran Church Missouri Synod's 2009 CPH Catalog features 10 books by Bonhoeffer and one about him.

CN has shown for more than 50 years that Bonhoeffer's Christ is not the Christ of the Bible. When Detroit area Lutherans almost 50 years ago had more praise for Bonhoeffer than Luther at a Reformation Rally, *CN* documented Bonhoeffer's anti-Christian theology directly from Bonhoeffer's last writings.

In 2006 at the 100th anniversary of Bonhoeffer's birth Concordia Seminary, Ft. Wayne and Concordia Seminary, St. Louis had conferences where Bonhoeffer was held up to students and others attending the gathering as a great confessional Lutheran. A news release from Concordia Seminary, St. Louis said that perhaps Bonhoeffer is "the most important Lutheran theologian since Martin Luther" and that he is the most widely admired and respected theologian in America. (*CN*, July 3, 2006, p.1)

Christian News maintains that a theologian who denied such doctrines as the resurrection of Jesus Christ should not be considered "the most important Lutheran theologian since Martin Luther." The October 2, 2006 *Christian News* referred to C.F.W. Walther, the first president of the Lutheran Church-Missouri Synod, as "the American Luther" and Dr. Kurt Marquart, as "The International Luther." *CN* said that Concordia Seminary should have awarded Marquart a D.D. degree. *CN* claims that the writings of Walther and Marquart have been far more helpful for Christendom than anything Bonhoeffer wrote.

The February 2006 *Lutheran Witness* published an article by Dr. Uwe Simeon Netto which said that Bonhoeffer was a "confessional Lutheran." The *Lutheran Witness* refused to publish a letter from the editor of *Christian News* showing that Bonhoeffer rejected such doctrines as the resurrection of Christ. Only one side was allowed to be heard. *CN*'s letter was published in the July 3, 2006 *CN* together with the *Lutheran Witness* article which insisted that Bonhoeffer was a confessional Lutheran. *CN* also published a review of a CPH book praising Bonhoeffer. The review was by Dr. Matthew Becker, a member of Jesus First who promotes evolution and women pastors.

The review appeared in the *Concordia Journal* of Concordia Seminary, St. Louis. The *Concordia Journal* would not publish an article by a Lutheran theologian who mentions that Bonhoeffer's Christ is not the Christ of the Bible but it did publish a review by DayStar and a Jesus First liberal. *CN* challenged both seminaries to publish or at least respond to "An Evaluation of Dietrich Bonhoeffer's Life and Theology After Half a Century" by Dr. Raymond Surburg, who had long been a professor at Concordia Seminary, Ft. Wayne. Surburg, on the basis of Bonhoeffer's own writings, showed that Bonhoeffer's Christ was not the Christ of the Bible. Those who praised Bonhoeffer at both seminaries ignored Surburg's thoroughly documented article. It was again reprinted in the July 3, 2006 *CN*. This same issue of *CN* quoted from a book published by Yale University which showed that Bonhoeffer rejected the Christ of the Bible. When the AAL financed a movie praising Bonhoeffer and his theology, *CN* sent Surburg's article to each member of the AAL Board of Directors, including Dr. Tom Zehnder, a member of Jesus First and Executive Director of Lutheran World Missions. *CN* invited each member of the AAL Board of Directors to show where Surburg was in error and where he misquoted Bonhoeffer or quoted him out of context. Not one member of the AAL responded.

"The Most Widely Admired and Respected Theologian In America" in the July 3, 2006 *CN* noted: "Bonhoeffer has long been particularly praised by Lutherans who want to let Jews and others know that they are anti- Nazi, oppose anti-Semitism, and do not deny that during World War II the Germans executed some six million Jews, most of them by gassing. Many of those who praise Bonhoeffer seldom have as much praise for any Christian martyr who opposed Communism. When *CN* visited the Holocaust memorial in Berlin and viewed the exhibits in Buchenwald showing the horrors of the Holocaust, *CN* asked some who praised Bonhoeffer and insist that the Germans exterminated six million Jews during World War II: 'Where are the memorials for the many millions murdered by the Communists?' The Bonhoeffer defenders knew of no such memorials."

CN has often insisted on the importance of studying documentation and the actual evidence. *CN* has frequently photographed as evidence articles of liberals. What a tragedy that even so many who claim to be confessional Lutherans refuse to study the evidence. They simply follow the crowd and promote what is politically correct. The "great confessional Lutheran scholars" refuse to read any evidence published in *CN* showing that Bonhoeffer's Christ is not the Christ of the Bible. The following item appeared in the September 11, 1972 *Christian News:*

"...the Christ of Bonhoeffer is not the Christ of the Scriptures, is not the Christ of the Reformers..." says Dr. Cornelius Van Til in the *Westminster Theological Journal*, May, 1972

Van Til writes in a review article on Bonhoeffer: "The Christ of Bonhoeffer, in contrast to the Christ of Calvin, is constructed in terms of post- Kantian philosophy and theology. This is factually incontrovertible. The consequence of this fact implies a reinterpretation, and UMDEUTUNG, of every word of the vocabulary of biblical and confessional teaching. However much evangelical- and notably, Reformed-Christians may wish to incorporate Bonhoeffer in the list of their heroes of the faith, together with Calvin, Kuyper, Bavinck, Hodge, Warfield, and Vos, they have no right to do so. Bonhoeffer must be placed in the line of Kant, of Schleiermacher, of Ritschl, and of Barth. It is the theological descendants of such men as these who rightfully claim Bonhoeffer as their own.

"Modern, neo-orthodox theologians know that the two Christs, the Christ of Luther and Calvin and the Christ of Bonhoeffer stand mutually opposed to one another."

Van Til documents his article with quotations from the writings of Bonhoeffer to show that Bonhoeffer's Christ is not the Christ of the Bible. Bonhoeffer has been highly praised by such Lutheran liberals as Martin Marty and in parts of the Lutheran Church- Missouri Synod's Mission Life curriculum. The *Westminster Theological Journal* is published by Westminster Theological Seminary, Chestnut Hill, Philadelphia, Pennsylvania 19118, $7.50 per year, $2.50 a copy. Van Til's analysis of Bonhoeffer's theology is one of the most perceptive we have seen.

The August 7, 2006 *Christian News* published several articles showing that the Christ of Karl Barth is not the Christ of the Bible. One of the articles was "Christianity and Crisis Theology" by Cornelius Van Til. It appeared in the August, 1948 *Concordia Theological Monthly* of Concordia Seminary, St. Louis.

Bonhoeffer also greatly admired Soren Kierkegaard. The Easter, 2006, *Logia* of the Luther Academy praised Kierkegaard and urged Confessional Lutherans to "follow Kierkegaard for a distinctly Lutheran and scholarly view of teaching and scholarship." *Christian News*, April 25, 2006 published what *Logia* said about Kierkegaard and then showed that Kierkegaard's Christ was not the Christ of the Bible. J. T. Mueller wrote in the December, 1945 *C.T.M.* of Concordia Seminary that "Kierkegaard's Christ was of his own making."

Van Til's article in the May 1972 *Westminster Theological Journal* showing that Bonhoeffer's Christ is not the Christ of the Bible was published in the October 16, 2006 *Christian News*. Lutherans and others praising Bonhoeffer as a great Confessional Lutheran never mention what Surburg or Van Til wrote about Bonhoeffer after carefully studying Bonhoeffer's writings.

Bonhoeffer and the Holocaust
A CHRISTIAN NEWS SURVEY
"'Holocaust' Debate" on p. 1 should be carefully read by thinking Americans
Christian News, July 12, 2010

20 years ago *Christian News* published a notice to find someone who actually read what *CN* had written about the Holocaust who still believes the evidence indicates Germans exterminated 6 million Jews (May 7, 1990). *CN* has repeatedly found that most of *CN*'s critics had never actually read what *CN* said. Not one person who had actually read what *CN* published about the holocaust still accepted the 6 million figure.

This issue reports that *Christianity Today* and *World* have joined Concordia Seminary, St. Louis and Concordia Seminary, Ft. Wayne in their high praise of Dietrich Bonhoeffer as an orthodox Christian theologian. The *Lutheran Witness* of the LCMS insisted that he was "a confessional Lutheran." Concordia Seminary, St. Louis said that Bonhoeffer is "the most important Lutheran theologian since Martin Luther" and that he is "the most widely admired and respected theologian in America" (*CN*, July 3, 2006, p. 1). *CN* has noted as the Holocaust story grows, the Bonhoeffer story grows. During the editor's student days at Concordia Seminary little was said about the "six million Holocaust" or Bonhoeffer. Now the seminary has said Bonhoeffer is the most important Lutheran theologian since Martin Luther. The former great professors at the St. Louis Seminary must have been uninformed like Churchill and Eisenhower who were for not mentioning the six million Holocaust in their voluminous writings or WWII.

CN has noted for almost 50 years that Bonhoeffer repudiated historic Christianity. Several times *CN* published "An Evaluation of Dietrich Bonhoeffer's Life and Theology After A Half Century" by Dr. Raymond Surburg of Concordia Seminary. The October 16, 2006 *Christian News* reprinted from the May 1972 *Westminster Theological Journal* "Dietrich Bonhoeffer" by Cornelius Van Til.

Christian News has yet to find one person who has actually read what Surburg and Van Til wrote about Bonhoeffer's theology who still maintains that Bonhoeffer was a Christian whose Christ was the Christ of the Bible and that Bonhoeffer accepted such Christian doctrines as the physical resurrection of Christ.

Here are *CN*'s questions for all Bonhoeffer fans.

1. I have read "An Evaluation of Dietrich Bonhoeffer's Life and Theology" by Raymond Surburg and "Dietrich Bonhoeffer" by Cornelius Van Til. Yes ___ No ___

2. I still maintain that Bonhoeffer was an orthodox Christian theologian. Yes ___ No ___

You may e-mail your response to *Christian News* at cnnewsnandinfo@yahoo.com.

Bonhoeffer: A True Believer
By Cal Thomas
The Chronicle-Telegram, June 23, 2010
Christian News, August 30, 2010

June 18, 2010, marked the 70th anniversary of Charles de Gaulle's historic call to arms for the French to resist the Nazis and also Winston Churchill's "finest hour" address.

Another anniversary might have gone unnoticed were it not for a brilliant new biography of a man who gave his life in a failed plot to assassinate Adolf Hitler. "Dietrich Bonhoeffer: Pastor, Martyr, Prophet, Spy" by Eric Metaxis, is a major biography of this giant of faith published 65 years after his death. . . .

In an age (then and now) full of "cheap grace," here is a book that will challenge Christians and non-Christians alike. Few books can claim to be a "must-read." This is one:

Ed. *Bonhoeffer - Pastor - Martyr - Prophet, Spy* was reviewed in the May 10, 2010 *Christian News*. The May 10, 2010 *CN* also published "An Evaluation of Dietrich Bonhoeffer's Life and Theology After Half of a Century", by Raymond Surburg. Surburg shows on the basis of Bonhoeffer's own writings that Bonhoeffer rejected such Christian doctrines as the resurrection of Christ and that his Christ was not the Christ of the Bible. The October 16, 2006 *CN* reprinted an article by Cornelius Van Til on Bonhoeffer which appeared in the May, 1972 *Westminster Theological Journal*. Van Til showed that Bonhoeffer radically departed from Christianity. *CN* has yet to find anyone who has actually read the Surburg and Van Til articles who still maintains that Bonhoeffer accepted historic Christianity. Those who praise Bonhoeffer refuse to read what Surburg and Van Till wrote.

BONHOEFFER AND KING
Christian News, November 1, 2010

Bonhoeffer and King – Their Legacies and Import for Christian Social Thought. Willis Jenkins and Jennifer M. McBride, Editions. Fortress Press, Minneapolis.

The back cover of this latest issue of the ever increasing number of books on Martin Luther King, Jr. and Dietrich Bonhoeffer says:

"Assessing the Legacy and Potential of TWO PROPHETIC GIANTS Dietrich Bonhoeffer and Martin Luther King Jr. – these giants of recent Christian social thought are here reassessed for a new context and a new generation. Each combined activism, ministry, and theology. Each took on public roles in opposition to prevailing powers of their time. Each professed a kind of Christian realism and ended as a martyr to his respective cause. Here many of the leading Christian social thinkers of our own day revisit the insights, causes, and strategies that Bonhoeffer and King employed for a new generation and its concerns, race, reconciliation, nonviolence, political violence, Christian theological identity and ministry. Along with the editors, the illustrious gathering of theologians, ethicists, and historians includes:

"Michael Battle, M. Shawn Copeland, Jean Bethke Elshtain, Stephen R. Haynes, Timothy P. Jackson, Geffrey B. Kelly, Charles Marsh, Rachel Muers, Larry L. Rasmussen, Stephen G. Ray, Jr., Gary M. Simpson, Craig J. Slane, Glen H. Stassen, Emilie M. Townes, Raphael G. Warnock, Andre C. Willis, Richard W. Wills, Sr., Josiah U. Young III.

"Willis Jenkins is Margaret Farley Assistant Professor of Social Ethics at Yale Divinity School and author of Ecologies of Grace: Environmental Ethics and Christian Theology (2008). Jennifer M. McBride is a Visiting Lecturer at Candler School of Theology, Emory University and Director of the Atlanta Theological Association's Certificate in Theological Studies at Metro State Prison for Women. She is author of the forthcoming work The Church for the World: A theology of Public Witness.

Chapter 2 "King and Bonhoeffer as Protestant Saints" by Stephan R. Haynes says: "Dietrich Bonhoeffer and Martin Luther King Jr. must be numbered among the most prominent and influential Christians of the twentieth century" (21).

On p. 23 there are "Portraits of King and Bonhoeffer as Saints."

Charges of marital infidelity and plagiarism

"For King, the alleged failures of integrity concern private behavior. The charges of marital infidelity are perhaps best known, but these charges are discredited to some extent by the means used to obtain the information on which they are based. The matter of King's alleged plagiarism is different, it seems to me. In the case of his dissertation in particular, the offense is demonstrable and amounts to a moral failure that scholars cannot easily dismiss' (24).

"Like the other authors in this book, I have immense respect for Dietrich Bonhoeffer and Martin Luther King Jr., a respect that only grows with time. I hope they are the first two people I meet in heaven; and if they are I will stand in awe and in silence" (30).

Josiah U. Young III writes in a chapter titled "Theology and Racism":

"King did not hold that god the Son became flesh in any literal sense. The ancient theologians Bonhoeffer upheld were thus to King archaic in their worldview. When, therefore, King asserted in one of his sermons that 'the ultimate meaning of [doctrine of] the Trinity' is its affirmation that 'God and Christ are one in substance,' and that to experience 'one is to experience the other,' he was not upholding Nicaea (325) and Constantinople (381), but demythologizing them. Bearing more of an affinity to Schleiermacher than to Barth, King held that Christ's consciousness of God rather than his preexistence was the redemptive factor. For King, in addition, Christ's personality, wisdom, and ethical correctness, which King understood à la Alfred Knudson as self-consciousness and self-direction, is the image of God. By contrast, Bonhoeffer's interpretations of the imago Dei entailed his conviction that Christ mirrors the Creator because he was truly God and truly human" (73).

Christian News has often shown that Martin Luther King rejected such doctrines as the virgin birth, deity and resurrection of Christ. When the *National Observer* published an interview article with King, King clearly did not uphold basic Christian doctrines. *CN* wrote to King, King's Southern Leadership Conference and the *National Observer* asking to be informed if King was not correctly quoted. The *National Observer* responded that King never voiced any objections to the article. King said the same thing in some of his writings (see the sections on King in *The Christian News Encyclopedia*). Yet King has many supporters, even among Lutherans. Father Richard Neuhaus, who marched with King, wanted the Lutheran Church to declare King a saint. ELCA's Lutheran Book of Worship includes King on its list of saints.

Paul McCain of CPH has vigorously defended King when *Christian News* and other took sharp issue with King's theology and moral standards.

Several times *Christian News* has published long scholarly articles by Raymond Surburg of the Lutheran Church-Missouri Synod and Cornelius Van Til of the Orthodox Presbyterian Church where they show that Bonhoeffer's Christ was not the Christ of the Bible and historic Christianity and that King repudiated the Lutheran Confessions and theology of Martin Luther. *CN* has yet to find a Bonhoeffer defender who says he has read the articles by Surburg and Van Til on Bonhoeffer's theology. *CN* has shown for almost 50 years that Bonhoeffer in his own writings repudiated the resurrection of Christ and demythologized the Bible more than Rudolf Bultmann.

A Revolution

Young says:

"King was a peacemaker, a nonviolent reconciler; but we should never forget that King intended to bring about nothing short of a revolution" (75).

Timothy Jackson writes in a chapter titled "Church, World, and Christian Charity:"

"Dietrich Bonhoeffer and Martin Luther King are rightly our heroes for helping Christians to atone for this regrettable past, for teaching us to be in the world and for the world but not simply of the world. Together with likenesses of Saint Elizabeth of Russia, Archbishop Oscar Romero, and others, their statues now properly grace the façade of Westminster Abbey in the heart of London. Just above the Great West Door, Bonhoeffer and King symbolically bless those going into, but also those coming out of, the historic church. This loving ability to stand with both insiders and outsiders, both believers and atheists, is a gift to the wide world worthy of the Son of God. We can only try to go and do likewise" (105).

Glen H. Stassen writes:

"Both Bonhoeffer and King were committed to following the way of the incarnate Jesus—and followed him to death. Both were committed to embodying Jesus' way holistically –not only in one narrow part of life, but in ever-expanding dimensions of life. Both continue to lead us to repent for the racism, authoritarianism, domination, and militarism of ideologies that hijack Christian faith for their self-serving schemes. This is what many of us call the way of incarnational discipleship.

"Both Bonhoeffer and King were murdered in April of the year when they had reached age thirty-nine, depriving us of the leadership we so badly needed for healing our shame, and for recovery from authoritarianism and domination. Assassinations always seem to come from the authoritarian and reactionary side, not the peace and justice side, and to deprive us of the leadership for justice and peacemaking that we long for. They deprive us of our future, assassinating the leaders of healing and justice: Abraham Lincoln in 1865, Dietrich Bonhoeffer in 1945, Mohandas Gandhi In 1948, John Kennedy in 1963, Robert Kennedy In 1968, Martin Luther King in 1968, Anwar al Sadat in 1981, Yitzhak Rabin in 1995. This means that the Jesus-following believers in justice rather than racism, and peace rather than violence, need to keep raising up more leaders like Dietrich Bonhoeffer and Martin Luther King Jr. to compensate for the violence of injustice, and to persuade yet more people to follow the way of peacemaking and healing rather than domination, exclusion, violence, and injustice. We will do it" (204-205).

Geffrey B. Kelley writes:

"This Christ-centered attitude was for Bonhoeffer and King the very center of their spirituality, as they committed themselves to work in communion with Jesus Christ for peace, justice, and the liberation from the oppression of their people" (213).

Here is another Bonhoeffer book published by Fortress Press for the LCMS's CPH to list in its catalog and include in its promotional display of Bonhoeffer books.

Fortress Press should have included in Bonhoeffer and King the essays by Surburg and Van Til which document the fact that the Christ of both King and Bonhoeffer was not the Christ of the Bible.

Surburg, Maier, Bonhoeffer, and the Holocaust
Christian News, November 8, 2010

Walter A. Maier Still Speaks – Missouri and the World Should Listen by Herman Otten, 476 pages. $16.95 plus $4.00 s/h.

Now is the time for professors at the LCMS's two seminaries and other champions of Dietrich Bonhoeffer to read chapter XII in *Walter Maier Still Speaks – Missouri and the World Should Listen*. It is titled "Surburg, Maier, Bonhoeffer, and the Holocaust."

"Worse Than Promoting Pietism" in the November 1, 2010 *CN* noted that "a student reports that these small group worship events 'grew out of last winter's campus wide reading of Bonhoeffer's Life Together.'"

The evangelical *World* magazine is currently offering a copy to new subscribers of a recent biography by Eric Metaxis praising Bonhoeffer as a great Christian theologian.

The errors in the book were mentioned in a review in the May 10, 2010 *Christian News*.

The October 19, 2010 *Christian Century* said:

"Bonhoeffer's ideas have somehow seeped deeply into much contemporary Christian thinking outside of the fundamentalist world, and what appeared radical in his day is now widely accepted. It might also be concluded that Bonhoeffer's inquiry about religion in a 'world come of age' is passé in a postmodern global context, where religion has made a remarkable comeback and religious pluralism is, for many, a theological sine qua non."

It is considered a mark of up-to-date scholarship by both liberals and conservatives to quote Bonhoeffer as some great religious guru. LCMS President Matthew Harrison's latest book *On Joy* includes more boxed quotations from Bonhoeffer than any other theologian, except Martin Luther.

Both liberal and conservative professors in the LCMS during the 1950s said virtually nothing about Bonhoeffer. The LCMS's Concordia Theological Journal said no more about Bonhoeffer than Winston Churchill and Dwight Eisenhower said in their many writing on WWII about the Holocaust. The Bonhoeffer "myth" continues to grow with the 6 million Holocaust.

Those who are promoting Bonhoeffer have been able to get many millions from Thrivent (formerly AAL and LB) and the Schwan Foundation. Such major donors refuse to support those who champion Maier, and his forthright opposition to theological modernism and communism, his defense of the inerrancy of the Bible and the Christ of the Bible.

A supplement from the Commission on Worship of the LCMS in the March, 2008 Reporter of the LCMS announces that Dr. Dean Wenthe will be a keynote speaker at the third national worship conference to be held at Concordia, Seward, July 22-25. The report says: "For each of the four days of the conference, a keynote address will be offered. Speakers include:

"Dean Wenthe, President of Concordia Theological Seminary, Ft. Wayne, Indiana, will speak on 'The Psalter: A Prayer Book', working from ideas suggested by Dietrich Bonhoeffer to explore the authenticity, beauty, and clarity of the Psalms for individual and corporate prayer." Bonhoeffer denied that the Psalms were God's inerrant word revealed to man and that at least some of them directly predicted the Messiah, Jesus Christ, the God-Man. Wenthe is an editor of the Old Testament section of the Concordia Self-Study Bible – New International Version which says in its comments on Psalm 16:9-11 that "David speaks here, as in the rest of the Psalms, first of all of himself. . ." St. Peter in Acts 2:25 ff quotes Psalm 16 and says that David is not at all speaking about himself but only speaking about Jesus Christ.

Maier took sharp issue with liberals at Union and elsewhere who denied that David when he wrote Psalm was first of all speaking about Christ. *Walter A. Maier Still Speaks* includes what Maier wrote about Psalm 22 and Messianic prophecy (pp. 33-77). Maier took sharp issue with the position taken by the *RSV*, *ESV* and *NIV* translators.

Bonhoeffer is held in high regard at both LCMS seminaries where Maier is seldom mentioned. The LCMS's future pastors are taught to have a high regard for Bonhoeffer and told virtually nothing about Maier. At the hundredth anniversary of the birth of Walter Maier neither seminary had any special commemoration. At the 100th birthday of Bonhoeffer, both seminaries sponsored a seminar on Bonhoeffer where Bonhoeffer was highly praised.

A news release from Concordia Seminary, St. Louis, said that Bonhoeffer was perhaps "The most important Lutheran theologian since Martin Luther." A review of a book on Bonhoeffer published by the LCMS's Concordia Publishing House appearing in the Concordia Journal of the St. Louis seminary said that Bonhoeffer was "the most influential theologian of the Twentieth Century." "Welcome Back, Dietrich," an article in the *Lutheran Witness* by Dr. Uwe Simeon-Netto of Concordia Seminary, St. Louis, said that Bonhoeffer was a "confessional Lutheran." Netto makes the same statement in a book published by CPH. the *Lutheran Witness* refused to publish a letter quoting from Bonhoeffer's writings which showed that Bonhoeffer rejected historic Christianity.

While *CN* publishes books praising Bonhoeffer and sells books by Bonhoeffer, it no longer sells any of the some 20 books by Maier which CPH formerly published. Paul McCain and CPH refused to publish *Walter A. Maier Still Speaks – Missouri and the World Should Listen*, even though McCain has asked David Benke to write another book for CPH to publish.

Only a few years after his death, Maier became almost a forgotten man at the seminary where he taught. Most professors seldom mentioned or recommended Maier's writings. Some said there was a certain amount of envy involved. However, a more important reason is that the scriptural position Maier took on the inerrancy of the Bible, direct Messianic prophecy, a six 24 hour day creation and his outspoken opposition to communism was no longer being affirmed by many professors. They preferred that their students read books by Karl Barth, Paul Tillich, Dietrich Bonhoeffer, Gustav Aulen, Reinhold Niebuhr, Gerhard Forde and other liberal and neo-orthodox theologians.

The March 31, 2008 *Christian News* reported that *Walter A. Maier Still Speaks* was sent to all LCMS Seminary professors.

Chapter XII "Surburg, Bonhoeffer and the Holocaust" in *Walter A. Maier Still Speaks* says:

Dr. Raymond Surburg, a Lutheran Church-Missouri Synod Old Testament scholar, who taught at Concordia University, Seward, Nebraska, and Concordia Seminary, Ft. Wayne, repeatedly defended the position Dr. Walter Maier took on the inerrancy of the Bible, the historicity of Genesis, higher criticism, evolution, the Old Testament etc.

Some of the many articles Surburg sent *Christian News* for publication are in *The Christian News Encyclopedia*. Dr. Walter Maier Jr. regularly visited and watched over Surburg during Surburg's final years. Dr. Walter Maier III preached the sermon at Surburg's funeral.

"The CTCR vs. THE LCMS – The History of Messianic Prophecy in the Lutheran Church-Missouri Synod from 1847 Till the Issuing of the CTCR's 'Prophecy and Typology' in 1996" were the title and subtitle of an article by Dr. Raymond Surburg in the September 30, 1996 *Christian News*.

The LCMS's CTCR adopted a statement in 1996 which took issue with the position on messianic prophecy which Luther, Maier, Beck and the LCMS in former years defended. It supported the position of the Concordia Publishing House Self Study Bible (*NIV*) which says in its comments on Psalm 16:9-11: "David speaks here, as in the rest of his psalms, first of all of himself." The CTCR took issue with the Apostle Peter who said that David is here not speaking about himself but only about Jesus Christ (Acts 2:25-26).

Surburg wrote:

"Walter A. Maier, Sr. and Messianic Prophecy" "Walter A. Maier, Sr. (1893-1950) followed the views on Messianic prophecy held by Luther, Walther, Stoeckhardt, L. Fuerbringer, Laetsch and other contemporaries. In his Notes on the Genesis Seminary Course[38] and in his Notes of Selected Psalms[39] he defended rectilinear prophecy and was opposed to the substitution of typological prophecy in place of rectilinear. In opposition to many scholars of his day he accepted Psalm 8 as a rectilinear prophecy dealing with Christ and not having as its purpose the praise of the greatness of man as God's creature. He vigorously defended the Christo-centricity of the Old Testament.[40] In a published Christmas sermon he claimed that there were over three hundred Messianic prophecies in the Old Testament. Maier relied upon the clear statements of the New Testament for the establishment of numerous Old Testament predictions about Christ's life and work. L. Fuerbringer and Th. Laetsch were two other contemporary exegetes who agreed with Maier about rectilinear prophecy.

[38] W. A. Maier, Notes on the Book of Genesis (St. Louis Concordia Mimeograph Company, 1930)
[39] Exegetical Notes on the Psalms (St. Louis: Concordia Mimeograph Company, 1930), cf. especially his arguments for rectilinear prophecy and rejection of typological prophecy in Ps. 2, 8, 16).
[40] Walter A. Maier, Sr., The Radio For Christ (St. Louis, Concordia Publishing House, 1939), 50 in a sermon for Christmas on Isaiah 9:6,7.

CN hopes to be able to publish at least some of Surburg's writings on a wide variety of subjects. One of them is "An Evaluation of Dietrich Bonhoeffer's Life and Theology After Half of a Century." Bonhoeffer was executed at the age of 39 on April 9, 1945 for his part in a plot to execute Adolf Hitler. Surburg wrote in the September 13, 1995 *Christian News,* as many Christians were marking the 50th anniversary of Bonhoeffer's death: "While in prison Bonhoeffer came to the conclusion that mankind no longer needs God. What amounts to theoretical atheism was Bonhoeffer's assertion that God is teaching us that we must live as men who can get along very well without him." Surburg based his article upon Bonhoeffer's writings, particularly his last writings. Surburg wrote: "Although he claimed to be a Lutheran and is so called in the literature of our day, Bonhoeffer was not a Lutheran, for he rejected and abandoned the theology and teachings of the Book of Concord." "His Christology is considerably different from that found in Luther and in the Lutheran Confessions." Bonhoeffer's "Christology is not what the New Testament sets forth, but was the product of his philosophical thinking." "Van Til in his book, *The Great Debate*, contended that the Christ of Bonhoeffer is not the Christ of Scripture and can hardly be distinguished from the Christ of Karl Barth (pp. 42-76 of Van Til's book.)" "Later he (Bonhoeffer) adopted the Bultmann view on 'Mythology' of the New Testament." "In Bonhoeffer's opinion Bultmann's demythologizing of the Bible did not go far enough."

Christian News has exposed the anti-scriptural and anti-Christian nature of Bonhoeffer's theology for some 45 years. No Bonhoeffer defender has shown where *CN* or Surburg misquoted Bonhoeffer. While Concordia Publishing House no longer publishes or sells any books by or about Walter Maier, it sells and even publishes books by and about Bonhoeffer. While both LCMS seminaries commemorated the 100th birthday of Bonhoeffer by inviting outside speakers to praise Bonhoeffer, neither seminary had any commemoration of the 100th birthday of Maier. The LCMS's *Portals of Prayer* has quoted Bonhoeffer as some great authority who has much wisdom to offer, but does not quote Maier in the same manner. In 2006 when both LCMS seminaries had a conference marking the 100th birthday of Bonhoeffer, *CN* suggested that the conference should have at least one speaker respond to such critics of Bonhoeffer as Raymond Surburg. What Surburg wrote and what *CN* has exposed about Bonhoeffer's anti-Christian theology was totally ignored. When the *Lutheran Witness* praised Bonhoeffer as a great Christian in an article by Uwe Simeon Netto, the *Lutheran Witness* refused to publish a letter from *Christian News* telling the truth about Bonhoeffer's theology. *CN*'s letter included quotes from Bonhoeffer's writings. One of them was: "Belief in the resurrection is not the solution of the problem of death," from Bonhoeffer's Letters and Papers From Prison, reviewed in the November 15, 1965 *Christian News*. (The *Lutheran Witness* article and *CN*'s letter are in the special July 3, 2006 *Christian News* issue on Bonhoeffer).

When the Aid Association for Lutherans sponsored and widely distributed to Lutheran congregations a film praising Bonhoeffer as a great Christian, *Christian News* asked the members of the AAL's Board of Directors if they believed a person who denied the deity and resurrection of Christ could be considered a Christian. No member of the AAL Board of Directors responded. Several times *CN* has noted that Franklin L. Baumer in his Modern European Thought: Continuity and Change in Ideas, 1600-1950 (Diers College, Yale University, 1977, MacMillan publishing Company) came to about the same conclusion about Bonhoeffer that Surburg did.

As the story of the Germans exterminating 6 million Jews during World War II, most of them by gassing, grew, Lutherans particularly increased their publicity and praise for Bonhoeffer. Honoring a theologian executed by the Germans was one way to make it known that Lutherans opposed Hitler and accepted as fact the ever growing story that the Germans executed six million Jews during World War. Maier did not praise Dietrich Bonhoeffer as some great Christian martyr as he is now being praised in the LCMS. It is true that he did not mention or accept as fact the six million Holocaust figure. However, Prime Minister Winston Churchill, President Dwight Eisenhower and the Red Cross, which investigated German prison camps during World War II, also did not mention the 6 million figure. During World War II when this editor went from door to door in a predominately Jewish neighborhood in the Bronx, New York, collecting newspapers for the war effort, none of the tenants of the hundreds of apartments he visited ever mentioned anything about their relatives in Eastern Europe being exterminated in gas chambers. For information on the Holocaust and Revisionism, see *The Christian News Encyclopedia*.

Those in the LCMS, who have referred to themselves as "hypereuros" or "high church," just as the Bonhoeffer enthusiasts, have also held conferences commemorating anniversaries of their heroes. But they have never conducted any such conference to preserve the memory of Walter Maier.

Christian News has asked many: "Why?" "Why Bonhoeffer and not Maier?"

Intellectual Snobs Ignore *Christian News*
BONHOEFFER: DENIED RESURRECTION OF CHRIST
Christian News, November 8, 2010

"Surburg, Maier, Bonhoeffer and the Holocaust" on page one again shows how highly Dietrich Bonhoeffer is being praised in the Lutheran Church-Missouri Synod. Concordia Seminary, St. Louis has said in a news release that Bonhoeffer is "the most important theologian since Martin Luther" and "the most important theologian of the 20th Century." Last week *CN* noted that a Bonhoeffer book was used for devotions by the entire seminary. The LCMS's *Lutheran Witness* insisted that Bonhoeffer was a confessional Lutheran. The LCMS's Concordia Publishing House, in its catalog has a full page featuring some ten books by Bonhoeffer and one published by CPH praising Bonhoeffer as a great Christian and Lutheran. One of CPH's biggest displays is the one on Bonhoeffer's books.

Christian News has repeatedly published evidence that Bonhoeffer demythologized the Bible, rejected the resurrection of Christ as a fact which actually happened in ordinary calendar history, and repudiated historic Christianity.

Kurt Marquart noted that intellectual snobs simply refuse to accept as fact something in a publication they despise regardless of how truthful it is. They refuse to read anything by someone they despise. *Concordia Seminary, St. Louis vs. Otten Case Book of Documentation* arranged by Kurt Marquart includes "A Respectful, Friendly, But Urgent Appeal to the Faculty." It says: "NEO-ORTHODOXY, EXISTENTIALISM, LUNDENSIANISM: Through their written works such men as Barth, Brunner, Tillich, Aulen, Nygren, and others, are teaching almost as effectively on this campus as if they had been formally called to this seminary as theological professors."

Bonhoeffer was not on the list because the St. Louis professors 50 years ago were so ignorant about the most important Lutheran theologian since Luther and the most influential theologian of the 20th Century they never mentioned him. Today Bonhoeffer should be added.

CPH should publish another book on Bonhoeffer. This one should include the lengthy scholarly articles *CN* has published on Bonhoeffer's theology by 1) Raymond Surburg and 2) Cornelius Van Til, 3) Valen Sendstad's *The Word That Can Never Die,* formerly published by CPH and 4) *Scripture and Myth* In Dietrich Bonhoeffer, by Richard Weikhart of the University of Iowa in *Fides et Historia 25, 1* (1993): 12-25.

Valen Sendstad showed in his book that Karl Barth, who greatly influenced Bonhoeffer and was praised by him, denied the Trinity.

Here are a few statements in the *Fides et Historia* article about Bonhoeffer:

"Bonhoeffer was thoroughly imbued with biblical criticism and always rejected attempts to dispense with it. In 1933 he wrote that the doctrine of verbal inspiration of scripture must be rejected in favor of biblical criticism."

"Barth considered the Bible a testimony to the history of God (*Geschichte*), not a record of events in the world. Thus he called the resurrection of Jesus an 'unhistorical event.' He asserted in 1920 that 'it is beside the point even to ask whether they [miracles in the Bible] are historical and possible. They make no claim to being either. They signalize the unhistorical, the impossible, the new time that is coming.'"

"Barth's distinction between *Historie* and *Geschichte* also translated into a dichotomy between time and eternity."

"The Barthian influence on Bonhoeffer's conception of biblical history is evident already in the summer of 1925. Concerning the resurrection of Jesus, Bonhoeffer wrote that 'it is . . . senseless and crude to make of it a bare historical (*historische*) fact, for God wants to appear in history (*Geschichte*). The resurrection occurs in the sphere of faith, of revelation; every other interpretation takes for it its decisive character: God in history (*Geschichte*).' In a lecture in 1928 Bonhoeffer stated that the Bible is filled with material that is historically unreliable. Even the life of Jesus is 'overgrown with legends' and myth so that we know little about the life of Jesus. Bonhoeffer concluded that '*Vita Jesu scribi non potest*' (the life of Jesus cannot be written). Barthian influence is especially pronounced in *Act and Being*, in which Bonhoeffer explained that Christian revelation and proclamation is never concerned with events of the past, but rather with those occurring in the present and oriented toward the future."

"Other writings of the middle period of Bonhoeffer's life make clear that he had no intention of upholding the historicity of scripture. In discussing the first three chapters of *Genesis in Creation and Fall* (1933) he criticized the idea of verbal inspiration and maintained that the biblical author was restricted by the state of knowledge when it was written. The Garden of Eden is a mythical world and the story is picture language to convey truths which can never be grasped in themselves."

"To avoid misunderstanding he added a clarifying note denying the literal resurrection of Jesus in the past."

"According to Bonhoeffer, the resurrection and other events in the Bible are thus not true as empirical facts of history."

"Picture language of the sort suggested by Bonhoeffer might also be called myth, and he explicitly made this connection. He welcomed the works of Bultmann and deplored the negative reaction accorded to his project of demythologization. Bonhoeffer wrote:

> "My view of it [demythologizing the New Testament] today would be, not that he went 'too far,' as most people thought, but that he did not go far enough. Not only the 'mythological' concepts, such as miracle, ascension, etc. (which are not in principle separable from the concepts of God, faith, etc.) but 'religious' concepts generally are problematic. You cannot, as Bultmann supposes, separate God and miracles, but you must be able to interpret and proclaim both in a 'non-religious' sense."

"Thus Bonhoeffer saw all biblical language as problematic and in need of demythologizing. The entire Bible is myth, not just the miracles."

"Bonhoeffer identified the resurrection and all biblical history as mythology, but 'this mythology is the thing itself!'"

"Bonhoeffer's stance toward God's role in the world seems just as paradoxical as his stance toward scripture. In the case of scripture, he denied any necessary metaphysical reality behind language, while in the present world, he denied any metaphysical reality beyond the world. God's transcendence is not some metaphysical transcendence, but is a transcendence within the world. In explaining his position Bonhoeffer used extremely paradoxical language:

> "God would have us know that we must live as men who manage our lives without him. . . The God who lets us live in the world without the working hypothesis of God is the God before whom we stand continually. Before God and with God we live without God."

"It is little wonder that conflicting interpretations of Bonhoeffer abound." "He still conceived of the Bible as a book of religious truths in mythological language that had no necessary connection with empirical historical or scientific truths. His rejection of Barth's 'positivism of revelation' and his desire to move beyond Bultmann make him a strange ally indeed of American evangelicals."

Father Richard Neuhaus, who was highly praised in the St. Louis seminary's Concordia Journal by David Benke, commended Bultmann's demythologizing. Neuhaus denied the inerrancy of the Bible, justification by faith alone, and was a universalist. It is time the great scholars of the LCMS's seminaries start reading articles and books which expose the truth about such liberals as Bonhoeffer and Neuhaus.

A Call to Refute "Scripture and Myth in Dietrich Bonhoeffer"
BONHOEFFER DENIED THE RESURRECTION AND DEITY OF JESUS CHRIST
Christian News, November 15, 2010

Dietrich Bonhoeffer, who denied the resurrection of Jesus Christ, is now considered by Concordia Seminary, St. Louis as "perhaps the most important Lutheran Theologian since Martin Luther" (p. 8). When the Bonhoeffer centennial was celebrated in 2006 at both LCMS seminaries those who said they had the evidence to show that Bonhoeffer's Christ was not the Christ of the Bible were denied an opportunity to present their evidence. The great scholars were not interested in the evidence. Both seminaries refuse to consider what Raymond Surburg, Cornelius Van Til and Richard Weikart had written about Bonhoeffer's theology.

Richard Weikart of the University of Iowa wrote in "Scripture and Myth In Dietrich Bonhoeffer" (*Fides Historia* 25,1 [1993]): "Thus Bonhoeffer saw all biblical language as problematic and in need of demythologizing. The entire Bible is myth, not just miracles."

"Bonhoeffer identified the resurrection history as mythology but 'this mythology is the thing itself' Bonhoeffer said he out-demythologized Rudolf Bultmann, the famous demytholigizer of the Bible. The entire article is in this issue (pp. 9ff).

Concordia Publishing House, particularly under Paul McCain, has been an enthusiastic promoter of Bonhoeffer. Its current catalog includes a full page of Bonhoeffer books, 10 published by ELCA's Fortress Press and one by CPH. *Christian News* has sent "Scripture and Myth In Dietrich Bonhoeffer" to both LCMS seminaries and LCMS President Matthew Harrison, inviting them to respond. How is it possible for them to promote a theologian who denies the deity and resurrection of Christ and the historic Christian faith?

CN wrote to Concordia Seminary, Ft. Wayne, where Bonhoeffer has been hailed a theologian of the Word of God:
November 4, 2010
To the Faculty of Concordia Seminary
Ft. Wayne , Indiana
Dear Gentlemen:
"Professor Says Plagiarism Cover Up In CUS" on page one of the November 1, 2010, *Christian News* reports that an article published in your Concordia Theological Quarterly was plagiarized and basically not written by the author the CTQ says wrote the article. On April 22, 2010 I wrote to Dr. Dean Wenthe and Dr. David Scaer and several others: "Some thought this case of flagrant plagiarism had been settled years ago. Is Jastram correct in what he says about no correction or apology appearing in CTQ and that the top officials of the LCMS did not allow this plagiarism to stop them from promoting Johnson?"

Christian News received no response from Drs. Wenthe or Scaer. Does the faculty maintain that it was proper for the CTQ to publish no correction and apology about this flagrant plagiarism?

The November 8, 2010, *Christian News* includes "Surburg, Maier, Bonhoeffer, and the Holocaust" and "Intellectual Snobs Ignore *Christian News* – Bonhoeffer Denied Resurrection of Christ." This article quotes from the attached "Scripture and Myth in

Dietrich Bonhoeffer." Bonhoeffer was highly praised at your seminary and in the *Concordia Theological Quarterly*.

Christian News intends to reprint the entire "Scripture and Myth in Dietrich Bonhoeffer." Richard Weikart of the University of Iowa came to the same conclusion that Raymond Surburg ("An Evaluation of Dietrich Bonhoeffer's Life and Theology", *CN*, September 13, 1995), Cornelius Van Til (*Westminster Theological Journal*, May, 1972, *CN*, October 16, 2006), Franklin L. Baumer (*Modern European Thought: Continuity and Change in Ideas, 1600-1950*, Yale University Press, 1977), and this editor did when he first read Bonhoeffer some 50 years ago. Bonhoeffer repudiated historic Christianity and denied such basic Christian doctrine as the resurrection of Christ. Is it proper to praise someone as a great Christian and Lutheran theologian if he denies the resurrection of Christ?

Christian News will be glad to publish a statement from any Bonhoeffer defender on your faculty who would like to show where "Scripture and Myth in Dietrich Bonhoeffer" is in error or where Surburg, Van Til, Baumer, and this editor are in error about Bonhoeffer when they maintain that Bonhoeffer rejected historic Christianity. *CN* has often said that the LCMS needs scholars who follow the evidence and not the crowd. God's blessings, Herman Otten

----

A somewhat similar letter was sent to the faculty of Concordia Seminary, St. Louis. Neither Seminary responded.

Suggestion for CPH Book Which Tells the Truth About Bonhoeffer
November 4, 2010
Board of Directors
Concordia Publishing House
Mrs. Elaine M. Graff,
Chairman
wwgraff@gmail.com
Dear Members of the Board of Directors of Concordia Publishing House:
Greetings in the name of the Lord Jesus.

The 2010-2011 Resource Catalog of Concordia Publishing House lists ten books published by ELCA's Fortress Press by Dietrich Bonhoeffer and one book published by CPH which commends Bonhoeffer. CPH now has a big display of Bonhoeffer books. The general impression is that CPH agrees with what our seminaries have been saying about Bonhoeffer. The November 1, 2010 *Christian News* reviewed *Bonhoeffer and King* recently published by Fortress.

Attached from the November 8, 2010 *Christian News* is "Surburg, Maier, Bonhoeffer, and the Holocaust" and "Intellectual Snobs Ignore *Christian News* – Bonhoeffer Denied Resurrection of Christ" and "McCain Joins Baker and Bohlmann." The article on McCain explains why I am not sending this letter to him. He simply refuses to accept anything from *Christian News*.

Attached is also "Scripture and Myth In Dietrich Bonhoeffer" by Richard Weikart of the University of Iowa.

Note the suggestion *CN* makes in "Bonhoeffer: Denied Resurrection of Christ" about another book published by CPH on Bonhoeffer, whom, according to a press release from Concordia Seminary, St. Louis, is "the most important theologian since Martin Luther."

This editor recognized, after reading Bonhoeffer some 50 years ago, that he rejected historic Christianity and denied such Christian doctrines as the resurrection of Jesus Christ. He demythologized the Bible even more than Rudolf Bultmann. Raymond Surburg of Concordia Seminary, Ft. Wayne, Cornelius Van Til of Westminster Seminary, and Richard Weikart of the University of Iowa, similarly noted that Bonhoeffer's Christ was not the Christ of the Bible and did not rise from the dead.

At the present time CPH is helping to mislead the LCMS about Bonhoeffer and praising him as the greatest theologian since Martin Luther, a theologian who denied the resurrection of Christ as an event which took place in real calendar history. Praising and following Bonhoeffer will help continue the LCMS down the road to becoming one more of America's "anything goes" denominations.

Would CPH be willing to publish a book on Bonhoeffer which would includes Raymond Surburg's "An Evaluation of Dietrich Bonhoeffer's Life and Theology After a Half Century"; Cornelius Van Til's article on the theology of Van Til in the *Westminster Theological Journal*; sections of Franklin L. Baumer's, Modern European Thought: Continuity and Change in Ideas, 1600-1950, where he shows Bonhoeffer did not accept historic Christianity; parts of Olav Valen Sendstad's, *The Word That Can Never Die* (CPH), which show that Barth greatly influenced Bonhoeffer and denied the Trinity; and Richard Weikart's "Scripture and Myth in Dietrich Bonhoeffer"?

It is not enough for an orthodox church body to publish long, fine orthodox commentaries and reprint the works of orthodox theologians of the past if at the same time it promotes as thoroughly Christian and Lutheran the writings of a liberal theologian whose Christ was not the Christ of the Bible and who demythologized the Bible and denied such doctrines as the resurrection of Christ.

God's blessings,
Herman Otten, editor
Christian News
cc. Dr. Bruce G. Kintz, President and Chief Executive Officer, Concordia Publishing House
Christian News received no response.

Seeking Reaction From Bonhoeffer Centennial Committee
November 4, 2010
Rev. Eric R. Andrae
era@firsttrinity.net
Member, Bonhoeffer Centennial Committee of America
Dear Pastor Andrae:

The January, 2008 *Concordia Theological Quarterly* of Concordia Seminary, Ft. Wayne, published your "Pro Deo et Patria: Themes of the Cruciform Life in Dietrich Bonhoeffer." A small section was reprinted in the June 9, 2008 *Christian News* with comments. You refer to Bonhoeffer as "a man of the Word of God."

Your Bonhoeffer Centennial Committee of America was invited to show where such critics of Bonhoeffer, as Raymond Surburg and Cornelius Van Til, did not tell the truth about Bonhoeffer's demythologizing of the Bible and denial of the resurrection of Christ and the Christ of the Bible. None responded.

Attached from *Fides et Historia* is "Scripture and Myth in Dietrich Bonhoeffer" by Richard Weikart. *CN* intends to reprint it in the November 15, 2010 *Christian News*. You or any other defenders of Bonhoeffer's theology are invited to show where

Weikart, Surburg and Van Til misrepresented Bonhoeffer.

God's blessings,
Herman Otten

Christian News received no response.

World Promoting Metaxas Book on Bonhoeffer

November 4, 2010
Nick Eicher
World Publisher
neicer@worldmag.com

Dear Mr. Eicher:

Just received your letter mentioning that World is offering as a bonus with a subscription *Bonhoeffer, Pastor, Martyr, Prophet, Spy* by Eric Metaxas. *CN*'s review in the May 10, 2010 *Christian News* took sharp issue with Bonhoeffer's theology. *CN* has published evaluations of Bonhoeffer's theology by Cornelius Van Til, Raymond Surburg, Franklin Baumer, and others who all conclude that Bonhoeffer rejected historic Christianity, including such doctrines as the resurrection of Christ. This was the conclusion I came to when I first read Bonhoeffer some 50 years ago and met Van Til at Westminster Seminary.

Attached is "Scripture and Myth In Dietrich Bonhoeffer" by Richard Weikart, University of Iowa. It would be helpful if *World* would have someone show where the critics of Bonhoeffer, such as Weikart, are in error. *Christian News* would be happy to publish anything World has to say in defense of Bonhoeffer's theology.

God's blessings,
Herman Otten

Call For Fairness Concordia Theological Quarterly

November 4, 2010
Dr. David Scaer, Editor
Concordia Theological Quarterly
Ft Wayne , Indiana

Dear Editor Scaer:

An article in the January, 2008 Concordia Theological Quarterly on Dietrich Bonhoeffer said he was "A Man of the Word of God". Your CTQ presented him as a faithful Christian and Lutheran.

In the interest of truth, fairness and real scholarship, *Christian News* suggests that the Concordia Theological Quarterly publish the attached "Scripture and Myth in Dietrich Bonhoeffer" by Richard Weikart or "An Evaluation of Dietrich Bonhoeffer's Life and Theology After Half a Century" by Raymond Surburg.

Sincerely yours,
Herman Otten

Call for True Scholarship Concordia Journal

November 4, 2010
Travis Scholl, Editor
Concordia Journal
Concordia Seminary, St. Louis
Dear Editor:

Since the Concordia Journal has published a review article by Matthew Becker praising Dietrich Bonhoeffer as some great Christian and Lutheran, *Christian News* suggests that in the interests of truth, fairness, and true scholarship the Concordia Journal now publish "Scripture and Myth in Dietrich Bonhoeffer" by Richard Weikart (attached) or "An Evaluation of Dietrich Bonhoeffer's Life and Theology After Half a Century" by Raymond Surburg.

Sincerely yours,
Herman Otten
No Response

LCMS Needs Scholars Who Follow Evidence and Not the Crowd

November 4, 2010
Rev. Matthew Harrison,
President Lutheran Church-Missouri Synod
Dear President Harrison:

You have highly praised both LCMS seminaries as the greatest seminaries in the world. Both have joined the growing crowd of theologians who now regard Bonhoeffer as the greatest Lutheran theologian since Martin Luther.

The November 8, 2010 *Christian News* includes "Surburg, Maier, Bonhoeffer, and the Holocaust" and "Intellectual Snobs Ignore *Christian News* – Bonhoeffer Denied Resurrection of Christ." This article quotes from the attached "Scripture and Myth in Dietrich Bonhoeffer." Your book On Joy boxed quotes from Bonhoeffer and gives the reader the impression you have a regard for Bonhoeffer's theology.

Christian News intends to reprint the entire "Scripture and Myth in Dietrich Bonhoeffer." Richard Weikart of the University of Iowa came to the same conclusion that Raymond Surburg ("An Evaluation of Dietrich Bonhoeffer's Life and Theology", *CN*, September 13, 1995), Cornelius Van Til (*Westminster Theological Journal*, May, 1972, *CN*, October 16, 2006), Franklin L. Baumer (*Modern European Thought: Continuity and Change in Ideas, 1600-1950*, Yale University Press, 1977), and this editor when he first read Bonhoeffer some 50 years ago. The solid evidence indicates Bonhoeffer repudiated historic Christianity and denied such basic Christian doctrine as the resurrection of Christ. Is it proper to praise someone as a great Christian and Lutheran theologian if he denies the resurrection of Christ?

Christian News will be glad to publish a statement from any Bonhoeffer defender on your staff who would like to show where "Scripture and Myth in Dietrich Bonhoeffer" is in error or where Surburg, Van Til, Baumer and this editor are in error about Bonhoeffer when they maintain Bonhoeffer rejected historic Christianity. *CN* has often said that the LCMS needs scholars who follow the evidence and not the crowd.

God's blessings,
Herman Otten
No Response

Becker Invited to Respond to Weikart

November 4, 2010
Dr. Matthew Becker
matthew.becker@valpo.edu
Dear Dr. Becker:

You wrote in the Concordia Journal of Concordia Seminary, St. Louis, in a review of a book on Dietrich Bonhoeffer, published by CPH, that Bonhoeffer was "the most influential theologian of the Twentieth Century."

Attached is "Scripture and Myth in Dietrich Bonhoeffer" by Richard Weikart, published in Fides et Historia. *CN* intends to reprint it in the November 15, 2010 *Christian News*. You and other defenders of Bonhoeffer's theology are invited to show where Weikart misrepresents Bonhoeffer.

Sincerely,
Herman Otten

Becker's Response

Dear Editor Otten,

Stephen Haynes has demonstrated the limitations of Weikart's interpretation of Bonhoeffer. See his helpful book, "The Bonhoeffer Phenomenon: Portraits of a Protestant Saint" (Fortress, 2004). Weikart's criticisms of Bonhoeffer reveal more about Weikart and his conservative evangelical/fundamentalist criteria for determining his version of "normative orthodoxy" than they do about Bonhoeffer's eclectic mixture of liberal Protestantism, confessional Lutheranism, biblical Pietism, moderate Catholicism, and liberal Prussian Kultur.

Warm regards,
Matthew Becker
Prof. Dr. Matthew L. Becker
Associate Professor of Theology
Valparaiso University
219-464-6695

The *Lutheran Witness*

Editor
Lutheran Witness
Dear Editor:

The February 2006 *Lutheran Witness* published an article by Dr. Uwe Simeon Netto which said that Bonhoeffer was a "confessional Lutheran."

In the interest of truth, objectivity, and real scholarship, I suggest the *Lutheran Witness* publish the parts of "Scripture and Myth in Dietrich Bonhoeffer" by By Richard Weikart, University of Iowa (http://www.csustan.edu/history/faculty/weikart/Scripture-and-Myth-in-Dietrich-Bonhoeffer.pdf), which show that Bonhoeffer denied the resurrection of Christ, demythologized the Bible and proclaimed a different Christ than the Christ of the Bible. You may also want to ask Dr. Netto or any of the other LCMS professors praising Bonhoeffer to respond.

Sincerely yours,
Herman Otten

Dear Rev. Otten:

Thank you for contacting the *Lutheran Witness*.

Please know that your letter to the editor regarding Bonhoeffer's theology will be read carefully and given every consideration as we prepare our "Letters" page. However, please understand that we receive many more letters than we have space to print, and we are not able to publish every letter we receive. If we select your letter for publication, either in the magazine or on the Web, where we now offer an expanded "Letters" section, remember that your letter will be edited for style, clarity, and length.

Again, thank you for thinking of us and for your interest in the *Lutheran Witness*.

Yours in Christ,
Adriane Dorr
Managing Editor
The *Lutheran Witness*
The Lutheran Church—Missouri Synod
1333 S. Kirkwood Road
St. Louis, MO 63122-7295

Christianity Today

Christianity Today: Letter to the Editor
Letter to the Editor
Message: November 5, 2010
To David Neff Editor in Chief

An interview in the July 2010 *Christianity Today* with Eric Metaxas, author of *Bonhoeffer – Pastor, Martyr, Prophet, Spy* says that "Bonhoeffer is more like a theologically conservative evangelical than anything else. He was as orthodox as Saint Paul or Isaiah, from his teen years all the way to his last day on earth." Some have shown for some 50 years that in reality Bonhoeffer's Christ was not the Christ of the Bible and that he denied such doctrines as the resurrection of Christ which Paul proclaimed (1 Cor. 15) and the vicarious satisfaction of Christ which Isaiah predicted (Isaiah 53). In the interest of truth, fairness and real scholarship, *Christianity Today* may want to publish "Scripture and Myth in Dietrich Bonhoeffer", By Richard Weikart, University of Iowa
(http://www.csustan.edu/history/faculty/weikart/Scripture-and-Myth-in-Dietrich-Bonhoeffer.pdf)
Sincerely yours,
Herman Otten

Metaxas's Counterfeit Bonhoeffer: An Evangelical Critique

Review of Eric Metaxas, *Bonhoeffer: Pastor, Martyr, Prophet, Spy: A Righteous Gentile Vs. the Third Reich* (Nashville: Thomas Nelson, 2010)

**by Richard Weikart,
California State University, Stanislaus**

excerpts - entire review in January 24, 2011 *Christian News*

Though most evangelicals probably do not know it, most Bonhoeffer scholars dismissively reject the idea that Bonhoeffer's theology is compatible with American evangelical theology.

Metaxas, then, has presented us with a sanitized Bonhoeffer fit for evangelical audiences. Evangelicals can continue to believe comfortably that Bonhoeffer is one of them, and that his heroic stance against Hitler was the product of evangelical-style theology. This view is naïve, but many wish it to be so. They might prefer Metaxas's counterfeit Bonhoeffer to the real, much more complex, German theologian who continued to believe in the validity of higher biblical criticism, who praised Rudolf Bultmann when he called for demythologizing the New Testament, and who in his prison writings called for us to live "as if there were no God." In 1944, toward the end of his life, Bonhoeffer admitted that he was a theologian who "still carries within himself the heritage of liberal theology."

Fides ethistoria 25,1 (1993): 12-25
SCRIPTURE AND MYTH IN DIETRICH BONHOEFFER
By Richard Weikart, University of Iowa
Christian News, November 15, 2010

Dietrich Bonhoeffer has become a mythic hero in the pantheon of late twentieth-century Christianity. Admiration for him flows from such diverse and contradictory movements as fundamentalism and radical death-of-God theology, as well as from most groups located between these poles. American evangelicals[1] have joined the chorus of his praise and actively promote his works. A recent review of *A Testament of Freedom: The Essential Writings of Dietrich Bonhoeffer in Christianity Today* enjoins a predominantly evangelical audience to "sit... at the feet of Dietrich Bonhoeffer," whose life "rings with Christian authenticity."[2]

Two guidebooks to evangelical literature list Bonhoeffer's writings as important reading material for evangelicals.[3] My own contacts with evangelicals and fundamentalists confirm that Bonhoeffer enjoys widespread approbation among them.

Numerous factors have contributed to the popularity of Bonhoeffer among evangelicals. Unlike so many of his contemporaries, he showed great courage in opposing Hitler's policies. However, this could also be said of Karl Barth, the theologian exercising the greatest influence on Bonhoeffer. Barth took a decisive stand against Nazism and penned the Barmen Declaration, which was the manifesto for the Confessing Church, yet most evangelicals reject his neoorthodox theology. Of course, Bonhoeffer gained great stature by his death at the hand of the Nazis, which is usually described as a Christian martyrdom.

Bonhoeffer's reputation among evangelicals, however, does not rest solely on his political involvement. Two of his theological works, *The Cost of Discipleship* (1937) and *Life Together* (1939), are favorite books in evangelical circles.[4] Since Bonhoeffer was so closely allied with Barth, it is not surprising that evangelicals sympathetic with Barth respect Bonhoeffer's work so highly.[5] However, even evangelicals hostile to Barth's theology endorse Bonhoeffer's works.[6] The evangelical attacks on neo-orthodoxy have generally ignored Bonhoeffer, concentrating instead on Barth, Rudolf Bultmann, Emil Brunner, and others.

By their uncritical support for Bonhoeffer, evangelicals have created and perpetuated a myth. The depiction of Bonhoeffer as an evangelical is no closer to the truth than the presentation of him as an atheist, which is how the death-of-God theologians tend to portray him. Evangelicals often misread Bonhoeffer because they are unaware of the theological and philosophical context of his work. Words that mean one thing to Bonhoeffer can mean something quite different to evangelicals. Further, evangelicals tend to read Bonhoeffer's works the way they read the Bible—literally, if possible. In Bonhoeffer's case, this is problematic, as I will demonstrate.

In order to illustrate the chasm separating Bonhoeffer from evangelical—and especially fundamentalist—theology, I will explore Bonhoeffer's view of scripture in this essay. My analysis will demonstrate Bonhoeffer's simultaneous acceptance of biblical criticism and the primacy and authority of all scripture. His views concerning history, myth, and language must be understood in order to explain his paradoxical stance.

While emphatically rejecting a dualistic ontology that separates the spiritual from the secular or the earthly from the heavenly, an epistemological dualism underlay Bonhoeffer's view of scripture.[7] Although he rejected many aspects of liberal theology, he continued its tradition of distinguishing between religious and secular truth as two completely distinct realms of knowledge.

Bonhoeffer's career can be divided into three periods: (1) pre-1931, during which time he studied under liberal theologians at the University of Berlin, embraced Earth's dialectical theology, and wrote his first two theological works; (2) 1931-1939, the period including the Church Struggle, during which he published *The Cost of Discipleship* and *Life Together*, (3) 1939-1945, the time of Bonhoeffer's prison writings. Bonhoeffer's attitude toward the scriptures changed some from one period to the next. Even a superficial reading of his major works reveals this. In his doctoral dissertation, *Sanctorum Communio* (1927) and in his "Habilitationsschrift," *Act and Being* (1930), scriptures play a subordinate role and Bonhoeffer cited philosophers more often than scripture to substantiate his points. *The Cost of Discipleship* and *Life Together* provide quite a contrast, since in them scripture is everything and philosophers are rarely if ever mentioned. Further these latter two works enjoin the use of scripture and hold it up as a standard and authority. In his prison writings scripture remained important, but Bonhoeffer began grappling with the question of interpretation of scripture, a theme absent from earlier writings.

The change in Bonhoeffer's life and thought in 1931 was so pronounced that his friend and biographer Eberhard Bethge described it as a conversion experience. (This should not be confused with the contemporary evangelical understanding of conversion, for which Bonhoeffer had no sympathy.) Although Bonhoeffer rarely mentioned his experience, in 1936 he claimed it "transformed my life to the present day. For the first time I discovered the Bible.... It was a great liberation."[8] From that time forward Bonhoeffer was captivated by the Bible, especially the Sermon on the Mount.

The transformation to the third period was not so clear-cut and 1939 is only an approximation. Nevertheless during this final period Bonhoeffer appears to have lost some of his earlier zeal for the Bible. In January 1941, June 1942, and March 1944 he admitted to Bethge that he went days and weeks without reading the Bible much, though sometimes he would read it voraciously.[9] He wrote:

I am astonished that I live and can live for days without the Bible—I would not consider it obedience, but auto-suggestion, if I would compel myself to do it. ... I know that I only need to open my own books to hear what may be said against all this .... But I feel resistance against everything "religious" growing in me.[10]

As he wrestled with the problem of interpreting scripture, his attention shifted from the Sermon on the Mount and the New Testament to the Old Testament.

These shifts in the treatment of scripture, however, important as they are, represent differences in emphasis and attitude more than doctrinal differences. Underlying the superficial twists and turns of his theology were important continuities, which are apparent when one compares his early works with his *Letters and Papers from Prison*.[11]

Although some of his views submerged during the middle period, they were never entirely absent. Toward the end of his life Bonhoeffer denied that he had changed much: "Neither of us [Bonhoeffer and Bethge] has really experienced a break in our life."[12] He also acknowledged in 1944 that he "still carries within himself the heritage of liberal theology."[13]

Indeed liberal theology dominated the University of Berlin theological faculty while

Bonhoeffer studied there from 1924 to 1927 under Reinhold Seeberg. The famous church historian Adolf von Harnack was not only one of his teachers, but a personal friend whom he admired.[14] Bonhoeffer was thoroughly imbued with biblical criticism and always rejected attempts to dispense with it. In 1933 he wrote that the doctrine of verbal inspiration of scripture must be rejected in favor of biblical criticism. However, he indicated that biblical criticism is not decisive in interpreting scripture. According to Bonhoeffer, even though historical criticism has proved that Jesus did not speak some words ascribed to him in the Bible, this makes no difference. We must still preach the whole Bible and keep moving, like one crossing a river on an ice-pack that is breaking up.[15] In all his works, including *The Cost of Discipleship*, Bonhoeffer stood on the Bible as on a breaking ice-pack. However, he ignored the fissures, since he had full confidence that the ice would support him long enough to get across.

His attitude toward biblical criticism remained constant throughout his career.[16] During the time that Bonhoeffer was working on *The Cost of Discipleship*, he wrote to his brother-in-law that he had nothing against textual criticism, but thought that it only scratched the surface.[17] Not only did he find biblical criticism relatively unimportant for exegesis, but he also thought it could be dangerous. He warned, "Criticism should surely guard against thoughtlessly giving offense to the congregation," because the bible has comforted and helped many.[18] For this reason Bonhoeffer often masked his views on biblical criticism. His stance is reminiscent of David F. Strauss, who in the conclusion of *The Life of Jesus* (1835), recommends that preachers adopting his view of the scriptures as myth nevertheless retain the outward semblance of traditional views and preach on the significance of scriptures without referring to their unhistorical character.[19]

Bonhoeffer's lack of emphasis on biblical criticism stemmed from his acceptance of Barth's dialectical theology while studying in Berlin. Barth's famous early work, the second edition of *The Epistle of the Romans* (1922), was widely discussed at that time and Bonhoeffer also greatly enjoyed *Das Wort Gottes und die Theologie* (1924). Bonhoeffer was more heavily influenced by Barth's early work than by his *Church Dogmatics*. While he did show some appreciation for the volumes of *Church Dogmatics* he was able to read, in *Letters and Papers from Prison* he also became more critical of Barth's stance toward scripture.

In *The Epistle to the Romans* Barth issued an appeal to faith in the whole Bible as the Word of God without reference to the historical or scientific accuracy of its statements. Barth's call resonated with the intellectual currents and the needs of Germany in the early Weimar period. Germans groped for faith in the wake of the horrors of World War I and their devastating defeat, which undermined belief in human reason and progress. An intellectual reaction against positivism had begun before the war among such important figures as Friedrich Nietzsche, Sigmund Freud, and Max Weber, but it reached new heights during the Weimar period in various forms of irrationalism, such as Lebensphilosophie, Nietzscheanism, Spengler's philosophy, Heidegger's existentialism, the Conservative Revolution, volkisch thought, and, of course, Nazism.[20]

Irrationalism, i.e., the view that knowledge or truth is primarily non-rational and non-conceptual, was an important aspect of both Barth's and Bonhoeffer's thought. Both men were heavily influenced by Nietzsche, who was extremely popular in Weimar Germany. They shared an anti-conceptual mentality that captivated many of their contemporaries. Bonhoeffer continually emphasized the need for faith and revelation, because truth "is not the clear sky of concepts and ideas."[21] Their irrationalism affected their understanding of the Bible by providing them with radically new ways of conceiving of biblical history and language.

During the nineteenth century liberal theology, based on rationalistic foundations, had increasingly called into question the historical accuracy of scripture and rejected large portions of it as mythical. The task of F. C. Baur, David F. Strauss, Albrecht Ritschl, Adolf von Harnack, and others was to sort out the mythical from the historical and retain only the latter. The supernatural stories in scripture were usually categorized as mythical and no longer taken seriously. The myths may have been necessary to communicate to previous ages, but in the modern scientific age they were superfluous, according to the liberals.

Under the influence of Nietzsche, Franz Overbeck, and others, Barth came to conceive of history and myth in an entirely different way. Nietzsche, instead of contemptuously dismissing myths, valued them as a form of non-conceptual knowledge derived through instinct or intuition. He advocated the recovery of myth to solve the problems of society and to unify modern culture. This is no peripheral point in Nietzsche's thought, but is, according to Allan Megill, "the focus of his entire enterprise."[22] Nietzsche deplored the role of history in destroying illusions and myths and considered primitive Christianity a vibrant myth that degenerated when Christians began believing in Jesus as a historical figure instead of a myth-maker.[23] For Nietzsche Jesus is not a temporal reality at all, but "an 'eternal' factuality, a psychological symbol redeemed from the concept of time."[24]

A new appreciation for myth permeated the *Zeitgeist* of Weimar Germany, partly through the influence of Nietzsche. Thomas Mann and other literary figures grappled in their works with the significance of myths.[25] Carl Jung investigated the role of mythical thought in the human psyche. Ernst Cassirer, a prominent neo-Kantian philosopher, incorporated ideas about myth in his theory of symbolic forms in the 1920s. Since Cassirer thought all knowledge was constructed by the mind and did not refer to external reality, the symbolic forms—language, myth (including religion), and art—were all valid means of communicating knowledge.[26]

Like Cassirer, Barth was a neo-Kantian, at least at the time of his early writings. During his student days, he was captivated by Kantian philosophy and went to the University of Marburg to study under Wilhelm Hermann, a neo-Kantian theologian. Barth's early dialectical theology was heavily impregnated with Kantian concepts. Kant had denied the possibility of knowledge about the noumenal realm, including God, and thus created an epistemological division between the noumenal and phenomenal realms. Barth's emphasis on the transcendence of God and his radical otherness in relation to humans flowed from this epistemological dualism.[27]

Barth's division of knowledge into two realms together with his affirmation of myth spawned his new conception of biblical history. In his early work, Barth drew a radical distinction between scientific or empirically verifiable history (Historie) and God's history (*Geschichte* or *Heilsgeschichte*), which corresponds to the phenomenal/noumenal dichotomy. According to Barth, "There is . . . not only a transcendent truth, but transcendent events, a world history (*Weltgeschichte*) in heaven, an inner movement in God. What we call 'history' ('*Geschichte*') and 'events' is only a confused reflection of transcendent developments."[28] Barth considered the Bible a testimony to the history of God (*Geschichte*), not a record of events in the world. Thus he called the resurrection of Jesus an "unhistorical event."[29] He asserted in 1920 that "it is beside the point even to ask whether they [miracles in the Bible] are historical and possible. They make no claim to being either. They signalize the unhistorical, the impossible, the new time that is coming."[30]

Barth's distinction between *Historic* and *Geschichte* also translated into a dichotomy between time and eternity. In the 1919 edition of *The Epistle of Romans* Barth informed his readers that their relationship with Jesus and Abraham is timeless and averred that the Bible, when speaking about the "past" is also speaking about that which is both present and future.[31] In the more influential 1922 edition, Barth introduced Overbeck's concept of *Urgeschichte* (pre-history or primal history) to explain his position. Overbeck had claimed that *Urgeschichte* was a history of events that were not perceptible and were not tied to time.[32] In 1920 Barth wrote a sympathetic extended review of Overbeck's posthumously published *Christentum und Kultur* (1919), in which he explained that Overbeck excluded Christianity from history and history from Christianity. Christianity exists only in the timeless realm of *Urgeschichte*.[33]

The Barthian influence on Bonhoeffer's conception of biblical history is evident already in the summer of 1925. Concerning the resurrection of Jesus, Bonhoeffer wrote that "it is . . . senseless and crude to make of it a bare historical (*historische*) fact, for God wants to appear in history (*Geschichte*). The resurrection occurs in the sphere of faith, of revelation; every other interpretation takes from it its decisive character: God in history (*Geschichte*)."[34] In a lecture in 1928 Bonhoeffer stated that the Bible is filled with material that is historically unreliable. Even the life of Jesus is "overgrown with legends" and myth so that we know little about the life of Jesus. Bonhoeffer concluded that "*Vita Jesu scribi non potest*" (the life of Jesus cannot be written).[35] Barthian influence is especially pronounced in *Act and Being*, in which Bonhoeffer explained that Christian revelation and proclamation is never concerned with events of the past, but rather with those occurring in the present and oriented toward the future.[36]

Bonhoeffer's 1931 conversion did not erase the dichotomy in his mind between history and revelation or time and eternity. However, he obscured this distinction in some of his works by confining his focus to revelation and scripture, while ignoring its relationship to empirical history. One scholar sympathetic with Bonhoeffer criticizes *The Cost of Discipleship* as a dangerous piece of writing on the New Testament because the author's intention and method can so easily be misunderstood. For one thing, *The Cost of Discipleship* can be read as a sectarian tract, as a call for the Church to "get back to the Bible" and follow its injunctions just as they stand. . . .[37]

Bonhoeffer himself later admitted that his book had a dangerous side to it, though he did not repudiate it.[38]

Other writings of the middle period of Bonhoeffer's life make clear that he had no intention, of upholding the historicity of scripture. In discussing the first three chapters of Genesis in *Creation and Fall* (1933) he criticized the idea of verbal inspiration and maintained that the biblical author was restricted by the state of knowledge when it was written. The Garden of Eden is a mythical world and the story is picture language to convey truths which can never be grasped in themselves.[39] In *Christology* (1933) Bonhoeffer claimed that through faith historical facts were not past, but present; not contingent, but absolute; not historical, but contemporary. He further asserted that "the Jesus that cannot be historically grasped is the object of resurrection faith."[40]

Only two passages in *The Cost of Discipleship* clearly reveal Bonhoeffer's view on the unhistorical character of the Bible. One is only part of a sentence: "We cannot and may not go behind the word of scripture to the real events...."[41]

The other is a footnote that is couched in philosophical language, and, while comprehensible to those having studied theology or philosophy, it is probably unintelligible to the average non-philosophically inclined evangelical reader. The footnote is enlightening, because it occurs in a passage in which Bonhoeffer affirmed the truth, reliability and unity of the scriptures in the strongest possible way. To avoid misunderstanding he added a clarifying note denying the literal resurrection of Jesus in the past.[42] He wrote:

The confusion of ontological statements with proclaiming testimony is the essence of all fanaticism. The sentence: Christ is risen and present, is the dissolution of the unity of the scripture if it is ontologically understood.... The sentence: Christ is risen and present, strictly understood only as testimony of scripture, is true only as the word of scripture.[43]

According to Bonhoeffer, the resurrection and other events in the Bible are thus not true as empirical facts of history. Closely related to his view of history and springing from the same irrationalist bent was Bonhoeffer's conception of language, which depended heavily on Nietzsche and Barth. Barth and Bonhoeffer were by no means alone in viewing language as problematic. Indeed language and hermeneutics was a central problem for philosophy and theology in the early twentieth century and continues to be so. Barth and Bonhoeffer both embraced the need for contradiction and paradox in the Bible and theology, because they rejected the idea that biblical statements could be metaphysical or ontological statements.[44] Since they saw truth as non-conceptual, language could not adequately convey God's revelation.[45]

Before *Letters and Papers from Prison* Bonhoeffer only occasionally broached the topic of biblical interpretation. In *Christology* he drew a distinction between the word of man and the Word of God, which differ not only in content, but in their very essence. The word of man is in the form of ideas, but this is not true of the Word of God. "The truth is not something resting in itself and for itself, but is something that happens between two persons."[46] Later Bonhoeffer explained that when the Word of God is preached, it differs from the word of man, since the Word of God is not the expression of something lying behind it, but it is the very presence of Christ.[47] The truth of God is thus tied to relationship, not ideas or principles.

Another characteristic of biblical language that Bonhoeffer emphasized was that it is essentially a language of action. This theme emerged in *Act and Being*, where Bonhoeffer called the Word of God the word of decision (*Entscheidungswort*) for those who hear it.[48] Decisionism is also a dominant theme in *The Cost of Discipleship*, where interpretation of the Bible is divorced from all scientific or historical considerations and simple obedience to the command of Jesus is enjoined. The anti-rationalist disposition of Bonhoeffer caused him to replace critical questioning of the biblical text with a practice-oriented simple understanding of scripture.[49] The concept of the simple understanding of scripture, which is mistranslated as "literal interpretation" in *The Cost of Discipleship*, does not refer to the conveyance of any kind of historical, scientific, or ontological knowledge; thus it does not correspond in any way with the evangelical conception of a literal understanding of scripture.[50] Rather Bonhoeffer conceived of the simple understanding of scripture as something that captivates the will and demands a decision.[51]

Decisionism was an important aspect of the Weimar Zeitgeist and once again Nietzsche was an important precursor. Indeed Nietzsche's *Antichrist* contains a passage foreshadowing Bonhoeffer's *Cost of Discipleship*. I do not know to what extent Bonhoeffer was actually influenced by this particular passage and doubt that he consciously relied on it. However, it clearly demonstrates the affinity between his and Nietzsche's ideas. Nietzsche stated, "It is not a 'faith' that distinguishes the Christian: the Christian acts, he is distinguished by acting *differently*." Then he enumerated actions that set the Christian apart, all of which he drew from the Sermon on the Mount.[52] Nietzsche consistently stressed the primacy of the deed and the will and rejected all dogmas, formulas, and ontology. Bonhoeffer's clarion call to obedience to the Sermon on the Mount in *The Cost of Discipleship* should not be confused with a fundamentalist view of scripture, but is actually closer to a Nietzschean view of language and the deed.

Bonhoeffer's stance toward the scriptures, history and language becomes even clearer when we turn to *Letters and Papers from Prison*, since Bonhoeffer began to write a theological work on the interpretation of scripture while he was in prison. His manuscript never surfaced after the close of World War II, but he expressed many of his ideas in letters to Bethge, so we do have access to many of his innermost thoughts during this period. In the writings of his final years, Bonhoeffer pulled together many of the threads I have already traced in his earlier works. There are some new departures, but the groundwork for them had already been laid.

While he was in prison, Bonhoeffer grappled with the problem of how to communicate the truths of Christianity to an increasingly secular world or, as he termed it, "the world come of age." This was not merely a theoretical question for him, since he now had to relate to fellow prison inmates rather than fellow Christians. In April 1944 Bonhoeffer first broached the subject with Bethge, and in subsequent letters Bonhoeffer called for a "non-religious" or "secular" interpretation of the Bible.

A new way of interpreting the Bible was needed, Bonhoeffer thought, because of the problematic nature of language and because the world could no longer relate to the biblical language. In April 1944 he wrote that his main question was "who Christ really is for us today." Then he continued, "The time when people could be told everything through words, whether theological or pious, is over...."[53] How then can Christians communicate with the world?

Bonhoeffer posed the question to himself in this way:

How do we speak of God—without religion, i.e. without the temporally conditioned presuppositions of metaphysics, inwardness, etc.? How do we speak (or perhaps now we cannot even "speak" as we used to) in a "secular" way about "God"?[54]

From his definition of religion in this passage, it is apparent that his non-religious interpretation must involve a non-temporal and non-metaphysical language.

In May 1944 Bonhoeffer renewed his call for a new non-religious language. He considered the old terminology of Christianity problematic:

But also we ourselves are again thrown back entirely to the beginnings of understanding. The meaning of reconciliation and redemption, regeneration and the Holy Spirit, love for our enemies, cross and resurrection, life in Christ and Christian discipleship is so difficult and distant, that we scarcely dare to speak of them any longer.[55]

Bonhoeffer wanted the old religious interpretation of the Bible, which involved metaphysical and individualistic interpretation, to give way to a non-religious interpretation.[56] Indeed he did not consider Sheol, Hades, or Christian redemption metaphysical realities that exist somewhere in the past or will exist in the future. Rather they are pictures of that which exists in the here and now.[57]

Picture language of the sort suggested by Bonhoeffer might also be called myth, and he explicitly made this connection. He welcomed the works of Bultmann and deplored the negative reaction accorded to his project of demythologization. Bonhoeffer wrote:

My view of it [demythologizing the New Testament] today would be, not that he went "too far," as most people thought, but that he did not go far enough. Not only the "mythological" concepts, such as miracle, ascension, etc. (which are not in principle separable from the concepts of God, faith, etc.), but "religious" concepts generally are problematic. You cannot, as Bultmann supposes, separate God and miracle, but you must be able to interpret and proclaim both in a "non-religious" sense.[58]

Thus Bonhoeffer saw all biblical language as problematic and in need of demythologizing. The entire Bible is myth, not just the miracles.

In a later letter he expressed opposition to Bultmann's attempt to distinguish myth from truth in the scriptures:

My view is that the full content, including the "mythological" concepts, must be kept—the New Testament is not a mythological clothing of a universal truth!; rather this mythology (resurrection, etc.) is the thing itself!—but the concepts must be interpreted in such a way as not to make religion a precondition of faith.[59]

Bonhoeffer identified the resurrection and all biblical history as mythology, but "this mythology is the thing itself!" By this Bonhoeffer meant that the mythological language had no metaphysical truth standing behind it. Thus the mythological language stood as truth in its own right and could not simply be replaced with other words as Bultmann tried.[60] Despite Bonhoeffer's disagreement with Bultmann many scholars have noted the proximity of Bonhoeffer's non-religious interpretation to Bultmann.[61]

His attempt to move beyond Bultmann by introducing a non-religious interpretation of scripture brought Bonhoeffer into opposition to Barth. While lauding Barth for initiating a critique of religion, he criticized Barth's later attempts in *Church Dogmatics* to reinstate all the supernaturalist language of the scripture, such as upholding the virgin birth. Bonhoeffer lamented this restoration and characterized it as a "positivism of revelation."[62] Whether or not Bonhoeffer misconstrued Barth's position—as Barth complained that he did—it is clear that Bonhoeffer's sympathy lay more with Barth's earlier dialectical theology rather than with his *Church Dogmatics*.

Bonhoeffer's stance toward God's role in the world seems just as paradoxical as his stance toward scripture. In the case of scripture, he denied any necessary metaphysical reality behind language, while in the present world, he denied any metaphysical reality beyond the world. God's transcendence is not some metaphysical transcendence, but is transcendence within the world. In explaining his position Bonhoeffer used extremely paradoxical language:

God would have us know that we must live as men who manage our lives without him. . . . The God who lets us live in the world without the working hypothesis of God is the God before whom we stand continually. Before God and with God we live without God. It is little wonder that conflicting interpretations of Bonhoeffer abound.

Bonhoeffer's concern for locating God in this present world rather than in some transcendent realm caused him to shift his interest from the New Testament to the Old Testament. He saw the Old Testament as more this-worldly than the New Testament, since Israel was concerned mostly with deliverance in the here and now. He criticized any redemption myths that imply there is some salvation for us outside of this present age.[63]

As we have seen, Bonhoeffer's irrationalist view of language encouraged paradox, and one final paradox concerning scripture emerged in Bonhoeffer's writings. Evangelicals usually construe Bonhoeffer's stress on scripture as a summons for every

Christian to read, interpret, and obey scripture. *Life Together* especially seems to convey this message, since Bonhoeffer admonished his readers to meditate daily on the scriptures and even asserted, "Whoever does not want to learn to independently handle the scriptures is no evangelical Christian."[64]

However, in most of his works Bonhoeffer rejected the idea that interpretation of scripture is an individualistic enterprise. Rather he saw it rooted in the community of believers.[65] In his doctoral dissertation, *Sanctorum Communio*, he identified the Word of God with the word preached in the church and equated this word with the very presence of Christ.[66] Bonhoeffer again identified the Word of God with preaching in *Act and Being* and maintained that the preaching office ensures that the preacher speaks for God.[67]

In *The Cost of Discipleship* Bonhoeffer spent many pages urging obedience to the commands of Jesus before informing his audience how to hear the voice of Jesus and how to know what Jesus is saying. Because he was expounding scriptural commands of Jesus, such as the Sermon on the Mount, it seems at first that Jesus' commands should be sought in the scriptures. However, when Bonhoeffer finally explicitly addressed this important question, he directed people to listen to the church rather than to seek personal revelation through studying the scriptures.

If we want to hear his [Jesus'] call to discipleship, we must hear him where he himself is. The call of Jesus Christ goes forth in the church through his word and sacrament. Preaching and sacrament of the church is the place of the presence of Jesus Christ. If you want to hear the call of Jesus to discipleship, you do not need any personal revelation. Hear the sermon and receive the sacrament![68]

Bonhoeffer was even more emphatic on this point in Ethics, where he asserted that scripture essentially belongs to the preaching office and the preaching belongs to the congregation. Scripture must be interpreted and preached. In its essence it is not a book of edification for the congregation.[69]

Bonhoeffer has been criticized by some as elitist, and surely his understanding of the preaching office and the subordination of the congregation to preaching reinforces this image.[70] If the Bible is not for the congregation to interpret, then they are at the mercy of whomever happens to be filling the pulpit. Further, in Ethics Bonhoeffer altered his view of where the command of God could be heard. He came to believe that God's command could be heard not only in the church, but also in the family, the work place, and through the government.[71] Therefore, it is in the authority structures of this world that God is heard and not through personal Bible study and the revelation of the Holy Spirit to the individual. I find this conception of hearing the voice of God through earthly authorities highly ironic in light of Bonhoeffer's own experiences with Nazism and the German state church.

Bonhoeffer's insistence in the final year of his life that God is firmly situated in this world is a denial of ontological dualism. However, he never rejected the epistemological dualism inherent in his earlier work.[72] He still conceived of the Bible as a book of religious truths in mythological language that had no necessary connection with empirical historical or scientific truths. His rejection of Barth's "positivism of revelation" and his desire to move beyond Bultmann make him a strange ally indeed of American evangelicals.

Richard Weikart is professor of history at California State Univ., Stanislaus, and author of *From Darwin to Hitler: Evolutionary Ethics, Eugenics, and Racism in Ger-

many, Hitler's Ethic: The Nazi Pursuit of Evolutionary Progress, and The Myth of Dietrich Bonhoeffer: Is His Theology Evangelical?

For a good scholarly review of Metaxas' *Bonhoeffer* see: http://journal.ambrose.edu/ojs/index.php/acchquarterly/article/view/46/92

Endnotes

1 The words evangelical and evangelicalism will be defined in this essay as pertaining to the movement in the late twentieth century (especially in the United States) that emphasizes the inerrancy of scripture and is exemplified by Carl F. H. Henry and *Christianity Today.*

Bonhoeffer was an evangelical in the sense of belonging to the German Evangelical Church, which is the official title of the Lutheran church in Germany, but this is not the sense in which I am using the term.

2 Kevin A. Miller, "A Man for Others," *Christianity Today* 35.8 (22 July 1991): 58.

3 Edith L. Blumhofer and Joel A. Carpenter, *Twentieth-Century Evangelicalism: A Guide to the Sources* (New York: Garland, 1990), 327; Mark Lou Branson, *The Reader's Guide to the Best Evangelical Books* (San Francisco: Harper and Row, 1982), 2, 104, 149.

4 Blumhofer, *Twentieth-Century Evangelicalism*, 327; Branson, *Reader's Guide*, 2, 149.

5 Donald G. Bloesch, *Freedom for Obedience: Evangelical Ethics in Contemporary Times* (San Francisco: Harper and Row, 1987), 10-11.

6 John Warwick Montgomery, *The Suicide of Christian Theology* (Minneapolis: Bethany Fellowship, 1971), 476.

7 On ontological dualism, see Eberhard Bethge, *Dietrich Bonhoeffer: Man of Vision, Man of Courage*, trans. Eric Mossbacher et al. (New York: Harper and Row, 1970), 777.

8 Ibid., 154-55.

9 Bonhoeffer to Bethge, 31 January 1941, in *Gesammelte Schriften* (hereafter cited as GS), ed. Eberhard Bethge (Munich: Christian Kaiser Berlag, 1958 ff.), 5:397; 25 January 1942, in GS, 5:420; and 19 March 1944, in *Widerstand und Ergebung: Briefe und Aufzeichnungen aus der Haft* (hereafter WE), (Munich: Christian Kaiser Verlag, 1954), 163 (Eng. trans., *Letters and Papers from Prison* [hereafter LPP], trans. Reginald Fuller et al. [New York: Macmillan, 1971], 234).

10 Bonhoeffer to Bethge, 25 June 1942, in GS, 5:420.

11 Scholars upholding continuity in Bonhoeffer's thought include John D. Godsey, *The Theology of Dietrich Bonhoeffer* (Philadelphia: Westminster Press, 1960), 264; Andre Dumas, *Dietrich Bonhoeffer: Theologian of Reality*, trans. Robert McAfee Brown (New York: Macmillan, 1971), 154; Ernst Feil, *The Theology of Dietrich Bonhoeffer*, trans. Martin Rumscheidt (Philadelphia: Fortress Press, 1985), 54; and others. David H. Hopper, however, in *A Dissent on Bonhoeffer* (Philadelphia: Westminster Press, 1975), 97, argues for discontinuity in Bonhoeffer's thought, but does not show discontinuity in the area of scripture interpretation.

12 Bonhoeffer to Bethge, 22 April 1944, in WE, 174 (LPP, 275).

13 Bonhoeffer to Bethge, 3 August 1944, in WE, 257 (LPP, 378).

14 Dietrich Bonhoeffer, "Rede zum Gedachtnis Adolf von Harnacks," in GS, 3:59.

15 Dietrich Bonhoeffer, "Christologie," in GS, 3:204-6; see also Bethge, *Dietrich Bonhoeffer*, 56-57.

16 Richard Grunow, "Dietrich Bonhoeffers Schriftauslegung," in Die mundige Welt (Munich: Christian Kaiser Verlag, 1955), 1:64-66.

17 Bonhoeffer to Riidiger Schleicher, 8 April 1936, in GS, 3:26-27.

18 Bonhoeffer, GS, 4:256.

19 Horton Harris, *David Friedrich Strauss and His Theology* (Cambridge: Cambridge University Press, 1973), 56-57.

20 On the reaction against positivism and the embracing of irrationalism, see H. Stuart Hughes, *Consciousness and Society: The Reorientation of European Social Thought, 1890-1930*, rev. ed. (New York: Vintage Books, 1977), ch. 2 and passim; Kurt Sontheimer, *Antidemokratisches Denken in der Weimarer Republik: Die politischen Ideen des deutschen Nationalismus zwischen 1918 und 1933* (Munich: Nymphenburger Verlagshandlung, 1962), chs. 2 and 3; Jeffrey Herf, *Reactionary Modernism: Technology, Culture, and Politics in Weimar and the Third Reich* (Cambridge: Cambridge

University Press, 1984), 46 and passim; and Karlheinz Dederke, *Reich und Republik: Deutschland, 1917-1933*, 5th ed. (Stuttgart: Klett-Cotta, 1984), 137-38.

21 Bonhoeffer, GS, 4:83.

22 Allan Megill, *Prophets of Extremity: Nietzsche, Heidegger, Foucault, Derrida* (Berkeley: University of California Press, 1985), 65, 76, 82; Friedrich Nietzsche, *The Birth of Tragedy*, section 23.

23 Friedrich Nietzsche, Werke (Berlin and New York: Walter de Gruyter, 1972), 3, bk. 1:291-92; *Birth of Tragedy*, section 10.

24 Friedrich Nietzsche, *Antichrist*, section 34.

25 Eberhard Kolb, *The Weimar Republic*, trans. P. S. Falls (London: Unwin Hyman, 1988), 88; Richard Hinton Thomas, "Nietzsche in Weimar Germany—and the Case of Ludwig Klages," in *The Weimar Dilemma: Intellectuals in the Weimar Republic*, ed. Anthony Phelan (Manchester: Manchester University Press, 1985), 74-75.

26 Ernst Cassirer, *Language and Myth*, trans. Susanne K. Langer (New York: Dover, 1946), 8; David R. Lipton, Ernst Cassirer: *The Dilemma of a Liberal Intellectual in Germany*, 1914-1933 (Toronto: University of Toronto Press, 1978), 116.

27 Eberhard Busch, *Karl Barth: His Life from Letters and Autobiographical Texts*, trans. John Bowden (Philadelphia: Fortress Press, 1976), 34-35, 38-40, 44-45, 49.

28 Karl Barth, Der Romerbrief (1919 edition), ed. Hermann Schmidt (Zurich: Theologischer Verlag, 1985), 161.

29 Karl Barth, *Der Romerbrief* (Munich, 1922; repr. Zurich, 1984), 175,183; *Romerbrief* (1919), 182; *The Word of God and the Word of Man*, trans. Douglas Horton, (n.p.: Pilgrim Press, 1928), 90; Tjarko Stadtland, *Eschatologie und Geschichte in der Theologie des jungen Karl Barth* (Neukirchen-Vluyn: Neukirchener Verlag des Erziehungsvereins, 1966), 120-21, 132-34.

30 Barth, *Word of God and Word of Man*, 91.

31 Barth, *Romerbrief* (1919), 106-7.

32 Franz Overbeck, *Christentum und Kultur: Gedanken und Anmerkungen zur modernen Theologie*, ed. Carl Albrecht Bernoulli (Basel, 1919; repr. Darmstadt: Wissenschaftliche Buchgesell-schaft, 1963), 25.

33 Karl Barth, "Unsettled Questions for Theology Today (1920)," in *Theology and Church: Shorter Writings, 1920-1928*, trans. Louise Pettibone Smith (New York: Harper and Row, 1962), 61-62.

34 Dietrich Bonhoeffer, *Jugend und Studium*, 1918-1927, ed. Hans Pfeifer et al., in *Werke*, vol. 9 (Munich: Christian Kaiser Verlag, 1986), 319.

35 Dietrich Bonhoeffer, "Jesus Christus und vom Wesen des Christentums," in GS, 5:137-38.

36 Dietrich Bonhoeffer, *Akt und Sein: Transzendentalphilosophie und Ontologie in der systematischen Theologie*, ed. Hans-Richard Reuter, in Werke, vol. 2 (Munich: Christian Kaiser Verlag, 1988), 107-8, 110.

37 Walter Harrelson, "Bonhoeffer and the Bible," in *The Place of Bonhoeffer: Problems and Possibilities in His Thought*, ed. Martin E. Marty (New York: Association Press, 1962), 123-24.

38 Bonhoeffer to Bethge, 21 July 1944, in WE, 248 (LPP, 369).

39 Dietrich Bonhoeffer, *Schopfung und Fall*, ed. Martin Riiter and Use Todt, in *Werke*, vol. 3 (Munich: Christian Kaiser Verlag, 1989), 46-47, 75-77.

40 Bonhoeffer, "Christologie," in GS, 3:203, 205.

41 Dietrich Bonhoeffer, *Nachfolge*, ed. Martin Kuske and Use Todt, in *Werke*, vol. 4 (Munich: Christian Kaiser Verlag, 1989), 75 (English trans., *The Cost of Discipleship* [hereafter CD], trans. R. H. Fuller [New York: Macmillan, 1959], 93).

42 Ibid, 219-21 (CD, 254-56).

43 Bonhoeffer, *Nachfolge*, 219-21 (CD, 254-56).

44 Feil, *Theology*, 47.

45 For Bonhoeffer's position, see Feil, *Theology*, 47. For Barth's position, see Gordon H. Clark, *Karl Barth's Theological Method* (Philadelphia: Presbyterian and Reformed, 1963), 136-37; Klaas Runia, *Karl Barth's Doctrine of Holy Scripture* (Grand Rapids: Eerdmans, 1962), 61-62; and Harold Lindsell, *The New Paganism* (San Francisco: Harper and Row, 1987), 182-83.

46 Bonhoeffer, "Christologie," in GS, 3:185.

47 Bonhoeffer, GS, 4:240-42.

48 Bonhoeffer, Akt, 131.

49 Ernst Georg Wendel, *Studien zur Homiletik Dietrich Bonhoeffers: Predigt-Hermeneutik Sprache* (Tubingen: J. C. B. Mohr, 1985), 115, 125, 133.

50 Bonhoeffer, *Nachfolge*, 75 (CD, 93).

51 See also Bonhoeffer, GS, 4:243.

52 Nietzsche, *Antichrist*, section 33; see also sections 32 and 35.

53 Bonhoeffer to Bethge, 30 April 1944, in *WE*, 178 (LPP, 279).

54 Ibid, 180 (LPP, 280).

55 Bonhoeffer, *WE*, 206 (LPP, 299-300).

56 Bonhoeffer to Bethge, 5 May 1944, in *WE*, 183-84 (LPP, 285-86).

57 Bonhoeffer to Bethge, 27 June 1944, in *WE*, 266 (LPP, 336-37).

58 Bonhoeffer to Bethge, 5 May 1944, in *WE*, 183 (LPP, 285).

59 Bonhoeffer to Bethge, 8 June 1944, in *WE* , 220-21 (LPP, 329).

60 Gotz Harbsmeier, "Die 'Nicht-Religiose Interpretation biblischer Begriffe' bei Bonhoeffer und die Entmythologisierung," in *Die mundige Welt* (Munich: Christian Kaiser Verlag, 1956), 2iJ 2:85-86.

61 Bethge, *Dietrich Bonhoeffer*, 777; Dumas, *Dietrich Bonhoeffer*, 17-18; Gerhard Ebeling, "Die 'Nicht-Religiose Interpretation biblischer Begriffe,'" in *Die mundige Welt* (Munich: Christian Kaiser Verlag, 1956), 2:51; Harbsmeier, " 'Nicht-Religiose Interpretation/ " 82; Gerhard Krause, "Dietrich Bonhoeffer und Rudolf Bultmann," in *Zeit und Geschichte: Dankesgabe an Rudolf Bultmann zum 80. Geburtstag*, ed. Erich Dinkier (Tubingen: J. C. B. Mohr [Paul Siebeck], 1964), 458; Heinrich Ott, *Reality and Faith: The Theological Legacy of Dietrich Bonhoeffer*, trans. Alex. A. Morrison (Philadelphia: Fortress Press, 1972), 114, 120.

62 Bonhoeffer to Bethge, 30 April 1944 and 5 May 1944, in *WE*, 179, 184-85 (LPP, 280, 286).

63 Bonhoeffer to Bethge, 27 June 1944, in *WE*, 225-26 (LPP, 336); Dumas, *Dietrich Bonhoeffer*, 142; James W. Woelfel, *Bonhoeffer's Theology: Classical and Revolutionary* (Nashville:Abingdon Press, 1970), 223-24.

64 Dietrich Bonhoeffer, *Gemeinsames Leben*, ed. Gerhard Ludwig Miiller and Albrecht Schonherr, in Werke, vol. 5 (Munich: Christian Kaiser Verlag, 1987), 47.

65 Clyde E. Fant, *Bonhoeffer: Worldly Preaching* (Nashville: Thomas Nelson, 1975), 35; Feil, Theology, 14, 75; Grunow, "D. Bonhoeffers Schriftauslegung," 64.

66 Dietrich Bonhoeffer, *Sanctorum Communio: Eine dogmatische Untersuchung zur Soziologie der Kirche*, ed. Joachim von Soosten, in Werke, vol. 1 (Munich: Christian Kaiser Verlag, 1986), 159, 172.

67 Bonhoeffer, *Aft*, 131.

68 Bonhoeffer, *Nachfolge*, 218; cf. 215 (CD, 250, cf. 249-53). A mistranslation in CD, 253, 9 Z obscures this point slightly. "Hore die Predigt" is rendered "Hear the Word" instead of correctly as "Hear the sermon."

69 Dietrich Bonhoeffer, *Ethik* (Munich: Christian Kaiser Verlag, 1953), 228-29 (Eng. trans. *Ethiks*, trans. Neville Horton Smith [New York: Macmillan, 1965], 294-95).

70 Hopper, *Dissent*, 99-103.

71 Bonhoeffer, *Ethik*, 214-16 (*Ethiks*, 277-78).

72 Geffrey B. Kelly, *A Bonhoeffer Legacy: Essays in Understanding*, ed. A. J. Klassen (Grand Rapids: Eerdmans, 1981), 90, 102, contradicts me on this point. Harrelson, in "Bonhoeffer," 136, sees another form of dualism, i.e., a dualism of proclamation.

Religionless Christianity
from Association of Contemporary Church Historians
Christian News, November 15, 2010

Review of Eric Metaxas, Bonhoeffer: Pastor, Martyr, Prophet, Spy: A Righteous Gentile vs. the Third Reich (Nashville: Thomas Nelson, 2010), pp. 608, ISBN 1595551387.

(excerpts only)

This is a badly flawed book. On one level it is simply a popular retelling of Bonhoeffer's life drawn from familiar sources such as the Dietrich Bonhoeffer Works English edition, the Bethge biography, and Love Letters from Cell 92. Metaxas has also looked at the outtakes of the Doblmeier documentary interviews with Bonhoeffer's students, so there are a few new anecdotes here. Much of the book, however, is a familiar patchwork of lengthy direct citations from the DBWE volumes, the Bethge biography, and Love Letters. It is also a consciously evangelical (in the U. S. context) interpretation of Bonhoeffer, his life, and times. . . .

x x x

In 1942 he wrote of "a Christendom enmeshed in guilt beyond all measure" and I personally think that any interpretation of his famous discussion of "religionless Christianity" needs to start there. A thoughtful and honest evangelical analysis of the complete Bonhoeffer, not just the parts that go down easy, would be useful.

But Metaxas has simply pulled together the passages he likes and ignored anything that might complicate the picture he wants to create—the same thing of which he accuses others, when he writes on page 466: "Many outré theological fashions have subsequently tried to claim Bonhoeffer as their own and have ignored much of his oeuvre to do so ... (they) have made of these few skeletal fragments something like a theological Piltdown man, a jerry-built but sincerely believed hoax." Yes, indeed.

Victoria J. Barnett, General Editor, Dietrich Bonhoeffer Works, English Edition and Director of Church Relations, U. S. Holocaust Memorial Museum

A Man Ahead of His Time
SAFFEN'S BONHOEFFER HOUSE
Christian News, December 6, 2010

A pastor in the Evangelical Lutheran Church in America called *Christian News* last week to thank *CN* for all the material *CN* has been publishing on Dietrich Bonhoeffer, particularly Richard Weikart's "Scripture and Myth in Dietrich Bonhoeffer" (*CN*, November 15, 2010).

The ELCA pastor told *CN* that when he was a student at the Lutheran School of Theology in Chicago he was invited to visit the Bonhoeffer House directed by Lutheran Campus Pastor Wayne Saffen.

The ELCA pastor said that the Bonhoeffer House attracted "druggies," alcoholics and all sorts of liberals who held far out theological views while opposing a truly Lutheran congregation. *Christian News* published many articles by Wayne Saffen which came from the Bonhoeffer House. Saffen was a man ahead of his time. During the 1950s not too many Lutherans were praising Bonhoeffer. Neither liberal nor conservative professors at either LCMS seminary had much to say about Bonhoeffer. The index for the St. Louis seminary's *Concordia Theological Monthly* 1930-1959 shows no articles by or about Bonhoeffer.

Today the St. Louis seminary says that perhaps Bonhoeffer is the most important Lutheran theologian since Martin Luther and the most influential Lutheran of the 20th century. Concordia Seminary Ft. Wayne highly praised Bonhoeffer at its Bonhoeffer centennial. The LCMS's *Lutheran Witness* said Bonhoeffer was a confessional Lutheran. *CN* has shown, ever since the 1960s when Saffen at his Bonhoeffer House was lauding Bonhoeffer, that Bonhoeffer rejected such doctrines as the virgin birth and resurrection of Christ and that his Christ was not the Christ of the Bible. The LCMS seminaries now agree with Saffen on Bonhoeffer. Will they now praise Saffen?

CN sent "Scripture and Myth in Dietrich Bonhoeffer" by Richard Weikart to both LCMS seminaries, Matthew Becker, LCMS President Matthew Harrison, *Christianity Today*, *The Concordia Theological Quarterly*, and *World* since they all praise Bonhoeffer. *CN* invited them to respond to Weikart. *CN* also asked the faculty of the Ft. Wayne Seminary if the seminary ever insisted that its theological quarterly should correct the flagrant plagiarism published in this faculty journal. An article attributed to Concordia University Chicago President John Johnson, former president of the St. Louis Seminary, published in CTQ, was plagiarized to a large extent from another source. For years after the plagiarism was exposed the Ft. Wayne seminary still listed the article on its web site as written by Johnson.

The Bonhoeffer supporters at both LCMS seminaries and in the LCMS bureaucracy should now praise Wayne Saffen for being a man ahead of his time. One of the articles in *CN*'s large file on the Bonhoeffer's House Wayne Saffen is the February, 1968 critique where the Bonhoeffer House director wrote:

"The five year old bi-weekly publication, *Lutheran News*, has gone ecumenical (to the right) and weekly effective January. Now titled, *Christian News*, it has widened its strategy from dividing or conquering the Missouri Synod and the Lutherans to dividing or conquering the visible churches of Christ on earth. Its own realignment of Christendom calls for division between 'liberals' and 'conservatives' with a super-church (or conventiclers) for each. The 'real' Lutherans and Christians are to go with the editor. He doesn't care where the rest of us go, since we are all going to the same place anyhow." "We repeat. It is an impressive record. Concerns which had been generated when the editor was still a student have almost all been validated by convention resolution: affirming a 6 day creation, a historical Jonah, an inerrant Scripture, Adam and Eve as real historic persons, etc. Missouri Synod in convention assembled has vindicated almost every doctrinal stand of Herman Otten as its official position. Now, that has to be impressive. How can the Synod, then, still withhold recognition of his ordination when it was carried out in strict accordance with the directions of C.F.W. Walther?"

The June 30, 1975 *Christian News* published on page one Saffen's "Don't Feed The Animal's: How to Deal With the 'Conservative' Beast (s) at the 'LCMS Disneyworld Convention.'"

"Lutheran Pastor Ousted by Manteca Congregation," in the October 10, 1975 Stockton Record reported: "An article written just before last summer's church convention in Anaheim may also have been responsible for the drive which led to his ousting. The Rev Wayne Saffen said the article entitled 'Don't Feed the Animals: How to Deal with the 'Conservative' Beasts at the 'LCMS Disneyland Convention,' had appeared in a conservative publication, *'Christian News,'* published in New Haven, Missouri. The article said in part: 'Conservatives will go through an electoral process to ratify the decisions made before at the St. Louis Computer Center which substitutes for a brain.'" CPH, which has a full page in its catalog featuring books by Bonhoeffer, whom CPH considers a great confessional Lutheran theologian should now publish a book on the Bonhoeffer House's Wayne Saffen. He was a man ahead of his time when it comes to recognizing that Bonhoeffer was such a great confessional Lutheran theologian. A professor at one of the LCMS's seminaries which considers Bonhoeffer, even though he denied the deity and resurrection of Christ, the greatest Lutheran theologian since Martin Luther, should write the book on the Bonhoeffer House's Wayne Saffen. There is plenty of helpful material on Saffen in *CN*'s research center. *CN*'s files of some 50 four draw filing units are open.

Christian News published many articles and letters by Saffen. LCMS President Jacob Preus was furious with *Christian News* for publishing Saffen's material. Preus said that at times Saffen was exposing what he was doing but there was no reason why *CN* should give a liberal like Saffen any space. Saffen was proud that *CN* at times went to Kurt Marquart for response to Saffen. The director of the Bonhoeffer House referred to Marquart as *CN*'s chief intellect.

At LCMS Seminary Insights for Preaching from Theological Liberals
BONHOEFFER, THIELICKE, AND EBELING REPUDIATED HISTORIC CHRISTIANITY
Christian News, November 22, 2010

A notice in the July, 2010 *Life* for The World of Concordia Seminary, Ft. Wayne says that Seminary Professor John Pless will be the presenter of an Advent Preaching Seminar on "Insights for Advent Preaching from Bonhoeffer, Thielicke and Ebeling."

CN has reviewed several of Thielicke's books. Thielicke denied the virgin birth of Christ and allowed for the evolutionary origin of man and the universe. The German theologian was highly praised by liberals and some uninformed evangelicals in the U.S. and Australia. Thielicke's theological liberalism was exposed in the July, 1980 Concordia Journal of Concordia Seminary, St. Louis by Professor Richard Klann. Are the current LCMS seminary professors familiar with what their own seminary's theological journal said in former years?

When Thielicke was invited to lecture at Seminex he said that Seminex is to the LCMS what the German protesting church was to the Nazis. He said that the LCMS was like the Nazis and "A No Church." Thielicke rejected the Mosaic authorship of the Pentateuch and denied the inerrancy of the Bible, claiming that even the accounts of the resurrection of Christ in the New Testament often contradict one another. Thielicke's anti-scriptural theology is documented on pages 1649-1650 of *The Christian News Encyclopedia*. It includes a "Thielicke-Montgomery" debate.

Along with Thielicke and Bonhoeffer, Ebeling is now hailed at both LCMS seminaries as a great confessional Lutheran who has much to offer to Lutheran preaching.

The Fall, 2009 *Concordia Journal* of the St. Louis seminary said that Ebeling was "The most influential Luther scholar of the 20th Century." The December 7, 2009 *CN* reprinted much of the article. *CN* said that "Concordia Seminary, St. Louis should be first promoting the actual writings of Luther and then such Luther scholars as Marquart, Preus and Montgomery." *CN* noted what Marquart said about Ebeling in his "Truth and Or Consequences" (*A Christian Handbook on Vital Issues*, pp. 407-440). The *CN* editor documented Ebeling's liberal anti-scriptural theology in an essay he presented at Moorhead State Teachers College, Moorhead, Minnesota in 1970 at the fifth Annual Convention of Lutherans Alert. John Montgomery in his "*Lutheran Hermeneutics and Hermeneutics Today*" (*Concordia Theological Monthly*, Occasional Paper No. 1, 1966 photographed in the September 5, 1966 *Lutheran News*) referred to Ebeling's position as "neo-liberalism." Cornelius Van Til in his The New Hermeneutics showed how far Ebeling had departed from historic Christianity (*Christian News*, April 28, 1975).

CN has exposed the anti-scriptural theology of Bonhoeffer from his own writings for almost 50 years. *CN* quoted Bonhoeffer. *CN* reprinted a long article on the theology of Bonhoeffer by Cornelius Van Til which appeared in the May, 1972 *Westminster Theological Journal*. Van Til showed that Bonhoeffer's Christ is not the Christ of the Bible although at times he sounds quite orthodox. Several times *CN* published "An Evaluation of Dietrich Bonhoeffer's Life and Theology After Half a Century" by Raymond Surburg. Neither the *Concordia Theological Quarterly* of the Ft. Wayne Seminary nor the *Concordia Journal* of the St. Louis seminary would publish Surburg's article even though he was a professor at the Ft. Wayne seminary. Neither seminary would publish any article which told the truth about Bonhoeffer. Surburg showed that Bonhoeffer rejected such basic doctrines as the deity and resurrection of Christ.

A news release from the St. Louis seminary said that Bonhoeffer was perhaps the most important Lutheran since Martin Luther. Paul McCain at CPH has highly praised Bonhoeffer and Richard Neuhaus. CPH has a big display of Bonhoeffer's writings. The CPH catalog lists 10 books by Bonhoeffer and one book about him. This book, published by CPH, was favorably reviewed by Matthew Becker in the Concordia Journal of the St. Louis seminary. Becker claims that Bonhoeffer was the most influential Lutheran of the 20th Century. Becker boldly promotes evolution and the ordination of women in *A DayStar Reader* sent to LCMS District Presidents and other LCMS leaders.

"A *Christian News* Survey", an editorial in the July 12, 2010 *Christian News* concluded:

"*Christian News* has yet to find one person who has actually read what Surburg and Van Til wrote about Bonhoeffer's theology who still maintains that Bonhoeffer was a Christian whose Christ was the Christ of the Bible and that Bonhoeffer accepted such Christian doctrines as the physical resurrection of Christ.

"Here are *CN*'s questions for all Bonhoeffer fans.

"1. I have read '*An Evaluation of Dietrich Bonhoeffer's Life and Theology*' by Raymond Surburg and '*Dietrich Bonhoeffer*' by Cornelius Van Til. Yes ____ No ____

"2. I still maintain that Bonhoeffer was an orthodox Christian theologian. Yes ____ No ____

"You may e-mail your response to *Christian News* at cnnewsandinfo@yahoo.com."

Both LCMS seminaries have also now been presenting Jaroslav Pelikan, Arthur Carl Piepkorn, and his follower, Father Richard John Neuhaus, as faithful Christians.

Uwe Simeon Netto, who had been associated with Concordia Seminary, St. Louis said that, although both Pelikan and Neuhaus left the Lutheran Church -Missouri Synod, neither left Luther. Netto wrote in the *Lutheran Witness* that Bonhoeffer was a confessional Lutheran. Pelikan joined the Orthodox Church and Neuhaus the Roman Catholic Church. Their anti-scriptural theology is documented in *The Christian News Encyclopedia*. Pelikan was an evolutionist who undermined the historicity of the Christian faith. Neuhaus similarly denied the inerrancy of the bible and supported evolution. He denied justification by faith alone. He was a universalist who said no one was in Hell. Piepkorn's anti-scriptural theology is noted in the editor's *Walter Maier Still Speaks – Missouri and the World Should Listen*.

For intellectual snobs, as Kurt Marquart observed more than 40 years, facts in publications they despise simply do not exist.

50 years ago theologians like Barth, Emil Brunner, Reinhold and Richard Niebuhr, Gustav Aulen, Rudolph Bultmann and Paul Tillich were among the "great" theologians whose writings were praised at the St. Louis seminary.

"A Respectful, Friendly, But Urgent Appeal to the Faculty," one of the documents in Concordia Seminary, St. Louis vs. Otten Case – *Book of Documentation* Arranged by Kurt Marquart (available from *Christian News* for $20.00) noted:

"NEO*ORTHODOXY, EXISTENTIALISM, LUNDENSIANISM: Through their written works such men as Barth, Brunner, Tillich, Aulen, Nygren, and others, are teaching almost as effectively on this campus as if they had been formally called to this seminary as theological professors. We believe that the influence of these individuals will never be broken unless and until the faculty takes a public and unanimous stand regarding their errors, and makes systematic efforts to implement this stand."

Now its Bonhoeffer, Martin Marty, Thielicke, Ebeling, Gerhard Forde, Piepkorn, Carl Braaten, Neuhaus, Walter Wangerin, Leonard Sweet, and Robert Jenson "teaching" at the LCMS's Seminaries.

CN has never opposed reading the writings of the liberals or inviting them to serve as guest speakers provided informed and articulate theologians who reject their theology are given the opportunity to respond. They seldom are. Students generally hear only one side. Those who oppose the theology of the liberals are not given the opportunity to expose their theology. The same favorable attitudes toward liberals exposed in "Concordia Seminary vs. Otten Case - Book of Documentation" arranged by Kurt Marquart 50 years ago has returned to both LCMS seminaries.

MARTIN LUTHER KING

First Article on King in Lutheran
Lutheran (Christian) News, September 23, 1963
Rev. King Will Speak at Temple Israel
St. Louis Globe-Democrat September 12, 1963

The Rev. Martin Luther King Jr., Negro integration leader, will preach the sermon at the regular Sabbath service at Temple Israel, Ladue and Spoede roads, Creve Coeur, at 8:15 p.m. Friday, Sept. 20, it was announced Wednesday by Rabbi Martin Katzenstein.

Rabbi Katzenstein said Dr. King had accepted his invitation to occupy the pulpit on that date, known as the Sabbath of Repentance, occurring during the most solemn period in the Jewish religious calendar, the High Holy Days.

Rabbi Katzenstein emphasized that Dr. King will be guest preacher at a regular Sabbath service, not a community meeting. Admission will be limited to congregation members until 8:05 p.m., he said, after which the general public will be admitted.

The High Holy Days, annual 10-day period of repentance, start with Rosh Hashonah, the Jewish New Year, and culminate in Yom Kippur, the Day of Atonement. Rosh Hashonah, ushering in the Jewish new year 5724, begins this year at sundown Sept. 18.

Assassination of President Kennedy
Lutheran (Christian) News
December 30, 1963

(We have already commented on the assassination of President Kennedy in our issues of December 2 and 16. We felt our readers would be interested in the following statements which we are presenting without comment. Ed.)

A Marxist Communist

6. "The President of the United States has been murdered by a Marxist-Communist within the United States.

"It has been pointed out by the Hon. Martin Dies, since the assassination, that 'Lee Harvey Oswald, was a Communist,' and that when a Communist commits murder he is acting under orders. The former Congressman, head of the original Dies Committee, is probably second only to J. Edgar Hoover in firsthand knowledge acquired from early and long experience in investigating Communist activities."

The John Birch Society

7. "The only commentator to match Warren's bold stroke was Professor Henry Steele Commager of Amherst who concluded the ultimate blame for the President's murder rested with those who had, inter alia, stirred up antagonism toward Russia. If a Communist murders our President, the fault belongs with those who tell us we should worry about Communism.

"These pronouncements, in addition to their unseemliness, are roughly comparable as logical exercises to blaming Laocoon for the fall of Troy, Paul Revere for the British invasion, and Churchill for the disaster of Munich." M. Stanton Evans, National Review Bulletin, December 10, 1963.

8. "Who, in the last period, has defied law and order, has called for direct opposition to the law—if we are going to take the position that lawlessness leads to assassination? Is it just the universally condemned Ross Barnestt? Let us look at others of the law-defiers.

"Martin Luther King. He has said that laws that are bad are immoral laws, and therefore are not really laws at all; and under his leadership, and that of his many followers, Americans have directly flouted the law.....

"There are the peace marchers, and assorted left-activists, e.g., the heroes of Berkely who by physical and vocal obstructionism tried to halt the legal activities of the House Committee on Un-American Activities." William F. Buckley, Jr. The St. Louis Globe Democrat.

Prizewinner
There is reason to thank God for the like of Martin Luther King
Lutheran (Christian) News

The *Lutheran Witness* (**November 10, 1964**) Official organ of The Lutheran Church-Missouri Synod. Published biweekly by Concordia Publishing House, O.A. Dorn, General Manager, 3558 S. Jefferson Ave., St. Louis, MO. 63118. Subscription: $1.75 a year. Second-class postage paid at St. Louis, MO.

THERE ARE THOSE IN AMERICA who view the selection of Martin Luther King Jr., as 1964 Nobel Prize winner as being a travesty, because the young Negro clergyman's rise to prominence had been associated with conflict, strife, and even violence.

In reviewing the high, international honor that has come to a fellow citizen, perhaps all Americans ought to ponder what could be happening in the Negro's struggle for dignity and justice if the rights movement had centered about a personality and motivating force other than those represented by Martin Luther King.

Plaudits over the Norwegian Parliament committee's choice have poured in from all corners of the world. Though the selectors customarily cite no reasons or explanations for their choice, many recognize that their action has again served notice to the world that in the strife-igniting frictions among men and nations the peacekeeping methods of the Prince of Peace might just be the most workable after all.

By preachment and by action Dr. King has demonstrated that he is a committed humans rights leader but is first of all a committed Christian. In fact, as must be the case with every Christian, he is the former just because he is the latter.

Dr. King has said that he learned the effectiveness of the nonviolence principle as a weapon from Mahatma Grandi. But as a pastor's son and pulpiteer of no small ability he knows that the theme of overcoming through patient continuance in well-doing, of not rendering evil for evil, of the wrath-turning soft answer, of patient firmness looms large on almost every page of the New Testament.

By exhibiting an all-too-rare brand of Christian humbleness and tenacious courage Dr. King has, as the New York Times editorialized, "symbolized the fine balance between impatience and restraint needed to bring about a social revolution without a bloody upheaval."

Something of the measure of the man may be seen in the words with which the hospitalized clergyman greeted the news: "I do not consider this merely an honor to me personally but a tribute to the discipline, wise restraint, and majestic courage of the millions of gallant Negro and white persons of goodwill who have followed a nonviolent course in seeking to establish a reign of justice and a rule of love across this nation."

America has good reason to thank God that Dr. King is the man he is-wise, able, humble, inspired and moved by a spirit that has roots in the Gospel of reconciliation. (Emphasis added)

The Theology of Martin Luther King
'The Essence is Love'
Christian News, **April 6, 1964 and December 14, 1964**

DANVILLE, VA.
NATIONAL OBSERVER DEC. 30, 1963

Mention the name "Martin Luther King." Into most minds springs the image of an activist, a Negro rights general who'll lead renewed demonstrations in 1964.

The image is valid, but so is another image. It is the image of a Christian minister. Perhaps, as some say, Dr. King perverts the Christian message; perhaps, as others maintain, he captures its very essence. Whatever the case, he bases his actions on his Christian convictions.

Here, deeply involved in a racial dispute, Martin Luther King chatted not long ago about his Christian convictions. Now and then he thumbed through his red-letter edition of the New Testament to illustrate his comments with an appropriate Bible verse.

"The essence of the Christian gospel? To me it's very simple," he said in his measured, mellifluous tones. "The essence of the Christian gospel is love."

Love Theme Is Dominant

The word "love" flows freely in his conversation. It's part of the title of his only book of sermons, *Strength to Love*. To him the traditional issues of theology—sin and salvation, the divinity of Christ, His virgin birth, His bodily resurrection—are peripheral. Love is central.

By love, he means neither romantic love nor love for friends, but good will and understanding for all men. The Greek New Testament, he notes, uses three words for love: *Eros*, romantic or aesthetic love; *philia*, affection between friends, and *agape*, a redeeming good will that "cleanses" both the person who is loved and the one who loves.

"*Agape* is the highest form of love," said Dr. King. "It's completely unselfish; it seeks nothing in return." When the apostle Paul spoke of love in his first letter to the

Corinthians, he used the word *agape*: "And now abideth faith, hope, and love, these three; but the greatest of these is love."

"Certainly the supreme example was the experience of Christ on the cross," Dr. King went on. "'Father, forgive them, for they know not what they do.' This was real redemptive love. Here was a symbol of crime, the cross. Yet redemptive love transformed it into a symbol of salvation."

No Fundamental Fervor

Other religious beliefs of Dr. King bear few marks of the fundamentalist Baptist tradition in which he was raised. With his father, a preacher in the old Baptist tradition, he's co-pastor of Atlanta's Ebenezer Baptist Church. But his sermons contain no "hard" preaching on Heaven and Hell, no preoccupation with sin and salvation.

He rejects, for example, the idea that men are innately sinners. He defines sin as "the estrangement that always develops when man misuses his freedom and revolts against God." Men inevitably sin, but this doesn't mean they're innately bad. Nor are they innately good. They have potentialities for both bad and good.

What set Jesus apart, he believes, was Jesus' unique goodness. "I don't think anyone else can be Jesus. He was one with God in purpose. He so submitted His will to God's will that God revealed His divine plan to man through Jesus."

In this sense, says Dr. King, Jesus was divine. But Dr. King rejects the virgin birth of Christ as a literal fact. The early Christians he says, had noticed the moral uniqueness of Jesus; to make this uniqueness appear plausible, they devised a mythological story of Jesus' biological uniqueness.

A Messenger of Ideas

Dr. King, of course, did not originate these ideas. Essentially, he's not a creative theologian but a clergyman, not an originator of ideas but a messenger of them. His ideas are a synthesis of thoughts culled from other men's minds. In fact, he describes his "intellectual pilgrimage" in precisely these terms.

In his seminary studies at Crozer Theological School in Pennsylvania and at Boston University School of Theology (where he earned his Ph.D.) he was influenced first by religious liberalism, which stresses the social rather than the spiritual concerns of man. Reading philosopher Reinhold Niebuhr, however, he soon concluded that "liberalism is all too sentimental in its analysis of man, and doesn't grapple sufficiently with the problem of evil."

Yet the revolt of Niebuhr's "neo-orthodoxy," he found, went too far in stressing a hidden, unknown God and man's capacity for evil. Today he believes in "neither liberalism nor neo-orthodoxy, but in a synthesis that combines the truth of both and avoids the extremes of both."

'Love Your Enemies'

Thus, in speaking about Christian love, Dr. King acknowledges that it may never be completely fulfilled. "Men have a tragic inclination to yield to selfish impulses. But one always has the capacity to strive for love. It remains the regulating ideal."

He takes this ideal from a literal reading of Christ's words on love. "This is my commandment," John reports Christ as saying, "That ye love one another, as I have loved you." Luke quotes Jesus: "Love your enemies, do good to them which hate you." In Matthew's account of the Sermon on the Mount, Jesus tells His disciples: "Resist not evil: But whosoever shall smite thee on thy right cheek, turn to him the other also."

Fundamentalists tend to take everything in the Bible literally; yet when pressed, many of them write off the phrase "Love your enemies" as unrealistic. <u>Dr. King writes off a literal view of the virgin birth</u>; yet he insists that Jesus' words, as reported in the New Testament, be interpreted literally.

In doing so, he has made what many clergymen consider a singular contribution to modern religious thought. Using the words of Christ and the example of Gandhi in India, he was the first—and remains the foremost—to really articulate the concept of nonviolent resistance for Christianity in America.

Doctrine of Nonviolence

Gunnar Myrdal committed no oversight when, in writing *An American Dilemma*, considered by many the definitive work on the American Negro, he omitted mention of Gandhi, nonviolence, or passive resistance. He was writing in 1942. The doctrine of nonviolence wasn't applied to the Negro movement until 1955, when Dr. King, 26 and a year out of seminary, assumed the leadership of the bus boycott in Montgomery, Ala.

Dr. King's sermons, lectures, and conversation all show a strong preoccupation with the race issue. Just one example: He turns to race to illustrate his point that Christians must "love" people even though they don't "like" them: "I wouldn't like to have dinner with Sen. (James O.) Eastland (Mississippi Democrat) every night. But I have to love him, like every man, because God loves him."

Some of Dr. King's critics, of course, question his intention when he speaks of *agape* love, particularly in the context of the racial issue. They argue that "Love your enemies" can prove an effective tactic, that Dr. King and his followers actually seek something in return—recognition of their equality.

Unquestionably many Negroes do regard nonviolence more as a tactic than as a guiding principle. Dr. King and his closest associates insist that they deplore this attitude: "The minute you allow race to become a factor in your relationship with another person, you've lost the *agape* quality."

As a Christian minister, Dr. King follows a two-part formula: First, relentlessly proclaim that love is the essence of the Christian gospel. Second, carry this conviction to the street and store.

The formula has won him countless epithets – and countless accolades. "On the basis of his deep Christian commitment and courage," says Methodist Bishop John Wesley Lord of Washington, D.C., Dr. King is nothing less than the "moral leader of the nation."

Dr. King, as is natural, takes a more modest view as he tells his visitor goodbye in Danville. "I'm glad to see," he says, "that someone recognizes that I'm a preacher."

--Lee E. Dirks
(Emphasis added)

Lutheran Pastors Told to Pay Heed to Negro Leaders
The *Minneapolis Star* (Jan. 6, 1965)
Reprinted in *Lutheran* (now *Christian*) *News*, January 13, 1965

By Willmar Thorkelson
Minneapolis Star Writer

Lutheran pastors should be <u>more interested in reading everything by Martin Luther King Jr. than by Martin Luther</u>, a California clergyman told a convocation of American Lutheran Church pastors today in St. Paul.

And they can also find a lot of <u>penetrating theology</u> in the writings of two other Negro authors, <u>James Baldwin</u> and <u>Dick Gregory</u>, said the Rev. Ross F. Hidy, pastor of St. Mark's Lutheran Church (LCA) in San Francisco, in a talk at Luther Seminary.

Pastor Hidy told the ALC pastors he is worried that the Lutheran Church may have become like "Rip Van Winkle" and may be sleeping through revolutions involving race, technology, urban development and religious unity. (Emphasis added)

Religious Socialism
By Kurt Marquart
Toowoomba, Australia
Lutheran (now *Christian*) *News*, January 11, 1965

"Christian Social Action", a LUTHERAN WITNESS editorial of Dec. 8, 1964, might just as well have appeared in THE CHRISTIAN CENTURY. It certainly does not say anything that is particularly Scriptural. On the contrary, the Social Gospel outlook seems to be taken for granted by such expressions as "the degree of involvement the church ought to seek in social issues." In other words, it is only a question of degree. "The church's" right to be involved in "social issues" at all is not even questioned.

What is entirely overlooked is Luther's Biblical distinction between God's "Kingdom on the Right," the Church, and His "Kingdom on the Left," the socio-political order. It is a Roman and Calvinistic delusion that the Church must guide, influence, and, if possible, direct the functioning of society. No such programmer will be found in the New Testament! The Church has its tasks and methods, and the State has different tasks and methods. The former administers supernatural treasures, the Gospel and the Sacraments, for men's salvation, while the latter takes care of temporal order and justice, on the basis of Natural Law, reason, and experience—not revelation! The things of God and the things of Caesar should not be mixed.

It is true that Christians, as subjects or citizens, owe their governments and countries loyal service and support (see the Table of Duties in the Catechism). This means that Christians will, in their capacity as citizens, advocate, support, and promote such policies and measures as are most conducive to public order and justice (Augsburg Confession XVI). The Church as Church, however, has nothing to say to the State as such, nor has it any divinely-given blue-print for society.

Intellectual Snobs
When the WITNESS appeals to Martin Luther King, the National Lutheran Coun-

cil, the L.C.A.'s "Board of Social Ministries," and the World Council of Churches, it becomes very clear that it is not just a general Calvinistic Church-State mixture, but the specific, rather unsavory Religious Socialism, known as the Social Gospel, which is being worked into the Missouri Synod.

Dr. Martin Luther King has himself recorded his indebtedness to Walter Rauschenbusch (THE CHRISTIAN CENTURY, April 13, 1960, p. 440). Now who was Rauschenbusch? He was the real founder of the Social Gospel in America. His "theology" was simply a religiously sugarcoated socialism. Stormer's NONE DARE CALL IT TREASON – for intellectual snobs of course facts contained in books they dislike simply don't exist; Orwell's memory Hole, you know! – traces the connection between Rauschenbusch and Fabian Socialism. And "Harry Ward, later identified as a communist, wrote the Methodist "Social Creed," the Marxist principles of which were repeated in the official social creed of the whole Federal Council of Churches by a committee of which Ward was a member! Transmission of Socialistic propaganda through the religious leadership of the country undoubtedly helped the "New Deal" considerably. And LUTHERAN NEWS has already reported the fact that the Religious Establishment campaigned against Goldwater in 1964, and undoubtedly played a major part in his defeat.

Contributing to Communist World Conquest

The ecclesiastical "Social Action" which the WITNESS is now recommending to its readers, has in the past been entirely misdirected and has unwittingly made a tremendous contribution to Communist world-conquest. The bitter irony is that many sincere people have been imagining that they were merely putting the Christian Faith into action socially and economically, when in actual fact Christianity was merely the verbal decoration on the Socialist ideology, which at bottom is atheistic, materialistic, and anti-Christian! The Christian Faith hasn't been applied to society at all; Socialist ideology has been applied to Christianity, instead! And modern theology itself—having jettisoned the historic Christian content in an effort to be "relevant" – is more irrelevant than ever! (See "The Irrelevance of Theology," THE CHRISTIAN CENTURY, Dec. 30, 1959).

And now comes something which should shock all sincere members of the Religious Establishment into sudden awareness of the horrible reality: Richard H. Rovere, the prominent political analyst, and himself certainly no Goldwater Tory, has published a book THE AMERICAN ESTABLISHMENT (London: Rupert Hart-Davis), the following statements of which are among the most significant written in this century:

"The Establishment is a general term for those people in finance, business, and the professions, largely from the Northeast, who hold the principal measure of power and influence in this country irrespective of what administration occupies the White House. . . (It is) a working alliance of the near-socialist professor and the internationalist Eastern banker calling for a bland bi-partisan approach to national politics. . .

"Summing up the situation at the present moment, it can, I think, be said that the Establishment maintains effective control over the Executive and Judicial branches of government; that it dominates most of American education and intellectual life; that it has very nearly unchallenged power in deciding what is and what is not respectable opinion in this country. <u>Its authority is enormous in organized religion (Roman Catholics and fundamentalist Protestants to one side)</u>, in science, and indeed, in all the learned professions except medicine" (my emphasis).

Clowns in a Farce

There we have it. Hundreds of well-meaning ecclesiastics are eagerly promoting the social (ist) programme of the National Council of Churches, in the belief that they are making Christianity "relevant," and that, like the prophets of old, they are announcing God's judgment upon society, etc. How galling to realize that far from being prophets courageously denouncing the iniquities of their times, these people are merely instruments subserving the purposes of the "working alliance of the near socialist professor and the internationalist Eastern banker" (isn't that exactly what the late Major C.H. Douglas, the founder of Social Credit, had been claming for years, in his brilliant books?) who decide "what is and what is not respectable opinion in this country," and whose "authority is enormous" – where? Among the "irrelevant," socially "irresponsible" Fundamentalists? No! In that very same "organized religion" which is supposed to be so prophetic and "socially responsible"! Perhaps Rovere's book will help sincere men here and there to realize that whereas they fancied themselves solemn heroes in a tragedy, they had not been given the whole script, which, in the larger perspective makes them but clowns in a farce!

Good Samaritans

There are of course sociopolitical issues with moral aspects, on which it is the Church's duty to speak—not for the State's benefit, as "conscience of the nation," but for the guidance of Christians. When, for example, an apostate, this-worldly ecclesiasticism advances, in the name of Christianity, some Socialist economic scheme, or some pro-Communist policy (disarmament, "peaceful co-existence," etc.) it is the duty of the faithful Church to tear the Christian mask off this hoax. And it is certainly the duty of the Church to warn her members against ideologies (Fabian and Marxist Socialism) which, no matter how "respectable" among the opinion moulders of "the near-socialist professor and the internationalist Eastern banker," are irreconcilably opposed to the Christian world view.

When it comes to specific issues – like the fashionable obsession with "race relations" – the Church too must demand of her members (not of the State) justice and charity. But this does not mean agitation for disastrously totalitarian "Civil Rights" legislation, as Dr. Hamann has pointed out in his penetrating article "Racism" (AUSTRALIAN THEOLOGICAL REVIEW, September, 1963).

And the WITNESS is quite right in saying: "More than sporadic charity is needed." But the solution proposed, that "the church" as such "must risk involvement in all areas of life that matter to people" is Calvinistic and unacceptable. Hospitals, relief-centers, welfare-clinics, etc., ought to be undertaken by societies within the Church. And it is important that our preaching be such as to inspire Christians to genuine compassion for all humanity—and not just abstractly, but concretely. Genuine Christian compassion, free of cant and pose, will never be "respectable," but must – like St. Francis—expect active opposition from the Establishment in Church and State. But, like St. Francis, it will find ways and means of being Good Samaritans to suffering humanity in the Name of the Son of Man!

A Communist Creation
Lutheran News, **March 8, 1965**

"The so-called civil-rights movement in the United State is a communist creation, and has been largely manipulated by communists since it was created.

"The National Association for the Advancement of Colored People (NAACP) is the primary civil-rights group—connected with others through interlocking directorates. The NAACP was founded in 1909. Its first five top officials were well-known socialists—one of whom (W.E.B. DuBois) later became a militant communist. In 1936, communists began infiltrating the NAACP. By 1956, at least 77 top NAACP officials were known to federal agencies as participants in communist or pro-communist activities....

"The Committee (The Joint Legislative Committee on Un-American Activities of the State of Louisiana ed.) reported that Martin Luther King's Southern Christian Leadership Conference is also substantially under the control of the Communist Party.' King (foremost personality in the civil-rights movement) is notorious for his association with communists, communist fronters communist organizations, and moral degenerates connected with communist causes" (THE DAN SMOOT REPORT, February 22, 1965, P. O. Box 9538, Lakewood Station, Dallas, Texas, Dan Smoot is a former F.B.I. agent).

King's Christian Ethics
Lutheran News, **September 30, 1965**

Dr. Martin Luther King recently called for a reversal of the American policy against the admission of Communist China to the United Nations and again asked for a suspension of American bombing missions against North Vietnam. He said he was offering his ideas on world peace "as a minister concerned with bringing Christian ethics to bear on the social evils of today."

Dr. King certainly has the right to express his convictions but we question whether he can be considered a spokesman of the "Christian" position. While the LUTHERAN WITNESS, official organ of The Lutheran Church-Missouri Synod, refers to Dr. King as "a committed Christian" and claims that "America has good reason to thank God that Dr. King is the man he is--wise, able, humble, inspired and moved by a spirit that has its roots in the Gospel of reconciliation" (November 10, 1964), we still believe a Christian is one who accepts such basic doctrines as the virgin birth and resurrection of Christ.

Evidently Dr. King does not consider the fundamental doctrines of the Christian faith very important. Earlier this year the NATIONAL OBSERVER published a "Newsbook" on RELIGION IN ACTION. A revealing article on Martin Luther King in this "Newsbook" said: "... his sermons contain no 'hard' preaching on heaven and hell, no preoccupation with sin and salvation.

"He rejects, for example, the idea that men are innate sinners. He defines sin as 'the estrangement that always develops when man misuses his freedom and revolts against God.' Men inevitably sin, but this doesn't mean they're innately bad. Nor are they innately good. They have potentialities for both bad and good.

"What set Jesus apart, he believes, was Jesus' unique goodness. 'Don't think anyone else can be Jesus. He was one with God in purpose. He so submitted His will to God's will that God revealed His divine plan to man through Jesus.'

"In this sense, he says, Jesus was divine. But he Rev. Dr. King rejects the virgin birth of Jesus Christ as a literal fact. The early Christians, he says, had noticed the moral uniqueness of Jesus; to make this uniqueness appear plausible, they devised a mythological story of Jesus' biological uniqueness' (128-9).

"An Unusual Look at Martin Luther King," the title of the article on King in RELIGION IN ACTION, said: "To him the traditional issues of theology- sin and salvation, the divinity of Christ, His virgin birth, His bodily resurrection -- are peripheral. Love is central" (128).

While the LUTHERAN WITNESS refers to Dr. King as "a committed Christian" and even though Dr. King continues to remain one of the darlings of the Lutheran Human Relations Association of America, some of our Bible believing Negro friends reject both Dr. King's liberal theology and radical political views. So do we.

It's Very Simple
Lutheran News, January 10, 1966

It's very simple – The True story of Civil Rights, by Alan Stang. Western Islands, Belmont, Massachusetts, 1965. Paper, 218 pp., $1.00.

IT'S VERY SIMPLE is not a book about segregation or integration but about "the REAL purpose of the Negro revolution." Alan Stang's first publications on the civil rights movement were written while he was a resident of Harlem in New York City. The author is a graduate of City College of New York and Columbia University. He is a former business editor for Prentice-Hall Inc., and has written, produced and done research for radio and television. Now a resident of mid-Manhattan, Stang devotes his time of journalism and is a frequent contributor to magazines.

Stang suggests that possibly those who were wrong about China and Mao, Cuba and Castro, Algeria and Ben Bella, Tanzania and Nyerere, and others, may possibly also be wrong about the real purpose of our nation's race revolution.

After presenting hundreds of documented facts, Stang concludes: "On the basis of all the gigantic evidence we have seen, I charge that America's 'race problem' and the 'civil rights movement' supposed to end it, have both been planned by the Communists, as we have seen, built up by the Communists, as we have seen, and, most important, CONDUCTED by the Communists, as we have seen.

"I charge—on the basis of what we have seen—that despite all of the idealistic and good people who have been deceived and pulled into the operation or into support of it, the 'civil rights movement' is for the most part a Communist operation under the cloak of which the Communists hope to capture this country…

"I charge that the Communists have done everything in their power to create this despair by convincing Negro and white Americans that black men can be nothing but incompetent, helpless and unmanly—that, in short, they are 'niggers'—and that the only way they can avoid starvation is for Massa Big Daddy government to feed them.

"I charge therefore that the Communists-under the cloak of civil rights-are trying to get American citizens who happen to be black to exchange the benevolent slavery of the Old Plantation for the malevolent slavery of the New Plantation.

"I charge that the growing hostility between black and white Americans IS real and that it is for the most part the work of the Communists-as we have seen" (212-213).

This is the kind of book the theological liberals who defend Dr. Martin Luther King Jr. will probably try to ignore. We would like to see the Lutheran Human Relations Association of American attempt to answer IT'S VERY SIMPLE. If Stang's documented facts are in error and he isn't telling the truth about Martin Luther King Jr., Bayard Rustin, Fred Shuttlesworth, the NCC, then the LHRAA should point this out.

The Southern Conference Educational Fund
Lutheran (Christian) News January 10, 1966

"Activities of the Southern Conference Educational Fund, Inc. In Louisiana," by The Joint Legislative Committee on Un-American Activities State of Louisiana, November 19, 1963. Old State Capitol, Baton Rouge, Louisiana. Paper, 124 pp.

Since several Lutherans have had some connection with the Southern Conference Educational Fund (SCEF), a communist front organization, this documented report by the Joint Legislative Committee on Un-American Activities of the State of Louisiana should be of more than passing interest to Lutherans interested in the current "civil rights" movement. According to CERTAIN ACTIVITIES AND AFFILIATIONS OF 181 LUTHERAN CLERGYMEN by J.B. Matthews and published by the Church League of American, Rev. Andrew... of the Lutheran Church Missouri Synod have cooperated with SCEF.

Many documents and letters are photographically reproduced in this report. On page 86 the signature of Sarah Patton Boyle appears under a petition seeking executive clemency in the case of Carl Braden, a known communist. Mrs. Boyle was a guest speaker at the 1964 Valparaiso University Workshop and Institute on Human Relations. Exhibit 43 for this official report is a "photograph of Martin Luther King and three officers of SCEF previously identified as Communists." (100). Exhibit 44 is a check paid to Martin Luther King by the SCEF.

The report concludes: "It appears from the evidence that seven or eight really run the SCEF. Five of these, namely Anne Braden, Carl Braden, Dombrowski, William Howard Melish, and Aubrey Williams have all been previously identified in sworn testimony as members of the Communist Party. The sixth, Benjamin E. Smith, is a national Officer in a cited Communist front, the National Lawyer's Guild, and the seventh, Rev. Fred L. Shuttlesoorth, is an ex-convict. This type of leadership speaks for itself," (120).

"By each and everyone of these tests, the SCEF is in fact a Communist front!"

It appears to us that the officials of the Lutheran Human Relations Association of America should repudiate any association with a known Communist front. They ought to study the documentation in this report if they still think they ought to defend the SCEF and its leaders.

The Negroes In a Soviet America
Lutheran News January 10, 1966

THE NEGROES IN A SOVIET AMERICA, by James W. Ford and James S. Allen. Workers Library Publishers, New York, 1935. 47 pp. Reproduced by American Opinion, Belmont, Massachusetts, 3 for $1.00.

James W. Ford, one of the authors of this pamphlet, had been several times the candidate of the Communist Party for Vice-President. "James S. Allen," the other, is the alias for Sol Auerbach whose activities were a matter of record before the Dies Committee. When this pamphlet was first reproduced by the National Economic Council in 1945, this council said: "This special offset edition of 'The Negroes in A Soviet America' has been brought out in order that the people may form a true understanding of what is back of the present, hullabaloo about 'Race Equality.'"

Civil Riots U.S.A.
Lutheran News, January 10, 1966

Civil Riots U.S.A., by Constructive Action, 701 East Whitier Boulevard, Whittier, California, 1965. 28 pp. $.50.

This booklet is based on a film strip directed and produced by Bill Richardson and written by Gary Allen. It seeks to explain what is behind some of the recent race riots in our nation.

The booklet contains some 50 pictures taken from the filmstrip together with explanatory comments. We are reproducing here one page of pictures from the filmstrip. Here are some of the comments accompanying these pictures: "One of the most active and widely traveled Civil Rights leaders is Bayard Rustin. Rustin, who is best known for organizing the March on Washington in 1963, was organizer for the Young Communist League. During World War II, Rustin spent twenty-six months in Federal Prison for Draft evasion. In 1953, he pleaded guilty to a sex perversion charge, in Pasadena, California.

"In 1957, while employed as Martin Luther King's personal secretary, Rustin attended the National Convention of the Communist Party. In 1958, while still in King's employ, Rustin went to Soviet Russia to participate in an anti-American propaganda show called the 'Non-Violent Action Committee Against Nuclear Weapons.' Rustin accompanied King in 1964, when King accepted the Nobel Peace Prize....

"Here is a check to King from the Southern Conference Educational Fund, the organization cited by both House and Senate investigating committees as the key Communist front in the South.

"In this picture taken at King's Southern Christian Leadership Conference meeting, the three in the background are the identified Communists who run the Southern Conference Educational Fund, Carl and Anne Braden, and James Dombroski."

The pamphlet concludes: "We must caution you—the Communist's game is hatred. They have labored industriously among Negroes to foment hatred of whites. If whites retaliate by stimulating hatred of Negroes, they are falling into the Communist's trap. Americans must put the blame where it belongs, on agitators, dupes and fellow-travelers. Unfortunately, in a situation such as existed in Watts, the majority of law abiding Negroes who were trapped in their homes were not as newsworthy as the hoodlums setting fires to a store.

"For the most part the numerous acts of heroism performed by Negroes in saving whites from being kicked to death by mobs have gone unnoticed.

"In addition to avoiding the Communist trap of race hatred, we must also follow the positive program of support of our local law enforcement agencies."

Here's a filmstrip which we recommend for the next Valparaiso University Workshop and Institute on Human Relations.

Color – Communism – And Common Sense
Lutheran News, January 10, 1966

COLOR COMMUNISM AND COMMON SENSE, by Manning Johnson. Alliance, Inc. New York, 1968. Reprinted by American Opinion, Belmont, Massachusetts. Paper, 80 pp. $.50.

In this short book the author, himself a Negro and for ten years a member of the Communist Party, exposes the Party's cruel deception of American Negroes and shows how the "Civil Rights" movement will benefit the Communists. Johnson was inducted into the Communist Party largely because of the preachings of a communist Bishop (retired) of the Episcopal church, William Montgomery Brown.

In his chapter on "Subverting Negro Churches" the former Communist official notes: "A large number of Negro ministers are all for the Communists. Some are prominent and influential; others are 'run of the mill.' They are in common belief that beating the racial drums is a short cut to prominence, money and the realization of personal ambitions even if the Negro masses are left prostrate and bleeding--expendables in the mad scramble for power" (14). According to Johnson, the Communists generally agreed "that the Church is the 'best cover for illegal work'" (16).

The Negro author says: "The fact that the reds have never contributed anything tangible to the progress of the Negro is overlooked though the reds have collected millions of dollars as a result of race incitement.

"Like the Communist Party, the N.A.A.C.P. has collected millions of dollars through exploitation of race issues. The bigger the race issue, the bigger the appeal and the bigger the contributions...

"Yet one cannot find any report of any of this money being spent for factories and shops to provide jobs, land and home construction, specialized training for talented youth, hospitals, convalescent homes, classes in sanitation and personal hygiene, care and upkeep of property, combating crime and juvenile delinquency, centers to aid Negro youth in preparing to meet stiff employment competition in science and industry.

N.A.A.C.P.

"It is then no accident that the N.A.A.C.P. is dubbed 'The National Association for the Agitation of Colored People.' The record speaks for itself. Millions for agitation; not one cent for those things that win respect and acclaim of other races and national groups" (45-6). "The main danger and handicap to the Negro is not the Southern school, but the persecution and hate complex the N.A.A.C.P. and the reds are trying to create" (50).

Some of the leaders of "human relations" societies should study what this patriotic Negro American has to say about "Modern Day Carpet baggers." Johnson writes: 'At the root of all the present day racial trouble is interference in the internal affairs of

Southern States by people not at all interested in an amicable settlement of any problems arising between Negro and white Americans. "This interference comes from organizations and individuals in the North seeking to use the Negro. Among them are found Communists, crypto-communists, fuzzy-headed, liberals, eggheads, pacifists, idealists, civil disobedience advocates, socialists, do-gooders, conniving politicians, self-seekers, muddleheaded humanitarians, addlebrained intellectuals, crackpots and plain meddlers. Like 'missionaries,' they descend on the South ostensibly to change or alter it to benefit the Negro" (51).

Manning Johnson, who has great pride in his race, observes: "Great Negro Americans such as Booker T. Washington and George Washington Carver should serve both as an inspiration and a reminder to the present and successive generations of Negro Americans that they too 'can make their lives sublime and in departing leave behind them footprints in the sands of time.'

"The great surge of progress of the Negro since slavery can be largely traced to the work and efforts of these two men, their supporters, their emulators and their followers. Theirs was a deep and abiding pride of race, a firm belief in the ability of their benighted people to rise above their past and eventually stand on an equal plane with all other races. Moreover, equality was to them, not just a catchword—the prattle of fools—but a living thing to be achieved only by DEMONSTRATED ABILITY" (56-7).

Lutherans Divided on King
Wave of Rioting Hits U.S. Cities
Schiotz Urges Lutherans to Back King
August 23, 1966

A wave of rioting that resembled guerrilla warfare swept across the United States in late July. Chicago, Cleveland and New York were among the cities hit.

The 4-day orgy of rioting on Chicago's explosive West Side cost two lives -- one a 14-year old Negro girl. Hundreds of persons were injured including 61 policemen.

Chicago police arrested 533 persons during the first three nights of rioting. Damage to property may run as high as 2 million dollars.

Dr. Fredrik Schiotz, president of the American Lutheran Church and the Lutheran World Federation, has called on members of the American Lutheran Church to rally behind Dr. Martin Luther King, Jr., and the Southern Leadership Conference as a way of avoiding violence.

Dr. Schiotz said, "Many well intentioned people have been critical of Dr. King, calling him a Communist." "The time for indulging in this luxury is over," the ALC president said. "It is time for all who believe in justice under law to pray for and speak well of the work of the Southern Christian Leadership Conference."

But Chicago's Mayor Richard J. Daley charged that the Chicago riots were due in great measure to staff members of Dr. Martin Luther King's Southern Christian Leadership Conference (SCLC).

The mayor's charge was made in a press conference on July 15 during which he also announced that Governor Otto Kerner had mobilized National Guardsmen to help the embattled police. Daley told newsmen that he has documented evidence that members of King's own SCLC staff in Chicago had actually inspired and instructed people in conducting racial violence.

Mayor Daley, when asked about possible links between the activities of King's staff and the disorders, stated that:

". . . surely some people who have come in here have been talking for the last year about violence, and how to conduct violence--and they are on his (King's) staff.

"They're responsible in great measure for the instructions that have been given in the training of youngsters.

"Who makes a Molotov cocktail? Someone has to be trained.

"People were in here training, and here are tapes and documentation, or anything else you want to show, that certain elements were in our city for no other purpose but to bring disorder to the streets of Chicago."

Violence Follows King

The mayor's accusation against King's staff was supported by Dr. J. H. Jackson, president of the 5.5 million-member National Baptist Convention, the nation's largest organized body of Negroes, and by other leaders. Dr. Jackson said: "I believe our young people are not vicious enough to attack a whole city. Some other forces are using these young people."

"Certain strangers" are in Chicago "to get youngsters to riot," Dr. Jackson added.

Joseph LeFevour, president of a Chicago policeman's association, criticized King's presence in Chicago. Lefevour said: "He (King) preaches non-violence, yet wherever he goes violence erupts."

Ernest R. Rather, president of an inter-racial civic organization, has urged King to leave Chicago and to go back to the South. Rather, a Negro public relations executive, said that some of Kings' statements during his current Chicago campaign "may have motivated the West Side riots" and that King actually may have planned his statements to have this effect.

Two days before the rioting erupted, King told a rally in Chicago's Soldiers Field: "This day we must decide to fill up the jails of Chicago, if necessary, in order to end slums."

On January 28, 1966, after meeting with Chicago's Police Superintendent O.W. Wilson, the Nobel peace Prize winner said:

"It may be necessary to engage in acts of civil disobedience (in Chicago) in order to call attention to specific problems. Often an individual has to break a particular law to obey a higher law, that of brotherhood and justice."

Police Superintendent Wilson, who had to dispatch 1000 policemen to the riot-torn West side area, has been critical of remarks by King concerning Chicago's alleged "police brutality."

The National Guard has been called out in Chicago on two occasions recently to put down racial riots in the same area. Approximately 4000 troops saw action in the latest riot.

Senator Frank J. Lausche (D., Ohio) told a Chicago audience on July 27, 1966 that "the rioting and looting in large metropolitan cities in past months are part of a national conspiracy executed by experts." Lausche added, in obvious reference to Martin Luther King, that this rioting "was generated and brought to the boiling point by those who are living in luxury by conducing so-called non-violent crusades."

Organize Teen Age Gangs

Columnists Robert Allen and Paul Scott reported recently that "lieutenants of King are contracting Chicago street gangs and bringing them into his civil rights movement to fight 'the power structure.'" They revealed that "an investigative report being circulated inside the Justice Department' indicates that "King plans to organize the teenage gangs into protest and marching groups in all major U.S. Cities if his Chicago experiment is a success."

King's organization is reported to be "studying the Buddhist use of street gangs in Saigon demonstrations."

The Southern Christian Leadership Conference and King have called on the United States government to abandon South Vietnam's Premier Nguyen Cao Ky and to consider withdrawing from the country altogether.

Rev. Albert Richard Sampson, a Baptist minister on King's staff, is in charge of organizing the youth gangs. Rev. Sampson is reported to be working with between 30 and 40 Chicago teenage gangs.

Members of King's staff held so-called workshops for youth gang members in Chicago prior to the rioting. Movies of the Watts riots were shown at these sessions.

Dr. King met last February in Chicago with Black Muslim leader Elijah Muhammad, who preaches that white men are "a race of devils." A spokesman for King said after the meeting that both men agreed that they had a "mutual area of concern" and would meet again.

The Chicago riots, according to Chicago's American (July 19, 1966) "appear to have been deliberately fanned and spread by the Revolutionary Action Movement (RAM)," a violent black nationalist subversive movement in the United States. RAM members follow the writings of Robert F. Williams, a Negro Communist expatriate, who has left the United States to take up residence in Red China.

Witt's SHURE Group

Robert F. Williams' book, NEGROES WITH GUNS, is included on the controversial "Negro History" bibliography printed and distributed by SHURE. Elmer E. Witt, executive director of the International Walther League, is chairman of SHURE. As indicated in LUTHERAN NEWS (May 16, 1966), this bibliography was distributed at SHURE's first open meeting following Witt's re-election as chairman and has created a stir among Lutherans. Witt was one of the three official Lutheran Church-Missouri Synod observers at last month's World Conference on Church and Society sponsored by the World Council of Churches in Geneva.

Witt's SHURE group has received Federal anti-poverty funds through its sub-group VISION for use in recruiting and training volunteers. It also has sponsored workshops and speeches by members of King's SCLC staff, including Rev. James Bevel and Albert A. Raby.

The LUTHERAN WITNESS, official organ of the Lutheran Church-Missouri Synod, referred to Martin Luther King on November 10, 1964 as "a committed Christian." it also claimed that "America has good reason to thank God that Dr. King is the man he is."

Leaders of the World Council of Churches advised King in a letter during the recent riots that "Christians belong in the midst of conflict and crises." They urged Christians to flinch "no longer from antagonism and violence."

This letter was signed by the general secretary-elect, Dr. Eugene Carson Blake; the present general secretary, Dr. W.A. Visser't Hooft; and conference presidents from eight countries.

William O. Walker, a Negro editor and the director of Ohio's industrial relations department, has placed part of the blame for the recent Cleveland riots on the white clergy. Walker said that white Protestant ministers working in Cleveland's slums "set up the Negro population for that other element all over America today that is ever ready to take advantage of a bad situation."

Evangelist Billy Graham recently appealed publicly to President Johnson to identify the groups inside America "who are teaching and advocating violence, training in guerrilla tactics and defying authority."

"The FBI and the President know who they (the extremist leaders) are and what they are up to. Now the people need to know," Graham added.

Dr. Graham further stated that "we are on the road to anarchy... In this country, and the symptoms are ominous and dangerous." He said that "our leaders should not ignore this threat any longer."

King's Critics

While prominent leaders of the World and National Council of Church have been ardent supporters of King, conservative theologians have charged that King denies such doctrines as the virgin birth of Christ and Christ's physical resurrection. Others have taken issue of King's support of civil disobedience.

George Schuyler, a Negro editor, has charged that the civil rights activities of King and other leaders have been "disastrous" to the American Negro. "He (King) made the Negro look ridiculous," said Schuyler. "He has produced the image of an impoverished, illiterate, undisciplined, and ignorant individual. This picture is simply not true."

J. Edgar Hoover, director of the FBI, has called King "the most notorious liar in the country." A St. LOUIS GLOBE DEMOCRAT staff writer said that "Martin Luther King Jr.'s civil rights group has worked jointly with the Southern Conference Educational Fund, Inc., a large Communist front organization, according to evidence forwarded to federal investigators in Washington" (December 28, 1963).

James S. Kemper, Jr., president of the Kemper Insurance group told the New York Mutual Agents Association, according to the October 4, 1965 U.S. NEWS AND WORLD REPORT: "More than any other single man, Dr. King is responsible for the development of mass crime in the civil-rights movement." Kemper said that "The spectacle of a Nobel Peace Prize sinner, supported by thousands of white and Negro clergymen, endorsing the breaking of any law is an open invitation to lawbreaking by anyone who chooses to do so."

Read King Not Luther

However, the Lutheran Church in America and leaders of the Lutheran Human Relations Association have endorsed King's program of civil disobedience. Rev. Ross F. Hidy, a clergyman of the Lutheran Church in America who is a member of the sponsoring committee of CHRISTIANITY TODAY'S World Congress on Evangelism, has been a prominent Lutheran supporter of King. The January 27, 1965 LUTHERAN, official organ of the LCA reported: "St. Paul, MINN.--Lutheran pastors should be more interested in reading everything by Martin Luther King than by Martin Luther, a California LCA pastor told a convocation of American Lutheran Church pastors here.

"They can also find a lot of penetrating theology in the writings of two other Negro authors, James Baldwin and Dick Gregory, said the Rev. Ross F. Hidy, pastor of St. Mark's Lutheran Church in San Francisco."

The January 28, 1965 LUTHERAN SENTINEL, official organ of the Evangelical Lutheran Church said that "This advice to be sure to read what Dr. Martin Luther King has written is not only nonsense. It is the sheerest blasphemy. For King, by his own documented statement, finds, like other so-called preachers of our day, no use of the blood atonement, the substitution atonement of Jesus. His interpretation of AGAPE, of the concept of charity, is apart from the love of the Good Shepherd that gave His life that we might live."

LUTHERAN NEWS wrote to King on December 16, 1964:

> The December 30, 1963, edition of the Dow Jones weekly NATIONAL OBSERVER published an article "The Essence Is Love--The Theology of Martin Luther King." Concerning your theology it said:
>
> "To him the traditional issues of theology--sin and salvation, the divinity of Christ, His virgin birth, His bodily resurrection--are peripheral. Love is central."
>
> "But his sermons contain no hard preaching on heaven and Hell, no preoccupation with sin and salvation."
>
> "He rejects, for example, the idea that men are innately sinners."
>
> "But Dr. King rejects the virgin birth of Christ as a literal fact. The early Christians, he says, had noticed that moral uniqueness of Jesus; to make this uniqueness appear plausible, they devised a mythological story of Jesus' biological uniqueness."
>
> Could you kindly tell me whether the NATIONAL OBSERVER has correctly represented your theology? Have you or the Southern Christian Leadership conference sent any protest to the NATIONAL OBSERVER?--

The letter was sent to both the headquarters of the Southern Christina Leadership Conference and to King's church in Atlanta but no reply was received. NATIONAL OBSERVER informed LUTHERAN NEWS: "We have received no comments, either favorable or unfavorable from Martin Luther King or any of his associates regarding this story."

The NATIONAL OBSERVER'S statements on Kings' theology were repeated in a 1965 NATIONAL OBSERVER NEWSBOOK titled RELIGION IN ACTION, 128-131.

Black and Conservative
Christian News, October 3, 1966

BLACK AND CONSERVATIVE. By George S. Schuyler. New Rochelle, New York; Arlington House Publishers, 1966. 362 pages. $5.95.

BLACK AND CONSERVATIVE is the autobiography of George S. Schuyler, a columnist for the PITTSBURGH COURIER and a contributor to the NORTH AMERICAN NEWSPAPER ALLIANCE, a syndicate that serves hundreds of dailies.

Schuyler, who began his active political life as a member of the Socialist Party in 1921 and has been a successful Negro journalist for more than 40 years, in his autobiography presses hard for an answer to this question: "Why has the Liberal press rendered millions of successful Negroes completely invisible? Why have the networks failed to acknowledge this part of our Negro population? People who want no government handouts... Need no charity. Negro people who, without sit-ins and marches and bloody riots, have long ago shown that they can be as 'equal' as anybody."

Referring to Schuyler, H.L. Mencken wrote in 1945: "I am more and more convinced that he is the most competent editorial writer in this great Free Republic." The publishers of BLACK AND CONSERVATIVE state: "The implicit message of George

Schuyler's life is heartening for all men of good will. He shows us how a Negro can make his way without favors, without condescension, without bitterness. And he shows us how a man can be both BLACK AND CONSERVATIVE."

Schuyler is not overly impressed with the "intellectuals" of our day. He writes: "During my time I have rubbed shoulders with hundreds of the best known 'intellectuals' in America and abroad, conversed with them, read their writings and juggled their theories, and in retrospect it is appalling how downright wrong so many have been and still are. At least the poor whom they chide for not reading more have led nobody astray!" (102).

The Negro journalist, who was aware of the spreading infection of Communist thought in education and government during the '30s, wrote on September 9, 1939, just a few days after the invasion of Poland: "The sudden waltzing together of Hitler and Stalin has shocked the liberals and starry-eyed fellow travelers, and greatly embarrassed the naïve majority of Communists, but it left me quite calm and chuckling.

"I have been saying all along that there is no difference between Fascism and Communism, and this position has brought shrill and frothy protestations from Comrades and their stooges, especially from the black Reds parked on the Communist payroll. And yet nothing has been more obvious to an impartial and sensible observer" (249).

Martin Luther King

We wholeheartedly recommend this book for such Lutherans as Dr. Fredrik Schiotz, president of the Lutheran World Federation, the editors of the LUTHERAN WITNESS, some members of the faculty of Concordia Seminary, St. Louis, officials of The Lutheran Human Relations Association of America, and the social action leaders of the Lutheran Church in America. These Lutheran officials are among those who believe the Church ought to support such radical agitators as Martin Luther King. Schulyer writes after more than 40 years of first hand experience: "From the beginning of the so-called Negro Revolution and the insane antics identified with it, I had taken the same position editorially and in my columns that I had through the years. I had opposed all of the Marchers on Washington and other mob demonstrations, recognizing them as part of the Red techniques of agitation, infiltration, and subversion. This was indicated by the fact that invariably they were proposed, incited, managed, and led by professional collectivist agitators, whose only interest in the workers was to exploit them; backed by the proliferation of 'liberals' of position and influence who always run interference for them by 'explaining' and defending their course.

"I had consistently warned Negroes for forty years that their miseries could not be alleviated in any way by mob action, nuisance provocations, and civil disobedience. The waving of empty pistols, accompanied by insults imprecations, and denunciations of white people, generally and specifically, was quite futile, and would simply create what Negroes could not afford: that is to say, more enemies. Week after week I pressed the point (as I had since 1923). But under the influence of their white (or Red) mentors, a contaminated Negro leadership snapped at the Communist bait, received the support of white 'liberal' charting a course of disaster, and like pied pipers led the lunatic fringe astray" (341-2).

According to Schuyler, "the Communist conspiracy" "touches millions who do not recognize its touch and who derisively deny being dupes" (347). Schyler, who has worked and lived in Harlem, blamed the 1964 Harlem race riots "on the incessant incitement of civil rights leaders" (348). When Dr. Martin Luther King was awarded the Nobel Peace Prize Schuyler "held that King was quite undeserving of any prize as an apostle of peace, either globally or domestically; that his entire activity was to the contrary" (350).

Schyler, who is no Uncle Tom, concludes: "Relegating spurious racism to limbo, in our future America we need to stress the importance of the individual of whatever color... We need to strive to become one people in our resolution, determination, and achievement instead of two peoples, colored and white" (352).

The Christian, of course, should recognize that it is only the saving Gospel of Jesus Christ which first restores peace with God and then establishes real peace between men of all races. Only in Christ Jesus are we all one.

King and the WCC
Christian News, December 11, 1967

The World Council of Churches has again shown that it is completely in the control of theological modernists. WCC officials have asked Dr. Martin Luther King to deliver the sermon at the opening worship service at the Fourth Assembly of the WCC on July 4, 1968 in Uppsala, Sweden.

King is a theological modernist. He considers such Christian doctrines as the virgin birth and physical resurrection of Christ open questions. He does not believe Christians have to accept such doctrines. King's Christ is not the Christ of Holy Scripture and the historic Christian faith. His Christ is not the second person in the Holy Trinity, true God and true man, who gave His life as a ransom for the sins of all men. In spite of his unbelief, King has the enthusiastic backing of such Lutheran liberals as Dr. Fredrik Schiotz, leaders of the Lutheran Human Relations Association, and the members of the staff of the LUTHERAN WITNESS. The Lutheran Church-Missouri Synod's official organ claims King is a "committed Christian" for whom we should be thankful. Evidently a "committed Christian" doesn't have to confess the physical resurrection of Christ.

Just a few months ago King said the United States was the greatest purveyor of violence in the world. The fact that the WCC can select as a worship leader a theological modernist, who constantly minimizes the menace of Communism and makes untruthful statements about the United States, should convince all Christians that they should sever ties with the WCC.

Both the Lutheran Church in America and the American Lutheran Church are members and active supporters of the WCC. If The Lutheran Church—Missouri Synod follows the lead of its officials and declares altar and pulpit fellowship with the ALC, then it won't be long before the Missouri Synod is also a member of the WCC. Then the entire Missouri Synod can join in worship with such modernists as King. Some of Missouri's liberals are already worshipping with him.

Reverend Martin Luther King
April 8, 1968
Editorial

Dr. Martin Luther King was shot and killed by a sniper last Thursday evening in Memphis, Tennessee.

Every True Christian and loyal American, whether he agrees with Dr. King's program of civil disobedience or not, will deplore this act of violence. They will sincerely sympathize with his family. As President Johnson said shortly after Dr. King's death, "we can achieve nothing by LAWLESSNESS, divisiveness."

Dr. King had the support of many churches and large numbers of clergymen. Last month the Department of Social Justice of the National Council of Churches and Church of the Brethren, Lutheran, Roman Catholic, and other clergymen in the Washington D.C. area announced support of Dr. Kings' Poor People's Campaign which was to begin this month.

Two years ago Dr. Fredrik Schiotz, president of the American Lutheran Church and Lutheran World Federation, urged Lutherans to back Dr. King. The LUTHERAN WITNESS, official organ of The Lutheran Church-Missouri Synod, referred to Dr. King as a "committed Christian" and said that "America has good reason to thank God that Dr. King is the man he is – wise, able, humble, inspired and moved by a spirit that has its roots in the Gospel of reconciliation" (November 10, 1964). Shortly after violence broke out in Memphis late last month during a demonstration by Dr. King, we asked Dr. Schiotz and the LUTHERAN WITNESS whether they still supported Dr. King. We have not yet received an answer to these inquiries.

> **Americans certainly have the right to participate in peaceful law-abiding demonstrations, but it is unfortunate that Dr. King and his associates elected not to pay any attention to a temporary injunction restraining them from leading a mass march in Memphis which was scheduled for today.**

We have always shared Dr. King's concern for the Negro and the poor. However, we could not agree with him when he branded the United States as "the greatest purveyor of violence in the world today" and accused our nation of "using poison water to kill a million acres of crops of the Vietnam people." We don't believe that Dr. King was telling the truth when he said that "U.S. soldiers may have killed a million South Vietnamese civilians—mostly children." Just a few days before Dr. King was shot, Congressman John M. Ashbrook noted in the April 1 CONGRESSIONAL RECORD that "last year I outlined the various statements of Reverend King which more than gave credibility to the charge by J. Edgar Hoover that he was the Nation's 'most notorious liar.'" Congressman Ashbrook noted that Dr. King had again twisted the truth during a speech he gave last month extolling the late Negro communist W.E.B. Dubois (CONGRESSIONAL RECORD, E 2506-2507).

Not all those who took issue with Dr. King can be accused of racism. After violence broke out in Memphis just a few days prior to Dr. King's death, responsible voices urged him to reconsider leading massive demonstrations. THE ST. LOUIS POST DISPATCH, which has long been a champion of Dr. King, said that the time had come to reconsider massive demonstrations. It noted IF the leaders of nonviolence cannot control violence, they have lost their basic tactic. If they know in advance that they cannot keep control, they are courting violence."

We had intended to reprint several items in this issue from last week's CONGRESSIONAL RECORD and an editorial and cartoon from THE ST. LOUIS GLOBE DEMOCRAT on Dr. King. However, now we will merely note that our primary objection to Dr. King was always theological.

We believe Dr. King's program of civil disobedience is contrary to Holy Scripture (Romans 13) and we regret that he refused to affirm such Christian doctrines as original sin, the full deity of Jesus Christ, and Christ's Virgin Birth and Resurrection.

We pray that prior to his death Dr. King repudiated his anti-Christian theology and came to a saving knowledge of Jesus Christ. This Christ alone breaks down all barriers between rich and poor, black and white. He is the world's only hope and all those, regardless of their color, who recognize their sin and place all their confidence in Christ's saving merits can be assured of eternal life in heaven. Only Jesus Christ can and did promise: "I am the resurrection, and the life; he who believes in Me shall live even if he dies, and everyone who lives and believes in Me shall never die" (John 11:25-26). Every Christian clergyman whose heart is filled with Christian love for all men will dedicate his life to proclaiming this Christ, the Christ whose glorious resurrection we celebrate this coming Sunday.

King and The King of Kings
April 15, 1968

Those who spoke at Dr. Martin Luther King's funeral last Tuesday missed a tremendous opportunity to exalt the KING OF KINGS, Jesus Christ, the world's only Savior from sin and eternal damnation. Dr. King was praised but not the KING OF KINGS. Dr. King was quoted more than the KING OF KINGS.

The funeral of every true Christian should stress that the deceased, regardless of how famous he may have been, was a sinner and in need of God's grace in Christ Jesus. No one who spoke at Dr. Martin Luther King's funeral mentioned that Dr. King confessed his sin and trusted only in the merits of the KING OF KINGS for eternal life.

Scores of our nation's top leaders were present at Dr. King's funeral. Millions upon millions throughout our nation and in other countries watched and listened to the funeral on television and radio. Dr. King's closest associates had a tremendous opportunity to present a real Christian testimony, but they failed to testify to the KING OF KINGS.

During the funeral a portion of a sermon King preached just a few weeks ago was played. Dr. King said in this sermon that at his funeral he didn't want anyone to mention his Nobel Peace Prize or the 300 and more other awards he has been given. However, Dr. King then went on to say that at his funeral it should be mentioned that he tried to love and serve humanity and that he tried to "make of the old world a new world." Dr. King said nothing about empha-

sizing his own sinfulness and God's grace. He did not say that at his funeral THE KING OF KINGS alone should be exalted.

Dr. King's death was said to be "one of the darkest hours in the history of all mankind." Dr. King was referred to as a "20th Century prophet" who was filled with the "philosophy of non-violence." He was hailed as "one of history's truest representatives" of God's will and it was stated by one of his associates that "like Jesus he had to die as a martyr for a cause." Dr. King's death was termed a "sacrificial death."

Dr. Harold DeWolf, Dr. King's mentor and major professor at Boston University School of Theology, delivered the funeral tribute. Dr. DeWolf frequently marched with Dr. King and spent many hours counseling Dr. King and claimed that he knew the innermost thoughts of the assassinated civil rights leader. DeWolf's tribute praised Dr. King but not the KING OF KINGS.

We hardly expected anything more from Dr. DeWolf, a prominent liberal theologian. Dr. DeWolf's Christ is not the KING OF KINGS, the second person in the Holy Trinity. Dr. King's mentor writes in his THE CASE FOR THEOLOGY IN LIBERAL PERSPECTIVE that "The Bible itself is by no means infallible. In it are to be found the erring words of men as well as the authoritative word of God. . ." (47). The liberal professor claims that the demonology of the New Testament is best regarded "as belonging merely to the pseudoscience of the first century, part of the erroneous human culture to which and through which the revelation came, and not as part of the revelation itself" (94). DeWolf, like King, casts doubt on the virgin birth of Christ (61) and says that "certainly we ought to repudiate the notion that God is unwilling to forgive any sin until blood has been spilled as propitiation. . . This is not a legal transaction required by God, in which God demanded his pound of flesh and took it from Christ instead of us" (77). De Wolf does not believe in the Christian God, the Holy Trinity (104 ff.).

He says that the Christian doctrine of tri-personality in unity is unchristian, unthinkable, and irrational mystery-mongering (104 ff.). There appears to be little difference between Dr. De Wolf's theology and the theological views of his most famous student. (See "THE THEOLOGY OF MARTIN LUTHER KING," p. 7).

Rabbi Abraham Heschel, a close friend of Dr. King, read Isaiah 53 during the funeral service at Morehouse College. Those who believe in the true message of the Old Testament recognize that Isaiah was here speaking about Jesus Christ, the God-Man who gave his life for the sins of all men. Heschel, however, rejects the God of both the Old and New Testament, and believes that Isaiah's words could just as well be applied to Dr. King as the KING OF KINGS, Jesus Christ. The Christian does not believe that Dr. King's death was a sacrificial death for the sins of anyone. Only the death of the KING OF KINGS was a vicarious satisfaction for the sins of the entire world. Jesus and no one else paid the ransom to free all men, black and white, from sin and eternal death.

Dr. Franklin Clark Fry, president of the Lutheran Church in America, participated in the funeral service by reading Matthew 3:3-12. The eulogy was delivered by Dr. Benjamin Mays who said that the "American people are in part responsible for Dr. King's death" and that the "Memphis officials must bear some of the guilt" for Dr. King's death. We don't believe all Americans are any more responsible for Dr. King's death than all Negroes are responsible for the murder and looting that has been going on in our nation. Those who commit the murders are responsible. Every true Christian and every loyal American deplores the assassination of Dr. King and sincerely sympathizes with his family. Such wild accusations as were made by Dr. Mays during the funeral eulogy do not help relations between white and black. He should have preached about the resurrected Christ, the Christ who alone can establish true harmony between white and black. The service closed with the singing of WE SHALL OVERCOME rather than with a Christian hymn which exalts the resurrected KING OF KINGS.

Only those, regardless of their color, who confess that they are sinners and believe that Jesus Christ is the resurrected Son of God will be with Christ in Heaven. Those who depend upon their own works and good life and who reject the Resurrected KING OF KINGS will be lost forever. THE KING OF KINGS alone should be at the center of every Christian funeral. While some of the hymns sung at Dr. King's funeral praised the KING OF KINGS and undoubtedly expressed the true Christian faith of many of those who sang them, those who spoke at Dr. King's funeral praised the wrong King.

May God grant that prior to his death Dr. King repudiated the anti-Christian theology of his mentor Dr. DeWolf and his own liberal theological views and that he truly confessed the words of one of the hymns sung at the morning funeral service:

> When I survey the wondrous cross
> On which the Prince of Glory died,
> My richest gain I count but loss
> And pour contempt on all my pride.
>
> Forbid it, Lord, that I should boast
> Save in the death of Christ, my God;
> All the vain things that charm me most,
> I sacrifice them to His blood.

A Cool Corrective
House Divided—The Life and Legacy of Martin Luther King
Christian News, October 14, 1968

(Review Article)
HOUSE DIVIDED – THE LIFE AND LEGACY OF MARTIN LUTHER KING. By Lionel Lokos. Arlington House: New Rochelle, New York, 81 Centre Street, 10801. October 26, 1968. 57 pages. $6.95.

Lionel Lokos, who is no racist or segregationists, in HOUSE DIVIDED has provided a cool corrective to the propaganda surrounding one of today's most emotional issues. The author, who was formerly a liberal Democrat, says: "I am writing this book not as a liberal, but as a conservative; not as a WASP, but as a Jew, and something of a rugged individualist; not as a champion of an American apartheid, but as one who now lives in a heavily integrated neighborhood; not as a long distance onlooker, but as one who has been in Harlem, and, more than that, part of whose family once lived and worked in Harlem" (12).

HOUSE DIVIDED is not another book hastily published following the assassination of Dr. Martin Luther King, Jr. The more than 2500 footnotes indicate that the author has carefully researched his subject. Liberal defenders of King will have a difficult time challenging this book. The author quotes from many of King's own writings and from sources generally favorable to King, such as THE NEW YORK TIMES.

Lokos notes that "Martin Luther King had a unique facility for opposing riots in the aggregate, and yet somehow, in some way, for some reason, excusing the individual rioters" (52-53). He quotes King as stating: "an unjust law is no law…the individual who discovers on the basis of conscience that a law is unjust, and is willing in a peaceful sense to disobey the unjust law and willingly and voluntarily suffers the consequences is expressing the highest respect for the law" (76).

After noting how King actually stole some private property, Lokos writes: "In his orations on civil disobedience, King acknowledged an obligation to comply with 'the moral law of the universe.' Among the most solemn of these are the Ten Commandments, but this in no way deterred King from elbowing the Decalogue aside to suit his convenience in Chicago. Certainly when Martin Luther King boldly walked right in and commandeered a slum dwelling, he was bending, if not breaking, the commandment: 'Thou Shalt Not Steal'" (230).

The author observes: "In his takeover of the slum dwelling, King was not fighting a burly Jim Clark, but an 81-year-old invalid who was confined to his home. The octogenarian landlord, John Bender, said that the building had not been profitable, and told the press that he would be willing to GIVE the building to King if he would take over the mortgage. King did not accept the offer" (231). Lokos adds: "While King asserted the right to receive the rent moneys, the landlord was still being charged with all the legal and financial responsibilities for the dwelling" (231).

J. Edgar Hoover, a man not given to hysteria, called King "the most notorious liar in the country." Lokos presents facts which show that King, who has been almost canonized by liberal churchmen, did not always tell the truth. King lied about his country when he said that the United States was the "greatest purveyor of violence in the world today" (380). He lied about our soldiers when he said that the South Vietnamese "watch as we poison their water, as we kill a million acres of their crops. They must weep as the bull dozers roar through their areas preparing to destroy the precious trees. They wander into the hospitals with at least 20 casualties from American fire-power for one Viet Cong-inflicted injury. So far we may have killed a million of them—mostly children" (38). King lied about U.S. soldiers when he asked: "What do they (the peasants) think as we test out our latest weapons on them, just as the Germans tested out new medicine and new tortures in the concentration camps of Europe?" (380).

In spite of the fact that King glorified the Communist rulers of Hanoi and lied about U.S. soldiers in Vietnam, liberal clergymen continue to praise this "notorious liar." Even the liberal WASHINGTON POST showed more sense than many clergymen when it noted that King "all but exonerated the Hanoi government and the Viet Cong for their roles in the war" (382). Lokos quotes a Presidential aide as shouting: "My God, King has given a speech on Vietnam that goes right down the Commie line!" (382).

According to the author, "The civil disobedience glorified by Martin Luther King – the concept that each man had the right to put a kind of Good Housekeeping Seal of Approval on laws that met with his favor, and reserve the right to disobey 'unjust' laws or even 'unjust' officers of the law – was more than enough to kindle the spark of rebellion, if not revolution among, young militants who simply stopped turning the other cheek, and started battling those who had been called their oppressors. It was King who, by the very nature of nonviolent dynamics, was compelled to FORCE reluctant police to arrest him. It was King who raised the cry of police brutality in the South, and thereafter made EVERY police action in EVERY ghetto racially suspect. As surely as the child is father to the man, non-violent resistance in the South sired the violent resistance in the North" (458).

The scholarly author says in his last chapter on "The Legacy of Martin Luther King:" "In the days following the tragic death of Martin Luther King, much was said about the legacy he left his country. Some called it a legacy of peace. For myself, I am perfectly willing to grant his brilliance, his basic sincerity, his charismatic effect upon perhaps hundreds of thousands of Americans – and still regretfully conclude that primarily Martin Luther King left his country a legacy of lawlessness. His concept of civil disobedience was exquisitely embroidered with 'love' and 'good will,' but stripped to its essentials it was the concept that every man could be his own judge and jury and legislator – that no law was binding upon any American unless he could 'conscientiously' obey it" (460). The author adds: "King's first act of civil disobedience created the first small crack in the wall of law enforcement. Each succeeding act of civil disobedience widened that crack in the wall, and weakened its foundations. Today, for the second time in our history, America is a house divided – but this time the division is not between freedom and slavery, but between law and lawlessness. In effect, these are two biracial societies, not physically separated, but often dwelling side by side in the same cities, the same neighborhoods, even the same families.

"Our house is divided for all the world to see, and now we are compelled to see it as well. We see it in the fanatical excesses of the anti-Vietnam movement. We see it in colleges where student body militants virtually seize power from the school administration. We see it in the rantings and ravings of Stokely Carmichael, who was practically permitted to incite the sacking of the nation's capital without spending so much as a day in prison. We see all this and more, and we know that the forces of law and order are on the defensive – and losing more and more precious ground each day to the forces of a civil disobedience, until it borders on anarchy. This is all part of the unhappy legacy left us by Martin Luther King – the doctrine that a man can invoke beliefs of conscience to place himself above the law. It is our American nightmare, and could some day be the death of our country and our democracy.

"It is only a short step from the doctrine of civil disobedience to the criminal disobedience of the Negro riots. The more articulate rioters would probably say that they are simply invoking their right to disobey 'unjust' policemen, exacting retribution from 'unjust' storekeepers, and in general, declining to cooperate with 'an unjust society.' The liberal's protest that the rioters are being violent, while Martin Luther King was nonviolent, wholly misses the point. Once you permit a man to disobey laws he dislikes, you cannot later disapprove of the FORM that disobedience takes or the MOTIVATION behind it" (461-462).

The author does not share the enthusiasm liberal and even some naïve conservative clergymen have shown for the Report of the National Advisory Commission on Civil Disorders. He writes: "Many liberals who long ago decided that 'God Is Dead' now worship a new Deity – the Report of the National Advisory Commission on Civil Disorders. This is their Holy Writ and they genuflect at its biracial shrine in their words, in their actions, and in the pressures they exert on local police to observe its dogma. To question the report has become an all but unforgivable blasphemy, which subjects the apostate to charges of 'racism,' 'backlash,' or worse. But as a matter of conscience, the author must live dangerously and express his view that there is little in the U.S. Riot Commission Report to command confidence" (464).

Lokos says that "what the Negroes need is something that no government, no people, no open-end checkbook can give them. They need self-respect, self-esteem, a sense of PERSONAL worth and PERSONAL achievement. It cannot be handed down by the courts. It must come from within the minds and hearts of some 22 million Negroes" (476).

Again it should be noted that Lokos is not a racist or a segregationist. He recognizes that King had some legitimate concerns. The publisher notes that the author "writes not in a spirit of hatred, or even anger, but rather in a spirit of sorrow at the tragedy that has fallen upon this nation because of false counsel." We suggest that particularly clergymen, who have been misled by the liberal propaganda concerning King, read this book.

While we generally agree with the author and similarly deplore King's civil disobedience, we primarily took issue with King because of his liberal Christ-denying theology. King, who posed as a Christian clergyman, rejected the historic Christian faith. His greatest failure as one who claimed to be a Christian clergyman was that he did not proclaim the saving Gospel of Jesus Christ, the only real message which can bring true peace into the hearts of all men regardless of their color.

Dr. King condemned the U.S. government as the "greatest purveyor of violence in the world today." Dr. King lied about U.S. soldiers when he said that the South Vietnamese "watch as we poison their water, as we kill a million acres of their crops…

Ministerial Students and Their Role in Community
By Herman Otten
Concordia Senior College, Ft. Wayne, Indiana
May 12, 1969 (Excerpt)
Christian News, June, 1969

Martin Luther King

Martin Luther King stated during an address at Riverside Church in New York on April 4, 1967 that America is "the greatest purveyor of violence in the world today." The Communist press gave considerable publicity to King's 1967 address in Riverside church. This year the April 13 issue of the Communist DAILY WORLD again quoted King as saying during this address: "It is worth noting that Abraham Lincoln warmly welcomed the support of Karl Marx during the Civil War and corresponded with him freely." The Communist press has been playing up this statement by King .The March 3, 1968 Communist WORKER quotes King as making the same statement about Marx and Lincoln. How much truth is there to this warm welcome King, whom FBI Director J. Edgar Hoover referred to as the nation's "most notorious liar," maintained Lincoln gave to the support of Karl Marx?

Following the re-election of Abraham Lincoln in 1964, the Central Council of the International Workingmen's Association sent a congratulatory address to Lincoln. Carl Sandburg in the WAR YEARS, vol. 3, p. 579, refers to this address as the work of Karl Marx. It was forwarded through Charles Francis Adams, the United States Minister in London, and on January 31, 1965, its receipt by Lincoln was acknowledged by Adams. THE COLLECTRED WORKS OF ABRAHAM LINCOLN (New Brunswick, Rutgers University Press, 1955) does not include or refer to any letter written by Lincoln to Marx. [11]

Father Daniel Lyons recently wrote in TWIN CIRCLE: "Another way in which the cause of religion and civil rights is hurt is when clergymen active in civil rights espouse the cause of the Far Left and even Communism. I was shocked when I heard Dr. Martin Luther King take the side of the Viet Cong. I sat dumbfounded in the Riverside Church in New York City two years ago as Dr. King condemned the United States as 'the greatest purveyor of violence in the world today' – not Moscow and Peking, but the United States. He praised Ho Chi Minh as an independent democratic leader, 'the only true leader' of the Vietnamese. 'We may have killed a million, mostly children,' he went on recklessly. He admitted the next day he got his research from Ramparts Magazine, now happily defunct. There was no need for him to espouse the cause of Communism, but he did. 'Only Marxism has the revolutionary spirit,' he said, and he urged that we 'get on the right side of the world revolution.' The late Dr. Martin Luther King alienated right-thinking people with his anti-American and pro-Communist remarks. In doing so he damaged the cause of civil rights severely. Responsible people lost confidence in him."

"I was also disappointed when Father James Groppi of Milwaukee described the Viet Cong terrorists as the true heroes in Vietnam, 'like the Revolutionary soldiers in 1776.' Stokely Carmichael, he said, is 'like Patrick Henry or Nathan Hale.' Father Groppi must know that Stokely identifies himself with Castro. He knows that Stokely urges Negroes 'to kill some white cops. . . There's not a right or wrong about killing. It's a matter of who has the power. . . It will be necessary to attack police stations and to kill policemen,' Stokely says." [12]

Every ministerial student, who may be tempted to follow the kind of civil disobedience urged by Dr. King, should recognize that King did not accept such Christian doctrines as the virgin birth and physical resurrection of Christ. The NATIONAL OBSERVER noted on the basis of an interview with Dr. King that to King "the traditional issues of theology – sin and salvation, the divinity of Christ, His virgin birth, His bodily resurrection are peripheral. Love is central." "He rejects, for example, the idea that men are innately sinners." "Dr. King rejects the virgin birth of Christ as a literal fact."[13]

When we wrote to the NATIONAL OBSERVER to find out whether any protests had been raised by Dr. King or his staff against the article, the paper replied: "We have received no comments, either favorable or unfavorable, from Martin Luther King or any of his associates regarding the story." We asked both Dr. King and the Southern Christian Leadership Conference about the article but did not receive any reply. If you study King's writings you will not find in them any clear affirmation of the Christian faith.

Rev. Uriah Fields, a black churchman who served as Dr. King's secretary during the early stages of the Montgomery bus boycott, wrote in the AMERICAN CHALLENGER that "King helps to advance Communism. He is surrounded with Communists. This is a major reason why I severed my relationship with him during the fifties. He is soft on Communism. I do not believe that he is a Communist or a Christian, for that matter.

"King's commitment to anti-American conspirators accounts for his position and outrageous anti-American pronouncements he made on Vietnam. Recently, he branded the U.S. 'the greatest purveyor of violence in the world today,' accused it of 'using poison water to kill a million acres of the crops of the Vietnam people' and asserted that 'U.S. soldiers may have killed South Vietnamese civilians – mostly children.'" [14] A committed Christian does not tell lies about the United States and its soldiers.

Julia Brown, a Negro and a former undercover agent for the FBI, writes in her discussion of the Watts riot in I TESTIFY: "Martin Luther King whom the Communists say heads the 'civil rights' revolution has sparked such insurrection under the guise of peace and non-violence. King is publicized on every occasion, put on television programs and on university platforms to stir hate against the respectable Negro people who are law abiding citizens, and who speak out against his kind."[15]

Rev. C. Fain Kyle, one of the evangelical Negro clergyman who opposed Dr. King, wrote to King in 1964 that "You are misleading God's people through false teaching with regard to what they should do in order to obtain for themselves equality and civil rights; . . . you are continually handling the Word of God deceitfully in your madness and folly to play and prey upon the unlearned, inexperienced and emotional type of both races for self aggrandizement; . . . you are reaping a great harvest from those who are gullible by promising them liberty."

George Schuyler, a Negro writer for the North American newspaper Alliance, wrote in his column shortly after King's tragic assassination; "The goal of the overwhelming majority of American Negroes is middle-class co-existence. Millions have obtained that status and more are doing so all the time. There is lessening economic discrimination and everywhere they wish to vote, they are doing so. It will not speed the process to continue tactics of harassment and annoyance, but may well cause retrogression in race relations to the disadvantage of all. Dr. King, tragically, never learned this. His followers had better."

If you are surprised that there were so many responsible Negroes who took issue with Dr. King's tactics and even his theology, then I suggest you read some of the books by the conservative Negroes I have mentioned.[16] If the ministerial student wants to be properly prepared for his role in their community he shouldn't limit his reading to just those books recommended by some liberal professors. I also suggest that you take the time to discuss the race problems with some ordinary hardworking Negroes.

Some of those who print our paper are Negroes. They had little use for the tactics of Martin Luther King. Just after I participated in Valparaiso University's WEEK OF CHALLENGE last year, I was taken from one Chicago airport to the other by a Negro taxicab driver. We soon became involved in a discussion of the riots in Chicago and Dr. King. This taxicab driver, as I recall, had at least a half dozen children he was trying to get through school. He deplored the tactics of Dr. King which he claimed actually helped to agitate some of the rioters. He rightly noted that King was actually guilty of breaking the law when he took over a Chicago tenement from an elderly sick landlord. He claimed that jobs were available for most of those who truly wanted to work but that too many had been led to believe that the government owes them a living. He didn't like war but he was proud to have a son standing up for his country in Korea. I didn't do too much talking because I wanted to learn from him, but as we parted I couldn't help but wish that such an ordinary black man could have addressed the students at Valpo. They would have heard more common sense from him than from most of the speakers they had during their WEEK OF CHALLENGE, a number of who were supposed to be experts on the racial revolution.

Footnotes

[11] See the "Martin Luther King: Master of Deceit" in the April 1, 1968 CONGRESSIONAL RECORD. Reproduced in the APRIL 15, 1968 CHRISTIAN NEWS.

[12] TWIN CIRCLE, April 13, 1969.

[13] "The Theology of Martin Luther King," NATIONAL OBSERVER, December 30, 1963. Reprinted in the April 15, 1968 CHRISTIAN NEWS.

[14] AMERICAN CHALLENGER, March, 1968. See "Idolatrous Praise," CHRISTIAN NEWS, April 15, 1968, 6.

[15] Julia Brown, I TESTIFY (Belmont, Mass.: Western Islands) 281.

[16] George S. Schuyler, BLACK AND CONSERVATIVE (New Rochelle, New York: Arlington House). Howard O. Jones, FOR THIS TIME (Chicago: Moody Press). Tom Skinner, BLACK AND FREE (Grand Rapids, Michigan: Zondervan). Julia Brown, I TESTIFY (Belmont, Mass.: Western Islands).

King and Fosdick
Christian News, April 3, 1978

Baptist Preachers with Social Consciousness. A Comparative Study of Martin Luther King and Harry Emerson Fosdick. Ardmore, Pa.; Dorance & Company, 35 Cricket Terrace 19003. 1978. 69 pages. $5.00.

Dr. Julius Scruggs has been the pastor of various Baptist churches and has been active in programs of the N.A.A.C.P., the Urban League and P.U.S.H. (People United to Save Humanity). He prepares **The Teacher**, a Sunday school quarterly published by the National Baptist Convention.

Dr. Scruggs says in his conclusion: "Harry Emerson Fosdick and Martin Luther King Jr., were decades apart in age, but extremely close in ideas. . . They were shaped and influenced by similar ideologies: evangelical liberalism, personalism, the Social Gospel Movement, and the ideology of Gandhi" (62).

Scruggs writes: "Just as men today search the pages of antiquity to study Socrates, Plato, Aristotle, Augustine, Martin Luther, and others, so will generations now and to come seek a deeper knowledge of Harry Emerson Fosdick and Martin Luther King, Jr. These two men will remain significant because they scratched where people itched.

"In an article in **Religion in Life**, Ralph Sockman summed up Fosdick's ministry in these revealing words: 'He has helped to make religion intellectually respected, socially responsible, and spiritually redemptive.' The **Atlanta Constitution** boldly printed: '...the greatest preacher in America during the past hundred years is Dr. Harry Emerson Fosdick'" (63). Scruggs evidently agrees. He adds: "Upon King's death, Rev. Eugene Carson Blake, general secretary of the World Council of Churches, wrote: 'By international consensus Dr. King was first citizen of the world. In the United States he was a main hope for a tortured nation'" (64).

Professor John Killinger of Vanderbilt Divinity School says in this book's introduction: "Nor can I think of either Fosdick or King without thinking of the other. That is perhaps the most surprising thing. Before Dr. Scrugg's work, it was easy enough to regard either of them alone. But now I see them as belonging to the same continuum" (viii). Scruggs says that "the stream of evangelical liberalism flowing through Fosdick and King was fundamentally the same.

"The social awareness of both King and Fosdick was also tremendously influenced by Walter Rauschenbusch and the Social Gospel Movement" (xiv). "….Gandhi, the Indian saint, influenced King tremendously and Fosdick to a lesser degree. Gandhi was Fosdick's hero and King's strategist" (xiv).

Scruggs quotes King as saying: "My liberal leaning may root back to the great imprint that many liberal theologians have left upon me and to my ever present desire to be optimistic about human nature." "Liberalism provided me with an intellectual satisfaction I had never found in fundamentalism…there are aspects of liberalism that I hope to cherish always; its devotion to the search for truth, its insistence on an open and analytical mind, and its refusal to abandon the best lights of reason. The contribution of liberalism to the philological-historical criticism of biblical literature has been of immeasurable value and should be defended with religious and scientific passion" (17).

According to the author, "It is easy to discern from both Fosdick and King that their embracing liberalism came as a result of their dissatisfaction with fundamentalism. Let us therefore look at what fundamentalism advocates in comparison and contrast to liberalism-especially evangelical liberalism.

"In its simplest form fundamentalism can be reduced to five cardinal doctrines: belief in an inerrant Bible, belief in the virgin birth of Jesus, belief in the theory of atonement (Jesus' death 'a sacrifice to satisfy divine justice'), belief in the physical resurrection of Christ, and belief in Christ's supernatural miracles.

"Belief in an inerrant Bible particularly caused many problems for the church and theology during the emerging of the new Darwinian theories of evolution and the rise of the German school of historical and textual criticism of the Bible. Many American Christians who sought to save the credibility of the word of God embraced biblical criticism and were quickly labeled as liberals. During his tenure at First Presbyterian Church in New York, Fosdick sought to conciliate fundamentalist and liberals by preaching a sermon called 'Shall the Fundamentalists Win?' The purpose of this sermon was to foster an inclusive fellowship of Christians both liberals and fundamentalists. However, Fosdick admitted that this was one of his sermons which failed to achieve its objective. After the sermon the liberal-fundamentalist controversy exploded and made headline news. From that moment forward the fundamentalist wing in the Presbyterian church, led by Clarence MacCartney and William Jennings Bryan, was in controversy with Fosdick until he resigned from Old First Presbyterian to assume work elsewhere (ultimately as pastor of Riverside Church in New York City).

"Fosdick and King both repudiated fundamentalism and embraced evangelical liberalism" (17, 18).

Scruggs observes that "Like fundamentalism, liberalism can be simplified in a few tenets. In its succinct expression, liberalism emphasizes: (1) The value of religious experience (2) Concern of God for all of life (3) Strong ethical orientation (4) Rights of reason and moral experience (5) Taking seriously the humanity of Jesus (6) The dynamic nature of history (7) The liberal spirit – open and tolerant" (18).

According to Scruggs, "One can see the stream of King's liberalism flowing all the way from Fosdick's day, …"(19)

Scruggs is correct. The god of Fosdick and the god of King is the same god. It is the god of theological modernism. Some fifty years ago during the time when Fosdick was creating a storm within the Presbyterian Church, the liberal Christian Century, which sided with Fosdick, said that "Christianity according to fundamentalism is one religion and Christianity according to modernism is another...There is a clash here as profound and grim as between Christianity and Confucianism. The God of the fundamentalist is one God, and the God of the modernist is another" (January 3, 1924).

The god of Fosdick, King, and *The Christian Century* is the god of modernism.

It is well known that Fosdick rejected such Christian doctrines as the deity of Christ, Christ's virgin birth and His physical resurrection from the dead. King did the same. Fosdick and King both rejected historic Christianity. Their god was not the God of historic Christianity.

Anyone who still believes King accepted historic Christianity and believed in the God of historic Christianity should read this book by a liberal theologian who admires both King and Fosdick.

Ed. The Lutheran Church-Missouri Synod's *Lutheran Service Book* includes a hymn by Harry Emerson Fosdick.

Saint King – Martyr of the Church
Christian News, December 8, 1975

The Council of Churches of the City of New York has expressed "great dismay and shock" at the Federal Bureau of Investigation's "harassment and persecution" of the late Dr. Martin Luther King, Jr.

"Martin Luther King in many minds and hearts is already counted among the saints of the church and we believe his name will appear in the official calendar of saints in an increasing number of churches as time goes on," the council said in a statement unanimously approved at its semi-annual meeting.

The statement was issued in response to testimony by an FBI official before the Senate Select Committee on Intelligence that the agency had conducted actions against Dr. King in an effort to discredit him.

Rev. Richard Neuhaus and other LCMS "moderates" have urged the LCMS to declare Martin Luther King a Saint. The April 24-April 7, 1972 NEWSLETTER of the Church of St. John The Evangelist, Rev. Richard Neuhaus and Rev. John Heinemeier, pastors, stated: "On Monday we will continue in our observance of the Stations of the Cross...but on this day, the day on which we remember the life and death of **Martin Luther King, Martyr of the Church**, we will stop at a 'fifteenth station,' the portrait of Dr. King which hangs on the back wall of church. This special Liturgy on the day of God's servant and martyr, Martin, will begin at 8 p.m. Tell your friends!

"On Tuesday we will do the stations of the cross outside the church, where Jesus is still dying today in his brothers and sisters. We will pause for mediatation and prayer in front of PS 49, the A & P, the Welfare Office, a burnt-out apartment building, a dark street corner, and then return to the church for the Meal of Hope, 8:00 p.m."

A number of years ago the Lutheran Church-Missouri Synod's **Lutheran Witness** highly praised King and said that he was "a committed Christian" even though King did not accept such Christian doctrine as the virgin birth and resurrection of Jesus Christ. The **Lutheran Witness** said that " America has good reason to thank God that Dr. King is the man he is- wise, able, humble, inspired and moved by a spirit that has its roots in the Gospel of reconciliation" (LW editorial reprinted in **A Christian Handbook**, p. 292. Other items on King are on pages 279-294).

The Inter-Lutheran Commission on Worship (LCA-ALC-LCMS), which has been working on a new Lutheran Hymnal, has listed Martin Luther King and Pope John

XXIII in a calendar of "lesser festivals." Some churchmen are not yet ready to honor King as a Saint and have a special day set aside for "Saint King." Father Daniel Lyons writes: "I went to hear this famous Christian leader when he spoke at Riverside Church on April 4, 1967, in New York City , I was never so shocked in all my life. He preached the straight Communist line. In elaborating on 'the madness of Vietnam,' Dr. King raised Ho Chi Minh as the only leader of the Vietnamese people. He condemned the United States as 'the greatest purveyor of violence in he world today.' He called Ho Chi Minh an independent democratic leader, and condemned the late President Diem as 'one of the most Vicious modern dictators.' We may have killed a million, mostly children, he said." (**The Story of Dan Lyons**, by John D. McCallum, p. 291-2).

The December 1975 **Time** noted in a report titled "The Crusade to Topple King:" "The FBI in 1964 anonymously sent to King's wife Coretta a tape of some bedroom conversation that had been secretly recorded while King was traveling. Such a tape was a prized possession of Hoover 's, and he once had it played for Lyndon Johnson, who in turn entertained reporters with his version of King's extramarital conquests."

The "moderate" churchmen who are now condemning Hoover and the FBI and coming to King's defense are not concerned about King's adultery and "extramarital conquests." Many of them are defenders of situation ethics and the "new morality. They are vigorously protesting the methods used by the FBI in exposing King. A man who had been faithful to his wife, had not lied about the United States and who repudiated the Communists would have had nothing to hide and fear.

The Inter-Lutheran Commission on Worship will be in deep trouble if it continues to exalt a liberal churchman who denied the Christian faith, lied about America , and led an immoral life. Neuhaus and his deluded followers can have their "Saint Martin," but faithful Lutherans are not going to stop at the "fifteenth station" before Saint Martin , "Martyr of the Church."

Leading Men to Hell
Christian News, **August 22, 1977**

When the National Conference of the New York based Black Theology Project (story p. 1) this month unanimously adopted a paper which endorsed violence, it clearly showed that it does not speak for the black Christians of America. This organization is controlled by radicals who repudiate the saving Gospel of Jesus Christ. They have been influenced by liberal theologians who support the social gospel rather than the saving Gospel of Jesus Christ.

Dr. James Cone of Union Theological Seminary is one of the chief spokesmen for this leftist group of black churchmen. Some have hesitated to protest against this black organization's support of violence for fear that they will be labeled "racists."

When either white or black churchmen endorse violence and the destruction of the American system they must be exposed and repudiated. The Christian doesn't recognize the validity of either "white theology" or "black theology." Only the saving Gospel of Jesus Christ has any scriptural basis. All other kinds of theology are phony and will only lead men to hell.

The Inspired Community: A Glance At Canon History
By Everet B. Kalin, professor Concordia Theological Seminary St. Louis. *Concordia Theological Monthly*, September, 1971.

"For whether one calls Martin Luther King's 'Letter from a Birmingham Jail' inspired or not, it still presents itself as a prophetic witness from God, and thus one needs to 'test the spirits to see whether they are of God.' It is there that the normative character of God's gracious actions in Jesus Christ, and of the apostolic witness to these actions, becomes important. One must ask whether King's letter or any other message today that claims to be a word from God conforms to what we know of God's intentions toward people and His will for people's lives as these are revealed in Jesus Christ and witnessed to by the apostolic testimony."

"If Scripture alone were inspired, then we would have the strange situation in which a saying of Jesus was used and rephrased and modified for many years in the oral tradition, but only as Mark or Matthew took this tradition and either used it as it was or further modified it would inspiration take over. This is both a strange and an unnecessary view. If we take seriously the thinking of the early church about inspiration, we see that the Holy Spirit was at work not only in Mark's writing but also in that process by which the Christians before him, many of them no longer known to us by name, received, reinterpreted, and handed on these words."

The editor of *Christian News* filed charges of false doctrine vs. Professor Kalin for denying the scriptural doctrine of the inerrancy and inspiration of the Bible and for placing King's letter on the same level of inspiration of St. Paul's letters. The St. Louis Seminary and LCMS bureaucracy defended Kalin. Kalin later left the LCMS with the Seminexers. He signed Faithful to Our Calling – Faithful To Our Lord which the LCMS's 1973 convention said contained false doctrine not to be tolerated in the LCMS.

A Response to Black Theology
By M.G. Jones
Christian News, September 26, 1977

As a black Christian, I am unable to agree with the position expressed in the paper recently adopted by the National Conference of New York Black Theology Project. (*Christian News*, August 22, p. 1). A part of one of a few statements to which I take exception is:

". . . the black church must lead the way in a new struggle for freedom from injustice, racism, and oppression."

Racism, oppression and injustice are all caused by sin. Freedom from sin is the only true liberating force in the world today. Freedom from sin is what liberates the heart and mind and banishes the need for racism, oppression and injustice. Freedom from sin is provided through Jesus Christ who will direct the heart and the mind to right motivation and also to right action. In learning to obey His commands, the oppressor finds true freedom for himself as he learns to "love his neighbor as himself." It must begin here. John in his letter asks the question of whether we can really love God who we have not seen without loving our brother whom we have seen.

As a black Christian, I can neither "accept nor affirm" the "whatever method they decide is best in their particular situation is the right way to fight or oppose injustices." God's word states, "There is a way that seems right unto man, but the end thereof are the ways of death" (Prov. 14:12). His word also states that our thoughts are not His thoughts, nor our ways His ways. His thoughts and ways are higher (Is 55:8 & 9). If we must enter the fight against injustice, we must use the higher ways of God. We as Christians are not free to use any method we like.

The issue of "white theology" failing to "view the physical as well as the spiritual nature of human beings", must be dealt with by white Christian ministers in white Christian churches. God's love must be preached as reaching down to all men through Jesus Christ. Even a slight perusal of the gospels will show changes in the lives of anyone really touched by Christ. White people touched by Christ will also exhibit changes in their lives toward their black children.

". . . the issue is black survival". In the black church as well as the white church, the issue should be salvation and redemption through Jesus Christ. Any other issue shows a departure from the teaching of God's word. This is the gospel that Christ gave man to preach in His church. When this gospel is preached, and reaches the heart social issues are dealt with.

The "black church" will not win the fight against racism, oppression, or injustice by deviating from Christ's standards. Theology cannot be colored black, white, or any other color that man may be. It is only as all people black, white, or any color they may study about God and His relation to the world, and allow that relationship to change their lives, that true liberation will be effected. "Ye shall know the truth and the truth shall make you free."

We as black Christians in black churches are not to march by the world's drummer. Our tune is different. We shall know the truth of Christ-dying for sin. This truth accepted, and changing our attitudes will begin the liberating process. The same truth must be applied to the lives of our white brothers and sisters who inflict the oppression, racism, and injustice. Once liberated in Jesus Christ, no man is able to bind us again. "If the Son shall make you free, you shall be free indeed." It is to this truth that the "black church" must lead the way.

This is the only way!

This is the real issue of "Black Theology."

One For "The Book"?
The Sword of the Lord, Friday, October 20, 1979
By Evangelist Robert L. Sumner, Contributing Editor

One of the most inane propositions to come down the pike in the last thousand years or so relates to the "Reverend" Muhammed Kenyatta and his Black Theology Project's proposal to add a 67th book to the Bible. The suggestion, although it has been timidly offered by various and sundry nuts before, came at the third annual conference of the group in Cleveland. Kenyata, a sociology instructor at Haverford College in Pennsylvania, founded Black Theology Project three years ago at Atlanta.

What valuable missive does "Muhammed" and his cohorts think deserves elevation to the status of Sacred Scripture? None other than Martin Luther King's "Letter From

Birmingham Jail"! No Fooling? (My youngest son wondered, facetiously, if they wanted it called "III Kings"!)

What an insult to Almighty God! What an affront to Jesus Christ! Surely such a suggestion does not border on blasphemy-it is blasphemy! Martin Luther King, in addition to being a pro-Communist rabble-rouser who left a trail of violence everywhere he took his "Non-violent" road show, was not even a Bible believer in the traditional evangelical sense. He was an out-and-out modernist, one who repudiated the teachings of the Word of God. He denied, for example, the virgin birth, the deity of Christ, the inspiration of Scripture, the reality of Hell, and just about everything else the Scriptures teach. In one of his books, which we have in our library, he totally and completely repudiated historic Christianity and gave his reasons for so doing. And his sexual immorality is so well documented it is not even debatable. To suggest placing a missive from his pen in the Word of God sinks as low in the religious gutter as is humanly possible.

King wrote his letter in April of 1963, responding to criticism from white Alabama clergymen that he was an outside agitator whose actions were both "unwise and untimely." Kenyatta's defense of his suggestion was: "We believe that God worked through Dr. Martin Luther King in that jail in Birmingham in 1963 to reveal His holy word. What we believe is that God continues to move people, with or without their conscious knowledge."

No, God does not continue to move people in writing Sacred Scripture. That series of divine revelation ended on the Isle of Patmos about 1,900 years ago with John's "Revelation of Jesus Christ." And it closed, incidentally, with a terrible curse upon anyone who would try to "add" something else!

We suggest to blacks everywhere that they cease attempting to elevate Martin Luther to some sort of sainthood, and admit he was the non-Christian unbeliever he really was. There are plenty of fine outstanding blacks who devotedly love and serve the Saviour who are deserving of the highest honors. Honor them!

Incidentally, Kenyatta frankly acknowledged that he and his group are "often out of step with mainstream black churches," and that they "operate a kind of laboratory where radical concepts can be tried."

So much for the radical concept!

The FBI and Martin Luther King Jr.
Christian News, **January 28, 1980**

"Few believed the FBI's official contention that King's organization, the Southern Christian Leadership Conference, was being infiltrated by Communists.

"But a new book about King and the FBI, by University of North Carolina scientist David J. Garrow, suggest that the FBI's claim was justified, at least in the beginning" says the September 28 *Newsweek* in a report of the recently published book The FBI and Martin Luther King, Jr. (320 pages. Norton. $15.95).

Newsweek says that surveillance "did give the FBI access to King's sometimes raunchy private life- the bawdy jokes and sexual adventures, the self-doubts and drinking bouts. There was a report that King once threatened to jump from a hotel window if the woman with him did not declare her love. Hoover, he reports, talked about

King's 'obsessive degenerates sexual urge.'

"Garrow believes that some officials were truly offended by King's private life. Others, like Hoover and President Lyndon Johnson, were more intrigued. But no one moved to stop the coverage until Congress began to ask about questionable FBI surveillance techniques-and bureau officials discovered that they could not interest the media in their salacious tapes. 'They're out to break me,' King said after being sent one of the FBI tapes anonymously."

Some of the methods the FBI has used in the Abscam case appear rather questionable but such methods were not needed to trap King and expose his immoral lifestyle.

Responsible blacks such as Julia Brown, an undercover agent for the FBI, have long shown that the Communists used Martin Luther King, that King's organization was infiltrated by Communists and that King refused to do anything about it.

CN has published numerous articles documenting King's record and his anti-Christian theology. King denied such Christian doctrines as the virgin birth of Christ, original sin, and the physical resurrection of Christ.

His mentor, Dr. Harold De Wolf, who preached at King's funeral, similarly rejects historic Christianity. Dr. Julius Richard Scruggs, a black theologian and supporter of King, in his Baptist Preachers with Social Consciousness, A Comparative Study of Martin Luther King and Harry Emerson Fosdick concludes that King and Fosdick had about the same theology. Scruggs is correct. Neither King nor Fosdick accepted the Christ of Holy Scripture. Fosdick publicly attacked the virgin birth and deity of Christ.

Although King was a theological modernist, an advocate of civil disobedience and morally degenerate, he was hailed as a great committed Christian by The Lutheran Church-Missouri Synod's *Lutheran Witness*. When Dr. Jacob Preus was president of Concordia Seminary, Springfield, Illinois, we had to take issue with him for suggesting that the seminary have a Martin Luther King Jr. scholarship. We warned President Preus about King's theology and record but Preus thought such a scholarship would gain him popularity among blacks.

The new *Lutheran Book of Worship* used by the Lutheran Church in America, the American Lutheran Church, and the Association of Evangelical Lutheran Churches has a special day set aside for King, who is featured as a great Christian saint in the *LBW*. Of course, there is forgiveness for every repentant sinner. But there is no record of King ever expressing any repentance for his anti-Christian theology and thoroughly immoral lifestyle. We wrote to King and his Southern Christian Leadership Conference about his theology after an article appeared in the *National Observer* showing that King denied basic doctrines of the Christian faith. The *National Observer* said King did not take issue with the article but neither King nor the SCLC answered *CN*. We'd be interested to hear from King's defenders how they now feel about King being included in the *LBW*'s list of great Christian saints.

* * * *

That fact that through the years *CN* has exposed the anti-Christian theology and lifestyle of King does not prove that we are racists as some of our critics contend. The record shows we were defending the black man and deploring racism long before this was the popular thing for churchmen to do. Already during our grammar school days we worked in Harlem, New York, in the homes of black people. Later we were the only white laborer on a crew of some 40 black farm workers. One of the first essays we ever wrote was in defense of blacks. We went to school and church with children from many races and nationalities. We were one of the first to recommend that the

LCMS elect responsible blacks to prominent positions in the synod. This was long before some of today's churchmen, who now like to pose as such great champions of the black man by praising King, even had any contact with blacks.

Happy Martin Luther King's Day...or NOT
By: Charles Hampton

Every January, the mainstream media goes into a frenzy of adulation, as we are encouraged to honor one of the most morally degenerate figures in all of modern American history. School children across the nation pause to reflect on the legacy of the so-called "Reverence Doctor Martin Luther King, Jr." A national holiday has been declared in King's honor. This is an honor accorded to no other American...not Washington, not Jefferson, not Lee or Lincoln.

Due to the hype that surrounds the life of Martin Luther King, a largely unsuspecting public now perceives the man as both a statesman and a saint. Nothing could be further from the truth. The King legacy is a myth beginning with the man's name.

When faced with King's socialism, communistic connections, moral perversion, and anti-American bias...most of King's fans either say they weren't part of his main philosophy or usually they simply ignore them. Slightly before the King Holiday was signed into law, Governor Meldrim Thompson of New Hampshire wrote a letter to Ronald Reagan expressing concerns about King's morality and Communist connections. Ronald Reagan responded, "I have the same reservations, however the perception of too many people is based on an image, not reality. Indeed, to them the perception is reality."

http://www.eboards4all.com/813467/messages/38626.html

Denied Historic Christianity – Honored in LBW
Martin Luther King, Jr., January 15, 1929 – April 4, 1968
Christian News, January 5, 1981

Should there be a Federal paid holiday in honor of the late Martin Luther King? Many churchmen answer: "Yes." Should Christian seminaries establish scholarships in honor of Dr. King? Does Dr. King deserve the recognition he is given in the New **Lutheran Book of Worship** where a special day is set aside for him along with the great saints of Christendom.

Julia Brown, a former under cover member of the Communist Party for the FBI, answers the first question with a firm "no" in a speech which appeared in the **Congressional Record**. It is reprinted in this issue. Other responsible black leaders have said much the same thing about King. Christian seminaries should not set up scholarships in honor of Dr. King. King does not deserve the recognition he is given in the LBW because he rejected historic Christianity.

Some dozen years ago we had to take issue with Dr. Jacob Preus, now president of the LCMS, when he suggested that the LCMS's Concordia Seminary in Springfield, Illinois, establish a Martin Luther King scholarship. We noted that King rejected historic Christianity. Here is part of an address we delivered at Concordia Senior College, Ft. Wayne, Indiana on May 12, 1969:

* * * * *

Congressional Record
PROCEEDINGS AND DEBATES OF THE 96TH CONGRESS, SECOND SESSION

AMERICANS, STOP THINKING LIKE COMMUNISTS
PLEADS A FORMER COMMUNIST AND PATRIOTIC AMERICAN NEGRO

REMARKS OF
HON. LARRY MCDONALD
OF GEORGIA IN THE HOUSE OF REPRESENTATIVES
Wednesday, June 18, 1980

Senate Testimony

Mr. Chairman, I, Julia Brown, joined the Communist Party in December, 1947, thinking I was joining a legitimate civil rights movement. Finding out that I was a true member of the Communist Party which advocated the overthrow of the U.S. Government, I decided to leave the organization, but I had to bide, my time to avoid suspicion. Subsequently I went to the FBI to report what I had heard and seen. In 1951, I was asked by the FBI to go back into the Communist Party as an undercover agent to report on their subversive activities.

While at the Communist Party meetings, which only Party members attended, I frequently heard Martin Luther King discussed, and was told by Frieda Catz that he was in training for a civil rights movement. Frieda Catz was a Party member from Cleveland, Ohio, who had been assigned to my training and education within the Communist Party. On learning this, I reported it to my contact in the FBI. He told me that the Bureau knew that Martin Luther King had high level connections with the Communist Party, and I should report anything else that I heard about his activities. I continued to report until 1960, over ten long years.

In Martin Luther King's early years of agitation, he was the hero of America's Communists. The cells that I was associated with in Cleveland were continually being asked to raise money for Martin Luther King's activities and to support his civil rights movement by writing letters to the press and influencing local clergymen, and especially black clergymen, that Martin Luther King was a good person, unselfishly working for the American Negro, and in no way connected with the Communist Party.

There are many great American Negroes such as George Washington Carver and Booker T. Washington who provide the youth of America with an example they can follow. Martin Luther King provides an example of agitation and manipulation for goals dictated by hatred and envy. The memory of Carver and Washington would be dishonored if your Committee acts favorably in this matter.

Mr. Chairman, while I was in the Communist Party, as a loyal American Negro, I knew Martin Luther King to be closely connected with the Communist Party. If this measure is passed honoring Martin Luther King, We may as well take down the stars and stripes that fly over this building and replace it with a red flag.

And that was my message to the Senate Judiciary Committee on June 2, 1979. I would like to believe that what I said would have been enough to stop the glorification of Martin Luther King. But we all know that, even if they never name a holiday after him, there are still too many Americans who hold that man to be like a god. What has happened, of course, is that there are too many of our fellow citizens who actually have been conditioned to think exactly the way Communists want them to think.

Dr. King's Birthday to be LCA Holiday
Lutheran Perspective, October 19, 1981

The Lutheran Church in America will recognize the birthday of Martin Luther King, Jr., as a holiday for its employees starting in 1982.

The denomination's Executive Council at its meeting in New York City, Sept. 26, added January 15 to the list of employee holidays, bringing the total to 11.

Delegates to the LCS biennial convention in Seattle last year recognized memorials from two synods by voting to have "all synods urge their congressional representatives" to declare the birthday of the civil rights leader who was assassinated April 4, 1968, a national holiday.

The action came in response to a request from the Minnesota Synod, which in 1979 called on the Minnesota state legislature to recognize the birthday as a state holiday. The Synod asked the church body to call upon the U.S. Congress to do likewise.

The Pacific Northwest Synod, which had taken similar action in states included in its district-Alaska, Idaho, Montana, Oregon and Washington – also called upon the LCA to encourage establishment of a national holiday.

The Pacific Northwest Synod, which had taken similar action in states included in its district – Alaska, Idaho, Montana, Oregon and Washington – also called upon the LCA to encourage establishment of a national holiday.

The Pacific Northwest memorial noted that the LCA is "a church that has continually worked for justice and against racism" and stated the recognition of the birthday as a national holiday "would be an appropriate way of proclaiming our continuing hope that racism will be eradicated."

Several council members expressed the desire that the birthday be "celebrated" in tribute to Dr. King and to his contributions in the civil rights efforts.

Patron Saint to Seminex
Christian News, February 8, 1982

Dr. Martin Luther King, Jr. has been almost like a patron saint to Seminex.
Dr. Holland Jones, Professor of Exegetical Theology at Seminex, writes in the February, 1982 Currents in Theology and Mission: "For the Lord who said through the prophet Joel, 'Your old men will dream dreams,' has through his inspired prophet, Martin Luther King, helped me to a dream a dream.

"These prophets of old couldn't make up their minds for sure on the issue of violence. Isaiah and Micah declared in the New Age that people will beat their swords into plows, their spears into pruners. Joel declared that the New Age people will beat their plow shares into swords, their pruners into spears.

"The dream Dr. King has inspired me to dream is not ambiguous on this issue. I foresee a time, when, the theological swords and spears so skillfully and courageously manipulate to cut up and down our brothers and sisters, will be permitted to fall from the hands of stalwart defenders of orthodoxy, even Lutheran orthodoxy.

"That's Father's plan. In his time, he'll do it."

Although King did not affirm such doctrines as the virgin birth and physical resurrection of Christ, liberal churchmen maintain that a person does not have to accept these doctrines in order to be considered a great saint of the Church.

Among the Files: Muck
Conservative Digest, **September 1983**
The Christian News Encyclopedia, **p. 2535**

What does the FBI have on King? An exhaustive 1981 study, well documented, offers a glimpse. While sympathetic to King and critical of the FBI for "dogging" him "ruthlessly," David Garrow's 320-page book **The FBI and Martin Luther King, Jr.** *offers these items on King, among others, often citing as sources specific documents in the FBI's files (page numbers refer to Garrow's book):*

*"The bug had recorded a lively party involving King, several SCLC colleagues, and two black women who worked at the Philadelphia Naval Yard." (Page 105)

*"A Las Vegas prostitute who was a regular (FBI) source...claimed that ..she had spent the evening with Dr. King...King had been extremely forceful, if not downright violent with her. She asserted....that never again would she have anything to do with someone like King." (Page 16)

*"The Bureau had learned from its New York wiretaps of several lively incidents that had occurred during King's trip to Europe to accept the Nobel Peace Prize. These incidents had disturbed several members of the King entourage who had not been accustomed to the style in which King and his closest colleagues partied, and these individuals had related their concerns to others over wiretapped phone lines." (Pages 132-3)

*"In letters. . . Sullivan claimed....four other solid grounds for the probe (of King): embezzlement, employing prostitutes, alienating wives affections from their husbands and violation of the Mann Act.... King, for instance, had embezzled or misapplied substantial amounts of money contributed to the civil rights movement. King also had violated prostitution laws in numerous places." (Pages 162-3)

* "The monograph...then summarized the four-year-old Willard Hotel happenings, which were termed a 'two-day drunken sex orgy.' The report added: 'Throughout the ensuing years and until this date King has continued to carry on his sexual aberrations secretly while holding himself out to public view as a moral leader of religious convictions.'

"The final portion was entitled 'King's Mistress' and described a supposedly long-standing affair that King had been carrying on with the wife of a California dentist. One of the Bureau's major sources on this subject was the woman's own brother... (who) had complained to the Bureau about King, whom he called a 'hypocrite.' (p. 186)

*David Garrow, *The FBI and Martin Luther King, Jr.* (New York: Penguin Books, 1981), a 320–page paperback listed at $5.95.

Ignoring Reams of Documentation
Christian News, October 31, 1983

Why are those who were the most enthusiastic supporters of Martin Luther King, including churchmen who have urged their denominations to declare King a saint, opposed to the releasing of the FBI's files and tapes on King? If King was such an outstanding moral Christian and patriotic American, surely the tapes and files would show that King has no association with any communists and did not engage in any immoral sex with prostitutes and others in hotel rooms. If King was such a great American worthy to be honored even more that Abraham Lincoln, Booker T. Washington, George Washington Carver and many other famous Americans, surely the record would have shown that his critics, who claimed King associated with communists and was a sexual libertine, were slandering King.

Liberals, who want to suppress King's record, insisted that the Watergate tapes of the Nixon administration be unsealed.

Some congressmen did supply their colleagues with plenty of evidence documenting King's anti-American and pro-Marxist position. However, the documents were generally ignored. Some Senators strongly denounced the documentation but did not bother to show where it was in error. They were just like many church officials we have encountered through the years. They simply ignore the reams of documentation and go right on promoting liberal professors and clergymen who deny historic Christianity. There are none so blind as those who refuse to see.

Both Seeger and King Denies Historic Christianity
Folk Singer Seeger and Wife Win Reconciliation Fellowship's King Award
By Religious News Service, January 13, 1984
Christian News, January 23, 1984

Nyack, N.Y. (RNS) – Folk singer Peter Seeger and his wife, Toshi, are the winners of the 1984 Martin Luther King, Jr., Award of the Fellowship of Reconciliation.

The religious pacifist organization, on whose advisory committee Dr. King served, noted that both the Seegers had been associated with the civil-rights leader during his career. Pete sang for Dr. King during the Montgomery bus boycott in 1956, Pete and Toshi joined the 1965 Selma-to-Montgomery march, and they both took part in the 1968 Resurrection City campaign in Washington after Dr. King's assassination.

While Pete is the better known of the two, the Fellowship said that Toshi "has produced films documenting the folk-arts movement around the world," and has used "her skills as a potter and photographer in the cause of justice and peace."

The Lutheran Church-Missouri Synod's youth auxiliary was criticized for inviting Pete Seeger to sing at its 1965 national convention on the ground that he was "anti-Christian" and had sung "blasphemous" songs. The fellowship responded at the time that, while Mr. Seeger "is not a member of an organized church body, he has personally affirmed he believes in Jesus Christ and reads and studies the Bible regularly."

The Fellowship of Reconciliation has presented its King award each year since 1979, to a person or group "making a significant contribution to the non-violent struggle for a peaceful and just society."

* * *

Ed. *Lutheran News* (now *Christian News*) in 1965 published Pete Seeger's long record of support for Communists causes. Many pages of documents received from the House Committee on Un-American Activities were photographed in *Lutheran News*. Sworn public testimony of Harvey Matusow given before the HCUA identified Seeger as a member of the Communist Party. Seeger is referred to as an identified member of the Communist Party in the 1960 Annual Report of the HCUA. The 1961 HCUA Annual Report says that Seeger is "the best known of the Communist Party's entertainers."

Lutheran News also published Seeger's "To My Old Brown Earth," a song which he often sings at funerals. It says: "To my old brown earth and to my old blue sky I'll give these last few mol-e-cules- of 'I' – And you who sing – and you who stand nearby I do charge you not to cry – Guard well our human chain Watch well you keep it strong As long as sun will shine And this our hymn keep pure and sweet and green- For now I'm yours and you are also mine."

Correspondence with Seeger at the time the LCMS's youth organization invited Seeger to entertain LCMS youth revealed that Seeger was not a Christian and that he did not believe in any resurrection. LCMS officials, particularly its youth leaders, defended Seeger. Dr. John Tietjen, then editor of **The American Lutheran**, viciously blasted us for opposing Seeger. At an open hearing in 1965 at a Lutheran Church – Missouri Synod Convention in Detroit, we presented documentation to a convention committee clearly showing Seeger's Communist and anti-Christian record. LCMS youth officials said they had documents from a government committee refuting the government documents we submitted as evidence. We asked the LCMS officials to furnish the LCMS convention with the documents. Such LCMS liberals as Dr. Ralph Moellering and Dr. Otto P. Kretzmann defended Seeger but could not refute the documentation we submitted as various exhibits. Unfortunately, some LCMS officials at the convention smeared us as some sort of anti-communist radical who had never been certified for the ministry. The delegates by a 335-291 vote decided to allow the LCMS's youth officials to keep Seeger on the youth program. We suggested that the LCMS officials invite Herbert Philbrick, Fred Schwarz or some other anti-communist to have the opportunity to speak to the LCMS youth along with Seeger but the LCMS officials were not interested in this proposal.

Both Seeger and Martin Luther King rejected the physical resurrection of Christ and other basic doctrines of historic Christianity. See **The Christian News Encyclopedia** (Index) for further information on the views of King and Seeger.

A Marxist Is No Saint
Christian News, October 8, 1984

According to Rev. James H. Cone, a professor at Union Theological Seminary in New York and the acknowledged pioneer of "black theology," Dr. Martin Luther King, Jr., went from an "integrationist" who tried to reform the system to a "revolutionary, and said in private that he was a Marxist." According to Cone, who is an ardent supporter of King, "If white people knew what King was about, they would have never named a holiday for him" (See "Black church leaders told they fail to teach the gospel" p. 1).

Cone is one of the nation's most outspoken liberal black churchmen. Like Martin Luther King, he does not accept the saving Gospel of Jesus Christ. King never affirmed such doctrines as the virgin birth and physical resurrection of Christ. Cone identified the "white church" with the Anti-Christ and the Gospel with "black power" (**Encyclopedia**, p. 290). He says he is convinced that some still unrealized form of socialist democracy is the only answer to "liberating" the poor, both here and abroad. A Religious News Service story said: "Mr. Cone's political-economic views of blacks' problems apparently are not far from the Marxist-oriented analysis of Latin American theologians such as Gustavo Gutierres, who coined the phrase 'theology of liberation'" (*CNE*, 290).

Cone is an outspoken supporter of the killing of unborn infants (*CNE*, 24).

We said in "Leading Men to Hell," an editorial in the August 22, 1977 *CN*: "When the National Conference of the New York based Black Theology Project (story p. 1) this month unanimously adopted a paper which endorsed violence, it clearly showed that it does not speak for the black Christians of America. This organization is controlled by radicals who repudiate the saving Gospel of Jesus Christ. They have been influenced by liberal theologians who support the social gospel rather than the saving gospel of Jesus Christ.

"Dr. James Cone of Union Theological Seminary is one of the chief spokesmen for this leftist group of black churchmen. Some have hesitated to protest against this black organization's support of violence for fear that they will be labeled 'racists.'

"When either white or black churchmen endorse violence and the destruction of the American system they must be exposed and repudiated. The Christian doesn't recognize the validity of either 'white theology' or 'black theology.' Only the saving Gospel of Jesus Christ has any scriptural basis. All other kinds of theology are phony and will only lead men to Hell."

The **Lutheran Book of Worship** has a festival day set aside for Dr. Martin Luther King, Jr., the self-acclaimed "Marxist" Rev Richard John Neuhaus and other liberal churchmen want declared Christian saints of this century. Anyone who says he is a "Marxist" and refused to affirm such Christian doctrines as the virgin birth of Christ and Christ's physical resurrection is not a Christian saint.

Neuhaus writes in the October 5, 1984 *Christianity Today* that "Those of us who received the grace of working with Martin Luther King, Jr., know how profoundly his life and work were empowered by religious faith."

King not only rejected the doctrines of historic Christianity but also its moral standards. Liberal preachers may excuse his extramarital affairs, but they clearly show that he should not be hailed as some great Christian saint.

King Admitted in Private He Was a "Marxist"
Black Church Leaders Told They Fail to Teach Gospel
By Religion News Service, September 28, 1984
Christian News, October 8, 1984

WASHINGTON (RNS) -- A group of 100 black church leaders were told here that they have superficially "idealized" the late Dr. Martin Luther King without following the example he provided as a religious leader of both "intelligence" and faith.

The Rev. James H. Cone, the acknowledged pioneer of "black theology," said church leaders have failed to "teach" themselves and young people to systematically "analyze" the causes of poverty and injustice, as did Dr. King and Malcolm X.

"We preach the gospel, but we don't teach it," he said at the annual meeting of Partners in Ecumenism, which is affiliated with the National Council of Churches. The meeting drew both Protestant and Catholic black leaders.

"It is disgusting to see lazy black preachers who have time to do everything but read a book," declared Mr. Cone, a professor of systematic theology at the prestigious Union Theological Seminary in New York.

"Our seminaries and church denominations have failed to instil within our ministers the need to continue to develop their intelligence through a disciplined program of study."

He said the black community was in "dire need" of leaders like Mr. King, who had the "courage to stand up against the odds, and the intelligence to know how to analyze the causes of injustice."

A minister in the African Methodist Episcopal Church, Mr. Cone's first book was published in 1969, when he was 30, and it has become a premier treatise on black theology, also known as black liberation theology. At the time, his appeal for blacks to go beyond the issue of race in America to a concern for economic injustice both here and abroad was revolutionary.

Recently, Mr. Cone has begun to urge blacks to "seriously study" the lives and thinking of two very different black leaders -- Dr. King, an "integrationist," and Malcolm X, a "separatist" -- as the starting point for a new theological vision of "black struggle and global freedom." The appeal is made in his most recent book, "For My People," published this year.

In several lectures and informal sessions to strengthen ecumenical black church meeting, held here Sept. 25-27, Mr. Cone continued his reputation for challenging respected figures in the black community, such as civil rights leaders and the black church.

He visibly stunned some of the churchmen, in one session, when he said, "Most gods have not been useful" to poor and oppressed people throughout the world.

Mr. Cone, who has traveled to Third World countries during the past year, asked the black church leaders: "Can you imagine what would happen if we started doing in the black church what is going on now in the Basic Christian Communities of Latin America?"

He was referring to the thousands of small groups throughout Latin America which meet regularly to study the relevance of the scripture to their social conditions.

"There is really teaching going on there," he said. "They are analyzing the world in which they live, in the light of faith and scripture."

Remarking that black churches have no serious "teaching ministry," he said: "I don't believe any people can be free if they don't analyze what the nature of their oppression is."

As a new way to inspire this type of analysis, Mr. Cone has been lecturing widely on Dr. King and Malcolm X, whose writings and speeches he has been studying for the past five years.

"Although black civil rights leaders and church people did a lot of talking about Martin and Malcolm following their assassinations during the 1960s," he said, "our failure to study them and to reflect on their lives and thought critically have led to their disappearance from the black masses and the black young."

Mr. Cone said that, in the last few years of his life, Dr. King, founder of the Southern Christian Leadership Conference, began to realize that his civil rights movement was helping middle-class blacks, but not "the masses" of blacks and poor whites.

"We are all tokens," he told his audience of middle-class blacks. "My being at Union Theological Seminary is not going to put food on anyone's table."

For that reason, Mr. King went from an "integrationist" who tried to reform the system to a "revolutionary, and said in private that he was a Marxist," Mr. Cone said. "If white people knew what King was about, they would have never named a holiday for him."

Asked by one clergyman if he believed the conservative presidency of Ronald Reagan would "galvanize" black church leaders, Mr. Cone added: "I wish I could believe that. But Ronald Reagan is prepared to let all of us in this room do all right. If we were going through what people are going through in Harlem, Central America, and South Africa, we would do it."

Honoring "A Marxist" With a Mass
Christian News, **January 14, 1985**

A report reprinted below from the St. Louis Review, a Roman Catholic newspaper, says that a Mass will be held at the St. Louis Cathedral on Sunday, January 13 honoring Dr. Martin Luther King, Jr.

King did not affirm such Christian doctrines as original sin and the virgin birth and resurrection of Christ. He never expressed any repentance of his totally immoral and anti-Christian lifestyle. One of his most ardent supporters, a prominent black theologian, wrote a book stating that King's theology was similar to that of Harry Emerson Fosdick. Fosdick repudiated historic Christianity. He was one of the Twentieth Century's most outspoken liberals. Recently Rev. James Cone, a friend and supporter of King and who is known as the father of "black theology," reported that King "said in private that he was a Marxist." According to Cone, "If white people knew what King was about, they would have never named a holiday for him." (*Religious News Service*, September 28, 1984. *CN* October 8, 1984).

The Christian News Encyclopedia, pp. 1123-1126, has a section on King's theology and views.

A number of years ago Rev. Richard John Neuhaus wanted The Lutheran Church-Missouri Synod to declare King a saint. The LCMS's **Lutheran Witness** defended

King, insisting that King was a committed Christian. According to liberal churchmen, it is not necessary to affirm such doctrines as the virgin birth and resurrection of Christ to be considered a great Christian saint and to be honored with a cathedral mass.

What a churchman does for the welfare of mankind is regarded as far more important than what he may believe about Christ. "Deeds and not Creeds" is the cry of the hour.

Perhaps we should add that those who insist on creeds, sound doctrine, particularly the scriptural doctrines of the resurrection of Christ and justification by faith alone in the merits of Christ, which liberals deny, are concerned about works. They recognize that works are the fruits of the faith.

An Immoral Character
Christian News, February 4, 1985

"Archdiocese Honors Martin Luther King As 'Great Gift' to All" was the lead headline on page one of the January 18 St. Louis Review of the Roman Catholic Archdiocese of St. Louis.

A mass was held "in honor of" Martin Luther King at the St. Louis Cathedral.

The St. Louis Review said: "In every age there is a person who hears the word of God and acts upon that calling, Father Herbert Harrison told a nearly full St. Louis Cathedral congregation last Sunday, Martin Luther King, Jr., he said, was one of those people."

Father Harrison said: "Martin Luther King took his baptism seriously." "Martin Luther King understood the implication of his incorporation into the mystical body of Christ."

Father Harrison is entirely wrong. King did not take his baptism seriously. He did not believe that Jesus Christ was born of a virgin, rose from the dead, or is God. He repudiated historic Christianity. Even some of the most ardent supporters of King admit that King did not accept the Christ of the Bible. King told some of his friends that he was a Marxist. Even King supporters now acknowledge that King was a flagrant adulterer. Patrick G. Coy, Director of Peace and Justice Ministry at St. Louis University, reviews **Let the Trumpet Sound – The Life of Martin Luther King, Jr.** in the Jan./Feb. 1985 **New Catholic World**. The book was written by Stephen Oats and published by Harper & Row. Coy says that "Oats does not shy away from certain areas of King's personal life, employing a sensitive frankness when recounting King's lack of sexual fidelity and the problems that eventually caused him when J. Edgar Hoover was bent on discrediting him."

It is simply amazing that both Roman Catholic and Protestant liberal churchmen continue to praise and even make a saint out of such an immoral character who admitted that he was a Marxist and who denied the Christian faith.

MLK Friend Said He Was A Communist
Calvary Contender, January 1, 1986

– James Cone, pioneer of "black theology" and a prof at Union Theol. Seminary, said Martin Luther King in his late years began to realize the civil rights movement was helping middle class blacks but not the poor masses. For that reason King went from an integrationist trying to reform the system to a revolutionary saying in private that he was a Marxist. Cone said "If white people knew what King was about, they would have never named a holiday for him." King led an immoral lifestyle and rejected basic Christian doctrines. FBI director Hoover called him "the most notorious liar in America."

King's Adultery "Well Documented" an Impenitent Adulterer Is No Christian Saint
The Double Standard of the Liberals
Christian News, January 27, 1986

Both the secular and religious press have recently given considerable publicity to the adultery committed by a prominent Fundamentalist clergymen, in Bangor, Main.

An Associated Press story, which appeared in the January 17 **Washington Times**, mentioned "the Oct. 15 announcement by the Rev. Herman C. 'Buddy' Frankland that he had committed adultery. Mr. Frankland a conservative political force, was a one-time independent candidate for governor." Frankland was the pastor of Bangor Baptist Church, "the biggest fundamentalist congregation in the Northeast before the crisis thinned its ranks." Dr. Jerry Falwell is now trying to rebuild this congregation.

The AP reported that "Mr. Frankland first gained prominence beyond Bangor in 1974 through his vocal opposition to the formation of a gay-rights group at the University of Maine." "Mr. Frankland lost a three-way race for governor in 1978 and more recently led a legal battle that won Main's Christian schools some independence from state regulation."

The January 17 **Washington Times** published the story on the adultery of this Fundamentalist just beneath an article on the theology of Dr. Martin Luther King. The article commends King and relies heavily on the testimony of Rev. Richard Neuhaus, an associate of King who wanted The Lutheran Church-Missouri Synod to declare King a Christian saint.

Several years ago, when a prominent anti-communist preacher became involved in sexual immorality, the press saw to it that his effectiveness was destroyed.

CN has opposed adultery, sexual immorality, and homosexuality whether it was committed by liberals or conservatives. It is particularly a great tragedy when conservative clergymen, who have spoken out against adultery and homosexuality, themselves become involved in immorality. It is unfortunate that some of them then make all sorts of excuse to defend their action and even divorce. Impenitent adulterers and homosexuals should be removed from the ministry whether they are liberals or conservatives. There should be no double standard.

When the adultery and immoral life style of Paul Tillich, whom many liberals still consider the greatest theologian of the Twentieth Century, was related in a book by Tillich's wife, liberals didn't deny that Tillich was an adulterer. Yet they excused Tillich and continued to hail him as a great Christian. Does the fact that liberals defend the immorality of their heroes tell something about their own standards?

Adulterous churchmen, who refuse to repent of their immorality, should not be hailed as great Christian saints. In recent weeks many churchmen, including the Pope, have been praising Dr. Martin Luther King as a noble Christian saint who has set a good example for all of us to follow.

Years ago *CN* protested when the Lutheran Church-Missouri Synod's **Lutheran Witness** said King was a "committed Christian." Any informed Christian, who has read some of King's writings, and his sermons, should recognize that King did not affirm historic Christianity. His Christ was not the Christ of Holy Scripture.

While the **Washington Times** this month has had many articles praising King, it said nothing about King's immorality. We do not excuse Frankland's adultery, which the **Washington Times** and other papers mentioned, but King's immoral lifestyle was far worse.

The press has from time to time referred to King's immorality but most liberals excuse it. They maintain that such gross immorality, even when no repentance is expressed should not disqualify one of their liberal heroes from being considered a great American and committed Christian saint.

The true Christian and real American patriot has different standards.

Here are just a few references to King's immoral lifestyle. Not all of them are found in "right-wing" publications.

1. The October 20, 1979 **Sword of the Lord** noted that King's "sexual immorality is so well documented it is not even debatable."

2. The September 28, 1981 **Newsweek** noted in a story on David's Garrow's **The FBI and Martin Luther King** that FBI surveillance of King "did give the FBI access to King's sometimes raunchy private life-the bawdy jokes and sexual adventures, the self-doubts and drinking bouts. There was a report that King once threatened to jump from a hotel a window if the woman with him did not declare her love. Hoover, he reports, talked about King's 'obsessive degenerate sexual urges.'

"Garrow believes that some officials were truly offended by King's private life. Others, like Hoover and President Lyndon Johnson, were more intrigued."

3. The December 1, 1975 **Time** noted in a report titled "The Crusade to Topple King:" "The FBI in 1964 anonymously sent to King's wife Coretta a tape of some bedroom conversation that had been secretly recorded while King was traveling. Such a tape was a prize possession of Hoover's, and he once had it played for Lyndon Johnson, who in turn entertained reporters with his version of King's extramarital conquests."

4. Tamara Henry writes in a United Press International review of the recently published **Martin Luther King Jr.** by Wm. Roger Witherspoon, an ardent admirer of King: "Witherspoon does bring out some facts that renew interest in a frequently told story. For example, King developed a love affair with a white woman and 'was in a quandry' about what to say moments before he delivered his memorial 'I Have A Dream' speech."

5. Walter Scott wrote in **Parade (St. Louis Post Dispatch**, December 29, 1985): "Mrs. King and the former Mr. (John F.) Kennedy are both alert, intelligent, sensitive

and perceptive women who were aware of their late husband's proclivites. Sad to say, the extramarital alliances of both men have tarnished their reputations."

6. Walter Scott wrote in the **Sunday Parade (St. Louis Post Dispatch**, March 28, 1982)that "J. Edgar Hoover, head of the FBI, had King's extracurricular sexual activities recorded and sent the tapes to various newsmen." According to Scott, "enthralled by King's sex life – Hoover turned the FBI into a voyeuristic collective of sorts, charged with detailing King's infidelities."

7. A tract now being widely circulated by some labeled as "right wing extremists" who are opposed to declaring a holiday for King and titled "ABOLISH THE KING HOLIDAY – King's Record Has Been Sealed By Court Order Until The Year 2027 – Why????" says:

"J. Edgar Hoover called King, 'the most notorious liar in the country.' He also said King posed a 'danger' to the nation?

"The FBI wired King's offices, and hotel rooms from 1963 to 1968. These tapes not only recorded his transaction with Communist agents but also wild interracial sex orgies which included acts of perversion. King's aide would use SCLC (tax exempt) money to hire White prostitutes to perform sexual acts with him. King often would use two prostitutes at the same time. These shocking tapes were ordered sealed for 50 years by Federal Judge John Smith, Jr., on January 31, 1977. In other words we will not be able to learn all the gory details until the year 2027. Some 90 Congressmen, led by the late Rep. Larry McDonald, urged Congress to find out what was on these tapes before they approved the disgraceful King Holiday Bill. A cowardly and spineless Congress voted 338 to 90 approving the "King Holiday."

What this pamphlet then says about King's bizarre "sex acts" is too disgusting to print. FBI Director Hoover had plenty of evidence to call King far more than a notorious liar.

CN will gladly publish any response King defenders want to make to the charges of King's adultery.

King's misled supporters, who are still convinced that King led a moral life, was faithful to his wife, and was indeed a "committed Christian" and a patriotic American should ask that the FBI files on King be opened.

Many of King's leading supporters recognize that King was indeed guilty of gross immorality and this is one reason why they want to keep the FBI files on King sealed.

Vote conscious politicians, liberals and conservatives, who know about King's blasphemous attacks against the U.S. his association with Marxists and his immoral lifestyle may now praise King. Informed Christians, blacks and whites, who are not out to win any popularity contest, can not join the crowd of King enthusiasts who want to declare him a great Christian saint. The U.S. should have a day to honor a black man. George Washington Carver should have been a much better choice.

The Feast of St. Martin
By Joseph Sobran
Wanderer, February 6, 1984
Christian New, February 10, 1986

Washington D.C. - The holiday brought very little rejoicing, except in the media, where it was an article of faith that Martin Luther King was a saint. For most Americans, Dr. King's birthday was "their" holiday, not "our" holiday. It represented one more victory by an aggressive minority lobby, which pilloried opposition as bigotry. The technique still works.

Consider the ironies. Dr. King was an inveterarte philanderer. We know this thanks to a scurrilous FBI campaign to spy on him, harass him, even blackmail him; but we do know it. Nobody disputes it, though Taylor Branch, in an admiring piece on Dr. King in The New Republic, skates lightly over it.

Now ordinarily, liberals delight in exposing the gulf of hypocrisy between the public moralist, especially the clergyman, and the private sinner. Elmer Gantry is an euphony for the Christian preacher who carries on like a riotous pagan. Most Americans still regard adultery, especially habitual adultery, as a serious character flaw, a betrayal of the most serious obligation a man or woman assumes in a lifetime. Imagine the merry ribaldry that would ensue if it were revealed that a fundamentalist preacher, prominent in conservative politics, was playing around on the side.

Which is to say, Dr. King's religion is not taken seriously by his own admirers. If it were, they would cease to be his admirers. He is, among other things, the first man of the cloth to be honored with a federal holiday. There has been no protest from ACLU types who might be expected to warn of the breach of the "wall of separation" between church and state.

The whole subject of Dr. King's personal conduct is pretty nearly taboo. So is the subject of his Communist associates. This story has actually been partly ventilated by a sympathizer of Dr. King's, David J. Garrow, in his book The FBI and Martin Luther King, Jr. According to Garrow, Dr. King privately described himself as a "Marxist."

It seems relevant to make these facts available to a nation that was being asked to establish a national holiday in honor of Dr. King. Instead, the liberal community forgot its cherished shibboleths of full disclosure and the public's right to know, and did its best to cover up the truth. The debate over the holiday was conducted in the dark.

Beyond that, Dr. King was simply a man of controversy. People in his lifetime disagreed with him, and he expected them to. To this day there is no unanimity about his version of "civil rights" or his predilection for state intervention.

And yet we are given the impression, by all the media celebrants, that Dr. King only opposition came from Bull Connor, the Ku Klux Klan, and a few German shepherds. This is depressingly crude hagiography.

For an illuminating contrast, take the Catholic Church – an institution despised by liberals as hopelessly illiberal. To its credit, it is – at least in the sense that "liberal" has acquired in our time.

Still, a candidate for Catholic sainthood has to pass a few hurdles that Dr. King was spared by modern liberalism. There is a full inquiry into the candidate's life the details of which are fully and ruthlessly exposed. A "devil's advocate" is appointed to make the strongest conceivable case against him. Firm proof of sanctity, including miraculous intervention after death, is required.

Dr. King is not known to have performed any miracles, except perhaps depriving his followers of their critical faculties. Which is why he has been accorded his huggermuggfer canonization. A fair examination of his life discloses a remarkable man, but not one who most people would regard with unqualified admiration, let alone with that special sense of common possession that belongs to a national hero.

Let me be personal. I didn't look up to him. I didn't agree with him. His life was not a life I would be proud to have led. I wouldn't even expect his views on any subject to be very interesting. I did admire his courage, but I admire the courage of many people. And I think that most Americans feel the same way I do.

If some people especially admire him, I understand. He spoke for millions of people who needed a spokesman at just his moment. They love and honor his memory. His is a charismatic symbol of their social advancement. That is all to the good.

But all this doesn't add up to a common hero for Americans. The way he has been honored is itself a dishonor. Even his admirers knew he couldn't stand up to a real inquiry. Is this how we choose our heroes now?

Pope Cites Dr. King's Views
St. Louis Review, January 17, 1986
Christian News, February 10, 1986

Washington (NC) – Pope John Paul II said he hope the new U. S. Holiday commemorating the Rev. Martin Luther King Jr. will help advance Dr. King's "worthy ideals" of peace, justice and nonviolence.

Cardinal Agostino Casaroli, papal secretary of state, sent a message on the Pope's behalf on the King observance to the people of the United States.

In the message, Cardinal Casaroli said the Pope was "mindful" of the significant contribution made by Dr. King in the quest for peace through justice and in search for universal solidarity through the elimination by nonviolent means of every form of unjust discrimination."

Dr. King, a Baptist preacher from Atlanta, GA, steadfastly insisted on nonviolent protest as he led the civil rights movement through the turbulent 1960s achieving major changes in U.S. Laws and attitudes before he was assassinated in 1968.

Cardinal Casaroli said the Pope "hopes that this observance" of Dr. King's birthday, "will serve to further the worthy ideals exemplified by his life."

King Not a Christian
The Christian News Encyclopedia, p. 2539

"Martin Luther King-Was He a Black Red?" is the title of a front page article by Dr. Don Boys in the January 1, 1987 Biblical Evangelist.

Boys says that "As a Member of the Indiana General Assembly, I cast the only vote against a resolution memorializing King out of 100 House members and 50 members of Senate." Dr. Boys shows how King had been used by the Communists and that some of King's closest associates were Communists.

While many churchmen agree with Rev. Neuhaus that King should be declared a great Christian saint, Boys concludes:

King Not a Christian

It distresses me to see honest, Conservative Christians "buying" the King propaganda. Are they so desperate for a hero? Many are not aware that King was a theological Liberal (trained at the ultra-liberal Crozer Seminary in Boston). King never used his talent to tell his followers that Jesus Christ was the hope of the world, that the New Birth would solve the hatred problem, that the Bible was the infallible Word of God, or that it was not a skin problem but a sin problem.

He did not because he did not believe those truths. King was probably not even a believer in Jesus Christ as his personal Savior! That will astound those people who think that salvation comes by church membership, baptism, good works, etc. Of course, only God knows those who are genuine Christians, but we know, according to the Bible, that one is not a Christian unless he believes in the substitutionary death of Christ and His bodily resurrection. King did not accept either tenet.

Should I mention the fact that King had numerous girl friends in various cities, and J. Edgar Hoover had taped phone calls of King and his "lady" friends? That hardly recommends such a man to be honored with a national holiday.

'Denying the Bodily Resurrection of Jesus'
To See the Promised Land
The Faith Pilgrimage of Martin Luther King, Jr.
Christian News, June 22, 1987

To see The Promised Land. The Faith Pilgrimage of Martin Luther King, Jr. by Frederick L. Downing. With a Foreword by James W. Fowler. Macon, Georgia: Mercer University press 31207. 298 pages.

Fred Downing, a great admirer of Dr. Martin Luther King, Jr., considers King one of the few authentic heroes and great Christian saints of the Twentieth Century. Donald Capps of Princeton Theological Seminary says that "To See the Promised Land is the first of its kind -- the first full-length application of faith development theory and the first genuine psycho historical study of Martin Luther King, Jr."

Many churchmen consider King one of the greatest Christians of this century. *The Lutheran Book of Worship* has a special festival day commemorating King as a Christian saint. Dr Richard Neuhaus, an associate of King who marched with King, urged the Lutheran Church-Missouri Synod to declare King a saint. LCMS President Jacob Preus suggested that the LCMS establish a scholarship fund in the name of Dr. King.

Rev. Sun Myung Moon of the Unification church has called King the greatest American of the Twentieth Century.

The Faith of Dr. King

Downing writes: "having written a doctoral dissertation on Tillich and Wieman at Boston University, King was a man of intellectual accomplishment" (38). According to Downing, King has a 'mythic-literal faith" during his early years. At first he was a "literalist" who believed the Bible stories his grandmother told him (88 ff.).

Quoting from King's "Autobiography" 9-10, Downing observers that King has this to say about the transition in his faith:

> "The lessons which I was taught in Sunday School were quite in the fundamentalist line. None of my teachers ever doubted the infallibility of the Scriptures. Most of them were unlettered and had never heard of Biblical Criticism. Naturally I accepted the teachings as they were given to me. I never felt my need to doubt them, at least at that time I didn't. I guess I accepted Biblical Studies uncritically until I was about twelve

years old. But this uncritical attitude could not last long for it was contrary to the very nature of my being. I had always been the questioning an precocious type. At the age of 13 I shocked my Sunday school class by denying the bodily resurrection of Jesus. From the age of thirteen on, doubts began to spring forth unrelentingly" (100).

Downing then comments;

> "One thing that is quickly apparent in this paragraph is the correlation of his uncritical attitude with his Mythic-Literal faith. But at age twelve--precisely his age when his grandmother dies - -King remembers that his faith begins to change. No longer can he accept the literal interpretation. And by age thirteen, he seems to have rejected the literalism of his former faith stage. The episode in Sunday School concerning the denial of the bodily resurrection of Jesus seems to imply a different stage of faith from that of his Mythic-Literal faith (101).

While Downing notes that in later years King did affirm his faith in some form of personal immortality, there is no evidence that King ever returned to his early faith in Christianity and to such doctrines as the physical resurrection of Jesus Christ.

The December 30, 1963 *National Observer* published an interview with King which noted that "to King the traditional issues of theology--sin and salvation, the divinity of Christ, His virgin birth, His bodily resurrection are peripheral. Love is central." "He rejects, for example, the idea that men are innately sinners." "Dr. King rejects the virgin birth of Christ as a literal fact." When we wrote to the *National Observer* to find out whether any protests had been raised by Dr. King of his staff against the article, the paper replied: "We have received no comments, either favourable or unfavourable, form Martin Luther King or any of is associates regarding the story." We asked both Dr. King and the Southern Christian Leadership conference about the article but did not receive any reply. (See the section on King in **The Christian News Encyclopedia**, pp. 1123 ff.).

According to Downing, "Up until the age of twelve, he recognized an 'uncritical attitude' in his reading of the Bible. King also remembered that for a long time he had accepted the 'fundamentalist' teachings of is church. But at the age of thirteen, he began to deny the literal nature of the Bible. This early period, dominated by King's 'uncritical attitude,' reflects Fowler's Mythic-Literal stage. But at age thirteen the Synthetic-Conventional stage is evident already" (102).

"The death of his grandmother brought on a crisis in his life in which the previously held principle of moral reciprocity was called into question. During this crisis, he became profoundly concerned with the doctrine of immortality. But a few months later, as he wrote, he was able to 'shock' his Sunday School class with his denial of the bodily resurrection of Jesus. This movement in his life can be understood as the transition from a Mythic-Literal form of faith to that of Synthetic-Convention faith, which typically has its rise in early adolescence" (122).

"Therefore, using King's own judgments about the growth and development of his life, one can see that from early adolescence to the era of his study at Crozer Seminary his faith and identity were characterized by a form of Synthetic-Conventional faith. That is, it was not until his time at Crozer that, as he said, he began to think deeply or to find a sense of the self apart from the traditional worlds that he had come to know in Atlanta" (123).

The "Ladies Man"

"Unwilling to confront his strong father openly, M.L. began to rebel in subtle ways. His comment in Sunday School about the bodily resurrection of Jesus can be understood in that light" (125).

"Tweed" King, says Downing, had the reputation of being quite a "ladies man." He writes:

> "And because of his love for clothes, especially his choice of stylish suits, M.L. was given the nickname, 'Tweed.' For at time 'Tweed' was content to roam up and down 'Sweet Auburn' with his friends 'Mole,' 'Sack,' and 'Rooster.' Known as quite a 'ladies man' within his group, 'Tweed' like his friends enjoyed practicing the art of courtship at every opportunity. And his brother A.D. could not remember a time when M.L. was uninterested in girls. Since M.L. was 'just about the best jitterbug in town,' and 'kept flitting from chick to chick,' A.D. decided early that he could not compete with him and gave up trying. Later, King himself admitted that his two major weaknesses were women and food. But in those early teenage years, M.L. was much like many of his peers; he was two persons. There was the mild-mannered, though often moody young student who deferred to his elders. And then there was the smooth-talking teenager who danced to every tune. Not unlike his friends, he smoked his first cigarette behind a fence and he seemingly changed girl friends almost as often as the dark suites.
>
> "At the age of fourteen King was sensual young man who loved 'soul' food, young women, and the street life of 'Sweet Auburn'" (127).

Profound Truths Behind Bible Myths

While at Moorehouse College King was exposed to biblical criticism and learned that behind the "myths" and "legends" of the Bible there were profound truths even if such miracles as the physical resurrection of Christ never actually happened in ordinary history. Downing writes:

> "George Kelsey, chairman of the Religion Department, became King's favorite classroom instructor. Prior to meeting Kelsey, King's only formal training in religion had been that of his Sunday school, where he was taught along the 'fundamentalist line.' in his first autobiographical essay, King wrote that the Sunday school teachers were 'mostly unlettered' and knew nothing of biblical criticism. His first teachers never 'doubted the infallibility of the Scriptures and for a time King did not either. 'Naturally,' he later wrote, 'I accepted the teachings as they were being given to me. I never felt my need to doubt them, at least at that time.' But, a time of doubt did come for King during his early adolescence. For a time the gap between Sunday school religion and what he learned in college grew wider. Then King wrote that 'this conflict continued until I studied a course in Bible in which I came to see that behind the legends and myths of the Book were many profound truths which one could not escape.' This course in the Bible was taught by George Kelsey. In addition to his college degree from Moorehouse, Kelsy held degrees from Andover Newton and Yale University. And under his instruction and that of others at Moorehouse King began to loosen the 'shackles of fundamentilism'" (137-138).

Downing says that "under the influence of professors like Kelsey, Chandler,

Chivers, and his mentor, Dr. Mays, King came to a new understanding of what the church could be. Its work could be socially relevant and intellectually stimulating" (139).

King's denial of historic Christianity did not just begin at Crozer Seminary. When we noted years ago that King denied such doctrines as the virgin birth of Christ and Christ's physical resurrection, Dr. Martin Simon, the father of Senator Paul Simon, and Dr. Arthur Simon of Bread for the World, sought to excuse King by saying that white evangelicals were to blame for King's liberal theology and denial of various Christian doctrines because no evangelical seminary would accept King. King's denial of historic Christianity began before his seminary days. Downing mentions nothing about any evangelical seminary denying King admittance. When he graduated from Moorehouse, he was not looking for an evangelical seminary.

King had learned, like so many other liberals who reject Christianity and yet become ministers, that one could deny such doctrines as the physical resurrection of Christ and still be a clergyman. Downing writes: "At thirteen he had 'rejected' the bodily resurrection of Jesus and vowed not to enter the ministry and soon became 'a strong believer in personal immortality'" (p. 140). "Although he said that the 'shackles of fundamentalism' came off at Moorehouse, King's ready acceptance of liberalism in his early days at Crozer does not mean a stage of transition for him" (151).

Downing observes that "In his biography of King, David Lewis suggests that at Crozer King carried on a rather busy night life. Lewis indicates that on the day of King's graduation from Crozer there were several young ladies -- each one unknown to the others -- each of whom anticipated that she would by Martin's fiancée. So they all came to the ceremonies to be represented as the one to whom Martin had committed himself" (154). Downing mentions a love affair King had with an attractive white woman (p. 154).

King and Marxism

Downing writes:

"During his Christmas break in 1949, King began to read the works of Karl Marx, including Das Kaptial and The Communist Manifesto. Admitting that 'Marx had raised some basic questions' for him, King went on to write that 'I was deeply concerned from my early teen days about the gulf between superfluous wealth and abject poverty, and my reading of Marx made me ever more conscious of this gulf.' Yet King attempted to read Marx with a critical eye. And in so doing, he became convinced that truth was to be found neither in Marxism nor in capitalism. As he saw it, both represented partial truth. As King summarized his struggle with Marx,

In so far as Marx posited a metaphysical materialism, an ethical relativism, and a strangulating totalitarianism, I responded with an unambiguous "no"; but in so far as he pointed to the weaknesses of traditional capitalism, contributed to the growth of a definite self-consciousness in the masses, and challenged the social conscience of the Christian churches, I responded with a definite 'yes'" (157).

King's Adultery and the Tapes

Downing writes that "a family friend wrote to Martin to remind him that a famous man had to beware lest he succumb to the attempts of others to discredit him. The friend called Martin's attention to 'one of the most damning influences' which he saw as 'that of women.' Some women 'too often delight in the satisfaction they get out of affairs with men of unusual prominence,' he wrote. Such women must be seen as 'enemies.' Then the friend said, 'White women can be lures. You must exercise more than care. You must be diligent indeed'" (235).

Much has been written about King's adultery and many sex affairs with both black and white women. At first his supporters attempted to deny them even though the FBI taped some of King's bedroom conversations. The evidence is overwhelming. President Lyndon Johnson is reported to have even played some of these tapes for reporters. Downing does not deny King's many extra-marital sexual affairs, but he, like many of King's supporters, now excuse them. Downing writes:

"Relying on the memory of Bayard Rustin, Stephen Oates wrote that after the March on Washington and the success of his 'I Have a Dream' speech, King was completely outside of his normal self. Oates describes how, some time after the March when Mrs. King had returned to Atlanta, King decided to 'entertain friends of both sexes' in his room at the Willard Hotel. Oates goes on to suggest that what King did not know that night was that the FBI had begun a long period of systematic electronic surveillance of his activities. After that night, according to Oates, a message was sent to J. Edgar Hoover that King was involved in 'sexual activities' in the room. But David Garrow has shown that the first such embarrassing tape was not recorded until January 1964, when King once again stayed at the Willard Hotel. Earlier suspicions of King within the FBI 'paled,' Garrow reports, 'besides information concerning King's own personal life that was picked up on the tapes.' Though King was grieved and appalled by the compounding violence of the summer of 1964 he was personally threatened by the efforts of the FBI. In November of that year, J. Edgar Hoover in a public statement called King "the most notorious liar in America." Three days later, one of Hoover's chief assistants wrote and mailed an anonymous letter to King along with a copy of an 'incriminating tape' which the FBI had gained through relentless surveillance schemes. Both the letter and the tape were discovered by Coretta King in January 1965. King was seriously threatened and said, 'they are out to break me.' But another of the FBI tapes confirmed that he also saw this episode as a 'warning from God' that he had not lived up to his role in history.

"The biographers suggest that there is little doubt that King cared for his wife and that they shared many tender moments together. But in the later years, he traveled so much - -by his own estimate, King spent only about ten percent of his time at home - - and those absences did take their toll. Publicly, Coretta King and his aides defended King by denying the charges leveled by the FBI. The consensus seems to be, however, that these were words intended to maintain a certain image in the larger public. The biographical judgment seems to be that King sometimes, when lonely and troubled, went against the moral instruction of his early years.

"How does one understand this phenomenon in the structure of a life that in other aspects seems to have been so totally dedicated to moral sobriety? Stephen B. Oates in his recent biography tended to attribute this aspect of King's personality to his vital nature. As Oates saw the situation, King 'needed love, personally, needed companionship, acceptance, and approval.' Therefore, Oates understood that in these private episodes King 'surrendered himself to his passionate nature and sought intimacy and reassurance in the arms of other women.' Arthur Schlesinger tended to agree with Oates. As Schlesinger summarized the situation, 'King was not only a great and honorable citizen and a noble leader; he was also, like other distinguished leaders, a passionate man. This was well known to his close associates and did not disturb them.' Marshall Feady saw it differently; however. He suggested that 'one senses that for King, inextricably caught in the duress and fear and solitude of the unremitting moral struggle he had to sustain, those episodes were an almost unthinking reflex of escape, complete and obliterating, into the luxurious sweet swimming anarchy of the flesh.'

"Put in the context of Erikson's theology of the 'negative identity,' these two views are not antithetical. For King, in the midst of life-threatening trials, these sexual episodes represent something of a regression for the passionate confirmation of one's selfhoods and the affirmation of a vital nature. Is this not in some way a thread that binds the story of a strong man and a troubled soul -- a story of one's patient-hood seeking consolation and affirmation of one's worth and personhood in cares maternal and tender? But on the other hand, did not this man know more than most mortals the struggles and tension that lies in the polarities of existential nothingness and metaphysical allness? So for King, those times away from the cameras may well have been something of a form of escape and the rejection of an identity that had brought so much pain. In both cases, these views represent the 'negative' of a larger identity but also something of a 'surrendered identity.'

"But if the need to escape is a plausible first interpretation of King's sexual activities, is there not more that must be said psycho dynamically? That is, if it is true that King's sexual exploits can be viewed within the context of Erikson's theory of negative identity, then the issue is rooted much more deeply in King's long-term conflicts as a human being" (238-240).

"And as M.L. or 'Tweed' tried to win the confrontations with Daddy King through a submission that was only apparent, so Martin the adult tried to beat Hoover by refusing both a defiant attitude on his own part and respect for Hoover's authority. In fact, the confrontations with both the father and with Hoover made King only more determined to find a form of autonomous freedom. But the price that he paid as a child and later as an adult was the price of an agonizing conscience.

"If then it is true that King's sexual exploits show him as a chauvinist, a rebel against socially and culturally defined mores, and a sinner against his own cherished values and teachings, does not this issue also show Martin Luther King, Jr., as intense 'quester' for human freedom and a sense of atonement that one finds only in the gracious, open arms of a benevolent God?" (241).

Downing says that "in less than a week after King's selection for the Nobel Prize was made public, Hoover called King a liar. This incident provoked King to send a telegram to Hoover. In a press conference, King suggested that Hoover must be beginning to falter under the pressure of his job. But a few days later, King met James Farmer in a New York airport and was told by Farmer that Hoover was spreading a 'story' about King. In essence, Hoover was on a campaign to discredit King publicly with 'information' about King's personal life, his financial dealings, and his association with Communists" (246).

Did King ever repent of his adultery? Downing writes: "on 4 December, King and a party of twenty-six persons left for Norway to receive the Nobel Peace Prize. On the plane, King sat with a friend and talked openly and honestly about his life. There had been some things in his personal life in the past. But he vowed that those episodes would not happen again. For he now realized how difficult such a problem could be. King made an effort toward a new resolve. 'Now that the Nobel award had placed him on a world stage as a moral leader, he had to live more carefully. Even if it deprived him of something he needed, he was gong to be 'Spartan' in his conduct'" (247).

King's resolution to change his life style, according to his critics, lasted until he got to his hotel in Norway.

Downing writes: "When King and his family returned form Norway, Coretta King found the letter and tape sent by the FBI several weeks earlier. Probably the package had been received at SCLC headquarters and added to a pile of other tapes to be sent to King's house, where Coretta traditionally had gone through them. But in this letter King found the most serious type of intimidation. King was told to look deep into his heart and to realize that he was a 'complete fraud.' He was told that he was an 'evil, vicious' fraud who could not believe in God and who had no moral principles. 'Your end is approaching,' the note read. King was told that 'there is only one thing left for you to do.' And supposedly, King was to know what that was. There was only one way out, this message indicated. And he was told, 'You better take it before your filthy, abnormal fraudulent self is aired to the nation.' With the note was compilation of several of the FBI tapes from the surveillance of King's travels across the country. King was stricken with grief over this harassment from the FBI. Distressed and frightened at what was the most in tense kind of intimidation he had ever faced, King fell into a 'serious and prolonged' period of 'mental anguish'" (250).

Downing says that "the King of this last period became more radical in his thinking about tactics and came to be perceived as a threat to the very structures of society, power, and stability.

"The radical faith that King slowly developed in his last years seems to have been a response to the convergence of forces in his life that he understood theologically as the will of God" (251).

"By 1965, King's words begin to reflect a deeper sense of faith, but it is not until early 1967 that he truly begins to actualize the dimension of commitment that Fowler describes as Universalizing faith" (251).

"King's movement toward Universalizing faith was gradual yet perceptible. And with the unfolding of his more radical faith, one can also trace a change in the way that he was received as a leader of the American public. As David Halberstein has noted, in the decade from 1956 to 1966 Martin Luther King, Jr., was the kind of radical with whom many Americans were comfortable. But after 1966 King began to be perceived as a threat to his own country. It was at that point that King's stances on economics and American foreign policy came to be seen as revolutionary. Charles Fager rightly saw at the time that the war issue was King's 'gravest challenge' and, to some extent, the culmination of his career'" (260-261).

A September 28, 1984 Religious News Service story said in a report of speech made to a group of black church leaders by Dr. James Cone, a professor at Union Seminary in New York and known as the "father of black theology," "Mr. King went from an 'integrationist' who tried to reform the system to a 'revolutionary, and said in private that he was a Marxist,' Mr. Cone said. 'If white people knew what King was about, they would never have named a holiday for him'" (*CN*, October 8, 1984).

This book by an admirer of King shows that King did not accept historic Christianity, led an immoral lifestyle, does not deserve to have a national holiday named after him, and should be removed from the calendar of saints in *The Lutheran Book of Worship*.

"Fred Downing explores the faith pilgrimage of Martin Luther King, Jr., with remarkable analytical power and deep empathy. We finally have a biography of Dr. King that contributes greatly to disclosing the deep contours of his spiritual genius. No one who reads this book could possible continue to ignore Dr. Kings' revolutionary, prophetic faith. Downing puts us all in his debt for this careful, compassionate, and path breaking book."

--James Melvin Washington, editor,
A Testament of Hope: The Essential Writings of Martin Luther King, Jr.

"I found *To See the Promised Land* to be a thoughtful and stimulating study that correctly emphasizes the central role of religious faith in the life of Martin Luther King, Jr." -- David J. Garrow,
author of *Bearing the Cross: Martin Luther King, JR., and the Southern Christian Leadership Conference*

"*To See the Promised Land* is the first of its kind-- the first full-length application of faith development theory and the first genuine psycho historical study of Martin Luther King, Jr. What's remarkable is that Fred Downing has succeeded in wedding these two scholarly enterprises. By doing so he has proven that the methods of psychohistory can serve the objectives of faith development research. He has demonstrated that psychology, in the hands of a diligent researcher and perceptive observer, can deepen our appreciation for the life of the individual studied, and sharpen our image of what his life signifies for those who share his vision. Through this powerful analysis of the life of Martin Luther King, Jr., Downing has established his own credentials as a faithful, though not uncritical, follower of one of Christianity's great knights of faith."

---Donald Capps,
Princeton Theological Seminary

Bearing the Cross: Martin Luther King, Jr. and the Southern Christian Leadership Conference
The Banner Of Truth (England), November, 1987

by David Garrow
William Morrow and Co., 800 pp, 1986

Martin Luther King could be a spellbinding orator and in an inarticulate age this was a highly visible feature. His memorable Washington speech can still wield an emotional punch whenever it is replayed. Its main thrusts, that men of every race should have equal status in the eyes of the law, and that dogmas of racial inferiority are an abomination, should be zealously acknowledged by every single Christian. His grievous murder makes him a tragic figure enobled by the dignified bearing of his wife. Understandably he has become a folk hero.

Yet there is another side. King was not, after all, a politician but a Baptist minister of Christ's gospel. He thus came under a higher scrutiny than those who make no profession to speak in Jesus' name. Paul asks, 'What business is it of mine to judge those outside the church? Are you not to judge those inside? God will judge those outside' [1 *Cor.* 5:12].

David Garrow is an associate professor of political science at the City College of

New York. He has had access to King's personal papers, and interviewed 700 of his associates. The picture that emerges is not an attractive one and scarcely one of the life of a Christian minister.

King's humanism is well-known. One of his convictions was that Ghandi was 'the greatest Christian of the modern world.' He believed that Marx 'had analyzed the economic side of capitalism right.' Hegel's dialectic captured him as a student and was reflected in his writings.

Martin Luther King's double standards in sexual morality, and the subsequent and related dark depressions that characterized the final years of his life are some of the revelations of this book. They have been the stuff of rumor for many years but Garrow has interviewed all those involved in the so-called Southern Christian Leadership Conference and built up this picture of a man who from student days was attracted to women. There were three particular relationships which were more than brief, one of these lasting for almost two years. Of that liaison Morrow writes: "That relationship, rather than his marriage, increasingly became the centerpiece of his life, but it did not eliminate the incidental couplings that were a commonplace of King's travels".

King's double-mindedness caused him to be guilt-ridden, depressed and obsessed with the spectra of his death. At one five-day retreat he told Joan Baez, after a couple of whiskies, that he was sick of everything and just wanted to be a preacher. But preach what? He said: 'People expect me to have answers and I don't have any answers. I don't feel like speaking to people. I don't have anything to tell them'. Andrew Young, the major of Atlanta and a long-term associate of King's, says, 'In the later years he was given to a kind of depression that he had not had earlier. He talked about death all the time. He couldn't relax and he couldn't sleep.'

With his enormous potential to be a leader and preacher of Jesus Christ, King turned his back on all of that to guide his people into the wilderness of political action where he deserted them and where so many of them forlornly wander until today. We must be thankful that Black American ministers are beginning to preach again the whole counsel of God unintimidated by humanist pressures to preach another gospel. The betrayal of the black pulpit in America is King's legacy.

The British press are currently obsessed with American 'fundamentalism' and what prominence would they have given to the biography of Luther King had he been a professing evangelical! But, as it is, we may expect no mention of it and the reviewer will be dismissed as another bigot for drawing attention to it.

GEOFFREY THOMAS

Teaching of King ideals stressed
The Washington Times, **September 21, 1988**

By Carol Innerst

Three hundred educators concluding a three-day "mini-summit" here today are pushing to have materials related to the Rev. Martin Luther King Jr. included in the curriculum of the nation's schools.

"Teaching young Americans about Dr. King is as important as teaching them about Madison, Jefferson or Lincoln, since students are not born knowing or committed to the values of our democratic society," said Albert Shanker, president of the American

Federation of Teachers and one of the conference planners.

Said Coretta Scott King, chairwoman of the Martin Luther King Jr. Federal Holiday Commission, which is sponsoring the conference: "The best way to make sure our youth learn and practice Dr. King's principles of racial equality and non-violent social change is to institutionalize them into our educational approach."

Among the districts that already have woven Dr. King's principles into their curriculum are Montgomery County, District of Columbia, Oklahoma City and Atlanta, said AFT spokeswoman Ruth Whitman.

"Those school districts have done a great deal to successfully infuse material regarding Dr. King into history, social studies, English and language arts," she said. "They have shown that his principles can be approached in a context other than history, and do not need to be departmentalized."

Sister Catherine McNamee, president of the National Catholic Education Association, called on schools to take advantage of telecommunications to link classrooms and share their best curriculum practices on the subject of the late civil rights leader.

By addressing issues such as the homeless and drug abuse – issues that Dr. King Likely would have addressed – school districts can further help students to understand the principles he stood for, National Education Association President Mary Futrell said.

A working relationship between school districts, teachers and administrators interested in disseminating information on teaching about Dr. King is expected to evolve from the conference, according to Ms. Whitman.

Also participating in the conference were the Council of Chief State School Officers. Carnegie Foundation for the Advancement of Teaching, Association for Supervision and Curriculum Development, U.S. Department of Energy, Council of Great City Schools, American Association of School Administrators and National Association of Elementary School Principles.

Teach Youth About King
Christian News Encyclopedia, p. 3759

"Three hundred educators concluding a three-day 'mini-summit' here today are pushing to have materials related to the Rev. Martin Luther King Jr. included in the curriculum of the nation's schools" reports the September 21 Washington Times.

The Washington Times quotes Albert Shanker, president of the American Federation of Teachers and one of the conference planners as saying: "Teaching young American's about Dr. King is an important as teaching them about Madison, Jefferson or Lincoln, since students are not born knowing or committed to the values of our democratic society."

The Washington Times added: "Said Coretta Scott King, chairwoman of the Martin Luther King Jr. Federal Holiday Commission, which is sponsoring the conference: 'The best way to make sure our youth learn and practice Dr. King's principles of racial equality and non-violent social change is to institutionalize them into our educational approach.'"

Educators who hold King up to youth as some wonderful hero are doing a great disservice to them. It is now well know and recognized even by some of King's most ardent supporters that he long was a gross adulterer. When youth read about King's adultery and see that he is still so highly praise, it is inevitable that they will soon conclude that there is nothing wrong with pre-marital and extra-marital sex. When they read that even one of King's staunches friends, Dr. James Cone, the father of black theology, said that King admitted he was a Marxist, many youth will soon conclude that Marxism can't be all that bad if such a great hero as King said he was a Marxist and worked side by side with Communists. Christian youth have nothing to learn from King's thoroughly anti-Christian theology. He accepted evolution, denied original sin, and rejected such doctrines as the virgin birth and deity of Christ. *The Christian News Encyclopedia* has plenty of information documenting King's position.

The Lutheran Book of Worship of the Evangelical Lutheran Church has a special festival day set aside for this great "Christian saint." The Lutheran Church –Missouri Synod's *Lutheran Witness* years ago said that King was a "committed Christian" even though King rejected the fundamental doctrines of the Christian faith. Some of King's admirers have recognized in books about King that King didn't accept the historic Christian faith.

Sun Myung Moon, publisher of the *Washington Times*, says that King is the greatest American of this century.

Martin Luther King Praised As A Great Christian and Martyr
Christian News, **January 23, 1989**

Dr. Martin Luther King, Jr. was again praised this month by many churches and religious leaders throughout the nation as a great Christian, noble martyr, and moral leader.

An annual liturgy "in honor of Dr. Martin Luther King Jr." was held in St. Francis Xavier (College) Church in St. Louis. Dr. King is "an example for all of us of someone whose faith motivated him to seek the justice that the Gospel calls for," said Tom Nolan of the Archdiocesan Human Rights Order.

Various denominations sent suggestions to their congregations for worship services honoring King. Liberal churchmen, who praise King, contend that one can be a great Christian without believing in such doctrines as the virgin birth, deity, and resurrection of Christ. They also maintain that it is possible to lead an adulterous life style and still be considered a fine moral example to follow.

Sun Yung Moon's Washington Times again published a special section honoring King. Moon has said that King is the greatest American of the Twentieth Century.

The January 23 U.S. News & World Report commented in an item titled "The greening of a martyr:"

"Both King and JFK were closet smokers, quick catnappers and skirt chasers, and both had overbearing fathers whose politics were sharply at odds with their own. In fact, Daddy King probably had more in common with old man Kennedy than Jack Kennedy had with the young King. Daddy King went from semiliteracy to learning how to read. Then he forces his way into college and took over a bankrupt church. While still not able to speak properly, he became the pastor of the biggest black church in Atlanta, largely by naked ambition, guile and force of will. His is almost a compressed version of the Kennedy family history.

"In 1934, Daddy King changed his first name and that of his 5-year-old son from Michael to Martin. The change took place after the senior King visited Germany, where Martin Luther had defied the Catholic Church. There's a thread of serendipity in this event. Somehow, the whole resonance of the civil-rights movement would have seemed so different if it had been led by Michael Luther King, Jr."

The Lutheran Book of Worship of the Evangelical Lutheran Church includes under "Lesser Festivals and Commemorations:" "January 15. Martin Luther King Jr., renewer of society, martyr, 1968." Some leaders of the LCMS have been among those who praise King. Not all LCMS pastors have been pleased with all the favorable publicity given to King. Dr. John M. Drickamer, an LCMS pastor in Kansas, wrote to Rev. Eugene Schmidt, president of the LCMS's Kansas District on January 12:

January 12, 1989
President Eugene Schmidt
The Kansas District of the Lutheran Church-Missouri Synod
2318 West Tenth Topeka, Kansas 66604
Dear Pres. Schmidt:

It is very distressing to read on the calendar included with the Kansas District publication, "Workers Together," for January 15: "We remember: Martin Luther King, Jr. 1968. Renewer of society, martyr."

It is public knowledge that King was a frequent adulterer and a Communist sympathizer. According to his own words, he was theologically very liberal, retaining little of the historic Christian faith. The documentation has often been presented in **Christian News.**

Even if the above were not known, the very fact that he was officially a Baptist preacher and therefore a false teacher would be enough to exclude him from commemoration by orthodox Christians.

There is no reason to commemorate him as a Christian saint and martyr. There is no excuse for including him as such in an official district publication. A retraction and an apology are in order.

Sincerely,
Dr. John M. Drickamer

Copy: **Christian News**

Dr. James Cone, the father of black theology and a close associate of King, said that King told him not long before his death that he was a Marxist. Cone, a defender of King, said that if Americans knew what King really stood for they never would have designed a holiday in his name. Even some of King's strongest supporters now recognize that King led a grossly adulterous life style. The **Christian News Encyclopedia** shows that King repudiated Christianity and the Christ of the Bible and that he was closely associated with some Communists.

"Inside FBI Files On The Rev. Martin Luther King" in the latest **CDL Report** says in part:

MUCK AND SMUT

There are many other unsavory revelations in the King files; things so offensive that an aide to Lyndon Johnson compared those files to "an erotic book." When F.B.I. Director Hoover said that "King is a 'tom cat' with obsessive degenerate sexual urges," he was not speculating. And insiders of the civil rights movement worried as to how much would become known about King's "unholy trilogy of sex, Communism, and finances." In the worshipful King biography by Stephen Oates, Let the Trumpet Sound, it is revealed that the F.B.I. had several editions of a monograph on Martin Luther King "with still more stories about sex, Communism and embezzlement..." These were widely distributed in intelligence and military circles.

The investigation of Dr. King by the F.B.I. uncovered activity at which one can only hint in a family publication. There was what the files call a "two day, drunken sex orgy" at the Willard Hotel involving Dr. King, S.C.L.C. colleagues, and two women from the Philadelphia Naval Yard. There was a dentist's wife, "King's Mistress" in California, whose brother complained bitterly about the celebrated minister being a "hypocrite." And there was the attempted S.C.L.C. group ravishing of an under-age worker.

Then there was the Los Angeles Hyatt House Motel episode in which Dr. King made filthy, explicitly sexual references to the recently assassinated President Kennedy, to Mr. Kennedy, and to J.F.K.'s funeral. Noted was a $100-a-night white woman in a Midwesten city who wasn't there for choir practice. A Las Vegas prostitute complained in another report about the violence to which she had been personally subjected to by the "Reverend" Dr. King. Yet another F.B.I. report refers to a time when an "Intoxicated" King threatened to "leap from the 13th floor of the hotel if the woman would not say she loved him." And members of the King entourage in Oslo, when he received the Nobel Prize, "expressed their concerns to others over wiretapped phone lines." They were not, as Professor Garrow described it, "accustomed to the style in which King and his closet colleagues partied."

It is interesting to note that the F.B.I.'s assistant director in charge of domestic intelligence, William C. Sullivan, thought there were four solid grounds for Bureau investigation of King, reported Professor Garrow: "embezzlement, employing prostitutes, alienating wives' affections from their husbands, and violation of the Mann Act" – a federal crime which involves taking women across state lines for immoral purposes. Little wonder that a typical bureau memo on this man spoke of exposing "King for the clerical fraud and Marxist he is at the first opportunity."

In its review of the Garrow book in 1981, *Newsweek* naturally downplayed the Communist connections, but talked about how he complained at the time that "if this self-seeking rabble-rouser is allowed to go through with his plans there, Washington may well be treated to the same kind of violence, destruction, looting, and bloodshed" as occurred in Memphis.

Was the murder of King supposed to change that, or was he now so clearly compromised that the Communists decided to make a martyr of him rather than risk exposure?

In any case, there are lots of reasons why Dr. King does not deserve to be honored with the national holiday, and his sins of the flesh are not paramount among them. An F.B.I. memo which we have seen refers, for example, to a fifteen-page document dated April 10, 1967, and sent to the White House. It "was a scathing indictment of Martin Luther King, Jr. ...clearly showing the surveillance gave the FBI access to King's sometimes raunchy private life-the bawdy jokes and sexual adventures, the self-doubts and drinking bouts." Cute. But all this private debauchery was but a sidebar to the reason for the Bureau's real concerns about subversion. And, recall, there were liberals a'plenty in Washington who snickered at the tapes when they were played behind closed doors-vile and scabrous material gathered on the orders of a liberal Attorney General and distributed by liberal President Lyndon Johnson. "G-damn it," David Garrow quotes L.B.J., "if only you could hear what that hypocritical preacher does sexually."

But when Senator Jesse Helms asked that the entire truth be told only about Dr. King's subversive connections, Senator Edward Kennedy and other liberals such as Pat Moynihan made a show of calling Helms a racist and scandal-monger. This from the brother of one man who ordered that King be tapped, and another who warned him to get rid of his Communist comrades.

Forgotten is the fact that at the time of his death Martin Luther King already had been making plans – which presumably are still in the intelligence files collected on King's trip to Communist East Germany-involving a mass-movement effort for yet another march on Washington. Director Hoover had already given secret congressional testimony about some of King's troublesome projections, and West Virginia's Senator Robert Byrd communist influence he is operating under. This document has not been released because of the liberal court's gag order. The liberals are determined to keep a lock on the truth until the year 2027, giving themselves another forty years to gild their King myth. Just how big will the myth be then?

Meanwhile, happy Martin Luther King Day.

Extra-Marital Sex Life
Parade, St. Louis Post-Dispatch
Christian News, January 29, 1989

Q. Did the FBI under J. Edgar Hoover ever try to get the late Rev. Marin Luther King Jr. to commit suicide by threatening to expose his extra-martial sex life? Did the FBI really follow the civil rights leader from hotel to hotel, recording his bedroom exploits? – A.N., Compton, Calif.

A. "Yes" is the answer to both questions. The late J. Edgar Hoover despised Dr. King. He insisted that King, who won the Nobel Peace Prize at age 35, was under Communist influence. In 1963, he pressured U.S. Attorney General Robert Kennedy to approve wiretaps on King's home and office in Atlanta. The FBI then embarked on a rigorous schedule of recording King, who was no angel and in fact had confessed to a friend: "I'm away from home 25 to 27 days a month. [Extramarital sex is] a form of anxiety reduction." In November 1964, an FBI agent sent a package to King at the headquarters of the Southern Christian Leadership Conference. It contained a reel of "sex" tape and an anonymous threatening letter. The package found its way to King's wife, Coretta. She opened it, played the tape and read the letter, which said in part: "King, there is only one thing left for you to do…You better take [your life] before your filthy, abnormal, fraudulent self is bared to the nation."

For further details of Dr. King's relationship with the FBI, you may care to read "Bearing the Cross," the comprehensive, Pulitzer Prize-winning book by David J. Garrow. Another excellent King biography is "Parting the Waters," by Taylor Branch.

Bush: King Was 'A Great Gift' From God
Rescind the Martin Luther King, Jr. Federal Holiday
Christian News, **January 30, 1989**

Statement by Carl McIntire
President of the International
Council of Christian Churches
Collingswood, New Jersey
January 20, 1989

For four years the Federal holiday in behalf of Martin Luther King, Jr., has given an opportunity to observe the celebration and where it is taking the nation.

Its development now calls for the repeal of this Federal holiday. Among the reasons are the following most objectionable developments which concern millions of Christians.

1. On Saturday, November 15, in the Riverside Church in New York City, the Rev. Wyatt T. Walker, chief of staff for Martin Luther King in the early 60's, compared Dr. King to Jesus and said King was "the only authentic spiritual genius that Western religion has produced." This account in quotes is an Associated Press story from the Philadelphia Inquirer, Monday, January 16. Ecumenical Press Service, January 11-15, said "Riverside has functioned as a sort of national cathedral of liberal Protestantism."

There is no way that anyone can be compared to Jesus. He was sinless. He was the Son of God sent from Heaven, virgin born, and was raised out of the grave. "For God so loved the world that he gave his only begotten Son...." To exalt King in this manner and put him on the highest pinnacle as "the only authentic spiritual genius produced by Western religions" elevates him to a position which is very offensive to many.

2. In Washington, Vice-President Bush attended an ecumenical breakfast on Monday, January 16, made up of many blacks supporting the Reagan administration, and praised the civil rights leader as " 'a great gift' from God." This was reported on the front page of **The New York Times**, Tuesday, January 17. For a political leader, just stepping into the White House for the next four years to appraise King as "a great gift from God" which elevates him into the area depicted by King's chief of staff.

For this occasion to be used for such a judgment of Martin Luther King, Jr. by a man who is stepping into the presidency means that this Federal observance has the top political leader offering a judgment that God sent King as His great gift to the nation.

3. A State-sponsoring of a religious service transgresses the Constitution of the United States and the separation of church and state. The State of New Jersey presented and sponsored, January 15, in the Capital, Trenton, the "Fourth Annual Ecumenical Service." The program featured the State seal and listed the Commemorative Commission, including the Honorable Thomas H. Kean, Governor, the Honorable Richard J. Hughes, former Governor and Chief Justice of the Supreme Court. Hughes with Constance Woodruff is Co-Chairman.

Published as a "state-wide ecumenical service," is opened with an invocation by Rabbi Norman Patz, Spiritual Leader of Temple Sholom, West Essex, N.J. It concluded with a benediction by Father Francis McGrath, Director of the Office of Ecumenism, Roman Catholic Diocese. The speaker was the Rev. Buster Soaries of the Shiloh Baptist Church, Trenton. The Call to Commemoration was by the Rev. Caleb

Oates, President of the General Baptist Convention of New Jersey. The Litany of Commemoration was led by the Rev. Winton Hill, Ill, of Mt. Teman A.M.E. Church of Elizabeth, N.J.

For a secular state to sponsor a religious service, and for such a development to come as a part of the King Federal holiday by public officials is a serious fracture of the oath of office all take to maintain and defend the Constitution with its First Amendment. A senator representing the State legislature brought greetings and the Governor sent his. For the King Anniversary to have already been responsible for four of these religious services, with no challenge thus far being made to it, reveals how far afield the political leaders have moved from honoring the prohibition against such religious involvement by a State.

4. The use of the word "ecumenical" in connection with these services and anniversaries is a great offense to the religious communities that reject and oppose the ecumenical movement. Historically it is a credible religious term, but has been taken and perverted to promote the ecumenical movement, which is represented by those churches and leaders in the country that participate in the ecumenical church bodies such as the National Council of Churches and the World Council of Churches.

The breakfast which Mr. Bush attended January 16 was publicized as an "ecumenical" prayer breakfast and so described in the Associated Press article which caries Walker's characterization of King's being compared to Jesus.

The word, "ecumenical," and its use promotes a religious movement and the churches committed to it. To use the Federal commemoration of King to this end impinges on the religious bodies in the country that oppose the ecumenical movement and are seeking to get Christian groups to disassociate themselves from it in order to maintain the historic Christian faith in the land.

5. The use of interfaith worship services including Jews, Roman Catholics, and Protestants for the commemoration involves a de facto rejection of the claim and position of Jesus Christ and historic Christianity. The 11 a.m. worship service announced for the Washington Cathedral at the conclusion of the inauguration was heralded as such a service. The State of New Jersey's ecumenical service included the interfaith emphasis where the Jew who does not accept Jesus Christ invoked God's blessing but not in His name; and the Roman Catholic in his services of worship daily administers the mass, which takes the wine and changes it into the real blood of Christ. The mixing of these beliefs together with the Protestant participation nullifies the requirement of Scripture that all worship be in Spirit and in truth. The King celebration has moved over into these realms where Christians in the country believe that Jesus Christ died once and for all and that He said: "I am the way, the truth, and the life: no man cometh unto the Father, but by me."

6. The "Litany of Commemoration" of Martin Luther King is entitled, "Let My People Go." It was used in Trenton, January 15, with the audience standing and the leader then presenting the pronouncement and the congregation vocally responding "Let my people go." The words are taken from Exodus and were used by Moses and Aaron calling upon Pharaoh to release the Hebrew slaves from 400 years of bondage. This litany revived the Civil War and used it to generate emotions unhealthy for the country. In the responses of the people, there was, "In the name of the Promised Land, let my people." That is the land of Canaan, the Holy Land. Another was, "In the name of the spirit of the Lord, let my people go," and finally, "In the name of Martin Luther King, Jr., let my people go."

Of the approximately 450 people in attendance, not more than 30 were white. To use such a litany and as presented by the State of New Jersey does great damage to the unity and well being of the United States.

7. King's dream, which is emphasized, was related to his words, that he envisioned a nation where a man would be judged not on the basis of his color but on the basis of his character. But the polarization that has just been seen in the 1988 election finds a contributing factor in these Federal King anniversaries. The blacks, thousands of them, vote for a man on the basis of his color, not his character and wherever there is a community where the blacks are in a majority, before long a black is elected to that office because he is a black. This holiday has generated such emotions!

This does not contribute to the unity of the nation, and it offers a temptation to political leaders to appeal to the "black community" to vote its color. The King anniversary in its over-all impact is undermining the unity of the nation and contributes to more racial tensions which is hardly desirable.

8. The place which the Communists have had is this whole area of agitating the blacks and the manner in which they used Martin Luther King Jr. and his association with them still has its effect and consequences which cannot be ignored. There is the testimony of two influential blacks. It still stands. It is that of Manning Johnson and Julia Brown. For nine years Mrs. Brown was a member of the Communist Party in Cleveland. She became an undercover operator for the FBI and she described how the Communists were operating in the black circles. Manning Johnson, who also served in the Communist apparatus, then served the FBI and gave his testimony at great length concerning how the Communists were using the blacks and worked particularly through their churches.

The Communists have not abandoned these areas, but are no longer being exposed by the Congressional Committees for the benefit and the security of the country. Communism is no longer an issue following these King Federal holidays.

For these and other reasons, it is apparent in the four years since the Federal holiday was established that what is taking place involves serious religious offenses violating the Constitution on separation of Church and State and contradictions, and favors certain religious groups as opposed to others, and is contributing to a political polarization which is unhealthy for the Land.

In outlining these reasons, I do so from a position as President of the International Council of Christian Churches, where there are more black churches and black Christians in its membership than any of the other five colors, red, brown, yellow, white. In this fellowship there is no color line. All are received, not on the color of their skin but in their oneness in Christ Jesus as they are members of his body, leaders in His churches, and are standing together to advance the cause of Biblical Christianity throughout the world.

This call to have Congress rescind the Federal holiday request the prayers and also the support of all who are in sympathy and appreciate the position here outlined which has resulted from the four years of the celebration. There are millions of Christians who are black, who love the Lord Jesus Christ in spirit and truth who will never dishonor Him when they learn these facts. It is in the best interests of all the American people and their representative in political assemblies and in keeping with their oath of office and their desire for the unity, security and well being of the county, that this Federal holiday be revoked. All those groups, churches and others who desire to commemorate the day are free to do so on their own in their right of free exercises of religion, free speech, free assembly.

Let steps be now taken to repeal the act of Congress authorizing the Federal holiday.

Former U.S. attorney says book right about King
The Huntsville Times, October 15, 1989
The Christian News Encyclopedia, p. 3759

By Mike Paludan
Times Staff Writer

FBI records back up the Rev. Ralph David Abernathy's newly published claims that Dr. Martin Luther King Jr. had extramarital affairs, including liaisons the week he was slain, says a former U.S. attorney who had access to the files.

Macon Weaver of Huntsville, who served in Birmingham as the U.S. attorney for North Alabama during the 1960's, said Saturday that Abernathy's book "And the Walls Came Tumbling Down" contains information on King's sex life that can be backed by FBI records obtained during surveillance of the civil rights leader.

Weaver had direct access to those FBI files because it was his office that had responsibility for issuing the arrest warrant for James Earl Ray, King's assassin.

Abernathy last week was labeled by former colleagues in the civil rights movement as an insane man simply trying to sell his book. The Rev. Jesse Jackson, state Rep. Alvin Holmes of Montgomery, and others called on Abernathy to repudiate the book.

But FBI records and other published histories of King back the claims, said Huntsville's Weaver.

"What he says in his book is verified by FBI reports, and I've read every one of them," Weaver said. The FBI files indicate that King had one such liaison with a Kentucky woman legislator on April 4, 1968, the afternoon he was assassinated in Memphis, Weaver said.

The former prosecutor said the files leave no doubt that King "was a womanizer. He had the women there in the Loraine Hotel when he got shot. The FBI's got plenty of records that go beyond this. They had his bed bugged in many places."

Weaver said the information contained in the FBI files is probably public record and could be examined.

"That investigation is over, so I don't know why they wouldn't be subject to the Freedom of Information Act," Weaver said.

Details of King's liaisons have come out before, Weaver said, "but nobody paid any attention to it." Weaver, now 70, left the U.S. Attorney's Office in late 1969.

Weaver was critical Abernathy's recent detractors.

"They're all saying nobody knows if that's true or not. Well, I know it is.

"They're saying (Abernathy's) a liar, and he's insane, he's losing his mind and all those kinds of things, and I just thought somebody ought to speak up who knows and say that he's telling the truth and that it can be verified by the reports of the FBI," Weaver said.

"That's what needs to be stopped. They're just making a fool out of Abernathy. And what he's saying is the truth. That's absolute factual information that he put in his book," Weaver said.

Weaver said he believed the FBI records to be accurate as well.

Weaver said his office issued the warrant on Ray because authorities were having difficulties dealing with Memphis law enforcement. Another factor was that King lived in Birmingham, Weaver added.

"In a conspiracy count, any place that an overt act has occurred has venue," he said.

As U.S. attorney, Weaver received written updates of the continuing FBI surveillance every couple of days, he said.

After King's assassination, the FBI investigated where King had been staying before arriving in Memphis, said Weaver.

"A lot of people checked out of the motel and ran over to the Howard Johnson's, and Abernathy and some with cooler heads told them they better get back where they belonged or it would look suspicious," Weaver recalled from the FBI files.

"That did look suspicious and that's why they (FBI) backtracked and found out that they (King and the Kentucky woman) had been in Panama City (Fla.) and also that he had been with her all afternoon when he got shot," Weaver said.

While Abernathy's book reported that King had had a liaison the night before his death, Weaver said the FBI reported a liaison that day.

"He (Abernathy) said that he (King) had been with her the night before, but the FBI report says he was there and had a liaison with her in her room during the afternoon when they were having a rest period. He was in that room with her. He walked out on the balcony, according to the report, while she freshened up and they were all going to somebody's house to eat," Weaver recalled from the FBI files.

The controversy last week over the book helped place it on the best-seller list, its publisher said.

Fueling the controversy have been public jabs by Jesse Jackson, Andrew Young and others close to King in the 1960s.

The Associated Press has quoted a group of Alabama state lawmakers as saying Abernathy is either insane, had been forced to write the book or let someone else write it using his name.

"I think some white folks put him up to it," state Rep. Holmes was quoted as saying.

King's Adultery
Can Unrepentant Adulterers Get to Heaven?
Christian News, October 23, 1989

God tells us: "Nobody who lives in sexual sin or worship idols, no adulterers or men who sin sexually with other men, who steal, are greedy, get drunk, slander, or rob will be heirs of the kingdom of God." 1 Corinthians 6:9,10.

Last week papers all over the country reported that Dr. Martin Luther King spent his last night with two women and then fought physically with a third. His close friend and associate, Dr. David Abernathy, in his recently published book, " And the Walls Came Tumbling Down" (Harper & Row) revealed that King was guilty of adultery right up until the time of his death. Others, both friends and foes, have written about King's flagrant adultery.

Christian News for more than 25 years has published articles about King's anti-Christian theology and lifestyle and his association with some prominent Communists.

Some of these articles are in **The Christian News Encyclopedia**. Years ago The Lutheran Church-Missouri Synod's **Lutheran Witness** referred to King as a "committed Christian" even though King rejected such doctrines as the virgin birth and resurrection of Christ.

The Lutheran Book of Worship, which is used in the Evangelical Lutheran Church in America and a good number of congregations in The Lutheran Church-Missouri Synod, includes a special festival day on its list of Christian saints for Dr. Martin Luther King, Jr. even though King, who repudiated historic Christianity, was an unrepentant adulterer.

One of the hoaxes that *CN* has repeatedly exposed is the hoax that prominent churchmen who live in adultery, such as Paul Tillich, Martin Luther King and Karl Barth were great **Christian** leaders. The "new morality" defended by liberal churchmen allows for the adultery of such great church leaders as King, Tillich and Barth. God tells us that unrepentant adulterers go to hell.

"Abernathy Book Bombshell – DR. KING'S LAST NIGHT –Account of women, violence in Memphis" was the headline which took up most of the front page of the October 12 New York Daily News.

In recent years Abernathy has been associated with Sun Myung Moon. He serves on two Moon dominated boards (**The Christian News Encyclopedia**, p. 2713). Moon has said that King is the greatest American of this century.

When the *National Observer* published and interview article with King in which King is supposed to have denied basic doctrine of the Christian faith, we asked King and also the Southern Christian Leadership Conference (SCLC) about the article. *CN* received no response. The **National Observer** told *CN* that neither King nor his Southern Christian Leadership Conference ever registered any protests against what the **National Observer** reported about King's theology.

CN also wrote to Ralph Abernathy after a report appeared in the **Congressional Record** which indicated that he was an unrepentant adulterer. The **Congressional Record** indicated that he was an unrepentant adulterer. The Congressional Record reprinted an editorial from the **Montgomery Advertiser**. It said that Abernathy is "best remembered here for what may have been a record dash from his church office on the night of Aug. 20, 1958. Panic stricken and screaming, he was pursued by an irate, hatchet wielding husband who had accused him of having a relationship with his wife more suited to the pages of Krafft-Ebing's PSCYOPHATICA SEXUALIS than a family newspaper.

"The wife of his assailant told a Montgomery Circuit Court jury in November 1958 that she had submitted to unnatural sex acts with the Reverend before her marriage, beginning at the age of 15, and that 'he never stopped chasin' me' even after her marriage to Edward Davis. She had been a member of Abernathy's church.

"On the day Davis accosted Abernathy in his office, armed with pistol and hatchet, Abernathy had called her, Mrs. Davis testified. The jury deliberated only 10 minutes, obviously invoking the unwritten law, before acquitting Davis of attempting to do in the preacher. Yet, basking in the reflected glory of King, Abernathy emerged from the revolting case unscathed in the eyes of SCLC."

We commented in the June 10, 1968 **Christian News**: "Now that Abernathy claims to be such a great spokesman for the nation's poor people, the time has come for him to explain the story of the 'record dash' which is beginning to receive wide circulation. We have seen no denial or explanation of the affair now included in the **Congressional**

Record. The leader of the Poor People's Campaign should not be an unrepentant adulterer. Furthermore, Abernathy is not going to 'redeem the soul of America' with his Poor People's Campaign. He should try preaching the saving Gospel of Jesus Christ, the only message of redemption for all sinners. This leader should preach on 2 Thess. 3:10 to the masses gathered in 'Resurrection City.' 'If any would not work, neither should he eat.' We have written to Rev. Ralph Abernathy and asked him for any statement he may have released with regard to the charges inserted into **The Congressional Record**."

The July 15, 1968 *CN* reprinted part of a story from **Human Events** which exposed how Abernathy and some other spokesman for the nation's poor were wasting thousands of dollars with their fancy lifestyle. The money had been given to help the poor. Human Events wondered how Abernathy could claim that his "Resurrection City" had spent 1.5 million dollars when almost everything had been donated. **Human Events** said that "The only known SCLS expenses were: 'Hotel and motel charges for Abernathy and numerous SCLS officials and their families. None of them spent a night in 'Resurrection City'. They lived in the best hostelries, ate in the best dining places, and shopped in the best stores. At one motel alone they paid a bill of $20,000. Mrs. Abernathy bought $400 dresses in one of Washington's most expensive stores.

"Three trucks and nine automobiles purchased in the capital to provide transportation for the SCLC officials and, on some occasions, shantytown demonstrators. The 12 vehicles were paid for in cash."

CN commented: "Why should Christians finance such waste?"

Paul Harvey in a column on the " 'Reverent' Rev. Abernathy" exposed Abernathy's adultery and extravagance. Then he quoted Abernathy as saying: "And believe me, Ralph Abernathy, this nation is going to have hell on its hands." "We're going to turn this nation upside down….I won't be nice the next time I go to Washington." And the man Abernathy appointed as the new "field director" of Abernathy's SCLC poor people's march said on June 3, 1968 in Washington: "The picnic is over; we're going to share in this nation's wealth or there won't be any wealth." (*Christian News*, July 1968)

Better Late Than Never
By Rev. Henry H. Mitchell
A Conservative Black Pastor Who Sent Articles to *Christian News* to Publish
Christian News, **November 6, 1989**

Truth comes to light: The **Star News** honors the Reverend Ralph Abernathy for having the courage to write this book, "And the Walls Camp Tumbling Down," regarding the hidden life of Martin Luther King, Jr. As we all know, Rev. Abernathy was one of the closest associates of Martin Luther King during his lifetime.

Some of Martin Luther King's associates are asking Rev. Abernathy for a retraction of his book regarding the womanizing (adultery) that Martin Luther King perpetrated during his life-time. To those who are asking for a retraction of the book, the Bible teaches that whatsoever is done in the dark will come to the light.

In 1966, along with a group of west-side ministers, I sent Martin Luther King a letter before he moved his crusade to Chicago to "end slums." We requested a meeting to get him to understand that slums are not ended by marching and to show him the proper direction for putting an end to them. Slums are created by slum-minded people and cannot be ended by marching, but rather by educating the people. It is the responsibility of the community to help keep their neighborhoods clean.

Martin Luther King refused to meet with us at that time, so we asked him to get out of Chicago. In April of 1966, he was very much alive.

It is high time for Americans to start lifting up Jesus. Jesus taught us to lift Him up and Him only . He said if we lift Him up, He will draw all men unto Him. The Bible teaches to put your trust not in man because man will deceive you. Many people have put their trust in black and white religious and political leaders, only to be deceived by them.

The **Star News** urges all of its readers to read Rev. Abernathy's book, "And the Walls Came Tumbling Down." The man is speaking the truth. To those who are asking Jesus for a retraction of His Word when He said that which is done in dark will come to the light.

I disagree with any person who will enslave another and deprive him of his God-given rights of freedom to do whatever he wants to, as long as it does not infringe upon the rights of others. I am against any kind of slavery, but I declare before God this day that the conditions of the mass of blacks have gotten worse after the so-called civil rights movement.

I agree with James Meredith who said, "They are the black bureaucrats who perpetuate and administer the policies of the white liberals. They are destroying the black community."

He cited the welfare programs, the low-cost housing programs, the affirmative action programs, busing of school children and other "supposedly" liberal reforms as examples of taking away self-control of the black community and putting it in the hands of government.

He further charged that "This plan for black progress" was never intended to work.

"It was designed to take control of the black community from the hands of blacks and put it into the hands of white liberals – the government – to make us dependent on them. To make us dependent on the government as a source of revenue instead of ourselves as the source of revenue."

Meredith said he blamed himself. "At first, while I did not approve, I did not perceive these policies as dangerous. I got sucked in lie a lot of others. Unfortunately, there is a whole black bureaucracy so dependent on the administration of these policies that they are now completely dependent on their existence. The worst danger, he said, is that it has destroyed the moral fiber of the black community. Families are disintegrated; there is unemployment; drugs, crime and a lack of community pride and involvement has disenfranchised blacks.

The solution?

"It is not simple. You can overcome the financial setbacks, the political setbacks; but, it is very difficult to mend what has happened to the morals.

"We need to return to the family as a source of strength, hard work instead of handouts and a pride in our schools and communities. We must assert ourselves as responsible first class citizens and take back control."

Meredith is the man most remembered as the first black to enter and graduate from the University of Mississippi in 1963; and the man who in 1966, while on a "Walk Against Fear," was wounded by three shotgun blasts fired by would-be assassins.

Star News, 1414 South Independence Blvd., Chicago, Illinois 60623

Was King a Plagiarizer?
Christian News, January 21, 1991

Some of the defenders of Dr. Martin King Jr. have been insisting that the reports about King being a plagiarizer are not true.

At one time King's defenders insisted that King was not an adulterer. Now even his most ardent friends have had to admit that the reports are true and that he had a "womanizing" problem for many years.

King's supporters long insisted that King was not sympathetic towards Marxism. Now Dr. James Cone, "the father of black theology" and a close friend of King, says that King told him that he (King) was a Marxist.

At one time even such publications as the *Lutheran Witness* of The Lutheran Church-Missouri Synod said that King was a "committed Christian" yet today the evidence shows that King did not accept historic Christianity.

The following letter by Dr. Westling, President ad interim of Boston University, appeared in the January, 1991 *Chronicles*, published by the Rockford Institute, 934 N. Main Street, Rockford, Illinois 61103:

On Martin Luther King, Jr.

In "Revolution and Tradition in the Humanities Curriculum" (September 1990), Thomas Fleming repeats the false story that Dr. Martin Luther King, Jr. plagiarized his Boston University doctoral dissertation. The charge has been made several times in the last year and appears to be spreading like whooping cough among the unvaccinated. Allow me to introduce some penicillin.

Dr. King's dissertation has, in fact, been scrupulously examined and reexamined by scholars, including scholars who are thoroughly familiar with the "personalist" theological tradition to which Dr. King's dissertation was a contribution and who would stand the best chance of catching any nonattributed quotatioris. Not a single instance of plagiarism of any sort has been identified.

The apparent source of this defamatory rumor was an article that appeared last December in a London newspaper-an article that was refuted by its supposed primary source in a subsequent issue. To my knowledge, the reappearance of this rumor in a recent issue of *Chronicles* is the first time that any reputable journal has stumbled into this pseudo-controversy.

To set the record straight, since 1955, when Dr. King submitted his dissertation, "A Comparison of the Conceptions of God in the Thinking of Tillich and Henry Nelson Wieman," not a single reader has ever found any nonattributed or misattributed quotations, misleading paraphrase, or thoughts borrowed without due scholarly reference in any of its 343 pages. If you or anyone else have evidence to the contrary, it should be presented.

Jon Westling
President ad interim
Boston University
Boston, MA

Theodore Pappas, the assistant editor of *Chronicles*, responds in a carefully documented article titled "A Doctor in Spite of Himself-The Strange Career of Martin Luther King, Jr.'s Dissertation."

Pappas shows by direct quotes from King's doctoral dissertation titled "A Comparison of the Conceptions of God in the Thinking of Paul Tillich and Henry Nelson Wieman," that King copied much of his dissertation from a dissertation by Jack Stewart Boozer titled "The Place of Reason in Paul Tillich's Concept of God." Pappas bases his arguments on evidence and solid fact not emotion and the opinion of the majority.

Pappas observes that some of the editors of Kin's papers at first denied any plagerizing. He notes that "Despite the serious nature of the charge, more than nine months have passed and no scholarly article has appeared and no discussion of the charges has occurred in our nation's press." The December 3, 1989 **London Telegraph** appears to be the first publication to print the story. **The Spotlight, Christian News**, and some other small publications picked up the story. (See the November 11, 1990 *Sunday Telegraph*, reprinted in the January 14, 1991 *CN*, p. 2).

Pappas lines up quotes from King and Boozer and shows how they are almost verbatim and that King even copied Boozer's mistakes. Pappas writes: "It is not merely that King's arguments, language, and choice of words run parallel with Boozer's, but that whole phrases, sentences, and even paragraphs are lifted verbatim from Boozer text." "There is virtually no section of King's discussion of Tillich that cannot be found in Boozer's text, and often the parallels are not simply similarities but downright duplications." "King has not only lifted this entire passage from Boozer's text, but he has even copied an error in punctuation."

"The story of King's plagiarism has been suppressed for one simple reason: fear-fear of the massive retaliation that will be visited upon anyone who attempts to set the historical record straight, not just on King and his dissertation but on any historical incident on which the powers that be have declared an official position. Perhaps the editors of this magazine would have been wiser had they ignored this entire matter. But evidence of a cover-up made up our minds. We have learned, for example, that high-level administrators at several major universities have attempted to suppress this story and that at least one scholar has been bullied into silence. We also wonder why the National Endowment for the Humanities, which funds the King papers project and is well aware of the charge of plagiarism, has yet to take any action."

"Then there is the reproof administered by the 'ad interim' president of Boston University... Mr. Westling insists that scholars have 'scrupulously examined and re-examined' King's dissertation without being able to identify 'a single instance of plagiarism' – no 'misattributed quotations,' no 'misleading paraphrases' and no 'thoughts borrowed without due scholarly reference.' He concludes his letter with this challenge: 'If you or anyone else have evidence to the contrary, it should be presented.' We issue a similar challenge to Mr. Westling, the editors of the King papers, and all other interested scholars: if you have any genuine evidence that might exonerate King, it should be presented."

Chronicles says in another article titled "Historical Update:"

"Following *Chronicles*' denunciation of King's plagiarism in mid-August (Perspective, September 1990), the *Wall Street Journal* broke the story on November 9, after we had already put together the January issue. The New York Times then followed with its own version of the story on November 10. The editors of King's papers apparently believed the cover-up had continued for long enough.

"In fact, Mr. Clayborne Carson now admits that he and some twenty other members and associates of his advisory board have known about the plagiarism for over three years, but chose to suppress the story until now."

"Second, David Garrow, a member of the project's advisory board and author of the Pultizer Prize-winning biography of King, Bearing the Cross, also now admits to having known about King's plagiarism and deliberately suppressing the story. Shouldn't he give back his Pulitzer?

"Third, if Jon Westling as ad interim president of Boston University was acting under his own initiative in concocting the story of King's innocence, then he is either incompetent or a liar. In either case, he should resign from the university he has disgraced. If he was acting as an agent for President John Silber, then the next move is up to Silber-who could, at the very least, strip King of his degree.

"Fourth, the National Endowment for the Humanities has known about the plagiarism for over a year. Instead of coming clean with the American taxpayers, who have funded the King papers project with a reported half million dollars, the Endowment simply sat on the facts. Mr. Cheney owes us a full explanation of the role she and the NEH played in this matter.

"Finally, the time has come for a frank and open debate on the significance of the King legacy. Unfortunately, the evidence is locked up in sealed FBI files. Instead of subjecting the nation to an unending series of disclosures and scandals, the government should unseal the documents. The issue is integrity-not of Martin Luther King, but of an American regime that refuses to tell the truth."

Scholars confirm plagiarism in King thesis
Washington Times, October 11, 1991
The Christian News Encyclopedia, p. 3789

Boston (AP) –A committee of scholars said yesterday that Martin Luther King Jr. plagiarized passages in his dissertation for a doctoral degree at Boston University.

"There is no question but that Dr. King Plagiarized in the dissertation by appropriating material from sources not explicitly credited in notes, or mistakenly credited, or credited generally and at some distance in the text from a close paraphrase or verbatim quotation," the panel said in a report.

Despite its findings, the committee said: "No thought should be given to the revocation of Dr. King's doctoral degree from Boston University" because that would not affect "academic or scholarly practice."

But the group did recommend that a letter stating the committee's finding be placed with the official copy of King's dissertation in the university's library.

University Provost Hon Westling accepted the report's recommendations. He said the committee "conducted the investigation with scholarly thoroughness, scrupulous attention to detail, and a determination not to be influenced by non-scholarly consideration."

Boston University established the committee nearly a year ago to determine whether plagiarism allegations against King who was assassinated in 1968 were true.

King wrote "A Comparison of the Conceptions of God in the Thinking of Paul Tillich and Henry Nelson Wieman" in 1955 as part of his requirements for a Ph.D. He received his degree after completing his studies at the division of religious and theological studies.

Committee member John Cartwright, the university's Martin Luther King professor of social ethics, said the initial rumors about the plagiarism did more harm than the panel's findings will.

"I think it is so good to get this behind us," Mr. Cartwright said.

He said the committee refrained from speculating about the reasons King may not have properly attributed material.

"We felt that because he is dead, to conjecture about his motives or any of that would be fruitless."

Mr. Cartwright said the committee determined the dissertation to be an academic contribution and found "no blatancy" in King's plagiarism.

"There is no obvious indication in the dissertation that he inappropriately utilized material," Mr. Cartwright said. "It's only when one really begins to look carefully that it becomes apparent. And none of the sources were very far removed from the material."

Lutheran University Calls King a "Christian"
King "Preaches" at Valparaiso University
Christian News, February 10, 1992

Although Dr. Martin Luther King, Jr., was a theological modernist who refused to affirm such Christian doctrines as original sin and the virgin birth and physical resurrection of Jesus Christ, Valparaiso University still insists that King was a great "Christian" pastor and preacher. Liberal religion professors at the Lutheran school have long insisted that Christianity is not the only divinely revealed and saving faith. According to these liberal Valparaiso religion professors, people can get to heaven without believing that Jesus Christ is the only way to heaven. They approved of a Rabbi who totally rejects Christianity, preaching in a regular chapel service at Valparaiso University commemorating the Holocaust.

The January 19 Alive newsletter of the Valparaiso University's Chapel of the Resurrection announced: "Special Morning Prayers for week of Martin Luther King, Jr. Commemoration-Although there will be no Morning Prayer on Monday, January 20, because of the special Martin Luther King, Jr. Convocation, that remembrance will set the theme for the following four days of Morning Prayer. We will remember Martin Luther King as a Christian pastor and as a preacher.

"Each day in the context of Morning Prayer, a sermon of Dr. King will be delivered in abbreviated form as the homily for the day."

The Order of Worship for January 24 of Valparaiso Chapel of the Resurrection, which was built primarily from money given by members of The Lutheran Church-Missouri Synod, features King on the front cover as "Pastor and Preacher." It says: "'I See the Promised Land,' presented today in Morning Prayer, was the Reverend Martin Luther King's last and most apocalyptic sermon. He preached it at the Bishop Charles Mason Temple, headquarters of the Church of God in Christ, in Memphis, Tennessee, on April 3, 1968, the eve of his assassination."

The order of worship says: "Leader: Traci Bendewits, Chapel Intern, Senior Deaconess Student-Reader: Hattie Calloway, Assistant Director, Dining Services – Presenting Dr. King's Sermon: Professor John Paul."

Valparaiso University religion professors have supported the theology of Seminex, including the ordination of women. The liberals maintain that man and the universe gradually evolved from primary substances and were not directly created by God as taught in the book of Genesis. Confessional Lutherans in many sections of the Lutheran Church-Missouri Synod have long protested against the promotion of liberal theology at Valparaiso University. Valparaiso University, which formerly expelled unrepentant homosexuals, now allows them to meet on campus.

Although Valparaiso University insists that it supports freedom of speech, most of the guest speakers invited to speak at the school are either political or theological liberals. Evolutionist are permitted to influence students but not creationists. *CN* has often suggested that a creation vs. evolution debate be held on campus between a Christian creationist scholar and some of the evolutionists at Valparaiso University. The school was not interested in giving its students an opportunity to hear both sides.

(See **The Christian News Encyclopedia** for documentation on King's theology and the theology promoted and tolerated at Valparaiso University.)

A Booker T. Washington Day
No Day for King – A Marxist, Adulterer, Plagiarizer and No Christian Saint
Christian News, January 9, 1995

(Editorial)

Martin Luther King Day is again being celebrated by many churches throughout the U.S. The Council of Lutheran Churches of Greater St. Louis is sponsoring its second annual Martin Luther King Jr. Prayer Breakfast on January 14. Roman Catholics are again having special masses honoring King.

Christian News has often said that the U.S. should celebrate a Booker T. Washington Day rather than a Martin Luther King, Jr. Day.

The January, 1995 **Lutheran Witness** of the Lutheran Church-Missouri Synod published an opinion column titled "Thoughts On Dr. Martin Luther King Jr." The LCMS's official publications, along with the official publications of almost all major denominations, have long praised King. **Lutheran Book of Worship**, the hymnal used in the churches of the Evangelical Lutheran Church in America and in many LCMS churches lists a special day for King, leaving the impressions that King was a great Christian Saint....

What kind of message is the **Lutheran Witness** and all the other denominational publications praising King sending to America's youth, particularly black youth, when they praise King and refuse to condemn his well known disgusting adulterous life style? This is the message: "Extra-marital and premarital sex is O.K. boys and girls. King did it many times ever since he was a teen-ager and right up until he was killed and yet he is today remembered as a 'Great committed Christian.' One doesn't have to accept such outdated truths as the virgin birth, deity and resurrection of Christ to be considered a great Christian saint. King never affirmed these doctrines and yet is hailed by leading denominational publications and churchmen today as a 'Great committed Christian.'" "Marxism isn't bad and it's O.K. to be linked up with the Communists. King said he was Marxist and he was associated with Communists and yet leading church papers and church leaders today still say King was a great patriotic

American and Christian." *CN* has often said that our nation should have a Booker T. Washington Day rather than a Martin Luther King Day. Official denominational publications should be letting their readers know what **Destiny Magazine: The New Black American Mainstream**, 809 Center Street, Lansing, MI 48901, has been saying. See "Self-Help, Strong Families, Religion, Patriotism – DESTINY PROMOTES THE 'OTHER' BLACK HISTORY" in the March 21, 1994 *Christian News*. It is a tragedy that official church papers never tell their readers about **Destiny**, which is published by conservative blacks.

The U.S. does not need a special day for a Marxist adulterer. Let's have a Booker T. Washington Day rather than a Martin Luther King Jr. Day.

Catholic Bishops Want Vatican to Name King a Martyr
Christian News, January 24, 2000

(RNS) American Catholic bishops have asked the Vatican to name slain civil rights leader Martin Luther King Jr. a 20th century martyr for Christianity, according to the Boston Globe.

King, along with four church women murdered in El Salvador in 1980, is among 10,000 people around the world nominated for recognition as 20th century martyrs by Pope John Paul II.

"To think that his life of service and giving has been recognized, it's very humbling to me," said Christine King Farris, sister of the Baptist minister who was assassinated in 1968.

Those chosen as martyrs will be selected by a special Vatican commission, and will be honored in Rome in a May 7 ceremony, part of the Jubilee 2000 celebration marking Christianity's 2,000th anniversary.

The group honored in Rome will include both Catholics and non-Catholics, and will be separate from the martyrs officially granted sainthood by the Roman Catholic Church.

Paul Henderson, director of the U.S. bishop's office for Jubilee 2000, said the recognition granted to non-Catholics represents the pope's wish for an inclusive celebration of Christianity.

"One of the Holy Father's emphasis for the jubilee years is that is it not just a Catholic event but a celebration of 2,000 years of Christianity, for all," said Henderson.

Daniel Boyarin, a professor at the University of California at Berkeley and author of "Dying for God: Martyrdom and the Making of Christianity and Judaism," hailed the pope's decision.

"For the pope to recognize non-Catholic martyrs is a very important ecumenical move," Boyarin said. "It was only a few centuries ago when Catholics and Protestants were burning each other at the stake."

Ed. King denied such Christian doctrines as the virgin birth of Christ, His deity and resurrection. Some of his closet friends have noted that King was an unrepentant adulterer who had sex with many women. Dr. James Comb, a professor at Union Seminary, New York, and a close friend of King, said that King told him that he (King) was a Marxist.

Says King Was a Communist Traitor
Christian News, January 24, 2000

Dear Editor, WASHINGTON TIMES:

Why do we celebrate Martin Luther King, Jr.'s, birthday? He was a . . . communist, and there is ample evidence to prove this. Mrs. King had the records kept on him sealed for 50 years "to avoid embarrassment." The FOA act allowed a few to slip through the cracks, however. The tapes that have been released to Sen. Helms are very revealing.

It was not some "right-winger" who had King's office and hotel rooms bugged. This order was signed by then U.S. Attorney General Bobby Kennedy on October 10, 1963. Evidence proved that King was under the direct orders of Soviet spies and financed by the Communist Party. The Kennedy tapings continued for five years and also developed shocking revelations regarding King's sexual practices.

African-American Hayard Rustin is a former organizer for the Young Communist League. He spent 60 days in a California jail on a 1953 conviction for performing lewd homosexual acts in public. He also served 20 months in prison for draft evasion. Today Rustin is paid by Jewish organizations for the use of his name as a "signer" of ads urging "Black-Jewish Unity." He was King's secretary and advisor from 1956 to 1960.

During this period Rustin attended the National Convention of the Communist Party in 1957 as an "honored observer." King called him "a brilliant, efficient, and dedicated organizer." It was Rustin who introduced King to a Soviet spy named Stanley D. Levison. He was a New York lawyer, and vice-president of the N.Y. Council of the American Jewish Congress. Levison's job was to launder the $1 million subsidy Soviet Russia gave to finance the U.S. Communist Party. Levison provided important financial, organizational and public relations services for King.

After King's death, his wife, Coretta Scott King, described Levison's role as "always working in the background. His contribution has been indispensable." Levison wrote an obituary for King and described America as "a nation tenaciously racist...sick with violence...and corrosive with alienation. The civil rights liberation struggle is the most positive and rewarding area of work anyone could experience."

The money which the Soviet Union funneled to Levison came from the Isidore G. Needleman. He was a KGB secret police agent who fronted as an officer of AMTORG, the trading company in New York City which buys U.S. goods for shipment to Russia.

Martin Luther King Jr., is no American hero, he was a communist traitor, and should not be honored with a national holiday.

Edward J. Toner, Jr.
LCDR USNR (Ret.)
481B Jason Place
Brick, NJ 08724
(732)840-4203

King's Sexual Orgies
Christian News, January 24, 2000

Dear Editor:

The Martin Luther King National Holiday shows just how much the general public has been kept in the dark on the character of this man, who pleaded for us to judge a man not by his color, but the content of his character. What a hypocrite.

The FBI wired King's offices and hotel rooms from 1963 to 1968. These tapes not only recorded his transactions with communist agents but also wild interracial sex orgies which included acts of perversion.

King's aids would use SCLC, (tax exempt) money, to hire white prostitutes to perform sexual acts on him. King often would use two prostitutes at the same time. These shocking tapes were ordered sealed for 50 years by U.S, Federal Judge John Smith, Jr., on January 31, 1977. In other words we will not be able to learn all the gory details until the year 2027.

Some 90 congressmen, led by the late Rep. Larry McDonald, urged Congress to find out what was in these tapes before they approved the disgraceful King Holiday Bill. A cowardly and spineless Congress voted 338 to 90 approving the King Holiday.

Still, we have been able to learn some of the shocking incidents recorded on the King tapes, thanks to the efforts of Sen. Helms and the FOA. Washington's old Willard Hotel was the scene of King forcing white women to drink "Black Russians" and performing sexual acts upon him. In Las Vegas, King's aids paid $100 each to prostitutes to join him in orgies. In New York City, King got drunk and threatened a white girl working for civil rights to submit to his strange sexual tastes or he would jump from the 13th floor window. She succumbed to prove her loyalty to King.

In Norway, King was nude when stopped by police while chasing a woman down a hotel corridor. In Los Angeles a dentist supporter of King was outraged when he discovered his wife engaged in weird sexual acts with the civil rights leader. King was forced to flee the city after the dentist threatened to kill him. This escape was taped on February 20, 1968. Is this the kind of man we want to hold up before our children to be honored as a national hero?

For publication,
Edward J. Toner Jr.

King Honored at ELS's Bethany College
Denied Resurrection of Christ, Was a Gross Adulterer, Plagiarist and Communist Sympathizer
Will LCMS Give $250,000 For Martin Luther King National Memorial?
Christian News, August 23, 2002

Although Dr. Martin Luther King, Jr., rejected the Christian faith, including such doctrines as the physical resurrection of Jesus Christ, was an adulterer who regularly cheated on his wife, a plagiarizer and a Communist sympathizer, many Lutherans continue to hail King as a great Christian.

The August 2002 Reporter of The Lutheran Church-Missouri Synod said in a report of the LCMS's Black Ministry Family Convocation, July 24-28, in Orlando, Fla.: "During business sessions, delegates adopted nine resolutions. Among those actions, they voted to:

"Request the LCMS Directors to authorize a Black-ministry campaign, in cooperation with the LCMS Foundation, to raise $250,000 by Sept. 1, 2003., as a contribution to the proposed national memorial to Dr. Martin Luther King, Jr., planned for Washington, D.C."

Although King denied the basic doctrines of the Christian faith, the LCMS's **Lutheran Witness** already years ago said that King was "a committed Christian." **The Lutheran Book of Worship** used in ELCA and some liberal LCMS churches has King on its list of Christian saints. Father John Neuhaus, who marched with King, wanted the LCMS to declare King a great Christian saint.

Dr. James Cone, the father of "black theology" and a close friend of King, said that King told him that he (King) was a Marxist. When the **National Observer** interviewed King and published an article on King's theology noting that King denied the basic doctrines of the Christian faith, *CN* asked King and his Southern Christian Leadership conference to let *CN* know if the *National Observer* had misrepresented King. The **National Observer** told *CN* that neither King nor anyone with King's organization expressed any disagreement with the article on King's theology. It is in **The Christian News Encyclopedia**.

King's extramarital sexual exploits have been widely publicized by his friends and opponents. Ralph Abernathy, one of King's closet aides, wrote in his book on King and the civil rights movement that King had sex with several women the night he was assassinated.

Liberal churchmen have long excused King's flagrant adultery, insisting that King makes a fine role model for youth. Major foundations and insurance companies have not hesitated supporting those who praise King even though King was a socialist who strongly opposed free enterprise and the free market, the very system which enabled the foundation to make money.

Many Lutheran colleges have long hailed King as a great Christian, a patriotic American and a good role mode. This year even the conservative Bethany Lutheran College of the Evangelical Lutheran Synod praised King at a special observance for King. Students were not told that King repudiated the Christ of the Bible and was a flagrant adulterer. Those who tell the truth about King are considered right-wing fanatics who are not worthy of support. It does not pay to tell the truth about King or liberals and adulterous and unscripturally divorced clergymen in any denomination.

Archdiocese of St. Louis Celebrates the Life and Work of Dr. Martin Luther King, Jr.

http://archstl.org/category/tags/mass

WHAT: Archbishop Robert J. Carlson will celebrate the thirty-fifth annual Archdiocesan Mass and lead the commemoration for the life and work of Dr. Martin Luther King, Jr.

WHEN: Sunday, January 16, 2011, at 2:30PM

WHERE: Cathedral Basilica of St. Louis, 4431 Lindell in the Central West End

ST. LOUIS — As part of its annual national observance of Martin Luther King, Jr. Day, the Archdiocese of St. Louis celebrates Dr. King's words, acts, and deeds for social justice. Mass will include a choir consisting of parishioners from across the Archdiocese of St. Louis, brought together solely for this event.

Myths of Martin Luther King
Christian News, February 3, 2003
By Marcus Epstein

There is probably no greater sacred cow in America than Martin Luther King Jr. The slightest criticism of him or even suggesting that he isn't deserving of a national holiday leads to the national holiday leads to the usual accusations of racist, fascism, and the rest of the usual left-wing epithets not only from liberals, but also from many ostensible conservatives and libertarians.

This is amazing because during the '50's and '60's, the Right almost unanimously opposed the civil rights movement. Contrary to the claims of many neocons, the opposition was not limited to the John Birch Society and southern conservatives. It was made by politicians like Ronald Reagan and Barry Goldwater, and in the pages of Modern Age, Human Events, National Review, and the Freeman.

Today, the official conservative and libertarian movement portrays King as someone on our side who would be fighting Jesse Jackson and Al Sharpton if he were alive. Most all conservative publications and Web sites have articles around this time of the year praising King and discussing how today's civil rights leaders are betraying his legacy. Jim Powell's otherwise excellent the Triumph of Liberty rates King next to Ludwig von Mises and Albert J. Nock as a libertarian hero. Attend any IHS seminar, and you'll read "A letter from a Birmingham Jail" as a great piece of anti-statist wisdom. The Heritage Foundation regularly has lectures and symposiums honoring his legacy. There are nearly a half dozen neocon and left-libertarian think tanks and legal foundations with names such as "The Center for Equal Opportunity" and the "American Civil Rights Institute" which claim to model themselves after King.

Why is a man once reviled by the Right now celebrated by it as a hero? The answer partly lies in the fact that the mainstream Right has gradually moved to the left since King's death. The influx of many neo-conservative intellectuals, many of whom were involved in the civil rights movement, into the conservative movement also contributes to the King phenomenon. This does not fully explain the picture, because on many issues King was far to the left of even the neo-conservatives, and many King admirers even claim to adhere to principles like freedom of association and federalism. The main reason is that they have created a mythical Martin Luther King Jr., that they constructed solely from one line in his "I Have a Dream" speech.

In this article, I will try to dispel the major myths that the conservative movement has about King. I found a good deal of the information for this piece in "I May Not Get There With You: The True Martin Luther King" by black leftist Michael Eric Dyson. Dyson shows that King supported black power, reparartions, affirmative action, and socialism. He believes this made King even more admirable. He also deals frankly with King's philandering and plagiarism, though he excuses them. If you don't mind reading his long discussions about gangsta rap and the like, I strongly recommend this book.

Myth #1: King wanted only equal rights, not special privileges and would have opposed affirmative action, quotas, reparations, and other policies pursued by today's civil rights leadership.

This is probably the most repeated myth about King. Writing on National Review Online, There Heritage Foundation's Matthew Spalding wrote a piece titled "Martin

Luther King's Conservative Mind," where he wrote, "An agenda that advocates quotas, counting by race and set-asides takes us away from King's visions."

The problem with this view is that King openly advocated quotas and racial set-asides. He wrote that the "Negro today is not struggling for some abstract, vague rights, but for concrete improvements in his way of life." When equal opportunity laws failed to achieve this, King looked for other ways. In his book **Where Do We Go From Here**, he suggested that "A society that has done something special against the Negro for hundreds of years must now do something special for him, to equip him to compete on a just and equal basis." To do this he expressed support for quotas. In a 1968 Playboy interview, he said, "If a city has a 30 percent Negro population, then it is logical to assume that Negroes should have at least 30 percent of the jobs in any particular company, and jobs in all categories rather than only a menial areas." King was more than just talk in this regard. Working through his Operation Bread-basket, King threatened boycotts of businesses that did not hire blacks in proportion to their population.

King was even an early proponent of reparations. In his 1964 book, **Why We Can't Wait**, he wrote,

> No amount of gold could provide an adequate compensation for the exploitations and humiliation of the Negro in America down through the centuries..... Yet a, price can be placed on unpaid wages. The ancient common law has always provided a remedy for the appropriation of the labor of one human being by another. This law should be made to apply for American Negroes. The payment should be in the form of a massive program by the government of special, compensatory measures which could be regarded as a settlement in accordance with the accepted practice of common law.

Predicting that critics would note that many whites were equally disadvantaged, King claimed that his program which he called the "Bill of Rights for the Disadvantaged" would help poor whites as well. This is because once the blacks received reparations, the poor whites would realize that their real enemy was rich whites.

Myth #2: King was an American patriot, who tried to get Americans to live up to their founding ideals.

In National Review, Roger Clegg wrote that "There may have been a brief moment when there existed something of a national consensus – a shared vision of eloquently articulated in Martin Luther King Jr.'s 'I Have a Dream' speech, with deep roots in the American Creed, distilled in our national motto, E pluribus unum. Most Americans still share it, but by no means all." Many other conservatives have embraced this idea of an American Creed that built upon Jefferson and Lincoln, and was then fulfilled by King and libertarians like Clint Bolick and neocons like Bill Bennett.

Despite his constant invocations of the Declaration of Independence, King did not have much pride in America's founding. He believed "our nation was born in genocide," and claimed that the Declaration of Independence and Constitution were meaningless for blacks because they were written by slave owners.

Myth #3: King was a Christian activist whose struggle for civil rights is similar to the battles fought by the Christian Right today.

Ralph Reed claims that King's "indispensable genius" provided "the vision and leadership that renewed and made crystal clear the vital connection between religion and politics." He proudly admitted that the Christian Coalition "adopted many elements of King's style and tactics." The pro-life group, Operation Rescue, often compared their struggle against abortion to King's struggle against segregation. In a speech titled The Conservative Virtues of Dr. Martin Luther King, Bill Bennett described King, as "not primarily a social activist, he was primarily a minister of the Christian faith, whose faith informed and directed his political beliefs."

Both King's public stands and personal behavior makes the comparison between King and the Religious Right questionable.

FBI surveillance showed that King had dozens of extramarital affairs. Although many of the pertinent records are sealed, several agents who watched observed him engage in many questionable acts including buying prostitutes with SCLC money. Ralph Abernathy, who King called "the best friend I have in the world," substantiated many questionable acts in his autobiography, **And the Walls Came Tumbling Down**. It is true that a man's private life is mostly his business. However, most conservatives vehemently condemned Jesse Jackson when news of his illegitimate son came out, and claimed he was unfit to be a minister.

King also took stands that most in the Christian Right would disagree with. When asked about the Supreme Court's decision to ban school prayer, King responded, I endorse it. I think it was correct. Contrary to what many have said, it sought to outlaw neither prayer nor belief in God. In a pluralistic society such as ours, who is to determine what prayer shall be spoken and by whom? Legally, constitutionally or otherwise, the state certainly has no such right.

While King died before the Roe vs. Wade decision, and, to the best of my knowledge, made no comments on abortion, he was an ardent supporter of Planned Parenthood. He even won their Margaret Sanger Award in 1966 and had his wife give a speech titled "Family Planning – A Special and Urgent Concern" which he wrote. In the speech, he did not compare the civil rights movement to the struggle of Christian Conservatives, but he did say "there is a striking kinship between our movement and Margaret Sanger's early efforts."

(Ed. King rejected historic Christianity. "He did not affirm such doctrines as the virgin birth, deity and resurrection of Jesus Christ." See "A Booker T. Washington Day – Not a Martin Luther King Day," *CN*, Jan. 20, 2002, and **The Christian News Encyclopedia**.

Myth #4: King was an anti-communist.

In another article about Martin Luther King, Roger Clegg of National Review applauds King for speaking out against the "oppression of communism!" To gain the support of many liberal whites, in the early years, King did make a few mild denunciations of communism. He also claimed in a 1965 Playboy that there "are as many Communists in this freedom movement as there are Eskimos in Florida." This was a bald-faced lie. Though King was never a Communist and was always critical of the Soviet Union, he had knowingly surrounded himself with Communists. His closest advisor Stanley Levison was a Communist, as was his assistant Jack O'Dell. Robert and later John F. Kennedy repeatedly warned him to stop associating himself with such subversives, but he never did. He frequently spoke before Communist front groups such as the National Lawyers Guild and Lawyers for Democratic Action. King even attended seminars at The Highlander Folk School, another Communist front, which taught Communist tactics, which he later employed.

King's sympathy for communism may have contributed to his opposition to the Vietnam War, which he characterized as a racist, imperialistic, and unjust war. King claimed that America "had committed more war crimes than any nation in the world."

While he acknowledged the NLF "may not be paragons of virtue," he never criticized them. However, he was rather harsh on Diem and the South. He denied that the NLF was communist, and believed that Ho Chi Minh should have been the legitimate ruler of Vietnam. As a committed globalist, he believed that "our loyalties must transcend our race, our tribe, our class, and our nation. This means we must develop a world perspective."

Many of King's conservative admirers have no problem calling anyone who questions American foreign policy a "Fifth columnist." While I personally agree with King on some of his stands on Vietnam, it is hypocritical for those who are still trying to get Jane Fonda tried for sedition to applaud King.

Myth#5: King supported the free market.

OK, you don't hear this too often, but it happens. For example, Father Robert A. Sirco delivered a paper to the Acton Institute titled "Civil Rights and Social Cooperation." In it, he wrote,

> A freer economy would take us closer to the ideals of the pioneers in this country's civil rights movement. Martin Luther King Jr. recognized this when he wrote: "With the growth of industry the folkways of white supremacy will gradually pass away," and he predicted that such growth would "Increase the purchasing power of the Negro [which in turn] will result in improved medical care, greater educational opportunities, and more adequate housing. Each of these developments will result in a further weakening of segregation."

King of course was a great opponent of the free economy. In a speech in front of his staff in 1966 he said,

> You can't talk about solving the economic problem of the Negro without talking about billions of dollars. You can't talk about ending the slums without first saying profit must be taken out of slums. You're really tampering and getting on dangerous ground because you are messing with folk then. You are messing with captains of industry…Now this means that we are treading in difficult water, because it really means that we are saying that something is wrong…with capitalism… There must be a better distribution of wealth and maybe America must move toward a Democratic Socialism.

King called for "totally restructuring the system" in a way that was not capitalist or "the antithesis of communist." For more information on King's economic views, see Lew Rockwell's "The Economics of Martin Luther King Jr."

Myth #6: King was a conservative.

As all the previous myths show, King's views were hardly conservative. If this was not enough, it is worth noting what King said about the two most prominent postwar American conservative politicians, Ronald Reagan and Barry Goldwater.

King accused Barry Goldwater of "Hitlerism." He believed that Goldwater advocated a "narrow nationalism, a crippling isolationism, and a trigger-happy attitude." On domestic issues he felt that "Mr. Goldwater represented an unrealistic conservatism that was totally out of touch with the realities of the twentieth century." King said that Goldwater's position on civil rights were "morally indefensible and socially suicidal."

King said of Reagan, "When a Hollywood performer, lacking distinction even as an actor, can become a leading war hawk candidate for the presidency, only the irrationalities induced by war psychosis can explain such a turn of events."

Despite King's harsh criticism of those men, both supported the King holiday. Goldwater even fought to keep King's FBI files, which contained information about his adulterous sex life and Communist connections, sealed.

Myth #7: King wasn't a plagiarist.

OK, even most of the neocons won't deny this, but it is still worth bringing up, because they all ignore it. King started plagiarizing as an undergraduate. When Boston University founded a commission to look into it, they found that 45 percent of the first part and 21 percent of the second part of his dissertation was stolen, but they insisted that "no thought should be given to revocation of Dr. King's doctoral degree." In addition to his dissertation many of his major speeches, such as "I Have a Dream", were plagiarized, as were many of his books and writings. For more information on King's plagiarism, The Martin Luther King Plagiarism Page and Theodore Pappas' Plagiarism and the Culture War are excellent resources.

When faced with these facts, most of King's conservative and libertarian fans either say they weren't part of his main philosophy, or usually they simply ignore them. Slightly before the King Holiday was signed into law, Governor Meldrim Thompson of New Hampshire wrote a letter to Ronald Reagan expressing concerns about King's morality and Communist connections. Ronald Reagan responded, "I have the reservation you have, but here the perception of too many people is based on a image, not reality. Indeed, to them the perception is reality."

Far too many on the Right are worshiping that perception. Rather than face the truth about King's views, they create a man based upon a few lines about judging men "by the content of their character rather than the color of their skin"-something we are not supposed to do in his case, of course-while ignoring everything else he said and did. If King is truly an admirable figure, they are doing his legacy a disservice by using his name to promote an agenda he clearly would not have supported.

January 18, 2003

Marcus Epstein [send him mail] is an undergraduate at the College of William and Mary in Williamsburg, VA, where he is president of the college libertarians and editor of the conservative newspaper, The Remnant. A selection of his articles can be seen here http://www.lewrockwell.com/orig/epstein9.html Copyright 2003 LewRockwell.com

An International Church
Better Than $250,000 For The Martin Luther King Memorial
Christian News, June 7, 2004

Testimony by the editor of *Christian News* to be presented to Committee Four of the LCMS's 2004 convention in St. Louis at its open hearing on July 10.

An overture before your committee (**Convention Workbook**, pp. 219-220) from the Lutheran Church-Missouri Synod's Black Ministry Convocation is asking for $250,000 from the LCMS for building the Martin Luther King Monument on the Capital Mall, Washington D.C. Our black fellow Christians should be commended for their concern for justice.

The Black Ministry Convocation says in its overture that "we thank and praise God for a leader like Martin Luther King, Jr., who was committed to a determined but non-violent struggle for justice and Christian brotherhood." Our black fellow Christians should be commended for their concern for justice and Christian brotherhood. This has not always been shown in America to those of various races and nationalities.

The LCMS's *Lutheran Witness* has referred to King as a "committed Christian" even though he refused to affirm such doctrines as original sin, the virgin birth, deity and resurrection of Jesus Christ. Dr. James Cone, "the Father of Black Theology" testified that King told him that he (King) was a committed Marxist. Ralph Abernathy, King's closest aid, said that King had sex with several women who were not his wife the night before he was assassinated. *The Christian News Encyclopedia* includes articles on the theology and morals of Martin Luther King.

CN and Christian blacks have long said that it would be more fitting to have a "Booker T. Washington Day" rather than a "Martin Luther King Day." It is true that ELCA's Lutheran Worship honors King as a great Christian saint even though King rejected historic Christianity.

There is a much better way for the LCMS to show that orthodox Lutherans oppose the racism of the evolutionists, the racism of the White Identity cult, and the racism of the Israel First Millennialist who believe that God has some special chosen people today and that present day Israel by divine right owns all the land of Palestine.

Why not use the money with which the Black Ministry Convocation wants to honor Martin Luther King for a statue or statues of some prominent blacks in the LCMS such as Rosa Young, the famous educator who was advised to go to the LCMS by Booker T. Washington, or Marmaduke Carter, the author of Lutheran Customs, Peter Hunt, Albert Dominic, or Robert King. Perhaps all of them could be included on a bronze panel like that at Our Savior Lutheran Church, Houston, Texas (p. 1). The panel is patterned after a smaller panel at the famous Luther memorial in Worms, Germany. Between Luther and leading figures of the Reformation are the pastors who have served Our Savior Lutheran Church.

More would see the statue or relief panel if it were at Concordia Seminary, St. Louis, possibly next to the Luther statue or on the wall of some building rather than at Concordia, Selma. Perhaps some prominent Lutheran native American like John Johnson, a Chinese person, a Korean like the Korean Luther, Won Yong Ji, and Indian like Victor Raj, a converted Jew like Ed Balfour, and prominent Lutherans from other races could be included on the relief panel all gathered around Martin Luther.

Let the world know that the LCMS is truly an international church for all people, and preaches the saving Gospel and Luther's scriptural doctrine to all. It has no racial or nationality boundaries and champions justice and true freedom for all.

READ - READ - READ
Christian News, October 4, 2004

"ELCA Published Book Defending Cone's Black Theology" on p. 1 shows that ELCA's Fortress Press is promoting the anti-scriptural theology of Dr. James Cone, the "Father of Black Theology." *CN* has exposed the anti-Christian, pro-abortion, pro-homosexual views of Cone for decades. Cone was a close friend of Martin Luther King. Cone says that King insisted he (King) was "a Marxist." According to Cone, whites never would have named a day after King if whites knew what King really believed.

The father of "Black Theology" says the white church is the anti-Christ. Read the quotations in this issue taken from the ELCA published book. LCMS President Jerry

Kieschnick wants his LCMS to draw closer to ELCA. Has he read this ELCA book? How many of the books published by ELCA attacking basic doctrines of the Christian faith have many pastors read? *CN* seldom sees them reviewed in any liberal or conservative publications. During the last 42 years *CN* has reviewed scores of them. Most reviews included lengthy quotes. Some reviews are in *The Christian News Encyclopedia*. When Concordia Seminary President John Johnson commended ELCA's Fortress Press for its publishing work, *CN* listed some of the many liberal books published by Fortress. Several promote homosexuality.

Cone, however, is correct when he complains about the lack of reading by many pastors. Note the item on reading on p. 22. *CN* has observed that there are pastors who can spend hours with their computers and in front of their TV sets. Some can debate via-email for hours on some rather insignificant fine liturgical point. They have little interest in such subjects as the articles in this issue about the bombing of innocent civilians (see Grace Otten's photos on Dresden and the articles on the bombing of Dresden, pp. 12-16), or what Dr. Jabs refers to on this page as "the greatest humanitarian crisis in the world today." What *CN* writes about the importance of physical fitness (Save the Pederson Field house and related articles, pp. 1-11), should not even be covered by a Christian newspaper, according to some *CN* critics.

If more LCMS pastors and laymen would read the truth about what is happening today in Christendom and the LCMS, the LCMS would not now be in danger of being completely taken over by the liberals who are working for women pastors, the acceptance of evolution, etc. READ-READ-READ.

Says King Claimed to be "A Marxist"
Attacks the Christ of the Bible
ELCA PUBLISHED BOOK DEFENDING CONE'S BLACK THEOLOGY
Christian News, October 4, 2004

Living Stones In The Household of God - The Legacy and Future of Black Theology. Edited by Linda Thomas. Fortress Press, Box 1209, Minneapolis, MN 55440. 2004, 234 pages. paper.

The front and back cover of this book published by Fortress Press of the Evangelical Lutheran Church in America are reproduced here.

Dr. James Cone, a professor at Union Theological Seminary known as "the Father of Black Theology" and not the Christ of the Bible is the hero of this book. *CN* has exposed the anti-scriptural theology of the Father of Black Theology for decades. The "Record of James H. Cone in *The Christian News Encyclopedia*" in this issue has some items about Cone in the *CNE*. Cone was a close friend of Dr. Martin Luther King. He claims that King told him that he (King) was a Marxist. Cone said that if most churchmen really knew what King beleived they would never have praised him or named a day after him.

Editor Linda E. Thomas, an ELCA professor, writes in the book's preface:

"What is exciting about this book is that black theology is examined as public theology not only addressing the historically black churches but also in dialogue with various theologies - Asian, Native American, Latino/a and white - and the corresponding faith traditions represented by these theologies" (vi).

"Finally, I want to thank my teacher and mentor, James H. Cone, who weathered the storms, continues to fight, and has gifted the world with a theology that makes faith take risks as no other theology has done before" (viii).

Thomas writes in the introduction:

"In **Black Theology and Black Power** (1969), James H. Cone, the father of black theology, criticized the white church. He wrote, 'If the real Church is the people of God, whose primary task is that of being Christ to the world by proclaiming the message of the gospel (Kerygma), by rendering services of liberation (diakonia) and by being itself a manifestation of the nature of the new society (koinonia), then the empirical institutionalized white church has failed on all counts'" (xi).

"The future of black theology will also have to deal with sexual orientation in the black community and the church. Black heterosexuals enjoy privilege virtue of their sexual orientation; this societal structure oppresses and fractures the lives of black lesbians, gays, bisexuals, and transgender persons. In addition, black theology will articulate the reasons that it is unjust for heterosexuals to use the Bible to condemn homosexuals while at the same time expect verses that sanction slavery to be thrown out, put aside, or reinterpreted.

"The future of black theology will articulate the importance of treating black children as full human beings. The future of black humanity is embodied in black children. They must be nurtured from their earliest days. Black parents must have quality child care that is free or affordable. Children must have free health care. Children must be the investment of choice for the black church as it relates to education and housing. In the future for the future, black theology must be a theology of liberation for black children" (xiv).

Martin Luther King

"In the tradition of the Hebrew prophets and against the advice of his closest associates in black and white communities, King stood before a capacity crown at Riverside Church on April 4, 1967, and condemned America as 'the greatest purveyor of violence in the world today'" (7).

James Cone writes in Chapter One:

"In 1903 W.E.B. DuBois said: 'The problem of the twentieth century is the problem of the color-line - the relation of the darker to the lighter races of men in Asia and Africa, in America and the islands of the sea.' That message is as true today as it was when he uttered it. There is still justice in the land for black people. 'No justice - no peace' proclaimed blacks to whites during the 1992 Los Angeles riot and the years that followed. 'No love - no justice' was Martin King's way of proclaiming to all who would listen" (12).

W.E.B. Dubois was a Communist.

Jeremiah A. Wright Jr. writes in a chapter on "Doing Black Theology in the Black Church:" "United Black Christians and the Commission for Racial Justice represent caucuses in another white denomination. Also, Albert Cleage, a United Church of Christ minister, wrote **The Black Messiah and Black Christian Nationalism** and founded the Shrine of the Black Madonna. The National Black Episcopal Caucus, the Black Lutherans, the Black United Presbyterians - all of those folk leading fight for black theology are in white denominations" (17).

Rev. Albert Cleage, a United Church of Christ clergyman, promoted the Marxist

Black Manifesto. He wrote in his The Black Messiah that everything about traditional Christianity is false and that Jesus never really rose from the dead. (*The Christian News Encyclopedia*, p. 285, p. 555).

Rosemarie Radford Reuther

Rosemary Radford Reuther is the author of a chapter titled "A White Feminist Response to Black and Womanist Theologies." *CN* has often noted that Reuther repudiates historic Christianity. In this book she continues to promote her anti-scriptural universalism. She defends speaking of God as "goddess."

She writes:

"One of my great delights is the increasing emergence of feminist theologies in many different contexts: womanist, Mujerista, Asian-American, and lesbian theologies in the United States, as well as diverse feminist theologies in Africa, Asia, Latin America, and the Middle East. Buddhist, Hindu, Jewish, and Muslim women are doing feminist theology in their distinct religious contexts. I have been deeply involved in the last twenty years with both first-third world dialogue between Christian feminists and inter-religious feminist dialogue.

"This pluralism is coming to be assumed, although we are still learning how to collaborate and not be used to undercut one another" (58).

D. Stephen Long writes in a chapter titled "What I Learned from James Cone and Black Theology:

"Cone's work is significant precisely because he breaks through the bourgeois sentimentality that too often masquerades in and through the language of contemporary theological education, where the language of the white church dominates the language of pluralism, inclusion, diversity, and dialogue. Cone transgresses the boundaries this language establishes, boundaries that seem to invite the production of civic and civil theology. In the midst of that language Cone tells us:

> The time has come for white America to be silent and listen to black people.
> All white men are responsible for white oppression.
> Theologically, Malcolm X was not far wrong when he called the white man "the devil."
> To love the white man means that black man confronts him as though without any intentions of giving ground by becoming an it.
> Any advice from whites to blacks on how to deal with white oppression is automatically under suspicion as a clever device to further enslavement.
> The task of black theology is to take Christian tradition that is so white and make it black, by showing that whites do not really know what they are saying when they affirm Jesus as the Christ.

"Cone's work is neither sentimental invitation for dialogue nor liberal pleading for inclusivity. For those of us in the white church there is no way out of the judgment these statements render" (60, 61).

Long speaks about what he considers to be the "neo-Lutheranism" of Paul Tillich. He says that "Tillich drew upon Martin Luther as the example par excellence of the 'courage to be'" (68). Tillich repudiated the existence of any personal God. He denied the Trinity and the entire Christian faith. He was, according to his wife, also a pornographer and adulterer. See the **The Christian News Encyclopedia**.

Iva E. Carruthers writes in a chapter on "Black Theology and Ecumenism:" "The evolving corpus and legacy of the works of James H. Cone are seminal and central to late twentieth - and twenty first century ecumenism within both the African American religious context and the larger Christian church. In the halls of academia, within the walls of the black church, and at the table of ecumenical discourse, the man and message of James Cone has been like a burning bush - for some reflecting the light of God, for others a smoldering thorn of discomfort that will not die out" (116).

"In 1968 Albert Cleage, a United Church of Christ minister, published **The Black Messiah**. In 1969 James H. Cone published **Black Theology and Black Power**. When NCBC met at Interdenominational Theological Center (ITC) on June 13, 1969, they looked specifically to Cone to shape their foundational consensus document. From that moment on, there was no turning back the influence Cone would have upon the leadership and ecumenical organizations active on the threshing floor of theologizing and human social justice activities, including people of all hues, political persuasions, genders, sexual persuasions, and classes" (119).

The authors reject the inerrancy of the Bible. Although Peter says he wrote 1 and 2 Peter, M. Shawn Copeland says this is uncertain (183). Copeland says:

"Black theology been here; black theology still here! Black theology is the Spirit's gift: Black theology takes us down lifts us up, carries us over! Black theology been here; black theology still here; black theology became a natural, walking man in James Hal Cone. What the Spirit showed him and through him showed us is that black theology must meet the anguish of chronos with the power of kairos" (186).

"What the Spirit showed James Cone and through him showed us is that black theology must meet the anguish of this chronos with the power of God's kairos" (187).

"What the Spirit showed James Hal Cone and through him showed us is that black theology is the daring deep black, blue-black, black and blue protest of liberation for oppressed and oppressor! What the Spirit is showing him and is showing us is that black theology must meet the chaos of imperial globalization with the order of divine truth. What the Spirit is showing him and showing us is that in embracing the cross black theology must address the suffering of our people. What the Spirit is showing him and showing us is that standing before the cross of our people's suffering, black theology must resist evil. This is our mandate for black theology's community; this is our hope for ourselves and our students. Yet, first and foremost, always, this is God's doing: it is a wonder to behold" (188)!

Cone writes in the final chapter of this ELCA book:

"Watching and listening to my parents, I soon discovered that God's Spirit makes you say things you would rather not say because the truth is hard-hitting. It makes people angry because it exposes their hypocrisy. While writing **Black Theology and Black Power**, I often said to myself, 'Oh, s***, white folks ain't going to like that.' When I got to the chapter on the black church, it broke my heart to have to make public what everybody knows to be the truth about it" (206).

"Bennett, as president of Union, called me into his office and asked whether my second book was theological hyperbole. 'You don't really believe that the white church is the antichrist, do you?' I looked John in the eye and told him that I was not dealing with theological exaggeration. 'If you really believed that the white church is the antichrist, why are you teaching at Union?' he asked. 'My dad was a woodcutter,' I said, 'and I worked at Union. I see little difference between the two workplaces since whites control both. As long as I seek justice in the system, I might as well work at Union. There is no more spiritual significance to working at Union than any other white supremacist institution.' John Bennett was a little surprised that I meant what I said in my theological texts and that I was not simply engaging in shock therapy. I was not kind to white theologians who wanted dismiss black theology as overstatement"

(208).

"Many of my former students are not only writing about black theology but also mentoring doctoral students who will follow in their steps as they are following in mine. I am not worried about black theology's survival. It inspired and was inspired and challenged by both feminist and womanist theologies; queer theology; the theologies of Native, Asian, and Hispanic Americans; Dailit theology in India; Minjung theology in Korea; black theology in South Africa and Britain; and many other theologies among the poor throughout the world. Through mutual inspiration and challenge, black theology in South Africa and Britain; and many other theologies among the poor throughout the world. Through mutual inspiration and challenge, black theology stays alive and active in the world. Wherever people of color in the churches have been struggling for justice against white supremacy, black liberation theology has been there (210).

"I can whip white theologians intellectually anytime and anywhere because they are so ignorant about black history and culture.

"I read a variety of writers - especially black theologians, historians, biblical scholars, the whole field of religion. Read as widely as you can. Don't let a day go by without reading a serious book or essay. Reading is food for thought. I try to read and write about eight hours per day. In my younger days, it was about fourteen to sixteen" (211). How many in ELCA will protest that their official press has highly approved the black theology of Dr. James Cone, the father of "Black Theology" who repudiates the Christian faith.

How long will LCMS President Jerry Kieschnick promote his program of the LCMS drawing closer to ELCA. He should follow Cone's advice and read some books including books like Cone's published by ELCA.

Record of James H. Cone
in *The Christian News Encyclopedia*
Christian News, October 4, 2004

1. Signer of "A Call to Concern" published in the October 24, 1977 Christian Century. Document supports abortion. "5. We call upon the leaders of religious groups supporting abortion rights to speak out more clearly and publicly in response to the dangerously increasing influence of the absolutist position."

2. Cone was a leading spokesman for the National Conference of the New York based Black Theology Project. This organization promoted violence and social gospel rather than the Saving Gospel of Jesus Christ. See "Leading Men to Hell" and "A Response To Black Theology" reprinted here from the *CNE*, 286. (*Christian News*, September 26, 1977 and August 22, 1977).

3. "Mr. Cone's political-economic views of blacks' problems apparently are not far from the Marxist-oriented analysis of Latin American theologians such as Gustavo Gutierrez, who coined the phrase 'theology of liberation.'

"Mr. Cone said that socialism should not be rejected just because the communist have not produced an acceptable model." "Black Theologian Cone Retains His Ability To Provoke Controversy." *Religious News Service, CNE*, 209.

4. **"James H. Cone reviews Martin Luther King, Jr. The Making Of A Mind**

in the July/August, 1985 New Catholic World. John J. Ansboro is the author of this book published in 1984 by Orbis Books, Maryknoll, New York.

"Cone is a professor at Union Theological Seminary and generally known as the father of 'black theology.' He was a close friend and supporter of King. Cone claims that King told him not too long prior to his death that he was a Marxist. The father of black theology maintains that if most churchmen really knew what King stood for they would never have praised him. King has been highly lauded even by such anti-communists as Sun Myuing Moon. King did not affirm such doctrines as the virgin birth and physical resurrection of Christ. Nevertheless, the LCMS's *Lutheran Witness* said King was 'a committed Christian'" (*The Christian News Encyclopedia*, p. 2523).

5. "Cone recently told a gathering of black church leaders that Dr. Martin Luther King Jr. went from 'integrationist' who tried to reform the system to a 'revolutionary and said in private that he was a Marxist.' According to Cone, who, along with Sojourners, is an ardent supporter of King, 'If white people knew what King was all about, they would never have named a holiday after him.'" *The Christian News Encyclopedia*, p. 3043. *Christian News*, October 8, 1984.

A BOOKER T. WASHINGTON DAY RATHER THAN MARTIN LUTHER KING JR. DAY
Christian News, **January 31, 2005**

Churchmen of all stripes continue to defend the celebration of Martin Luther King Day. The conservative Roman Catholic Archbishop of St. Louis celebrates a Mass in honor of King. The Evangelical Lutheran Church in America's Lutheran Book of Worship in its calendar of "Lesser Festivals And Commemorations" lists such "Christian saints" as Martin Luther, "renewer of the Church" and Martin Luther King, Jr. a "renewer of society, martyr." The LCMS's Portals of Prayer mentions Martin Luther King. Jr., Day. The LCMS's *Lutheran Witness* referred to King as "a committed Christian" even though King did not affirm such doctrines as the virgin birth and resurrection of Christ. Rev. Paul McCain, interim president of the LCMS's Concordia Publishing House, when he publicized a column by R. Albert Mohler from the conservative Southern Baptist Press noted: "I for one am thankful for Martin Luther King's work and I would echo and affirm these comments by Dr. Alfred Mohler." Mohler concluded a column titled "The Content of Our Character -- King's Dream and Ours": "This much is clear. When Martin Luther King, Jr.. spoke that day from the Lincoln Memorial, he demonstrated true moral courage and spoke as a prophet. His dream was the right dream. His dream must be our dream. Our response to that dream reveals the true content of our character."

Anyone who takes the time to check the long record of *Christian News* will not find any defense of racism of any kind in the some 2,000 issues of *CN*. For more than 42 years *CN* has opposed the racism of the white supremacists, Identity cult, British Israel, evolutionists, the Israel First Millennialists, etc. *CN* has often noted that the Bible teaches that God "hath made of one blood all nations of men" (Acts 17:26 KJV). "From one man He made every nation to have the people live all over the earth" (Acts 17:26 *AAT*).

The *CN* editor grew up in New York City where there was no segregation. He worked in Harlem, the home of thousands of blacks, with his father as a housepainter. He saw how the blacks loved his father, "Painter Herman", a fair man who fought for the rights of all.

One of the first papers the editor wrote for a college course defended the rights of blacks. The editor quoted from newspapers published in Harlem. One summer he worked with a farm crew of about 40 blacks from Jamaica where he was the only white laborer. The editor worked with blacks on construction in New York. He went to New York public schools with children from many nationalities and races. When his home church, the oldest continuing Lutheran Church in the U.S., celebrated its 300th anniversary, the pastor noted in a commemorative pamphlet that the congregation included people who came from some 30 nationalities and several races. One of his roommates, when he began preparing for the ministry at Concordia Prep, Bronxville, New York, shortly after World War II, was a Chinaman.

Booker T. Washington has long been one of the editor's heroes. *CN* has published articles about him. It was Booker T. Washington who advised Rosa Young, the famous black educator, to go to the LCMS for help.

CN has documented the career, theology and lifestyle of Martin Luther King ever since King began as a young liberal churchman who rejected the basic doctrines of Christianity, was a plagiarizer, was associated with Communists and was setting a poor example for youth by having numerous extra-marital affairs. Now even some conservatives, who may not have any record of championing the cause of blacks during their youth, are climbing on the King bandwagon. They excuse his anti-Christian theology and lifestyle. FBI Director Hoover rightly referred to King as one of the nation's greatest liars. Dr. James Cones, the father of "black theology," a professor at Union Seminary in New York and a close friend of King said that King had told him that he (King) was "a Marxist." Ralph Abernathy, King's closest associate, wrote that King even the night before he died had sex with several women. Any married man like King who regularly commits adultery is not only an adulterer but a horrendous liar. He regularly broke his promise of being faithful to his wife. How can such a liar be trusted? King's liberal theology is documented in **The Christian News Encyclopedia**. When the **National Observer**, published by the **Wall Street Journal**, printed an interview with King in which King expressed his liberal theology, including a denial of original sin and the virgin birth of Christ, *CN* asked both King and his Southern Christian Leadership Council to let *CN* know if the **National Observer** had misquoted King. Neither the Southern Christian leadership Council nor King ever said that King was misquoted or misrepresented. An ardent admirer of King wrote a biography of King which noted that King's theology was much like that of Harry Emerson Fosdick, a famous preacher who denied the deity of Jesus Christian and historic Christianity. When King died, *CN* noted that one of King's liberal professors, who preached the funeral sermon, said nothing about sin and salvation only in Jesus Christ. *CN* noted that the entire service "praised King but not the King of Kings, Jesus Christ."

Christians who champion King as some great moral Christian martyr are not helping the nation's youth. "If King did it, why can't I", youth, both black and white, argue.

Once again *CN* says: "Down with all racism. Defend the oppressed and persecuted. Celebrate a Booker T. Washington Day and not a Martin Luther King Day."

Anyone who takes the time to check the long record of *Christian News* will not find any defense of racism in the some 2,000 issues (now more than 2,250) of *Chris-*

tian News.

Time To Drop The Martin Luther King Day
A BOOKER T. WASHINGTON AND GEORGE WASHINGTON CARVER DAY
Christian News, January 23, 2006

Evidence continues to mount that the time has come to drop the Martin Luther King day. No womanizer, adulterer, and unpatriotic person should be set before the nation's youth as some great role model.

Churchmen, including Archbishop Raymond Burke of St. Louis, who this year led the annual Mass for King, and who maintains that King was a great Christian, should study King's theology. He rejected historic Christianity and did not affirm such Christian doctrines as the virgin birth and resurrection of Jesus Christ. (See *The Christian News Encyclopedia*).

Remembering Martin Luther King Jr., the lead story in the January 16 St. Louis Post-Dispatch had a picture of King being kissed by his wife. "King family feud, book are seen as distraction" a story on page two of the St. Louis paper noted:

"On what would have been the Rev. Martin Luther King Jr.'s 77th birthday, his legacy is under attack and its greatest defender is unable to speak."

"And the spotlight is again hitting King's more human side in a new book that alleges extramarital affairs and a nasty split with a civil rights colleague, the Rev. Jesse Jackson. The story threatened to overshadow King's humanitarian contributions on the 20th anniversary of the national King holiday today.

"Despite all the distractions, those who stood by King's side as soldiers in the civil rights movement say his memory is untouchable.

"Rumors of womanizing by King and feuds with Jackson and others have long been popular topics in media and books like 'And the Walls Came Tumbling Down,' the memoir written decades ago by King's former right-hand man, the Rev. Ralph David Abernathy.

"Historian Taylor Branch's book 'At Canaan's Edge,' released last week, is the latest. In the book, the third in Branch's series detailing King's life and the civil rights movement, the author writes of a long-standing affair King allegedly revealed to Coretta Scott King the year before his 1968 assassination."

King's right hand man Abernathy reported in his book that King had sex with several women just before he was assassinated. King is no role model for youth. Drop the King Day and substitute it with one honoring two great American blacks, Booker T. Washington and George Washington Carver.

A DISGUSTING ADULTERER
Martin Luther King
Christian News, December 3, 2007

"The Secret Agony of Martin Luther King Jr. - An exclusive book excerpt tells the inside story of his troubled final days - By Taylor Branch" are the words on the front cover of the January 9 **Time**.

Time says that "The turbulence of King's final days comes vividly to life in **Time's** exclusive excerpts from **At Canaan's Edge**: America in the King Years 1965-68, the final volume of Pulitzer prize winner Taylor Branch's three-part history of the civil rights movement and its most charismatic leader. In this portrait of King as a man under siege, his passion and his rhetoric reach new levels of grace." "Taylor Branch has spent the past 24 years researching and writing about King's life."

Here is one of the excerpts which is in the January 9, 2006 Time:

His affairs had been an open secret for years, but two weeks after his birthday, King confessed one of them to his wife Coretta.

AS A NEWCOMER, RUTHERFORD STOOD AT THE PERIPHERY OF SCLC'S most private drama. He saw the swirling, teasing flirtations of its inner circle, and he discouraged prurient speculation suits elsewhere. Rutherford could only guess about what he called a "double life," marveling at burdens King must carry beyond the superhuman pressures and expectations of the movement. King's formidable armor wore down in midlife, draining assurance from his glib mantra as a young scholar that many great men of religion had been obsessed with sex – St. Augustine, St. Paul, Martin Luther, Kierkegaard, Tillich – and his self-reproach spilled over when Coretta underwent surgery for an abdominal tumor on Jan. 24. He disclosed to her the one mistress who meant most to him since 1963 – with intensity almost like a second family even though she lived in Los Angeles – a married alumna of Fisk, of dignified bearing like Coretta, but different. The result was painful disaster. On hearing the news, Juanita Abernathy, SCLC co-founder Ralph Abernathy's wife, exploded with the fury of a trusted second that King had picked Coretta's most vulnerable moment just as she recovered from her hysterectomy, to ambush her sanctuary of willful, silent discretion. If he was truly desperate to be honest, she said, King should purge himself privately to God or a psychiatrist. Ralph Abernathy grew so alarmed about King's confession that he canvassed the regular mistresses for hidden fits of jealousy or romantic blackmail, but he found no conventional clues to explain the rash new fatalism in King.

MARTIN LUTHER KING JR.
Christian News, April 27, 2009

Martin Luther King Jr. for Armchair Theologians. By Rufus Burrow Jr. Westminster John Knox Press, 100 Witherspoon Street, Louisville, Kentucky 40204-1396. 194 pages.

CN has been accused of racism because *CN* has long maintained that Martin Lutheran King Jr. rejected such doctrines as original sin, the virgin birth, and resurrection of Jesus Christ. This book by an admirer of King shows *CN* has been telling the truth about Martin Luther King's theology for more than 45 years.

The back cover of "Martin Luther King, Jr." says:

"Burrow succeeds brilliantly in making King's ideas accessible and comprehensible for people in both the academy and the public square. It is the perfect text for all who wish to better understand the intellectual ideas, sources, and categories that grounded King's struggle for a better nation and world." – Lewis V. Baldwin, Professor of Religious Studies at Vanderbilt University and the author of There is a Balm in Gilead: The Cultural Roots of Martin Luther King, Jr.

"One imagines Rufus Burrow Jr., a masterful, engaging storyteller, sitting in his own armchair narrating the powerful, poignant, passionate account of the life of Rev. Dr. Martin Luther King Jr. This is a superb book." – Cheryl Kirk-Duggan, Professor of Theology and Women's Studies and Director of Women's Studies, Shaw University Divinity School, and the author of Misbegotten Anguish: A Theology and Ethics of Violence.

Written by experts but designed for the novice, the Armchair series provides accurate, concise, and witty overviews of some of the most profound moments and theologians in Christian history. This series is an essential supplement for first-time encounters with primary texts, a lucid refresher for scholars and clergy, and an enjoyable read for the theologically curious.

Rufus Burrow Jr. is Indiana Professor of Christian Thought and Professor of Theological Social Ethics at Christian Theological Seminary, Indianapolis. Among his many books is God and Human Dignity: The Personalism, Theology, and Ethics of Martin Luther King, Jr.

Ron Hill is a freelance illustrator and cartoonist living in Cleveland, Ohio.

Resurrection of Christ

The author writes:

Fundamentalist teachings regarding the Bible were basically conveyed to King and other Ebenezer Baptist Church youth by Sunday school teachers and through his father's sermons. They were taught the inerrancy and infallibility of the Bible, as well as the truth of the virgin birth and the bodily resurrection of Jesus. Youth were not permitted to question these or any other orthodox Christian teachings. However, by age thirteen King was already doing just that. For example, he doubted the truth of the literal bodily resurrection of Jesus. He recalled growing increasingly 'skeptical of Sunday-school Christianity' and was embarrassed by the 'unbridled emotionalism' in his father's church. These were the types of things that initially led King to reject ministry as the best means of helping his father fight racism and discrimination" (24).

"Martin Luther King acknowledged that his religious ideas were shaped by his childhood experiences and beliefs. These included…(6)fundamentalist religious beliefs that shaped his early religious ideas until he rejected them beginning at age thirteen;" (25-26).

Getting Behind the Myths in the Bible

"While in high school King rejected the ministry. He had grown up with fundamentalist teachings and what he perceived as too much emotionalism in worship services. He wondered 'whether religion could be intellectually respectable as well as emotionally satisfying.' When he came under the influence of President Mays and Professor Kelsey at Morehouse College, he saw ministry and the minister in a much more favorable light.

"Kelsey challenged King to look behind the myths in the Bible stories to get at the deep abiding truths that many of them contained. He was inspired by Kelsey's belief that modern times called for ministers who were well educated and committed to social Christianity. King was grateful to Kelsey for removing 'the shackles of fundamentalism' from him" (43, 44).

Walter Rauschenbusch

"The social gospel writings of Walter Rauschenbusch (1861-1918) provided the formal theological rationale. Mohandas K. Ghandhi's philosophy of nonviolence supplied the method, although King was not at that time a Ghandian," (46).

Rauschenbusch promoted the social gospel and not the Saving Gospel. He rejected historic Christianity. *The Christian News Encyclopedia*, p. 2257, ft. 10.

Hegelian

"Second, despite its shortcomings, King was impressed with Hegel's analysis of the dialectical process. Hegel saw this process at work in reason, history, and the universe as a whole. Simply put, the dialectical process entails a necessary movement from thesis to antithesis, and then to a synthesis of the two. Since this process rejects the 'either-or' approach in favor of the 'both-and' approach, it allowed King to see that some truth, however miniscule it may be at times, may exist in quite opposite ideas or viewpoints, and that taken together one may arrive at a fuller, more reasonable view of truth – that is, as synthesis of the strong points in the two opposites. To put it another way, one may be able to arrive at a middle or compromise position, which King often did in his civil rights ministry" (p.49, 50).

Hegel did not believe in a concrete historical Jesus and in the Neo-Heglian school his philosophy led to a destruction of the historical foundation of the Christian faith. (*The Christian News Encyclopedia*, p. 120). Karl Marx learned much from Hegel.

Social Gospel

"Although King received a good dose of social gospel teachings under Mays, Kelsey, and Williams at Morehouse, his first formal systematic reading of social gospel literature occurred in seminary. Indeed, even before King read social gospel literature he declared in a paper in a preaching class during his very first semester, 'I am a profound advocate of the social gospel' (51).

Bayard Rustin and Communism

"Bayard Rustin had been a member of the Young Communist League, imprisoned for three years as a conscientious objector during World War II, and arrested on a charge of publicly engaging in a homosexual act in California two years before the boycott. Because of these things, some black leaders urged that he not be sent to Montgomery, since his background might prove detrimental to the movement. His prior affiliation with the Communist Party and his arrest for a public homosexual act would be potentially devastating for the campaign if word got into the hands of white authorities in Montgomery. Significantly, there is no evidence that King was personally troubled about these aspects of Rustin's life" (82).

Women, Capital Punishment and Homosexuality

"King was on record early regarding his opposition to capital punishment. And although there was no overt gay rights movement in his day, there is disagreement within the King family and among others as to whether he would be supportive of gay rights were he alive today. Bernice King, the youngest of King's children, has spoken and marched against gay rights. The two sons, Martin and Dexter, believe that everything about King's theology and practice unequivocally places him in the camp of supporting gay rights. This opinion was shared by King's late wife, Coretta, and late daughter,

Yolanda" (142).

"Remember, Coretta and Martin deleted the promise to 'obey' from their wedding vows" (146).

"King applauded Christianity for helping to lift the status of women from that of mere childbearers to one of dignity, honor, and respect" (147).

The author does not mention King's adultery and having sex with many women which shows that in actual practice he had a low regard for women and was unfaithful to his wife. See *The Christian News Encyclopedia* for documentation of King's anti-Christian theology and adultery.

Homosexuality

"Rustin was homosexual and had been arrested for a public homosexual act in California in 1953. When Rustin met King he was up-front about the matter, as well as having once been a member of the Communist Party. King gave no indication of being troubled by his sexuality. On reflection, Rustin said he did not know for certain how King felt about his sexuality, adding in 1987 that King 'would have been sympathetic and would not have had the prejudicial view. Otherwise he would not have hired me.' Only when his orientation became a concern to the movement did it become an issue for King, said Rustin. When the talk and innuendoes began, King set up a committee to advise him. The group decided that both King and the movement would be harmed if Rustin remained. Rustin was convinced that King was never happy about his leaving Montgomery" (153).

"Indicators are that King simply accepted Rustin as a human being who was committed to the cause of civil rights. At least one biographer on Rustin contends that King preferred that Rustin be a closeted homosexual. Indeed, Rustin himself said that he was genuinely accepted in the movement 'so long as I didn't declare that I was gay'" (154).

Christian News has long told the truth about the anti-Christian theology, lifestyle and Marxism of Martin Luther King. Yet the Lutheran Church-Missouri Synod's *Lutheran Witness* said King was a "committed Christian" even though he denied the resurrection of Christ. The *Lutheran Witness* similarly praised Dietrich Bonhoeffer, one of King's heroes, as a Christian and a confessional, although Bonhoeffer, like King, denied the resurrection of Jesus Christ.

Happy Martin Luther King Day!
By Paul McCain
Cyberbrethren: A Lutheran Blog
Christian News, January 25, 2010

It is time once again for me to make my annual comments about Martin Luther King day. Sadly, every year when I do this I get the same sort of responses, no matter how hard I try to be clear on why this day is so important to so many of our African-American brothers and sisters, and, why it is so important for all of us in this nation.

Sure enough there are those quite happy to entirely ignore the point of my post and gas on about how Martin Luther King was this, that, or another thing, about how his theology was bad, or how he was 'liberal' and on and on. I've even had a Lutheran pastor opine, on this day, about the nature of the Civil War and if owning slaves is a Biblically justified practice. I kid you not.

I will again however say that such comments display an astounding lack of sensitivity and concern about the feelings of our fellow Americans who look to Martin Luther King as a significant figure in advancing civil rights in this nation. And please do not, please, do not say, "Some of my best friends are Black." Oh, really? Then try to be a bit more sensitive, please. Some of my best friends are left handed, but I don't go out of my way to offend left-handed people by denigrating honoring a left-handed person for whom they have high regard. But, seriously, some of my best friends are left-handed. I even married a left-handed person. See how hollow that sounds?

I do wonder how many of us with pale skin have ever shared a meal with a Black person, in their home, actually spoken at length with them as people, not as "Blacks." Similarly, how many Blacks have had Whites into their homes and hosted them for a meal and spoke to them as people, not White? I know the problem cuts both directions, but on MLK day, this is not the appropriate time for White folk to go on and on about their gripes with Black folks.

And then, I hear from people telling me how terrible the civil rights movement has been for African-Americans, and how it has only led to what is now a permanent underclass in this country, etc. etc. There is plenty to talk about here. But that the Civil Rights movement was a good thing in many ways is undeniable.

Would you have preferred the continuation of Jim Crow laws, lynchings and telling people they can't drink from certain water fountains, use certain bathrooms or ride only in the back of the bus or not be served a meal just because their skin is dark? Would you feel the same if the laws were in reverse and it was the white-skinned who could not do these things? "Good Christians" are not immune are they? I still have a vivid memory of angst being expressed by some members of my home congregation when Black folks showed up once for Holy Communion, from the common cup! And that was only in the late 1960s, not that too far long ago.

After the Civil War and well into the 1960s many, many African-Americans were still treated nearly like slaves in so many places. Despite the Civil War, many states made it impossible for blacks to vote and via indentured servanthood [aka sharecropping] created a serfdom across the South. Can we be a bit sensitive to the bitter, hard and long struggle of a people brought to this country as slaves?" [Yes, yes, I know blacks sold other blacks into slavery in Africa...and yes, African-Americans can be as prejudiced against others because of race as anyone else].

So, I apologize for what appears to be a gloomy post, but it is always sad that whenever anyone tries to say anything about Civil Rights, particularly on MLK day, we have to have a litany from white folks criticizing, whining and complaining, thus quite entirely missing the point of MLK and his meaning for our nation and for so many of our fellow citizens.

Ed. Paul McCain of the LCMS's Concordia Publishing House posted virtually the exact same message on his January 17, 2011 Cyberbrethren: A Lutheran Blog. The CPH Board of Directors has not asked McCain to cease his praise and promotion of Dietrich Bonhoeffer and Martin Luther King.

C.F.W. Walther told the Truth About the Civil War
The Real King And the Real Lincoln
RESPONSE TO MCCAIN'S "HAPPY MARTIN LUTHER KING DAY"
Christian News, February 1, 2010

Rev. Paul McCain of Concordia Publishing House in his "Happy Martin Luther King Day" (*Christian News*, January 25), complains about those who "go on about Martin Luther King was this, that, or another thing, about how his theology was bad, or how he was 'liberal' and on and on. I've even had a Lutheran pastor opine, on this day, about the nature of the Civil War and if owning slaves is a Biblically justified practice, I kid you not."

Evidently McCain maintains that those who express concerns about King's repudiation of such doctrines as the virgin birth, deity and resurrection of Christ, King's horrendous adulterous lifestyle, his Marxism and plagiarizing have no concern for advancing civil rights. Does McCain really think King is a fine role model for youth of any race? This is how Lutheran churches in St. Louis have presented King with an annual essay contest on Martin Luther King Day. *The Lutheran Book of Worship* hails King as some great Christian martyr. Richard John Neuhaus, who marched with King, wanted the LCMS to declare King a saint.

The editor of *Christian News*, who expressed concerns about King's theology and lifestyle years before he was assassinated and there was a Martin Luther King, Jr. Day, has been accused by critics of racism and anti-Semitism. Yet the record clearly shows that the editor championed the rights of all men, including blacks and Semites ever since his grade school days in New York City. He worked in Harlem as a house painter with his father who was loved by blacks. They frequently asked for "Painter Herman" to paint their apartment. When the editor and his father were working in Harlem during what may have been the last major race riot in Harlem they experienced no harm from blacks.

During his college days the editor wrote a paper in defence of blacks in Harlem. When his home congregation celebrated its 300th anniversary, the pastor wrote in the anniversary booklet that the members of the congregation came from some 32 nationalities and several races. Growing up in the Bronx it was no big deal to play with youth from many nationalities and races. One summer the editor was the only white on a farm crew of some 40 blacks who came from Jamaica. The editor travelled to St. Louis by bus when he attended Concordia Seminary, St. Louis in 1952. When he transferred to a public transportation bus in St. Louis for the last few miles to the seminary, he sat in the back of the bus so his two large suitcases would not get in the way of other passengers. He was shocked when the bus driver hollered "whites up front, blacks in the back." He had never heard of this in New York City.

During its early days in the 1960s *CN* published the columns of several black columnists who sharply disagreed with King's political and theological liberalism and immoral lifestyle.

Several times *CN* suggested that the U.S. celebrate a Booker T. Washington or a George Washington Carver Day, two of America's finest black patriots.

Several times the editor's congregation submitted an overture like the following one Trinity, New Haven submitted on January 10 to be sent to the LCMS's 2010 convention.

To Repudiate Racism

Whereas, The theory of evolution has often led to the racist notion that the white man is higher on the evolutionary scale, and

Whereas, Some maintain that God has some special race such as the "Jews"; and

Whereas, Some believe that Anglo-Saxons are God's special race; and

Whereas, The Bible teaches that all men come from Adam: "From one man He made every nation to have the people live all over the earth" (Acts 17:26); and

Whereas, The Bible teaches that all Christians, regardless of race, color, nationality, social status, or sex are God's chosen people ("You are a chosen people" [I Peter 2:8-9]); therefore be it

Resolved, That the Lutheran Church-Missouri Synod repudiate all racism including the racism of the white supremacists, the evolutionists, and the Israel First Millennialists who believe that God has a chosen race.

Some of what *CN* has said about King is in *The Christian News Encyclopedia*. When the December 30, 1963 *National Observer* published an interview with Martin Luther King titled "The Theology of Martin Luther King," *CN* asked King and his Southern Christian Leadership Conference to let *CN* know if the *National Observer* misrepresented King's theology. This newspaper reported that King did not affirm such Christian doctrines as the virgin birth, deity and resurrection of Christ. The *National Observer* informed *CN* that it had received no objections from King and his Southern Christian Leadership Conference about the interview article. Through the years *CN* has documented King's anti-Christian theology and his utterly disgusting treatment of women, including prostitutes. Yet, the *Lutheran Witness* referred to King in a major editorial as "a committed Christian." CPH, under McCain, refuses to consider the evidence about King just as he refuses to consider the evidence about the Revised Standard and English Standard Versions of the Bible.

His comments on the Civil War indicate that he hasn't read what *CN* has published about the Civil War, Abraham Lincoln and what Walther wrote about the Civil War and slavery. It's high time the bureaucracy stop acting like intellectual snobs and start studying the facts even if they are in *Christian News*. McCain should study what *CN* has written about such wars as the Civil War, the "intellectual snobs" should read *The Real Lincoln - A New Look at Abraham Lincoln, His Agenda and an Unnecessary War*." (Reviewed in the October 21, 2002 *Christian News*.) *Christian News* published the entire foreword by Walter Williams, one of *CN*'s favorite black columnists.

Photographed in this issue is the foreword by Walter Williams and comments from the book's jacket about the author.

The October 21, 2002 *Christian News* said:

The Real Lincoln -- *A New Look at Abraham Lincoln, His Agenda, and an Unnecessary War.* By Thomas J. DiLorenzo. Foreword by Walter E. Williams, John M. Olin Distinguished Professor of Economics, George Mason University. Prima Publishing, Roseville, California. www.primapublishing.com 2002, $24.95.

"*The Real Lincoln* contains irrefutable evidence that a more appropriate title for Abraham Lincoln is not the Great Emancipator, but the Great Centralizer" writes Walter Williams in the foreword of this book. Williams, some of whose columns have appeared in *CN*, says: "As DiLorenzo documents -- contrary to conventional wisdom, books about Lincoln, and the lessons taught in schools and colleges--the War between the States was not fought to end slavery."

Some members of the Lutheran Church-Missouri synod have been embarrassed with the position C.F.W. Walther took toward Lincoln and the Civil War. This book shows that Walther was right. Unlike some religious leaders Walther did not consider the Civil War some righteous holy crusade for freedom. He did not share Lincoln's enthusiasm for Julia Ward Howe's Battle Hymn of the Republic. Note "The Civil War" reprinted here from *"The Messianic Character of American Foreign Policy"* by John W. Robbins, *The Christian News Encyclopedia*, pp. 4120-4122. Comments by Concordia Seminary Professor Alfred Rehwinkel on Walther's views of slavery and the Civil War are in *Salt, Light and Signs of the Times -- An Intimate Look at the Life and Times of Alfred (Rip) Rehwinke*l by Ronald Stelzer, pp. 222-224. (The American Luther Today, *Christian News*, November 8, 1999, pp. 25-26). Walther's writings on slavery were published in the August 5, 1996, December 9, 1996, and June 23, 1997, issues of *Christian News*.

The foreword to *The Real Lincoln* by Walter Williams appears in this issue together with comments on the jacket. The following tributes are on the back cover.

Bonhoeffer and King
Christian News, November 1, 2010

Bonhoeffer and King – Their Legacies and Import for Christian Social Thought. Willis Jenkins and Jennifer M. McBride, Editions. Fortress Press, Minneapolis.

(Excerpt)

Josiah U. Young III writes in a chapter titled "Theology and Racism": "King did not hold that God the Son became flesh in any literal sense. The ancient theologians Bonhoeffer upheld were thus to King archaic in their worldview. When, therefore, King asserted in one of his sermons that 'the ultimate meaning of [doctrine of] the Trinity' is its affirmation that 'God and Christ are one in substance,' and that to experience 'one is to experience the other,' he was not upholding Nicaea (325) and Constantinople (381), but demythologizing them. Bearing more of an affinity to Schleiermacher than to Barth, King held that Christ's consciousness of God rather than his preexistence was the redemptive factor. For King, in addition, Christ's personality, wisdom, and ethical correctness, which King understood à la Alfred Knudson as self-consciousness and self-direction, is the image of God. By contrast, Bonhoeffer's interpretations of the imago Dei entailed his conviction that Christ mirrors the Creator because he was truly God and truly human" (73)....

Paul McCain of CPH has vigorously defended King when *Christian News* and others took sharp issue with King's theology and moral standards.

WHAT DO THESE TWO MEN HAVE IN COMMON?
Raymond Richardson, a black man from the Virgin Islands and *CN* Editor Herman John Otten

Both are Christians and Lutherans. Both have college graduate degrees. Both are fathers of seven children. The children of both have won numerous academic, athletic and music awards. Both are grandparents of the infant in the photo, Isaac Herman John Otten.

Christian News, August 2, 2010

CONCORDIA SEMINARY, ST. LOUIS VS. OTTEN CASE

BOOK OF DOCUMENTATION

ARRANGED BY KURT MARQUART

BECAUSE THEY SOUGHT FREEDOM TO WORSHIP GOD, A COMPANY OF SAXON EMIGRANTS LEFT THEIR FATHERLAND IN 1838 AND BUILT A HOME IN THE NEW WORLD. THEY SETTLED IN PERRY COUNTY, MISSOURI, THEN A WILDERNESS UNTRODDEN BY WHITE MEN. THE FOLLOWING YEAR THREE OF THEIR YOUTHFUL LEADERS, CANDIDATES OF THEOLOGY, FOUNDED AT ALTENBURG AN INSTITUTION, CONCORDIA COLLEGE, DESTINED TO BECOME THE PARENT OF NEARLY A SCORE OF SOUNDLY LUTHERAN COLLEGES IN THIS AND OTHER LANDS.

REMOVED TO ST. LOUIS IN 1849, TWO YEARS AFTER THE FOUNDING OF THE EVANGELICAL LUTHERAN SYNOD OF MISSOURI, OHIO AND OTHER STATES, CONCORDIA COLLEGE BECAME THE DIVINITY SCHOOL OF THAT CHURCH BODY. AFTER SEVERAL REBUILDINGS AND ENLARGEMENS, THE SEMINARY WAS RELOCATED ON A NEW SITE AND ITS PRESENT GROUP OF BUILDINGS CONSECRATED TO THEIR PURPOSE JUNE 13, 1926. IN MEMORY OF THIS EVENT ITS BOARD OF CONTROL HAS AUTHORIZED THE STRIKING OF THIS MEDALLION. EZEKIEL 47:12.

(Statement on back of medallion)

The "Marquart Otten Team" at the Lutheran Church-Missouri Synod's convention in San Francisco in 1951

PART I
Christian News **Challenges the Concordia University System and All Christian Youth – Work for A 21st Century Reformation**
FIGHT FOR THE FAITH
By Herman Otten, Pastor
Trinity Lutheran Church
Editor, *Christian News* and *An American Translation of the Bible*
Concordia University, Wisconsin, February 3, 2011

"While I've been eager to write you, dear friends, about the salvation we share, it's now necessary that I write you and urge you to fight for the faith once entrusted to the holy people" (Jude 3).

Thank you for your invitation. It's good to be here at your fine school which the special January 3, 2011 issue of *Christian News* on higher education said was the "Largest and Best" Lutheran university.

In November, when Dr. James Burkee, Chair of the Faculty, invited me, at the request of CUW President Patrick Ferry, to speak, I asked him what I should speak about. He suggested perhaps something on the Concordia University System. He noted that the November 1 *Christian News* had commented on the school system of The Lutheran Church-Missouri Synod.

The lead headline of this issue of *CN* was "The Dying Concordia University System." Then there are photos of each one of the ten schools in CUS. The subtitle is "LCMS PROFESSORS ALLOWED TO DEFEND EVOLUTION, WOMEN PASTORS, AND HOMOSEXUALTY."

The Dying of the Light

Each week *Christian News* generally features a new book. This time *CN* again reported on "*The Dying of the Light – The Disengagement of Colleges & Universities From Their Christian Churches*," an 868 page book published by Eerdmann in 1998. Here it is. The author is James Tunstead Burtchaell. The preface says: "Countless colleges and universities in the history of the United States were founded under some sort of Christian patronage, but many which still survive do not claim any relationship or denomination. Even on most of the campuses which are still listed by churches as their affiliates, there is usually some concern expressed today about how authentic or how enduring the tie is; and often wistful concern is all that remains. This book is an attempt to narrate and understand the dynamics of these church-college campuses relations, the ways they have tended to wither, and the why.[1]

Author Burtchaell has extensive experience in American higher education. The November 1, 2010 *Christian News* said:

"Twelve years ago *Christian News* urged all LCMS officials who were defending the theological orthodoxy of all professors in the Concordia University System to study *The Dying of the Light*. Many are so busy traveling, attending meetings, raising funds, keeping the bureaucracy afloat and implementing all sorts of programs, conducting workshops etc. They say they have no time to read such big scholarly books as *The Dying of the Light* or to bother to study what *Christian News* is saying and documenting about the Concordia University System."

The chapter on "The Lutherans" in *The Dying of the Light*[2] shows that the "light" of Jesus Christ is dying in most Lutheran colleges in the U.S. as it is in the colleges begun by other denominations.

Gettysburg and Lutherans – The Mother of Popular Education

Some thirty years ago *Christian News* was urged to reprint *The Conservative Reformation and Its Theology* by Charles Porterfield Krauth. *CN* had long promoted this great classic but did not have the funds to reprint the 840 page book. *CN* commended CPH for reprinting it in 2007.[3] C.F.W. Walther had a high regard for Krauth who joined the faculty of the Lutheran Theological Seminary in Philadelphia in 1864 and the University of Pennsylvania in 1866. Burtchaell in his *The Dying of the Light* mentions that Krauth was part of a caucus of conservative faculty which included H. Louis Baugher and Henry Eyster Jacobs. McKnight was president of Gettysburg from 1884 – 1905. After mentioning some confessional Lutherans in the old General Synod (now ELCA), Burtchaell writes:

"Together they speak to the same themes as McKnight. The Reformation has made Lutherans the mother of popular education and Germany the schoolmistress of the world. In the atmosphere of intellectual freedom in America, where all power must devolve upon persuasion, influence and progress belongs to whoever masters education, and the Lutherans are best able to do that: not narrow like the Calvinists, nor foreshortened in their perspective like the secularists, nor authoritarian like the Catholics, the Lutheran colleges offer religious culture before all else. This they describe in the by-now familiar terms: suffused with the Christian spirit, broad enough (i.e., free of sectarian imposition) to commend itself to the public at large. But just as surely, their schools are 'ministers of good to the State.' They offer education at a lower cost than the state colleges (this was still the case). And they give the church the capacity to educate 'the leaders and chief actors of the coming generation.'

"Thus far their calling. But the results had been disappointing."[4]

The Dying of the Light then goes on to report what has happened at Gettysburg and other Lutheran colleges. Many non-Lutheran and even non-Christian faculty were hired. Only a minority of the students were Lutheran, at Gettysburg about 10 percent. "As late as 1953, among the 115 periodicals received by the (Gettysburg) library only three were in the field of religion (Bible)."[5] "There is accordingly a course on Martin Luther King, Jr., but none on Martin Luther."[6]

ELCA's January, 2011 *Lutheran* reports: "Gettysburg (Pa.) College will establish a Middle East and Islamic Studies program with a $532,000 grant from the Andrew W. Mellon Foundation." Through the years, *Christian News* has noted that far too frequently foundations and individuals who become wealthy because of the free market system give their money to schools which promote socialism, evolution, and universalism.

The Dying of the Light says:

"And when the ELCA was unabashedly proclaiming that on campus 'the integrating element is the assurance that in Christ all things hold together,' only 10 percent of the students left were Lutheran and might understand how that was meant.

"The only way for a college to be effectively Lutheran by 'suffusion,' or 'atmosphere,' would be to admit and appoint students and faculty who were as prepared for solidarity in faith as for solidarity in scholarship."

"In recent years about one in every nineteen young Lutherans of college age has matriculated at a Lutheran-related college. By this reckoning one might discount the traditional claim that the Lutheran colleges are training Lutheran church members for leadership, in the church or in society at large."[7]

Hindu Heads St. Olaf Religion Department

ELCA's St. Olaf's College is one of the ELCA colleges mentioned in *The Dying of the Light*. In 1970 Dr. Sidney Rand, President of St. Olaf, who also served as U.S. ambassador to Norway, invited me to meet with members of the religion department at St. Olaf. I accepted the invitation since I already had some speaking engagements in Minnesota. Members of the religion department made it clear that they rejected the inerrancy of Scripture, supported evolution, and such destructive notions of liberal higher critics of the Bible as the J-E-D-P source hypothesis. Fundamental doctrines as the virgin birth and vicarious satisfaction of Christ were not considered binding. They insisted that officials of the LCMS who were supporting fellowship with the American Lutheran Church were less than honest when they were telling members of the LCMS that there were no doctrinal differences between the ALC and LCMS. Since the 1970s the religion department, which was controlled by liberals, has gone down hill. ELCA's November, 2008 *Lutheran* reported that Anantanand Rambachen, a Hindu, has become head of the religion department at St. Olaf. This Hindu scholar has blasted historic Christianity. He is the author of "The Advata World View: God, World, Humanity." He says "I have tried to give my students an understanding of what it means to see the world through Hindu eyes." The November, 2008 *Lutheran* reported, after noting that a Hindu was now the head of the Department of Religion at an ELCA college: "Openness, independence and variety are also important to ELCA's institutions of higher education. The [ELCA] proudly claims its 20 colleges and universities and sometimes ignores them," writes Stanley N. Olson, executive director of Vocation and Education, in the fall 2006 *Intersections Journal*.[8]

First Things On U.S. Colleges

The January 3, 2011 special issue of *Christian News* on Higher Education mentions what a *First Things* survey of more than 2,000 U.S. colleges, published in the November *First Things*, says about Gettysburg and Concordia University, Wisconsin. The December *Forum Letter* noted in its summary of the *First Things* report on U.S. colleges:

"The bad news is that only three Lutheran schools were mentioned in the commentary section – or maybe that's good news, considering the comments. Valparaiso topped their list of 'declining schools,' largely because 'some of the faculty is trying hard to undo the school's Lutheran heritage.' On the other hand, students also report relatively low levels of sexual activity and alcohol, tobacco, and recreational drug use. And relatively little studying, for that matter. St. Olaf got somewhat higher ratings, though it was panned for its website which says that religion is studied at St. Olaf 'because religion has always been a major influence on the development of human societies.' Yeah, that's rather a low view of the purpose of a church college religion department. The most damning comment was reserved for Gettysburg College, where, FT tells us, 'religious convictions are not unknown.' Concordia University Wisconsin made the list of 'Schools on the Rise Filled with Excitement,' though there was no commentary to tell us what is so exciting; still, good for them."

The January 3 *Christian News* published excerpts from the November *First Things* in stories titled "*First Things* Publishes Special Issue on Higher Education," "*First Things* Reports on Moral Standard in U.S. Higher Education," and "College Descriptions." "Concordia Wisconsin – Biggest and Best" lists ten reasons why Concordia University, Wisconsin is the biggest and also the best (if the small schools of the WELS, ELS and CLC are not considered large enough to rank) Lutheran University.

The list begins with CUS's excellent statement on "Worship in a Collegiate Setting" prepared by the CUW faculty and Board of Regents during the 1995-96 school year. It ends with a report noting that the chairman of the Department of Theology at CUW is the only LCMS professor who had the courage to expose a blatant case of plagiarism covered up by CUS leaders and LCMS seminaries and bureaucrats. Reason 7 quotes what was said in the April 30, 2001 *Christian News* when CUW awarded Professor Kurt Marquart of Concordia Seminary, Ft. Wayne a D.D.:

"Concordia University, Wisconsin, and its fine president, Dr. Patrick Ferry, should be commended for awarding Professor Marquart a D.D. Concordia Seminary, St. Louis, should have given it to him long ago. The fact that Concordia, Wisconsin, is awarding Professor Marquart a D.D. is just one more reason why youth should consider attending Concordia, Wisconsin."

A CALL FOR THE HIGHEST ACADEMIC STANDARDS

"A Call for the Highest Academic Standards" in *CN*'s special issue on Higher Education begins by mentioning *Who Really Wrote the Bible* by two Jewish scholars. It is featured on page one of the January 3, 2011 *Christian News*. This book exposes the myth that the liberals who deny that God is the real author of the Bible and claim that the first five books of the Bible came from sources designated as J-E-D and P by the liberals are the real scholars.

The December 20, 2010 *Christian News* noted in "New Book by *Christian News* – BONHOEFFER AND KING": "The great LCMS Bonhoeffer praising scholars should be telling their students to read '*Who Really Wrote the Bible? And Why It Should Be Taken Seriously Again*' by Eyal Rav-Noy and Gil Weinreich."

Every U.S. seminary, which wants to keep up with the latest textual scholarship, should make this book required reading for all students. The organized conservatives in the LCMS who want "out-of-date far right" *Christian News* to cease should be urging their followers to get this book. They should stop spending so much time at their computers and read the books *CN* has been promoting. They might get off the Bonhoeffer bandwagon. *CN*'s *Bonhoeffer and King* will show that both were anti-Semites because they rejected the God of the Old Testament, the only true God who actually exists, and did not believe Moses wrote the first five books of the Bible.

Biblical Criticism Not Dead

Some of our uninformed Lutheran professors claim that biblical criticism and the J-E-D-P Source Hypothesis are dead and therefore there is no need to speak to students about it. They contend the editor of *Christian News* is living in the past and just fighting the same old battle for more than 50 years, not realizing that times have changed since his seminary days. "He should keep up with what is going on in the church and world." John Barton writes in his *The Nature of Biblical Criticism*, published by Westminster Knox Press in 2007[9]: ". . . the present book has as one of its aims to argue that biblical criticism is not dead. It is important that it should survive and proper." This liberal goes on to reject the Mosaic authorship of the Pentateuch, the unity of Isaiah, the 600 B.C. dating of Daniel, and the historicity and inerrancy of the Bible, antiscriptural critical views which undermine the foundation of historic Christianity as this editor has noted since his student days.

Christian News has published stories on the "Great Courses."[10] This widely hailed teaching company regularly offers courses on religion taught by higher critics of the Bible. It claims: "The Teaching Company is a unique publisher. For nearly 20 years, we've produced The Great Courses – college level courses taught by the most engaging professors that universities like Harvard, Stanford, Princeton, Vanderbilt, and Georgetown have to offer." Even politically conservative *Human Events* and *Washington Times* have been publishing full page advertisements from the "Great Courses."[11]

The Great Courses say:

"We've created a 'university of the best' designated careful collaboration with our customers. We identify the top 1% percent of college professors based on teaching awards, published evaluations, newspaper write ups, and other sources. Only those who score highest on our customers' review of auditions are chosen for The Great Courses." The Great Courses does not offer courses by such great Christian scholars as Paul Maier, Alvin Schmidt, Nathan Jastram, John Eidesmoe, Kurt Marquart, Robert Preus, Raymond Surburg, Henry Koch, John Warwick Montgomery, etc. Instead it's chief religion teacher is Bart Ehrman, a skeptic and higher critic of the Bible who totally rejects historic Christianity. The 2011 Spring Sale Catalog of The Great Courses says: "The Great Courses – Now enjoy brilliant lectures in your home or car."[12] It begins with a painting of Jesus. However it's Jesus is not the Jesus of the Bible but the Jesus of modern unbelief who did not rise from the dead and saves no one. Those who claim the editor of *CN* is out of date for regularly attacking higher criticism of the Bible are the ones who are out of date.

"A Call For the Highest Academic Standards" in the January 3, 2011 *Christian News* mentions that at an open hearing on doctrinal matters, attended by some 1400 prior to the LCMS' 1962 convention in Cleveland, I challenged the liberal St. Louis professors at the hearing to defend their notion that "the Hebrew word **almah** does not have to be translated 'virgin' because in one Bible passage **almah** is used where it obviously does not mean 'virgin.'" The exegetical department of the seminary had adopted a statement declaring that **almah** in Isaiah 7:14 need not be translated virgin and that when it was first written it did not apply to the Virgin Mary but rather to some woman living at Isaiah's time. The faculty was not able to answer. I asked the faculty at the open hearing to give the Bible passage using **almah** where it obviously does not mean 'virgin'. There was dead silence at the hearing. A member of the St. Louis exegetical department then said that at the moment the faculty could not recall the Bible passage but would show me the passage after the hearing. The faculty never did because there is no such Bible passage. The Hebrew word **bethulah**, which some say would have been used by Isaiah if he meant "virgin", is used in Joel 1:8 for a woman who was married in her youth. I didn't gain any points with the faculty by challenging not only their theology but also their scholarship.[13]

I challenged the "great scholars" at the seminary to debate their higher critical notions with Dr. William Beck, translator of *An American Translation of the Bible*. Beck agreed to debate. The liberals supporting the *Revised Standard Version of the Bible* and opposing Beck's *AAT* refused to debate. Today those in the LCMS and at CPH promoting the *ESV*, which is 91% *RSV*, similarly refuse to debate defenders of the *AAT*. When the same unscholarly and anti-scriptural notions were promoted by the keynote speaker at a symposium on Scripture at the St. Louis seminary in 2010, I was told by some at the symposium that he was not challenged.

Is The Higher Criticism Scholarly?

When the press in 1974 reported the battle at the St. Louis seminary was supposed to be one between "power and scholarship," the conservatives having the power and the liberals the scholarship, *CN* showed that true Biblical scholarship was on the side of the Bible believers rather than the Bible doubters. *CN* published the entire 62 page pamphlet *Is The Higher Criticism Scholarly?* by Robert Dick Wilson. It is in *The Christian News Encyclopedia.*[14] The pamphlet includes a series of questions the liberal higher critics, who promote the J-E-D-P source hypothesis and other critical notions, would never answer. *CN* included these questions in an open letter to the students at the St. Louis seminary who were defending their liberal professors. *CN* challenged the students to ask their liberal professors these questions. The liberals were miffed that a young pastor they refused to certify was challenging their scholarship. Being accused of liberalism did not particularly bother them, but they did not want to be accused of being poor scholars.

Who Really Wrote the Bible?[15] by Eyal Rav-Noy and Gil Weinreich is just one of many books which show that in some areas the liberals were poor scholars clearly outclassed by such great Lutheran scholars as George Stoeckhardt, Theodore Laetsch, Walter Maier, Ludwig Fuerbringer, William Beck, Siegbert Becker, Kurt Marquart and others who rejected the critical views of the Bible championed by those who left the LCMS in 1974 and formed Seminex. Some 45 out of 50 faculty and staff members left the St. Louis seminary, taking with them about 450 students, many in the LCMS's mission department and eventually more than 400 pastors and 100,000 members.

The Foolishness of God –
The Place of Reason in the Theology of Martin Luther

"A Call For the Highest Academic Excellence" mentioned that confessional Lutherans have a long history of promoting high academic standards. Siegbert Becker, who along with Kurt Marquart served as a counselor in the Concordia Seminary vs. Herman Otten Case, is the author of *The Foolishness of God – The Place of Reason in the Theology of Martin Luther*. This book by a real scholar, who earned his doctorate under liberal scholars, shows how it was possible for Luther to call reason both the devil's bride and yet the good gift of God. He showed that Christianity is intellectually defensible. "It is not Christianity that needs to be made reasonable. It is reason that needs to be made Christian."

Intellectual Respectability

"Intellectual Respectability, Si! Pseudo-Intellectual Aping, No!" in the January 3, 2011 *Christian News* noted:

Christian News has long emphasized the importance of the highest intellectual standards, a careful examination of the evidence, documentation and facts, in all areas, including Bible manuscripts, textual criticism, evolution, archaeology, theology, wars, alleged appearances of Mary, the Shroud of Turin, visions of charismatics, the Holocaust religion, etc.

The editor still affirms the same position expressed in "Intellectual Respectability, Si! Pseudo-Intellectual Aping, No!" an editorial in the January 12, 1964 *Lutheran News*, which became *Christian News* in 1968. This editorial said:

> Conservatives sometimes imply that "intellectual respectability" is a bad thing. It is not. We must distinguish between genuine intellectual respectability, or better, integrity, and its mass produced imitation. The former is characterized by substance, toughness of mental fiber, interior consistency, breadth of perspective, and a firm ultimate anchorage in reality—which to the Christian can only mean submission to divine revelation. Pseudo-intellectualism, on the other hand, is a mere craven subservience to fashion, which mistakes (1) learning for truth, (2) academic standing for learning, and (3) "hi-fidelity" reproduction of the latest literary "hit parade", for academic standing!

The pompous vulgarity of the proverbial "newly rich" invades also the realms of the mind. Unlike genuine intellectual integrity, which is rarely "respectable," the false kind, shining with the splendor of Establishment, possesses a high degree of snob-value, because it seeks, and receives, honor from men, not from God. The mediocre mind automatically follows the course of least resistance. Three hundred years ago that meant being orthodox. Today it means sliding through theological school, and perhaps into prominence, on the airy, post-Barthian clichés obligingly dispensed by "up-to-date" professors. It means also throwing one's pinch of incense to the statue of St. Pontius ("What is Truth?") Pilate, and participating in the Academic Litany: "Holy Immanuel (Kant), so teach us to question, that at the Last Critique...."

Intellectual Snobs

Reason No. 9 "Upholding Creation" in my list of reasons why Concordia University, Wisconsin is the biggest and best Lutheran university is that Ben Stein's "Expelled: No Intelligence Allowed" was recommended in the Spring 2008, *Concordian* of CUW.

Ben Stein's "EXPELLED" exposed the "intellectual snobs" of our day who refuse to even consider the evidence for intelligent design. *Christian News* has published several favorable reviews of "EXPELLED" and for decades has opposed the intellectual snobs who refuse to consider the evidence which refutes their pet ideas. *CN* has rejected the anti-scriptural and unscientific myth of evolution ever since *CN* began in 1962. *CN* sells many books and videos which refute the intellectual snobs. When *CN* suggested that Valparaiso University and some other Lutheran colleges, which have evolutionists on their faculty, debate scientists who are creationists, the intellectual snobs refused to debate the creationists after the first debates where the creationist showed that the evolutionists did not have real scholarship on their side. They would not even tell their students about such groups as the Creation Research Society which includes several hundred scientists who reject evolution and affirm a six 24 hour day creation.

Kurt Marquart

The first time *CN* used the term "intellectual snobs" was in an editorial by Dr. Kurt Marquart titled "Religious Socialism" in the January 11, 1965 *Lutheran* (now Christian) *News*. This issue of *CN* reprinted an editorial from the Lutheran Church-Missouri Synod's December 8, 1965 *Lutheran Witness* titled "Christian Social Action." Marquart wrote in response: "'Christian Social Action', a *Lutheran Witness* editorial of December 8, 1964, might just as well have appeared in *The Christian Century*. It certainly does not say anything that is particularly scriptural. On the contrary, the Social Gospel outlook seems to be taken for granted...." *The Christian Century* has long been a leading voice of Protestant liberalism. It has repeatedly attacked basic Christian doctrines. It supports abortion and homosexuality.

Marquart wrote in "Religious Socialism" that "for intellectual snobs, of course, facts contained in books they dislike simply don't exist; Orwell's Memory Hole, you know." Marquart mentions the favorable opinion the *Lutheran Witness* had of Martin Luther King, Jr. The November 10, 1964 *Lutheran Witness* insisted that King was "a committed Christian" even though *Christian News* and others had published evidence showing that King did not affirm such Christian doctrines as the virgin birth and resurrection of Jesus Christ. The intellectual snobs at the *Lutheran Witness* ignored the evidence. The *Lutheran Witness* excused King's horrendous adulterous life style, insisting that he was still "a committed Christian."

The "intellectual snobs" at the *Lutheran Witness* and liberals elsewhere in the LCMS simply refused to read articles by Marquart and others in *Christian News* which took issue with their liberal and Social Gospel views. The Hungarian Revolution took place when the editor and Marquart were roommates at Concordia Seminary, St. Louis. They noted that the intellectual snobs ignored the horrors of the communists and the "Butcher of Budapest" while they often praised the communists and attacked the anti-communist Joe McCarthy.[16]

William Beck

Dr. William Beck was another orthodox LCMS theologian who exposed the "obscurantism" of the intellectual snobs who were defending the *Revised Standard Version* of the National Council of Churches and the destructive higher critical views of the translators responsible for the *RSV*. These intellectual snobs at Concordia Publishing House and Concordia Seminary, St. Louis refused to publish articles he wrote which exposed the *RSV* as both unreliable and not in the language of the people. The intellectual snobs refused to participate in any debate with him. One of Beck's articles they refused to publish was "What Does **almah** Mean?" It was published in the April 3, 1967 *Christian News*. It is in *The Christian Handbook on Vital Issues*. The intellectual snobs refused to respond and acted as if they never even read it. "If it appears in *Christian News* it is not worth reading" is the attitude of many intellectual snobs. It was beneath the intellectual snobs to read articles in *Christian News* by even such orthodox scholars as Raymond Surburg, George Stoeckhardt, Robert Preus, William Beck, William Arndt, John Warwick Montgomery, Kurt Marquart, Siegbert Becker, Henry Koch, Walter A. Maier Sr., Paul Burgdorf, Ludwig Fuerbringer, and a host of others. The intellectual snobs have for decades ignored just about anything published by *Christian News*. This includes Beck's *An American Translation of the Bible*, *Baal or God*, *The Christian News Encyclopedia*, C.F.W. Walther's *Pastoral Theology*, Peter Krey's *Devotions of the Apostle's Creed*, Ricaldo Montecroce and Luther's *Islam in the Crucible*, *Walter A. Maier Still Speaks*, *Marquart's Legacy*, *Luther Today*, *Crisis in Christendom*, *Seminex Ablaze*, *Servant Captains*, etc.

When Beck gave me his CPH published tract on the Jehovah's Witnesses New World Translation, he commented:

"This Jehovah's Witnesses pamphlet is a fascinating item showing the *RSV* bias of our church. Because the Jehovah's Witnesses are involved, everybody in the faculty and at CPH immediately and self-evidently let me damn it any way I wanted to and are praising me for having done a good job. If anybody will check carefully my references, he'll see that I'm damning the *RSV* without mentioning it. The *RSV* has as many and bad errors as this Jehovah Witnesses' Bible; I sometimes believe it's worse than the ones treated here. In my writings that are now breaking through if I make a little mention of an error in the *RSV* or the *NEB* that is scratched, and one article is now being held up completely, I believe for that reason. We must have obscurantism to protect our introduction of the *RSV* as the Mo. Synod Bible. You may want to use this in LN."

Beck's tract on the Jehovah's Witnesses' *New World Translation* is in the August 7, 1967 *Lutheran News* and *The Christian News Encyclopedia*.

English Standard Version

The *New English Standard Version*, now used by CPH instead of the *RSV* and *NIV*, is 91% *RSV* which is copyrighted by the ultra-liberal National Council of Churches. While some of the weaknesses of the *RSV* are removed, (Isaiah 7:14 etc.) most of the doctrinal errors in the *RSV* are still in the *ESV*. The *ESV* has the same approach to the actual text as the *RSV* translators had. Beck showed that the *RSV* translators "corrected" the Hebrew text in more than 1,000 places. They simply rejected the inerrancy of the Bible and other Christian doctrines. Today the "intellectual snobs" refuse to consider the massive evidence Beck presented about the *RSV*, the theology of its translators and their use of stilted outmoded language. CPH insists that both the *RSV* and *ESV* are reliable. CPH still refuses to debate its use of the *ESV* version with any defender of Beck's *AAT*. The intellectual snobs refuse to publish any survey which includes a comparison of passages in the *ESV* with those in the *AAT*.[17] The *ESV* defenders display the same obscurantism as the *RSV* defenders Beck opposed. They simply ignore the voluminous evidence published in *Christian News*. They have the big money behind them. In today's world it is often the money and power which counts and not truth and real scholarship.

Banning *Christian News*

Intellectual snobs on the faculties of some LCMS seminaries and colleges have from time to time tried to have *Christian News* banned from distribution to their students. The same issue of *CN*, which published Marquart's "Religious Socialism" with its comments about intellectual snobs, published "*Lutheran News* Found in Seminary Fireplace." Some 140 copies of *Lutheran* (now *Christian*) *News* addressed to students on campus were tossed into a fireplace. The post office told *CN* that this was a clear violation of government regulations.

Covering Up Theological Liberalism

Intellectual snobs have often refused to consider evidence showing that theological liberalism is being defended and promoted in their denomination. They ignored the voluminous evidence published in Paul Burgdorf's *Confessional Lutheran* and later in *Christian News* and Paul Neipp's *Through to Victory*. They acted as if these publications simply did not exist. They seldom made any reference to them even in footnotes.

In 1964 in Alhambra, California I debated a prominent Lutheran liberal theologian before some 600 people. The debate lasted four hours. It was titled: "Doctrinal and Practical Issues Facing the Lutheran Church Today." Some of the material later appeared in *Baal or God*. Congregations in various sections of the nation then invited me to debate prominent officials of the church, including district presidents and synodical vice-presidents on whether or not theological liberalism was being defended and promoted in the denomination. I generally came with a trunk suitcase of books and documentation. I would show the district president a book, ask him to read the name of the book, author and publisher and then some marked quotations in the book where the author clearly attacked a basic Christian doctrine. Then I asked the official if the author was on the denomination's clergy roster. The church official would have to admit the author was on the clergy roster. Then I would ask: "Is anything being done to discipline the author?" Each time the church official would have to admit that nothing was being done and that the author was considered in good standing in the denomination. It didn't take a rocket scientist to show that officials were covering up false doctrine in the denomination. After this happened in several sections of the nation, the intellectual snobs refused to appear in any debate with me. The intellectual snobs refused to face the facts.

Refusing to Consider the Evidence

The last time this happened was when a panel of the LCMS's Council of Presidents heard a case involving me and Dr. Charles Mueller, Sr., a prominent leader of Jesus First and close friend of LCMS President Kieschnick. The panel of LCMS district presidents found me guilty of breaking the 8th Commandment vs. Mueller when I said that Mueller wanted the LCMS to be open for clergymen who support women serving as pastors. I brought a suitcase of documents with me to the hearing in St. Louis to prove I told the truth about Mueller. I invited Mueller to the hearing in order to answer questions and authenticate the documents I intended to present at the hearing. Mueller refused to come to the hearing and the panel of district presidents dismissed me from the hearing even before I could say one word. I was not allowed to face my accuser. Rev. Herbert Mueller, Chairman of the COP panel and now LCMS First Vice-President, showed me some new regulation, I believe from the CCM, and told me I had to leave the hearing. I said I wasn't familiar with all these new man made regulations of the bureaucracy, but I do know even the pagan Romans recognized the right for a man to speak in his own defense and face his accuser, which the COP denied me (Acts 25:16). I do know it is a fundamental Scriptural and American principle that the accused has the right to face his accuser, regardless of what the LCMS's COP and CCM says.

I then mailed some of the documents I intended to present at the hearing. The panel of district presidents simply ignored the evidence I gave them. The LCMS district presidents then found Mueller innocent of all charges and declared that Jesus First leader Mueller was always an orthodox Lutheran.

I sent the COP panel documents showing that Mueller had written in 1974 when he was a district president that he defended the theology of Seminex. The COP panel ignored the evidence. LCMS President Jerry Kieschnick mailed the findings of the panel to all members of the COP stating that I am an impenitent sinner whose congregation should be removed if I do not repent for "sinning" vs. Charles Mueller. Kieschnick furnished no evidence for the serious charges he widely circulated. Intellectual snobs do not have to consider evidence. They have the power and that is what counts, not the evidence.

Recovered Memory Therapy

Intellectual snobs refused to consider the evidence that there is no scientific basis for the kind of recovered memory therapy promoted by some psychologists. In 1996 a professor at Concordia Seminary filed a lawsuit vs. me and *Christian News* after I said he practiced "voodoo psychology." The professor came to my circuit to drive demons out of a house where the owners refused to live because of the alleged existence of demons in the house. The professor "exorcised" the house. The seminary professor then led the daughter of a staff member at the St. Louis seminary to believe her father had raped her and sacrificed the fetuses to the devil. There was solid evidence in medical records that proved the girl was a virgin after the confused girl was led by the seminary professor with his voodoo psychology to believe her father raped her. The district president and seminary defended the seminary professor and his "voodoo psychology". During the months the case dragged on *CN* published many articles by competent psychologists who discredited the "voodoo psychology" of the Concordia Seminary professor. Among the books *CN* urged the defenders of the St. Louis professor, who led the daughter of a seminary faculty member to believe she had been raped by her father, to read were these books by Martin and Deidre Bobgan: *Against 'Biblical Counseling' for the Bible, Competent to Minister, Christ Centered Ministry, The End of 'Christian Psychology'*, and *12 Steps to Destruction*. *CN* urged the defenders of the "voodoo psychologist", who filed a lawsuit vs. *Christian News*, to read *How Christian Is Christian Counseling?* by G.L. Almy, M.D., *Lost Daughters* by R. Van Til, *Victims of Memory* by M. Pendergast, and *Why Christians Can't Trust Psychology* by

Ed Bulkley. All these books are still available from *Christian News*.

When the case involving the "voodoo psychologist" at the seminary came up during hearings of a seminary faculty committee considering whether or not to certify me for the ministry, the faculty defended the "voodoo psychologist" and insisted that I should not be certified for the ministry. Although I had repeatedly urged the faculty to read books refuting the erroneous notions of the "voodoo psychologist" on the faculty, it appeared as if hardly any member of the faculty had read any of the books. When the psychology department at Washington University heard for themselves the "voodoo psychologist" at the seminary promote his "voodoo psychology", the seminary faculty went down in the estimation of some Washington University professors when they discovered the seminary faculty defended the "voodoo psychologist" *CN* had rightly exposed.

The seminary professor recommended in the LCMS's *Lutheran Witness*, *The Courage to Heal* by Ellen Bass and Laura Davis, two lesbians. The book promotes recovered memory therapy and immoral sex. Concordia Seminary President John Johnson strongly defended the seminary professor and the book *The Courage to Heal*. He said the book contains "redeeming features." Johnson insisted that the seminary was unanimously supporting the seminary professor who sued me and unanimously opposed my certification for the ministry. The seminary professor was featured on the LLL's "On Main Street" television program hosted by Lutheran Hour Speaker and now Concordia Seminary President, Dale Meyer. I asked seminary President John Johnson, after he commended *The Courage to Heal*, if he had read the book. This great scholar whose flagrant plagiarism was covered up by the LCMS's seminaries and bureaucrats said he had not read the book.

Reason 10 in my list of reasons why CUS is the biggest and best Lutheran university mentions that the chairman of the theology department of CUW had the courage to expose Johnson's plagiarism. He is now president of Concordia University, Chicago. Such courage on the part of scholars in the LCMS is a rarity. Some professors also teach their students "Cooperate and graduate. Learn from what we did to Herman Otten, who did not cooperate."

Liberals and Conservatives

Intellectual snobs, who refuse to consider the evidence are found both among liberals and conservatives.

The conservative high churchmen in the LCMS, who at times have worn buttons referring to themselves as hyper-euros and Loehe and Graubau men, refuse to consider the Scriptural evidence that ordination is not a sacrament in the same sense as baptism and the Lord's Supper. The intellectual snobs will not debate the issue in any arena where both sides are given an opportunity to defend their position and question the other. Intellectual snobs who insist there is solid evidence that the Germans during World War II exterminated some 6 million Jews, most of them in gas chambers, refuse to read books and articles by such revisionist scholars as Robert Faurison, Arthur Butz, Charles Weber, David Irving, Robert Countess, Wilhelm Staeghlich, Thies Christopherson, Fred Leuchter, Paul Rassinier, Rabbi J.B. Burg, R. Clarence Lang, etc. The intellectual snobs simply ignore evidence which refute their notions.

Dietrich Bonhoeffer and Martin Luther King

Many "scholars" in the LCMS take issue with and ignore the evidence that Dietrich Bonhoeffer and Martin Luther King rejected such Christian doctrines as the resurrection of Jesus Christ and denied the historic Christian faith in some of their writings.

CN has repeatedly found that intellectual snobs are only interested in presenting their side. The long history of *CN* shows that *CN* has always been willing to publish letters and articles from anyone who wanted to refute what *CN* published. *CN* has often listed the addresses of publications which oppose *CN*'s position, besides photographing their articles in *CN*. They never list *CN*'s address or reprint what *CN* says.

Ever since it's beginning a *CN* motto has been: "Put all the facts on the table and let the chips fall where they may."

THE DYING CONCORDIA UNIVERSITY SYSTEM

"The Dying Concordia University System," the five column heading of the November 1, 2010, *Christian News* was followed with a full color photo of each one of the ten schools in CUS. An editorial in this issue noted:

> How can anyone say that the Concordia University System is dying? (p. 1) It has more students and professors than ever before. It pays its presidents about as much as the LCMS President receives, has costly buildings, and charges $30,000 a year.
>
> Read this issue and you will find out why the Lutheran Church-Missouri Synod's Concordia University System is dying.
>
> It is following the pattern of the "Christian" schools analyzed in the massive *The Dying of the Light – The Disengagement of Colleges and Universities from Their Christian Churches* (p. 1).
>
> "LCMS Professors Allowed to Defend Evolution, Women Pastors, Homosexuality" on p. one includes a letter *CN* sent to CUS President Kurt Krueger and LCMS President Matthew Harrison on September 30 after receiving "Concordia University System Viewbook" promoting the 400 million dollar "For the Sake of the Church" fund raising drive. Note on page 13 what *CN* said about this drive when it first began. *CN* asked Presidents Krueger and Harrison: "Do you believe that the professors in CUS should be required to oppose evolution and women serving as pastors and that they should be removed after a fair hearing if they do not?" [Neither Krueger nor Harrison responded.]
>
> *Christian News* has for decades supplied LCMS officials with plenty of documentation showing that there are LCMS professors in the CUS who promote evolution, women pastors, homosexuality, and some of the destructive views of the higher critics of the Bible. The bureaucrats still claim they have no evidence. They say they have no time to read *Christian News*. There are none so blind as those who do not want to see. Some of what *Christian News* has published about the Concordia University System is in *The Christian News Encyclopedia*. Among the LCMS intellectual snobs the *CNE* is considered not worth reading. *Christian News* is the unprofessional, cheap print "cut and paste" product of a computer illiterate, country pastor who was never certified by any LCMS seminary.
>
> "LCMS School System May Soon Be In Same Disarray as Public Education," reprinted on page 14 from the October 24, 1998 *Christian News* comments on a Lutheran Educators Conference. The schools in the CUS are moving away from traditional education approaches. *CN* said twelve years ago: "LCMS now stands at a crossroads. It can choose to clean house or accept the creeping liberalism that is rotting away its education and Christian mission." The LCMS bureaucrats chose not to clean house. Creeping liberalism was allowed to continue. No professor who promoted evolution, women pastors or homosexuality was removed. Homosexuals were allowed to continue teaching. See "Are Homosexuals Permitted to Teach in the LCMS's Concordia University System" on page 14. CUS President William Meyer never answered *CN*. The cover up of homosexuals and their sympathizers continued. Now Daystar, which includes CUS professors, boldly champions a change in the LCMS's official opposition to homosexuality.
>
> The Concordia University System is not dying because of a decrease in the number of students and professors and beautiful buildings and campuses. It is dying be-

cause it includes many professors who do not accept the scriptural position of the LCMS. They promote evolution, women pastors, homosexuality, and the destructive notions of liberal higher critics of the Bible.

WHAT SHOULD BE DONE ABOUT THE DYING CUS?

"What Should Be Done About the Dying CUS" in the November 1, 2010 *CN* said in part:

> The Lutheran Church-Missouri Synod simply does not have enough qualified confessional Lutheran professors to fill all the positions in the Concordia University System.
>
> All CUS professors should be asked where they stand on justification by faith alone, evolution, the inerrancy of the Bible, homosexuality, abortion, the J-E-D-P source hypothesis, etc.
>
> If a CUS school will not insist that all of its professors affirm justification by faith alone, the inerrancy of the Bible, oppose evolution and the destructive notions of liberal Bible critics, the LCMS and this school should come to a parting of the way.
>
> *CN* has suggested that one solution would be to combine the two LCMS seminaries and have the present Concordia Seminary, Ft. Wayne serve as a college for all those preparing for the pastoral ministry. One of the CUS schools, which would only have truly confessional professors, could serve as the college for all those preparing to become Christian Day School teachers.

"A MILLION DOLLAR EDUCATION"

The November 1, 2010 issue of *Christian News* with the rather pessimistic lead headline "The Dying Concordia University System" included "Pastor William Bischoff – A PRODUCT AND CHAMPION OF OLD MISSOURI." It was a speech I gave at the dedication of Bischoff Hall at Trinity Lutheran Church, Bridgeton, Missouri. The church's sign says "Old Missouri." Pastor Bischoff and I began Concordia Prep, Bronxville, New York in 1946 (I was 13 and he was 14). We were roommates one year at Concordia College, Bronxville, and a year at Concordia Seminary. When I preached the sermon at his funeral in 2009, I noted that he was a product and champion of "Old Missouri" and its educational system, now referred to as the Concordia University System.

A fellow Bronxville alumni said that "we received a million dollar education." In high school besides the regular science, math and history courses future LCMS pastors had four years of German, three years of Latin, two years of Greek and four years of religion and then more Latin, Greek and German in college. Hebrew began at the Seminary.

Sports and music events were limited to afternoons, Friday evenings and Saturdays. All students had to be in their rooms studying each evening from 7 to 9:30 p.m.

No major denomination had a better schooling program for its future pastors and Christian day school teachers than the LCMS. No professor, as far as I know, in any of the dozen relatively small LCMS Prep Schools and Junior colleges throughout the nation promoted evolution, women serving as pastors or homosexuality. Even a member of the "liberal" "44", such as Dr .Thomas Coates at Concordia, Portland, Oregon strongly defended direct rectilinear messianic prophecy.

The system was not perfect but it helped develop a great sense of loyalty to God's Word and congeniality.

When Pastor Bischoff and I came to St. Louis we were thrilled to meet fellow future pastors coming from the other LCMS prep schools throughout the nation. Almost all the approximately 700 students lived on campus. Seminarians were generally not permitted to get married. Most did not have the luxury of a car. Pastor Bischoff and I sang in the Lutheran Hour chorus and participated in the seminary's great intramural sports program. I also took part in the seminary's varsity sports program during the years the seminary played against some fine competition, including Valparaiso University, Washington University, Indiana State, Southeast Missouri State, etc.

Students who lived frugally could get by on about $900 a year during prep school years and then $1300 dollars a year at the seminary. The LCMS took care of most of the tuition for all future pastors. Few began their first year in the pastoral ministry with a debt. When I received my M. Div. from the seminary in 1957, a few days later I received an M.A. in history from Washington University. The masters degree cost me only $250 since I had my "room and board" at the seminary where I took classes during the day and attended Washington University in the evening.

Many seminary graduates were like Pastor Bischoff, products and champions of Old Missouri, not because of any non-thinking shoddy traditionalism but because Old Missouri was nothing more nor less than the theology of C.F.W. Walther who followed Martin Luther, who followed only Scripture.

My father, a union house painter in New York City, encouraged his three boys to attend Concordia, Prep and Junior College, Bronxville, and his daughter Concordia, Bronxville, Junior College. When we came home on some weekends he was more interested in how the Greek and Latin were going than what the athletic teams were doing. He encouraged independent thinking and wasn't always impressed with the scholarship of some professors. When he was steel wooling the floors in the home of one of the professors preparing them for shellacking, the professor asked the common laborer if he were related to the Otten boys at the school. "Yes, they're my boys." The professor responded: "They must have a smart mother." Dad Otten wasn't impressed with this professor's knowledge of the causes of WWII and defense of President Franklin Roosevelt. Dad read various newspapers and magazines. One of them was The Walther League Messenger, edited by Lutheran Hour speaker, Walter Maier. *The Crime of Our Ages*, by Dr. Ludwig Fritsch, was one of the books my father urged me to read.

When I did some graduate work in history at Columbia University and Columbia Teachers College in New York, my father was a member of a crew painting Butler Library at Columbia. At times I ate my bag lunch with the painters. I soon found out that some of these ordinary working men knew more in some areas and had more common sense that some of my highly acclaimed professors.

A recent reprint of this book, "The Crime of the Century," first published in 1947, by the National Justice Research Institute, includes this item:

"Pastor Herman Otten Remembers Dr. Fritsch
Editor, *Christian News*, New Haven, MO

"During my senior year [at Concordia College Institute in Bronxville, New York], I gave a talk on Roosevelt, Pearl Harbor, and the forced repatriation of millions of Eastern Europeans back to the Communists. One of the resources I used was *The Crime of the Ages*, by Ludwig A. Fritsch. The book included a pamphlet with an endorsement from Dr. Walter A. Maier, who at that time was speaker on the 'International Lutheran Hour' and a professor at Concordia Seminary, St. Louis.

"My history professor, who was an ardent fan of Roosevelt, almost exploded after I completed the speech. I had previously expressed some disagreement with this professor's views of the causes for the war and Roosevelt's part in the war, but this was the final straw. A few of my classmates were prepared for a confrontation. I was sent to the principal to get 'straightened' out. It didn't do much good and only led me to read more books by such Revisionist historians as Charles Tansill, George Morgenstern, Percy Greaves, John T. Flynn, Charles Beard, Admiral Theobald, etc. I was determined to read all I could about WWI and WWII. When I graduated from Concordia Seminary, St. Louis, in 1957 I also received a Master's Degree in history from Washington University. One reason for majoring in history was because I was interested in writing a textbook on American history which would tell the truth about the origins of World War I and II."

Christianity, Truth and Fantasy: The Holocaust, Historical Revisionism and Christians Today, The Journal of Historical Review, Fall 1989 (Vol. 9, No. 3), pages 321-360.

The "history professor" was the prof who told my father his boys must have a smart mother.

Christianity, Truth and Fantasy

"Christianity, Truth and Fantasy," the speech I gave at the Institute for Historical Review in Los Angeles in 1989 and now mentioned in a reprint of a book I read at Concordia, Bronxville, shortly after WWII, concluded:

> For over 25 years *CN* has been exposing a good number of hoaxes, even those held by many church members. Some have asked: Do you believe there is any absolute truth. Is there anything, in your estimation that is not a hoax? You publish all sorts of opinions. Just where do you stand? Each week we state in our masthead: "CHRISTIAN NEWS is not a doctrinally neutral observer, but is committed to the full historic Christian faith, as it is authoritatively revealed in the written Word of God, the Holy Scriptures, and correctly set forth in the Confessions of the Orthodox Church to wit, the Book of Concord in 1580."
>
> I commend to all revisionists and everyone else nothing neither more nor less than historic Christianity. God by "raising Christ from the dead has given everyone a good reason to believe" (Acts 17:31).
>
> In spite of the many attempts to falsify history, the Christian Church has always struggled for the truth. This was true for the first Christians. It was also the basic issue of the Reformation. One of the greatest confessors of the faith in this century, Dr. Herman Sasse, who was also avidly anti-Nazi, pointed out in his book *Here We Stand* that the "reformation emphasized the profound seriousness of the truth."
>
> So, as an Evangelical Lutheran pastor, in the tradition of the early church and the Reformation, I stand before you today again to make strong appeal for the struggle for the truth.
>
> The subject of the holocaust is not my primary concern in life. It is not my main message. As stated in the masthead the paper we founded and have served as editor for the past 26 years, we preach Jesus Christ and Him crucified. Never-the-less, Christians must not only strive to proclaim the saving Truth of the Gospel. We are obligated by this same Gospel to tell the truth in all areas of life, including events of politics, economics, war, and Church and secular government.
>
> "These are the things which you should do: speak the truth to one another; judge with truth and judgment for peace in your gates" Zechariah 8:16.[18]

The statement in the masthead I quoted at the Institute of Historical Review, a group which includes many non-Christians, was written by Professor Kurt Marquart. It has now appeared in more than 2,250 issues of *Christian News*.

When Kurt Marquart and I were roommates at the St. Louis seminary, a liberal professor referred to "the Otten-Marquart team" where Otten was the mouth and Marquart the brains. Kurt responded: "Herman can think for himself. Anyone who can get a Masters Degree from the seminary and a few days later an M.A. from Washington

University and still play on some varsity teams can't be stupid."

Professor Kurt Marquart An Earned D.D.

I've already noted that one of the reasons why I wrote *"Concordia University – Biggest and Best" Lutheran University* was because CUS awarded Kurt Marquart a D.D. Marquart also graduated from Concordia, Bronxville. When my brother Walter, during a chapel devotion at the college, read a letter I sent him, Marquart asked if I would be his roommate at the seminary even though I was two years ahead of him and first year students were generally not placed with third year students. Walter thought it would be good for me to spend less time with sports and more time with a real scholar. God's hand was at work getting two students together, who in some respects were very different and had never met each other. As a first year student Marquart had to arrive a week earlier for an orientation week. When I arrived in our room he was not there. He had set up a small table with candles and a crucifix. His desk was surrounded by ancient books, some in Latin, he had gathered from the cage in the sem's library. Very few students made use of these books. Only a few professors, such as Arthur Carl Piepkorn, did. On Kurt's desk was a long letter of some 20 pages in a language I did not understand. It for sure was not German, Greek, Latin, French, Spanish, or English. Later I found out that the letter was a defense of the scriptural doctrine of justification in Russian to be sent to a prominent Orthodox theologian (Father John Meyendorf), who was a step-cousin of Marquart's. (Marquart's brother George told me that "Father John Meyendorf was probably the best educated, intelligent and erudite clergyman of the Russian Orthodox Church in the latter part of the 20th Century.") Hanging on the wall was a framed sign quoting Thomas Jefferson: "I have sworn on the altar of God eternal hostility against every form of tyranny over the mind of man." During his college years at Bronxville, Kurt made hundreds of copies of the Jefferson statement to pass out. His czarist step-father was somewhat of a tyrant who demanded young Kurt agree with him. The step-father could not cope with the fact that young Kurt was his intellectual superior.

When Marquart was on a panel at a Walther Conference at Concordia Seminary, St. Louis, which included former Minnesota Governor and Congressman, Albert Quie, a California U.S. Congressman and the pastor of one of the largest churches in the Evangelical Lutheran Church in America, he brilliantly answered questions from the floor. When the moderator asked if any other panelists wanted to comment, Bill Dannemeyer, the California Congressman responded that after 14 years in Congress he had learned to keep his mouth shut when someone more brilliant had answered a question. This is the way I felt when Marquart was present even though he was two years younger. I was smart enough to keep silent when we were discussing theology with liberal students and professors and later reporting to officials of the Lutheran Church-Missouri Synod about the liberal theology which began infiltrating the St. Louis seminary during the 1950s. Contrary to some reports about Otten and Marquart being primarily responsible for "an ugly time" at the St. Louis sem and using underhanded, secret and backdoor methods, "the Otten-Marquart team" worked completely above board, was open, kind, courteous and practiced no deception or double-talk, even though both Otten and Marquart were, of course, sinners and not perfect.

Marquart's Legacy Speech Banned

When Marquart died in 2006, it was announced that Otten was to speak on Marquart's Legacy at a Walther Conference at the St. Louis seminary. The seminary then received a call from the International Center that the Walther Conference was not to be held at the seminary. LCMS President Kieschnick had previously protested when several congregations in the Texas District asked me to speak.

The speech I prepared for delivery at the seminary is in *Marquart's Legacy*, a book which includes many testimonials about Marquart and a list of the Marquart writings published in *Christian News, The Christian News Encyclopedia, Luther Today – What Would He Do or Say?*, and *Crisis in Christendom – Seminex Ablaze*. The speech on Marquart's Legacy, which I was banned from delivering at the seminary, said in part:

WHO IS THE GREATEST THEOLOGIAN OF THE TWENTIETH CENTURY

A news release from this seminary announcing a Dietrich Bonhoeffer conference held here this year said that Bonhoeffer is "the most important Lutheran theologian since Martin Luther" and that he is the most widely admired and respected theologian in America (*CN*, July 3, 2006, p. 1). The *Lutheran Witness* published an article by Uwe Simeon Netto of this seminary which said that Bonhoeffer was a confessional Lutheran theologian. (*Christian News* has repeatedly shown that on the basis of Bonhoeffer's own writings he denied the resurrection of Christ, the Christ of the Bible and historic Christianity, *CN* October 16, 2006). This editor was only a young boy growing up in New York when Bonhoeffer was at Union Seminary in New York. However, some 40 years ago, when Bonhoeffer was praised at a Reformation rally in the LCMS more than Luther, he read Bonhoeffer's latest writings.

"A Servant of Jesus Christ" lists some of the many great theologians, churchmen and pastors with whom the editor has had contact during his almost 50 years as pastor and 44 years as editor of a Christian weekly. Then the article says: "While *CN* maintains that much of the talk about who is the greatest theologian of the 20th Century is rather foolish, *CN* rates no theologian in the last half of the Twentieth Century higher than Professor Kurt Marquart. Some may know more in their individual field: Hebrew, Greek, History, Archaeology, textual criticism, etc., but few, if any, have such a broad knowledge of matters in so many areas, including world affairs, and particularly Communism. *CN* has said that while there are other theologians who have been gifted with great intellects, they often do not have what is so important for every theologian who teaches future pastors, and that is the kind of humility and pastoral spirit Marquart has shown during his years as pastor, professor, and father." Marquart was certainly far more important and should be more respected than a liberal like Bonhoeffer praised this year at both LCMS seminaries.

"A Servant of Jesus Christ" mentions that during Marquart's first year at this seminary I introduced him to many of the leading "liberal intellectuals" among the 700 students at the seminary whom I had gotten to know my first two years at the seminary. It says: "When the older liberal intellectuals attempted to back me into a corner with their vast learning, Kurt would bail me out with his keen intellect and tremendous logic. The older students were baffled with this first year man with the perpetual clerical collar whom Otten now has 'enlisted' to support his 'confessional,' 'patriotic,' 'anti- communist' and 'out of date' views. They had met their match and knew it.

If all these silly, untrue stories which have been passed around through the years, about Otten and Marquart, by those who have been misinformed, were true, Concordia Seminary, St. Louis would not have lost the Seminary vs. Otten case. Trinity Lutheran Church, New Haven, where I have been the pastor since 1958 would never have been reinstated in the LCMS after church bureaucrats, under the direction of liberals at the St. Louis seminary, several times suspended the congregation and eventually expelled it from the LCMS. The true story is told in "*Concordia Seminary, St. Louis vs. Otten Case – Book of Documentation* arranged by Kurt Marquart." [cover on page p.250]

We worked together on the book at the St. Louis seminary and in Weatherford, Texas, where Marquart was a pastor before he went to Australia.

Dr. Martin Noland, former director of the Concordia Historical Institute, is one of the few who actually studied the more than 1,000 page transcript of the Seminary vs. Otten case directed by Marquart. Noland is working on a book about Marquart. In "Dr. Martin Noland – Marquart's Defense Exonerated Otten," in the January 18, 2010 *Christian News*, Noland wrote: "My first impression is that you did the right thing in choosing Dr. Marquart as your advocate. He outclassed and out-argued the lay attorney representing the seminary. It looked to me like the seminary attorney did the best he could, under the circumstances, but he had a weak case to start with and a strong opponent (Marquart) at the finish." "My conclusion, based on first reading of the reports, is that you were exonerated by Marquart's defense and that you should have been certified. The rest of what has happened since that time has been political maneuvering by your enemies."

"Kurt Marquart – God's Chosen Instrument in the LCMS's 'Great Battle for the Bible'" on pages 17-20 includes Noland's questions and my answers. This article includes letters from Kurt Marquart and Robert Preus explaining how it happened that Marquart came back to the U.S. to teach at Concordia Seminary, Springfield, Illinois which moved to Ft. Wayne, IN.

Power, Politics, and the Missouri Synod, By James Burkee

The January 3 special *Christian News* issue on higher education included a full page on *Power, Politics, and the Missouri Synod* to be released by Fortress Press on February 1. Dr. James Burkee, the personable chairman of the CUW faculty, is the author, Dr. Martin Marty, associated with *The Christian Century* for more than 50 years, is the author of the foreword. *CN*'s report included enthusiastic endorsements. *Forum Letter* noted that Fortress Press bills it as "the first full scholarly account of the rise of political conservatism" in the LCMS. The book is available from *Christian News* for $26.00 plus s/h. Organized conservatives in the LCMS may not be too happy with the book. It certainly exposes the double talking and deception and power politics practiced by LCMS President Jacob Preus, the hero of most organized conservatives. He had the full support of the Schwan Foundation with its millions. *Fortress Press* announced:

> *Power, Politics, and the Missouri Synod* follows the rise of two Lutheran clergymen—Herman Otten and J. A. O. Preus—who led different wings of a conservative movement that seized control of a theologically conservative but socially and politically moderate church denomination (LCMS) and drove "moderates" from the church in the 1970s. The schism within what was then one of the largest Protestant denominations in the United States ultimately reshaped the landscape of American Lutheranism and fostered the polarization that characterizes today's Lutheran churches.

"Kurt Marquart – God's Chosen Instrument" in the January 18, 2010 *Christian News* noted:

> The 1973 LCMS's convention, a highlight of the LCMS's great "Battle for the Bible", in resolution 3-09 declared that the theology of those who formed Seminex was false doctrine which was not to be tolerated within the LCMS. Hundreds of liberals at the convention demonstrated against the Bible believers in the LCMS who opposed theological liberalism, evolution, universalism and the destructive criticism of the Bible promoted by liberal Bible higher critics. Kurt Marquart was one of those who took issue with LCMS President Jacob Preus and others in the LCMS bureaucracy, for not following through on 3-09 of the LCMS's 1973 convention. The liberal professors and officials like Charles Mueller, Sr., who supported the theology of the Seminexers but remained in the LCMS, were not disciplined. Only a few district presidents, who broke a by-law when they ordained uncertified Seminex graduates,

were removed.

Anyone who has studied what was happening theologically within the LCMS for twenty years prior to the LCMS's 1973 convention knows that God's chief instrument, and the real hero in this battle, was no one in the LCMS's bureaucracy, no LCMS president, no seminary president, no professor or anyone else whose salary came from the LCMS. It was no one associated with any secret group working and meeting behind the scenes planning political strategy and forming voting guides.

It was a highly, intellectually gifted and articulate refugee from communism. It was no "Johnny-come-lately." It was a young, highly dedicated and Christ-centered, spiritually minded student who had just left his teenage years. He was "the brain" behind a few students who protested in the 1950's against theological liberalism, evolution and universalism creeping into the LCMS, particularly at Concordia Seminary, St. Louis. He was the chief and often sole author of the documents in the "Seminary vs. Otten" case. He was the young man who faced experienced seminary lawyers and mature faculty administrators who tried their best to show the LCMS's highest court of adjudication, its Board of Appeals, that all seminary professors were orthodox Lutherans and that student Herman Otten, his seminary roommate, had not told the truth about seminary professors he said were liberals. He showed that Otten told the truth.

None of this history is mentioned in any publication by CPH or financed by the Schwan Foundation. *Christian News* noted in its review of CPH's "A Seminary In Crisis" that those who have the money often write the history of a denomination.

Marquart's Legacy,[19] published by *Christian News*, shortly after Marquart died in 2006, lists the hundreds of writings by Kurt Marquart which *Christian News* has published. Once all the issues of *CN* are scanned any computer literate person will be able to read them.

Although Marquart accepted a call to Australia in 1961, his influence continued within the LCMS through his writings. After attending the Lutheran World Federation's Fourth Assembly in 1963 as a reporter for *Christian News*, Marquart lectured in some 20 U.S. cities from coast to coast. The LCMS paid 20 observers to attend this LWF Assembly. It was about to join the LWF, when Marquart's reports in *Christian News* (formerly *Lutheran News*) and lectures about the LWF and liberalism creeping into the LCMS became the chief factor in turning the tide in the LCMS away from the LWF. At that time no one salaried by the LCMS or any of its schools dared openly to challenge the liberalism in the LCMS and world Lutheranism as boldly, effectively, and intelligently as Kurt Marquart. ["What the LCMS Has to Offer Former Captive Nations – JESUS FORGIVES YOUR SINS – Justification by Grace Alone," the lead story in the January 10, 2011 *Christian News* includes some of Marquart's articles on Communism.]

Again in 1967 he exposed and challenged liberalism and Communism and the new morality in a lecture tour in the U.S.

Rev. Paul McCain, who had the support of the Schwan Foundation, was among the "respectable" conservatives who tried to drive a wedge between Marquart and Otten by telling Marquart that Otten refused to meet with LCMS President A.L. Barry. The exact opposite was the truth. When the Barry-McCain administration issued a ruling, later followed by LCMS conventions, that the Seminary vs. Otten case was closed, Marquart wrote in the July, 1998 *Reporter* of the LCMS: "For the convention to pronounce the Herman Otten case 'closed' (again!) would be to perpetuate blatant injustice and to signal shameful kinship with corrupt power cliques which habitually punish whistle-blowers rather than wrong doers."

When an LCMS convention called for a special committee to study the Seminary vs. Otten case, Marquart wrote to this committee in an effort to explain the clear meaning of the ruling of the LCMS's highest court, its Commission on Appeals, in this case:

"Anywhere else but in the Soviet Union and in other dark corners of unchallenged bureaucratic arrogance, it would have been self-evident that the Seminary had failed to show just cause." "The whole 'Seminex' development vindicated Pastor Otten's concerns many times over." (LCMS's COP violated LCMS's *Handbook* – The Seminary Case vs. Otten Is Simple Not Complex).[20]

The COP, which has the support of the LCMS's new administration, still rejects the clear meaning of the final ruling of the LCMS's Commission on Appeals, in the Seminary vs. Otten case where Marquart was one of Otten's counselors. The LCMS's *Handbook* required the bureaucrats to accept the ruling.

Marquart's dealings with the LCMS bureaucracy, led him to tell the Walther Conference meeting at Concordia Seminary, St. Louis in 2003: "Our tragedy is that this absolute priority of the divine truth has before displaced in our Synodical life. By what? By organizational, bureaucratic concerns. Our disease is, you might say, 'bureaucratitis.'"[21]

During his years at Concordia Seminary, St. Louis, Marquart was the theological leader of those who opposed LCMS membership in the LWF. When Martin Marty in 1957 supported LCMS membership in the LWF and LCMS President John W. Behnken opposed it at a student body meeting at the old chapel at Concordia Seminary, St. Louis, Behnken was not pleased that it appeared that Marty had the support of the majority of students and faculty who heard the Behnken-Marty discussion on the LWF. Marty is the author of the foreword of Professor James Burkee's *Power, Politics and the Missouri Synod*. After the Behnken-Marty LWF dialogue (debate) in the old seminary chapel, I was a member of a group Behnken invited to meet with him to inform him and Herman Harms, the LCMS's First Vice-President, what was going on at the seminary. My report to Behnken also commented on the "Seminarian Controversy." It noted that "Conservatives have not been adequately represented since Dr. Marty was editor." Marquart and I had served on the Seminarian's staff, constantly opposing the liberal majority. One of them defended by the faculty joined the Unitarian church after graduation and another first joined the U.L.C. and then the Unitarians. He was defended and certified for the ministry by the faculty.   Seminex administrators said that Marquart and I were not sufficiently theologically advanced to understand the liberals at the seminary and such "shining stars and lights" in the LCMS as Jaroslav Pelikan and Marty. Later Richard Neuhaus and Robert Wilken also associated with the *Seminarian*, cheated Marquart through underhanded tactics out of becoming the editor of the *Seminarian*. I told them at the time: "You liberals claim to promote honest ethics and yet through unethical tactics you robbed Kurt, who was the most qualified, of becoming editor next year when he returns from vicarage." Both Neuhaus and Wilken denied the inerrancy of the Bible, justification by faith alone and that Jesus Christ is the only way to heaven. Years later they joined the Roman Catholic Church. I had said during our seminary days that these followers of Arthur Carl Piepkorn might one day join the Roman Catholic Church.

"CUW Alumnus and Nationally Recognized Scholar Come to Campus to Talk About the Breakdown of Trust"

The November 22, 2010 *Christian News* published a press release from CUW announcing that Dr. Marty was to speak here on November 17, 2010. The CUW release said that Dr. Marty "is the author of more than 50 books, recipient of several distinguished awards and over 70 honorary doctorates." I know of no other Lutheran who has written as many book and received as many honorary doctorates. Years ago *Christian News* commended him for his work ethic. When Dr. Marty wrote an article in 1957 in *The Christian Century* attacking the inerrancy of the Bible, Dr. J.T. Mueller at the time was a retired professor at Concordia Seminary, St. Louis. Among his many books and hundreds of published articles was *Christian Dogmatics*, an epitome of Francis Pieper's 3 volume *Christian Dogmatics*. When Dr. Mueller read my response to Dr. Marty's "Fundamentalism and the Church"[22] he urged me to become a journalist. I planned to become an agricultural missionary or athletic coach and teacher at one of our colleges. Mueller wanted someone who would stand up in public to the liberals creeping into the LCMS, particularly its colleges and seminaries. Someone who would put his concerns in writing. He asked me to visit Dr. Henry Grueber, a classmate of his and LCMS President John W. Behnken. Grueber was living in retirement in Milwaukee. He had been a former First Vice-President of the LCMS. He had asked J.T. Mueller for information about what was going on theologically at the St. Louis Seminary. Mueller, who no longer had tenure because of his age, feared he might be relieved of teaching some graduate classes if he reported the truth about the rise of theological liberalism at the seminary. Upon Grueber's request I characterized the doctrinal position of several faculty members, as he read me their names from the *Lutheran Annual*. To help him remember the mass of details, I returned the next day, November 30, 1957, and gave him a confidential written resume of what I had told him. I gave much the same report to Ralph Bohlmann, when I met with him in his room at Concordia College, Milwaukee, now CUW, where he had been teaching. Bohlmann, who became president of the St. Louis Seminary and then the LCMS, said he shared similar concerns about the rise of liberalism at the St. Louis Seminary but advised that to get ahead in the LCMS it was wisest not to go public.

Grueber took my report to the Milwaukee pastoral conference. The Milwaukee pastors then sent a letter of concern to the St. Louis Seminary. The Seminary invited the Milwaukee pastors to send a spokesman to the Seminary. They sent Grueber. When he came to St. Louis, he asked me to visit him in the room the Seminary had arranged for him. Grueber asked me if he could reveal the source of material which led the Milwaukee pastors to write their letter. I told him he was free to use my name. I regarded classroom teaching as public and not secret. The Seminary faculty disagreed. The faculty said classroom teaching was not public and insisted a student had no right to report even to his parents or the president of the LCMS what was being taught in the classroom. I argued that every man, woman, and child, who supported the Seminary had a right to know what their future pastors were being taught. In a certain sense my report in Milwaukee to Grueber was the beginning of the long Seminary vs. Otten case which Professor Burkee writes about in his book scheduled to be released on February 1, 2011 by ELCA's Fortress Press.

I wrote the report to Greuber in the home of a good friend and supporter of Dr. Walter Stuenkel, president of Concordia, Milwaukee at the time. He was a major supporter of Concordia, Milwaukee.

Kurt Marquart, vicared for English District President Hugo Kleiner in North Tonawanda, New York. When Marquart and I picked up this district president at the St. Louis train station during one of his visits to St. Louis, he said that he would have less concerns about the liberalism creeping into the LCMS if there were more students like Marquart and Otten. Marty was a member of Kleiner's English District. Kleiner was concerned about his theological liberalism.

When 45 out of 50 professors and staff members left Concordia Seminary, St. Louis in 1974 at the height of the LCMS's "Battle for the Bible," taking with them some 450 seminarians to form Seminex, Marty also left the LCMS, writing in *The Christian Century* that both Concordia Seminary and the LCMS had "gone to ashes". When the liberals left the Seminary, *Christian News* said that it was once again becoming "the world's finest seminary." Years later when the seminary again began shifting away from the conservative position of those who rebuilt the seminary in the 1970s and 1980s after the big walkout in 1974, Marty was invited to speak at the seminary. A group of laymen in California, including a U.S. congressman who received a D.D. from the St. Louis seminary and Christ College, Irvine, then attempted to arrange a debate at the seminary between Marty and Otten. Marty was to argue why seminarians should attend an ELCA seminary, where Marty was a member, and Otten why they should attend an LCMS seminary, which Marty wrote had "gone to ashes." Then each would be given time to question the other about anything they had written. Marty was to be given the opportunity to refute what Otten wrote about him in a seven part series during 1997 in *Christian News*. Otten agreed to debate, Marty declined.

A TWENTY-FIRST CENTURY PLATFORM FOR CONCORDIA UNIVERSITY WISCONSIN, OTHER SCHOOLS IN THE CONCORDIA UNIVERSITY SYSTEM, AND THE YOUTH OF AMERICA FIGHT FOR THE FAITH
PART II

In the name of God the Father, God the Son and God the Holy Spirit.

When Dr. James Burkee chairman of your faculty last November invited me to speak here on February 3 he suggested that I speak on the Concordia University System. Dr. Burkee informed me that the invitation came from CUW President Patrick Ferry. The headline of the November, 2010 *Christian News* was "The Dying Concordia University System." *Christian News* reviewed The *Dying Light* at considerable length when it first appeared in 1998 and now again featured this 869 page book *The Dying of the Light – The Disengagement of Colleges & Universities From Their Christian Churches*." There are almost 50 pages on the Lutherans and some of their colleges. The November 2010 *First Things* was a special issue on higher education. *First Things* claims to have surveyed more than 2,000 U.S. colleges, among them CUW. Several pages in the December 20 *Christian News* were devoted to the report in *First Things* on U.S. colleges.

My research led me to review not only what was in my files at the *Christian News* Research Center but also what *CN* has said about the Concordia University System and particularly Concordia University, Wisconsin. *Christian News* published in a special issue (January 3, 2011) on education "Concordia University, Wisconsin, Biggest and Best." I listed 10 reasons. Having a U.S. President speak at CUW, honest home run champion Henry Aaron speak, having our St. Louis Rams use your great facilities for their training camp or that your Greenbay, Wisconsin Packers are in the Superbowl were not among the reasons. I mentioned: 1) Statement on Worship, 2) A Lutheran Worldview, 3) Leaders in Pre-Seminary Enrollment 4) Liberal Professors Removed, 5) A Christ Centered, Articulate President, 6) Confessional Lutheran Lectures, 7) "Professor Kurt Marquart – An Earned D.D.", 8) CUW Make the Grade, 9) Upholding Creation, and 10) Plagiarism Cover Up. Point 10 showed that Dr. Nathan Jastram, Chairman of your theology department, was about the only LCMS scholar to expose a serious case of plagiarism in CUS. When a former professor from CUW read what I had said in "Concordia University, Wisconsin – Biggest and Best", he called to tell me some bad things about your school. I asked him to put his views in writing. No school is perfect. All can improve. CN plays no favorites and is open to publish all sides. So far I have not received a statement from the professor.

CN reprinted your entire statement on "Worship in a Collegiate Setting." *CN* said when it first appeared in 1996 that it should be used in all schools in CUS. While *CN* has not always been enthusiastic about the awarding of D.D.'s to theologically incompetent and unscholarly district presidents and others in the bureaucracy, *CN* said:

"Concordia University, Wisconsin, and its fine president Dr. Patrick Ferry, should be commended for awarding Professor Marquart a D.D. Concordia Seminary, St. Louis, should have given it to him long ago. The fact that Concordia, Wisconsin, is awarding Professor Marquart a D.D. is just one more reason why youth should consider attending Concordia, Wisconsin."

In Part One, I mention that Marquart was the theological and intellectual leader of the conservatives at the St. Louis seminary while the leaders of the liberals were such bright "shining stars and lights" as Jaroslav Pelikan and Martin Marty. However, Part One became far too long for delivery here this evening. I have e-mailed it to Dr. Burkee in case he wanted to give it to faculty members on the panel.

I have included it as an appendix to a book I have been preparing on Dietrich Bonhoeffer and Martin Luther King, Jr., since the book exposes the poor scholarship and refusal to study clear evidence of those in the bureaucracy, including LCMS seminaries, CUS and CPH, who praise Bonhoeffer and King as great Christians who believed in the resurrection of Christ and are role models for those in CUS to follow.

A Twenty-First Century Reformation

When Kurt Marquart and I were roommates, during the 1950's at Concordia Seminary, St. Louis, we discussed the need for a Twentieth-Century Reformation and Formula of Concord.

After the LCMS's Council of Presidents, including LCMS President Jacob Preus, in October, 1969, unanimously repudiated *Christian News* and warned against lending any credence to *Christian News*, 850 laymen, pastors and professors attended a testimonial banquet for *Christian News* held at the Marriott Motor Hotel in Chicago on February 22, 1970. There I presented "A Twentieth Century Platform for Lutherans." It included a call for "a new TWENTIETH CENTURY FORMULA OF CONCORD, an orthodox statement of faith around which all loyal Christians could rally." The keynote speaker, Pastor Alvin Wagner, a member of the LCMS's Commission on Theology and Church Relations read a letter from Kurt Marquart's friend in Australia, Dr. Hermann Sasse, a leading Lutheran theologian. Sasse wrote for the group at the testimonial banquet to hear: "Somebody should rise and publicly thank Herman Otten for his brave fight . . . why was it left to a young pastor to speak where others should have spoken." I concluded by asking the group: "Ponder this message from Rev. Kurt Marquart, one of our contributors in Australia, and in my estimation one of the real theologians in Christendom today." Marquart's message said in part: "The Church today is alive and is Church only where she thinks in terms of Christ's 'New Maths.' If we try to calculate our Christian life and work, as individual, as families, and as congregations, on the basis of our own resources, the odds against us are staggering: Our own sins, our weaknesses, our lack of qualifications, and even our funds, doom us from the start. But the Lord wants us to do His work in bold, even reckless reliance on Him as divine supplier of all our needs. . . It is up to Christians to see themselves not as the 4000 comfortably seated on the grass, waiting to be served, but as the dozen men working in the multiplication and sharing of the Bread of Life."

A few months after I presented this Twentieth Century Platform for Lutherans including the Call for a Twentieth Century Formula of Concord, I spoke on "Victory and Joy with Christ – THE UPSURGE OF AUTHENTIC LUTHERANISM"[23] at Walther Memorial Church in Milwaukee. The pastor of this church, Dr. Edwin Suelflow, became president of your district and chairman of the Board of Regents of CUW. I began: "As we lecture in various sections of the country we have noted that all too frequently conservatives are too pessimistic. They act as if in a free contest truth must lose. They have lost the joy and optimism of the Christian faith. Some who consider themselves conservative have no real positive program." I concluded at the crowded Milwaukee church: "My fellow Lutherans, let's not run away from the liberals. We have the truth on our side. We have real scholarship on our side. Above all, God is on our side and he has promised us the victory."

"Urges 'Peaceful Reorganization' of Synod," a long report in the November 12, 1970 *Badger Lutheran*,[24] mentioned the 10 point platform for "authentic Lutheranism" I presented. The *Badger Lutheran* said in part: "Conservatives must 'learn to work together and stop wasting time and energy attacking one another,' the speaker emphasized. Too often he said, conservatives have 'failed to show true love' to those within their ranks who support other courses of action." "He enlarged on tactical methods throughout the question period: 'Fight out in the open . . . no behind the scenes meetings, no contact men. I don't think God supports underhanded maneuvering. 'Use tact – don't try to roll over people like a steam roller. Win them in a loving and friendly manner.'"

Some 40 years later Dr. James Burkee in his *Power, Politics and The Missouri Synod* exposes some of the tactics of organized conservatives, particularly LCMS President Jacob Preus, which Marquart and I deplored. The *Badger Lutheran* noted: "(9) after a peaceful reorganization or after the liberals are driven out, then, said Otten, the conservatives should build the finest church body in all history – one that is truly mission minded, truly catholic, evangelical and progressive; one that has the finest schools and colleges; one that will re-establish fellowship with the Wisconsin Synod and the Lutheran Churches of the Reformation; one that will present to the world an orthodox statement of faith."

After reporting that "Between 350 and 400 persons attended the talk," the *Badger Lutheran* concluded by publishing the entire statement of the LCMS's Council of Presidents repudiating *Christian News* and warning against lending any credence to the editor.

Through the years my congregation has petitioned LCMS conventions to promote a Twentieth Century and now Twenty-First Century Formula of Concord. Each time tunnel vision bureaucrats have stopped the move in one way or another.

A delegation from the Lutheran World Federation recently met with the Pope and urged him to help plan a 500th Anniversary Celebration of the Reformation. *CN* has often said that the liberal Lutherans and the Pope might as well unite. Today neither affirms the scriptural doctrine of justification by faith alone, the vicarious satisfaction of Christ and the inerrancy of the Bible. Both allow homosexuals to serve as pastors. Both promote universalism, the anti-scriptural notion that all religions worship the true God. Both support evolution and deny the historicity of the Genesis account of creation. Both deny that Moses, under the inspiration of God the Holy Spirit, wrote the first five books of the Bible. Both insist these books came from the fictitious J-E-D and P sources centuries after Moses died.

Here are some reasons why all of Christendom should fight for the faith (Jude 3) and needs a 21st Century Reformation and Formula of Concord today far more than it did 500 years ago in Luther's day:

WHY A 21ST CENTURY REFORMATION TODAY
The American Luther – C.F.W. Walther,
First President of The Lutheran Church-Missouri Synod.

1. "The Church has no choice but to be at war. It is ecclesia militans, the Church Militant, and will remain such until the blessed end. Wherever a Church is seen to be, not ecclesia militans, but ecclesia quiescens, a Church at ease, that – you may rely on it! – is a false Church." C.F.W. Walther's *Law and Gospel*, p. 266.

2. "Christianity, according to fundamentalism, is one religion and Christianity, according to modernism, is another. . . There is a clash here as profound and grim as between Christianity and Confucianism. The God of the fundamentalist is one God, and the God of the modernist is another . . . Which is the true Christian religion is the question to be settled by our generation for future generations." *The Christian Century*, January 3, 1924.

The Christian Century has long been a voice of modern liberalism advertising itself as "Protestantism's leading non-denominational journal". The "god" of *The Christian Century* is the "god" of most major denominations today. Confessional Lutherans are not Fundamentalists but their God is the God of those who affirm the Fundamentals of the Christian faith.

3. "Modern theology, represented also by some Lutherans, has become dynamic Unitarianism." Francis Pieper, Former President of the Lutheran Church-Missouri Synod, *Christian Dogmatics*, Vol. 1, p. XI, April, 1924.

4. "Should the majority of liberal Protestant ministers ever decide to be intellectually honest with their congregations, the Lutheran Reformation would seem altogether mild by comparison. Protestant parishioners would, I am convinced, leave their churches wholesale." Jesse J. Roberson, a liberal Protestant clergyman, *Christianity Today*, January 17, 1964.

5. "We repeat the appeal to American Protestantism is: 'BACK TO LUTHER!' And if this be a battle cry that is to summon the latent forces of complacent laity to action; if it be the rallying summons to a spiritual crusade for Christ; if it means the splitting of the church into two groups, one liberal and unbelieving, and the other conservative and faithful unto death; if it requires the breaking of conventional ties, the banishment of pulpit Judases, then we will repeat the cry: 'BACK TO LUTHER!'" – Dr. Walter A. Maier, Lutheran Hour Speaker, *Walther League Messenger*, November 1933, at 450th anniversary of birth of Martin Luther.

6. "No longer is it this or that aspect of revelation which is questioned, but all revelation, and the very idea of revelation. Not this or that particular truth is rejected, but all truth, and the very possibility of truth. Herein lies the intensive, vertical radicalism of the current crisis. Extensively, horizontally, the crisis is equally radical: the conflict is and must be fought on a global scale, owing to the great advances in transportation and communication and the resultant 'ecumenical' developments. The front cuts across most synodical and denominational lines." Kurt Marquart, "The International Luther", *Crisis In Christendom, Lutheran News*, December 16, 1963. Reprinted from *The Australian Theological Review*, September 1962.

7. "A Call for a Twentieth Century Reformation and Creed. *CN* Editor Presents Twentieth Century Formula of Concord at International Council of Christian Churches in Vancouver at the University of British Columbia, July 30, 1990." Delegates from nations around the world greeted this call with a standing ovation and voted to send the Twentieth Century Formula of Concord to all their churches. The vast majority were non-whites. *Christian News*, October 25, 2010.

8. "Christianity is dying. It was once the bastion of Western Civilization. Now, Christianity is a pitiful remnant of its former greatness. Across the West, it is in full retreat." Columnist Jeffrey T. Kuhner, *Washington Times*, April 2, 2010.

9. "Plans are afoot for thousands of abuse victims and their loved ones to travel to Rome in October for a 'Reformation Day' to pressure the Vatican to act. McDaid, who met Benedict in Washington in 2008, is one of the prime organizers of the march on St. Peter's, and he envisions a massive democracy movement to transform Rome. 'It's the people's church,' he says. 'We have to take it back.' McDaid talks about priests and nuns who are raising travel money for 'victims who can't rub two nickels together to get to Rome. This is way bigger than [Martin Luther's] Reformation.'" Cover Story of the June 7, 2010 *TIME*.

10. "What can the righteous do as the foundations of Christianity are being destroyed? We need a new reformation in our churches. Christians need to be figuratively nailing Genesis chapters 1-11 on the doors of churches and Christian colleges/seminaries, challenging God's people to return to the authority of the Bible." Ken Ham, "Calling for Reformation," *Answers in Genesis Update*, Vol. 17, No. 10, October, 2010.

11. "When it comes to salvation, just 30 percent of all Americans embrace the belief that good works do not earn salvation, but that it is a gift of God through the atoning death and resurrection of Jesus Christ. People attending Assembly of God (64 per cent), Pentecostal (62 percent) are most likely to share this view; while Catholics are least likely (9 percent). Lutherans are below the national average, at 27 percent." From "Poll: Most Christians' beliefs out of sync with Bible." *Reporter* (Lutheran Church-Missouri Synod) July 2001, reprinted in July 23, 2001 *Christian News*).

12. "Most colleges and universities no longer have a serious, valued, or functional relationship with their Christian sponsors of the past." From *The Dying of the Light – The Disengagement of Colleges & Universities from their Christian Churches* by James Tunstead Burtchaell, Eerdman, 1998.

The World Church of 2017

13. Lee Penn, the author of "The World Church of 2017," the year of the 500th anniversary of the Reformation, writes in the latest *Spiritual Counterfeit Journal*:

"By the end of 2000, many observers had consigned the mainline Protestant churches in North America to the dust-bin of history. They had been losing members since the mid-1960s; declining donations forced lay-offs of Church staff and closures of parishes and seminaries. Meanwhile, mainline Church leaders closed overseas missions, blessed society's politically favored vices, and denounced only the sins that were out of fashion at the New York Times, CNN, and MTV--believing that this was the way to be 'relevant' and popular.

"The turn-of-the-century travails of the Episcopal Church in the USA were the clearest example of the perilous condition of the mainline Protestant churches. The survival strategies that the Episcopalian leadership adopted in response have worked for other mainline Protestants, too.

"Since 1965, the Episcopal Church had lost more than one-third of its membership, while the US population grew by one-third. In the summer of 2000, the Episcopalian General Convention-- the highest decision-making authority for the denomination--had officially recognized heterosexual and homosexual 'life-long committed relationships' outside of marriage."

"Polls show that today's UCA (United Church of America) members are:
- "20% Wiccan and neo-pagan
- "20% pantheist or, to use a term favored by UCA Bishop Matthew Fox, 'panentheist'.
- "50% 'Broad Church'--they say the old Creeds and read the Bible, and interpret them according to their own desires.
- "10% are traditional Evangelicals and high-church Protestants. Some say that they remain in the UCA as missionaries to their errant brethren; others refuse to leave the parishes where they were baptized and married, or where their ancestors are buried.

"Recent Gallup polls show the following--roughly identical--demographics for the UCA and the American Catholic Church:
- "20% age 75 and over.
- "20% actively homosexual, bisexual, or Transgender.
- "35% divorced heterosexuals who cannot remarry under Catholic, Orthodox, or Evangelical rules. Most have remarried, or are 'partnered.'
- "15% young heterosexual 'swinging singles.'
- "10% young and middle-aged married couples, half of whom have children. . .
- "Only 10 percent of UCA members reject their churches' radical worship services. The UCA hierarchy holds that the 'old truth' is valid for the reactionaries; the 'new truths' -- and the corresponding liturgies --are valid for everyone else. As Episcopal Presiding Bishop Griswold had said in 2000, 'Truth is purifier.' The UCA hierarchy feels secure in its control of its churches, and no longer fears concerted opposition from those who believe the traditional Christianity expressed by the old rites. UCA conservatives can have their staid, comfortable parishes and worship as they wish--as long as they don't publicly criticize what occurs in other parishes or what is done by the UCA hierarchy. . ."

The Worldwide Uprising Against Sex Abuse Within the Church, particularly within the Roman Catholic Church

14. Protestantism, including especially the charismatics, has had its share of sex abusers and adulterous womanizing and divorced clergymen, including the much publicized televangelists. *Christian News* has published many reports about this scandal.

A *Catholic News Service* story in the January 7, 2011 *St. Louis Review* of the archdiocese of St. Louis reports in a story titled: "Milwaukee Archdiocese files for bankruptcy over abuse claims:"

"Milwaukee is the largest archdiocese to file for Chapter 11. The archdiocese of Portland, Ore., with approximately 390,000 Catholics, filed for bankruptcy in July 2004. In February 2007, the Diocese of San Diego, with nearly 900,000 Catholics, filed for Chapter 11 protection."

"Archbishop Listecki wrote that, since the late 1980s, the archdiocese had worked 'to meet the needs of victims/survivors without taking this drastic action (Chapter 11 reorganization).'

"'We have directed increasing resources toward providing financial, psychological, pastoral and spiritual support to victims/survivors. . . . We have spent more than $29 million to cover costs associated with this tragedy,' the archbishop said.

"Since 2002, the archdiocese has sold property, liquidated savings and investments, eliminated ministries and services, cut staff by nearly 40 percent, and put all available real estate on the market in order to provide resources.

"'As a result, we have succeeded in reaching mediated settlements with more than 190 individuals,' Archbishop Listecki said. 'But in the end, our available resources fell short.'"

The primary cause of the great sex abuse scandal in the Roman Catholic Church is its decades long cover up of the tremendous number of homosexual priests, bishops, archbishops, seminarians, and even a Pope. Some Roman Catholic authorities have estimated that as many as 50 percent of Roman Catholic priests and seminarians may be homosexuals. Its difficult to give an exact figure. The September 26, 2005 *Newsweek* reported that "The Rev. Donald Cozzen, in his book, '*The Changing Face of the Priesthood*' estimated that 23 to 58 percent of Catholic clerics have homosexual orientations."

Some 40 years ago my congregation petitioned The Lutheran Church-Missouri Synod to support what the Bible teaches about homosexuality. It is a sin. (Romans 1) Homosexuals should not be permitted to serve as pastors. The LCMS did adopt this position. It actually showed more love to homosexuals than the Roman Catholic Church and all those major Protestant denominations which now permit homosexuals to be pastors and who commune homosexuals. The Bible teaches that homosexuals, who continue in their sinful lifestyle, are going to hell. By refusing to commune homosexuals and have them serve as pastors, the LCMS is showing them true love. We want them to go to heaven. Hopefully, they will repent of their sin if we do not commune them, and then confess Jesus Christ as their Savior from sin and go to heaven when they die.[25]

Christian News has noted for some 30 years that Milwaukee Archbishop Rembert Weakland was a pro-homosexual, who was covering up for homosexual priests. Father Enrique T. Rueda in his *The Homosexual Network – Private Lives & Public Policy* published by Devin Adair in 1982 and reviewed in *Christian News* exposed the famous Milwaukee Archbishop. Liberal churchmen appreciated Weakland's socialist notions and attack on America's free enterprise system.

"'The Wisconsin Lutheran Synod's Favorite RC, a Homosexual Predator,' Dr. Gregory Jackson --Archbishop Signed $450,000 Agreement to Hush Sex Abuse Claim" was the title of a headline in the June 3, 2002 *Christian News*. The story noted that Gregory Jackson, Ph.D. Notre Dame, S.T.M., Yale, wrote: "Roman Catholic Archbishop Weakland was the featured speaker at Wisconsin Lutheran College, WELS."

The June 3, 2002 *Christian News* reprinted "An Archbishop's Fall from Grace," from the June 3, 2002 *Newsweek*. "A Gay Culture in the Church" and "More coverups, more shame, from the June 34, 2002 *U.S. News and World Report*, and "Milwaukee bishop admits he paid off accuser," from the May 24, 2002 *St. Louis Post Dispatch*. "Marty and Archbishop Weakland at Wisconsin Lutheran College" in the June 3, 2002 *Christian News* was a letter *CN* wrote to the presidents of the WELS and ELS about Martin Marty and Archbishop Weakland speaking at Wisconsin Lutheran College.

The June 8, 2009 *Christian News* said in a review:

AMCHURCH COMES OUT.
The U.S. Bishops, Pedophiles Scandals and the Homosexual Agenda.

Paul Likoudis, the author of this book, writes in a front page story titled "The

Shameless Archbishop. . . Weakland's Self-Revelations are A Cautionary Tale," in the May 28, 2009 *Wanderer*, a Roman Catholic Weekly:

"Today, we have the spectacle of the former archbishop of Milwaukee, Rembert Weakland, OSB, proudly bragging about his sin, recalling his past sexual affairs with other men and objecting to the Church's teaching that homosexuality 'is objectively disordered.'

"Those are bad words because they are pejorative,' he told The New York Times' Laurie Goodstein in an interview heralding the May 29 release of his autobiography.

"Weakland's public proclamation that he is 'gay' American and the attention he is drawing to himself with his new narcissistic, tell-all book, *A Pilgrim in A Pilgrim Church*, one Milwaukee Catholic told the *Wanderer*, 'is opening a can of worms. Even worse, it is like he is ripping off all the scabs from the still-festering wounds he left in this Arch-diocese.'

Now the Roman Catholic Arch-diocese of Milwaukee has become the largest Arch-diocese in the nation to declare bankruptcy because the Roman Catholic Church from the Pope down has covered up the tremendous homosexual scandal in Rome and not removed homosexuals from their priesthood.

Randy Engel, a Roman Catholic scholar, in her *The Rite of Sodomy - Homosexuality and the Roman Catholic Church* has much to say about homosexual churchmen like Archbishop Weakland. The 1300 page book concludes:

"There can be no question that Pope Paul VI's homosexuality was instrumental in the paradigm shift that saw the rise of the Homosexual Collective in the Catholic Church in the United States, at the Vatican and around the world in the mid-20th century.

"Pope Paul VI played a decisive role in the selection and advancement of many homosexual members of the American hierarchy including Joseph Cardinal Bernardin, Terence Cardinal Cooke, John Cardinal Wright and Archbishop Rembert Weakland and Bishops George H. Guifoyle, Fancis Mugavero, Joseph Hart, Joseph Ferrario, James Rausch and their heirs.

"The knowledge that a homosexual sat in the Chair of Peter—knowledge that spread like wild-fire on the 'gay' gossip circuit—would certainly have served as an inducement for homosexual men to aspire to the priesthood and even prompt them to contemplate the unthinkable—a religious order or community composed exclusively of sodomites.

"Most importantly, the long-guarded quasi-secret of Paul VI's homosexual life has, for decades, contributed to the silence and cover-up by the American hierarchy on the issue of homosexuality in general and the criminal activities of pederast priests in particular.

"But it is a secret no longer.

"The final piece of the puzzle has been put in place" (1157).

Destructive Criticism of the Bible In All Major Denominations

15. Christendom today is in far greater need of a Reformation than it was 500 years ago. The Roman Catholic Church of Luther's day was much closer to the Bible and historic Christianity than the Roman Catholic Church of our day. 500 years ago there were no liberal theologians in the Roman Catholic Church denying the Trinity, the virgin birth, the deity and resurrection of Christ. The Church affirmed the inerrancy of the Bible. It did not promote evolution. It taught that Christianity is the only saving faith and non-Christians like the Jews and Muslims worship a god who does not exist.

500 years ago Rome had not adopted its official statements on the Immaculate Conception of Mary, The Infallibility of the Pope, and the Assumption of Mary. It had not yet fabricated all this utter nonsense of Mary appearing to some all over the world. "Rome Promotes Another Hoax as Fact" in the January 17, 2011 *Christian News* reported that, according to a *Religion News Story* in the January 11, 2011 *Christian Century*, the Roman Catholic Bishop of Green Bay, Wisconsin, recently declared that it is absolute fact that Mary appeared three times in Wisconsin. The story also mentions that Mary appeared to the Mexican peasant Juan Diego in 1531. Pope John Paul II canonized Juan Diego, declaring him to be a saint even though reputable Roman Catholic scholars warned the Pope that there is no evidence Juan Diego actually lived much less that Mary appeared to him. An advertisement of *Raised From the Dead, True Stories of 400 Resurrection Miracles* by Father Albert Herbert, a book with Rome's Imprimatur, says: "The raising of the dead is a miracle which, astounding as it is, has been performed hundreds of times since the days of Christ."

Dr. Burkee mentions in his *Power, Politics and the Missouri Synod* my book *Baal or God*. It says little about the Lutheran Church-Missouri Synod but it shows that within almost all major Protestant denominations theologians were allowed to deny the great fundamental truths of historic Christianity. Not much is said about theological liberalism within the Roman Catholic Church. The book was published in 1965. Far more destructive than the homosexual scandal in Rome is that today Rome has caught up with modern liberal Protestantism. The same destructive notions of liberal Bible critics in Protestantism now prevail within Rome, including almost all its colleges and seminaries. Pope Benedict XVI, former Cardinal Ratzinger, clearly promotes the notions of Bible scholars who undermine the historicity and inerrancy of God's Word. *Christian News* has reviewed some of the Pope's books, including his *Introduction to the Christian Faith*. Since 1965, *Christian News* has reviewed such authoritative Roman Catholic works, which have Rome's Imprimatur, as the 15 volume, 15 million word *New Roman Catholic Encyclopedia*, *The New Jerome Biblical Commentary*, the *Jerusalem Bible* and hundreds of books by Roman Catholic theologians and leaders. I've seen very few reviews of these books in the theological publications of Lutheran seminaries and in the writings of the organized conservatives who say the editor of *Christian News* is out-of-date, fighting the same battle he's fought for more than 50 years. The February, 2011 U.S. Catholic is a "Special Issue on Catholic Education. "Let's get a BIG BANG out of science" is the title of the cover story. Roman Catholic schools throughout the nation now promote evolution. It says that "95% of U.S. Catholic readers surveyed accept evolution as a legitimate theory." Theological liberalism and higher criticism has taken over the Roman Catholic Church. Such conservative Roman Catholic Bible scholars as the late Father John Steinmueller, whose books on Scripture were formerly used as textbooks in Roman Catholic seminaries, greatly appreciated our defense of the inerrancy and historicity of the Bible and also *CN*'s exposing of theological liberalism in Rome.

America's Youth Following Europe

16. Those known as the "hyper-euros" in Lutheranism want the Lutheran church to return to the hierarchical church government the founders of The Lutheran Church-Missouri Synod wanted to leave in Europe. Those founders, along with Walther, championed "congregationalism" and the rights of laymen. Far more serious, however, is America's youth who are following the attitude toward Christianity and the Christian Church of the youth of Europe. When I spoke in a school in Germany, I asked how

many go to church. Only about 5% of those who had been confirmed in a Lutheran church were still attending church. When I asked why so few still attend church, I was told that the pastors themselves don't believe in Christianity. I soon found out that the school was about average for Europe. *Already Gone* is the title of a valuable book by Ken Ham of Answers in Genesis & Britt Beemer. 125,000 copies have already been sold. The back cover says "The next generation is already calling it quits on traditional church... If you look around in your church today, two-thirds of the young people who are sitting among us have already left in their hearts; soon they will be gone for good. This is the alarming conclusion from a study commissioned from America's Research Group, led by respected researcher Britt Beemer. The results may unnerve you – they may shake long-held assumptions to the core – but these results need to be taken seriously by the church."

As one who has been a full time pastor for more than 50 years, I can testify from first hand experience and numerous contacts around the nation that many youth in America are following the pattern of Europe's youth when it comes to interest in regularly attending worship services, Bible study and Christian youth gatherings. More congregations are closing. Hundreds of vacant congregations in The Lutheran Church-Missouri Synod are not calling pastors because they simply can no longer afford a full time pastor. The election of a new president is not going to stop the loss of more than 30,000 members in the LCMS each year and the closing of more congregations.

Communism – The Captive Nations and Kurt Marquart

The January 2011 President's News Letter in the LCMS's January *Reporter* had a photo of pastors and deacons of the Siberian Evangelical Lutheran Church together with some leaders of the LCMS. During the last 50 years *Christian News* has published hundreds of articles on Communism, the Captive Nations, and the persecution of Christians in Communist lands. My congregation repeatedly petitioned conventions of the LCMS to adopt a resolution on Communism and the Captive Nations basically written by Kurt Marquart, who had escaped the Communist when they took over his native Estonia. Finally in 1975 the LCMS adopted Marquart's overture submitted by Trinity, New Haven. During the 1990s, with the fall of the Iron Curtain, pastors from the former Captive Nations visited *Christian News* and my congregation. They were greatly interested in the work of *Christian News* in part because of the articles *CN* published vs. Communism and theological modernism and for the Captive Nations. When a group of them attended a worship service at Trinity I told them:

"What Does the LCMS Have to Offer Today?"

Now that the Communists no longer control most of the former Captive Nations, what does the LCMS have to offer today that so many of these other groups and churches sending hundreds of missionaries and workers to Russia, Ukraine, Latvia, Slovakia, Poland, Estonia, Lithuania, Kazakhstan, etc., do not clearly present?

The LCMS, far more than any other major church body, proclaims the saving Gospel of Jesus Christ, the forgiveness of sins. Listen again to our second text...

"But God has done it all. When we were His enemies, through Christ He made us His friends and gave us the work of making friends of enemies. In Christ, God was getting rid of the enmity between Himself and the people of the world by not counting their sins against them, and he has put into our hands the message how God and men are made friends again. Since God is pleading through us, we are ambassadors for Christ. We ask you for Christ, 'Come and be God's friends.' God made Him who did not know sin to be sin for us to make us God's righteousness in Him" (2 Corinthians

5:18-21).

This evening dear students and faculty members of Concordia University Wisconsin I tell you the same thing I told those from former Captive Nations. You made the right choice attending or teaching at a confessional Lutheran University, which clearly proclaims the central doctrine of the Christian faith, justification by faith alone in the saving merits of Jesus Christ and the other fundamentals of the historic Christianity, the doctrine of the Holy Trinity, the virgin birth, deity, vicarious satisfaction, bodily resurrection of Christ, the inerrancy and historicity of the entire Bible in all matters, a school which also affirms a six 24 hour day creation, a young earth, and teaches that Christianity is the only faith which is founded on solid historic evidence and not myth and fairy tale. In this age of relativism and universalism, when many deny objective, propositional truth and say your god is whatever you make him, you are attending a school which insists that Jesus Christ is the only way to heaven and all other religions are false and lead only to Hell as Jesus says (John 14:6), "I am the way, the truth and the life, no man comes to the Father except by me." Peter confesses (Acts 4:12), the Athanasian Creed affirms: "Whosoever will be saved, before all things it is necessary that he hold the Catholic (i.e., universal Christian) faith. Which faith except everyone do keep whole and undefiled, without doubt he shall perish everlastingly. And the catholic faith is this, that we worship one God in Trinity and Trinity in Unity." "This is the catholic faith; except a man believe faithfully and firmly, he cannot be saved." All schools in the Concordia University System are expected to affirm the Lutheran Church-Missouri Synod's Statement on Faith and Scriptural and Confessional Principals affirmed by the LCMS in 1973 at the height of its great Battle for the Bible: "We believe that Jesus Christ is the only way to heaven and that all who die without saving faith in Him are eternally damned." Today some fail to recognize that the LCMS's great Battle for the Bible involved far more than the inerrancy of the Bible, the ordination of women, evolution, homosexuality, the historicity of Genesis and Jonah, but also the vicarious satisfaction of Christ, the teaching that Jesus paid the ransom price to God the Father for the sins of all, and the doctrine that Jesus Christ is the only way to heaven was also involved.

Unlike some other conservative non-Lutheran schools, which may affirm the fundamentals of the Christian faith, capitalism, free enterprise, a confessional Lutheran school also accepts what the Bible teaches about Christ's body and blood being in with and under the bread and wine in Holy Communion and Baptism being a washing away of sins, a regeneration. They do not teach the silly anti-scriptural notions of the millennialists, particularly the Israel-First millennialism of Christian Zionists which gets many to support unjust wars. The list of schools mentioned in the November *First Things* in its survey of some 2,000 colleges includes some conservative Protestant and Roman Catholic Schools which do oppose evolution, abortion, socialism, humanism, affirm free enterprise and oppose the Global Warming nonsense, support American patriotism, etc.

If all the schools in CUS were teaching what the founding fathers of the LCMS affirmed in all areas there would be no need for conservative parents to send their children to non-Lutheran schools. The LCMS would once again have the finest school system in the nation. While I never professed to be some great scholar and intellect like Kurt Marquart, I am proud to be a product, starting at age 13, and champion of the school system of "Old Missouri" even though like all human organizations it was not perfect.

In Part One, I mention the long history of Christianity and the LCMS of championing the highest academic standards. I commented on Luther's use of reason, noting what Marquart wrote in "Intellectual Respectability, Si! Pseudo-Intellectual Aping, No!" ("A Call for the Highest Academic Standards.")[26]

The November, 2011 *First Things* mentions some conservative Roman Catholic schools, which are supposed to promote patriotism and support free enterprise and oppose socialism. Yet these conservative Roman Catholics fail to recognize what John Robbins in his massive *Ecclesiastical Megolomania* reveals about Rome and the Popes having a long history of opposing free enterprise and supporting socialism. During the last 50 years there have not been many pastors who have spoken to more non-Lutheran groups which included many fine Christians. I have also read their books and publications. There are those who contend that the LCMS learned to oppose evolution and promote the inerrancy of the Bible in all matters from the Fundamentalist. The record shows and the fact is the LCMS was defending the inerrancy of the Bible in all matters, opposing the destructive notions of higher criticism, the J-E-D-P source hypothesis, Deutero-Isaiah, the 160 dating of Daniel long before the Fundamentalists. LCMS scholars were urging the use of the finest Biblical manuscripts. Informed LCMS scholars, such as William Beck, opposed the obscurantism and unscholarly notions promoted by the *RSV* translators and now continued in part by the *ESV* promoters of CPH.

Anyone who wants information about what the LCMS has said since its founding should check the 8 Volume *Eckhardt's Reallexicon* and the *Index to the Concordia Theological Journal*. Read the sections on evolution and the Bible.

When I left New York City on bus to enter Concordia Seminary at the age of 19, my father went with me on a subway to the bus station in downtown Manhattan. Our family did not have an automobile. As I entered the bus, my father, who was not one to always follow the majority and often said the masses are the _____ , told me not to blindly follow such LCMS theologians as C.F.W. Walther or Francis Pieper, but to "make sure everything you are taught is based on the Bible." I took his advice, studied Walther and Pieper, and what other churches and theologians were saying and came to the conclusion the founding fathers of the LCMS were correct in almost all areas.

Walther was correct when he did not join the abolitionists in promotion of the bloody and unnecessary Civil War with its more that a million casualties. After examining the evidence, I found out that I had been misled during my Bronx public school days about such an American "hero" as Abraham Lincoln. John Robbins wrote in "The Messianic Character of American Foreign Policy:" "The Civil War, to a large extent, may be blamed on the clergy of both the North and the South."[27] C.F.W. Walther was not among these clergymen. Walter Williams, a great black columnist, writes in the foreword to *The Real Lincoln*, by Thomas J. Dilorenzo: "The War between the States was not fought to end slavery." "*The Real Lincoln* contains irrefutable evidence that a more appropriate title for Abraham Lincoln is not the Great Emancipator, but the Great Centralizer"(*Christian News,* February 1, 2010).

Such well informed Lutheran theologians as Walter Maier, Alfred Rehwinkel, and Henry Koch did not swallow the pro-war policy of Franklin Roosevelt. The November 22, 2011 *Christian News* commented on this in its leading story titled "Bipartisan Warfare State" taken from the November 8, 2010 *New American* published here in Wisconsin. Lutherans are not pacificist. They support Luther's view of a "just war." Many of the wars the U.S. has fought have not been "just wars."

Years ago when I was a speaker at Valparaiso University during its Week of Challenge on a panel discussing poverty, I showed the group what the founding fathers of the LCMS had to say about work, labor unions, in defense of the poor etc. Rev. Arthur Simon, a panel member who founded Bread for the World, was sympathetic towards socialism just like his brother Paul, who became a pro-abortion U.S. Senator. He said he was surprised the LCMS said so much against the "robber barons."

STEWARDSHIP AND CONSERVATION

This evening we are in your new Center for Environmental Stewardship. Currently the "in thing" to promote at many schools is to get on the environmental global warming band wagon. Even the LCMS' Commission on Theology and Church Relations in its recent report titled *Together With All Creatures – Caring For God's Living Earth* endorses an environmental group which promotes abortion as Rev. Peter Speckhard, Associate Editor of *Forum Letter*, observes in "Missouri's Magisterium Strikes Out" reprinted in the January 3, 2011 special issue of *Christian News* on education. When the 160 page CTCR document sent to all LCMS churches first appeared, *CN* said it again showed why the LCMS should save money and abolish the CTCR. This pastor has had a lifelong interest in environmentalism and proper Christian stewardship involving stewardship of the land, body, money and above all the doctrine God has given man. Many times I showed what Luther and the fathers of the LCMS said about good stewardship, land, animals, plants, nutrition, etc. Some of it is in *The Christian News Encyclopedia*. There is no reason why good health conscious youth and those interested in environmentalism have to join the Seventh Day Adventists or some other antiscriptural group which promotes sound principles of health.

During my years in the ministry I've planted thousands of trees. My wife, Grace, a graduate of Concordia College, St. Paul and Valparaiso University, is a member of the National and State Walnut Council. She canned and froze as many as 900 quarts a year from our "organic garden," when our seven children were still at home. One daughter milked her own cow; we raised our meat, ground wheat for flour, etc. I don't have such a great lake as your Lake Michigan for swimming, but as I regularly swim (six months a year) around one of the "lakes" we built at Camp Trinity where we live in a log house, I have a wonderful view of some of the trees we began planting 40 years ago as tiny seedlings. One year when I was young and foolish I swam just about every day in the year, even when it was snowing. That year the lakes didn't freeze over. When our family for five summers went on a tenting tour of five provinces of Canada and every state except Hawaii and Maine, camping in state and national parks and forests, we studied the environment as I read to the children along the way books from National Geographic, the Little House on the Prairie series, history books, etc. We invited the conservation and forestry department to help us make proper use of the soil and land at Camp Trinity. One of our mottoes at the camp is "give a hoot don't pollute." *Christian News* has long promoted the fitness program of the Creation Health Foundation: Health Fitness = (+) nutrition (+) exercise (+) exercise (+) rest (-) stress (-) drugs (-) pollution, where (+) means optimal, and (-) means minimal. The true Christian has the advantage of another factor, Namely, (+) prayer, Bible reading and Christian fellowship.

Pastor Peter Krey, the pastor/theologian whose writings during the 1960s and 1970s often appeared as the leading doctrinal devotional on page one of *Christian News* was written up in a national conservation magazine because of his work in soil conservation and stewardship of the land. The LCMS's *Lutheran Witness* then noted that what this pastor was doing was also done hundreds of years ago by orthodox Lutheran pastors.

Bible believing Christians do not have to take a back seat to the liberals when it comes to proper emphasis on environmentalism and stewardship. We do not have such a fine Center for Environmental Stewardship as this but we do have a fitness center and a 5k trail through the woods around the "lakes" and along the creek surrounding the camp on two sides where we have through the years constructed habitats and feeding plots for wildlife. Christians do not have to take a backseat to the liberals when it comes to a proper emphasis on environmentalism and stewardship.

BIRTH CONTROL AND REAL CHURCH GROWTH

Christian News has often said in this day of all kinds of church growth schemes that the best answer to improving church growth is a return to what the Bible, Martin Luther and the founding fathers of the LCMS teach about birth control. An overture from Trinity, New Haven submitted to the LCMS's 2011 convention calling for real church growth by a return to the position the LCMS formerly held on birth control was buried by the LCMS bureaucracy. "It only came from a congregation", not some prestigious group such as a faculty of CUS. God does not bless every man with a wife and woman with a husband, yet a women's highest career is still in the home having children regardless of how many college degrees she has. Thos e of you who are going to be pastors, remember that in the 1890's the average pastors family had 6.7 children.

Surveys taken of youth at LCMS youth conventions show that a high percentage of them have had sex outside of marriage. Although in former years the youth of the LCMS did not always practice what the LCMS taught about having sex, the time has come for our entire Concordia University System to promote the kind of morality, no sex outside of a heterosexual marriage, regularly affirmed in the former *Walther League Messenger*, the LCMS' youth magazine, and in such CPH publications as Lutheran Hour speaker Walter Maier's *For Better Not For Worse*. Unfortunately, *Christian News* could not get permission from CPH to reprint this manual on marriage with its section opposing the use of contraceptives. *CN* had a great young scholar willing to update the statistics and make it more current.

One of the reasons I listed in "Concordia University, Wisconsin the Biggest and Best" was CUW's excellent statement on music. No church body has a greater musical heritage than the Lutherans. Next to theology, Luther placed good music. No church has taken a better and longer stand vs. abortion, the sinful killing of unborn infants. Following the fathers of the LCMS, *CN* has been campaigning vs. abortion long before the Supreme Court ruling of 1973 and right to life groups began.

DON'T WASTE TIME

Do not waste your years here at Concordia. When I was attending the graduate school at Columbia University in New York I figured out that it was costing me about five dollars an hour to sit in class. Use your library, read at least some of the periodicals in the reading room. Computers are helpful, yet, often they take the place of reading books and good magazines and newspapers. At times some of these chat rooms on the computer remind me of the bull sessions we had at Concordia, Bronxville. They were fun, but the time came to get down to real learning by reading books. The November 15, 2010 *Christian News* quoted at some length from the recently released book by Nicholas Carr, *What The Internet Is Doing to Our Brains: The Shallows*. Carr writes: "The Net's cacophony of stimuli short-circuits both conscious and unconscious thoughts, preventing our minds from either thinking deeply or creatively."

One of the helpful books I read during my days in CUS, some 60 years ago, was Andrew Carnegie's *How To Win Friends and Influence People*. Carnegie gives tips on how to remember names. Learn the names of your classmates and try to greet as many of them as possible by name and with a smile. This is one way to help develop a friendly, cordial atmosphere at all of the CUS schools. In Part One, I mentioned how

Kurt Marquart and I became roommates after my brother read a letter in chapel from me. It was just some simple advice for those preparing for the ministry, including not wasting time in bars. Marquart thought that this kind of advice was important and needed. All Christian youth have a high calling whether or not they are preparing for the Holy Ministry, "Fight the Good Fight of Faith" in this day of skepticism, relativism, universalism, and immorality.

I'll conclude this section for students in CUS by urging them to follow the example of Dr. Kurt Marquart: "Place Scripture above all, think for yourself, do not bow to the bureaucracy, examine the evidence, and do not swallow hoaxes."

Faculties – No Warrens of Cowering Rabbits

Now a word for the faculty of Lutheranism's biggest and best university.

Kurt Marquart, whom you rightly honored with a doctorate, said that seminary faculties "should not be warrens of cowering rabbits but men of God speaking their convictions regardless of image" (*Christian News*, August 7, 1989). What he said about seminary faculties should also be said about all the faculties in the Concordia University System.

When Kurt Marquart was a member of the faculty of Concordia Seminary, Ft. Wayne, Indiana, this faculty submitted some excellent overtures to LCMS conventions. The faculty of the St. Louis seminary did not submit such overtures.

While many LCMS professors are hesitant to oppose by name liberal theologians in the Evangelical Lutheran Church in America and quote from the works of these theologians, Marquart has done this from his student days. When ELCA published *Christian Dogmatics* edited by Carl Braaten and Robert Jenson, the faculty of Concordia Seminary, Ft. Wayne submitted an overture to an LCMS convention showing that ELCA could hardly be considered a Lutheran Church. It quoted from *Christian Dogmatics* to show that this ELCA textbook used in ELCA seminaries denies such doctrines as the Trinity and Virgin Birth. The faculty quoted ELCA's *Christian Dogmatics*: "Truly, the Trinity is simply the Father and the man Jesus and their Spirit as the Spirit of the believing community" (102). Nothing in *Christian Dogmatics* has been retracted. Letters *CN* wrote to Braaten, Jenson, ELCA Bishop Herbert Chilstrom and others responsible for the book are in *The Christian News Encyclopedia*.[28] Marquart in some of his writings attacked the Braaten - Jenson *Christian Dogmatics* for opposing the deity of Christ. Braaten spoke at the 2007 Symposia of Concordia Seminary, Ft. Wayne. CPH is now publishing a book which includes a chapter by Braaten, who is now hailed as a great conservative in ELCA. Jenson spoke at the 2005 Ft. Wayne Symposia. While some LCMS professors now maintain that Braaten and Jenson are sound Lutheran theologians, Marquart remained concerned about their theology. After Jenson spoke at the 2005 Ft. Wayne Symposia, *CN* was told that Jenson claimed that he and Braaten said: "Don't buy any of our books that we wrote in earlier years because we were wrong..." Jenson told *CN* he never made such a statement.[29] He and Braaten are still backing their *Christian Dogmatics*. Jenson wrote in *The Christian Century* that he has now been attending an Episcopalian church.

The influence of Kurt Marquart at the Ft. Wayne seminary is to a large extent responsible for the vast difference between overtures submitted to LCMS conventions from Concordia Seminary, Ft. Wayne and Concordia Seminary St. Louis. Marquart was primarily responsible for overtures opposing theological liberalism.

"To Declare Church Fellowship with ALC No Longer Exists," submitted to the 1981 convention of the Lutheran Church-Missouri Synod, is an example of the kind of documented overtures from the Ft. Wayne faculty for which Marquart was at least in part responsible. This overture on p. 178 of the LCMS's 1981 convention workbook says: "There is even open endorsements, at an official level within the ALC, of E. Kaesemann's radical thesis that the New Testament canon cannot support doctrinal unity among the churches because the New Testament itself already contains contradictory theologies ('Differences,' pp. 8, 15, 16)." Overtures from the Ft. Wayne faculty showed that at least some there were keeping up with what was going on in the theological world and urging a clear articulate response from the LCMS.

"To Ask ALC for Official Position on Two Recent Publications of Augsburg," an overture to the LCMS' 1979 convention, from the Ft. Wayne faculty said that "Two recent ALC-related books leave no doubt about the gravity of the issues at stake: Paul Jersild, Invitation to Faith (Augsburg, 1978), and James Nelson, Embodiment (Augsburg, 1978), represent outright attacks on the central Gospel - mystery of the divine - human Person of the Savior Himself, and on Biblical Ethics." The Ft. Wayne faculty observed that Jersild maintains that "Pagan religions also convey the saving grace of God." The faculty said that Jersild ridiculed and rejected the two-nature doctrine of Christ. The faculty added about the Nelson book, published by Augsburg, that the book maintains that "New Testament teachings about sex are partly wrong." "Sexual intercourse between single/unmarried adults is not wrong." "Homosexual behavior is not wrong; rather Paul's condemnation of it is wrong." "Churches should not 'bar' avowed and practicing homosexuals from ordination and the public ministry." The faculty lists the page numbers in the Nelson and Jersild book which attack Christian doctrine.

"To Secure Sound and Consistent Fellowship Position," an overture submitted by the Ft. Wayne faculty to the LCMS' 1977 convention (1977 LCMS Convention Workbook), is another example of the kind of overtures from the Ft. Wayne faculty which carry the Marquart imprint. The overture noted that the *Lutheran Quarterly*, published jointly by the seminary faculties of the ALC and the LCA, printed a blatant denial of the Holy Trinity and of the divinity of Christ and portrayed the Transfiguration as 'an occasion on which Jesus, who had deep rapport with his psychic disciples, hypnotized them, and presented them with illusions of Moses, Elijah and the voice of God, in order to convince them of his unusual messiahship. . .' We ask whether the routine treatment and publication of such blasphemy, without public rebuke, simply as a piece of historical-critical scholarship, can be described as anything short of boundless apostasy."

Other overtures from the Ft. Wayne faculty during the Marquart years asked the LCMS to take a stand vs. the Church Growth Movement, the ordination of women, abortion, historical-criticism, the LWF, fellowship with the ALC, etc.

Similar overtures were not submitted to LCMS conventions by the St. Louis seminary or the faculties of any LCMS college. Marquart was at least in part responsible for the fact that Concordia Seminary, Ft. Wayne, took an outspoken public stand on so many current issues.

Bretscher's Denial of Deity of Christ

When Dr. Paul G. Bretscher of Valparaiso University wrote "The Sword of the Spirit", the department of systematic theology of the Ft. Wayne seminary concluded an evaluation of Bretscher's work: "The essay's doctrines of Holy Scripture and of the Church cannot be squared with the Lutheran Confessions' understanding of the Word of God." The St. Louis seminary did not register any similar protest. One of the committees of the St. Louis seminary, while Ralph Bohlmann was president, which ruled against certifying the editor of *CN* for the pastoral ministry in the LCMS, said that the *CN* editor as the pastor of a rural congregation had no calling to register concerns about the theology being taught at Valparaiso University or elsewhere in the LCMS.

Dr. Paul Bretscher blamed *Christian News* for "bringing down Concordia Seminary." He wrote in 1992 in his *"Christian News* and Me" sent to all LCMS churches: "I grew up in the piety which *CN* has praised to its wrathful end these 30 years." When he denied the deity of Christ in his *Christianity's Unknown God*, as the pastor of an LCMS church, I filed charges against him. The bureaucrats were remaining silent. Bretscher was eventually removed from the LCMS after the charges were filed.

Through the years, including the years Marquart was in Australia, my congregation submitted hundreds of overtures to LCMS conventions on a large variety of issues. Many were patterned after Marquart's method. Liberals were miffed that so many overtures pertaining to the inerrancy of the Bible were adopted by LCMS conventions (Christ being the only way of salvation, the historicity of Genesis, a six day creation, the unity of Isaiah, the vicarious satisfaction of Christ, the immortality of the soul, affirming capital punishment; opposing the new morality, euthanasia, and historical criticism, promotion of *An American Translation of the Bible*, and calling for the discipline of those who promote women pastors and evolution).

Unfortunately, today the LCMS bureaucracy often buries overtures which only come from a congregation. This has discouraged congregations from submitting overtures. Very few congregations, even the congregations of the leaders of the many divided organized conservatives in the LCMS, seldom now submit overtures. Congregations are not being informed by their pastors. At the last LCMS convention only about one-third were interested enough to return their ballot for LCMS president and vice-presidents.

The time has come for your faculty to submit the kind of overtures the Ft. Wayne faculty sent to conventions during the Marquart years.

Reason 4. In "Concordia Wisconsin – Biggest and Best" noted that your faculty decisively voted down a move to declare LCMS Atlantic District President David Benke "alumnus of the year." He is an outspoken liberal, a hero of Jesus First, a group of liberals, moderates and charismatics in the LCMS which maintain that the LCMS should allow its clergymen to promote women pastors and evolution. Benke said that "The Muslim God is also the true God." Concordia Seminary, St. Louis, on the other hand, asked Benke to write an article in the seminary's *Concordia Journal* praising Father Richard Neuhaus as a great Christian theologian. Ever since his student days at the St. Louis seminary Neuhaus denied the inerrancy of the Bible, justification by faith alone and that Jesus Christ is the only way to heaven. Neuhaus was similarly praised at Concordia Seminary, Ft .Wayne when he was invited to speak at this seminary. Neither LCMS seminary today can be expected to submit the kind of overtures to LCMS conventions the Ft. Wayne seminary submitted when Marquart was alive.

What kind of overture should your faculty submit? You could start with the overtures from Trinity, New Haven which the Kieschnick administration banned at the 2010 LCMS convention. They are:

1. "Return to Former Adjudication System – Laymen Belong in Church Courts."
2. "Curb the LCMS Bureaucracy."
3. "Disband Jesus First and DayStar." (This overture called for having all members of Jesus First and DayStar affirm the LCMS' scriptural position or be honest and leave

the LCMS).

4. "Elect Members of Commission on Constitutional Matters at Synodical Convention."

5. "Time for LCMS to End 50 Year Injustice."

6. "To Repudiate Racism."

The January 11, 2010 *CN* listed the kind of overtures a solidly committed Lutheran theology department at a CUS school like CUW may want to consider submitting to the next LCMS convention. Among them are: "Oppose Evolution and Command Creation Research Society and Creation Museum." This overture included: "Resolved that the 2019 convention of the LCMS declare that all of the professors in LCMS colleges and seminaries must teach that evolution is contrary to the Bible and true science and that God created the world in six 24 hour days and not in millions or billions of years."

1. "To Publish an Orthodox Christian Translation of the Bible in the Language of Today." This overture concluded with these resolves: "Resolved, that the 2010 Convention of the LCMS authorize the publication of an orthodox Christian translation of the Bible by confessional Lutheran scholars in confessional Lutheran church bodies, and be it further

"Resolved, that *An American Translation of the Bible* be used as the basis for this orthodox Christian translation."

Dr. Timothy Maschke of your theology department said in a review of the English Standard Version of the Bible in the April, 2005 *Concordia Journal*: "The *AAT* provides a more readable and understandable translation." A survey comparing the *ESV* and *AAT* showed that some 90% of those who responded preferred both the language and doctrinal accuracy of the *AAT*. Promoters of the *ESV* in the LCMS are winning, not because they have the truth but because they have the money and power. My preface in the *AAT*, when it was published by *Christian News* in 1975 said: "No translation is perfect. Suggestions for revision in any future printing will be gratefully accepted and considered." Through the years many improvements have been made in the *AAT* by confessional Lutheran scholars.

2. "To Advocate Withdrawal from LWF." This overture concludes: "Resolved, that the 2010 convention of the LCMS request that all churches in fellowship with the LCMS withdraw from the LWF."

3. "To Reaffirm Justification by Faith Alone in the merits of Christ." This overture concludes: "Resolved that this convention authorize a professional survey of just the LCMS to find out the percentage of members of the LCMS congregations who accept the Scriptural doctrine of justification; and be it further

"Resolved, that the convention urge all LCMS congregations and schools regularly affirm the importance of the doctrine of justification alone in the merits of Jesus Christ."

4. "To Repudiate Racism." This overture concludes: "Resolved that the Lutheran Church-Missouri Synod repudiate all racism, including the racism of the white supremacists, the evolutionists, and the Israel First Millennialists who believe God has a chosen race." The LCMS bureaucracy refused to say why it banned this overture.

5. "Telling the World Christ Is the Only Way to Heaven and Christianity Is the Only Saving Faith." This overture concluded: "Resolved, That all District Presidents of the LCMS insist that every pastor in his district maintain that 1) Jesus is the only way to heaven; 2) those that do not trust in Christ for salvation are damned; and 3) Christianity is the one and only divinely revealed and saving faith."

6. "LCMS in 2010 Still Opposes the Destructive Higher Criticism of the Bible." One of the resolves in this overture is: "Resolved, That all professors or pastors on the LCMS clergy roster must believe and teach that the entire books of Genesis and Jonah present historic fact; Moses wrote the first five books of the Bible; the known 8th Century Prophet Isaiah wrote the entire book of Isaiah, the Exodus took place in the 15th Century, B.C. as the Bible teaches; the J-E-D-P and Q source never existed and Jesus is the only way to heaven."

The back cover of the December 28, 2011 *Christian Century* again shows why it is so important in our day for Concordia University, Wisconsin, and all of the schools in the Concordia University System and the Lutheran Church-Missouri Synod to take a solid stand against the destructive higher criticism of the Bible. The entire back cover of *The Christian Century* promotes "2011 Washington Island Forum with Marcus J. Borg, July 27 – July1, 2011." It says "Marcus Borg is canon theologian at Trinity Episcopal Cathedral in Portland, Oregon. Internationally known in both academic and church circles as a biblical and Jesus scholar. . ." The *Washington Island Forum* featuring Marcus Borg, according to *The Christian Century* is "Co-sponsored by *The Christian Century* and the Wisconsin Council of Churches." Most of the major denominations in Wisconsin, including the Evangelical Lutheran Church in America, are members of the Wisconsin Council of Churches. Borg's thoroughly anti-Christian theology is quite acceptable within most of the major denominations in Wisconsin in the Wisconsin Council of Churches. Borg, who grew up as a Lutheran in North Dakota, believed at one time that the Bible was God's directly revealed and inerrant Word.

He wrote in ELCA's June, 2007 *Lutheran* that Jesus came to establish a Kingdom on earth and not in heaven. Borg is leader of the Jesus Seminar, which claims that Jesus did not say 80% of the words attributed to him in the Bible. Borg says Jesus is not God, He did not die for the sins of all men, and never rose from the dead. *Christian News* has published many articles which documented Borg's anti-Christian theology.[30]

"No Virgin Birth or Resurrection – Views of Jesus Seminar Scholars Adopted at Roman Catholic and Protestant Seminaries" said:

"The critical scholarship and views held by 'The Jesus Seminar' has been adopted by most of the seminaries of the Roman Catholic Church and mainline Protestant denominations say a recent report of The Jesus Seminar. More than one hundred religious scholars and seminary professors from almost all the major denominations are members of the Jesus Seminar.

"According to the Jesus Seminar, the Lord's Prayer, passages in the Bible which say that the Jews crucified Jesus, many of the parables of Jesus, and other statements in the Bible attributed to Jesus, were never said by Jesus. The Jesus Seminar scholars say they were fabricated by the early church years after Jesus lived and died. The Jesus Seminar is now planning to produce a movie which will present a Christ who was not born of a virgin and who did not rise from the dead. (*The Christian News Encyclopedia* has several articles on the 'findings' of the Jesus Seminar)."[31]

I have been reading *The Christian Century* since the 1950s. It is pro-abortion, pro-homosexual, and has regularly attacked such doctrines of the Christian faith as the resurrection of Christ. It is cited on more than 75 pages of *The Christian News Encyclopedia*. Borg's anti-Christian theology is quite acceptable to *The Christian Century* and the Wisconsin Council of Churches jointly sponsoring Borg's appearance here in Wisconsin.

7. "Selecting Convention Committee Members and Committee Chairman." This

overture calls for a curbing of the power of the LCMS president to select all convention committee members and committee chairmen. Even the U.S. government does not give its president so much power.

8. "Promoting Church Growth by Returning to Luther's and the LCMS's Former and Scriptural Position on Birth Control." This buried overture concludes: "That the 2010 convention of the LCMS still accepts the Scriptural position of Martin Luther on birth control and the position long promoted in the LCMS by such orthodox LCMS theologians as John H.C. Fritz, Walter Maier, Martin Nauman, Theodore Laetsch and many others."

9. Curb the Bureaucracy. This overture received no attention at the LCMS's 2010 convention, where much of the time at the 4.5 million dollar convention was spent on restructuring. It was published in the January 4, 2010 *Christian News*. "Curb the Bureaucracy" quotes Dr. Kurt Marquart: "Our tragedy is that this absolute priority of divine truth has become displaced in our synodical life. By what? By organizational concerns. Our disease, you might say, is 'bureaucratitis." During the 1960s the LCMS began having full-time district presidents, losing members and at the same time increasing the bureaucracy. Since 1964 the LCMS has shown a gain of more than 500 clergymen on the LCMS roster not serving congregations but "Synod, Districts, and others." "Curb the Bureaucracy" shows the long theologically liberal position of the LCMS's Council of Presidents. The COP opposed the investigation of Concordia Seminary, St. Louis, supported the liberal professors who formed Seminex and appointed an outspoken evolutionist to the LCMS's Commission on Theology and Church Relations. This overture concludes with a resolve to end full time district presidents and have them become pastors of a congregation.

10. Publish Marquart writings. The 2010-2011 CPH resource catalog has a full page promoting some 10 books by Dietrich Bonhoeffer and one book about him. It lists no books about Kurt Marquart and only one book by him, **Confessional Lutheran Dogmatics, The Church and Her Fellowship, Ministry and Governance**. The hundreds of Marquart writings listed in **Marquart's Legacy** should be published in a series of volumes. They have more popular appeal and are far more helpful than Bonhoeffer's writings, which undermine historic Christianity. Marquart wrote an entire series for a Lutheran youth publication. Your faculty could petition the next LCMS convention to ask CPH to publish Marquart's writings and rather than giving Bonhoeffer so much space in CPH's display room, give Marquart's writings the prominence they deserve. The book on **Bonhoeffer and King** Christian News plans to publish will clearly show that Bohnoeffer denied such doctrines as the resurrection of Christ.

A Twenty-First Century Reformation

Above all as the 500th Anniversary of the Reformation approaches in 2017, faculties in CUS should call for a 21st Century Formula of Concord and 21st Century Reformation. *CN* has published many reasons for such a 21st Century Reformation and 21st Century Formula of Concord. Unfortunately, among the tunnel vision minded organized conservatives and in the LCMS bureaucracy little interest has been expressed in a 21st Century Reformation and Formula of Concord which speaks to the issues of our day. My book, *Walter Maier Still Speaks – Missouri and the World Should Listen*, includes a tentative 20th Century Formula of Concord (pp. 296-316), I presented to the International Council of Churches meeting at the University of British Columbia. Sections on Baptism, the Lord's Supper, Millennialism, etc. could be added. There is no reason why your theology department with its solid Lutheran chairman could not get the ball rolling for such a 21st Century Formula of Concord. It certainly would arouse more interest than something coming from a person who has just been a country pastor since he graduated from the St. Louis seminary in 1957.

Set Up a Series of Debates

The Concordia University Wisconsin press release announcing my appearance here this evening quotes CUW President Patrick Ferry as saying: "Concordia is a place where dialog, discussion, and debate are encouraged." Every school in CUS and the LCMS' seminaries should arrange for a series of friendly debates. Dr. Burkee, in his *Power, Politics, and the Missouri Synod*, which once again I encourage you to read, mentions: "My mother, Jan, who met my father for their first date, of all places, at a lecture by Herman Otten at her San Diego church, has been a life-long source of inspiration and encouragement. So too has my wife, Susan, for over twenty years." This may have been at the time I spoke in some churches in Southern California which invited a liberal ALC theologian and me to debate the doctrinal and practical issues facing all of Christendom. Most of the 600 who attended the debate remained the entire four hours. Debates should now be held at CUS schools. First on evolution and creation, then on higher criticism of the Bible, the J-E-D-P hypothesis, etc. Debates draw the interest of students and faculty. A good start would be to have a debate on creation vs. evolution by such an outspoken defender of evolution as Dr. Matthew Becker of Valparaiso University and Dr. David Menton of the Creation Museum of Answers in Genesis or Dr. David Kaufmann of the Creation Research Society. When I was invited to participate in a debate at Westminster College on Satanism with Michael Aquino, Ph.D., the intellectual leader of the Satanists, the cite of the debate had to be moved to the schools largest auditorium because of the interest. *Christian News* has never opposed having a liberal such as Martin Marty speak at a CUS school provided that an articulate, intelligent, confessional spokesman familiar with the liberal's position is given opportunity to show where the liberal, evolutionist, pro-abortionist, pro-homosexual, etc., is wrong and time to question him. Not even the 6 million figure of the Holocaust should be considered beyond debate. Our CUS youth should be taught to examine the evidence and not swallow hoaxes as fact just because a thousand books and hundreds of movies portray the hoax as fact. They should not become like such cultists as the Mormons or Jehovah's Witnesses, who refuse to examine the evidence that their religion is founded on fiction and myth.

Just because almost all seminaries, including the LCMS's, now praise Dietrich Bonhoeffer as a great Christian martyr doesn't mean it is true. Let's have debates at CUS schools on whether or not Bonhoeffer and Martin Luther King, Jr. are the great Christians the vast majority of Christian seminaries now claim. My new book on Bonhoeffer and King exposes the lack of scholarship of those who champion Bonhoeffer and King as great Christians who set a fine example for youth in both faith and practice. At the present time the most outspoken critics of *Christian News* who want *CN* to close up shop, are those hyper-euros who want the LCMS to return to the hierarchical church government the founding fathers of the LCMS left behind in Europe. Lets have a debate between John Pless of our Ft. Wayne seminary, who is a leader of the Loehe Society, and Jack Cascione, a leader of the Walther Conference. Loehe with his hierarchical notions opposed Walther's congregationalism and defense of the rights of laymen.

In Part I of my presentation I noted that the real hero, God's chief instrument in the LCMS's great Battle for the Bible, about which Dr. Burkee writes in his book, was no one in the LCMS bureaucracy, no double talking LCMS president, no seminary president, no professor or anyone whose salary came from the LCMS. It was no one associated with any of the organized conservative groups working behind the scenes, planning political strategy and voting guides. "It was a highly, intellectually gifted and articulate refugee from communism. It was no 'Johnny-come-lately.' It was a young, highly dedicated and Christ centered, spiritually minded student who had just left his teenage years. He was 'the brain' behind a few students who protested in the 1950's against theological liberalism, evolution and universalism creeping into the LCMS, particularly at Concordia Seminary, St. Louis."

I know of no one in the LCMS since the days of Walter Maier who was more highly recognized outside the LCMS than Kurt Marquart. When Marquart appeared on the Manion Forum of Dean Clarence Manion of the Notre Dame School of Law, Dean Manion commented (Manion Forum, December 3, 1967): "My friends, in my 13 years at this microphone, I have never heard a more precise and learned analysis of the conflict now raging between Communism and organized religion, namely, the churches of all denomination."

Al Schmidt, who taught at Concordia Seminary, Ft. Wayne, with Marquart, wrote: "His presentations are understood and admired in contexts outside of the church. For several years, Kurt and I were members of the Board of Directors of the Allen County Right to Life organization in Fort Wayne. This group had a lot of Catholic members, but when Kurt spoke, the people listened. Many times I heard them say: 'He surely know how to discern the major issues.' He was liked so well they even elected him as president of the organization."

Crisis in Christendom – Seminex Ablaze, p. 130.

When Kurt Marquart died, Hon. Tom McVeigh referred to him as "America's gift to Australia" (Christian News, January 8, 2007. "He came to us on the 'Darling downs, Australia, like a great searchlight from across the Pacific Ocean."

I wish that this evening he would be speaking to you instead of me, and that then every school in the Concordia University System would invite him to speak. What a tragedy that when Kurt Marquart was running for the presidency of the LCMS shortly after your school awarded him a doctorate, the organized, tunnel vision conservatives refused to support him for LCMS president. When *Christian News* tried to get these organized conservatives to back Dr. Marquart for president, they totally ignored *Christian News*. They did not share Dr. Marquart's broad vision, including his promotion of a Twentieth Century Formula of Concord and Reformation. Dr. Marquart's broad vision included his promotion of a Twentieth Century Formula of Concord and Reformation. Their focus was often only on the LCMS. Dr. Marquart, who was always a strong champion of C.F.W. Walther and his defense of congregationalism and the rights of laymen, lost the support of the Loehe supporting hyper-euros in the LCMS when he opposed their sacerdotalism.

The organized conservatives ignored the wishes of many congregations. They were not going to support someone who made it clear that if he were elected president, evolutionists and supporters of the theology of Seminex and women pastors, would get removed form the LCMS. Marquart wrote in his statement for the *Lutheran Witness* when he was on the LCMS presidential ballot: "The single most crucial issue facing our Synod, in my view, is the progressive loss of doctrinal unity. There is, for instance, the acceptance of evolution by some within the Concordia University System and there is the neo-Pentecostalism of 'Renewal in Missouri.'" (*Lutheran Witness*, May, 2004. *Christian News*, May 17, 2004).

No other candidate for LCMS president spoke as clearly as Marquart did vs. "evolution, theological liberalism, and neo-Pentecostalism" in the LCMS. He didn't get to first base with the "tunnel vision" organized conservatives and hyper-euros in the LCMS who were working behind the scenes with their United List. *Christian News* published "Luther Today – What Would He Do or Say" (220 pages) and "Crisis in Christendom – Seminex Ablaze" (512 pages). They included some of Marquart's writings. Both were ignored by the organized conservatives. *Christian News* prepared two videos on Marquart. These were also totally ignored by the organized conservatives. They never recommended that convention delegates read Marquart's writings or watch the Marquart videos.

They were professionally done and showed Kurt Marquart in action and making speeches. The organized conservatives simply did not want a man who insisted that resolution 3-09 of the LCMS's 1973 convention (reaffirmed at the 2010 convention) should be implemented. This resolution said that the theology of Seminex was false doctrine and should not be tolerated within the LCMS. Marquart regretted that 3-09 was never implemented in the LCMS. The Seminex supporting liberals, pro-evolutionists and pro-woman pastor liberals and charismatics were permitted to stay within the LCMS. To this day 3-09 of the 1973 convention, reaffirmed at the 2010 convention, remains unimplemented. Charges of false doctrine filed vs. an outspoken evolutionist and supporter of women pastors are ignored. The organized conservatives never even mention that 3-09 of the 1973 convention was reaffirmed in 2010.

For those of you here preparing for the ministry, permit me to recommend to you Kurt Marquart, rather than Dietrich Bonhoeffer, now championied by many seminarians, as a fine role model. Far too many students, including seminarians, show little interest in what is going on in the church, the nation, and the world. They read little beyond what their professors tell them to read. They live in their own little world, just like far too many professors live in an Ivory Tower.

Kurt Marquart fought the good fight of faith from his student days until he died. When we were roommates he had little time to go to bars, or even talk about girls. He was on a crusade fighting the good fight of faith once he recognized what was happening in all of Christendom and particularly at Concordia Seminary, St. Louis. He saw the need for a Twentieth Century Reformation.

About the only time we talked much about girls was when he showed me a picture of a church secretary to whom he sold his car when he was on the way to Australia. He took her out to lunch to show her how to drive the car. She gave the young pastor her photo. It was the picture of a beautiful girl with the words on the back: "Perhaps our paths will cross again some day." All I could say when he visited me on his way to Australia, was: "Kurt, follow up on that one." He didn't need my advice. They corresponded and became engaged. She traveled to Australia and they were married. All of his five children were born in Australia before he returned to the U.S. to teach at Concordia Seminary, Springfield, Illinois which then moved to Ft. Wayne, Indiana.

When I asked Kurt about retiring as I walked to his car parked outside the *Christian News* office, he said: "Herm, can you imagine St. Paul or St. Peter saying that now that they had reached a certain age they were going to retire to the sunny beaches of Cyprus?" They had a calling and would not quit until God called them home. Marquart fought the good fight right until shortly before he died of Lou Gehrig's Disease.

He could hardly write on the classroom blackboard. He baptized a great-grandchild shortly before he died. This great champion of the faith was least of all impressed with his own abilities, saying at the presentation of the festschrift with which he was honored on his 65th birthday as the audience applauded, "Thank you for putting up with me."

Now finally, as one who has had all his years in the ministry not been sitting in some ivory tower but baptizing infants, confirming youth and adults, being with them in their dying moments and finally made that walk with them to the grave, permit me to tell you that these issues we have been talking about concern the most important matters all men must face: "Where did I come from; why am I here and where am I going." May God grant that all of you here, students and faculty trust only in the merits of Christ for your eternal salvation and in Him who said: "I am the resurrection and life, he that liveth and believeth in Me though he were dead yet shall he live." Each day as I take my regular 4 a.m. morning walk (formerly run), I have a program of first praying Luther's morning prayer, then for my wife, myself and each one of my seven children, their spouses, and all the grandchildren, etc. Then I go into a pattern of singing in my mind some of the hundreds of hymns I have memorized during my years in the pastoral ministry, many of them on my former 16 mile weekly run to the *Christian News* printer in Washington, Missouri to set up *Christian News*. About the time I pass a cemetery on the border of Camp Trinity, I'm praying the last verses of "O God, Thou Faithful God" TLH, 395. They are:

Let me depart this life
Confiding in my Savior;
Do Thou my soul receive
That it may live forever;
And let my body have
A quiet resting-place
Within a Christian grave;
And let it sleep in peace.

And on that solemn Day
When all the dead are waking,
Stretch o'er my grave Thy hand,
Thyself my slumbers breaking.
Then let me hear Thy voice,
Change Thou this earthly frame,
And bid me aye rejoice
With those who love Thy name.

Any athlete knows that as the years go on he becomes slower and weaker. There was a time that I could easily beat all of my children in running, biking, and swimming. A daughter, when she was about 6 complained about the heat while running with me on a hot summer day. She asked for an umbrella. Some years later she became the National College Marathon champion in Los Angeles. It won't be long and her children will beat her even though she is a cross country and track coach. Now some of my grandchildren pass me in all events. Several times at the closing award banquet at an Iron Man triathlon, I've told the athletes, who come from all over the U.S. and a good number of other nations, that regardless of their training program, good nutrition, and all the gimmicks various groups pedal at such events, they are all going to slow down because of one three letter word: S-I-N. All men are sinners. The wages of sin is death. But thank God the Christian who trusts only in the merits of Jesus Christ has eternal life.

May you leave CUW after your years at the largest and best Lutheran University with a firm conviction of faith in Christ, His resurrection and eternal life in heaven forever with all those who love His name. Fight for the true Christian faith until the grave.

Endnotes

1 James Tunstead Burtchael, *The Dying of the Light – The Disengagement of Colleges & Universities from their Christian Churches* (Grand Rapids, Michigan, William B. Eerdmans Publishing Company, 1998), 14.

2 Ibid. pp. 459-555.

3 *Christian News*, June 9, 2008.

4 Burtchael op. cit. p. 471.

5 Ibid., p. 494.

6 Ibid., p. 494.

7 Ibid., p. 498.

8 *Christian News*, November 10, 2008.

9 Reviewed in the December 10, 1997, *Christian News*.

10 *Christian News*, October 9, 2009. "Media Puffs Bart Ehrmann – Attacks Bible and Historic Christianity." "Jesus, Interrupted: Revealing The Hidden Contradictions in the Bible." *Christian News*, November 16, 2009.

11 *Washington Times*, January 3, 2011.

12 *Christian News*, January 17, 2011.

13 William Beck, "What Does Almah Mean." *Christian Handbook on Vital Issues*, pp. 537-548; John E. Steinmueller, "Etymology and Biblical Usage of 'Almah'", *Catholic Biblical Quarterly*, *Christian Handbook On Vital Issues*, pp. 551-554.

14 Robert Dick Wilson, "Is the Higher Criticism Scholarly" *The Christian News Encyclopedia*, Volume V, pp. 3285-3288.

15 *Christian News*, January 3, 2011.

16 The January 10, 2011, *Christian News* includes some articles Kurt Marquart wrote on Communism and the Captive Nations.

17 "*ESV* or *AAT* – The People's Language – *The Christian's Travel Guide to World History*," Henry Koch, pp. 349-351.

18 *Christian News*, February 20, 1989.

19 *Marquart's Legacy*. By Herman Otten, 2006. 76 pages. $5.00.

20 *Christian News*, November 23, 2009, pp. 4 and 5.

21 *Crisis In Christendom – Seminex Ablaze*, p. 412.

22 Martin Marty, "Fundamentalism and the Church," *Christian Century*, November 27, 1957.

23 *A Christian Handbook on Vital Issues*, pp. 749-755.

24 Ibid., pp. 756-757.

25 Randy Engel, *Homosexuality and the Roman Catholic Church*. New Engel Publishing, Box 356, Export, Pennsylvania 15632, p. 1157.

26 *Christian News*, January 3, 2011, pp. 15-17.

27 *Christian News Encyclopedia*, pp. 4120-4122.

28 *Christian News Encyclopedia*, pp. 3540-3545.

29 *Christian News*, July 25, 2005.

30 *Christian News*, June 18, 2007.

31 *Christian News Encyclopedia*, p. 3298. See also "Seminar Says Only 20 Percent of Jesus' Sayings Were Authentic." "A Fairy Tale Religion," The Bible – 'God's Story' or a 'Human Composition'", "Marcus J. Borg – Different Ways of Looking at the Bible" *The Christian News Encyclopedia*,

Index

pp. 3299-3300.

3-09 - 294
Aaron Henry - 272
Abernathy, Ralph - 214, 217, 230, 240
Abolitionists - 283
Academic Standards - 254
Act and Being - 72
Aczel, Amir D. - 88
Adjudication System - 288
Adulterer - 242
Adultery - 192, 200, 215
Advent Preaching - 107
Affirmative Action - 228
Aid Association for Lutherans (AAL) - 38, 40, 45, 48, 55, 95, 109
Allen, Gary - 156
Allen, James S. - 156
Allwardt, Theodore F. - 104
Almah - 255, 258
Almy, G.L.- 260
Already Gone - 281
America - 171
American Lutheran Publicity Bureau - 101
America's Youth - 280
An American Translation of the Bible - 255, 289
Andrae, Eric A. - 90, 123
Anti-Communist - 230
Anti-Semites - 2
Anti-Semitism - 65
Aquino, Michael, PhD. - 292
Arndt, William - 258
Ashbrook, John M. - 165
Assumption of Mary - 280
Aulen, Gustav - 24, 90, 119
Australia - 288
Australian Theological Review - 152
Badger Lutheran - 274
Baldwin, James - 150, 161
Baptism - 282
Barmen Declaration - 24, 31
Barry, A.L. - 269
Barth, Karl - 9, 13, 24, 43, 51, 90, 98, 110, 119
Bass, Ellen - 261
Baumer, Franklin L. - 50, 53, 62, 122
Beard, Charles - 265
Beck, William - 6, 91, 255, 256, 258
Becker, David - 46, 55
Becker, L. - 44
Becker, Matthew - 55, 91, 97, 125, 126
Becker, Siegbert - 256, 258
Beemer, Britt - 281
Behnken, John W. - 270, 271

Benke, David - 120, 288
Bennett, Bill - 229
Bennett, John - 237
Bernardin, Joseph Cardinal - 279
Berrigan, Father Daniel - 60
Bertram, Robert W. - 23, 41
Bethany College, Mankato, MN - 226, 227
Bethel Confession - 106
Bethge, Eberhard - 16, 18, 42, 44, 56, 71
Bethulah - 255
Biblical Criticism - 254
Biblical Discernment Ministries - 21
Bibliotheca Sacra - 22
Birth Control - 285, 291
Bischoff, William - 263
Black and Conservative - 162
Black Ministry Convocation - 233
Black Theology - 178, 179, 233, 234
Black Theology Project - 177
Blecker, LaMarr - 33
Bobgan, Martin and Deidre - 260
Bonhoeffer - Agent of Grace - 40, 44
Bonhoeffer House - 41
Bonhoeffer, Dietrich - 4, 43, 48, 106, 261, 267, 273, 292
Bonhoeffer's Christology - 27
Bonhoeffer's Theology - 26
Booker T. Washington Day - 223, 239
Borg, Marcus - 290
Bormann, Martin - 99
Boyle, Sarah Patton - 155
Boys, Don - 196
Braaten, Carl - 286
Braden, Anne - 155
Braden, Carl - 155
Brains - 285
Brauer, Jerald C. - 33
Bretscher, Paul G. - 287
Brown, Julia - 173, 182, 183
Brunner, Emil - 24, 90, 119
Buchenwald - 102
Buckley, William F. Jr. - 146
Bulkley, Ed - 261
Bultmann, Rudolf - 5, 8, 16, 24, 101, 135
Bureaucracy - 288, 291
Burg, Rabbi J.B. - 261
Burgdorf, Paul - 49, 258, 259
Burkee, James - 251, 268, 272
Burrow, Rufus - 242
Burtchaell, James Tunstead - 251
Butz, Arthur - 261
Calvin - 79
Calvinism - 79
Camp Trinity - 284

297

Capital Punishment - 244
Capitalism - 282
Capps, Donald - 204
Captive Nations - 281
Carberry, Cardinal - 43, 65, 67
Cardinal Ratzinger - 280
Career - 240
Carmichael, Stokely - 172
Carnegie, Andrew - 285
Carr, Nicholas - 285
Carruthers, Iva E. - 236
Carter, Jimmy - 14
Carver, George Washington - 186, 241
Casaroli, Cardinal Agostino - 196
Cascione, Jack - 292
Center for Environmental Stewardship - 284
Chardin, Teilhard de - 88
Cheap grace - 59
Christian - 207, 222
Christian Century - 18, 37, 38, 44, 151, 257, 271, 275, 290
Christian Dogmatics - 271
Christian News - 259, 272, 274
Christian News Encyclopedia - 23, 32
Christian Zionists - 282
Christianity Today - 21, 41, 107, 127, 161, 275
Christopherson, Thies - 261
Church Growth - 285, 291
Churchill, Winston - 1, 93, 104, 115
Civil Riots - 156
Civil War - 171, 249, 283
Clauss, Dennis - 40
Cleage, Albert - 235, 237
Cloud, David - 36
Coates, Thomas - 263
Colson, Charles (Chuck) - 21, 35
Columbia University - 285
Communio Sanctorum - 72
Communism - 244, 281
Communist - 192, 225
Communist Party - 157, 183, 187
Computers - 285
Concordia College Ann Arbor - 7
Concordia College Bronxville - 263, 285
Concordia College Portland - 263
Concordia Journal - 56, 124
Concordia Publishing House - 1, 50, 122
Concordia Seminary, Ft. Wayne - 57, 90, 107, 121, 286
Concordia Seminary, St. Louis - 55, 63, 66, 122, 178, 283
Concordia Senior College, Ft. Wayne, IN - 171
Concordia Theological Monthly - 55, 104, 110
Concordia Theological Quarterly - 90, 124
Concordia University System - 262, 293
Concordia University, Wisconsin - 251, 253, 272
Cone, James - 177, 188, 189, 208, 234, 235, 238
Confessing Church - 54
Confessional Lutheran - 49, 259
Congregation - 285
Connell, Hugh J.O. - 65
Conrad, David - 7
Conservation - 284
Conservative - 231
Cooke, Terence Cardinal - 279
Council of Presidents - 259, 273
Council on Biblical Inerrancy - 15
Countess, Robert - 261
Cozzen, Donald - 278
Creation and Fall - 5, 6, 73
Creation Health Foundation - 284
Creation Museum - 289
Creation Research Society - 257, 289
Crucible - 49
CTCR - 91
Cullmann, Oscar - 13, 24
Dachau - 103
Dannemeyer, Bill - 266
Davidheiser, Bolton - 16
Davis, Laura - 261
DayStar - 108, 288
Debate - 259
Debates - 292
DeGruchy, John W. - 37
Delloff, Linda-Marie - 19
Destructive Criticism - 279
DeWolf, Harold - 167, 181
Dialectical Theology - 71
Diego, Juan - 280
DiLorenzo, Thomas J. - 248, 283
Dirks, Lee E. - 149
Doblmeier, Martin - 97
Dodd, C.H. - 24
Dohnany - 25
Dorr, Adriane - 127
Douglas, Major C.H. - 152
Downing, Frederick L. - 197
Dresden - 234
Drickamer, John M. - 208
DuBois W.E.B. - 153, 235
Dying Light - 251
Ebeling, Gerhard - 107
Ecclesiastical Mania - 283
Eckhardt's Reallexicon - 283
Eden, Anthony - 31
Eidesmoe, John - 255
Eisenhower, Dwight - 1, 93, 104, 115
Engel, Randy - 279
English Standard Version - 255, 258, 259

Episcopal Church - 277
Epstein, Marcus - 228, 232
Estonia - 281
Ethics - 78
Evangelical Lutheran Church in America - 48, 286
Evangelical Lutheran Synod - 227
Evans, M. Stanton - 146
Evolution - 289
Expelled: No Intelligence Allowed - 257
Extra-Marital Sex Life - 210
Eyal Rav-Noy - 254
Faculties - 286
Faith of Dr. King - 197
Falwell, Jerry - 192
Faulstick, R. - 6, 8
Faurison, Robert - 261
FBI - 180
Fellowship of Reconciliation - 187
Ferrario, Bishop Joseph - 279
Ferry, Dr. Patrick - 254, 273, 292
Fides et Historia - 119
Fields, Uriah - 172
First Things - 272, 283
Fletcher, Joseph - 8
Flossenberg prison - 25
Floyd, Wayne Whitson Jr. - 20
Flynn, John T. - 265
For Better Not For Worse - 285
Ford, Charles - 58, 61, 65
Ford, James W. - 156
Fortress Press - 114, 122, 234, 268, 271
Forum Letter - 253, 284
Fosdick, Harry Emerson - 101, 174, 181, 190
Fox, Matthew - 277
Frankland, Herman C. 'Buddy' - 192
Free Enterprise - 282
Free Market - 231
Fritsch, Ludwig - 264
Fritz, John H.C. - 291
Fry, Franklin Clark - 167
Fuerbringer, Ludwig - 256, 258
Fundamental Baptist News - 36
Fundamentalist Digest - 22
Gandhi - 100, 114
Garow, David - 180, 185, 193, 195, 210
Gaulle, Charles de - 111
Georgetown - 255
Geschichte - 131
Gettysburg - 252
Girls - 294
God - 29
Gogarten, Friedrich - 24
Grabau - 261
Graff, Elaine M. - 122
Graham, Billy - 94

Great Courses - 254
Greaves, Percy - 265
Greenfield, Gary - 53
Gregory, Dick - 150, 161
Griswold, Bishop - 277
Groppi, James - 172
Grueber, Henry - 271
Grunow, Richard - 11
Guifoyle, Bishop George - 279
Gutierrez, Gustavo - 60
Halberstein, David - 203
Hale, Nathan - 172
Ham, Ken - 276, 281
Hamann Dr. - 152
Hampton, Charles - 182
Hanged on a Twisted Cross - 53
Harrison, Matthew - 95, 115, 121, 125, 262
Hart, Bishop Joseph - 279
Harvard - 255
Haynes, Stephan R. - 112
Health Fitness - 284
Hedrich, Reinhard - 99
Hegelian - 244
Heinemeier, John - 176
Henry, Patrick - 172
Henry, Tamara - 193
Herbert, Albert - 280
Heritage Foundation - 228
Heschel, Rabbi Abraham - 167
Hidy, Ross F. - 150, 161
Higher Criticism - 255, 290
Himmler, Heinrich - 99
Hindu - 253
Historie and Geschichte - 119, 132
Hoffmann, Oswald - 101
Holl, Karl - 71
Holocaust - 65, 69, 110, 256, 292
Holy Communion - 282
Homosexual Priests - 278
Homosexuality - 100, 244
Homosexuals - 262
Hoover, J. Edgar - 161, 165, 169, 197, 210
Human Events - 53, 255
Hunnex, Milton D. - 88
Huntemann, Georg - 60
Huntsville Times - 214
Hyper-euors - 280
Index to the Concordia Theological Journal - 283
Indiana State - 264
Infallibility of the Pope - 280
Institute of Historical Review - 265
Intellectual Respectability - 256
Intellectual Snobs - 86, 95, 108, 118, 150, 257, 259
International Council of Christian Churches - 211
Irving, David - 261

Isaiah 7:14 - 255
Islam in the Crucible - 258
Israel First Millenennialism - 282
Israel First Millinnialists - 289
Jackson, Gregory - 278
Jackson, J.H. - 159
Jackson, Timothy - 113
Jasmin, Don - 22
Jastram, Nathan - 255
J-E-D and P - 254, 283
Jefferson, Thomas - 266
Jehovah's Witnesses - 258
Jenkins, Willis - 112
Jenson, Robert - 286
Jerusalem Bible - 280
Jesus First - 49, 53, 108, 288
Jesus Seminar - 290
Jews - 98
Johnson, John - 234
Johnson, Manning - 213
Johnson, President Lyndon - 181, 193, 209
Jones, M.G. - 178
Just War - 283
Justification - 282, 289
Kalin, Everet B. - 178
Kant - 80
Kazakhstan - 281
Kelley, Geffrey B. - 114
Kelsey, George - 199
Kemper, James S.
Kennedy, Bobby - 225
Kennedy, John - 114
Kenyatta, Muhammed - 179, 180
Kierkegaard, Soren - 4, 13, 26, 62, 77, 110
Kieschnick, President Gerald - 55, 94, 259, 260, 267
Killinger, John - 174
King Henry VIII - 99
King Holiday - 226
King, Coretta Scott - 205
King, Martin Luther - 48
King, Martin Luther Jr. - 161, 176, 257, 261, 273, 292
Kintz, Bruce G. Dr. - 123
Kirschbaum, Charlotte von - 52
Kleinhans, Theodore J. - 49, 50, 55, 56
Koch, Henry - 105, 255, 258, 283
Koster, H. Lester de - 79
Krauth, Charles Porterfield - 252
Kretzmann, Otto P. - 187
Krueger, Kurt - 262
Kueng - 13
Kuhn, Harold - 11
Kuhner, Jeffrey - 276
Kyle, C. Fain - 173
Ladies Man - 198
Laetsch, Theodore - 256, 291

Lane, James N. - 97
Lang, R. Clarence - 261
Latvia - 281
Lehmann, Paul - 59
Lehmann, Robert - 7
Leibholz - 30
Letters and Papers from Prison - 4, 9, 133
Leuchter, Fred - 261
Library - 285
Likoudis, Paul - 278
Lincoln, Abraham - 86, 171
Lithuania - 281
Loconte, Joseph - 96, 98
Loehe - 261
Logia - 110
Lokos, Lionel - 168
Long, D. Stephen - 236
Luther Today - 258
Luther, Martin - 63, 91, 98, 256, 285
Lutheran - 253
Lutheran Book of Worship - 182, 207, 208
Lutheran Church in America - 184
Lutheran Forum - 17, 19, 42, 106
Lutheran Human Relations Association of America - 155
Lutheran Quarterly - 287
Lutheran Sentinel
Lutheran Witness - 46, 55, 59, 62, 68, 126, 146, 181, 193, 239, 257
Lutheran World Federation (LWF) - 274, 289
Lyons, Father Daniel - 172, 177
MacArthur, John F. Jr. - 21
Machen, Gresham - 71
Maier, Paul - 255
Maier, Walter A. - 39, 91, 101, 104, 258, 256, 264, 275, 283, 285, 291
Manhattan - 105
Marquart, Kurt - 39, 68, 86, 95, 108, 119, 150, 254, 255, 256, 258, 265, 266, 267, 268, 273, 275, 281, 286, 291, 293, 294
Marquart's Legacy - 258
Martin Luther King's Day - 182, 241, 245
Marty, Martin - 9, 14, 24, 41, 109, 268, 270, 271, 272, 273
Martyr - 207
Mary - 256, 280
Maschke, Timothy - 289
Mass - 190, 191
Matthews, J.B. - 155
Matusow, Harvey - 187
Matzat, Don - 21
McBride, Jennifer M. - 112
McCain, Paul - 49, 50, 57, 113, 121, 239, 245, 247, 249, 269
McDonald, H.D. - 30

McDonald, Larry - 183, 194, 226
McIntire, Carl
McKnight - 252
Melano, Beatriz - 60
Mencken, H.L. - 162
Messianic Prophecy - 91
Metaxas, Eric - 96, 97, 107, 114
Meyendorf, John - 266
Meyer, Dale - 261
Meyer, William - 262
Milwaukee Archdiocese - 277
Milwaukee Pastoral Conference - 271
Minh, Ho Chi - 172, 177
Mitchell, Henry H. - 217
Moellering, Ralph - 187
Mohler, R. Albert - 239
Moltmann - 13
Montecroce, Ricaldo - 258
Montgomery, John Warwick - 255, 258
Moon, Sun Yung - 207
Morgenstern, George - 265
Mother Teresa - 48
Muck and Smut - 208
Mueller, Charles, Sr. - 259
Mueller, Herbert - 260
Mueller, J.T. - 52, 70, 110, 270
Mugavero, Bishop Francis - 279
Muggeridge, Malcolm - 35
Music - 285
Myrdal, Gunner - 149
Myth - 135
Mythology - 135
Myths - 4, 199
National Association for the Advancement of Colored People (NAACP) - 153, 157
National Holiday - 209
National Observer - 1, 147, 153, 162, 172, 181
National Review - 228, 229
Nauman, Martin - 291
Nazi - 100, 101
Nazi Theology - 99
Neff, David - 127
Negroes - 156
Neipp, Paul - 259
Neo-Pentecostalism - 294
Neuhaus, Father Richard John - 66, 90, 94, 107, 120, 176, 188, 190, 197, 227, 247, 270, 288
New Roman Catholic Encyclopedia - 280
New York Times - 211
Newsweek - 180
Niebuhr, Reinhold - 24, 43
Niemoeller, Martin - 24, 31
Nobel Peace Prize - 166, 202, 209
Noland, Martin - 268
Norway - 202

Not a Christian - 196
Nygren, Anders - 24, 90, 119
Oates, Stephen - 201
O'Connell, Hugh J. - 65, 67
Oesch, Wilhelm - 49
Old Missouri - 263
Olson, Stanley - 253
Organized Conservatives - 2, 268, 293
Otten, Grace - 234, 284
Otten, Herman - 94, 171, 251, 264, 269
Otten-Marquart Team - 266
Overtures - 288
Pannenburg - 13
Parade - 194
Patz, Rabbi Norman - 211
Peerman, Dean - 24
Pelikan, Jaroslav - 66, 90, 273
Penn, Lee - 276
Philbrick, Herbert - 187
Pieper, Francis - 91, 104, 275
Piepkorn, Carl - 266
Plagiarizer - 219, 221, 232
Pless, John - 292
Poland - 281
Poor People's Campaign - 165
Pope Benedict XVI - 276, 280
Pope John Paul II - 90, 196
Pope John XXIII - 48
Pope Paul VI - 279
Portals of Prayer - 239
Powell, Paul W. - 17
Power, Politics, and the Missouri Synod - 268
Premarital Sex - 223
Preus, Jacob - 181, 182, 268, 273, 274
Preus, Robert - 39, 255, 258
Princeton - 255
Private Property - 169
Prostitute - 209
Psalm 16:9-11 - 91
Quie, Albert - 266
Rabin, Yitzhak - 114
Racism - 2, 242, 248, 289
Rambachen, Anantanand - 253
Rand, Sidney - 253
Rassinier, Paul - 261
Rauff, Edward - 7
Rausch, Bishop James - 279
Rauschenbusch, Walter - 151, 244
Rav-Noy, Eyal - 2, 256
Ray, James Earl - 214
Reagan, Ronald - 190, 232
Reason - 256
Recovered Memory Therapy - 260
Red Cross - 93
Reese, George C. - 12
Reformation Festival - 6
Reformation Sunday - 48
Rehwinkel, Alfred - 39, 283

Religious Socialism - 257
Renewal in Missouri - 294
Resurrection - 5, 9, 11, 22, 28, 135, 147, 198
Retiring - 294
Reuther, Rosemarie Radford - 236
Revised Standard Version of the Bible - 255
Riverside Church - 171
Robbins, John - 283
Roberson, Jesse - 275
Robertson, Edwin H. - 47, 75
Robinson, Bishop John - 8, 11, 21, 65
Roosevelt, F.D. - 264, 283
Rudin, A. James - 37
Rueda, Enrique T. - 278
Russia - 281
Rustin, Bayard - 156, 201, 244
Saase, Hermann - 66, 100, 265
Sadat, Anwar al - 114
Saffen, Wayne - 41
Scaer, David Dr. - 121
Schenck, Berthold von - 101
Schiotz, Fredrick - 158, 165
Schmidt, Alvin - 255
Schmidt, Eugene - 208
Scholl, Travis - 124
Schultz, Hans Jouchim - 33
Schuyler, George - 161, 162, 173
Schwan Foundation - 49, 115, 269
Schwarz, Fred - 187
Schweitzer, Albert - 55, 62
Scott, Walter - 193
Scruggs, Julius - 174, 181
Seeger, Pete - 186
Seminarian Controversy - 270
Seminex - 23, 256
Sendstad, Valen - 119
Seventh Day Adventists - 284
Sex - 285
Sex Abusers - 277
Sexual Orgies - 226
Sexual Urge - 181
Sherman, Franklin - 24
Shinn, Roger - 30
Shroud of Turin - 256
SHURE Group - 160
Shuttleswoorth, Fred L. - 155
Siberian Evangelical Lutheran Church - 281
Siegbert, Becker - 256
Simeon-Netto, Uwe - 59, 90
Simon, Arthur - 284
Simon, Martin - 200
Simon, Paul - 200
S-I-N - 296
Situation Ethics - 8
Six Million - 93, 104
Slovakia - 281
Smith, Benjamin E. - 155

Smith, Warren - 96
Smokers - 207
Sobran, Joseph - 194
Social Credit - 152
Social Gospel - 244
Sockman, Ralph - 174
Sojourners - 16
Solzhenitsyn - 48
Southeast Missouri State - 264
Southern Christian Leadership - 180
Southern Christian Leadership Conference - 1
Soviet Union - 269
Speckhard, Peter - 284
St. Louis Lutheran - 18
St. Louis Post Dispatch - 23
St. Louis Rams - 272
St. Louis Review - 43, 191, 277
St. Matthew Lutheran Church - 105
St. Olaf's College - 253
Staeghlich, Wilhelm - 261
Stanford - 255
Stang, Alan - 154
Starenko, Ronald - 7, 8
Stassen, Glen H. - 113
Stein, Ben - 257
Steinmueller, John - 280
Stelzer, Ron - 39
Stewardship - 284
Stoeckhardt, George - 256, 258
Stuenkel, Walter - 271
Sueflow, Edwin - 274
Sullivan, William C. - 209
Sumner, Robert L. - 17, 179
Surburg, Raymond - 23, 39, 42, 49, 117, 255, 256
Sword of the Lord - 179, 193
Tansill, Charles - 265
The American Lutheran - 187
The Banner - 79
The Christian News Encyclopedia - 262
The Conservative Reformation and Its Theology - 252
The Cost of Discipleship - 26, 35, 77, 128, 130, 136
The Courage to Heal - 261
The Crime of Our Ages - 264
The Dan Smoot Report - 153
The Dying of the Light - 262
The Lutheran - 12, 16, 17, 18, 19, 20, 23, 42
The Lutheran Cyclopedia - 1
The Nature of Biblical Criticism - 254
The New Jerome Biblical Commentary - 280
The New Modernism - 86
The New York Times - 169
The Real Lincoln - 283
The Rite of Sodomy - Homosexuality

and the Roman Catholic Church - 279
Theobald, Admiral - 265
Theology and Church Relations - 284
Thielicke, Helmut - 107
Thomas, Cal - 111
Thompson, Meldrim - 232
Thornbury, Greg PhD - 97
Through to Victory - 259
Tietjen, John - 187
Till the Night Be Past-The Life and Times of Dietrich Bonhoeffer - 50
Tillich, Paul - 8, 9, 24, 43, 119, 192, 221
TIME - 9, 41, 177, 193, 276, 285
Toner, Edward - 225
Trees - 284
Trinity - 282
Trinity Lutheran Church, New Haven, MO - 251
Twentieth Century Formula of Concord - 273
Twentieth Century Reformation and Creed - 276
Twenty-First Century Platform - 272
Twenty-First Century Reformation - 273, 291
Twenty-First Century Reformation Today - 275
Ukraine - 281
Union Seminary - 1, 12, 101, 105
Unitarianism - 275
United Church of America - 277
United List - 294
Valen-Sentatd, Olav - 52
Valparaiso University - 155, 173, 222, 257, 264, 283, 287
Van Til, Cornelius - 13, 14, 27, 69, 71, 86, 89, 122
Vanderbilt - 255
Vashem, Yad - 38
Vicarious Satisfaction - 282
Virgin Birth - 11, 22, 148, 282
Virgin Mary - 255
Vodoo Psychology - 260
Walker, William O. - 160
Wall Street Journal - 96
Walter A. Maier Still Speaks - 115
Walther C.F.W. - 264
Walther League Messenger - 264, 285
Walther, C.F.W. - 39, 55, 252, 275
Wannsee Conference - 102
Washington Times - 193, 207, 255, 276
Washington University - 261, 264
Washington, Booker T. - 186, 240, 241
Washington, James Melvin - 204
Weakland, Rembert Archbishop - 278, 279
Weber, Charles - 261

Weikart, Richard - 122, 119, 128, 136
Weinreich, Gil - 2, 254, 256
Weniger, G. Archer - 22, 43
Wenthe, Dean - 115, 121
Westling, Jon - 219
Westminster Theological Journal - 69, 71
Westminster Theological Seminary - 83
Who Really Wrote the Bible? - 2, 254
Wilken, Robert - 270
Williams Aubrey - 155
Williams Robert F. - 160
Williams, Walter - 249, 283
Wilson, Robert Dick - 256
Wisconsin Lutheran College - 53
Wisconsin Lutheran Synod - 278, 290
Witt, Elmer E. - 160
WORKER - 171
World - 96, 107, 114, 124
World Church - 276
World Council of Churches - 164
World War II - 1
Worship in a Collegiate Setting - 254, 273
Wright, John Cardinal - 279
Yale University - 109
Yale University Press - 53
Young, Josiah U. III - 112
Young, Rosa - 240
Zehnder, Thomas - 53, 69
Zerner, Ruth - 19

Books Published by *Christian News*

An American Translation of the Bible
Translated by William F. Beck

This Bible translation, known as the "Beck Bible," is also called The Holy Bible;An American Translation(AAT).

AAT, of course, is not only a Bible for Lutherans. Being a faithful translation, not a paraphrase, of Hebrew, Aramaic, and Greek manuscripts, it is a Bible for every Englishspeaking person who needs to learn of Jesus and His redemption. As such, the Lord used His servant, the late Dr. Beck, to do the major work on AAT, and other living servants to continue the work of polishing, publishing, and most importantly, preaching it.

Crisis in Christendom Seminex Ablaze
By Herman Otten

"Crisis in Christendom has lasting interest for all those who are concerned about preserving the scriptural and confessional position of the LCMS and documentary information about the history of the LCMS's "Battle for the Bible II."

Marquart's Legacy
By Herman Otten

Marquart's Legacy begins with a brief biography of Kurt Marquart. Then follows "Remembrances of a Former Seminary Roommate." Finally, the reader is introduced to Marquart's legacy as a professor, pastor, and theologian. See why he is the International Luther.

Walter A. Maier - A Man Speaks Missouri and the World Should Listen
By Herman J. Otten

Dr. Maier's delivery…is characterized by prophetic boldness…The Gospel is proclaimed as though there were only twenty minutes left to bring millions to Christ. That kind of delivery is powerfully persuasive, for under it lies the terrific earnestness of a dying man talking to dying men."—Dr. Lester Zeitler

Islam In The Crucible
by R. da Montecroce and Luther

Ricoldo, a 14th century Dominican monk, studied the Qur'an in Arabic before refuting it. In 1542 Martin Luther translated the Confutatio Alcorani from Latin into German. In 2002 Thomas Pfotenhauer translated Luther's German version of Ricoldo's book and added copious notes.

Ricoldo went to Baghdad in order to present the case for Christianity to the Muslim intellectuals. Overwhelmed and depressed by the task, he wrote the Confutatio to persuade those misled by the Qur'an to return to the true God. Martin Luther shared Ricoldo's desire to recover the straying. Luther asked, "How is one to proceed in an attempt at converting these Muslims?" If Muslims could not be converted, Luther at least wanted Ricoldo's book to guard Christians against the teachings of Muhammad.

In seventeen chapters Ricoldo attacks the authenticity, accuracy, and ability of the Qur'an to reflect either the will or the gospel of God.

Pfotenhauer's notes balance some of the statements of Ricoldo and Luther with portions of the Qur'an and Hadith.

Prayers for The Worship Service
By Arthur J. Clement

Includes prayers for the entire Church Year (Advent-Trinity). An alphabetical listing of prayers topically to cover subjects discussed in sermons through the Trinity or Post-Pentecost Season. Special Prayers for Holy Communion, The injured, Ill, Military Personnel, Motherhood, Synod, and much more.

Devotions on the Apostles Creed
By Peter Krey
These devotions will inform and inspire. They can be used as a guide for daily meditation or for more intensive Bible study. Peter Krey writes in a clear and understandable manner for both laymen and pastors. His meditations on the Apostles Creed and other writings are solidly based on God's Word, Holy Scripture.

Pass the Salt
by J.B. Romnes
This "Evangelical Feast of Satire" is a compilation of the many cartoons that have been featured in Christian News. Through these cartoons the artist provides commentary on the current issues that are affecting the Christian church.

Luther Today
by H. Otten
Luther Today gives answers to many current issues such as abortion, evolution, homosexuality, and much more using the writings of the Martin Luther as he speaks to us today.

Christian News Encyclopedia, Volumes 1-5
A collection of articles from Christian News that are organized by topics which are easy to find.

How To Start Or Keep Your Own Missouri Synod Lutheran Church
by J.M. Cascione
GOALS OF THIS BOOK:
1. To provide a resource for lay people who want to start or keep their own LCMS congregation
2. To preserve the practice of congregational self-government in all LCMS congregations
3. To encourage the LCMS Convention to reaffirm congregational voters' assemblies as the official policy of all LCMS congregations.
4. To serve as a reference book for basic quotes from the Bible, the Lutheran Confessions, Luther, and Walther on how to start or keep your own LCMS congregation.

Baal or God
by Herman J. Otten, Ed.
Beliefs and Practices of the Churches of the World Today-Back to Christ and the Bible - A Call for a Twentieth Century Reformation 500 Years After Luther.

C.F.W. Walther's Pastoral Theology
Answering Questions on:
The Call
Preaching
Holy Communion
Funerals
Visitations
Baptism
Marriage
Discipline
The reader today will find that the book is very practical and helpful, and not out of date. Why? Because Walther's book is not a "how to" book for developing skills…but truly a pastoral theology." –Dr Robert Preus

Luther's Small Catechism
Luther's Small Catechism with questions and answers in the An American Translation of the Bible text.

The Christian Travel Guide to World History
by Henry Koch
"This book is the product of a lifetime of advanced study in both secular and theological fields, including actual travel to the lands of the Bible and the Reformation. Recent discoveries in the filed of archaeology now equip us to understand the Biblical narratives covering 4,000 years of human history better than every before. It literally makes the Bible come alive and personal when we begin to view the Scriptures in their chronological, historical and geographical setting." William Bischoff

Two Rivers to Freedom
by Stella Wuerffel
A historical-romantic novel about courageous Saxon Christians emigrating to America in the 1800's. Up the Elbe River in Germany to the sea, across the wide ocean in small ships, then up the Mississippi to Altenburg and St. Louis.

The Lutherans Catechism on Homosexuality
by Dr. David Kaufmann
Ever since Sodom and Gomorrah, history has demonstrated that the rise of homosexuality in a culture is the last step before God brings His final judgment and the demise of that culture. We must wake up and not only pray for a great repentance, reformation and revival to take place in the Church, we must actively seek it by honoring the inerrancy, infallibility and authority of God's Word, the Holy Bible, and obey it!

Salt, Light and Signs of the Times
By Ronald W. Stelzer
An Intimate Look at the Life and Times of Alfred (Rip) Rehwinkel

Dr. Alfred Rehwinkel was one of a kind in American Christendom. I was among a multitude of students who could listen endlessly to this spellbinder in classroom and chapel. We shall not see his like again.
Dr. Paul Maier, Author, Professor; Western Michigan University

Servant Captains for the Good Ship Missouri
By Herman Otten
This book includes some of the many writings of Dr. John Wohlrabe ("Navigating a Course for the Good Ship Missouri", "How We Got Into This Mess: A Brief Survey of LCMS History", "What is Clear!", "Power in the Word of God Alone", "On the Way To Episcope", "Ministry of a Military Chaplain"), a brief biography, the testimony of others about him, and some information about his work.

Reclaiming the Gospel in the LCMS
How to Keep Your Congregation Lutheran
By Jack Cascione
This book exposes: 1.) the workings of the Church Growth Movement; 2.) why this movement is so dangerous; 3.) names and groups promoting and networking the change in LCMS congregations; 4.) the marketing, mind control, information management, and behavior modification techniques they use instead of Christian doctrine; 5.) how far the "change agents" have progressed; 6.) the agenda for the future; 7.) and how it is funded. This book is designed to inform, educate and help you.

Lutheran News, Inc.
684 Luther Lane
New Haven, MO 63068
573-237-3110
www.ChristianNewsmo.com

www.ingramcontent.com/pod-product-compliance
Lightning Source LLC
Chambersburg PA
CBHW051419290426
44109CB00016B/1356